Religious and Political History and Thought in the Byzantine Empire

Professor Paul J. Alexander

Paul J. Alexander

Religious and Political History and Thought in the Byzantine Empire

Collected Studies

VARIORUM REPRINTS
London 1978

80- 1217
ISBN 0 86078 016 3

Published in Great Britain by   *Variorum Reprints*
                                 21a Pembridge Mews London W11 3EQ

Printed in Great Britain by   *Kingprint Ltd*
                                 Richmond Surrey TW9 4PD

VARIORUM REPRINT CS71

CONTENTS

ICONS AND ICONOCLAST CONTROVERSY

BYZANTINE APOCALYPTIC

This volume contains a total of 360 pages

PREFACE

The articles on the religious and political history and thought of the Byzantine Empire brought together in this volume were written over a timespan of more than thirty-five years. They appeared in a variety of journals, *Festschriften*, etc., in the United States and abroad, some of them in rather inaccessible publications. It is therefore a matter of great satisfaction to me that they will henceforth be available between two covers. Except for my books, reviews, occasional writings, and a few studies on problems of ancient history and patristics, this volume will comprise all my scholarly writing.

As indicated by the title and structure of this collection, the articles here reproduced group themselves fairly naturally under three headings: the ideology and practice of Byzantine imperialism; the Byzantine theory of religious images and the course of the Iconoclastic Controversy; and the nature and development of Byzantine apocalyptic literature and thought. For each of these three themes, the articles are arranged not so much in the order in which they were written as according to the chronology of the materials discussed in them, at least where the contents have a chronological focus. Of the three themes mentioned, the first has interested me throughout my scholarly career, not only in the articles here reproduced but also in my larger publications. The studies belonging to the second theme are all related, in one way or another, to my book *The Patriarch Nicephorus of Constantinople. Ecclesiastical Policy and Image Worship in the Byzantine Empire* (Oxford, 1958) and should be considered in conjunction with it. Finally, with regard to the third theme, I have devoted a monograph to the first edition and explanation of a Greek text: *The Oracle of Baalbek. The Tiburtine Sibyl in Greek Dress, Dumbarton Oaks Studies* 10, Washington, D.C., 1967. Moreover, I have been engaged for a number of years on a comprehensive work tentatively entitled: *Byzantine Apocalypses. History and Prophecy.* In this work I hope to assign the principal Byzantine apocalypses to their proper time, place and milieu and to investigate their literary relationships and purposes ("The Texts"); to extract the historical information they may contain ("The Events"); and to investigate the origin and development of eschatological and other ideas that they use ("The Ideas"). Drafts for several chapters have been completed and the articles in Part Three of the present volume will give some indication as to methodologies, purposes and results of the larger project. I should like to add that two essays now in process of publication are related to the third theme: an article on "The Medieval Legend of the Last Roman Emperor and Its Messianic Origins," to appear in the *Journal of the Warburg and Courtauld Institutes*, and another on "The Diffusion of Byzantine Apocalypses in the Medieval West and the Beginnings of Joachimism," to be published by Longmans Green in a volume entitled *Prophecy and the Millennium* in honor of Dr Marjorie Reeves.

The articles gathered in this volume were written under widely differing circumstances, under various influences and at separate stages in my intellectual development. It should therefore come as no surprise that they exhibit considerable dissimilarities in method, presentation and style. If I were to rewrite them today, I should certainly introduce a number of formal changes, but on the whole I see no reason to revise major substantive conclusions. There is, however, one exception. For a long time I was convinced that Pseudo-Methodius, the seventh-century author of the most influential Byzantine apocalypse, was a Monophysite. However, for the reasons indicated briefly in my addition to no. XII, I now believe that Pseudo-Methodius may have been either a Monophysite or a Nestorian.

The articles are reproduced as first published, but additional bibliographical remarks have been added in several cases. These additions do not lay claim to completeness but consist of items that came to my attention and seem to me to advance the discussion of the problems touched upon in my articles. Undoubtedly important contributions have escaped me. Recent editions of texts cited in my articles are not normally referred to (but see Additional Bibliography to no. XI). It is a matter of particular regret to me that it proved impracticable to substitute for the published Russian translation of my essay on "Pseudo-Methodius and Ethiopia" (no. XI) my (unpublished) English original. As a second best, I have appended to that article a brief English summary.

A word on the methodology and objectives pursued by me in these articles may be appropriate. As I re-read them, I noted that in many of them the core consists of a first or improved edition of a text or a commentary upon it, while in a smaller number of them I proceed in the opposite direction, from a historical problem to its textual source or sources. To some degree this orientation is due to the fact that many of these articles are closely linked with my books on larger subjects. In a book the road from problem to texts is frequently more appropriate and the detailed study of the textual evidence can thus easily be reserved for separate treatment. In a deeper sense, however, it seems to me that the prevalence of the textual approach in my articles is more than an accident. In fact, its strength became ever clearer to me as I gained experience in historical research. It enabled me to understand the past in terms of its own intellectual categories and problems. While this result has its shortcomings as well as its advantages and can easily degenerate into sterile antiquarianism, these perils can be overcome. One way of minimizing them is for the historian not to consider his task completed unless and until he has not only elucidated his text as a product of its time, but also answered a number of further questions: the relationship of the text in question to related sources, its evidential value for the political, social and other problems of the age when it was written, etc.

In general I found that respect for and patience with textual relics of past generations rarely failed to sharpen my understanding and my ability to reconstruct, with the aid of the combined skills of the philologist and the historian, major aspects of a bygone age. I know of no more satisfying experience than to free, by the application of the methods of textual criticism, an important ancient or medieval text from the dross of the centuries — I was privileged to perform this task, on a larger scale than in these articles, under the unforgettable guidance of the late Professor Werner Jaeger, in my edition of Gregory of Nyssa's *Homilies on Ecclesiastes*, Gregorii Nysseni Opera, volume V, Leiden, 1962; and by exercising the historian's craft, to learn to understand it, including all its allusions, metaphors and obscurities, as a meaningful product of its own political, social and religious environment. Experience further showed that the textual approach was likely to produce the best results if I freed myself from two kinds of limitations. I tried to go beyond the conventional sources for Byzantine history (chronicles, documents, etc.) and included more unusual iv

materials such as theological tracts, correspondence, saint's lives, apocalypses as well as non-literary evidence (for example language, place names, archaeology). Secondly, in editing Byzantine texts or commenting upon them, I frequently disregarded artificial barriers of a chronological, linguistic or cultural kind and compared my Byzantine materials with related documents from Classical Antiquity or from the Western, Slavic or Moslem Middle Ages. It is, of course, not my intention to lay a claim to any kind of originality for these reflections, which are in fact the daily bread of many a practising historian. I mention them merely to explain the subject matter and methodologies of these articles and to express my conviction that if the pre-modern historian allows the pendulum to swing too far in the direction either of the textual or of the topical approach, in the end the sources are likely to stand mute or the problems to yield no solution.

In my articles (and other publications) I have expressed my thanks to scholars who at various stages contributed to my intellectual development or otherwise assisted me in my work. These feelings of gratitude remain to the present day; in fact, in several instances the course of time has intensified them. For the compilation of this volume I received a generous grant from the Committee on Research at the University of California, Berkeley, which proved extremely helpful. I am also grateful to Mr Michael Maas, a student in the University Graduate Program in Ancient History and Archaeology, for composing the index, primarily of names of persons and places, and assisting me conscientiously and energetically in many other tasks.

Finally, I feel honored and indebted to Mrs Eileen Turner and the firm of Variorum Reprints for including the present volume in their program of publications.

PAUL J. ALEXANDER

Department of History,
University of California,
Berkeley, CA 94720
August 1977

ACKNOWLEDGMENTS

I wish to express my thanks to a number of journals, other publications and institutions for kindly granting permission to reproduce the articles in this volume. They include: *Speculum*; President and Fellows of Harvard College; Princeton University Press; *Dumbarton Oaks Papers*; *Medievalia et Humanistica*; *American Historical Review*; *Actes du XIIe Congrès International des Etudes Byzantines*.

BYZANTINE EMPEROR AND EMPIRE:
IDEOLOGY AND PRACTICE

I

SECULAR BIOGRAPHY AT BYZANTIUM[1]

I

CLASSICAL secular biography[2] died a spectacular though lingering and somewhat disreputable death with productions like the *Historia Augusta* written at the end of the fourth century A.D.,[3] or the Life of the Neoplatonist Isidore, written by his pupil Damascius at the beginning of the sixth century A.D.[4] Even biographical secular panegyrics, the history of which cannot be separated from that of biography proper since the days of Isocrates' *Euagoras*, are not preserved in the East after the sixth century A.D.[5] When classical biography was far gone in years, perhaps already moribund, it had engendered a progeny which was to perpetuate the memory of the parent all through the Middle Ages: this was hagiography.[6] But secular biography itself was reputed to be dead, so dead that Krumbacher[7] listed the works that should have been classified under this heading in his chapters on historical writing.

Nevertheless secular biography and secular panegyric were not unknown at Byzantium. We hear of them first in connection with Basil I, the Macedonian (867–886 A.D.). His biographer and grandson, the Emperor Constantine VII Porphyrogenitus (912–959 A.D.) mentions among the deeds which Basil per-

---

[1] The author wishes to express his thanks to Professor R. P. Blake and Professor G. La Piana. He prepared this paper under their direction and is indebted to both for a great number of valuable suggestions. In particular, private and seminar discussions with Professor Blake gave him ample opportunity to correct errors and avoid rash judgements.

[2] F. Leo, *Die Griechisch-Römische Biographie nach ihrer literarischen Form* (Leipzig, 1901); D. R. Stuart, *Epochs of Greek and Roman Biography* (Berkeley, California, 1928). — I am using the term 'secular' for biographies or biographical panegyrics where some emphasis, at least, is placed on the hero's worldly achievements.

[3] Short résumé of the problems involved in A. Rosenberg, *Einleitung und Quellenkunde zur Römischen Geschichte* (Berlin, 1921), pp. 231–241.

[4] R. Asmus, *Das Leben des Philosophen Isidoros von Damaskios aus Damaskos* (Leipzig, 1911).

[5] The last were those delivered in the School of Gaza. H. Leclercq. 'Panégyrique,' in Cabrol et Leclercq, *Dictionnaire d'Archéologie Chrétienne et de Liturgie*, XIII, 1016–1045.

[6] On the classical models of Greek hagiography see J. List, 'Das Antoniusleben des hl. Athanasius d. Gr. etc.,' *Texte und Forschungen zur Byzantinisch-Neugriechischen Philologie*, XI (1930), and the literature listed in the introduction. Add P. Bezobrazov, 'Drevneišija grečeskija žitija,' *Žurnal Ministerstva Narodnago Prosveščenija*, N. S., LXXI (October, 1917), 147–173.

[7] K. Krumbacher, *Geschichte der byzantinischen Literatur etc.*, in I. von Müller, *Handbuch der klassischen Altertumswissenschaft*, IX, 1 (2nd ed., Munich, 1897). He calls the fifth book of the Theophanes Continuatus 'die Geschichte' of Basil I (p. 253), the work of Nicephorus Bryennius a 'Familienchronik' (p. 272), and Anna Comnena's *Alexias* 'die Geschichte des Alexios Komnenos' (p. 274). The comments of E. Gerland, 'Die Grundlagen der byzantinischen Geschichtsschreibung,' *Byzantion*, VIII (1933), 98 on the Byzantine 'Kaiserbiographie' and 'Kaiserporträt' refer to short characteristics in the histories and chronicles rather than to extensive biographies. — Mr. G. Downey kindly calls my attention to the fact that in his article entitled 'Imperial Building Records in Malalas,' *Byzantinische Zeitschrift*, XXXVIII (1938), 10, note 3, he had shown building records to be one of the items mentioned in Byzantine panegyrics and imperial biographies.

formed αὐτουργός, in person, that 'occasionally he directed righteous affairs (τὰ πρὸς τὸ δέον) with prudent handling, but at other times he lent his ear, and listened attentively, to historic narrations, political precepts, ethical teachings, patristic and spiritual admonitions and imitations; at other times he led and trained his hand toward the writing pen (τὴν χεῖρα πρὸς τὸν γραφικὸν ἐξεπαίδευε καὶ κατηύθυνε κάλαμον), now he examined the mores, lives, handling of affairs, and military exploits of both generals and emperors, and after careful consideration, selecting the basic and laudable points of these, he endeavored to carry out in his own actions an imitation *thereof*; while on the other hand he carefully studied the careers of those who had been outstanding in the mode of life agreeable to God.'[1] We may, perhaps, doubt how veracious this account is in the case of Basil.[2] For our purpose, it is sufficient to note that two generations later his grandson could *imagine* his grandfather as studying deeply both secular and ecclesiastical biography, and that this first mention connects biography with hagiography.

Our second testimony is a fully preserved specimen of secular biography, that of Basil I, written by his grandson Constantine VII Porphyrogenitus,[3] which will be discussed at length below. This biography, however, is all that was ever carried out of a much more ambitious plan. In his preface, Constantine states:

For a long time my urge and desire had been to implant a practical experience and knowledge of affairs in the minds of the more seriously minded through the never-forgetful and immortal mouth of history, and I wished, should I perchance have been capable thereof, to have recounted some of the deeds of the emperors, their marshals, generals, and their lieutenants throughout the whole period of the Roman rule at Byzantium. But since this matter demanded not only much time and uninterrupted work, but also an abundance of books and surcease from affairs, and since all those I did not have, I was forced to choose the second course, namely to narrate, for the time being, the deeds and the entire development of one Emperor (i.e., Basil) etc., so that the generations to come would not ignore the primary source and root of the royal stem which stretched over a long period. If, then, haply a further space of time be yet measured unto us, and some slight respite from infirmities, and should no external circumstance stand in the way, it may be that we, in unbroken order, shall add the complete chain of the history of his progeny which comes down even unto us.[4]

[1] Theophanes Continuatus, ed. I. Bekker, *C(orpus) S(criptorum) H(istoriae) B(yzantinae)*, XXXII (Bonn, 1838), 314, 6–17.

[2] There is some evidence for the truth of parts of this account. Two hortatory works, addressed to Leo VI, are attributed, in our manuscripts, to Basil I (cf., however, Krumbacher, *Geschichte*, pp. 457 sq., and K. Emminger, *Studien zu den griechischen Fürstenspiegeln etc.* [Diss. München, München, 1913], pp. 23–73). Basil's interest in the cult of Saints is illustrated by the Georgian Life of St Hilarion (Latin translation by P. P. Peeters, 'S. Hilarion d'Ibérie,' *Analecta Bollandiana*, XXXII [1913], 236–269), chs. 33–44, and the note on St Menas in *Synaxarium Ecclesiae Constantinopolitanae*, ed. H. Delehaye, *Propylaeum ad AASS Novembris* (Brussels, 1902), col. 470; cf. H. Delehaye, 'L'invention des reliques de Saint Ménas à Constantinople,' *Analecta Bollandiana*, XXIX (1910), 117–150.

[3] It is incorporated as Book V in the anonymous collection which we are accustomed to call *Theophanes Continuatus* (see above note 1). On this work cf. F. Hirsch, *Byzantinische Studien* (Leipzig, 1876), pp. 175–302; K. Krumbacher, *Geschichte*, pp. 347–349; H. Nickles, 'The Continuatio Theophanis,' *Transactions of the American Philological Association*, LXVIII (1937), 221–227. On Book V, and its author in particular, see A. Rambaud, *L'Empire Grec au dixième siècle. Constantin Porphyrogénète* (Paris, 1870), pp. 137–164; F. Hirsch, *Byz. Stud.*, pp. 225–267.

[4] Theoph. Cont., p. 211, 18, to p. 212, 17.

Constantine's historical program thus developed in three stages: (1) the original scheme, an account of the deeds of all the Byzantine celebrities, (2) the present Life of Basil, (3) a continuation of the narrative down to his own period. The wording does not make it clear whether (1) and (3) would have had biographical form if they had been carried out; for the extant part (2), however, the biographical character is expressly stated.

Approximately to the same period belong eight books, written by a certain Manuel πρωτοσπαθάριος καὶ κριτής, and containing the military exploits of John Kurkuas. We may infer from the subject that the work had biographical form.[1]

By the close of the eleventh century we hear bitter complaints that the new methods had done considerable harm to historical composition. John Scylitzes states in the preface to his chronicle:[2] 'For Theodore Daphnopates, Nicetas the Paphlagonian, Joseph Genesius, and Manuel, all from Byzantium, Nicephorus the Deacon, from Phrygia, Leo, from Asia, Theodore, who became the head of the flock of Side, and his nephew and namesake who led the Church of Sebasteia, and, after him (?), Demetrius, Bishop of Cyzicus, and the Monk John of Lydia, each of them put forward his own topic, the one praising an Emperor, another blaming a patriarch, the third lauding a friend—all carrying into effect their individual purpose under the guise of history. . . . They discussed profusely the events of their own time, and describing in the form of history what had shortly preceded them, the one from a favorable, the other from an unfavorable, point of view, a third with a view to please, a fourth according to the commandment laid upon him, they have each compiled their own history, and as they differ violently in the accounts which they give they have filled their listeners with vertigo and disturbance.'

Of the men mentioned, some are known as the authors of histories, others as the authors of encomiastic biographies.[3] The passage shows, therefore, not only that together with strictly historical works encomiastic biography had appeared on the literary scene, but that the newcomer had introduced ἔπαινος and ψόγος, praise and blame, even into the realm of supposedly impartial history.

---

[1] Theoph. Cont., VI, 41 (p. 428[1]). The work is to be dated between the year 944 A.D. when John Kurkuas was dismissed (St. Runciman, The Emperor Romanus Lecapenus and his reign [Cambridge, 1929], p. 231) and the reign of Nicephorus Phocas (963–969) when the above passage was written (F. Hirsch, Byz. Stud., p. 272).

[2] Most convenient text of this part of the preface in K. Krumbacher, Geschichte, p. 367.

[3] A number of Church encomiums are attributed to Theodore Daphnopates cf. V. V. Latyšev, 'Deux discours de Théodore Daphnopatès,' Pravoslavny Palestinski Sbornik, LIX (1910), and, by one manuscript, the life of Theodore the Studite, Migne, PG, C, col. 113, note 1. F. Hirsch, Byz. Stud., p. 284 note 1, and p. 361, and K. Krumbacher, Geschichte, p. 459, consider the possibility that Theodore was the author of the last part of Theoph. Cont., Book VI, and their view seems to have been taken up by S. P. Šestakov, 'La question de l'auteur de la Continuation de Théophanes,' in D. Anastasijević and Ph. Granić, Deuxième Congrès international des études byzantines (Belgrad, 1929), pp. 35–45. If that view is correct, this would be the 'praise of an Emperor,' namely of Constantine Porphyrogenitus. (The publications of Latyšev and Šestakov were inaccessible to the writer). — On Nicetas the Paphlagonian see below p. 203, note 2. His Vita Ignatii could be appropriately called the 'blame of a patriarch.' — Joseph Genesius is the historian. — 'Leo, from Asia,' is, perhaps, the historian Leo the Deacon. — 'Manuel' is probably identical with the author of the work on John Kurkuas, see above, note 1. — The other writers are unknown.

But this diagnosis did not cure the evil. In the first half of the twelfth century Nicephorus Bryennius wrote his ὕλη ἱστορίας and his unfinished work was completed by his widow Anna Comnena in her *Alexias*. Nicephorus announces in so many words that he is going to record the πράξεις of Alexios I Comnenos (1081–1118). His work, in his own view is neither history nor encomium, it is nothing but a starting point for future authors, and therefore called modestly ὕλη ἱστορίας.[1] In reality, it is the beginning of a biography, starting out with the ancestry and discussing at length the career of Alexios before he came to the throne.

When Nicephorus died,[2] Anna used his unfinished work as a model for the *Alexias*.[3] Though again and again Anna poses as a historian, she is writing the πράξεις of an Emperor,[4] not the history of the Empire. It must be admitted that her work with its many digressions often exceeds the limits of biography proper; but it will be shown below that there was a tendency in biographical writing to assume a historical character.

A further survey of Byzantine literature would only add to the material. The data which I have adduced will suffice to prove that there existed at Byzantium, at least from the tenth century on, a considerable mass of encomiastic secular biography which has hitherto been erroneously classified as historical literature.

II

What brought about this revival of secular biography? To answer this question we shall examine more closely the earliest complete specimen, i.e., the *Vita Basilii*, written by Constantine VII Porphyrogenitus — in the hope that this study will lift the veil which hangs over the early history of this revival.

The first clue is offered by the plan of the work.[5] Its characteristic features are: (1) the πράξεις of Basil (28–101) are preceded by a venomous invective against his predecessor, (2) the account of the πράξεις is divided, and subdivided, according to the various spheres of life (civil administration, campaigns, private life), not according to the virtues which the πράξεις illustrate, (3) the account of the πράξεις is historical rather than biographical, in particular in the elaborate account of Basil's campaigns and building activities.

This structure is much too elaborate to be accidental. We may then assume

---

[1] *Nic. Bryenn.*, ed. A. Meineke, *C.S.H.B.*, xxv (Bonn, 1836), *praef.*, pp. 16 sq.

[2] Not before 1137 A.D., cf. G. Buckler, *Anna Comnena, A Study* (London, 1929), p. 34.

[3] Buckler, *Anna*, p. 230.

[4] Anna Comnena, *Alexias*, ed. A. Reifferscheid (Leipzig, 1884), *praef.*, *passim*. Miss Buckler does not discuss, *ex professo*, the literary form of the *Alexias*; in one place, however (p. 11), she calls it a 'Life of Alexius Comnenus.'

[5] It seems advisable to submit an analysis to the reader (the numerals refer to the chapters of the Bonn edition): Preface (1). Ancestry (2–4). Youth (5–8). Career down to co-emperorship (9–19). Digression on the evil conduct of Michel III (20–27). Basil's financial policy (28–30). Judicial reforms (31). Church affairs (32). Legal reforms (33). Rebellion, with an appendix on Basil's children as the safeguards for the dynastic succession (34–35). Basil's military exploits. Reforms in the army (36). Campaigns in the East (36–51). Campaigns in the West (52–71). Private Life. Literary interests and care for his people (72). Digression on Basil's benefactors (73–77). Building activities (78–94). Missionary work (95–97). Death of eldest son (98). Interest in the prosperity of the rural population (99). Estrangement between Basil and his son Leo (100–101). Death and successor (102).

that Constantine followed an established literary plan. The only work in Greek showing a similar plan *in nuce* is a Panegyric delivered by Procopius of Gaza in honor of the Emperor Anastasius I (491–518 A.D.) probably not much after 501 A.D.[1] The work is much shorter, but (1) the adventures of Anastasius are preceded by a description *in nuce* of the woeful conditions before he became Emperor, and (2) they are divided into military achievements, deeds of peace, and private affairs.[2] There is no specific evidence that Constantine knew, or used, Procopius' *Panegyric*.[3] But the similarity in structure will enable us to define more closely the nature of Constantine's work.

It is known[4] that Procopius' Panegyric is built in accordance with a classical type of rhetorical scheme, described by Menander the Rhetor(third century A.D.?) under the title of βασιλικὸς λόγος or 'imperial oration,'[5] but certainly as old as the age of Vergil and probably much older.[6] Now Constantine's work likewise agrees with the βασιλικὸς λόγος in a good many respects. The most important is that, strictly in accordance with Menander's precepts (p. 99, sect. 19), the πράξεις are divided into those of peace and those of war. Menander even provides for a comparison of the deeds of the hero with those of his predecessor (p. 104, sect. 36).[7]

It must be admitted, however, that serious divergences exist between the βασιλικὸς λόγος as described by Menander, and the *Vita Basilii*: (1) The deeds of war, according to Menander (p. 100, sect. 19) should precede those of peace. With Constantine, the deeds of war follow those of peace. To meet this objection, it

---

[1] Critical edition, with introduction and commentary, by C. Kempen, *Procopii Gazaei In Imperatorem Anastasium Panegyricus* (Diss. Bonn, 1918).

[2] An analysis of the plan will be found in Kempen, *Paneg.*, pp. xii–xiv. It should be compared with the plan of the *Vita Basilii*, as given above, p. 197, note 5. For (1) see ch. 5 (p. 4, 14): ἄμεινον δὲ τῶν προλαβόντων μικρὰ ⟨πρῶτον⟩ ὑμᾶς ἀναμνῆσαι καὶ δεῖξαι, πῶς ποτε τούτων ἐχόντων εἰς ὅσην ἡμῖν ἀφῖκται μεταβολήν etc. — The historical character of the πράξεις, so characteristic in Constantine's work does not appear in Procopius. Furthermore the deeds of war, with Procopius, precede those of peace; with Constantine, they follow them. On these divergences see below, pp. 198–200.

[3] The School of Gaza had, however, a considerable influence on subsequent Byzantine literature, Krumbacher, *Geschichte*, p. 454, and K. Seitz, *Die Schule von Gaza. Eine literaturgeschichtliche Untersuchung* (Diss. Heidelberg, Heidelberg, 1892), see the review of J. Draeseke, *Byzantinische Zeitschrift*, II (1893), 334–336. Add that Timotheos of Gaza's zoological work was copiously used by the poet George the Pisidian, and excerpted by — Constantine Porphyrogenitus, cf. M. Wellmann 'Timotheos von Gaza,' *Hermes*, LXII (1927), 179–204.   [4] Kempen, *Paneg.*, pp. xiv–xxii.

[5] On Menander the Rhetor see H. Radermacher, 'Menander (16),' *RE*, XXIX, 762–764. Edition by C. Bursian, 'Der Rhetor Menandros und seine Schriften,' *Abhandlungen der Philosophisch-Philologischen Klasse der Kgl. Bayerischen Akademie der Wissenschaften*, XVI (1882), No. 3. For the βασιλικὸς λόγος see pp. 95–105.

[6] E. Norden, 'Ein Panegyricus auf Augustus in Vergils Aeneis,' *Rheinisches Museum für Philologie*, LIV (1899), 466–482.

[7] Apart from these agreements in structure, there are a good many parallels: portent (σύμβολον) Menander p. 98, sect. 13 (at the birth)∽Constantine pp. 218 sq. (in early youth); dream of Cyrus' mother, Menander p. 98, sect. 13∽Constantine p. 222, l. 3; Achilles brought up by Cheiron, Menander p. 98, sect. 15∽Constantine p. 220, l. 4; capable lieutenants sent out by the Emperor, Menander p. 102, sect. 30∽Constantine p. 257, l. 20; fiscal policy Menander p. 103, sect. 30∽Constantine p. 260; legal policy, Menander p. 103, sect. 31∽Constantine p. 262, l. 16 ff.; general improvement of morale, Menander p. 103, sect. 32∽Constantine p. 315, ll. 10 ff.

suffices to point out that Vergil, *Aeneid* VI, 791–805,[1] Themistius in his orations,[2] and an anonymous encomium on Julian[3] follow the same arrangement. (2) Menander recommends subdividing the deeds of peace according to the three cardinal virtues of justice, temperance, and prudence (p. 100, sect. 20). Constantine's subdivision, however, takes account of the customary branches of governmental activity (financial, judicial, ecclesiastical, legal affairs). To this objection we can reply, first of all, that Menander's tortuous explanations, and in particular the hypothetical consideration that even deeds of war can fall under the heading 'prudence' (p. 100, sect. 21) make it probable that he is attempting to refute a rival type of βασιλικὸς λόγος. Furthermore, neither Tacitus' *Agricola*, nor Eusebius' *Vita Constantini*, nor Procopius' *Panegyric* follow the precept given by Menander:[4] the former two follow a chronological plan while Procopius of Gaza agrees with Constantine Porphyrogenitus in subdividing the deeds of peace according to the normal distinctions of statesmanship. (3) We saw that Constantine, before discussing the deeds of Basil, inserts a violent invective against Michael III, and we noted that the account of the πράξεις is historical rather than biographical. Menander provides for a 'polite' discussion of the reign of the predecessors,[5] but in a different place in his schema; and there is no indication in Menander that the account should, or may, be historical. Both these features are to be found, however, in Tacitus' *Agricola*.[6] The former point alone seems to occur in the anonymous encomium on Julian exactly at the place where Tacitus and Constantine insert it.[7]

Divergences therefore occur in the *Vita Basilii* from the type of βασιλικὸς λόγος as described by Menander, but in spite of them all we were able to refer to other works which are known to be βασιλικοὶ λόγοι and yet show these same deviations. We conclude, therefore, that there existed one, or several, rival types of βασιλικὸς

[1] E. Norden, *loc. cit.*, p. 467.   [2] W. Stegemann, 'Themistios,' *RE* A X, col. 1672.

[3] H. Gerstinger, 'Griechische Literarische Papyri I,' *Mitteilungen aus der Papyrussammlung der Nationalbibliothek in Wien* (*Papyrus Erzherzog Rainer*) (Vienna, 1932), no. IV. Cf. the review by A. Körte, *Archiv für Papyrusforschung*, XI (1935), 270–271 and *Mitteilungen etc.*, III (Vienna, 1939), 94.

[4] A. Gudeman claimed, and still claims — *Tacitus, De Vita Agricolae and Germania* (rev. ed., Boston, New York, Chicago, 1928), pp. 311–322 — that the *Agricola* follows, more or less closely, the plan of the βασιλικὸς λόγος. F. Leo, *Griech.-Röm. Biogr.*, p. 228 objected that Tacitus does not arrange the deeds according to virtues, and his objection has led most scholars to reject Gudeman's view, cf. H. Furneaux and H. G. C. Anderson, *Cornelii Taciti De Vita Agricolae* (Oxford, 1922), pp. xxiv–xxviii. See, however, below p. 200, note 1. On Eusebius' *Vita Constantini* as βασιλικὸς λόγος see the edition of J. Heikel in *Die griechischen christlichen Schriftsteller der ersten drei Jahrhunderte*, VII (1902), pp. xlvi–xlix.

[5] p. 104 sect. 36: ἥξεις δὲ ἐπὶ τὴν τελειοτάτην σύγκρισιν ἀντεξετάζων τὴν αὐτοῦ βασιλείαν πρὸς τὰς πρὸ αὐτοῦ βασιλείας, οὐ καθαιρῶν ἐκείνας — ἄτεχνον γάρ — ἀλλὰ θαυμάζων μὲν ἐκείνας, τὸ δὲ τέλειον ἀποδιδοὺς τῇ παρούσῃ.

[6] See the summary in the edition of Furneaux and Anderson. Before discussing Agricola's achievements in Britain, Tacitus inserts his famous chapters on the ethnology and geography of Britain (chs. 10–12) and follows them by an account of Agricola's predecessors (chs. 13–17). Furthermore, the account of the πράξεις is history, not biography, F. Leo, *Griech-Röm. Biogr.*, p. 231.

[7] P. 3: ⁵πρῶτον μὲν ο[ὖν? τῶν ἄλλω]ν ἁπάντων ⁶κέρδος τῆς [μον]α[ρ]χίας τὴν ⁷τρυφὴν ἡγουμένων καὶ ὥσπερ νό — ⁸μου τινὸς παραδεδωκότος τὸ τὰς ⁹τούτων ἡδονὰς παντοίαις μηχα — ¹⁰ναῖς θεραπεύεσθαι μό[ν]ος κατα — ¹¹λύσας τὸν νόμον καὶ ἐν [μικρο]ῖς καὶ ἐν μείζοσι [etc.

λόγος and that Constantine Porphyrogenitus, consciously or unconsciously, availed himself of one of them.[1]

III

How was this ancient schema handed down to the tenth century A.D.? Why was it that, after four centuries of sterility in the field of biographical literature, this rich crop grew up, and among it some of the masterpieces of Byzantine literature? In order to answer these questions, we must turn to a different set of observations.

The careful reader of the biographical framework of the *Vita Basilii* will notice that the rhetoric of these sections shows a striking similarity to that of current hagiography.[2] To begin with, a few generalities: πρόνοια, Providence, bulks large in the career of the hero both with Constantine and in hagiography.[3] The pun on the name of the hero is found in both.[4] The four cardinal virtues — temperance, manliness, prudence, and justice — are mentioned in nearly all the Saints' Lives of the eighth and ninth centuries.[5] Homoeoteleuta occur frequently.[6] Be-

---

[1] A consideration of the facts set forth in notes 4 and 6 on p. 199 leads us to reaffirm the theory of Gudeman as far as the *Agricola* is concerned. If works so far apart in time as Tactus *Agricola* and Constantine's *Vita Basilii* agree in many important parts of the general plan and if two points (precedence of the deeds of peace, and discussion of the predecessor) are furthermore confirmed by the anonymous encomium on Julian and Procopius' *Panegyric* respectively, there can be no doubt that Tacitus followed a rhetorical schema, particularly with an author imbued with rhetoric as Tacitus was. — J. Cousin, 'Histoire et Rhétorique dans l'*Agricola*,' *Revue des Etudes Latines*, XIV (1936), 326–336, came to a similar result by different methods.

[2] The following remarks will appear plausible to the reader if he keeps in mind the passage of the *Vita Basilii*, translated above, p. 195, where Basil is described as studying deeply both secular biography and hagiography. — For hagiographical works, we shall refer, for older publications, to the numbers of the Bollandists' 'Bibliotheca Hagiographica Graeca,' *Subsidia Hagiographica*, VIII (2nd. ed., 1909) = *BHG*. — In hagiography, rhetoric culminated with Symeon the Metaphrast, on whom see A. Ehrhard, 'Überlieferung und Bestand der hagiographischen und homiletischen Literatur der griechischen Kirche,' *Texte und Untersuchungen*, hrsgg. von E. Klostermann und C. Schmidt, I, II (1938), 306–318, and on his rhetorical methods, H. Zilliacus, 'Zur stilistischen Umarbeitungstechnik des Symeon Metaphrastes,' *Byzantinische Zeitschrift*, XXXVIII (1938), 333–350.

[3] *Vita Basilii*, pp. 257, 15; 221, 19; 222, 24; 316, 10. — *Vita Georgii episcopi Amastridos*, ed. V. G. Vasil'evski, *Trudy* (Petrograd, 1915), III, 5, 5; 10, 9; 25, 12; 28, 2; 34, 2; 41, 7; 63, 6; 65, 3 etc. — *Vita Ignatii* (*BHG* 817, Migne) coll. 524 B, 525 B, 533 A, 564 B, 572 C. — *Vita Constantini Judaei* (ed. H. Delehaye, *AASS. Novembris*, IV), 631 A, B, E (twice), 635 D, 639 E, 640 D, E, 642 F, 643 A, 644 F, 648 C, 648 F.

[4] P. 212, 7: ὃς καὶ τῆς βασιλείας ἐπώνυμος ἦν, and 331, 21: τὰ δὲ τῶν οἴκων κάλλη, ἅπερ ὡς βασιλείων βασίλεια ἐν αὑτοῖς τοῖς βασιλείοις ὁ βασιλεὺς Βασίλειος ἀνεδείματο. *Vita Nicephori* (*BHG* 1335, de Boor) p. 142, 10: Θεοδώρῳ γὰρ 'Ευδοκία πρὸς γαμικὴν συναφείαν ὁμιλήσασα τὸν ἀληθῶς εὐδόκιμον καὶ θεοδώρητον Νικήφορον ἐβλάστησε. — The most remarkable *jeu de mots*, on the name of the Empress Irene, is found in the *Vita Theophanis*, by the Patriarch |Methodius, ed. V. Latyšev, 'Žitie Prep. Feophana Ispovednika,' *Mémoires de l'Académie des Sciences de Russie, VIIIe série, Classe Hist.-Phil.*, XIII, 4 (1918), p. 14; it extends over more than a quarto page and threatens to commence when one thinks that all is over.

[5] *Vita Basilii*, p. 220, 11; 315, 8. — *Vita Georgi episcopi Amastridos* (ed. Vasilevski) p. 23, 1; *Vita Theophanis auctore Methodio* (ed. Latyšev), pp. 17, 17 and 18, 4; *Vita Ignatii* (*BHG* 817, Migne), p. 501, C; *Vita Theophylacti archiepiscopi Nicomediae* ed. A. Vogt, 'S. Theophylacte de Nicomédie,' *Analecta Bollandiana*, L (1932), p. 74, 3; *Vita Theodori Studitae* (*BHG* 1755, Migne), col. 120 B; *Vita Eudocimi* (*BHG* 606: Chr. M. Loparev, 'Žitie sv. Evdokima,' *Bulletin de l'Institut Archéologique Russe de Constantinople*, XIII [1908]), p. 237, 7 ff.

[6] P. 213, 3: καὶ χρόνου πολλοῦ καὶ πόνου συχνοῦ, 228, 30: καὶ τοῖς κτήμασι καὶ τοῖς χρήμασι. For hagi-

sides, a good many phrases and ideas occur which are found likewise in hagiographical writings:

Constantine	Hagiography
p. 212, 9: (Constantine is going to record Basil's deeds and life), ὡς ἂν...τοῖς ἐκγόνοις ἐκείνου οἰκόθεν εἴη ἀνεστηκὼς ὁ πρὸς ἀρετήν κανών τε καὶ ἀνδρίας καὶ τὸ ἀρχέτυπον τῆς μιμήσεως.	*Vita Nicephori* (*BHG* 1335, de Boor) p. 140, 25: τὰ τῷ θεοφόρῳ βεβιωμένα ὥσπερ τινὰ κοινὸν ἀρετῆς πίνακα τοῖς φιλοκάλοις προθήσωμεν. — *Vita Gregorii Decapolitae* (*BHG* 711, ed. F. Dvornik, *La Vie de Saint Grégoire Décapolite*, Paris, 1926), p. 46, 6:ὃς...πρόκειταιπᾶσιν ἀνθρώποις στήλη βιωφελὴς καὶ σωτήριος. — *Vita Antonii Cauleae* (*BHG* 139), p. 6, 2: καθάπερ τινὰ πίνακα τὰς αὐτοῦ προθεὶς ἀρετάς.
p. 212, 20: τὸ δὲ γένος εἷλκεν ἐξ Ἀρμενίων. — p. 230, 2: καὶ αὐτὸς ἐξ Ἀρμενίων ἕλκων τὸ γένος.	*Vita Constantini Judaei* (ed. H. Delehaye *AASS Novembris*, IV) p. 629 B: τὸ δὲ γένος εἷλκεν ἐξ Ἑβραίων.
p. 220, 4: (Basil was brought up by his father), οὔτε...Χείρωνος ἐδεήθη ὡς Ἀχιλλεὺς οὔτε Λυκούργου νομοθέτου καὶ Σόλωνος.	*Vita Tarasii* (*BHG* 1698) p. 396, 8 (Tarasius' father was), τὸ δίκαιον ἀδεκάστως πᾶσιν ἐπ' ἴσης νέμων Σόλωνος καὶ Λυκούργου.
p. 224, 7: τὸν γείτονα θανάτου ὕπνον, p. 252, 6: τῷ γείτονι τοῦ θανάτου ὕπνῳ.	*Vita Gregorii Decapolitae* (*BHG* 711), p. 46, 25: ὕπνον, θανάτου γείτονα. — *Vita Constantini Judaei* (ed. Delehaye), p. 636 A: τὸν ὕπνον θανάτου γείτονα.
p. 228, 1: (Danielis is kind to Basil), ὥσπερ τινὰ σπόρον εἰς ἀγαθὴν αὐτὰ καταβαλλομένη χώραν.	*Vita Theophanis* (auctore Methodio, ed. V. Latyšev, in *Mémoires de l' Académie des Sciences de Russie, VIIIᵉ série, Classe Hist.-Phil.*, XIII, 4 (1918) =*BHG* 1788), p. 3: κατιδώμεν οὖν...τὸν ἐξ αὐτῶν γεωργὸν, ὡς κατεβάλετο ἐν τούτῳ τὰ σπέρματα. — *Vita Methodii* (*BHG* 1278, Migne), col. 1245 D: ὥσπερ καλὴ γῆ τὸν σπόρον δεξαμένη.
p. 230, 13: ἀπ' ἐκείνης δὲ τῆς ἡμέρας ἤρξατο...ἡ τοῦ Βασιλείου φήμη εἰς πᾶσαν τὴν πόλιν διαφοιτᾶν, καὶ τοῖς ἀπάντων διεφέρετο στόμασιν.	*Vita Nicephori* (*BHG* 1335, de Boor), p. 154, 19: ἐξ ἐκείνου τε γὰρ ἐν παντὶ χείλει καὶ γλώσσῃ πάσῃ Νικηφόρος πατριάρχης ἀνηγορεύετο.
p. 240, 1: ὁ Βασίλειος περιτίθεται στέφανον, χειρὶ μὲν τοῦ τότε Μιχαὴλ βασιλεύοντος, ψήφῳ δὲ καὶ κρίσει Χριστοῦ τοῦ ἀεὶ βασιλεύοντος.	*Vita Ignatii* (*BHG* 817, Migne), col. 489 C: Μιχαήλ...ψήφῳ μὲν θεοῦ, ψήφῳ δὲ τῆς συγκλήτου πάσης τὰ σκῆπτρα τῆς βασιλείας ἐγχειρίζεται; col. 497 A: χειρὶ μὲν Βασιλείου..., τούτου χειρὶ τὸ φαινό-

---

ography see V. Vasilevski and P. Nikitin, 'Skazanija o 42 amoriskich mučenikach etc.,' *Mémoires de l'Académie Impériale des Sciences de St Pétersbourg, VIIIᵉ série, Classe Hist.-Phil.*, VII, 2 (1905), p. 224. Add *Vita Theophanis* (ed. Latyšev), p. 4, 18: χρήμασι καὶ κτήμασι; pp. 7, 10; 15, 24. *Vita Ignatii* (*BHG* 817, Migne), col. 556 A: κτήμασι καὶ χρήμασιν.

Constantine	Hagiography
	μενον, αὐτουργίᾳ δὲ τοῦ παναγίου Πνεύματος τὸ νοούμενον. — *Vita Theophylacti Nicomediae* (ed. A. Vogt, *Analecta Bollandiana* L [1932]), p. 74:εἰς χειροτονίαν προεκρίθησαν, οὐ ψήφῳ κενῇ καὶ ματαίᾳ..., ἀλλὰ ψήφῳ Πατρὸς, Ὑιοῦ καὶ ἁγίου Πνεύματος.
p. 243, 13: διηγήσομαι δέ τινα ἐξ αὐτῶν, οὐ πολλά, ἵνα ἀπὸ τῶν ὀλίγων γνῶτε καὶ τὰ λοιπά.	*Vita Ignatii* (*BHG* 817, Migne), col. 560 D: Ὀλίγα δὲ ἐκ πολλῶν...ἐπιτόμως ὑπομνήσαντες. — *Vita Josephi Hymnographi* (*BHG* 944), p.13, 9: ἐκ πλειόνων ὀλίγα διαγράφω.
p. 257, 17: καὶ νύκτωρ διηγρύπνει καὶ μεθ' ἡμέραν διεσκόπει.	*Vita Nicephori* (*BHG* 1335, de Boor), p. 148, 27: νύκτωρ τε καὶ μεθ' ἡμέραν. — *Vita Iosephi Hymnographi* (*BHG* 944), p. 3, 30: νύκτωρ καὶ μεθ' ἡμέραν. — *Vita Athanasii Methonae* (*BHG* 196), p. 5: νύκτωρ τε καὶ μεθ' ἡμέραν. —Theodorus Studites, *Laudatio in Matrem Suam*, Migne, *PG* IC, col. 897 D: νύκτωρ τε καὶ μεθ' ἡμέραν.
p. 280, 5: (Constantine is going to record well-attested facts only) μάλιστα ὅτι οὐδὲ ἐκεῖνος ἔτι ζῶν τὰ πρὸς χάριν θωπευτικῶς ὑποτρέχοντα ῥήματα ἐφαίνετο προσιέμενος.	*Vita Nicephori* (*BHG* 1335,de Boor) p. 141: (It would not be loyal to record the outward circumstances of the life of a person) τοῦ μηδεμίαν περὶ ταῦτα σχολὴν ἔχειν θελήσαντος, μόνοις δὲ τοῖς τῆς εὐσεβείας σεμνολογήμασιν ἑαυτὸν ... ὡραϊσάντος. — *Martyres XLII Amorienses* (*BHG* 1213), p. 28, 7: ἡγούμενον καὶ τοπάρχην πολυανθρώπου πόλεως (sc. σε προσείπω); ἀλλὰ τοῖς ἤθεσιν ὅλως τῶν ἀνακειμένων θεῷ κατακεκόσμησαι.
p. 316, 6: καὶ οὐδὲν θαυμαστὸν τοὺς...τὴν ἐπὶ τῆς γῆς ἐξουσίαν ἀνύοντας...ὑπὸ τῆς προνοίας παραθαρρύνεσθαι καὶ πρὸς τὸ συμφέρον ἰθύνεσθαι καὶ τὰ μέλλοντα προδιδάσκεσθαι (said to explain why Basil found solutions for his worries in sleep).	*Vita Ignatii* (*BHG* 817, Migne) col. 533 C: ἀλλὰ καὶ ὑπὸ ἀγγέλων θεοῦ ἔστιν ὅτε προστάγματι σχηματίζονται, καὶ ἐπὶ τοῖς ἄρχουσι δὲ μάλιστα καὶ βασιλεῦσι, εἰ καὶ μὴ εὐσεβεῖς εἶεν (said to explain a prophetic dream of Bardas).

Apart from these agreements there is one Saint's Life with a purpose strikingly similar to that of Constantine: the *Vita Ignatii*, written by Nicetas, ὁ καὶ Δαυίδ, ὁ Παφλαγών.[1] It is unique in hagiographical literature in that it combines the praise

---

[1] Migne, *PG, CV*, coll. 487–574. The work is not easy to date. If A. A. Vasiliev, 'Vizantija i Araby. Političeskija otnošenija Vizantii i Arabov za vremja makedonskoi dinastii,' *Zapiski Istor.-Fil. Fakulteta Imp. S. Peterburgskago Universiteta*, LXVI (1902), 85, and M. Amari, *Storia dei Musulmani di Sicilia* (2nd ed., Catania, 1933), I, 563, are right in dating the vision of Musilikes (col. 564 A) in 882 A.D., this is the latest *terminus post quem*; otherwise we have to content ourselves with the year 879 A.D., the death of Basil's son Constantine (col. 573 B; cf. A. Vogt, *Basile I etc.* [Paris, 1908], p. 58). A *terminus ante quem* is the second deposition of Photius in 886 A.D., which the biographer would scarcely have passed over with silence. This *terminus ante quem*, however, is based merely on an argument from silence.

of its hero Ignatius with blame of his great opponent, Photius.[1] This double purpose is comparable to that of the *Vita Basilii*, where the ἔπαινος of the hero, Basil, is combined with the ψόγος of Michel III; only, in the *Vita Basilii* the fact that the opponent was soon removed by murder enables the author to drop the ψόγος after his account of that event.[2]

IV

How should these parallels be interpreted? *A priori*, three solutions are possible: either hagiography is under the influence of secular biography, or secular biography is under that of hagiography, or both are under the influence of a third element. The first alternative can be excluded from the outset: all the Saints' Lives, on which we have drawn for the parallels, antedate the earliest mention of biographical writing at Byzantium.

Between the two remaining alternatives, it is hard to choose. It should be remembered that, at Byzantium, all instruction in rhetoric was secular,[3] and that the *Progymnasmata* of Aphthonius and similar works were still the basis of rhetorical education in the ninth century and later.[4] The rhetoric of the Saints' Lives proceeds ultimately from secular models. But down to the ninth and tenth centuries such a vast mass of Saints' Lives and Panegyrics had accumulated that it is impossible to see how much of their rhetoric goes back directly to the secular models which were taught in the schools, to early Christian literature so far as it had assumed secular forms, or to the hagiographical material which was influenced by both.[5] Suffice it to say that secular rhetoric was preserved, at By-

---

[1] This point was emphasized by Ch. Loparev, 'Vizantiskija Žitija Svjatych VIII–IX vekov,' *Vizantiskii Vremennik*, XIX (1912), 149. The double purpose is stated at the beginning when Nicetas expresses his desire to make his readers τὸν ἐργάτην μὲν ἀληθῶς τῆς δικαιοσύνης καὶ τῆς ἀρετῆς (i.e., Ignatius) εἰδέναι, καὶ ὑμνεῖν, καὶ ζηλοῦν· τὸν αὐτουργὸν δὲ τῆς κακίας καὶ τῆς ἀδικίας (i.e. Photius) ἐνδίκως ἀνωθεῖσθαι.

[2] If the author of the *Vita Ignatii* is identical with a Nicetas ὁ φιλόσοφος who wrote an encomium on St John Chrysostom by order of the Emperor Constantine Porphyrogenitus, as K. Krumbacher and A. Ehrhard, 'Der heilige Georg in der griechischen Ueberlieferung,' *Abhandlungen der Kgl. Bayer. Akademie der Wissenschaften, Phil.-Hist. Klasse*, XXV, 3 (1911), 182, as well as P. H. Delehaye, *AASS Novembris*, IV (1925), 13, believe (the latter while identifying the two names in which we are interested leaves the question open whether they should be distinguished from Nicetas Magister, the author of the Life of Theoctiste of Lesbos), it is indeed highly probable that the imperial Maecenas had knowledge of the earlier work of his protégé. But even if the two names refer to different persons — and this is the view of A. Vogt, 'Deux discours inédits de Nicétas de Paphlagonie,' *Orientalia Christiana*, XXIII, 1 (1931), 6, approved by A. Ehrhard, 'Niketas Paphlago,' *Lexikon für Theologie und Kirche*, VII (1935), 570 — there is still a good chance that Constantine knew a work which (1) dealt with the same period as his own, (2) was used by his contemporary and literary associate Genesios, cf. F. Hirsch, *Byz. Stud.*, p. 159, and (3) bore on a controversy between two individuals who served as models for the leaders of ecclesiastic parties until far into Constantine's own period.

[3] Krumbacher, *Geschichte*, p. 452.

[4] Cf. H. Rabe, *Joannis Sardiani Commentarium in Aphthonii Progymnasmata* (Leipzig, 1928), pp. xvi–xx; O. Schissel, 'Rhetorische Progymnasmatik der Byzantiner,' *Byzantinisch-Neugriechische Jahrbücher*, XI (1934/35), 1–10.

[5] On the secular models of early hagiographical literature see the bibliography above, p. 194, note 6. — On the influence of Gregory of Nazianzus on the hagiography of the ninth century, see P. Nikitin, 'O nekotorych grečeskich tekstach žitii svjatych,' *Mémoires de l'Académie Impériale des Sciences de St Pétersbourg, VIIIe série, Classe Hist.-Phil.*, I, 1 (1895), 36–51; V. Vasilevski and P. Nikitin, 'Skazanija o 42 Amoriskich Mučenikach et.,' *ibid.*, VII, 2 (1905), 133 and *passim* (see

zantium in two forms: in the schools, where the classical topics were dealt with
over and over again; in the churches, where homiletic and hagiographical literature was heard every day from the pulpit. It needed only the fresh breath of an
enlightened age where secular achievements and virtues were again appreciated
to make rhetoric leave the classes and churches and place itself once more at the
service of secular literature.

In the ninth century, indeed, secular learning was revived at Byzantium,[1] and
this revival found its expression, as in other fields, in hagiography: many Lives
which were written during this period record, with approval or disapproval, that
the Saint was instructed in secular knowledge.[2] One of them, the *Vita Nicephori*
(†829), written by Ignatius the Deacon during the second half of the ninth
century, has a feature which seems to be unique in hagiographical literature: it
does not contain a single miracle performed by the Saint.[3] This fact, together
with a certain emphasis on secular learning, entitles us to classify the work as
'semi-secular hagiography.'[4]

The connecting link between 'semi-secular hagiography' and wholly secular
biography, between the *Vita Nicephori*, by Ignatius the Deacon, and Constantine's *Vita Basilii*, is furnished by a funeral oration delivered by the Emperor
Leo VI the Wise (886–911) in memory of Basil I and Eudocia.[5] As far as I can see,

the index v° 'Gregorius Nazianzenus'); and F. Dvornik, 'Les Légendes de Constantin et de Méthode
vues de Byzance,' *Byzantinoslavica*, Supplementa, I (Prague, 1933), 33–34.

[1] J. B. Bury, *A History of the Eastern Roman Empire from the fall of Irene to the accession of Basil I*
(London, 1912), pp. 443–449; F. Dvornik, *Les Slaves, Byzance et Rome au IX⁰ siècle* (Paris, 1926),
pp. 106–123.

[2] The hagiographical texts are discussed, from this point of view, by Dvornik, *Légendes*, pp. 19–24.

[3] *BHG* 1335 (de Boor). — On Ignatius the Deacon, see the (incomplete) résumé in F. Dvornik,
La Vie de Sainte Grégoire Le Décapolite (Paris, 1926), pp. 14–19. In the *Vita Nicephori* no *post mortem*
miracles are mentioned at all. The reason may be that the Life was written immediately after the
the death of the Saint (F. Hirsch, *Byz. Stud.*, p. 20; V. Vasilevski, *Trudy*, III, p. xcvii; Ch. Loparev,
Vizantiski Vremennik XVII, [1910], 109–110; but cf. E. von Dobschütz, 'Methodius und die Studi-
ten,' *Byzantinische Zeitschrift*, XVIII [1909], 54). Even if that were the case, and if, accordingly, there
had not been much time for *post mortem* miracles to happen, it is all the more characteristic that
Nicephorus is not credited with a single miracle *inter vivos*: a man who had made a career in the administration service did not lend himself easily to miracles. We hear only of a number of prophetic
experiences, p. 164, 8 ff.: when touching the head of Leo V the Armenian at the coronation, Nicephorus
has the impression of touching thorns, pp. 189, 31–190, 11: prophecy of an evil outcome to Euty-
chianos, p. 201, 8–29: Nicephorus predicts to Bardas a fate as pitiable as his own. Even where an
incident could easily be given a miraculous turn, not much effort is made in this direction, p. 196, 13–
30: a plot against Nicephorus' life is revealed to him by a follower. It is characteristic that the one
clear case of a miracle, which is even called thus by Ignatius (p. 205, 8: θαυματουργία), viz., the dumb-
ness which befell an Iconoclast clergyman (p. 205, 6–21) has no connection whatsoever with Nicephorus.

[4] One would like to classify furthermore under this heading the Life of one of the rare Lay Saints
of the Byzantine Church St Eudokimos (†842 A.D.) But the published lives are metaphrastic (*BHG*
607) or postmetaphrastic (*BHG* 606; cf. A. Ehrhard, *Ueberlieferung und Bestand etc.*, I, 671, n. 7) and
the date of their source is uncertain.

[5] A. Vogt and I. Hausherr, 'Oraison funèbre de Basile I par son fils Léon VI Le Sage,' *Orientalia
Christiana*, XXVI, 1 (1932). See the important reviews by H. Grégoire, *Byzantion*, VII (1932), 626–633,
and F. D(ölger), *Byzantinische Zeitschrift*, XXXII (1932), 399–400, furthermore N. Adontz, 'La Portée
historique de l'oraison funèbre de Basile I, etc.,' *Byzantion*, VIII (1933), 501–513. There has not been,
to my knowledge, any study of the literary form of the work, except for the observations made by
the editors in the preface of this work.

this is the first[1] specimen of a biographical encomium dealing with a wholly secular hero. Nevertheless its connections with hagiography are obvious. First of all, it has come down to us in a corpus of Leo's church panegyrics.[2] Secondly, as the editors observed, the orations of Gregory of Nazianzus served as models for this work, just as for many contemporary Saints' Lives.[3] Thirdly, there are a fair number of parallels between Leo's oration and hagiography, in particular with the works of Ignatius the Deacon:[4]

Leo, *Funeral Oration*	Hagiography
p. 40, 16: πᾶς λόγος ἔργου ἐλάττων.	*Vita Antonii Cauleae* (*BHG* 139), p. 2, 13: φύσει γὰρ οἱ λόγοι τῶν πραγμάτων ἐλαττοῦσθαι πεφύκασιν.
p. 40, 29: ὅσα μὲν ὁ λόγος γράφοι, ὥσπερ εἰκόνα τινὰ ἢ σκιαγραφίαν ἐμφαίνεσθαι.	*Vita Nicephori* (*BHG* 1335), p. 142, 1: τῆς ἐκ τοῦ γένους τοῦ ἀνδρὸς σκιαγραφίας...ὅλον ὑμῖν τὸν ἀνδριάντα...διαγράψωμεν.
p. 42, 27: εἰ γὰρ καὶ τῶν ἐγκωμίων νόμοι πατρίδος καὶ γένους ἐπ' ἔρευναν παραπέμπουσιν, ἀλλὰ πρός γε τὴν παροῦσαν ὑπόθεσιν οὐδὲν ἂν ἡμῖν ὁ τοιοῦτος συνεισενέγκοι νόμος.	*Vita Nicephori* (*BHG* 1335), p. 141, 22: τὸ μὲν δὴ γένος καὶ περιφανείαν βίου, πατρίδα τε καὶ περιουσίαν, καὶ οἷς οἱ τῶν ἔξωθεν νόμοι ποιεῖσθαι τοὺς λόγους ὁρίζουσι, θαυμάζειν τε καὶ καθιστορεῖν ...οὐκ εὐαγὲς οὐδὲ ὅσιον οἶμαι.
p. 48, 14: (It would not be fit to praise Basil's beauty), ἐπεὶ μηδ' ἐκεῖνος... τούτοις ἐκαλλωπίσατο, ἀλλ' ἐνὶ μόνῳ τῷ τῆς ψυχῆς ἐσεμνύνετο κάλλει.	*Vita Nicephori* (*BHG* 1335), p. 141, 22: (It would not be fit to insist on the descent of a man) τοῦ μηδεμίαν περὶ ταῦτα σχολὴν ἔχειν θελήσαντος, μόνοις δὲ τοῖς τῆς εὐσεβείας σεμνολογήμασιν ἑαυτὸν... ὡραΐσαντος.
p. 50, 8: 'Αλλ' οἷόν με μικροῦ παρῆλθεν τῆς μνήμης διεκπεσόν κτλ.	*Vita Tarasii* (*BHG* 1698), p. 407, 1: Ὁ δέ με μικροῦ παρέδραμε καὶ τὴν μνήμην διαφυγὸν ἀνέκφορον ἔμελλε μένειν.

[1] A possible precursor is the Life of the Empress Theodora (*BHG* 1731) written during the reign of Basil i.

[2] A. Ehrhard, *Überlieferung und Bestand etc.*, ii, 230.

[3] For the influence of Gregory of Nazianzus on Leo, see pp. 24–30 of the editors' preface. Add Adontz, *loc. cit.*, p. 507. For hagiography see above, p. 203, note 5. It is interesting that both Ignatius the Deacon, in the *Vita Nicephori* (=*BHG* 1335, de Boor), pp. 141, 33 sq., and Leo, p. 44, 20 quote from the first strophe of Pindar, *Olymp.*, vi, from which Gregory of Nazianzus had quoted in the Funeral Oration on Basil the Great (=*BHG* 245, Boulenger), p. 100. — The plan of the oration is not rigorous and defies the attempt of a precise analysis. Yet it may be helpful to give at least the contours of this plan: Preface (pp. 38–42, 22). Descent (42, 22–46, 9). Mode of life (46, 9–21). Description (46, 22–48, 33). Career and portens (50, 16–28). Matrimony (52, 11–54, 12). Basil becomes Emperor (54, 26–56, 15). Wars (56, 16–28). Civil administration (56, 29–58, 30). Justice etc. (60, 1–23). Praise of Basil (60, 24–62, 5). Church Affairs (62, 6–64, 26). Death and θρῆνος (64, 26 to end).

[4] No inferences should be drawn, for the time being, from the fact that all the parallels antedating Leo are taken from the works of Ignatius the Deacon. The question whether this is a coincidence resulting from the particular direction of my reading in hagiography, or whether there are more specific relations between Ignatius the Deacon and Leo the Wise has to be reserved for further study. For the present purpose, it will be sufficient to point out the connections between Leo and hagiography in general.

Leo, *Funeral Oration*

p. 56, 7: ἀνεικάστοις κρίμασιν.

p. 60, 24: Ἔστι γὰρ δῆγε, ἔστι πρὸς εὐφημίαν ἀμύθητος ἡ εὐπορία.

p. 66, 29: Ἀλλὰ τί γέγονεν; εἰς μονῳδίαν ἡ εὐφημία μετέβαλεν κτλ.

Hagiography

Vita Nicephori (*BHG* 1335), p. 187, 12: κρίμασιν οἷς ἀγνοοῦμεν.

Vita Tarasii (*BHG* 1698), p. 411, 22: οὐκ ἔστι ταῦτα, οὐκ ἔστι.— See V. V. Vasilevski and P. Nikitin, 'Skazanija o 42 Amoriskich Mučenikach etc.,' *Mémoires de l'Académie Impériale des Sciences de St. Pétersbourg, VIII⁰ série, Class. Hist.-Phil.*, vii, 2 (1905), pp. 143–146.

Vita Nicephori (*BHG* 1335, de Boor), p. 139, 12: (ὁ λόγος), οἷα ναρκήσας εἰς εὐφημίαν τὴν γλῶτταν καθεῖναι, τὴν μονῳδίαν προείλετο.

Thus the rhetorical clichés as used by Leo are similar to those found in hagiographical writings.[1] Leo's work marks a further step in the direction of secular biography and may be classified as 'semi-secular biography.' In order to prove that Leo's work forms the connecting link between hagiography and secular biography, it will be necessary to show now that Leo's son, Constantine, depended on the earlier writing of his father, so far as the literary form is concerned. This thesis, plausible itself, can be confirmed by a comparison of the two works.[2] First of all the structure of Leo's speech, though being much less precise, resembles that of the *Vita Basilii*. Leo's account of the πράξεις is divided into those of war and those of peace; even the subdivision into Eastern and Western campaigns is mentioned (p. 56, l. 22). Most of the deeds of peace are mentioned by categories only (p. 62, 3), but Basil's ecclesiastical policy is discussed in detail (p. 63), much in the same way as in the *Vita Basilii*. Second, the two works agree in a number of details:

[1] Professor R. P. Blake kindly called my attention to, and gave me his unpublished notes on *Ms. Patm.* 254, containing the menologium for April. A description will be found in Ehrhard, *Ueberlieferung und Bestand etc.*, i, 611–614. Both Professor Blake and P. P. Peeters, 'Une Vie Grecque du Pape S. Martin i,' *Analecta Bollandiana*, li (1933), 226 would assign the Ms. to the tenth century, whereas Ehrhard dates it from the eleventh century. There is one text for each day and 18 of the 30 texts seem to be unpublished. The incipits as noted by Professor Blake show definitely the influence of rhetoric. For further information, we shall have to wait for the *étude d'ensemble* announced by P. Peeters.

[2] Where Leo and Constantine both record the same events — these cases have been discussed, from an *historical* point of view, by Adontz, *loc. cit.*, pp. 501–502 — the *literary* filiation between the two can be shown only if the two agree not only in general thought, but also in stylistic detail; for the mere facts, as circularized by pro-Macedonian propaganda, can proceed from any source, unless there is stylistic evidence that they are taken over from Leo. It is interesting to note how much more secure the Macedonian dynasty felt on the throne under Constantine than under Leo: Leo denies emphatically that Basil was privy to the murder of Michel iii (p. 56, l. 1: οὐ βιασάμενοι οὐδὲ ἅρπαγμα τὴν ἀρχὴν ποιησάμενοι, ἀλλ᾽ ἄκοντες ἐπὶ τοῦτο καταστάντες), whereas Constantine admits it by implication, for he tries to justify the murderers.

Constantine, *Vita Basilii*	Leo, *Funeral Oration*
p. 212, 20: τὸ δὲ γένος εἷλκεν ἐξ 'Αρμενίων.	p. 44, 27: ἕλκουσι γὰρ τοῦ αἵματος τὰς πηγὰς ἐκ τῶν 'Αρταξέρξου ναμάτων.
p. 219, 6: νομισθῶμεν ἴσως ἀπορίᾳ τῶν περὶ αὐτὸν καλῶν ἐν τούτοις (i.e., the portents that predicted Basil's coming to the throne) τὴν ἱστορίαν ἀπασχολεῖν.	p. 42, 29: οἷς ἄπορον ἐκ τῶν οἰκείων σεμνύνεσθαι, ἐκείνοις τὰ ἐκ τοῦ γένους ἀνάγκη συλλέγειν.
p. 223, 11: τῷ τοῦ ἁγίου μάρτυρος Διομήδους προσπελάζει μοναστηρίῳ καὶ ἀπὸ τῆς ὁδοιπορίας κατάκοπος ὢν αὐτοῦ που πρὸ τοῦ πυλῶνος ἐν τοῖς ἐκεῖσε βάθροις ἀτημελῶς οὕτως ἐπιρρίψας ἑαυτὸν ἀνεπαύετο.	p. 50, 26: δόξαν δὲ ἐν ἱερῷ οἴκῳ (ἦν δ'ἄρα τοῦ τῆς ἀληθείας ὑπασπίστου Διομήδους), ὡς εἶχεν, ἐπ' ἐδάφους ἐκλίθη.
p. 230, 13: ἤρξατο...ἡ τοῦ Βασιλείου φήμη εἰς πᾶσαν τὴν πόλιν διαφοιτᾶν, καὶ τοῖς ἁπάντων διεφέρετο στόμασιν.	p. 54, 18: ἡ...δόξα τρανῶς διὰ παντὸς ἐχώρει στόματος.
p. 240, 1: ὁ Βασίλειος περιτίθεται στέφανον, χειρὶ μὲν τοῦ τότε Μιχαὴλ βασιλεύοντος, ψήφῳ δὲ καὶ κρίσει χριστοῦ τοῦ ἀεὶ βασιλεύοντος.	p. 56, 3: πλὴν δίδωσι μέν, ὡς ἐδόκει, τοῦ τότε καιροῦ κρατοῦντος ἡ χεὶρ τὸ διάδημα· ἐδίδου δὲ αὐτὸ ἡ ἄνωθεν δεξία.
p. 257, 17: καὶ νύκτωρ...καὶ μεθ' ἡμέραν.	p. 52, 9: καὶ νύκτωρ καὶ μεθ' ἡμέραν.
p. 264, 15: τὸν δὲ τούτων νεώτατον Στέφανον, ὡς τὸν 'Ισαὰκ ὁ 'Αβραάμ, προσάγει θεῷ καὶ τῇ τοῦ θεοῦ ἐκκλησίᾳ ἐγκαταλέγει καὶ ἀφιεροῖ.	p. 64, 8: μιμεῖται τὸν πατριάρχην, πατριάρχην ἐκεῖνον ὃς ὁλοκάρπωσιν φέρει τὸν παῖδα Θεῷ..., καὶ τὸν παῖδα δωρεῖται τῇ ἐκκλησίᾳ.
p. 280, 6: οὐδὲ ἐκεῖνος ἔτι ζῶν τὰ πρὸς χάριν θωπευτικῶς ὑποτρέχοντα ῥήματα ἐφαίνετο προσιέμενος.	p. 38, 18: οὔτε τὸ πρὸς χάριν ἐκείνοις (i.e. Basil and Eudocia) εὑρίσκει χώραν, μάλιστα μὲν γὰρ ὅτι οὐδὲ περιοῦσιν τῷ βίῳ τοῦτο ἀγαπητὸν ἦν.
p. 280, 7: μηδὲ τὰ παρὰ πάντων ὁμολογούμενα δυνάμενοι ἢ σχολάζοντες παραδοῦναι γραφῇ.	p. 40, 2: ἃ δ'ἡμῖν εἰς γνῶσιν κατέστη, οὐδὲ ταῦτα ἀκριβῶς διεξιέναι σχολή.
p. 315, 10: καὶ ἐδόκει αὖθις ὁ βίος ἐπὶ τῆς ἀρχαίας γενέσθαι εὐταξίας καὶ καταστάσεως, κτλ. — See also p. 258.	p. 58, 27: ἃ ποτέ φασι χρυσᾶ ἔτη ἡ παλαιότης ἀνατεῖλαι, εἰς ταῦτα δοκεῖν αὐτὴν (sc. τὴν πολιτείαν) καταστῆναι.

Constantine, then, knew and used the work of his father.[1]

The subsequent history of secular biography at Byzantium follows the example set by Constantine Porphyrogenitus. Its peculiar characteristic is the elaborate and historical account of the πράξεις;[2] in the case of the *Alexias*, it all but bursts

---

[1] The fact that he does not quote it favors a conjecture of H. Grégoire, *loc. cit.*, p. 627, viz., that Leo's speech disappeared from most *corpora* of his works because of its allusions to the ecclesiastical schism.

[2] This feature is comparable to the history of description of works of art (ἐκφράσεις); being short interludes in official panegyrics in the beginning, they gradually grew in extent and precision and came to be the central part of the panegyric, P. Friedländer, *Johannes von Gaza und Paulus Silentiarius etc.* (Leipzig and Berlin, 1912), pp. 95–102.

the biographical frame which contains it. It was probably the historical character of this part of Byzantine biographies which misled Krumbacher to classify them as historical literature.

V

The preceding observations have shown that: (1) Constantine availed himself of a classical plan which was roughly a millennium old, (2) the hagiography of the ninth century, shows a tendency to assume an increasingly secular guise, and (3) Constantine used either the rhetoric of hagiography or that of its models, or both.[1]

Whether Constantine was influenced by what he had learnt in school, or by what he had heard in Church, or by both — the important thing is that now, for the first time, rhetoric and biographical form were applied once more to secular topics.

'No branch of literature has been more sensitive than biography to the "spirit of the age,"' says Sir Harold Nicolson.[2] The appreciation of secular ἀρετή had gradually faded when Christianity had become the State religion, and this appreciation slowly began to reappear from the ninth century on. Thus biography, as the type of literature which shows most faithfully the fluctuations of ethical concepts, had died a lingering death and was now witnessing a slow revival. It was helped by the ancient concept of the priestly character of kingship which reappears in the funeral oration of Leo the Wise. In connection with the heavenly rewards which he claims for his father (p. 74, 15) he says: 'If it is true that the *charisma* of kingship is not far removed from that of priesthood, why should it be given less than those (i.e., the priests)?' At the age of Constantine, the *charisma* had descended upon all the officers of the court, and they had all become potential heroes of biographical writing.

This development had a close parallel in the West. There the first specimen of secular biography was a product of the Carolingian renaissance, the *Life of Charlemagne*, written by Einhard, probably somewhat before 830–836 A.D.[3] Like Constantine Porphyrogenitus, he too used a classical model, Suetonius,[4] and the preface of his work at least is influenced strongly by a hagiographical work, the *Life of St Martin of Tours* by Sulpicius Severus.[5] Like Constantine's *Vita Basilii*, Einhard's biography was preceded by a piece of 'semi-secular hagiography,' i.e., a Saint's Life without miracles,[6] the *Life of Boniface* by Willibald.[7] Einhard's

---

[1] The assertion that Constantine used the work of his predecessors detracts in no way from his literary merits. If he borrowed the framework and the rhetoric — all the details, and in particular the central part of the book, the account of the πράξεις are his. The *Vita Basilii* is, in the writer's eyes, an extraordinary piece of literature, and it is precisely that blend of old and new which makes the fascination of Byzantine culture.

[2] H. Nicolson, *The Development of English Biography* (New York, 1928), p. 135.

[3] L. Halphen, *Eginhard. Vie de Charlemagne* (Paris, 1923), p. viii.   [4] *Ibid.*, pp. x–xi.

[5] M. Manitius, 'Zu Einharts Vita Karoli,' *Neues Archiv der Gesellschaft für ältere deutsche Geschichtskunde*, XII (1887), 205–206.

[6] M. Manitius, *Geschichte der lateinischen Literatur des Mittelalters*, I (München, 1911), in I. von Müllers Handbuch der klassischen Altertumswissenschaft, pp. 637 f.

[7] See the edition by W. Levison, *Vitae Sancti Bonifatii Archiepiscopi Moguntini* (Hannover and

Life of Charlemagne, in its turn, acted as godfather to the earliest secular biography on British soil, Asser's *Life of King Alfred*,[1] written 'at least as early as the first half of the tenth century.'[2]

At Byzantium, John Scylitzes had complained that praise and blame had ruined historical composition. Similar complaints had been raised by Polybius,[3] during the Hellenistic period, and by Lucian[4] in Roman times. Perhaps we need not take these complaints too seriously. The new type of literature itself appears to have been used exclusively in court circles and was earmarked so clearly as being *Tendenzliteratur* that it never deceived anybody. More harm was done when praise and blame penetrated into the field of history. Here, too, the tendency is usually obvious; but the intrusion cost us many of those impartial and objective descriptions which had contributed to the glory of classical literature.[5] It is this new element which, in the eyes of the writer, constitutes the fundamental difference between Byzantine historians before the Dark Ages and those thereafter.

HARVARD UNIVERSITY.

Leipzig, 1905), and the English translation by G. W. Robinson, *The Life of Saint Boniface by Willibald* (Cambridge, Mass., 1916).

[1] W. H. Stevenson, *Asser's Life of King Alfred* (Oxford, 1904), pp. lxxxi f.   [2] *Ibid.*, p. cxxvi.

[3] The passages are collected and discussed by Leo, *Griech.-Röm. Biogr.*, pp. 242–251. Cf. also P. Scheller, *De hellenistica historiae conscribendae arte* (Diss. Leipzig, 1911), pp. 48–56.

[4] Lucian, *De Historia Conscribenda*, 7, 38, 59, and *passim*.

[5] On many questions of literary criticism touched upon in this paper, it will be found both useful and stimulating to consult A. Maurois, *Aspects de la biographie* (Paris, 1928). On the distinctions between history and biography in particular, pp. 96–102.

ADDITIONAL BIBLIOGRAPHY

Romilly J.H. Jenkins,"The Classical Background of the Scriptores post Theophanem",Dumbarton Oaks Papers 8, 1954,11–30 (reproduced in his Studies on Byzantine History of the 9th and 10th Centuries", Variorum Reprints, London, 1970);Paul Lemerle, Le Premier Humanisme byzantin. Notes et remarques sur enseignement et culture à Byzance des origines au Xe siècle,Paris,1971,esp.268–300 (cf.my review Speculum 48,1973,770–776). To judge from the list of P.Paul Peeters'writings published in Analecta Bollandiana 59, 1951,pp.xlviii–lix,his study of cod. Patm. 254 (see 206n.1 above)never appeared.

II

THE PAPACY, THE BAVARIAN CLERGY, AND THE SLAVONIC APOSTLES*

In 1934 the bibliography of Constantine (Cyril) and Methodius filled a good sized volume of more than three hundred pages and comprised more than three thousand items,[1] and by now several important publications may be added to this list.[2] This interest in the activity of the Slavonic Apostles is not surprising inasmuch as Slavic religion and culture is due to a large extent to these two *praeceptores Slavoniae*: they meant for the Slavic world what Ulfilas and St Boniface combined meant for the Germanic. Nor can it be said that no further additions to the bibliography are to be expected and that all the problems raised by the story of Constantine and Methodius have been solved: it touches upon nearly all the aspects of medieval history and may be looked at with profit from various points of view.

During the last years or decades the chief interest has centered in a criticism of our sources, especially of the *Pannonian Legends*.[3] May we believe, so most scholars asked themselves, the information contained in our sources? The farther they probed into the laconic, often puzzling statements of the *Legends*, the more they realized that apart from certain peculiarities of emphasis and presentation required by the edifying purpose of these writings the *Legends* preserved a tradition of historical reality.[4]

* The writer wishes to thank Professor S. H. Cross in whose seminary on Old Slavonic the first draft of this paper was written and who encouraged the author to prepare it for publication. Professor R. P. Blake kindly read the manuscript and made a great number of valuable suggestions.

[1] G. A. Ilinski, *Opyt sistematičeskoi Kirillo-Mefodjevskoi bibliografii* (Sofia, 1934).

[2] The most important is that of F. Dvorník, *Les Légendes de Constantin et de Méthode vues de Byzance*, Byzantinoslavica, Supplementa, I (Prague, 1933); see the (unfavorable) review of A. Brückner, "Cyrill und Method," *Zeitschrift für osteuropäische Geschichte*, N. F., v (1935) 184–199. In a careful study P. Duthilleul, "Les sources de l' histoire des saints Cyrille et Méthode," *Echos d' Orient*, XXXIV (1935), 272–306 criticized the sources, especially the papal letters, and H. Schaeder, "Geschichte und Legende im Werk der Slavenmissionare Konstantin und Method," *Historische Zeitschrift*, CLII (1935), 229–255 emphasized the legendary or allegorical elements in some of our Slavic sources. P. Lavrov, "Materialy po istorii vozniknovenija drevneišei slavjanskoi pismennosti," *Trudy slavj. komissii*, I, Akad. Nauk SSSR (Leningrad, 1930), was not available to the writer. See also H. Weidhaas, "Methodius und die Mährer," *Jahrbücher für Geschichte Osteuropas*, II (1937), 183–200.

[3] They are used in the edition and translation of F. Pastrnek, *Dějiny slovanských apoštolů Cyrilla a Methoda* etc. (Prague, 1902); I can use only the sources printed in this book as I do not read Czech. French translation by Dvorník, *Légendes*, pp. 349–393.

[4] Dvorník's book centers around the reliability of the *Pannonian Legends*, whereas Duthilleul's important contribution is particularly instructive on the Latin side. The present writer cannot help feeling that (*pace* Brückner) Dvorník has succeeded in vindicat-

It may be expected that this "critical" method will continue to be followed by specialists and will yield further results. In the mean time we should not lose sight of the fact that the historicity of certain episodes of the story cannot be, and has never been, questioned. Those are incidents in which the *Pannonian Legends* (and sources dependent upon them) agree with Western sources. As there is not the slightest suspicion that these Western sources (papal letters, Frankish annals, etc.) depend on the Slavonic *Lives*, these facts are as well established as many others in medieval history, and even better than some. They require interpretation, not criticism, and in this field the student of the Slavonic Apostles may expect results as important as from the criticism of sources.

A series of such unquestionable (and unquestioned) facts may be educed if we investigate the data furnished by our Slavic and Western sources on the relations of Constantine and Methodius with the Popes. Here we shall not attempt to recount the course of the Moravian mission in any detail,[5] and in order to avoid complications we shall make it a point to use only such details from the *Pannonian Legends* as are borne out by independent sources.

The two brothers were natives of Thessalonica[6] and both had been closely connected with Photius before and after he became Patriarch.[7] The older, Constantine, was, for a while, librarian (*vivliotikar'*) of the Patriarch Ignatius, but it looks as if he had been forced upon Ignatius

---

ing the historicity of the *Pannonian Legends* and that these remarkable documents, so full of historical information for many sections of the medieval world, are easily among the best hagiographical writings. In fact one need only read the sixth and seventh volume in the *Epistolae* series of the *Monumenta Germaniae Historica* (henceforth abbreviated *Epistolae* VI and VII) to realize the excellence of the *Pannonian Legends*. This impression does not preclude (it even requires) a literary analysis of the *Legends* such as outlined by Miss Schaeder.

[5] Short resumés of the Pannonian and Moravian missions may be found in almost any general history of the Carolingian Period or of the Church in this period. Of them I have used particularly Hans von Schubert, *Geschichte der christlichen Kirche im Frühmittelalter* (Tübingen, 1921), and E. Amann, *L'Epoque Carolingienne*, in A. Fliche, and V. Martin, *Histoire de l'Eglise, etc.*, VI, 1937. — For the following narrative I shall use only those Western documents, especially papal letters, the authenticity of which has never been questioned. This does not imply that I consider other documents spurious.

[6] *V(ita) C(onstantini)*, ed. Pastrnek, ch. 2, p. 155; *V(ita) M(ethodii)*, ch. 2, p. 223; *Anastasii Bibliothecarii Epistolae sive Praefationes*, recc. E. Perels et G. Laehr, *Epistolae* VII, no. 15, p. 436 (A.D. 875): Constantinus Thesalonicenus philosophus.

[7] *V. C.*, ch. 4, p. 160· "Et didicit . . . apud Leonem et apud Photium dialecticam et omnes philosophicas disciplinas etc."; *V. M.*, ch. 4, p. 225 (the Emperor Michael and the Patriarch (Photius) try to make Methodius an archbishop and when he refuses they appoint him abbot in the monastery of Polychron). *Anastasii Epistolae*, no. 5, p. 407 (Photius is chided by his friend (*eius amico*) Constantine for having set forth the view that every man had two souls). — Constantine may even have succeeded Photius at the newly founded University of Constantinople (Dvorník, *Légendes*, p. 79 sq.)

by the court.[8] Although a recent assertion that after Photius had become Patriarch (858) he negotiated a reconciliation between the brothers and the regime of Bardas has no sufficient basis in the sources,[9] the facts mentioned above as well as their mission to the Khazars and Moravians[10] during the patriarchate of Photius make it probable that they were Photians rather than Ignatians. Leaving out all information attested by the *Legends* only, we find Constantine at Rome among the close acquaintances of Anastasius Bibliothecarius who had a very high opinion of the "philosopher."[11] When Constantine died in 869, he was buried in the Basilica of St Clement where his tomb with a fresco has been supposedly excavated in modern times.[12]

It was Constantine's brother Methodius who became a regular papal missionary to the Slavic lands. Whether or not we accept as genuine Pope Hadrian's letter to Prince Kocel of Pannonia,[13] it is a historical fact that in 869–870 Methodius was ordained archbishop of Sirmium and dispatched as a papal envoy (*legatus e latere*) to the Slavic districts.[14] After Methodius was tried and imprisoned for three years by

[8] *V. C.*, ch. 4, p. 162. Cf. Dvorník, *Légendes*, pp. 49–68 (where it is shown that *bibliothecarius* was the Latin equivalent of χαρτοφύλαξ. See, however, the "Older List of Papal Judges" edited by P. E. Schramm, "Studien zu frühmittelalterlichen Aufzeichnungen über Staat und Verfassung," *Zeitschrift der Savigny-Stiftung für Rechtsgeschichte, Germ. Abt.*, IL (1929) 203: "Bibliothecarius aput Grecos logothetio et referendarius interpretatur etc."

[9] Dvorník, *Légendes*, pp. 135–147, 210. See the review by H. Schaeder, *Jahrbücher für Kultur und Geschichte der Slaven*, N. F., x (1934), 589.

[10] Both embassies are mentioned in the *Legends* only, but without a previous Moravian mission one fails to understand why Pope Hadrian made Methodius archbishop of Sirmium.

[11] *V. C.*, ch. XVII, p. 211 (Anastasius "helps" when the Slavonic liturgy is sung at the sepulchre of St Paul); Epistolae VII (*Anastasii Epistolae*), no. 5, p. 407: "a Constantino philosopho magnae sanctitatis viro fortissimo," *ibid.*, no. 13, p. 433: Constantine apparently had "lectured" at Rome on the usefulness of St Clement's relics ("quantum utilitatis medulla eius habeat, auditoribus commendabat"), and Anastasius even takes the trouble of enlightening Charles the Bald as to the ambiguity of a Greek word which Constantine had used on such an occasion "*oxy* quippe et acutum signat et velox"; see also no. 15, p. 436 sq. — The brothers had come to Rome under Hadrian II (*ibid.*, p. 433: "Constantinus philosophus, qui Romam sub venerabilis memoriae Adriano iuniori papa veniens etc.") and if we may believe the *Legends* he has been called there by Hadrian's predecessor, Nicholas I (*V. M.*, ch. 6, p. 226).

[12] *V. C.*, ch. 18, p. 215. On the result of the excavations, see Wilpert, G., "Le pitture della basilica primitiva di S. Clemente," *Mélanges d'archéologie et d'histoire*, XXVI (1906), 251–303 and the important review by M. Rešetar, *Archiv für slavische Philologie*, XXVII, (1906), 421–429.

[13] *V. M.*, ch. 8, pp. 228–230=*Epistolae* VI (Hadrian), no. 43, p. 763.

[14] *V. M.*, ch. 8, p. 230; *Epistolae* VII (Johannes VIII), frgm. 22, p. 286 (A.D. 873): "O episcopum episcopo talia inferentem et ad hoc apostolice sedis manu sacrato et (e?) latere destinato; *ibid.*, frgm. 23 (A.D. 873): "Methodium, Pannonicum archiepiscopum legatione apostolice sedis ad gentes fungentem"; *ibid.*, no. 200, p. 160 (A.D. 879): "Methodius vester archiepiscopus ab antecessore nostro, Adriano scilicet papa, ordinatus vobisque directus."

the German King Lewis the German and the Bavarian bishops (870–873) who were unwilling to tolerate this encroachment of Rome into their sphere of missionary interest, it was Pope John VIII who insisted on, and obtained, Methodius' release and safe-conduct to Moravia.[15] In 879 Methodius was summoned to Rome to defend himself against certain accusations raised by his enemies, and he was entirely successful; he was also upheld by Pope John VIII on various other occasions.[16] It was Pope Stephen V, the successor of John VIII, who after Methodius' death in 885 prohibited the Slavonic liturgy and ruined to a certain extent the work of the brothers in Moravia.[17]

The facts mentioned above show beyond any doubt that Methodius enjoyed the protection of Pope Hadrian II and John VIII in his struggle against his enemies in Pannonia and Moravia. Who were those enemies? For a long time the Bavarian bishops, especially those of Salzburg and Passau, had been doing missionary work in Pannonia and Moravia. The history of this Bavarian mission in Slavic lands will be traced in more detail below; here it may suffice to point out that the Bavarian bishops and their missionaries were leading an active and successful opposition against Methodius from the moment when he first appeared on Moravian soil.

We are now prepared to formulate the problem of this paper. At the time when Methodius was sent as a papal missionary to his newly established archdiocese (869/870), the Slavic lands had been actively missionized by the Bavarian missions. It must have been obvious to the Holy See that the establishment of a new archdiocese in the territory of the Bavarian mission constituted an open declaration of war against the Frankish clergy. The person of the Byzantine monk, who was possibly even an adherent of Photius, at a time when the latter was condemned by the entire Church,[18] must have been a further provocation. What reasons did the Pope have to send such a person to the Slavic lands? Was he dissatisfied with the work done by the Bavarian bishops? Were there deeper reasons behind this step? After

---

[15] *V. M.*, ch. 9, p. 230–231; *Epistolae* (Johannes VIII) VII, frgms. 15–23 (all of A.D. 873).

[16] *V. M.*, ch. 12, p. 234; *Epistolae* VII, nos 200, 201, pp. 160 sq. (A.D. 879); no. 255, pp. 222–224 (A.D. 880, authenticity uncertain); no. 276, pp. 243 sq. (A.D. 881).

[17] *Epistulae* (Stephen V) VII, frgm. 33, p. 352 sq. and no. 1, pp. 354–358 (both of A.D. 885, but the authenticity of the latter document is uncertain, see G. Laehr, "Das Schreiben Stephans V. an Sventopulk von Mähren," *Neues Archiv der Gesellschaft für ältere deutsche Geschichtskunde*, XLVII (1927–28), 159–173.

[18] Methodius' relations to Photius are only of secondary importance in this connection. If Methodius was a follower of Photius, this did not mean at the time of his departure that he did not recognize the Pope (F. Dvorník, *Les Slaves, Byzance et Rome au IX⁰ siecle*, Paris, 1926, pp. 174–183). The main provocation for the Frankish clergy was that he was a Byzantine.

all, the Bavarian bishops themselves were subordinates of the Pope and the Bavarian mission should have benefited the Papacy, at least indirectly. The German king and the bishops of Salzburg and Passau, on the other hand, accepted the challenge and did not hesitate to do violence to the papal delegate, Methodius. How could they dare to attack the papal emissary in this way? We may suspect that the papal act of war was only an episode in a more comprehensive struggle against the Frankish clergy and that a general state of rebellion on the part of the latter against their ecclesiastical superior, the Pope, encouraged them to take up the gauntlet. We shall attempt to show that the *universal* Church as represented by the Pope, was attempting to break the growing power of the *territorial* churches as represented by an alliance between the various .princes and their great metropolitan archbishops, and that furthermore these *territorial* churches all over the medieval world were reacting vigorously against the pretensions of the Roman See (i). With regard to the Eastern Frankish Kingdom this struggle centered around the right of sending out missionaries: it became an established principle of the Popes that missionary work was their monopoly while the territorial churches claimed that the right of missions was a corollary deriving from the conquest carried out by their princes[19] (ii)).

I

To understand the situation of the Frankish church in the middle of the ninth century, one has to go back to the preceding period. After the death of Charlemagne (814) the dream of empire and unity had lingered on in the memory of men for a generation, and it was only after the death of Lewis the Pious (840) that it was abandoned. Just as in the case of Alexander's Empire, which broke up into three distinct territorial units after more than twenty years of continued attempts to restore its unity, the civil war between Lewis the Pious and his sons had ended in the constitution of a Western Frankish King-

---

[19] This interpretation has been touched upon by the scholar who has written by far the most penetrating study on the Slavonic Apostles from the Western point of view. H. von Schubert, "Die sogenannten Slavenapostel Constantin und Methodius. Ein grundlegendes Kapitel aus den Beziehungen Deutschlands zum Südosten," *Sitzungsberichte der Heidelberger Akademie der Wissenschaften, Phil.-Hist. Kl.*, 1916, Abh. 1, p. 12 writes: "Der Gegensatz der beiden Systeme trat immer wieder scharf zutage: die germanisch-landeskirchliche und die römisch-universale Fassung des Problems von Staat und Kirche." See also Dvorník, *Légendes*, p. 271 (following von Schubert); Laehr, *Schreiben Stephens V*, 170 sq. — It is due to Dvorník's studies that we now realize the importance of the papal claim on Illyricum for the problem of the Slavonic Apostles. Yet it remains to be explained why this claim was asserted so vigorously at this moment when this assertion meant a clash with the Frankish clergy.

dom, its Eastern parallel, and the intervening realm of Lothar I (843, Treaty of Verdun). The new territorial units are now constituted as individual states; they are diplomatic entities;[20] the Oaths of Strassburg (842) are the first monuments preserved in the vernacular languages; and the ties which bind the clergy to their respective rulers tend to bring about the development of territorial churches. The outstanding role which the Popes had assumed during the dynastic wars found its counterpart, both in Gaul and in Germany, in the development of the territorial churches grouped around their King and determined to keep the Pope in the position which he had held under Charlemagne. The Papacy, on the other hand, was anxious to establish its supremacy over the territorial churches of the Frankish Kingdoms and under the pontificate of Pope Nicholas I (858–868) energetic measures were taken in this direction.

The chief agent for the development of territorial churches on Frankish soil was the institution of the metropolitan archbishops.[21] Such prelates had existed in the Frankish Kingdom in the fifth century, but they had not survived the barbarian invasions. St Boniface had attempted to establish metropolitan archbishops under the direct guidance of the Papacy, but had failed to achieve his purpose. Finally metropolitan archbishops were appointed by Charlemagne in the last years of the eighth century. It has been said (and repeated) that they owed their existence to the introduction of the canonistic collection called the *Dionysio-Hadriana* (774): the canons spoke of metropolitans, and therefore metropolitans had to be created.[22] In his will of 811,[23] Charlemagne enumerates twenty-one *metropolitanae civitates*, all headed by an archbishop. During the generation which followed, two powers profited by the weakness of the body politic: the Papacy and the metropolitan archbishops. The metropolitan archbishops strengthened more and more the grip which they held over their province. If united behind the prince of their province, they were a potential danger to Rome, and as materially they depended to a large extent on the good will of the prince, such a

---

[20] J. Calmette, *La diplomatie carolingienne du Traité de Verdun à la mort de Charles Le Chauve* (843–877), Bibliothèque de l'Ecole des Hautes Etudes, fasc. cxxxv (Paris, 1901), p. 1 and *passim*.

[21] On the following, see the excellent book of E. Lesne, *La hiérarchie épiscopale. Provinces, métropolitains, primats en Gaule et Germanie depuis la reforme de saint Boniface jusqu'à la mort d'Hincmar, 742–882* (Lille and Paris, 1905).

[22] Lesne, *Hiérarchie*, pp. 62 sq., followed by P. Fournier and G. Le Bras, *Histoire des collections canoniques en Occident depuis les Fausses Décrétales jusqu'au Décret de Gratien*, I (Paris, 1931), p. 97. Is it not more probable that Charlemagne realized that metropolitan archbishops would allow the Emperor to exercise a firmer control over the clergy?

[23] Einhart, *Vita Caroli Magni*, ed. W. Wattenbach, Berlin, 1876, ch. 33, pp. 53 sq.

272

union was effected more often than not. It is not astonishing to see, therefore, that the Papacy, as well as the suffragan bishops, began to oppose the growing power of these metropolitan archbishops.

Nowhere has this opposition found a clearer expression than in the *Pseudo-Isidorian Decretals*, the famous forgery compiled either in the province of Reims or in that of Tours around the year 850.[24] One of the leading ideas of this collection is the protection of the bishop against the encroachments of the metropolitan archbishops:[25] Pseudo-Isidore is frankly hostile to the latter. The metropolitan archbishops surrounded by their suffragan bishops may try a bishop, but the sentence, being in such a case a *causa maior*, is reserved to the Pope and the accused may appeal against the decision of a provincial synod to the Pope. Although the compilers almost certainly had not intended primarily to strengthen the position of the Papacy, the decretals attributed to the Popes of the first and second centuries gave Rome such prominence in the Church that Rome recognized and used them, at least unofficially. Pope Nicholas I (857–868) and his successors availed themselves frequently of the spirit of the pseudo-canons in their fight against the power of the metropolitan archbishops. Certain episodes of this fight are well known. They will be sketched below in order to show more clearly the policy pursued by the Papacy with regard to the territorial churches and the metropolitan archbishops.[26]

It was Nicholas' first concern to prevent the rise of any possible ecclesiastical rival on Italian soil. Friction between the Papacy and the metropolitan see of Ravenna had been frequent long before Nicholas.[27] They became acute when John VIII became archbishop of

[24] On the many problems connected with Pseudo-Isidore, see for instance Amann, *L'Empire carolingien*, pp. 352–366; von Schubert, *Geschichte*, II, 415 sq; Fournier et Le Bras, *Collections Canoniques*, pp. 127–233.

[25] For the following, see Lesne, *Hiérarchie*, pp. 187–193; Fournier et Le Bras, *Collections Canoniques*, p. 132 sq.

[26] It hardly needs mentioning that in a good many cases the Popes urged the clergy to obey their archbishops. See for instance, *Epistolae* VI, no. 14, p. 281; no. 107, pp. 619–622 (both letters of Nicholas); no. 30, p. 734 sq. (Hadrian) etc. This is the rule which makes the exceptions mentioned in the text all the more remarkable.

[27] For this conflict, see E. Perels, *Papst Nikolaus I. und Anastasius Bibliothecarius. Ein Beitrag zur Geschichte des Papsttums im neunten Jahrhundert* (Berlin, 1920), pp. 44–52. — There exists a more recent biography of Pope Nicholas I, that by J. Haller, *Nikolaus I und Pseudoisidor* (Stuttgart, 1936). The value of Haller's book lies in its general thesis which is opposed to the traditional view. In his attractive style Haller argues that however high the ambitions of Pope Nicholas may have been, he was unable to carry into effect most of his program. There is some truth in this contention, but one need not follow Haller in his further conclusion that because of this the personality of Nicholas has been overestimated — "magnis tamen excidit ausis." See the reviews in *Vergangenheit und Gegenwart*, XXVII (1937), 451 sq. (P. E. Schramm); *Historische Zeitschrift*, CLIX (1938/9), 340–342 (Tellenbach); *Zeitschrift für Kirchengeschichte*, LV (1936), 688 ssq. (H. Koch); *English Historical*

Ravenna. Nicholas I took energetic measures when, among other things, John of Ravenna prevented the suffragan bishops of his province from complaining to Rome.[28] The incident ended in the complete submission of John, although the latter had the support of the Emperor; in his letter to the suffragan bishops (861) Pope Nicholas prohibited henceforth such abuses as had been practiced by Johannes "ne aliis metropolitanis episcopis talia praesumendi occasio remaneret et ecclesiae Dei tali inficerentur exemplo."[29] Thus this first episode ended with a program of threats directed against the power of the metropolitan bishops.

But the chief theater of war was to lie in Frankish territory, and the occasion for it was to be the divorce of King Lothar II.[30] Pope Nicholas intervened in this affair (862) on the ground that both parties, Lothar II himself and Theutberga whom Lothar had repudiated, had appealed to him. We may ignore here the course of events with regard to the royal couple, as we are interested rather in the affair of the archbishops Gunthar of Cologne and Thietgaud of Trier. These two men had played a prominent part in the various Lotharingian councils concerned with the royal divorce. In 863 they had been dispatched to Rome to obtain the papal consent to the decisions of the synod of Metz which had condemned Theutberga and declared valid Lothar's subsequent marriage to Waldrada. They did not achieve their purpose. Instead Pope Nicholas deposed[31] them both in a trial, the legality of which may be doubted. The Pope branded the archbishops as *tutores atque fautores* of Lothar II[32] and blamed them for having assumed jurisdiction ever the affair of Lothar II in violation of the apostical and canonical sanctions.[33] Other bishops who had sided with Gunthar and Thietgaud would share their fate, but they

---

Review, LIV (1939), 162 sq. (not available). As for the present purpose it is immaterial whether or not Nicholas achieved any given purpose (as long as this purpose itself is certain) and as in most other respects Haller's book is hardly an advance over the careful analysis of Perels, the latter's work will be used in the following discussion.

[28] *Liber Pontificalis*, ed. L. Duchesne, II, p. 155: (John of Ravenna) "quosdam temere excommunicabat, quosdam autem a visitatione sedis apostolicae avertebat, et quorundam res sine legali iudicio occupabat; necnon et sanctae Romanae aecclesiae plurima praedia auferebat, missos illius spernebat, et gloriam beati Petri apostoli, quantum in se erat, evacuabat." [29] *Epistolae* VI, no. 105, p. 616.

[30] On this complicated affair as a whole, see Perels, *Papst Nikolaus I*, p. 53 ssq.

[31] *Liber Pontificalis*, ed. Duchesne, II, p. 160.

[32] *Epistolae* VI, no. 18, p. 284. See also no. 22, p. 287: "Probat hoc Theutgaudi et Guntharii dudum episcoporum legitimus casus, qui pro eo, quod te minime competenter erudierunt, quin immo, quia praevaricationem tuam tegere argumentis suis et sub quadam iusticiae specie fucatis quibusdam exquisitis adinventionibus aequitatem obstruere studuerunt, nostra sunt apostolica auctoritate depositi et ab omni episcopatus regimine regulariter sequestrati." [33] *Ibid.*, p. 285.

would be pardoned if they declared in writing their agreement with the Holy See. And then in a seemingly casual remark the Pope reminds these other bishops that their own episcopate is derived from the Apostolic See! From other similar passages we learn the implication of this characteristic *argumentum ad hominem*; by undermining the authority of the see of St Peter, they deprive themselves of their one and only protector.[34] To prevent the repetition of such an alliance between Lothar II and the church of his territory, Nicholas demands categorically of Lothar II not to proceed to a new election at Cologne or Trier before reporting to Rome on this subject.[35]

The ensuing events are well known. Gunther and Thietgaud secured the help of the Emperor Lewis II. They complained to the Emperor "that they had been unjustly deposed, that the Emperor himself and the entire holy church had been offended, as it had never been heard of, or read anywhere, that a metropolitan bishop was deprived of his rank without the knowledge of the Prince or the presence of other metropolitan bishops."[36] Lewis II tried to break the resistance of the Pontiff by invading Rome in 864. The attempt ended in a complete victory of the Pope, who was prepared to suffer martyrdom rather than give in; the Emperor withdrew his protection from Gunthar and Thietgaud, and the latter were sent home. But during the

[34] *Ibid.*: "Ceteri autem episcopi, qui complices horum, Teutgaudi scilicet et Guntharii, vel sectatores esse feruntur, si cum his coniuncti seditiones, coniurationes vel conspirationes fecerint vel si a capite, id est a sede Petri, illis haerendo dissenserint, pari cum eis damnatione teneantur obstricti. Quodsi cum sede apostolica unde eos principium episcopatus sumpsisse manifestum est, sapere de cetero per semetipsos vel missis ad nos legatis cum scriptis suis se professi extiterint, noverint sibi a nobis veniam non negandam. See also, for the meaning of the *argumentum ad hominem*, no. 57, p. 360 (A.D. 863): "Nam quod Rothado hodie contigit, unde scitis, quod cras cuilibet non eveniat vestrum?"; no. 58, p. 363 sq. (A.D. 863), directed to Hincmar of Rheims in the affair of Rothad of Soissons): "Privilegia praeterea ab apostolica sede vestrae ecclesiae confirmanda depocitis, qui tamen nostra privilegia, quantum in vobis est, infirmare satagitis. Portum salutiferum sanctam Romanam ecclesiam appellatis, qui tamen, ne in eo aliqui salventur, quantum potestis, satagere procuratis. Quomodo ergo privilegia tua stare proterunt, si ita privilegia illa cassentur, per quae tua privilegia initium sumpsisse noscuntur? Aut cuius momenti erunt tua, si pro nihilo nostra pendantur? Si namque sal infatuatum fuerit, in quo salietur?; no. 71 p. 398 (A.D. 865, same affair): "Neque enim tam stolidus tamve poterit a rationis tramite devius inveniri, qui ceteris ecclesiis privilegia servari et soli Romanae ecclesiae adimi debere perhibeat, quae omnium ecclesiarum magistra, mater et caput est." Perels, *Papst Nikolaus I*, p. 252, has shown that such passages were dictated by Anastasius Bibliothecarius.

[35] Epistolae VI, no. 23, p. 288 (A.D. 863), to Lothar II: "Porro scias, quia relatum est nobis, quod, quicumque ad episcopatum in regno tuo provehendus est, nonnisi faventem tibi permittas eligi. Idcirco apostolica auctoritate sub divini iudicii obtestatione iniungimus tibi, ut in Treverensi urbe et in Agrippina Colonia nullum eligi patiaris, antequam relatum super hoc fiat nostro apostolatui.

[36] *Reginonis Abbatis Prumiensis Chronicon*, ed. F. Kurze (Hannover, 1890), anno 865, p. 83.

expedition against Rome these two archbishops issued a manifesto which they distributed everywhere and even deposited on the tomb of St Peter — one of the most curious documents of the period inasmuch as it illustrates the mental attitude of the ecclesiastical opposition. In the most vehement language they accuse Pope Nicholas of "making himself the emperor of the entire world."[37] They complain of the illegality of the trial staged by the Pope: they have been condemned in the absence of other bishops, by a motley crowd of clerics and laymen, "merely according to your arbitrary will and tyrannical madness."[38] They refuse to accept the Pope's sentence and emphasize, just as they had before Lewis II, that the reason for their indignation was not their person, but "the whole entirety of our rank which you are attempting to attack by force."[39] Thus Gunthar and Thietgaud, as well as the Pope himelf, realized that their affair was a test of the strength of the Papacy over against the metropolitan bishops. By attempting to win the support of the territorial clergies of the Frankish kingdoms[40] and their princes the two archbishops tried to build up an opposition between the universal church as represented by the Pope, and these territorial clergies. In this they were unsuccessful, and although attempts were made, time and again, of restoring Gunthar and Thietgaud, they never recovered their rank in the hierarchy.[41] When Pope Nicholas granted pardon to bishop Adventius of Metz who had claimed that during the synod of Metz (863) he had followed the authority of his metropolitan bishop, the Pope seasoned his pardon with a statement of principle which marks an advance over the

---

[37] *Annales Bertiniani*, anno 864, ed. G. Waitz, p. 68: "domnus Nicolaus, qui dicitur papa et qui se apostolum inter apostolos adnumerat totiusque mundi imperatorem se facit etc."

[38] *Ibid.*, p. 69 sq.; *Annales Fuldenses*, ed. F. Kurze (Hannover, 1891), anno 863, p. 61.

[39] *Ibid.*, "nec nostrae vilitatis personam attendentes, sed omnem nostri ordinis universitatem, cui vim inferre conaris, prae oculis habentes." Ruodolfus, the author of the part of the *Annales Fuldenses*, copies a somewhat more elaborate version of the manifesto where they accuse Nicholas of favoring their enemies and adds this characteristic clause: "sciesque nos non tuos esse, ut te iactas et extollis, clericos quos ut fratres et coepiscopos recognoscere, si elatio permitteret, debueras."

[40] See the preface to the manifesto preserved in the *Annales Bertiniani, loc. cit.*, p. 68 sq.

[41] Upon his return from Rome, Gunthar ignored the deposition and continued to act as archbishop of Cologne (*Epistolae* VI, no. 26, p. 291; no. 39, p. 313) whereas Thietgaud and the other participants in the synod of Metz submitted to the Pope. A.D. 864 the two archbishops proceeded to Rome in the hope of being restored, but they did not achieve anything (*Annales Bertiniani*, anno 864, p. 74). In 867 Lewis the German intervened in their favor, but Nicholas remained adamant (nos. 52 and 53, pp. 338–351). It would seem that Pope Hadrian II was contemplating a restoration of Gunthar, but nothing came of it (*Epistolae* VI, no. 25, p. 731, with the notes of the editor) and in 870 the old archbishop wrote a pitiful letter to the Pope in which he regretted his former actions ("considerans meorum multitudinem delictorum") and asked the Pope to confirm a certain Willibert as his successor (*Epistolae* VI, no. 5, pp. 246–249).

final act in the episode of Johannes of Ravenna with regard to the relation between the Papacy and the metropolitan bishops:

> Rursus si fatetur Antiochenum concilium: Per singulas regiones episcopos convenit nosse metropolitanum episcopum sollicitudinem totius provinciae gerere, quid praeiudicat sedi apostolicae sollicitudinem habenti non solum unius provinciae sed et totius ecclesiae, cum idem concilium magis metropolitas coerceat, refrenet et artet, dum eos non amplius quam suarum provinciarum dicat sollicitudinem gerere? . . . Ergo quia totius nos ecclesiae maxima cura praestolatur, nostrum praecipue debet ecclesia tota procul dubio iudicium promereri.

This second clash between the Carolingian clergy and the Roman See, then, concludes with a vigorous assertion of the papal authority over the metropolitan bishops.[42]

The vogue of the manifesto issued by Gunthar and Thietgaud during the Emperor's march on Rome was considerable. Ruodolfus of Fulda as well as Hincmar of Rheims knew it and inserted it in their Annals,[43] Gunthar and Thietgaud themselves had taken care that it was widely distributed. Certain passages in Nicholas' letters of 867 might lead one to believe that even in that year an ecclesiastical opposition party was still drawing its inspiration from Gunthar and Thietgaud's rebellion.[44] Nicholas knew that the two had distributed their proclamation all over the Occident.[45] It had come even to the knowledge of the Byzantine Patriarch Photius (858–867) who was pleased to avail himself of this Western protest against Nicholas in his famous encyclical to the three Eastern Patriarchs when he

---

[42] *Epistolae* VI, no. 31, p. 300.

[43] Above notes 37, 38; Rudolfus of Fulda who wrote the pertinent chapter in the year 863 itself (cf. the edition of Pertz and Kurze, p. 57, note 2) leaves it to his readers to decide whether the Pope or the deposed archbishop were right. His neutral attitude probably reflects that of the court at Regensburg.

[44] *Epistolae* VI, no. 52, p. 339 (A.D. 867, to Lewis the German): "Sed nunc pro reconciliandis Theutgaudo et Gunthario, totius huius mali fabricatoribus, satagitis, curritis, anxiamini et nobis crebro id ipsum mittere minime recusatis; quosque nescio quomodo amaricatos appelletis, dum certe illi pene cotidie potum amaritudinis propinare nobis non desinunt; nam quotiens eorum facti memoria inter aliorum dura quaeque nobis ingerentium infert, totiens nos absque multi meroris amaritudine remanere nequimus." The words "eorum facti memoria inter aliorum dura quaeque nobis ingerentium" might be taken to refer to Lothar II and Waldrada, but the parallel letter to the German bishops makes it probable, I think, that the *alii dura quaeque nobis ingerentes* are members of an ecclesiastical opposition, cf. *ibid.*, no. 53, p. 348: "Sint (i.e., Gunthar and Thietgaud) interim in signum et in portentum omnibus, quos vel ipsi deceperunt vel quibus audatiam persistendi in nequitia praestiterunt." It could hardly be said that Gunthar and Thietgaud gave Lothar and Waldrada "audatiam in nequitia persistendi."

[45] *Epistolae* VI, no. 53, p. 346 (A.D. 867): "vel qualiter ordinationi Dei in beato Petro ecclesiae Romanae collatae restiterint et contra privilegia sedis eius capitula obtrectationum conscripserint et per totum pene occidentale clima disseminaverint."

planned the deposition of the Pope (867): complying with a request of its authors, Photius sent it all over the Orient.[46] If Gunthar and Thietgaud had even asked Photius to send their manifesto all over the Orient, we may be reasonably certain that it was known also to the Bavarian bishops, in particular to the archbishop of Salzburg. This conclusion will help to explain the bold attitude of the Bavarian bishops towards the papal delegate, Methodius.

Shortly prior to the Lotharingian synod of Metz which led to the deposition of Gunthar and Thietgaud, the Pope had interfered in the province of the most powerful archbishop of the Western Frankish Kingdom, the great Hincmar of Rheims. In a synod at Soissons (862) Hincmar had deposed the oldest of his suffragan bishops, Rothad, the bishop of Soissons.[47] The Pope claimed that Rothad had appealed to Rome while Hincmar pleaded that after his appeal Rothad had agreed to a trial by his peers. Nicholas complained that Hincmar had acted contrary to the privileges of the Holy See;[48] the papal letters do not mention the situation of the metropolitan archbishops at all and look at the controversy rather from the point of view of relations between the See of St Peter and the territorial churches.[49] Hincmar, on the other hand, realized that the powers of the metropolitan bishops were under attack. While the Pope had written (in a letter which is not preserved) that he had been led to investigate the case of Rothad by the concern which he felt for all his brothers, Hincmar reminds him in pungent language that he, too, was included in this category although he was a metropolitan bishop. The Pope should be on the watch not only that the suffragan bishops are not unjustly condemned by their metropolitan bishops, but also that the metropolitan bishops are not harmed by their suffragans. He (Hincmar) does not object that, as long as the *vigor ecclesiasticus* remains unharmed, the Pope should have pity on Rothad. He warns him, however, that unless this *vigor ecclesiasticus* is upheld, others might be

---

[46] Migne, *Patr. Gr.*, cii, col. 737 C and D (see V. Grumel, *Les Regestes des actes du patriarcat de Constantinople*, i, fasc. ii (Chalcedon, 1936), no. 481): Νῦν δὲ καὶ γράμματα διάφορα, καὶ ἐκ διαφόρων ἐκεῖθεν ἀναπεφοίτηκεν, τραγῳδίας ἀπάσης καὶ μυρίων θρήνων γέμοντα· ὧν τὰ ἴσα, κατὰ τὴν ἐκείνων ἀξίωσίν τε καὶ ἐξαίτησιν (καὶ γὰρ εἰς πάντας τοὺς ἀρχιερατικοὺς καὶ ἀποστολικοὺς θρόνους διαδοθῆναι ταῦτα μετὰ φρικτῶν ὅρκων καὶ παρακλήσεων ἐδυσώπησαν), ὡς αὐτὰ ἐκεῖνα παραστήσει ἀναγινωσκόμενα, τῷδε ἡμῶν τῷ γραμματίῳ ἐνετάξαμεν κτλ.

[47] On this case, see Perels, *Nikolaus I*, 99–113, and the important memoir of Hincmar concerning the privileges of metropolitan bishops edited for the first time by E. Perels, "Eine Denkschrift Hinkmars von Reims im Prozess Rothads von Soissons," *Neues Archiv*, xliv (1922), 43–100 = *M. G. H.*, *Epistolae*, viii, no. 160, pp. 122–140.

[48] See for instance *Epistolae* vi, no. 55, p. 354; no. 58, p. 363; no. 64, p. 376 (all these letters date from A.D. 863).

[49] The *Liber Pontificalis* (ii, p. 163) says that Rothad was restored "ne talia sacerdotes et maxime sedem apostolicam appellantes ultra discrimina paterentur."

inspired by Rothad's example and be led into similar transgressions. Furthermore, he himself, and others in like positions, might either become weary in fulfilling their censorial functions or derive from Rothad's pardon the claim that they might now transgress the traditional limitations.[50] In spite of Hincmar's objections Rothad was restored to his see in 865. For our purpose it is interesting to note that by this incident the war between the universal Church and the territorial churches, between the Papacy and the metropolitan archbishops, had spread from Italy and the realm of Lothar II to the Western Frankish Kingdom.

There was to be, however, a sequel to the affair of Rothad: the *causa Wulfhadi*.[51] In 866 at the latest, the Pope took up the case of certain clerics of the province of Rheims who had been deposed in 853. Of these the most important was a certain Wulfhad who enjoyed the special protection of King Charles the Bald. Hincmar of Rheims had to yield to the unusual alliance between Pope and King,[52] and this alliance differentiates the *causa Wulfhadi* from the earlier clashes between the universal church and the territorial clergy. Nevertheless the upshot of this was another humiliation of Hincmar of Rheims — all the more so if a passage in the conciliar letter of Troyes (867) is genuine. In this passage[53] the Pope is asked by the Council to repress the presumptuous audacity of all the metropolitan bishops, and the connivance of other bishops, with the apostolical sword and to decree that henceforth no bishop may be deposed without a consultation with the Pope. A marginal note on this passage, in one of our manuscripts, claims that "certain bishops stung by their conscience had these (words) inserted because, being sincere, they did not reject (them) utterly on account of the scandal."[54]

---

[50] I am using Hincmar's letters in the hitherto anonymous edition which has begun to appear in *M. G. H., Epistolae*, VIII, fasc. 1 (Berlin, 1939) no. 169 (A.D. 864) pp. 157 sq.

[51] Perels, *Nikolaus* I, pp. 132–141.

[52] Hincmar instructs his emissary, the archbishop Egilo of Sens, to point out to the Pope that his policy of invalidating earlier decisions and of humoring the secular powers will weaken not only the bishops but also the Apostolic See; the Pope is also to be reminded of the way in which Gunthar of Cologne had taken his excommunication (Hincmar of Reims, *Epistolae* VIII, no. 186, p. 193).

[53] Mansi, XV, col. 795 D: . . . "exoramus magnificam beatitudinem, ut sapientissima indagine consideratis utriusque partis relatis, more beatissimorum praedecessorum vestrorum, quae de statu sacri pontificalis ordinis ab eis statuta et impraevaricabili auctoritate firmata sunt, ut immota de cetero maneant, mucrone apostolico quorumcumque metropolitanorum temeraria praesumptione suppressa, quin etiam reliquorum episcoporum quorumcumque, seu quantorumcumque, audaci conniventia penitus summota, privilegia et decreta servari innovata constitutione decernatis: ita ut nec vestris nec futuris temporibus praeter consultum Romani pontifici de gradu suo quilibet episcoporum deiciatur etc."

[54] Heinrich Schrörs, *Hinkmar, Erzbischof von Reims*, Freiburg i. Br., 1884, p. 288, note 74: "Haec quidam episcopi conscientia sua mordente inseri fecerunt, quod sinceri

There are indications that Nicholas had originally intended still further to humiliate Hincmar of Rheims by an investigation into the validity of his election.[55] At the same time (867), however, papal relations with Byzantium had taken a critical turn for the worse (see below, p. 279) and Nicholas realized that he could not wage war on so many fronts. A few weeks prior to his death, therefore, the Pope declared himself satisfied with the actions of Hincmar[56] and even asked for the literary aid of the Frankish clergy to refute Photius and present a united front against the attack from the East.[57] In this we need not see a reconciliation between the Papacy and the metropolitan bishops: it was no more than a truce[58] and when the danger from the Byzantine salient had passed, the war against the Frankish clergy was taken up anew.

Before leaving the pontificate of Nicholas, we have to cast a quick glance at the affair of Photius. It is impossible even to summarize here this well-known controversy,[59] which may be viewed from so many interesting angles. One of these is the Roman point of view, and there are indications that, according to Roman ideas, the Byzantine Patriarch was not essentially different from a Frankish archbishop and that, therefore, disobedience on the part of the former was to be regarded as just another manifestation by one of those territorial churches which were the target of Nicholas' attacks. It may be no coincidence that this view of the Pope was never more clearly expressed than in a letter addressed to Hincmar of Rheims (867) where Nicholas claims to have refused to recognize the validity of Ignatius' deposition *utpote a subiectis et ab imperiali potentia factam.*[60] In Nicholas' mind it was once more an unholy alliance between the prince of the territory and his clergy which obstructed the wishes of the Vicar of Christ. Just as in the case of the Frankish bishops, the Pope derives his right of interference from the fact that the successor of St Peter has power over the entire church.[61] He reminds the Byzan-

---

propter scandalum penitus non reiecerunt." This is one of the famous marginal notes in the *Cod. Laudun.* 407 which may go back to Hincmar himself, see E. Perels, "Die Briefe Papst Nikolaus I," *Neues Archiv,* XXXVII (1912), esp. 557–562. However that may be, this complaint seems to show that its writer considered the passage as a genuine (though regrettable) utterance of the Synod of Troyes. It has not been noted, however, that in his confirmation of the Synod of Troyes Pope Hadrian II does not mention our passage (*Epistolae* VI, no. 3, p. 699 sq.). On this problem, see Amann, *Epoque Carolingienne,* p. 393.

[55] Perels, *Nikolaus,* p. 140.

[56] *Annales Bertiniani, anno* 867, p. 89: "Nicolaus vero papa gratanter suscipiens quae Hincmarus scripserat ei, de omnibus sibi satisfactum esse rescripsit."

[57] Perels, *Nikolaus,* pp. 166–169.   [58] This is said against Haller, *Nikolaus,* p. 123.

[59] Good resumé in Amann, *Epoque Carolingienne,* pp. 465–483.

[60] *Epistolae* VI, no. 100, p. 601, Cf. also *ibidem,* no. 90, p. 509 (A.D. 866); no. 98, p. 563.

[61] *Ibidem,* no. 88, p. 475 (see the parallel passages in the note). Constantinople has not

tine Emperor that "no problem that may arise can be settled without the consent of the Roman See and the Roman Pontiff."[62] As in all the other cases, Nicholas was upholding the privileges of the Holy See against the encroachments of a territorial church and its prince; the only difference was that this time the Pope did not take under his protection a suffragan bishop against his archbishop, but the legitimate archbishop himself (Ignatius) against an invader (Photius), as well as against his imperial protectors and his ecclesiastical partisans.[63] The result was a victory of Nicholas, but it was a posthumous one.[64]

We can best gauge the effect of Nicholas' policy by examining the events which followed his death (867). In this respect we are particularly well informed by a letter of Anastasius Bibliothecarius, one of those rare documents which makes us realize and regret with particular bitterness the formal and official character of the sources on which we have to draw for most other historical problems. The letter is addressed to Ado, archbishop of Vienne, and informs him of the death of the Pontiff.[65] After his death, Anastasius continues, "rapacious wolves" are entering the scene, and Ado is asked to resist them. All those whom the deceased has rebuked for adultery or other crimes are joining forces to have his works destroyed and his writings burnt; they even bruit it about (falsely, Anastasius believes) that the Emperor (Lewis II) is going to support them. Of the new Pope, Hadrian II, Anastasius does not know yet whether he is going to attend to all the business of the Church or only to part of it. For our purpose the most interesting part of the letter is the postscript (*embolum*). In this Anastasius urges Ado to advise all the metropolitan bishops of the Gauls not to seek to restore their status by rushing forth to slight the deceased Pontiff.[66] Thus, along with those who had been

---

even the same rank as Rome, Alexandria, and Antioch, which are the *tres praecipuae ecclesiae* (*ibidem*).

[62] *Ibid.*, no. 82, p. 434: "absque Romanae sedis Romanique pontificis consensu nullius insurgentis deliberationis terminus daretur" (for parallel passages from the Frankish letters, see the note *ad locum*).

[63] In the East Nicholas carried out what he had intended to do, it would seem, in the Western Frankish Kingdom. If the Pope had actually investigated into the validity of Hincmar's election (above note 55) and deposed him, the case would have been very much the same. The difference was that Ebbo was dead whereas Ignatius was still alive.

[64] Haller, *Nikolaus*, p. 127, speaks of Nicholas' successor as of "ein Glückstreffer, der nicht seiner Kunst zu danken war."

[65] *Epistolae* VII, no. 3, p. 400 sq. On this letter, cf. W. Kremers, *Ado von Vienne. Sein Leben und seine Schriften*, Diss. Bonn (Steyl, 1911), pp. 43–45.

[66] *Ibid.*, p. 401: "Adiuro autem, ut omnibus metropolytis Galliarum haec intimetis, ne, si hic factum fuerit concilium, sic q(uidam?) recuperationem sui status assequantur, ut in derogationem defuncti praesulis prosiliant, etc."

involved in the affair of Lothar II and other similar cases, Anastasius fears above all the *metropolytae Galliarum* who may be seeking a restoration.

The letter of Anastasius introduces us into a world of which the foundations seem about to collapse. Indeed, Hadrian II (867–872) did not pursue the policy of his predecessor with the same vigor as the latter, but he was anxious to emphasize that he was inspired by the same principles.[67] In a letter to the bishops who had participated in the synod of Troyes (867), he asked them to resist any attack on the person or decrees of his predecessor on the part of the Greek Emperor or any member of the clergy, but at the same time he announced that the Apostolic See might be assuaged by a humble apology.[68] When Ado of Vienne, alarmed by the above letter of Anastasius Bibliothecarius, urged the new Pope to abide by the policy of his predecessor, the Pope answered much in the same tenor.[69] He may have compromised to some extent with regard to Lothar II and Waldrada, but with regard to the territorial clergies he followed the example of his predecessor.[70] This is shown by the incident of Hincmar, bishop of Laon.[71]

The latter claimed to have grounds of complaint against his King, Charles the Bald, and against his namesake, uncle, and archbishop, Hincmar of Rheims. The younger Hincmar, therefore, appealed to the Pope, and firm letters in his favor were dispatched to Charles the Bald and Hincmar of Rheims (868).[72] In the next year the tone of the papal letters, both to the King and to the Archbishop, become most violent.[73] For a moment Pope Hadrian seems to have believed that Hincmar of Laon did not mean his appeal to Rome seriously,[74] but when a Frankish synod of Douzy (871) deposed Hincmar

---

[67] It is with Anastasius' letter to Ado of Vienne in mind that we ought to read the account of the curious scene *Liber Pontificalis*, ed. Duchesne, II, 176 sq. When Hadrian thanked God that he had given the Church a man such as Pope Nicholas, the audience praised him for fulfilling, not tearing up the will of his father (Nicholas) and for following his decrees.

[68] *Epistolae* VI, no. 3, p. 700. Part of this letter agrees word for word with the above mentioned letter of Anastasius to Ado.

[69] *Ibid.*, no. 13, pp. 713–715 (A.D. 868). Same attitude in Photian affair, see *ibid.*, no. 37, p. 747; no. 38, p. 749; no. 39, p. 751 (all of A.D. 868); no. 41, p. 761 (A.D. 871).

[70] When Hadrian II (*Epistolae* VI, no. 7, p. 705, A.D. 868) refused to take up the case of the deceased Ebo of Rheims — a case which might have led to the deposition of Hincmar of Rheims — he was following the policy of the late Nicholas (above p. 279).

[71] On this affair, see Schrörs, *Hinkmar*, pp. 315–353.

[72] *Epistolae* VI, no. 14 and 15, pp. 715 sq.

[73] Only fragments of these letters are preserved, see *ibid.*, no. 20, p. 724 (A.D. 869) and the King's indignant references to papal letters quoted in the note *ad locum*.

[74] *Epistolae* VI, nos. 29, 30, p. 734 sq. (A.D. 871).

of Laon, Hadrian refused bluntly to confirm the decision of Douzy and declared his intention to try Hincmar of Laon at Rome.[75] This intention he upheld until his death (872) but in a more than mitigated form:[76] he claims that he wants to observe all the rights of the metropolitan bishops; that Hincmar of Laon should come to Rome, but would be tried in the province at Rheims; and that if he should refuse to come,[77] he would thereby condemn himself, and the Church should no longer be bothered by this affair. There can be no doubt about it that in the last year of his life Hadrian yielded to the alliance of the Western Frankish King and his clergy; there are, however, clear indications that this decision was due to political (not ecclesiastical) reasons. The false rumor of the death of the Emperor Lewis II in 871 had raised the question of the imperial succession[78] and in the letter to Charles the Bald, in the paragraph preceding the disguised retreat in the case of Hincmar of Laon, Pope Hadrian offered Charles the Bald the Empire after the death of his nephew, Lewis II.[79] Thus the Pope's ultimate retreat in the case of Hincmar of Laon does not mark the end of the concept of the universal church, but is an attempt to humor the prince whom he had chosen as the future protector of this institution. With Hadrian's letter of 872 he initiates a new policy of rendering the alliance between the Gallican clergy and its King innocuous by drawing the royal partner over into the papal camp — a policy which had been foreshadowed by the alliance between Pope Nicholas I and Charles the Bald in the *causa Wulfhadi* (above p. 278). The coronation of Charles the Bald at Rome (875) was the climax of the new papal policy which tried to obviate the danger of a Gallican Church by making its King the ally[80] and protector of the universal church.

The effect of this new alignment on the Western Frankish Church may be observed in a papal letter which Pope John VIII (872–882) dictated only a few days after the coronation of Charles the Bald.[81]

[75] *Ibid.*, nos. 34 and 35, pp. 739–742 (A.D. 871).

[76] *Ibid.*, no. 36, p. 745 sq. (A.D. 872).

[77] One cannot help wondering whether this is not an invitation to *make* Hincmar of Laon refuse to come. The secret instructions mentioned in the next sentence of the letters must have reassured the King even further that Hadrian had dropped Hincmar of Laon.

[78] *Annales Fuldenses, anno* 871, p. 74. See Calmette, *La Diplomatie Carolingienne etc.*, pp. 134–143.

[79] German and French scholars disagree (and will always disagree) as to the reason of preferring Charles the Bald to a member of the Eastern branch. For the German side, see Dümmler, *Geschichte des Ostfränkischen Reichs* (2nd ed.), II (Leipzig, 1887) 349 sq.; for the French side, A. Lapôtre, *L'Europe et le Saint Siège à l'époque carolingienne, première partie: Le Pape Jean* VIII (872–882) (*Paris*, 1895), ch. v.

[80] Lapôtre, *Europe*, p. 259, speaks of "l'alliance de l'Empire et de la papauté."

[81] *Epistolae* VII, no. 3, p. 315 sq.

It is well known that Hincmar of Rheims, undoubtedly the greatest among the Western Frankish archbishops, had disapproved of the imperial policy of Charles the Bald. In spite of this, his unbending loyalty may have contributed to the failure of the campaign undertaken by Lewis the German against the territory of the new Emperor. Yet John VIII did not select Hincmar when, in the above letter, he appointed a papal vicar *per Gallias et Germanias*, but chose the archbishop of Sens. Hincmar of Rheims saw in the establishment of the new papal vicar an encroachment on the rights of the metropolitan. bishops, and it was because of his stubborn resistance that the new institution soon sank into oblivion.[82] In this case the Gallican church was stronger than the Pope backed by its sovereign.

In summarizing our results, we may say that the Papacy from Nicholas I to the last moments of Hadrian II had fought against the territorial church on Western Frankish and Lotharingian soil. Initiating a new policy in 872 A.D. the Popes eventually succeeded in breaking the alliance between the territorial clergy of Gaul and its King by winning over one of the partners to its own side. But the war went on, and even gained new impetus, on Eastern Frankish territory.[83] Here the conflict turned on missionary work, and this brings us to the second part of our enquiry.

II

The barbarian invasions had given the Church a new task and new problems: the Christian religion had to be propagated anew and, in the beginning at least, this new start had to be undertaken by those ancient centers of Christianity which had not perished. It is not possible here to review the history of these missions, but we shall attempt to determine the papal attitude towards them.

It may be said that the great missionary centers of the period after the Barbarian invasions were Rome, Byzantium, and Celto-British Christianity. Wherever Rome sent its missionaries, it was bound to compete with rivals who represented one or the other of these centers

---

[82] For details, see Schrörs, *Hinkmar*, pp. 358–376.

[83] The first real conflict between Papacy and Eastern German church occurred in 866–67 when a papal mission ousted the Bavarians from Bulgaria. Why were there no clashes before and why did they happen then? Lewis the German had been the ally of the Emperor, Lewis II, from 857 on (Calmette, *Diplomatie Carolingienne*, p. 34) and the Pope could hardly afford to offend the ally of his protector. It seems furthermore that the long and prosperous reign of Lewis the German had unified the Eastern Kingdom to such an extent that the Pope realized the difficulty of an attack against the Eastern Frankish Church. Since 865, however, papal relations with Lewis the German had deteriorated (von Schubert, *Die sogenannten Slavenapostel*, p. 11) and there is a possibility that already in 867 A.D. Pope Nicholas had considered the transfer of the imperial dignity to Charles the Bald (Perels, *Papst Nikolaus*, p. 148).

of missionary work. The conversion of the Anglo-Saxons[84] begun by Pope Gregory the Great had to be undertaken despite the opposition of representatives of the Celto-Irish Church: in the first half of the seventh century the Celts not only refused to go over to the Roman side, but for thirty years (634–664) even succeeded in impressing their ecclesiastical ideas on their Anglo-Saxon conquerors. At the end of this period Rome won out, but the independent and even anti-Roman spirit of the Celtic Church, as represented by wandering missionaries, was to cause many difficulties to papal missions in other regions. While the Pope tried everywhere to establish new ecclesiastical provinces for the Roman Church, the natural tendency of the princes and their local clergies was to found their own churches.

This tendency of papal policy can be seen in the papal choice of missionaries. Augustine, sent to the Anglo-Saxons, was the prior of a Roman monastery; his immediate successors were also sent from Rome. The great archbishop Theodore of Canterbury was even a monk from Tarsus in Cilicia, and only in 692, a full century after the beginning of the Anglo-Saxon mission, do we find the first native at Canterbury.[85] Willibord and Boniface[86] were Anglo-Saxons strongly influenced by their Irish and British neighbors. Other examples might (and will) be added, but the above suffice to show that as long as possible the Popes were careful in the choice of their missionaries; they avoided sending to a new region of missionary activity a native of this same region. A foreigner was less likely to ally himself with local interests against the Roman See. He would depend in many respects on the Pope and would therefore remain an obedient servant of St Peter. Only when Roman Christianity was firmly implanted, or under strong pressure of a political kind, would the Popes agree to entrust the new province to native hands.

In the second part of the eighth century a new and vigorous competitor appeared on the missionary field, the Franks. Under Charlemagne, the victories of the Frankish arms were as a rule accompanied by an expansion of Frankish ecclesiastical influence: Frisia, Saxony, Bavaria, Aquitaine, even the Slavic lands (see below) were drawn into the orbit of the Frankish Church. For our purpose it will be sufficient to analyze in more detail Frankish missionary activities during the ninth century.

[84] For the Anglo-Saxon mission, see von H. von Schubert, *Geschichte*, I, 263–287; E. Caspar, *Geschichte des des Papsttums von den Anfängen bis zur Höhe der Weltherrschaft* (Tübingen, 1933), II, 676-688; R. Aigrain, in A. Fliche, and V. Martin, *Histoire de l'Eglise* v (Paris, 1938), 277–328. [85] Caspar, *Papsttum*, p. 862, and note 1.

[86] On St. Boniface, see Schubert, *Geschichte*, I, pp. 299–305; Caspar, *Papsttum*, II, pp. 694–723.

The Scandinavian mission had begun during the last years of Charlemagne.[87] The first serious attempt was made by Ebbo of Rheims in 822 and, although the mission was based on the result of imperial diplomacy, Pope Paschal I appointed him his legate and ordered him to consult on all problems with the Roman See; Paschal also entrusted a certain Halitgarius, Ebbo's companion, with the special mission of reporting from time to time to the Holy See on the progress of their mission.[88] The results of this mission were mediocre, and it was only when Ansgar (a monk of Corbie later transferred to its foundation of New Corbie and himself probably of Saxon origin) was active as a missionary in Scandinavia (826–830) that some success is recorded. When Hamburg was made an archbishopric in 831 and hence became center of the northern mission, Ansgar was made its first archbishop and received the pallium from Pope Gregory IV.[89] Complications arose when in 845 Hamburg was sacked and burned by the Danes. It was ultimately decided to unite Hamburg with Bremen but, as the bishop of Bremen was a suffragan of the archbishop of Cologne, the consent of the latter was deemed necessary for a measure which would place Bremen under the jurisdiction of another archbishop. When Gunthar, whom we have seen playing a prominent role in the affair of Lothar's divorce, had become archbishop of Cologne (850), he opposed the union of Hamburg and Bremen for some time on the ground that a suffragan see could not in fairness be transformed into an archbishopric and that he (Gunthar) could not diminish the privileges of his see.[90] In 862 at the latest, Gunthar yielded on this point reserving, according to the *Vita Anskarii*, confirmation on the part of the Pope.[91] Whether this reservation is historical or not,[92] Pope Nicholas certainly was of the opinion that Gunthar of Cologne had transgressed his powers; for, in answer to an enquiry of Lewis the German, he declared in 864 that Gunthar should never have been asked for and should never have given permission to make the bishop of Bremen an archbishop over Danes and

---

[87] von Schubert, *Geschichte*, II, pp. 501–510; Amann, *Epoque carolingienne*, pp. 247–255, 447–450

[88] *Epistolae* v, no. 11, pp. 68–70 (*ca.* A.D. 822). See von Schubert, *Geschichte*, II, p. 504.

[89] F. Curschmann, *Die älteren Papsturkunden des Erzbistums Hamburg*, etc. (Hamburg und Leipzig, 1901), p. 13, no. 1a.

[90] *Vita Anskarii*, ed. G. Waitz (Hannover, 1884), ch. 23, p. 48 sq.: "Qui primo quidem fortiter his reniti coepit, iustum non esse multipliciter asserens, ut sedes suffraganea in archiepiscopalem verteretur, nec se debere honorem sedis sui (sic!) in aliquo minuere."

[91] *Ibidem*, p. 49: "postremo tamen, et ipsis regibus et cunctis simul episcopis ibi aggregatis, pro hoc ipso eum rogantibus et omnino causa necessitatis id licitum fore dicentibus, respondit, si apostolica auctoritate firmaretur, ex se quoque ratum esse."

[92] On this point, see A. Hauck, *Kirchengeschichte Deutschlands* (Leipzig, 1890), II, pp. 625 sq., note 6.

Swedes.[93] This clause is of the greatest importance: it shows clearly that, in the eyes of the Pope, missionary activity was the special province of the See of Rome, and that no other member of the clergy had a right to interfere.[94] In spite of this rebuke, Nicholas supported the *votum* of Lewis the Pious and Lewis the German;[95] he confirmed the union of Hamburg and Bremen, forbade any archbishop of Cologne to exercise authority in the new diocese, and threatened any future opponent of his measure with the anathema.[96] At the same time Nicholas seems to have dispatched a letter directly to Ansgar in which he complied with his request, but announced at the same time that unless Ansgar followed in all respects the faith and decrees of the Apostolic See he would be deprived of his privileges.[97] Thus we find that, although the Scandinavian mission had been undertaken under imperial auspices, the Papacy did not miss any opportunities to bring it under its influence. In view of the balance of political powers, it was natural that the actual influence was small in the last years of Charlemagne and under Lewis the Pious, but tended to in-

[93] *Epistolae* VI, no. 26, p. 291 sq. (A.D. 864): "Ut episcopus Bremonensis, licet a Gunthario hæc non potuerit dari licentia nec ab eo tale quid peti debuerit, tamen pro amore domni regis, quia pia est eius petitio, cum nostra auctoritate in praedicto loco Bremon potestatem et honorem archiepiscopatus super Danos et Swevos habeat et simili modo sui successores per tempora futura perpetualiter teneant atque possideant."

[94] It might be argued that in 864 the Pope deposed Gunthar of Cologne and that this circumstance would explain his remark. I grant that in 864 Pope Nicholas would have used almost any argument to slight Gunthar, but even then he can hardly have blamed the archbishop of Cologne for an action which he had taken when he was still archbishop, and Ansgar and Lewis the German for requesting such action, unless this action itself, in the view of the Pope, lay outside the reach of an archbishop of Cologne.

[95] Curschmann, *Die älteren Papsturkunden*, no. 4a, p. 21: "magnorum principum uotum Hludouuici, uidelicet diuae recordationis augusti et aequiuoci eius filii excellentissimi regis, tam huius apostolicae auctoritatis praecepto, quam etiam pallii datione, . . . roborare decreuimus." The word *uotum* is used again with regard to the royal decision, see p. 22: "nostro hoc uotum roborante decreto," p. 23: "secundum reuerendissimi regis Hludouuici uotum."

[96] *Ibidem*, p. 23: "Nullus uero archiepiscopus Coloniensis ullam sibi deinceps in eadem diocesi uindicet potestatem . . . . Itaque omnia a dilecto filio nostro, rege Hludouuico, ad hoc deo dignum officium deputata, nostra etiam pia eius vota auctoritate firmamus. Et quia casus praeteritorum nos cautos faciunt in futurum, omnem quoque adversantem uel contradicentem atque piis nostris his studiis quolibet modo insidiantem, anathematis mucrone percutimus atque perpetuae ultionis reum diabolica sorte damnamus etc." The first part of this document (down to *muniamus*) is genuine, B. Schmeidler, *Hamburg-Bremen und Nordost-Europa vom 9. bis 11. Jahrhundert etc.* (Leipzig, 1918), pp. 128–159.

[97] The existence of this letter, of which only a fragment is preserved, has been proved by Schmeidler, *Hamburg-Bremen*, pp. 143–151, 248 sq.; see Curschmann, *Die älteren Papsturkunden*, no. 4a, p. 23: "Ueruntamen ista omnia superius annexa ab apostolica sede beatitudini tuae indulta agnosce, si a fide et decretis sanctae catholicae et apostolicae Romanae ecclesiae in nullo penitus declines. Quod si a fide et institutis aut sanctionibus te tanto sublimantis honore sedis apostolicae declinare studiose praesumpseris, his nostris tibi collatis careas benefeciis."

crease as time went on. The fact remains that from the first the Popes did everything in their power to bring the Scandinavian mission under their control: a papal "liaison officer" was to accompany Ebbo, the latter was to consult with Rome on all problems that might arise, the principle was proclaimed that the Holy See alone, and not the Frankish clergy, could authorize the placement of a bishopric under a new missionary archbishopric. Distrust of the Frankish clergy is the leitmotiv of the papal policy with regard to the Scandinavian mission.

This distrust was to flare up into open rivalry on the Bulgarian question,[98] and here it was to be crowned with the most spectacular success. King Boris of Bulgaria had been baptized in 863–64,[99] probably by Photius himself, but already in 866 the Bulgarian king felt dissatisfied when the Byzantines refused to create a Bulgarian patriarchate. Boris sent ambassadors to Regensburg, the residence of his ally, Lewis the German, and asked him for a bishop and priests.[100] At the same time the Bulgarian king, who was bargaining for the best offer, inquired of Pope Nicholas how the Bulgarian people could be baptized and asked for bishops and presbyters.[101] Both the Pope and the German king were only too glad to take the neophytes under their protection. Lewis the German sent the bishop Ermenrich of Passau, with presbyters and deacons, to Bulgaria and procured the sacred vessels and books from his brother Charles the Bald.[102] Pope Nicholas, on the other hand, answered the Bulgarian questions in a famous memoir[103] and dispatched two missionaries to Bulgaria: Paul, bishop of Populonia, and the famous Formosus of Porto.[104] The Frankish envoys, headed by Ermenrich of Passau, had been received with due respect (*cum debita veneratione*) by Boris, but they found to their great distress that the bishops sent by the Pope were already preaching and baptizing all over the country. Under these circumstances, the Frankish missionaries, with the proud bishop Ermenrich of Passau at their head, could do no better than return to their king. There can be no doubt that Lewis the German and the

[98] For details, see Lapôtre, *L'Europe et le Saint-Siège*, pp. 47–58; von Schubert, *Geschichte*, II, 514–518; Amann, *Epoque Carolingienne*, pp. 476–482; Perels, *Papst Nikolaus*, pp. 160–164; Dvorník, *Slaves*, ch. VI, pp. 184–195.

[99] On the date, see G. Ostrogorsky, *Geschichte des Byzantinischen Staates, ein Byzantinisches Handbuch im Rahmen des Handbuches des Altertumswissenschaft* (Munich, 1940), p. 161, note 1, and the references.

[100] *Annales Bertiniani*, anno 866, ed. Waitz, p. 85 sq.; *Annales Fuldenses*, anno 866, p. 65.

[101] *Liber Pontificalis*, ed. L. Duchesne, II, 164. The demand for bishops is mentioned *Annales Bertiniani, loc. cit*   [102] *Annales Bertiniani*, p. 86; *Annales Fuldenses*, p. 65.

[103] *Epistolae* VI, no. 99, pp. 568–600.   [104] *Liber Pontificalis, loc. cit.*

entire Frankish Church felt this failure to be a profound humiliation.[105]

We are now ready to direct our attention to the situation in Bavaria.[106] We have reserved this topic for the end of our discussion because it brings us back to our starting point, the Slavonic Apostles. The christianization of the Duchy of Bavaria had been completed around the year 700,[107] but Bavaria still lacked an ecclesiastical organization; only Frankish and Celto-British missions operating from Frankish territory were active among the Bavarians.[108] Against this expansionist tendency of the Franks the Bavarian Duke Theodo sought support with the Pope. In 716 Pope Gregory II despatched a bishop and two Roman clerics who were to make Bavaria an ecclesiastical province of the Roman church: new bishops were to be ordained *ex auctoritate beati Petri apostoli*; the right of appointing an archbishop is reserved to the Holy See; and if the papal envoys find a suitable candidate for this post, they are to send him to Rome, otherwise the Pope himself will send one to Bavaria.[109] This attempt of Pope Gregory at winning over Bavaria was unsuccessful: during the following decades the Frankish rulers won an ever increasing following in the Bavarian clergy and nobility.[110] So strong was Frankish propaganda in Bavaria that a second attempt of Rome to win influence in Bavaria with the help of St Boniface failed[111] and in 788 the duchy fell into the hands of Charlemagne without a fight and as a consequence of internal disintegration.[112]

The Bavarian dukes, and Tassilo in particular, undoubtedly had

[105] It is probable that this humiliation in Bulgaria made Ermenrich of Passau particularly violent when he tried another papal missionary who had interfered with a Bavarian mission, Methodius.

[106] Caspar, *Geschichte*, II, 691–694, 703–706; H. Löwe, *Die karolingische Reichsgründung und der Südosten. Studien zum Werden des Deutschtums und seiner Auseinandersetzung mit Rom*, Forschungen zur Kirchen- und Geistesgeschichte XIII, Stuttgart, 1937, esp. ch. I (see the review by H. W. Klewitz, *Historische Zeitschrift*, CLXI [1940], 341–344).

[107] Hauck, *Kirchengeschichte*, I, 336.

[108] Hauck, *Kirchengeschichte*, I, 337–343; Caspar, *Geschichte*, II, 692; Löwe, *Karolingische Reichsgründung*, p. 6.

[109] Migne, *Patr. Lat.*, LXXXIX, 332 B.C. See Brackmann, *Germania Pontificia*, I, pt. 2, p. 387, note 1; Caspar, *Geschichte*, II, 692–694. Against Caspar who states that "dieses Reorganisationsstatut für die bairische Kirche ging mit Schweigen über alle bisher dort tätigen wanderbischöflichen Kräfte weg," I should like to point out that by considering the possibility of finding a suitable candidate for the future Bavarian archbishopric in the Duchy itself the Pope must have thought precisely of these *Wanderbischöfe*.

[110] This development is well described by Löwe, *Karolingische Reichsgründung*, pp. 9–71. See also a very important article of A. Brackmann, "Die Anfänge der abendländischen Kulturbewegung in Osteuropa und deren Träger," *Jahrbücher für Geschichte Osteuropas*, III (1938), 185–215, esp. pp. 187 sq.

[111] Caspar, *Geschichte*, II, 704–706. Later attempts of the same type, *ibid.*, pp. 710 sq., 714.   [112] Löwe, *Karolingische Reichsgründung*, pp. 60–72.

encouraged missionary work among the Slavic Carantani, their neighbors to the south, whom Tassilo had defeated in 772, as well as among the Avars in Pannonia along with their Slavic subjects.[113] But while the Bavarian Dukes had had to concentrate most of their effort on the Frankish frontier and had been unable, accordingly, to embark on any large scale missionary propaganda in the east, the conversion by the sword and the gospel was to be much more successful and intensive under Carolingian auspices. In the midst of his wars against the Avars Charlemagne (796) had sought an *inviolabile foedus* with Pope Leo III, and it has been shown recently that this request for an alliance was motivated by the problems of Christian missions in the territories conquered from the Avars.[114] Two years later Charlemagne "ordered" (*mandare*)[115] the Pope to grant Bishop Arno of Salzburg the pallium and make him an archbishop in the province of the Bavarians.[116] Leo acted in accordance with this order, but in his letter of the same year and month addressed to the Bavarian bishops[117] the initiative for the new foundation is attributed to the Bavarian clergy, the act of founding itself is carried out by the Pope, and Charlemagne himself is only mentioned as having given his consent.[118] Evidently the Pope had to yield to an "order" emanating from the stronger partner of the alliance, but was at the same time upholding a legal claim. Now it has been maintained[119] that this papal claim concerned only the organization of the Bavarian clergy and had nothing to do with missionary activity. Against this view the most eminent expert

[113] The extent of Bavarian missionary activity has been exaggerated by Löwe, *Karolingische Reichsgründung*, pp. 51–55, 73, see Brackmann, *Abendländische Kulturbewegung*, p. 188 sq.

[114] See the articles of A. Brackmann, "Die Anfänge der Slavenmission und die Renovatio Imperii des Jahres 800," *Sitzungsberichte der Preussischen Akademie der Wissenschaften, Phil.-Hist. Klasse*, 1931, IX (brief résumé in his "Reichspolitik und Ostpolitik im frühen Mittelalter," *ibid.*, 1935, XXXII, esp. pp. 946–949) and the other article quoted above note 110. In this last article Brackmann has refuted the objections of Löwe, *Karolingische Reichsgründung*, pp. 72–86.

[115] It will be remembered (above note 95) that in A.D. 864 Lewis the German was to submit a mere *votum* (not a *mandatum*) that Pope Nicholas confirm the archbishopric of Hamburg. This change from *mandatum* to *votum* characterizes the shift which had taken place in the relations between Papacy and Franks since the time of Charlemagne.

[116] *Epistolae* V, no. 4, p. 59 sq. = W. Hauthaler, and F. Martin, *Salzburger Urkundenbuch*, II, fasc. 1 (Salzburg, 1910), no. 2 b, p. 4 sq. (Brackmann, *Germania Pontificia*, I, pt. 1, p. 9, no. 9): "... vestra a Deo protecta regalis excellentia mandasset nobis per ipsum [Fardolf, abbot of St Denis], quod Arnono episcopo [of Salzburg] pallium tribueremus et in provincia Baiowariorum archiepiscopum constitueremus."

[117] *Salzburger Urkundenbuch*, pp. 2–4, no. 2 a (Brackmann, *Germania Pontificia*, I, pt. 1, p. 8 sq., no. 8).

[118] Brackmann, *Slavenmission*, p. 79; Löwe, *Karolingische Reichsgründung*, p. 84; Brackmann, *Abendländische Kulturbewegung*, p. 204.

[119] Löwe, *Karolingische Reichsgründung*, pp. 83–86.

in Carolingian ecclesiastical history has pointed out that in his letters the Pope could not openly lay claim to the mission in the newly conquered territory because of the brilliant successes of Charlemagne against the Avars; all that he could do, therefore, was to reserve his legal claims to the new archbishopric and to pass over in silence[120] the question of the mission. This latter view of the papal policy is preferable, all the more so as Pope Leo did *not* pass over in silence the missionary problem. In a letter of April 11, 800, addressed to the Bavarian clergy, Leo urges the latter always to obey their archbishop (Arno) "whom you have received canonically from the holy catholic and apostolic Roman church." Then he continues: "For as the holy catholic and apostolic Roman church received authority from the holy fathers that *in a province expanded and widened with God's guidance in the way of Christianity* the apostolicus of the same church and vicar of the blessed Peter, the prince of the Apostles, has power of establishing a metropolis and of ordaining an archbishop, we have done so even in your parts."[121] It is certain then that in April, 800, at any rate, the Pope connected the creation of the archbishopric of Salzburg with the expansion of the Bavarian province and no other expansion can be meant but that brought about by the wars against the Avars.

During his imperial period Charlemagne launched a systematic attack against the Slavs which proceeded from the South to the North and extended the sphere of Frankish Christianity to the Vistula in the East and the Baltic Sea in the North.[122] It is understandable that as long as Charlemagne lived the Frankish Church retained the monopoly of converting the pagans and that it was Charlemagne himself who organized the missionary work. From a Bavarian source

[120] Brackmann, *Abendländische Kulturbewegung*, p. 204: "Sein (the Pope's) Schweigen über die Mission als eine der künftigen Hauptaufgaben des neuen Erzbistums erklärt sich aber unschwer aus der politischen Lage. Nach den glänzenden Erfolgen Karls im Avarenlande konnte er nicht gut Wünsche und Rechtsansprüche auf dieses Gebiet äussern."

[121] *Epistolae* v, no. 5, p. 61 = *Salzburger Urkundenbuch*, no. 2 d, p. 8 (Brackmann, *Germania Pontifica*, I, pt. 1, p. 9, no. 10): "Sicut enim a sanctorum patrum (sic!) sancta catholica et apostolica Romana ecclesia auctoritatem suscepit, ut in provintia, que Deo auspice in christianitatis more amplicata et dilatata est, licentiam habeat eiusdem ecclesiae apostolicus et vicarius beati Petri apostolorum principis constituere metropolim et ordinare archiepiscopum, ita et in partibus fecimus vestris." It is curious that Brackmann overlooked this passage: it is the strongest support for his thesis. Löwe, *Karolingische Reichsgründung*, 85 discusses this letter but does not mention our passage. — It is not impossible that we owe the only independent manuscripts of this letter, the "Rotulus" of the Vienna *Haus-, Hof- und Staatsarchiv*, to the desire of collecting the evidence against Methodius, see Brackmann, *Germania Pontificia*, I, pt. 1, p. 5; *Salzburger Urkundenbuch*, II, fasc. 1, first page of the (unpaginated) introduction.

[122] Brackmann, *Slavenmission*, pp. 80–82; *Abendländische Kulturbewegung*, pp. 205–208.

written in 870 we learn that Charlemagne and his son Pippin assigned the triangle between the rivers Raab, Drau, and Danube to the bishop of Salzburg.[123] While Arno of Salzburg was still on his return trip from Rome where he had received the pallium (798), he received instructions from Charlemagne to start his missionary work and from then on the latter proceeded smoothly until the time of Methodius.[124]

Under Charlemagne's weaker successors the Papacy begins to emphasize, ever more frequently and efficiently, the missionary claim which it had made shortly after the archbishopric of Salzburg was founded. This happened repeatedly at the time of the Scandinavian mission.[125] It happened again when the Bulgarians were converted to Christianity and when in the great clash between Roman and Frankish missionaries the former carried the day.[126] It was to happen again when Methodius appeared as papal delegate first in Pannonia and then in Moravia and was at loggerheads with the Bavarian clergy.

We may now return to our original problems which, in the course of our discussion, have not only found an answer but have also become much more pointed. Why did the Pope support the mission of a Byzantine abbot in a region which, for more than seventy years, had been actively missionized by the Bavarian clergy under the high protection of the Eastern Frankish king? How can it be explained that the Bavarian clergy in alliance with its king dared to imprison the papal delegate and archbishop of a new missionary province? How could they, later, succeed in ousting the disciples of this missionary from Moravian soil? By following up the papal policy towards the territorial churches from the pontificate of Nicholas I on, we have seen that their backing of Methodius lay in the general line of a long drawn fight against a dangerous alliance between the Frankish territorial clergies and their princes. Nicholas had announced his program in his fight against archbishop John of Ravenna. He had carried it further against King Lothar II and the Lotharingian clergy in the case of Gunthar and Thietgaud: the open rebellion of the latter allied with their king (and for a while even with the Emperor) found its expression in the great manifesto of 864. The violent language of this

---

[123] *Conversio Bagoariorum et Carantanorum*, ch. 6, *M.G.H.*, *SS.*, xi, 9. On the date, see Dümmler, *Ostfränkisches Reich*, ii, 376, note 1; W. Wattenbach, *Deutschlands Geschichtsquellen im Mittelalter* etc., i, ed. 7, (Stuttgart and Berlin, 1904), 291.

[124] *Ibid.*, chs. 8–14., pp. 9–14. The *Conversio* is a legal plea rather than an historical work (Wattenbach, *Deutschlands Geschichtsquellen*, p. 291), but the opposition which Methodius found in Pannonia shows that the general thesis presented by the *Conversio* is correct. See also von Schubert, *Die sogenannten Slavenapostel*, pp. 15 sq.

[125] Above p. 285 f., and Brackmann, *Abendländische Kulturbewegung*, 208 sq.

[126] Above p. 287.

invitation to disobedience towards the Pope must still have been ringing in the ears of the entire church when Methodius appeared in Pannonia and claimed for the Apostolic See a region into which the Bavarians prided themselves on having introduced Christianity. In the affairs of Rothad and Wulfhad Pope Nicholas had widened the theater of the conflict by attacking the same alliance on Western Frankish soil. The case of Wulfhad, however, had shown the territorial clergy fighting singlehandedly against a new alignment, their King allied to the Pope: on Western Frankish soil the Papacy was beginning to split the dangerous alliance between territorial clergy and King and to draw the King into its own camp. At the death of Nicholas I the specter of this dangerous alliance had once more shown its head, and during the major part of his pontificate Pope Hadrian II had continued the fight, as is evidenced by the affair of Hincmar of Laon. It was only when, in the last year of his life, Hadrian selected Charles the Bald as his candidate for Empire that he relinquished the struggle: with the senior partner of the territorial alliance drawn into his orbit and concerned with the problems of Empire, the opponent had become a *quantité négligeable*.

Yet the alliance between king and territorial church and the resulting danger had not vanished. On Eastern Frankish soil it had been more firmly cemented than in the West and down to the last year of Nicholas' pontificate the Papacy had not interfered effectively in territorial affairs. It had put its claims on missionizing the pagans on record during the Scandinavian mission of Hamburg and the Slavic mission of Salzburg, but had been unable to carry them into effect. In 866, however, Rome had expelled a Bavarian mission from Bulgaria and after 870 Rome through Methodius was trying to do the same in Pannonia. In the ninth century as before, Rome tries to establish a monopoly on missionary activity and to subject new fields of such activity to its influence by sending out its own missionaries.

From 870 to his death (885) Methodius had to fight against the Frankish clergy supported by the German king. Their attacks were essentially directed against what they considered Roman encroachment but, as the royal power was on the decline, this direction could not be admitted openly. The admitted targets of their attack, therefore, were the Slavonic liturgy and the orthodoxy of Methodius. Even when Pope Stephen V (885–891) withdrew his protection from the late Methodius's disciples in 885, his instructions for the delegates to Moravia show that the Holy See meant to retain its influence over the archbishopric.[127]

Thus Methodius and the Slavonic liturgy lost out. If, however, the main thesis which was developed above is true, we should expect that, even after dropping Methodius personally, the Papacy continued to apply the principles which had prompted it to support the Slavonic Apostle during his lifetime. By examining, therefore, the further ecclesiastical development of Moravia we may subject our argument to a crucial test of its correctness. We know nothing of the course of the papal delegation to Moravia in 885, but we do learn the events which followed it: the Swabian Wiching of Nitra, Methodius' arch-enemy, was given a free hand in Moravia and expelled Methodius' disciples.[128] This state of affairs lasted until 892, when Wiching went over to the Bavarian side and became chancellor of Svjatopluk's opponent, King Arnulf.[129] After the death of Svjatopluk (894) and a civil war between his sons,[130] a new papal delegation arrived; we do not know whether it was called by Moimir, son of Svjatopluk, or whether it came on papal initiative. We learn of this mission headed by an archbishop and two bishops from a letter addressed by the entire Bavarian clergy to Pope John IX in 900.[131] According to this interesting document the Moravians are boasting that by bribery they had persuaded the Pope to send the bishops to Moravia which, as the Bavarians claim in their letter, belongs to the diocese of Passau. The delegation, the Bavarian bishops aver, in violation of all the canons, ordained an archbishop and three bishops for Moravia. They assert furthermore that they are acting also in the name of their king, Lewis the Child. Here we recognize, fifteen years after the death of Methodius, the same forces at work which had supported and attacked him during his life time. The Papacy is trying again to assert its claim on the Moravian mission against an alliance between the Bavarian clergy and its king and the latter are opposing Pope John IX just as they had opposed his predecessors.

Neither the Popes nor the Bavarians were to reap the harvest of Methodius' work in Moravia: in the first years of the tenth century the heathen Magyars swept over Pannonia and Moravia. Youthful Christianity perished under their onslaught.

HARVARD UNIVERSITY

---

[127] See the *commonitorium*, *Epistolae* VII, no. 33, p. 352 sq.; it is unquestionably genuine. I abstain from relying on Pope Stephen's letter *Quia te zelo* (*ibidem*, pp. 354–358) as its authenticity is doubtful.   [128] Dümmler, *Ostfränkisches Reich*, III, 256–258.

[129] *Ibid.*, 362.   [130] *Ibid.*, 390–392.

[131] Brackmann, *Germania Pontificia*, I, pt. 1, p. 163 sq., no. 14. I am using the edition of H. Bresslau, in *Historische Aufsätze Karl Zeumer . . . dargebracht*, Weimar, 1910, pp. 22–26. German translation of large extracts in Dümmler, *Ostfränkisches Reich*, III, 510–515. The importance of this document for the papal policy has been emphasized by Laehr, G., "Das Schreiben Stephans V. an Sventopulk von Mähren," *Neues Archiv für ältere deutsche Geschichtskunde*, XLVII (1928), 172.

A full bibliography on the Slavonic Apostles down to
1969 will be found in the second edition of F.Dvornik,
Les Légendes de Constantin et de Métode vues de Byzance,Hattiesburg,Mississippi,1969,pp.xi-xxxviii;on
relations with the West and the Papacy in particular,
pp.xxxii-xxxviii;see also Dvornik's Byzantine Missions among the Slavs.SS.Constantine-Cyril and Methodius,Brunswick,New Jersey,1970,429-464. Succinct
and stimulating statement of the problems concerning
the Slavonic Apostles by Dimitri Obolensky,Cambrid-
ge Medieval History IV,Part I,Cambridge,1966,496-
501;fuller treatment in his book The Byzantine Com-
monwealth.Eastern Europe 500-1453,London,1974,
183-203 (bibliography pp.486-488). On the tomb of
Constantine at S. Clemente in Rome see Leonard Boyle
A Short Guide to St.Clement's,Rome,1968,50 (reproduction of Constantine's portrait fig.7,p.49)and by
the same author in the cooperative volume Cirillo e
Metodio,Rome,1964,159-193. Basic work on the Pseudo-Isidorian Decretals:Horst Fuhrmann,Einfluss und
Verbreitung der Pseudo-Isidorischen Fälschungen von
ihrem Auftauchen bis in die neuere Zeit,Schriften der
Monumenta Germaniae Historica 24,vols. I-III,Stutt-
gart,1972-1974,with discussion of many of the episodes touched upon in my article from the point of view
of the role of Pseudo-Isidore. Jean Devisse,Hincmar
Archevêque de Reims,Travaux d'histoire éthico-politi-
que 29,3 volumes,Paris,1975,was not accessible to
me.It is my impression that since the first edition of
Dvornik's Les Légendes in 1933 research on the Slavonic Apostles has concentrated on the investigation of
the textual tradition and on the linguistic and literary
evaluation of their work,rather than on the place of
their mission in the political and ecclesiastical history of the ninth century.

THE STRENGTH OF EMPIRE AND CAPITAL
AS SEEN THROUGH BYZANTINE EYES*

ONE of the best syntheses in the field of Byzantine history, Charles Diehl's famous *Byzantium: Greatness and Decline,* is devoted partially to an analysis of Byzantine strength.[1] In this work the author attributed the powerful position of the Byzantine Empire in the Middle Ages to elements such as the Byzantine autocracy, the high quality of its military establishment, the skill of its diplomats, the efficiency of its administrators, the economic and manpower resources of the territories controlled by Byzantium and the importance of the capital as its economic and social center. Naturally Diehl derived his factual information from the Byzantine primary sources, but it is noteworthy that the pragmatic linking of facts with the problem of Byzantine greatness is due in all cases to Diehl's historical judgment and was not expressed in the primary sources. Byzantine literature was permeated with the thought of the greatness of empire and capital, yet the Byzantine sources had, as will be seen, a simple explanation of Byzantine strength which allowed them to dispense with the kind of historical analysis to be found, for example, in Diehl's book. The Byzantines attributed the greatness of their empire and capital to their supernatural defenders and therefore had little incentive to develop either a historical analysis of their greatness or a secular theory of their political development. On the absence of political theory the late Professor N. H. Baynes remarked: "The subjects of the empire were convinced that their policy was approved by God . . . And if you believe that, what profits it to discuss other politics? It would be but a waste of breath."[2] For the same reason the Byzantines never explained in secular terms the strength of

---

* The substance of this paper was delivered orally at the meeting of the American Historical Association at Chicago in December 1959. In its present form it owes a great deal to the advice of Professor Ernst Kitzinger, to whom I wish to express my sincere gratitude.

[1] Charles Diehl, *Byzance, Grandeur et Décadence* (Paris, 1919). English translation: *Byzantium: Greatness and Decline* by N. Walford (New Brunswick, N. J., 1957).

[2] N. H. Baynes, "The Thought-World of East Rome," as reprinted in *Byzantine Studies and Other Essays* (London, 1955), p. 32.

mediaeval Byzantium. Yet Byzantine civilization, and especially its literature, is inspired by the conviction of Byzantine strength and can hardly be understood without a thorough grasp of its elements and presuppositions. It is the purpose of this paper to explain in detail the Byzantine view concerning the strength of capital and empire, as it existed before the crusades shattered Byzantine confidence in their historical destiny.

For the purpose of this discussion the Byzantine self-image may conveniently be divided into three components: a religio-political ideology or rhetoric; a theory of kingship based on a specific philosophy of history; and a justification of empire. Of these three components the most important in Byzantine eyes was the second. In the following discussion, however, the religio-political ideology will be placed first because here the classical roots can most clearly be demonstrated. It should be noted that in any given context these three components are apt to combine and intermingle. With regard to them, as in fact in most other respects, Byzantium was indebted to the Biblical tradition, to classical Greece and to ancient Rome. However, at Byzantium these three sources of inspiration did not prove of equal strength and authority. The Biblical fount was of course the strongest and its impact was felt whenever Greek or Roman materials were adopted at Byzantium. But it is also true that the Hellenic source was operative at Byzantium only as modified by the Romans. The Byzantine attitude towards Greece and Rome may be studied with the help of the Byzantine use of the words "Rome" and "Hellas" and "Greece." The Byzantines called their capital "Rome" or "Second Rome" or "New Rome." They referred to the inhabitants of the Byzantine Empire as *Romaioi* and to the Empire as *Romania*.[3] The term "Hellas" and some of its derivatives, on the other hand, had at an early time come to refer to paganism or more precisely to the Greek pagan tradition and normally retained its derogatory sense down to the twelfth century.[4] *Graecia* and *Graeci* were used occasionally in a neutral or favorable sense but normally they too had an uncomplimentary meaning. It is surely no accident that the

---

[3] Robert L. Wolff, "Romania: The Latin Empire of Constantinople," SPECULUM, XXIII (1948), 1–34, esp. 5 f.; F. Dölger's "Rom in der Gedankenwelt der Byzantiner," as reprinted in his *Byzanz und die europäische Staatenwelt* (Ettal, 1953), pp. 70–115, esp. pp. 77–98. Dölger's essay is basic for the topic of Byzantine ideology. Constantine Porphyrogenitus in the *Vita Basilii* (Theophanes Continuatus V, ch. 1, p. 211, ed. Bonn) calls the Byzantine period "the entire duration of Roman rule at Byzantium." A specific view of history, that of *translatio imperii* (cf. Dölger, pp. 98–101), underlies this terminology. According to it, the history of Roman rule may be divided into two historical phases distinguished by the shift of the capital from Rome to Byzantium, but in spite of this transfer it is the same Roman Empire that ruled from Rome first and from Constantinople afterwards. (Unless noted otherwise, all Byzantine historians and chroniclers will henceforth be cited from the Bonn Corpus.)

[4] K. Lechner, *Hellenen und Barbaren im Weltbild der Byzantiner: Die alten Beziehungen als Ausdruck eines neuen Kulturbewusstseins*, Diss. Munich, 1954; cf. the review by P. Lamma, *Byzantinische Zeitschrift*, XLIX (1956), 404–407, and the summary by Lechner in *Saeculum*, VI (1955), 292–306. On the pagan connotation of the Hellenic name and the emergence of the new term *Helladikoi* in the ninth century, see P. Charanis, "Hellas in the Greek sources of the Sixth, Seventh and Eighth Centuries," *Late Classical and Mediaeval Studies in Honor of Albert Mathias Friend, Jr* (Princeton, 1955), p. 172 f., n. 111. Constantine Porphyrogenitus seems to be the only mid-Byzantine author with a favorable view of the Hellenic name; cf. Lechner, *Hellenen und Barbaren*, pp. 51–53.

opprobrious meaning of *Graecus* makes its appearance in Procopius at about the same time when the term *Romania* is first found in the more popular language of Malalas to designate the Byzantine Empire.[5] *Graecia* was meant and felt to be a denial of all the positive values evoked by the term *Romania*. This hesitant or even negative attitude of the Byzantines towards the Hellenic heritage was due, at least partly, to the memory of Rome's victories over the Hellenistic states and of the incorporation of the Greek cities into the Roman Empire, a memory which compromised the prestige of Greece in the eyes of Rome and Byzantium. In the Byzantine self-image, then, Hellenic traditions were admitted only to the extent that they could be de-paganized and harmonized with the Byzantine claim of being the ruling power of a universal empire.

I. *The Religio-Political Ideology.*

The development of Constantinopolitan and imperial rhetoric is closely associated with the circumstances surrounding Constantinople's foundation. When Constantine the Great founded the Second Rome on the Bosporus, he thought of it as a second capital which he tried to make as similar to the first Rome as possible. It is well known that before the end of the fourth century resemblance to Rome was replaced by equality with Rome and that from the sixth century on *Rhomē* was used to designate Constantinople. Like every ancient city, Constantinople quickly acquired an official rhetoric by virtue of which it would be able to compete with the older cities of the Empire. Yet while there exist monographs on the literary praises of Athens, Rome, and Antioch, a collection and evaluation of the *Laudes Constantinopoleos* is still lacking[6] and only a few random

---

[5] Procopius, *Anecdota*, 24 §7 (p. 147, 5, ed. Haury) mentions among Justinian's and Theodora's injustices toward the military that "they accused them of being Γραικοί, implying that it was quite impossible for any person born in Hellas to be brave." Roman contempt for the Greeks is of course much older than the contemptuous use of the name (cf., for example, Juvenal, III, 58 ff.). Ducange's remarks (*Glossarium Mediae et infimae Graecitatis* [Lyons, 1688], *verbo* Γραικοί) are still instructive. For the neutral use of Γραικοί as "speaking Greek" (as opposed to "speaking a Slavic language") see Constantine Porphyrogenitus, *De Administrando Imperio*, ch. 49 (p. 228, 6, ed. Gy. Moravcsik and R. J. H. Jenkins [Budapest, 1949]). The term Γραικία seems to be used in a friendly sense in Theodorus Studita, *Epist.* 74 (ed. I. Cozza, *Nova Patrum Bibliotheca*, VIII, 60 f.).

[6] The bibliography on the literary glorification of cities will be found in A. D. Nock, "The Praises of Antioch," *Journal of Egyptian Archaeology*, XL (1954), 76–82, esp. 76, n. 3. A. P. Rudakov, *Ocherki Vizantiiskei Kultury po Dannym Grecheskoi Agiografii* (Moscow, 1917), ch. iii, pp. 110–137, collected some items on Constantinople from hagiographic sources. See also R. L. Wolff, "The Three Romes . . . ," *Daedalus* LXXXVIII (1959), 291–311, esp. p. 293 f. In the text following above I use in the first place an interesting text of the fourth century, Himerius' *Oratio* (VII) XLI, *In Urbem Constantinopolim*, ed. Aristides Colonna, Scriptores Graeci et Latini consilio Academiae Lynceorum editi (Roma, 1951), pp. 168–176. (Incidentally, this is the enigmatic "Aimonius Sophista" from whom a fragment is quoted by Leo Allatius in the Bonn edition of Georgius Acropolites, p. 205). Himerius' speech represents an attempt to adapt a Christian rhetoric, probably already developed for Constantine's city, to the pagan revival under Julian, but if one abstracts from this tendency, it may serve as an early inventory of the main topics of this rhetoric. The topics of Himerius' speech will be supplemented by some references to later authors dealing with the Praises of Constantinople, but the subject deserves full monographic treatment. I abstain from using the *Vita Ioannis Acatii* (*Bibliotheca Hagiographica Graeca*, ed. 3, Subsidia Hagiographica, no. 8a [Brussels, 1957], no. 829; henceforth abbreviated *BHG*[3]) because its date is unknown; it seems to be late.

examples can be given here. According to a fourth-century pagan example of literary "Praises of Constantinople," Constantinople is no ordinary city but almost a continent transformed into a city.[7] She is so large that she has made a large city out of the waters containing the continent. She extends over all beaches and all plains and has made land of the sea and forced it to become part of the city.[8] She is the beginning and end of Europe; she rules over as large a part of Asia as of Europe.[9] At Constantinople the Black Sea ceases to swell; at Constantinople the Aegean begins; the Bosporus is her neighbor, the Bosporus which, by being named after Zeus' mistress Io, foretold that he would nurse in his bosom a Zeus-born king.[10] The sea protects Constantinople,[11] a populous[12] city inhabited by a mixed race of natives and heroes who have made it truly an imitation of a kind of heaven,[13] a people from beginning to end purified by the gods.[14] The city is of great beauty, adorned with gold, by the arts, the senate house, baths, theaters, her greatest ornament is the emperor.[15] She is also the home of philosophy and literature.[16] A notion that is almost invariably found in the "Praises of Constantinople" is that of Constantinople the imperial city. Inherited from the first Rome on the Tiber, this epithet remains one of the designations of Constan-

---

[7] Himerius, *Oratio* (VII) XLI §4 (p. 170, 42, ed. Colonna).

[8] Himerius, *Oratio* (VII) XLI §6 (p. 171, 61, ed. Colonna). On Constantinople as the *megalopolis*, cf. Constantinus Porphyrogenitus, *Vita Basilii*, ch. 7 (Theophanes Continuatus, p. 221); *Vita Petri Episcopi Argivorum*, BHG³ 1504, ed. I. Cozza-Luzi, *Nova Patrum Bibliotheca*, IX, Part 3 (Rome, 1888), p. 2.

[9] Himerius, *Oratio* (VII) XLI §4 (p. 170, 45, ed. Colonna).

[10] Himerius, *Oratio* (VII) XLI §5 (p. 170, 48, ed. Colonna). Constantinople's location at the meeting place of two continents and the manifold advantages derived by the inhabitants from communications by sea remained a favorite topic, see Libanius Ep. 114 (ed. Foerster, x, 114); Procopius, *De aed.* I 5 (pp. 27–29, ed. Haury); cf. also Nock, *Journal of Egyptian Archaeology*, XL (1954), 80, n. 4.

[11] Himerius, *Oratio* (VII) XLI §10 (p. 173, 110, ed. Colonna). Cf. Nicephorus Phocas' harangue to his troops when he was on the point of capturing the capital, Leo Diaconus III 5 (p. 43).

[12] Himerius, *Oratio* (VII) XLI §11 (p. 173, 13, ed. Colonna). On the large number of houses (and consequently of inhabitants) at Constantinople see Nock, *Journal of Egyptian Archaeology*, XL (1954), 80.

[13] Himerius, *Oratio* (VII) XLI §11, (p. 173 f., 118 ff., ed. Colonna). The notion of Constantinople as the imitation of some kind of heaven seems an adaptation of the Christian topic of *Christomimesis*, see above n. 6.

[14] Himerius, *Oratio* (VII) XLI §13, (p. 174, 135, ed. Colonna).

[15] Himerius, *Oratio* (VII) XLI §8 (p. 172, 81, ed. Colonna). On the wealth and splendor of Constantinople, on its Senate and the beauty of its churches, see also the *Vita Petri Episcopi Argivorum* (above n. 8) p. 2.

[16] Himerius, *Oratio* (VII) XLI §12, (p. 174, 125, ed. Colonna). Cf. on literature §2, p. 169, 12 Colonna. On Byzantine pride in its learned men, see the career of the famous philosopher Leo, as told by several authors, e.g., by Theophanes Continuatus IV 27–29 (pp. 185–192) and Scylitzes-Cedrenus, vol. II, p. 169: the Emperor Theophilus refuses to loan Leo's services to the Khalif at Bagdad "because he considered it absurd to give others one's own treasure and to hand over to foreigners the knowledge of reality [i.e., philosophy] for the sake of which the Roman [i.e., Byzantine] people is admired and respected by all" (Theophanes Continuatus IV 27, p. 190). On Leo, see recently Cyril Mango, "The Legend of Leo the Wise," *Recueil des Travaux de l'Institut d'Etudes Byzantines* [Belgrade], VI (1960) 59–93, esp. 91. Another example of learning as a topic in the Praises of Constantinople in the *Vita Petri Episcopi Argivorum* (above, n. 8), p. 2.

tinople throughout the centuries, but in the mid-Byzantine period it is often combined with another, "god-protected."[17]

The concept of Rome and the Empire's eternity, however, could not simply be transferred to Constantine's city, as it conflicted with Christian doctrine. Consequently, it was modified into an expression of hope that capital and empire would last to the end of the world.[18] In this connection it is also worthwhile to mention the belief, also inherited from Rome, in *pignora imperii*, of which Constantinople was thought to possess for example the Staff of Moses, the Throne of Solomon, the Constantinian Cross. They related the emperors to their Israelite prototypes or to their Byzantine predecessors and thus were thought to guarantee the existence of the Empire for a long time to come.[19] In addition there existed at Constantinople a well-developed discipline devoted to the interpretation of astrological phenomena, of dreams, of omina and of the inscriptions and sculptural decoration of columns and statues. Columns and statues especially were popularly believed to prophesy not only the fate of individual emperors but also the end of city and empire. The *Patria Constantinopoleos*, written during the last years of the tenth century, are full of references to mysterious and threatening texts and sculptures found on columns at Constantinople. On the *Forum Tauri* for example stood an equestrian statue brought to Constantinople from Antioch. On its square base were engraved "stories of the last fate of the city when the Russians would be about to destroy the city itself." As Charles Diehl remarked a generation ago: "What makes [such accounts] interesting is the Byzantine belief in the certain and inescapable end of empire and city, this pessimistic feeling which knew and accepted, without resistance and complaint, a limited fate for capital and monarchy. . . . "[20] Yet even these Byzantine views of the end of world, capital, and empire, which the texts are fond of describing in terrifying tones, are colored, as it were, by the warm glow of pride in the capital, the monarchy, and the empire. One of the basic prophecies describing the end of the world, the *explanatio somnii* attributed to the Tiburtine Sibyl and going back to the fourth century A.D., mentions, during the reign of the Antichrist and immediately following upon the invasion of Gog and Magog, an interesting episode: the

---

[17] See for example Justinian's Constitution *De Conceptione Digestorum* §10, ed. Th. Mommsen and P. Krueger, Corpus Iuris Civilis, I, 8 (Cod. Iust., *ibid.*, II, 69, I, 17 §10): "Romam autem intelligendum est non solum veterem, sed etiam regiam nostram, quae deo propitio cum melioribus condita est auguriis." It appears frequently in Theophanes, as p. 485, 12; p. 486, 1 (ed. de Boor, vol. I) and regularly in Constantine Porphyrogenitus, *Vita Basilii* (Theophanes Continuatus, e.g., pp. 213, 221, 223, 227 etc.). In official documents this epithet appears frequently joined with another, "guarded by God," see for example the protocol of the first session of the Sixth Ecumenical Council (680 A.D.), ed. Labbé, tom. VII, 629 A. Same combination of epithets in Theophanes, p. 384, 25; 385, 1 (ed. de Boor).

[18] Otto Treitinger, *Die oströmische Kaiser-und Reichsidee* . . . , 2nd ed. (Darmstadt, 1956), p. 122. On this point a characteristic passage is found in Nicephorus Presbyter, *Vita Andreae Sali* (*BHG*³ 117) of the tenth (?) century (ch. 209, *P.G.*, CXI, 853 B).

[19] Treitinger, *Die oströmische Kaiser- und Reichsidee*, pp. 132–134. Interesting Russian data on *pignora imperii* in R. L. Wolff, "The Three Romes," *Daedalus*, LXXXVIII (1959), p. 301.

[20] *Patria Constantinopoleos*, II 47 (p. 176, 7, ed. Th. Preger). Cf. Ch. Diehl, "De quelques croyances byzantines sur la fin de Constantinople," *B.Z.*, XXX (1930), 192–196, esp. p. 195 f.

king of the Romans (i.e., the Byzantine emperor) will defeat Gog and Magog, will journey to Jerusalem, "will lay down his headgear and all his royal attire and hand over the Christian kingdom to God the Father and Jesus Christ his son."[21] In the prophecy of the Tiburtine Sibyl this episode follows immediately upon the appearance of Antichrist and the defeat of the tribes of Gog and Magog by the emperor; it precedes the end of the Roman (Byzantine) Empire.[22] In the *Revelation* of Pseudo-Methodius, probably of the seventh century, the same episode occurs, only that here the crown is deposited by the last emperor on top of the Cross and is taken into heaven together with the latter.[23] The same feature is found in a version of the *Visiones Danielis*, probably of the ninth century.[24] This motif of the surrender of royal rule by the last emperor, in fact the figure of this last emperor itself, is not of Christian origin but is derived from pagan Roman oracles (where the last emperor surrenders his power to the senate) which in turn may go back to an oriental prototype.[25] Whether of Roman or of oriental origin, the effect of this import into Christian prophecy was that it assigned to the Roman or Byzantine emperor and empire a central role within the divine plan of history. One might say — although of course no Byzantine would have said it — that in this view of history the kingdom of Heaven was no more than an improved, purified, and infinitely successful version of the *Basileus'* earthly kingdom. This figure of the last emperor and of the surrender of his power to God thus provided for at least a modicum of continuity from the familiar world of the Byzantine Empire to the strangeness of the heavenly kingdom and thereby deprived the events of the last

[21] Ernst Sackur, *Sibyllinische Texte und Forschungen* (Halle a.S., 1898), p. 186: "Cum autem audierit rex Romanorum [i.e., of the attack of Gog and Magog], convocato exercitu debellabit eos atque prosternet usque ad internicionem et postea veniet Jerusalem et ibi deposito capitis diademate et omni habitu regali relinquet regnum christianorum Deo patri et Iesu Christo filio eius." On the date of the text, see Sackur, p. 162. The Greek text of the Tiburtine Sibyl has been discovered in two manuscripts; cf. S. G. Mercati, "È stato trovato il testo greco della Sibilla Tiburtina," *Annuaire de l'Institut de Philologie et d'Histoire Orientales et Slaves*, IX (1949), 473–481. I plan to comment on these Greek texts in another context.

[22] Sackur, *Sibyllinische Texte*, p. 186: "et cum cessaverit imperium Romanum, tunc revelabitur manifeste Antichristus . . . ."

[23] *Revelatio Pseudo-Methodii* (*BHG*[3] 2036). Latin text ed. by E. Sackur, *Sibyllinische Texte und Forschungen*, pp. 60–113, esp. p. 93. Greek text edited by V. Istrin, *Otkrovenie Mefodia Patarskago*, etc. (Moscow 1897); this monograph was also published by Moscow University in *Chteniia* of the Imperatorskoe Obshchestvo Istorii i Drevnostei Rossiiskikh, 1897 and 1898, and it is to this last publication that reference is made here, see 1897, Part IV, Sect. iii, pp. 45 f. On Istrin's publication, see the review by C. E. Gleye, *B.Z.*, IX (1900), 222–228, and on Pseudo-Methodius the article by M. Kmosko, "Das Rätsel des Pseudomethodius," *Byzantion*, VI (1931), 273–296 (according to him, the original was written in Syriac under Muawiya, 661–680). The deposition of the *regalia* upon the Cross naturally presupposes that it is on earth (at Jerusalem). Ernst Kantorowicz, "The King's Advent and the Enigmatic Panels in the Doors of Santa Sabina," *Art Bulletin*, XXVI (1944), 207–231, esp. 226, has examined the ancient tradition of the ascent of the Cross at the time of Jesus' resurrection and connected it with the apocryphal *Gospel of Peter*. Unless Pseudo-Methodius represents a different tradition, it must be supposed that at the time of the Last Emperor the Cross has already descended to earth in preparation for Jesus' Second Coming.

[24] *Visio Danielis β* (*BHG*[3] 1872), ed. A. Vasiliev, *Anecdota Graeca-Byzantina* (Moscow, 1893), pp. 38–43, esp. p. 43. Cf. also the *Vaticinium de futuris rebus Byzantinis* (*Vita sancti Andreae Sali*, cf. n. 18 above), *ibid.*, pp. 50–58, esp. p. 54 (*BHG*[3] 117 d).

[25] Sackur, *Sibyllinische Texte*, p. 169 f.

days of some of their terror. The Roman notion of the eternity of capital and empire thus finds a late expression in this Byzantine idea of an orderly transfer of power from the last Byzantine emperor to God.

The religio-political rhetoric of Constantinople and the Byzantine Empire, then, which formed part of the Byzantine self-image, presents a curious mixture of elements. Partly it arose in clear competition with other cities of the Empire and emphasized Constantinople's superiority to the more ancient centers with regard to its location on the sea route from the Aegean to the Black Sea and on the land route from Europe to Asia, as well as the number of its dwellings. In other respects it adopted topics from the *Laudes Romae*, such as the epithets of *urbs regia* and *urbs aeterna*, both adjusted in various ways to the Christian religion. Nothing is as significant for the change from the early Byzantine to the mid-Byzantine period in this respect as a comparison of the official usage in the sixth and seventh centuries: Justinian I speaks of the [*urbs*] *regia*, the protocol of the sixth ecumenical council of the "imperial city guarded by God."[26] At pagan Rome the gods' concern for city and empire had been no more than one among many topics constituting together the Praises of Rome. At Christian Byzantium the Christian environment produced, at the latest in the mid-Byzantine period, a change of emphasis or better: the emergence of an emphasis where there had been none before.[27] At Christian Byzantium one feature came to overshadow all other items in the traditional repertory of religio-political rhetoric: Constantinople and the Empire are under the protection of God, Christ, and the saints. Of course the notion that a particular city had its divine protector or protectors was in no way novel and had been a standard item in the repertory of the praises of cities for centuries. The novelty consists in the fact that, beginning in the mid-Byzantine period, this one theme of the repertory grew in importance and frequency at the expense of the others. This idea had already received a classic formulation in the sixth century, when the African poet Corippus made the Byzantine Emperor Justin II reply to a haughty speech by an Avar envoy: "The Roman [i.e., Byzantine] state belongs to God."[28] In the seventh century, during the critical years of the Persian Wars, the poet George of Pisidia and his contemporaries represent God, Christ, the Virgin Mary, and the other saints as fighting on the Byzantine side, in fact sometimes taking an active part in combat, as the Homeric gods had done.[29] At the end of the tenth century the historian Leo the Deacon tells how the

---

[26] Note 17 above.

[27] Cf. W. Gernentz, *Laudes Romae* (Diss. Rostock, 1918). With the emergence of the emphasis on divine protection compare A. Grabar's remarks in *L'Empereur dans l'art byzantin* (Paris, 1936) on the disappearance of many themes from the repertory of Byzantine imperial art in the fourth to sixth centuries and the emergence of Christian symbols beginning with the late sixth century.

[28] Corippus, *In Laudem Iustini*, III 333 (ed. I. Partsch, MGH, Auct. Ant., III [Berlin, 1879], 145): "res Romana Dei est, terrenis non eget armis."

[29] *Georgius* Pisida, *Exped. Pers.* II 100 (p. 101, ed. Agostino Pertusi, Studia Patristica et Byzantina, VII, 1959): God the general of the Byzantine armies; III 385 (p. 133, ed. Pertusi): God the general of the heavenly and earthly armies; III 401 (p. 133, ed. Pertusi): Heraclius the *hypostrategos* under God's supreme command; *Bell. Avar.* 451 ff. (p. 196, ed. Pertusi): the Virgin Mary, in the thick of battle, fights invisibly, hits, inflicts wounds, deflects the sword of a Persian, overturns the enemy's ships. (Lines 457 ff. show that the poet considers the Virgin's military activities unusual. The same view is taken in *Chron. Pasch.*, p. 397). Theodorus Syncellus, the probable author of a homily preached

Emperor John Tzimisces, after his victorious return from Bulgaria, was received by the inhabitants of the capital urging him to enter the city in triumph upon a chariot inlaid with gold and drawn by white horses, but the emperor refused and placed instead upon the chariot's throne of beaten gold an image of the Virgin captured in Bulgaria.[30]

Byzantium's ambivalent attitude towards the Hellenic heritage, the modifications made to the belief in the eternity of city and empire, and the new emphasis on supernatural protection had been the logical consequence of the Empire's Christianization. The same process introduced into Byzantine ideology the entire repertory of Old Testament typology and prophecy. Byzantine emperors, for example, are regularly compared with Old Testament figures such as Moses, Elijah, David, etc.[31] In more general terms the emperor is frequently referred to as "the Lord's Anointed."[32] The fulfillment at seventh-century Byzantium of Old Testament narratives and prophecies is the pervading theme of a homily preached on 7 August 627 at St Sophia by Theodore Syncellus to commemorate the city's delivery from the Perso-Avar siege in the preceding year.[33] The speaker demonstrates that the Biblical account of the attack by the kings of Syria and Israel upon Jerusalem and Judah (735 B.C.) was a foreshadowing and a type of the Perso-Avar siege of Constantinople in A.D. 626. In the course of this demonstration Constantinople is expressly identified with Jerusalem.[34] The preacher takes this identification so seriously that he gives the three Byzantine envoys sent in

---

one year after the Perso-Avar siege of Constantinople in 626 (*BHG*³ 1061; on the authorship see F. Barišić, "Le siège de Constantinople par les Avares et les Slaves en 626," *Byzantion*, xxiv [1954], 373 f.) is more reserved than George of Pisidia. According to Theodore, the Virgin acts "through the hands of Christian soldiers" (L. Sternbach, *Rozprawy Akademii Umiejetnosci*, Wydial Filolog., ser. ii, tom xiv [Cracow, 1900, p. 306, 1). Note that after mentioning the magister Bonus' military preparations for the defense of the capital, Theodore Syncellus remarks (p. 303, 35, Sternbach): "for God rejoices even in these [military preparations] because he does not wish those that take refuge with him and pin their faith on him for their salvation to be inactive and idle." It sounds like an apology for military preparations; cf. Corippus' "terrenis non eget armis" (n. 28 above). On the emergence of the Virgin Mary as protectress of Constantinople see A. Florov, "La dédicace de Constantinople dans la tradition byzantine," *Revue de l'histoire des religions*, cxxvii (1944), 61–127.

[30] Leo Diaconus, *Hist.*, ix 12, p. 158. Cf. Scylitzes-Cedrenus, *Hist. Comp.*, vol. ii, p. 413, who adds that the emperor considered the Virgin the protectress of the city (πολιοῦχος). More than a century later John Cinnamus was to tell a similar story of the Emperor John Comnenus (*Hist.* i 5, p. 13). See Frolov, *loc. cit.* (n. 29 above), p. 105.

[31] Treitinger, *Die oströmische Kaiser- und Reichsidee*, p. 130.

[32] Thus Theophilus, upon his accession (828), called Leo V in order to show up the enormity of the crime committeed by Leo's murderers, cf. Theophanes Continuatus iii 1, p. 86; Scylitzes-Cedrenus, vol. ii, p. 100. On the messianic role of the king as the basis for a royalist political theory in the Western Middle Ages, see G. H. Williams, *The Norman Anonymus of 1100 A.D.*, Harvard Theological Studies, xviii (1951), esp. pp. 155–174, and R. W. Southern, *The Making of the Middle Ages* (New Haven, n.d.), pp. 92–94.

[33] Cf. n. 29 above.

[34] Theodorus Syncellus, p. 298, 25 ed. Sternbach (addressed to Prophet Isaiah: cf. Isaiah 7). On other Byzantine identifications of Constantinople with Jerusalem see Frolov, *loc. cit.* (n. 29 above), 86.

A.D. 626 to the Avar Chagan the names of King Hezekiah's ambassadors sent to Sennacherib of Assyria.[35] He is, however, not satisfied with this first level of typology but by means of complex chronological computations he discovers similarities between Constantinople's ordeal of A.D. 626, Jerusalem's fatal siege by Nebuchadnezzar (586 B.C.) and Titus' destruction of the Second Temple (A.D. 70).[36] Finally he adds a laborious proof that Ezekiel's prophecy of King Gog's and his northern people's attack on Jerusalem never found (nor could ever find) its fulfillment in historic Jerusalem and is rather to be considered a prophecy of the Perso-Avar siege of Constantinople in A.D. 626.[37] This cumulation of Old Testament links, considerably more elaborate than can be indicated here, undoubtedly is unusual and even betrays an element of intellectual playfulness, but it also reveals in a touching way the comfort and strength which a Byzantine preacher and his audience, not long after the dramatic events of 626, could derive from the equation of the New Rome with the ancient Jerusalem, more generally from the Old Testament as a source for Byzantine ideology and rhetoric.

This religio-political ideology, because it was an ideology and not a philosophical or religious system, could easily be manipulated for political ends. Thus in the tenth century the Emperor Constantine Porphyrogenitus advised his son and heir Romanos, in a confidential handbook of Byzantine diplomacy, the *De Administrando Imperio*, on how to deal with the greedy northern peoples (Khazars, Turks, Russians) and especially with their perennial demands for imperial vestments, for the liquid ("Greek") fire, or — most serious of all — for the hand of a purple-born princess. The father supplied his son with what he called 'plausible speeches and prudent and clever excuses.'[38] Romanos was to reply to barbarian requests for imperial vestments and diadems that God had sent them through an angel to Constantine the Great, charged him to deposit them in St Sophia and to curse anyone who should misuse or alienate them. The advice with regard to the Greek fire and the purple-born princess is cast in the same vein. Constantine Porphyrogenitus certainly was aware that these replies were specious, for in the case of the liquid fire he mentions in the same work that the Byzantines learned of this weapon from a refugee, Callinicus of Heliopolis, under Constantine IV Pogonatus (668–685).[39] Yet the general tendency of these replies is in keeping with Byzantine ideology: *res Romana Dei est*. Constantine's advice to his son was simply a new variation on an old theme, and this theme was in no way discredited because one or the other of the variations did not ring true.

[35] Theodorus Syncellus, p. 306, 20 (ed. Sternbach); cf. IV Reg. 18, 17 ff. He omits the name of the fourth envoy (probably Theodore himself, cf. Sternbach, p. 333; Barišić, "Le Siège de Constantinople," *Byzantion*, xxiv [1954], 374, n. 2, 383), because King Hezekiah of Judah sent three envoys only to King Sennacherib's commanders.

[36] Theodorus Syncellus, pp. 309 f. (ed. Sternbach).

[37] Theodore-Syncellus, pp. 314 ff. (ed. Sternbach).

[38] Gy. Moravcsik and R. J. H. Jenkins, edd., *Constantine Porphyrogenitus: De Administrando Imperio*, Magyar-Gorog Tanulmanyok, 29 (Budapest, 1949), ch. 13, pp. 64–76, esp. p. 66.

[39] Constantine Porphyrogenitus, *De. Adm. Imp.*, ch. 48 (p. 226, ed. Moravcsik-Jenkins).

II. *Theory of Kingship and Philosophy of History.*

In the preceding discussion of Byzantine ideology the Byzantine emperor played only a modest part. This is not accidental, for the ideology had been developed within a literary genre concerned with the praises of ancient cities, notably of Rome, and the ancient city as such had found it notoriously difficult to find a place for the rulers of kingdoms or empires. It will be remembered, however, that under the influence of the Old Testament the emperor as "the Lord's anointed [king]" emerged into Byzantine rhetoric, and this Old Testament view of the Byzantine monarchy remained basic throughout the Byzantine period. It was, however, combined at the time of Constantine the Great with a theory of Byzantine kingship which, as will be seen presently, was based on a profound philosophy of history. The Byzantine ideas concerning their emperor, the Byzantine *Kaisergedanke*,[40] have been treated in a series of excellent works and need only a summary here. In the Byzantine view the emperor was the only legitimate ruler over the entire Christian world in his capacity as God's image and representative on earth. As God's viceroy he was charged with the maintenance of peace in the Christian world, with the Christian mission to the "barbarians," and with the preservation of law. This sublime view of the Byzantine emperor's position constituted an element of enormous strength inasmuch as it assigned the emperor an easily understood place in the divine plan of history.[41] The emperor was selected by God and, as was seen above, at the end of time the last Byzantine emperor would bring about the transition from the earthly to the heavenly kingdom.

This Byzantine *Kaisergedanke* was based in the last resort on an interesting philosophy of history. In a remarkable book Professor Gerhard Ladner has emphasized the connection of the Byzantine *Kaisergedanke* with the concept of renewal.[42] He has demonstrated how, since the age of Constantine, Byzantine "political theology" based the renewal of man upon the role of the emperor as the imitator of Christ. Ladner's results will be utilized on the following pages for an explanation of the Byzantine views of the strength of empire and capital. It will be shown that it was not only the concept of the emperor as imitator of Christ but its connection with a peculiar notion of "newness" and consequently with a

[40] This term was used by F. Dölger, "Bulgarisches Zartum und byzantinisches Kaisertum," reprinted in *Byzanz und die europäische Staatenwelt*, pp. 141 f. (I know of no adequate English equivalent; "imperial idea" would stress the empire rather than the emperor). In the above article as well as in "Europas Gestaltung im Spiegel der fränkischbyzantinischen Auseinandersetzung des 9. Jahrhunderts," reprinted in *Byzanz und die europäische Staatenwelt*, pp. 291 f., Dölger has summarized the Byzantine *Kaisergedanke* in masterful fashion. Among the basic studies of the subject are: Erik Peterson, *Der Monotheismus als politisches* Problem (Leipzig, 1935); André Grabar, *L'empereur dans l'art byzantin* (Paris, 1936); Otto Treitinger, *Die oströmische Kaiser- und Reichsidee*, (above, n. 18).

[41] Cf. Dölger, "Bulgarisches Zartum" (above, n. 40) p. 143: "Despite its splendor, [this conception] was so simple that it was bound to be understood by the last peasant in the most out-of-the-way nook of the empire and that even the lowliest soldier would be willing to shed his blood for its sake."

[42] Gerhart B. Ladner, *The Idea of Reform: Its Impact on Christian Thought and Action in the Age of the Fathers* (Cambridge, Mass., 1959), esp. pp. 107–132.

particular philosophy of history that accounts for Byzantine self-confidence. The Byzantine idea of newness is a key concept of Byzantine political thought, for it was part (at least since the late fourth and fifth centuries) of the official designation for the capital, the "New Rome."[43] Not long ago it was observed that the notion of "newness" pervades one of the masterpieces of Byzantine prose, the biography of Basil I by Constantine Porphyrogenitus, and that Basil is here represented as the great "refounder and renovator of the Roman State."[44] It is worthwhile to attempt to define more closely the meaning of the "newness" brought about by Basil I.[45] One seventh of Basil's biography is concerned with the emperor's building activities. Here the language of "newness" occurs frequently, but curiously enough is not found where a modern reader would expect it: with regard to *brand*-new buildings. Basil's two most important new constructions were the New Church (*Nea*) and the New Building (*Kainourgion*), both within the imperial palace. Now it is obvious that the notion of "newness" appears in the name of both structures, yet Constantine Porphyrogenitus carefully explains that the New Church was dedicated by Basil to Jesus Christ, the Archangel Gabriel, the Prophet Elijah, the Virgin Mary, and St Nicholas, and that the name "New Imperial Church" represented not the official designation but the popular usage, perhaps of Constantine's own day.[46] The New Building, on the other hand, appears under no other denomination in the *Vita Basilii.*[47] With this important exception, however, the language of newness is conspicuously absent from Constantine's description of Basil's new constructions.[48] The situation is different where Constantine discusses Basil's repairs of earlier buildings. The entire section on Basil's building activities is introduced by the following statement:

At all times the Christ-loving Emperor Basil . . . showed concern for many of the holy and

---

[43] On Constantinople the New Rome, see the basic study by Dölger, cited n. 3 above, esp. pp. 83–98.

[44] R. J. H. Jenkins, "The Classical Background of the Scriptores post Theophanem," *Dumbarton Oaks Papers*, VIII (1954), 11–30, esp. p. 23.

[45] Dölger, in the article cited in note 3 above, has called attention to the meaning: "young" and "youthful" often given since the sixth century to the designation of "New Rome" in contrast to the Old Rome on the Tiber. In the present study the emphasis will be on another connotation of the word. In the translations of Greek texts following above it should be borne in mind, however, that the Greek word *neos* and its derivatives mean both "new" and "young."

[46] Constantine Porphyrogenitus mentions the *Nea* three times in the *Vita Basilii.* The fullest and most detailed account is found in chs. 83–86 (pp. 325–328) in the narrative of Basil's building activities. The other two instances are incidental. In ch. 68 (p. 308, 19) it is said that Basil kept the sailors busy by employing them in the construction of the church of Jesus Christ, the archangels (i.e., Gabriel and Michael) and the Prophet Elijah. Finally, in ch. 76 (p. 319) the author mentions the gifts offered by Basil's aged protectress Danelis to the church of Jesus Christ, the Archangel Michael and the Prophet Elijah "which we are accustomed to call the new imperial church." Cf. R. Janin, *La géographie ecclésiastique de l'empire byzantin*, I, 3: *Les églises et les monastères* (Paris, 1953), p. 374–378.

[47] Constantine Porphyrogenitus, *Vita Basilii*, ch. 89, (pp. 331–335). Cf. A. Vogt, *Basile Ier* (Paris, 1908), p. 408.

[48] The vocabulary used for the building process: ἀνοικοδομή (*Nea*, p. 308, 20); ἐγείρειν (*Nea*, p. 308, 20; 319, 14; = to build at least since Hellenistic times); οἰκοδομεῖν (*Nea*, p. 319, 12; 325, 9); δομεῖν (*Nea*, p. 325, 17); ἀναδέμεσθαι (*Kainourgion*, p. 331, 22); ἀνεγείρειν (*Kainourgion*, p. 332, 4):

divine churches. They had been damaged or completely destroyed by earlier earthquakes or were threatened with impending collapse because of cracks. By the generous supply and grant of the necessary materials he rebuilt some of them from the ruins and gave them beauty as well as safety. Others he strengthened by appropriate additions and repairs so that they would not collapse, but was responsible for their return to another bloom and youth.[49]

This same language of rejuvenation permeates the entire account of Basil's architectural activities. The western part of St Sophia was in danger of collapse, but Basil "himself, with the experience of craftsmen, strengthened and rejuvenated it and made it safe and durable."[50] At the church of the Holy Apostles, damaged by earthquakes, "he scraped off the [signs of old] age caused by time, removed its wrinkles and made it once again beautiful and young."[51] The church of the Mother of God at Pēgē "which was in ruins and had lost its ancient beauty [Basil] rejuvenated and made more splendid than before."[52] Similar formulae recur throughout the *Vita Basilii*.[53] For Constantine Porphyrogenitus, then, Basil's architectural activities, especially his repairs of earlier buildings, amounted to a renewal and rejuvenation of the city and a struggle against time's ravages, a judgment that finds expression especially in the statement with which he introduced the section on Basil's buildings. This view of imperial building activities was not invented by Constantine Porphyrogenitus but was traditional. For example, one of George of Pisidia's minor poems celebrates a "renewal" of a bath at Constantinople much in the same terms Constantine used three centuries later: Time had captured the bath, just as the barbarians (the Avars and Persians) had captured the cities of the Empire. Heraclius, the conqueror of Scythians and Persians, "rejuvenated" the cities as well as the bath.[54]

It is interesting to note that George of Pisidia's poem compares the "rejuvenation" of the bath with that of the cities of the Empire, i.e., with a political restoration. The same concept of political renewal permeates the *Vita Basilii*. The biographer mentions prominently, for example, that Basil legislated against the practice of Byzantine officials of supplementing their often meager salaries by demanding "tips" for the performance of public services. He speaks of Basil's edicts against this abuse in the following terms:

Striving to eliminate everywhere injustice, this most powerful [ruler, Basil] set up everywhere and dispatched edicts to every region. In them, all gifts which up to that time had

---

[49] Constantine Porphyrogenitus, *Vita Basilii*, ch. 78 (p. 321, 17 — 322, 5).

[50] Constantine Porphyrogenitus, *Vita Basilii*, ch. 79 (p. 322, 9).

[51] Constantine Porphyrogenitus, *Vita Basilii*, ch. 80 (p. 323, 4).

[52] Constantine Porphyrogenitus, *Vita Basilii*, ch. 80 (p. 323, 5). On this church cf. Janin, *Les églises et les monastères*, pp. 332–337.

[53] Church of Apostle Philip, ch. 80 (p. 323, 15; cf. Janin, *Les églises et les monastères*, pp. 508 f.). Church of Apostle Andrew (ch. 81, p. 324, 2; cf. Janin, pp. 32–35). Church of St Ann in Deuteron and church of Demetrius (ch. 81, p. 324, 4; cf. Janin, pp. 39–41, 94). Church of Martyr Aemilianus (ch. 81, p. 324, 6; cf. Janin, pp. 16 f.). Church of Martyr Nazarius (ch. 82, p. 324, 9; cf. Janin, pp. 372 f.). Church of Martyr Plato (ch. 82, p. 324, 16; cf. Janin, pp. 418 f.).

[54] Georgius Pisida, no. XLVIII (ed. L. Sternbach, *Wiener Studien*, XIV [1892], 56). R. Janin, *Constantinople byzantine: Développement urbain et répertoire topographique*, Archives de l'Orient Chrétien, IV (Paris 1930), does not discuss this poem in his section on baths at Constantinople (pp. 209–217).

seemed to be justified by wicked custom [established] by Time were cancelled and eradicated. Equality entire and Justice seemed to return to life as if from some foreign exile and to live among men.[55]

The rhetorical figures are not identical in George of Pisidia's poem and in Constantine Porphyrogenitus' prose, but they have this in common that in both works an emperor is celebrated as a political restorer and time as the great enemy. The last passage from the *Vita Basilii* is closely connected in thought with two others strategically located at the beginning and end of the discussion of Basil's political achievements. In the former it is said that Basil was concerned "to bring some good to his subjects and to have affairs take a visible and great change for the better."[56] With that purpose, Basil took the greatest care in his administrative appointments and selected officials who not only were above corruption but also would protect the poor against the rich.[57] Basil's appointees were eager that "men whom he [Basil] knew to have swooned and fainted because of those that had preceded him [Michael III] should recover and be restored to their ancient prosperity."[58] In a second passage, at the conclusion of Basil's domestic reforms, Constantine remarks that his grandfather manifested the four cardinal virtues and that "everything progressed towards the better. And once again life seemed to have returned to its ancient good order and condition."[59]

There emerges, then, from a study of the *Vita Basilii* a fairly consistent view of Basil's achievement. In his buildings as well as in his military and domestic activities, the emperor waged incessant war against time. Time threatens with senility both the body architectural of the capital and the body politic of the Empire. Time drives the virtues into exile beyond the frontiers of the Empire, weakens buildings and causes the inhabitants of the Empire to faint or to swoon. In his fight against this enemy, the emperor rejuvenates buildings and political institutions. He recalls the virtues from exile, especially by cultivating them himself and by selecting virtuous officials and he strengthens the edifices as well as his subjects. This "change for the better" he brings about by restoring the ancient status which had been corroded by time but which is now happily reproduced by Basil. Constantine Porphyrogenitus' view of the imperial mission, then, is essentially conservative. A good emperor such as Basil functions as the restorer of a splendid past, and the strength of capital and empire lies precisely in their potential for repeated imperial restorations. In conclusion it may be said that the newness of the architectural and political body of capital and empire, which in the *Vita Basilii* figures so prominently among the achievements of the emperor, implies restoration rather than innovation.

[55] Constantine Porphyrogenitus, *Vita Basilii*, ch. 30 (p. 259, 5). This edict is missing from Dölger's *Regesten*.

[56] Constantine Porphyrogenitus, *Vita Basilii*, cf. 30 (p. 257, 18). On the change for the better, see also ch. 72 (p. 315, 10) and ch. 29 (p. 256, 9). In the last passage the change is attributed to God.

[57] Here, as well as in other passages (e.g., ch. 99, pp. 346–348) Constantine Porphyrogenitus attributes to Basil the concerns of the tenth century, i.e., the hostility to large landholders expressed in the social and economic legislation of Romanos I Lekapenos and his successors.

[58] Constantine Porphyrogenitus, *Vita Basilii*, ch. 30 (p. 258, 7).

[59] Constantine Porphyrogenitus, *Vita Basilii*, ch. 30 (p. 258, 7, cf. also p. 256, 9: 257, 19).

What are the roots of this conservative confidence in the past, this fear of time, so characteristic of the Byzantines' view of their empire's greatness? It goes back ultimately to the view of Constantine the Great and of his circle, notably of Eusebius of Caesarea. This emperor's announcements contain indeed the philosophy of history found six centuries later in the *Vita Basilii*. It has not been sufficiently stressed that for Constantine the Great the Christian religion, which he was the first Roman emperor to favor after centuries of persecution, was not a new religion but as old as the world. Immediately upon the defeat of Licinius the emperor declared in a letter to provincials, which is especially interesting for his religious and political views and in which he addresses the Christian God: "Our [religion] is neither new nor novel but Thou hast ordained it with the worship proper to Thee ever since we have believed that the ordering of the universe had been firmly made. But the human race fell and was misled by errors of all kinds, yet Thou through Thy Son, lest Evil should further weigh us down, hast held up a pure light and reminded all men of Thyself."[60] In another letter of the same year 324 Constantine made it clear that the Incarnation was only one very important instance of mankind's recall by God and that he interpreted his own activities as another example of this same process:

He [God] sought my service and deemed it worthy for his will. I started out from the sea near Britain . . . , with the help of a higher power I repelled and scattered the terrors which beset the universe. In this way He recalled the human race, which through my service was taught the worship of the most august law, and at the same time the blessed faith was strengthened under the guidance of a greater power.[61]

Thus, in Constantine's view of history, mankind continued to err even after the Incarnation and had been recalled a second time by Constantine. The establishment of the true religion thus was not a sudden change but was a continuing process which in the days of Constantine had behind it a millennial history. Religiously Constantine's reign therefore brought a "universal renewal,"[62] just as by his military victory over Maxentius a decade earlier the emperor had "freed and restored the Senate and People of Rome to their ancient fame and splendor," as he

---

[60] Eusebius, *Vita Constantini*, II, ch. lvii (p. 64, 15 ff., ed. Heikel). On this letter see H. Dörries, *Das Selbstzeugnis Kaiser Konstantins*, Abhandlungen der Akademie der Wissenschaften in Göttingen, Philolog.-Hist. Kl., Dritte Folge, XXXIV (1954), 51–54, 250. On the authenticity of the letter, see p. 50, n. 2, but neither the authenticity of individual documents cited in *Vita Constantini* nor the vexed question of the Eusebian authorship of the entire work are of critical importance in the context of this paper, as at Byzantium they were never doubted.

[61] Letter to the Orientals, in Eusebius, *Vita Constantini*, II, ch. xxviii (p. 53, 7, ed. Heikel). Cf. Dörries, *Selbstzeugnis*, pp. 43–50, 250. Constantine had expressed a similar idea ten years earlier in a letter to the synod of Arles: "aeterna et religiosa incomprehensibilis pietas dei nostri nequaquam permittit humanam condicionem diutius in tenebris oberrare neque patitur exosas quorundam voluntates usque in tantum praevalere, ut non suis praeclarissimis luminibus denuo pandens iter salutare eas det ad regulam iustitiae converti" (ed. von Soden, *Urkunden zur Entstehungsgeschichte des Donatismus* [Bonn, 1913], No. 18, p. 23). Cf. Dörries, *Selbstzeugnis*, pp. 28–33.

[62] Constantine's letter to the Church of Nicomedia of A.D. 325 (ed. H. G. Opitz, *Urkunden zur Geschichte des arianischen Streites* [Berlin and Leipzig, 1934], no. 27, p. 59, 13). Cf. Dörries, *Selbstzeugnis*, pp. 70–74.

said in the inscription on his statue in Rome.[63] In religious and political terms Constantine interpreted his historical role not as an innovation but as the restoration of past glories.

Similar views are found in the works of Constantine's contemporary, Eusebius of Caesarea, where they form part of a philosophy of history derived through Eusebius' teacher Origen from Hellenistic philosophy. In his *Ecclesiastical History* Eusebius sets out to record the development of a Christian commonwealth antedating the age of Constantine.[64] According to Eusebius, it was no accident that the coming of Christ occurred simultaneously with the disappearance of many small states of the Hellenistic age and the establishment of a universal monarchy of Augustus. Without the Roman Empire the Christian mission would have been impossible and warfare between states and cities would have continued everywhere.[65] With the help of the *Logos*, the Emperor Constantine, God's friend, wears the image of the highest kingship; he imitates God, he steers and stands at the helm of all earthly things. The Saviour prepares the universe for his Father; his friend Constantine makes men ready for the saving *Logos'* kingship. The *Logos* wages war upon the demons; his friend Constantine upon the visible enemies of truth. The *Logos* enables his followers to understand his Father's kingdom; his friend Constantine "like some interpreter of the divine *Logos* recalls the entire human race to the knowledge of God."[66] In Eusebius' view the end of the persecutions and the many conversions of the Constantinian age to Christianity, "a second renewal much superior to the preceding," were brought about by Jesus Christ.[67] These consecutive renewals were rendered necessary by men misusing their freedom and denying God, i.e., by the Fall. Eusebius envisages the restoration of man not as a single historical event but as a historical process occurring in stages: the Fall, Jewish monotheism, the establishment of Augustus' monarchy as an image of the divine monarchy and the coming of Christ, the establishment of the Christian Empire by Constantine.[68] Eusebius does not state explicitly, as

---

[63] As cited in Eusebius, *Vita Constantini*, I, ch. xl (p. 26, 25, ed. Heikel). Cf. Dörries, *Selbstzeugnis* p. 215.

[64] Eusebius, *Historia Ecclesiastica*, V prooem. (p. 400, ed. E. Schwartz, ed. maior) describes his *Ecclesiastical History* as "the narrative concerning the body [of Christians living] according to God." I owe this point to the suggestive article by A. Pertusi, "L'atteggiamento spirituale della più antica storiografia bizantina," *Aevum*, XXX (1956), 134–166, esp. p. 145, n. 2.

[65] On Eusebius' theory of history and kingship the following works were especially helpful: Erik Peterson, *Der Monotheismus als politisches Problem*, etc. (Leipzig, 1935), esp. pp. 71–82 (where the Origenist inspiration of these views is demonstrated); F. Edward Cranz, "Kingdom and Polity in Eusebius of Caesarea," *Harvard Theological Review*, XLV (1952), 47–66; Gerhart B. Ladner, *The Idea of Reform*, esp. pp. 119–125. On the pagan antecedents of Eusebius' and Origen's views of kingship, see N. H. Baynes, "Eusebius and the Christian Empire," *Mélanges Bidez*, II = *Annuaire de l'Institut de Philologie et d'Histoire Orientales*, 1934, pp. 13 ff., reprinted in his *Byzantine Studies and Other Essays*, pp. 168–172.

[66] Eusebius, *Tricennalia*, chs. i (end) and ii (p. 199, 1–23 Heikel). Cf. Cranz, *Harvard Theological Review*, XLV (1952), 53 f.

[67] Eusebius, *Tricennalia*, ch. xvii 5 (p. 255, 6, Heikel). See Ladner, *Idea of Reform*, pp. 119 f. and the passages concerning the Constantinian renewal there quoted from Eusebius' *Ecclesiastical History*.

[68] Cf. Cranz, p. 52 f.

Constantine did in his letter to the provincials, that the Christian religion was co-eternal with the creation of the world, but this view seems to be implied in his philosophy of history. Neither Constantine nor Eusebius had occasion to be concerned with future stages of this historical process, yet throughout Byzantine history all imperial activities were understood as attempts to restore an earlier and better status along the lines of Constantine's and Eusebius' thought.[69]

Constantine's and Eusebius' ideas about history and kingship thus had decisive influence on Byzantine thinking. Their view of Constantine "restoring" his subjects to the state in which they had been created and from which they had been alienated by the Fall is responsible for the essential conservatism of Byzantine views of kingship. Forever after, positive achievements of Byzantine emperors such as Basil I were presented not as innovations but as restorations of man's first state. The connection with the doctrine of the Fall shows that the roots of the Byzantine view of *renovatio* derived from Christian doctrine based on the Old Testament account of the Fall. Byzantine emperors restoring their subjects to men's condition before the Fall — here was an aspect of Byzantine theory of kingship which in the eyes of the Byzantines both guaranteed and explained Byzantine greatness. Undoubtedly this greatness might as well have been reconciled with a philosophy of history which placed the achievement of true perfection in the future. Yet the Byzantine view of the Christian religion as created by God together with the world had this advantage over all future-minded philosophies of history that it presented the goal of history as anticipated by Adam at the time of his creation and before his fall. The Byzantine philosophy of history, thus, was immune against the doubt, which could be raised against any rectilinear philosophy, that the goal of history was unattainable: it had in fact been man's possession on the first day of history. No reason to doubt, therefore, that what had been possessed by man in the past could be restored to him in the present or in the future by a Christian emperor. The Byzantine view of history placed the attainability of the goal of history beyond doubt and thus established the Byzantines' conviction of the strength of their empire and capital on unassailable ground.

III. *Byzantine Justification of Empire.*

The theoreticians of Roman imperialism had not found it an easy task to justify in moral terms Rome's sway over her conquered provinces. Such Roman justifications have been examined in a remarkable article by E. von Ivanka down to the period of the Late Roman Empire.[70] Poets and prose writers in the Roman Empire had proclaimed that Roman government of the Mediterranean world was the deserved reward for her civilizing role: her political wisdom,[71] the military protection afforded by her armed forces and the respect for law shown by her

---

[69] Cf. Cranz, p. 47: "Byzantine imperial theory rests on assumptions similar to those of Eusebius," and Ladner, *Idea of Reform*, p. 120 f.: "This Eusebian conception of imperial *Christomimesis* . . . was to remain the basis of "political theology" in the Christian East."

[70] E. von Ivanka, "Zur Selbstdeutung des römischen Imperiums," *Saeculum*, VIII (1957), 17–31.

[71] Vergil, *Aeneid*, VI, 851.

administrators,[72] her concern for civilizing her subjects.[73] In the Hellenic half of the Roman Empire these "piecemeal" justifications culminated, at the latest in the second century A.D., in the overall theory that Rome ruled because she was morally perfect.[74] In the Eastern part of the Empire this preoccupation with the moral justification of empire seems to lessen in intensity or even to disappear after the fifth century. This was only natural in view of the development of Byzantine religio-political rhetoric and theory of kingship. If Byzantine rhetoric emphasized above all the supernatural protection of Constantinople and if the Byzantine philosophy of history saw in each emperor the image and agent of God charged with the mission of bringing fallen mankind back to God, who could then deny that a city and empire thus protected by superhuman forces and charged with a mission which knew no ethnic boundaries was bound to extend over all mankind? This point was so obvious that, if I am not mistaken, it was made rather rarely. Theodore Syncellus said in 627: "Constantinople is the eye of the Christian faith and an attack on it endangers the preaching of Christ's mystery to the ends of the world."[75] This view also underlay the Byzantine notion of a hierarchy of states. According to it, the Byzantine ruler ranked above even the most powerful kings of the mediaeval world in the "family of kings." This concept was of secular and political origin and derived ultimately from the notion of a family of courtiers in Ptolemaic Egypt.[76] In the mid-Byzantine period, however, this concept was "spiritualized" after the pattern of the monastic and secular clergies, where the bond of religious instruction by the abbot or the granting of the sacrament by the ecclesiastical superior, respectively, established degrees of rank.[77] Following these patterns, the Byzantine emperor was conceived of as the spiritual superior of all other rulers, no matter how powerful, because his mission was ecumenical.[78]

The Byzantines, then, found the bases of Byzantine greatness in a religio-political ideology inherited from late Antiquity and adapted in the mid-Byzantine period to the Christian environment by a strong emphasis on divine protection; in a theory of kingship which considered emperor and empire the images of the *Logos* of God and the kingdom of God, respectively, and assigned to the Byzantine emperor the task of periodically restoring man to the faith in which God had created him; and finally in a sense of Byzantine mission consisting in the preaching of the Gospel "to the ends of the world." This was a grandiose conception of

---

[72] Tacitus, *Historiae*, IV, 73 f.

[73] Claudianus, *De cons. Stilichonis*, IV 150–159.

[74] Von Ivanka, *Saeculum*, VIII (1957), esp. pp. 25–27.

[75] Theodorus Syncellus, p. 304, 17 (ed. Sternbach; see n. 29 above).

[76] On this concept see Georg Ostrogorsky, "Die byzantinische Staatenhierarchie," *Seminarium Kondakovianum*, VIII (1936), 41–61; F. Dölger, "Die Familie der Könige im Mittelalter," reprinted in this author's *Byzanz und die europäische Staatenwelt* (Ettal, 1953), pp. 34–69 (p. 62–66 on Ptolemaic antecedents).

[77] Dölger, *Byzanz und die europäische Staatenwelt*, pp. 67 f.; cf. pp. 55–59.

[78] Ostrogorsky, *Seminarium Kondakovianum*, VII (1936), 42: " . . . das Grunddogma der byzantinischen Staatslehre . . . von der oikumenischen Mission des byzantinischen Herrschers als des einzigen rechtmässigen Kaisers auf Erden. . . . "

Byzantine greatness which must have been infinitely reassuring in periods of imperial greatness and even during shorter periods of decline. In terms of this concept, it was always possible to account for setbacks on the battlefield or for temporary victories of an unorthodox theological doctrine by considering them examples of another fainting spell[79] or "falling asleep"[79a] soon to be followed by the reign of another restorer who would reawaken the state.

In evaluating the Byzantine self-image it is important, however, to note two principal shortcomings, one of them realized primarily by the modern historian and hardly by the Byzantines down to the Latin conquest, the other felt at Byzantium in the later periods of history. The first deficiency was the failure of Byzantine intellectuals to analyze the sources of Byzantine greatness in secular terms.[80] Secondly, the Byzantine self-image prior to the Fourth Crusade was of such a nature as not to offer psychological protection to the inhabitants of the Empire against a protracted period of internal disintegration and decline from the status of universal empire to that of a medium-sized or even small state. This situation prevailed at Byzantium since the end of the Macedonian dynasty. It is significant that the first expression of dissatisfaction with the prevailing self-image, so far as I am aware, dates from a few years after the Byzantine defeat at the hands of the Seljuqs at Manzikiert (1071), itself the consequence of internal disintegration and the cause of further decline. When in 1079/80 Michael of Attaleia composed his history of the years 1034–1079, he appended to his narrative of the battle of Manzikiert and of the ensuing troubles some general reflections on the reasons for Byzantium's defeats, indeed a frightening indictment of Byzantium's military and civil establishment.[81] He began with a contrast of Byzantium and ancient Rome. The Romans took the greatest care to ascertain and obey the will of the gods, Byzantine emperors and military commanders of the eleventh century, so Michael of Attaleia thought, were concerned only with enriching themselves. Their defeats were therefore well-deserved punishments for Byzantium's godless conduct. So far Michael's thinking followed the established pattern, but he continued:

Therefore I attribute the catastrophic outcome of events among the Romans [i.e., Byzantines] to divine Nemesis itself and to the judgment of an incorruptible sentence, for the following reason: the [other] nations are said to revere justice and to guard inviolate their ancestral customs and proclaim incessantly that all their prosperity is derived from the Creator. These [respect for justice and tradition, recognition of God's benefactions]

---

[79] N. 58 supra.

[79a] Χριστὸς καθεύδει is in the early ninth century Theodore of Studios' characteristic explanation for the predominance of Iconoclasm, Epist. ɪɪ 31 (*P.G.* xcɪx, 1204 A); ɪɪ 208 (*P.G.*, xcɪx, 1629D).

[80] P. 339 above.

[81] Michael Attaliotes, *Historia*, pp. 193–197. The passage is referred to in C. Neumann, *Die Weltstellung des byzantinischen Reiches vor den Kreuzzügen* (Heidelberg, 1894), pp. 120 f. It is replete with references to classical terminology. Compared with ancient Roman triumphs the return of Byzantine commanders is a clear example of divine infatuation (θεοβλάβεια, pp. 193 f.). The taking of the auspices and the Vestal Virgins are mentioned (p. 195). Byzantine emperors disregard the lessons of history which shows that misfortunes are due to divine anger or ignoble intentions (p. 194). The misdeeds of the Byzantine armies towards civilians are such that the latter feel relieved by Byzantine defeats (p. 196).

are achievements common to all men and are required of every religion; for the true and flawless faith of us Christians is nothing as much as a censure and condemnation, ever since we happened to lose those virtues, as is stated in the divine law of the command- ments: "He who knows the will of his master and does not do it will be stricken."[82]

The virtues of justice, traditionalism, and godliness are common achievements of mankind; they are possessed by other nations, are no longer a monopoly of the Byzantines; the Christian religion serves not to justify Byzantium but to condemn its depraved inhabitants! One thinks one hears one of the prophets of the Old Testament explaining to the Hebrews that their God is a universal and moral god, no more concerned with the people of Israel than with the gentiles, recognizing righteousness and condemning injustice wherever found. The passage clearly shows the shattering impact of Manzikiert and its sequel upon a Byzan- tine intellectual: Michael sees the Empire tottering and falling a prey to its Seljuq enemies and so he considers for a fleeting moment jettisoning and revising the traditional self-image. Yet it is as if he were afraid of his own courage. In the following paragraph he apologizes for his boldness. He offered his remarks, he continues, not in a spirit of insult or irreverence, but in order to convert Byzan- tine leaders, generals, and subjects back to the path of godliness, so that Byzan- tium may once more enjoy divine support.[83] It remains a fact that, faced by mili- tary defeat and social decay, this Byzantine historian had come to realize the insufficiency of the traditional explanations of Byzantine greatness.

University of Michigan

[82] Michael Attaliotes, *Historia*, p. 197. The last words of the passage are cited from memory, cf. Luke xii. 47. On Michael Attaliotes see the interesting comments by Pertusi, "L'Atteggiamento spiri- tuale" (n. 64 above), 164–166, esp. p. 165 f., n. 4, and on the text the same author's "Per la critica del testo della 'Storia' di Michele Attaliate," *Jahrbuch der Österreichischen Byzantinischen Gesselschaft*, vii (1958), 59–73.

[83] Michael Attaliotes, *Historia*, p. 197.

ADDITIONAL BIBLIOGRAPHY

On the Byzantine Kaisergedanke (p.348)see now the monu-
mental work by F.Dvornik,Early Christian and Byzantine
Political Philosophy.Origins and Background,2 vols.,Dum-
barton Oaks Studies 10,Washington,D.C.,1966,esp.chap-
ters XI and XII. The legend of the Last Roman Emperor
(p.343 f.)is treated more fully in no.XII below;see also my
Oracle of Baalbek (cf. Preface),116.The insistence of the
Vita Basilii on repairs of ancient buildings,rather then the
erection of new structures, as acts of renewal and rejuvenation (p.349 f.)is reminiscent of a similar tendency at the
court of the Ostrogothic King Theoderic,notably in the writings of Cassiodorus,as interestingly analysed by Herbert
Bloch,"Ein datierter Ziegelstempel Theoderichs des Gros-
sen",Mitteilungen des Deutschen Archäologischen Instituts,
Römische Abteilung 66,1959,196-203,esp.201-203.The parallel shows that this connotation of the concept is at least
as old as Late Antiquity.

IV

THE DONATION OF CONSTANTINE AT BYZANTIUM AND ITS EARLIEST USE AGAINST THE WESTERN EMPIRE

Professor George Ostrogorsky's publications have furnished inspiration for an entire generation of Byzantine historians. One of his major concerns in his books and articles has been the relationship of the imperial government at Byzantium with the rulers of Western and Eastern Europe. In at least one of his articles dealing with Byzantium's international relations Professor Ostrogorsky shed light on the problem of the use of the Donation of Constantine made by the Byzantines against Western powers[1]. It seems fitting therefore to present to him on his sixtieth birthday certain reflections on the evidence regarding the early role of this famous forgery at Byzantium.

The Donation of Constantine was frequently referred to in the great political debate between Byzantium and Western governments. This dialogue was reconstructed and examined in a remarkable essay by Professor F. Dölger first published in 1937[2]. Dölger showed how from the time of the Second Ecumenical Council (381) Constantinople claimed to be not only the Second Rome, as Constantine the Great had intended his new capital to be, but also the New Rome. In the seventh century at the latest, the term „New Rome" was interpreted in the East as distinguishing the youthful and flourishing capital in the East from the old and decaying Rome on the Tiber. Simultaneously, the Byzantines provided a historical and juridical basis for their claims: Byzantium was the New Rome because Constantine the Great had transferred the imperial power from Rome to Constantinople *(translatio imperii)*. The theory of the transfer of empire found its counterpart in the ecclesiastical field in Photius' view that the Roman see, because of its heretical opinions, had lost ecclesiastical primacy to the partiarchate of Constantinople. The papacy's reaction to these far-reaching Byzantine claims was embodied in the Donation of Constantine.

---

[1] George Ostrogorsky, „Zum Stratordienst des Herschers in der byzantinisch-slavischen Welt," *Seminarium Kondakovianum* 7 (1935) 187—205.

[2] F. Dölger, "Rom in der Gedankenwelt der Byzantiner," *Zeitschrift für Kirchengeschichte* 56 (1937) 1—42, reprinted in the same author's *Byzanz und die europäische Staatenwelt* (Ettal, 1953) 70—115. I shall henceforth refer to the pagination of this reprint.

This spurious document made the claim that Constantine the Great had bestowed on the pope as the successor of St. Peter the primacy over all the apostolic sees including that of Constantinople. According to Dölger, Byzantium responded to this Western step as early as the tenth century by using against the West the Donation of Constantine, the very document on which the papal claim for primacy was based.

Dölger's valuable and persuasive reconstruction has played a large role in recent studies of East-West relations during the Middle Ages[3]. There can be no doubt that on the whole Dölger's reconstruction of the great medieval dialogue between East and West is correct. Some of his conclusions about the use made at Byzantium of the Donation of Constantine though generally accepted[4] seem, however, unconvincing. The principal evidence on this matter will therefore be reviewed in this paper. Because the Donation of Constantine expressed eloquently and fully its Western authors' notions on the nature of *imperium* and *sacerdotium* and their proper relationship, it is important to examine the Byzantine attitudes towards this document, its long neglect in the East (even after it became known there) and the circumstances of its eventual adoption. The study will, I hope, shed light on some of the basic political ideas underlying and dividing the structures of the Western and Eastern Empires.

Dölger finds the earliest evidence for Byzantine use of the Donation of Constantine in Liudprand's *Legatio*. When, on 17 September 968, the militant bishop of Cremona was received at the imperial palace by the patrician Christophorus, he was told that pope John XIII had, in a recent letter, addressed the Byzantine Emperor Nicephorus Phocas as „Emperor of the Greeks“, rather than as „Emperor of the Romans“. At Byzantium this form of address was considered an insult because it denied the Byzantine claim to be the true Rome. To bring home to Liudprand the enormity of Pope John's crime, the patrician Christophorus and his associates addressed Liudprand as follows:

> „The stupid, silly pope does not realize that
> St. Constantine transferred to this city the
> imperial scepters, as well as the entire Senate
> and the entire Roman soldiery, but left at Rome
> only humble slaves, that is fishermen, cooks,
> fowlers, bastards, plebeians and servants“[5].

---

[3] I cite the works of W. Ohnsorge, especially his *Das Zweikaiserproblem im früheren Mittelalter* (Hildesheim, 1947), his collected papers: *Abendland und Byzanz* (Darmstadt, 1958) and his "Die Anerkennung des Kaisertums Ottos I. durch Byzanz," *Byzantinische Zeitschrift* 54 (1961) 28—52; Paolo Lamma, *Commeni e Staufer* (2 vols., Rome, 1957).

[4] Werner Ohnsorge, *Abendland und Byzanz*, p. 292 n. 17; "Die Anerkennung etc.," *B. Z.* 54 (1961) 43; Emil Herman, in *Das Konzil von Chalkedon* II (Würzburg 1953) 487; P. Lamma, I p. 5 n. 2. Dvornik, *Idea of Apostolicity and the Legend of the Apostle Andrew* (Cambridge, Mass., 1954) p. 288 n. 73 approves Dölger's views on the Donation of Constantine cautiously.

[5] Liudprand of Cremona, *Legatio*, ch. LI, p. 202, 20—25, ed. Joseph Becker: papa fatuus, insulsus, ignorat Constantinum sanctum imperialia sceptra huc transvexisse, senatum omnem cunctamque Romanam militiam, Romae vero vilia mancipia, piscatores scilicet, cupedinarios, aucupes, nothos, plebeios, servos tantummodo dimisisse.

Dölger sees no reason to doubt that Christophorus did speak these words. He points out correctly that a transfer of the entire Senate and of the entire Roman soldiery is not mentioned in the Byzantine narratives of the city's foundation and concludes that this strange and historically false conception must be based on a misunderstanding of the Donation of Constantine.

In fact a connection between Christophorus' words and this document is improbable. Dölger is aware that the patrician Christophorus did not reproduce accurately either the text or the meaning of the Donation of Constantine. He is, however, of the opinion that Christophorus misunderstood a passage from the introduction to this document[6]. This passage of the Donation of Constantine, according to Dölger, is supposed to state that Constantine moved the entire Senate and the entire hierarchy of officials with him to Constantinople[7], and it was this passage to which Christophorus was referring in his remarks to Liudprand. Now there are several difficulties in such a hypothesis. In the first place, Christophorus spoke of a transfer of the entire Senate but not of a transfer of the entire hierarchy of officials, as Dölger states. He mentioned instead the transfer of *cuncta Romana militia* which must refer to military men[8]. Secondly, the Donation of Constantine speaks of the Emperor Constantine acting in agreement *cum omnibus nostris satrapibus et universo senatu, optimatibus etiam et cuncto populo*[9]. The Donation's *omnes nostri satrapes* and its *optimates* can hardly have given rise to Christophorus' expression: *cunctam Romanam militiam;* for *satrapes* and *optimates* refer probably to high officials, *militia* to military men of all ranks. Finally, and most important, the introductory passage to the Constantinian Donation does not state that Constantine moved any part of the imperial government to Constantinople. It merely asserts that the Emperor, together with satraps, Senate, *optimates* and Roman people, was bestowing upon the Roman pontiffs supreme power[10]. Dölger does not make it clear whether he is thinking of a deliberate or erroneous misunderstanding of the Donation of Constantine at Byzantium, yet even the wildest misinterpretation of a document

---

[6] Dölger, *Rom in der Gedankenwelt*, p. 108, n. 64: Christophorus beruft sich nämlich darauf, dass Konstantin den ganzen Senat und die ganze Beamtenhierarchie (taxis) nach Constantinopel verlegt habe und spielt damit zweifellos auf den (missverstandenen) Wortlaut der Einleitung der Konstantinischen Schenkung ... an."

[7] Dölger, *Rom in der Gedankenwelt*, 110: "Die Konstantinische Schenkung spricht einleitend davon, dass Konstantin den *ganzen* Senat und die *ganze* hohe Beamtenhierarchie nach Konstantinopel mitgenommen habe ...."

[8] N. 5 above. Dölger seems to have combined Christophorus' words with those of Anna Comnena inadvertently (n. 17 below).

[9] Constitutum Constantini § 11 (I am using the most recent reprint of Zeumer's edition by Wolfgang Gericke, *Zeitschrift der Savigny Stiftung für Rechtsgeschichte, Kan. Abt.* XLIII (1957) 80—88): ... utile iudicavimus una cum omnibus nostris satrapibus et universo senatu, optimatibus etiam et cuncto populo Romano, ut .... pontifices ... principatus potestatem amplius, quam terrena imperialis nostrae serenitatis mansuetudo habere videtur, concessam a nobis nostroque imperio obtineant ....

[10] Constantine's own move to Constantinople is announced in § 18 (n. 31 below) but there the satraps, Senate, *optimates* and Roman people are not mentioned.

must possess some semblance of justification in the text which it supposedly misinterprets. Christophorus' claim that under Constantine the entire Senate and the entire *Romana militia* were moved from Rome to Constantinople can hardly have been based on a document which said that all of Constantine's satraps, the entire senate, his *optimates* and the entire Roman people collaborated in his bestowal of *principatus potestas* upon the Roman pontiffs.

Fortunately it is possible to go beyond probabilities. It can be proved that the words and ideas attributed by Liudprand to the Byzantine patrician Christoporus reflect an Italian tradition which was independent of the Donation of Constantine. So far as the wording is concerned, this is clear from the citation of Terence, one of Liudprand's favorite authors[11]. But there are indications that the thought of the passage as well is Liudprand's rather than Christophorus'. In his earlier work, the *Antapodosis*, Liudprand described the siege of Rome by King Arnulf of Carinthia in 896, attributing to the King a speech in verse. In it King Arnulf admonished his troops to fight valiantly, in terms borrowed by Liudprand from classical Roman poets. No military leaders, no Pompey or Caesar, were left in Rome. The military talents of a Julius Caesar had been taken to Greek lands by Constantine the Great. The present inhabitants of Rome were not interested in military matters (in „handling the shining shield") but in catching fat fish with their crooked rods[12]. These lines are not only consonant with Liudprund's unfavorable view of contemporary Romans[13], but also agree closely with the words attributed in the *Legatio* to Christophorus. The Byzantine patrician thought that Constantine the Great transferred the entire Roman soldiery to Constantinople; Arnulf said that Constantine brought Caesar's „talents" to Greek lands. Christophorus told Liudprand that only lowly people, especially fishermen, were left in Rome. King Arnulf told his soldiers that the inhabitants of Rome were inexperienced in the handling of arms and were interested in catching fish. Few scholars will be inclined to attribute much of the words and ideas contained in Liudprand's *Antapodosis* to King Arnulf, but for the present purpose it is immaterial whether the wording and thought is Arnulf's or Liudprand's. The decisive point is that the poem attributed by Liudprand to Arnulf, like the remarks put by the same author into the mouth of the Byzantine patrician Christophorus, states that Constantine the Great emptied Rome of soldiers and transported them to the East. Dölger claims that Christophorus' observations are based on a misunderstanding of the Donation of Constantine by the Byzantines. Is it really conceivable that a passage of the Donation was misunderstood in the same way by a

---

[11] See Becker's notes to the passage referred to (n. 5 above).

[12] Liudprand, *Antapodosis* (ed. Becker) XXVI, p. 22 ff: Non Pompeius adest, non Iulius ille beatus, / Qui nostros domuit proavos macrone feroces. / Indolis huius enim summos deduxit ad Argos, / Protulit in lucem quem sancta Britannica mater. / His torta studium pingues captare siluros/ Cannabe, non clipeos manibus gestare micantes. According to Bede and other Anglo-Saxon writers, Helen, mother of Constantine the Great, was the daughter of a British chieftain.

[13] Cf. *Legatio*, ch. XII p. 182 f. Becker.

Byzantine (Christophorus or his source) and a Westerner (Liudprand or Arnulf)? To raise this question implies a negative answer. Clearly the remarks of Christophorus are independent of the Donation of Constantine and are based on a Western tradition.

This Western tradition can be traced to the ninth century. It was shortly after 878 in all probability that a Neapolitan grammarian composed the *Versus Romae*[14]. The poet laments the decline of Rome. Rome's emperors forsook her a long time ago, her name and honor bas been transferred to the Greeks. None of her noble rulers remained at Rome and her free men till Pelasgian lands. Her masters are now the rabble brought there from the extremities of the world, slaves of slaves. Her empire has been transferred. As the patrician Christophorus claimed that Constantine the Great had transferred the entire Senate from Rome to Constantinople, the poet maintain that none of Rome's *nobiles rectores* remained in the city. According to the poet, Rome's free population cultivates „Pelasgian fields". Christophorus (or his source) has drawn a literal conclusion from the transfer of nobles and freemen to Constantinople mentioned in the ninth century poem: only slaves *(vilia mancipia)* are left in Rome. In the *Versus Romae* the foreign rabble and the slaves appear even as Rome's masters[15]. Just as in Christophorus' remarks, in the *versus Romae* Rome's decline is explicitly connected with the doctrine of the *translatio imperii*.

If, then, the words and thoughts attributed by Liudprand to the Byzantine patrician Christophorus are Liudprand's own[16] and based on a Western tradition, the question arises: what did Christophorus really say about Pope John XIII addressing Nicephorus Phocas as *Grecorum imperator?*

---

[14] Ed. L. Traube, *Monumenta Germaniae Historica, Poetae Latini Aevi Carolini*, III (Berlin, 1896) 554—556: Nobilibus quondam fueras constructa patronis/[2] Subdita nunc servis, heu male, Roma ruis./[3]Deseruere tui tanto te tempore reges, /[4] Cessit et ad Graecos nomen honosque tuus. /[5] Intenobilium rectorum nemo remansit /[6] Ingenuique tui rura Pelasga colunt /[7] Vulgus ab extremis distractum partibus orbis /[8] Servorum servi nunc tibi sunt domini. /....[17] Transit imperium mansitque superbia tecum. The poem was reprinted by William Hammer, "The Concept of the New or Second Rome in the Middle Ages," *Speculum* 19 (1944) 50—62, esp. 53 f., where the date is discussed (note 6) and the bibliography given. To the bibliography add: Fedor Schneider, *Rom und Romgedanke im Mittelalter* (reprinted Köln-Graz, 1959) 149 f., 263; Walter Rehm, *Europäische Romdichtung*, 2nd ed. (München, 1960) 39; Michael Seidlmayer, "Rom und Romgedanke im Mittelalter," *Saeculum 7* (1956) 395—412, esp. 398. I owe the last two references to the kindness of Professor Herbert Bloch, of Harvard University.

[15] Traube on p. 554 n. 3 of his edition (n. 14 above) interprets lines 7 and 8 of the poem (*Vulgus ab extremis* etc.) as referring to the Moslem attacks on Italy. He points out, however, that the expression *servorum servi* also is a pun on the papacy. The first two lines of the poem show that in the poet's view not only Rome's present masters but also all her contemporary inhabitants are slaves: none of her *nobiles rectores* has remained in the city and her free men live in Greek lands. This is exactly the view attributed by Liudprand to the patrician Christophorus.

[16] See Martin Lintzel, *Studien über Liudprand von Cremona*, reprinted in *Ausgewählte Schriften* II (Berlin, 1961) 351—398, esp. p. 383: So wird man die Unterhaltungen, die sie [Liudprand's *Legatio*] aufzeichnet, kaum als auch nur annähernd getreue Wiedergabe von wirklich geführten Gesprächen, sondern als polemische Auseinandersetzungen mit den Griechen in Dialogform zu bewerten haben, wobei Erinnerungen an echte Unterhaltungen mitklingen mögen."

No certain answer can be given to this question and only a guess is possible. Probably Christophorus stated the doctrine of the *translatio imperii*, perhaps in an emphatic or even exaggerated form. When Liudprand prepared the account of his embassy to Constatinople, he presented the patrician speaking in the words of Liudprand's favorite author Terence and expressing the doctrine of the *translatio imperii* in the form familiar to Liudprand from a Western tradition.

It has been demonstrated, then, that contrary to Dölger's view Liudprand's *Legatio* offers no evidence for the knowledge and use of the Donation of Constantine in tenth century Byzantium. A connection with the Donation of Constantine is also unlikely in the case of a twelfth century Byzantine text which played an important role in Dölger's argument. According to Dölger, Anna Comnena refers to the Donation of Constantine in her account of the beginnings of the Investiture Controversy. The Byzantine princess accepts a (false) rumor that Pope Gregory VII maltreated envoys of the German King Henry IV. To this account she appends an invective against Gregory and against the Latin claim that the pope was „the first archpriest and one who had become the president of the entire universe". She then continues:

> „For when the scepter and the Senate and
> simultaneously the entire officialdom
> were transferred from there [Rome] to this
> place, to our land, to our imperial city,
> the archepiscopal rank of the [ecclesiastical
> sees] was also transferred".[17]

She concludes that from the first the emperors had given preeminence (τὰ πρεσβεῖα) to the see of Constantinople. The Council of Chalcedon in particular had given first place to the see of Constantinople and had placed all dioceses in the universe under its authority.

Much has been written about this difficult passage, but in my opinion none of its difficulties are solved by the Donation of Constantine. Here it must suffice to discuss Dölger's contention that Anna's reference to the transfer of „the Senate and simultaneously the entire officialdom" is based on a misunderstanding of the Donation of Constantine. It should be pointed out first of all that Anna Comnena agrees with the words attributed by Liudprand to the patrician Christophorus only on one point: both claimed that the Senate was transferred from Rome to Constantinople. Otherwise the patrician mentioned the transfer of „the entire Roman

---

[17] Anna Comnena, *Alexias* I 13 (vol. I p. 47 Leib): Μεταπεπτωκότων γὰρ τῶν σκήπτρων ἐκεῖθεν ἐνθάδε εἰς τὴν ἡμεδαπήν τε καὶ ἡμετέραν βασιλίδα πόλιν καὶ δὴ τῆς συγκλήτου καὶ ἅμα πάσης τῆς τάξεως μεταπέπτωκε καὶ ἡ τῶν θρόνων ἀρχιερατικὴ τάξις. On this difficult and well-known passage, cf. for example A. Pavlov, "Podložna darstvennaia gramota Konstantina Velikago pape Silvestru v polnom grecheskom i slavianskom perevodie", *Vizantijskij Vremennik* 3 (1896) 18—82, esp. 35 f.; Georgina Buckler, *Anna Comnena*, London, 1929, 309—311 (curiously enough, in her translation of the passage, Mrs. Buckler omitted the crucial words: καὶ τῆς συγκλήτου καὶ ἅμα τῆς τάξεως); Father Leib in his edition of the *Alexiad* p. 171 f.

army" *(cuncta Romana militia)*, the imperial princess that of „the entire officialdom" (πᾶσα ἡ τάξις). Secondly, it can be shown that a connection between this passage from the *Alexiad* and the Donation of Constantine is a highly improbable and altogether unnecessary assumption. It is improbable for the same reason as with regard to Christophorus' words: the Donation of Constantine merely speaks of the Emperor Constantine, in cooperation with Senate, satraps, *optimates* and people, bestowing the *principatus potestas* on the pope. It is implausible that this passage should have been misunderstood to mean a transfer of Senate and officialdom from Rome to Constantinople. But such an assumption is also unnecessary, as Anna Comnena herself reveals in the very next sentence what the basis for her assertion is: the Council of Chalcedon, i. e. the famous twenty-eighth canon[18]. It is of course true that this canon had not spoken of a transfer of Senate and officialdom from Rome to Constantinople either, yet, if it is read against the background of the Byzantine doctrine of the *translatio imperii*, the twenty-eighth canon of Chalcedon could easily be understood to proclaim a transfer of Senate and officialdom. The Council of Chalcedon, following the precedent set by the Second Ecumenical Council, had explicitly based the privileges of the Constantinopolitan see on the fact that this city was „honored with kingship and Senate".[19] The notion of the *translatio imperii* means that of the two elements mentioned in the twenty-eighth canon, kingship and Senate, the former had left Rome and had been transferred to Constantinople[20]. What about the second, the Senate? During the period of the Roman Empire, emperors and Senate had normally resided together in the capital, Rome. When Constantine had founded his new capital, many senators had moved to Constantinople. In the Byzantine Empire known to Anna Comnena, Emperor and senate resided again in the capital city, Constantinople, and moreover this common location was proclaimed in the twenty-eighth canon of Chalcedon. Was it not in twelfth century Byzantium a plausible (though historically erroneous) inference from the twenty-eight canon of Chalcedon that the *translatio imperii* included a *translatio senatus?* The „officialdom" (τάξις), it is true, was not mentioned in the twenty-eight canon of Chalcedon. Yet this officialdom had clearly existed under the Roman Empire, and at Byzantium the exercise of imperial authority, of the *basileia* mentioned by the canon, was inconceivable without the officialdom to carry out the emperor's policies. So the transfer of the *basileia* proclaimed by the twenty-eighth canon could easily be interpreted as necessitating not only the transfer of the Senate but also that of the "officialdom". Anna Comnena's remarks, then, can be understood on the basis of the twenty-

---

[18] *ibid.*: Καὶ δεδώκασιν οἱ ἀνέκαθεν βασιλεῖς τὰ πρεσβεῖα τῷ θρόνῳ Κωνσταντινουπόλεως, καὶ μάλιστα ἡ ἐν Χαλκηδόνι σύνοδος εἰς περιωπὴν πρωτίστην τὸν Κωνσταντινουπόλεως ἀναβιβασαμένη τὰς ἀνὰ τὴν οἰκουμένην διοικήσεις ἁπάσας ὑπὸ τοῦτον ἐτάξατο.

[19] Eduard Schwartz, *Acta Conciliorum Oecumenicorum*, II 1, 3 (Berlin und Leipzig, 1935) p. [448] 89: ... εὐλόγως κρίναντες τὴν βασιλείᾳ καὶ συγκλήτῳ τιμηθεῖσαν πόλιν καὶ τῶν ἴσων ἀπολαύουσαν πρεσβείων τῇ πρεσβυτέρᾳ βασιλίδι ʻΡώμῃ κτλ.

[20] Dölger, *Byzanz und die europäische Staatenwelt*, 99—101.

eighth canon of Chalcedon, to which she explicitly refers, and of the *translatio imperii*, without recourse to a misinterpretation of the Donation of Constantine which, as we have seen, is improbable on independent grounds.

If neither Liudprand's *Legatio* in the tenth century nor Anna Comnena's *Alexiad* in the twelfth century contain evidence for Byzantine use of the Donation of Constantine, the question arises: when was the Donation of Constantine first appealed to by the Byzantines? A little more than a generation after Anna Comnena had completed her *Alexiad*, the Imperial Secretary John Cinnamus wrote a historical work covering the reigns of John and Manuel Comnenus[21]. In the fifth book of this work Cinnamus discussed the Byzantine war against King Stephen III of Hungary (1162—1164) and mentioned that King Stephen was given military aid by the ruler of Bohemia, Vladislav II. The historian then remarked that Vladislaw had been appointed ῥήξ by the first Hohenstaufen King of Germany, Conrad III, as a reward for the aid given on the Second Crusade (1147—1149). This was the occasion for a long and passionate outburst by Cinnamus against Western political claims which is as interesting as it is unusual in Byzantine historiography[22]. It has been analyzed several times, yet from this paper's point of view it will, I hope, prove possible to establish its main argument more sharply than has been possible hitherto. At the outset John Cinnamus declared that the bestowal of the royal title on the Bohemian Duke by the Hohenstaufen ruler was invalid. His reasoning was that Rome, from the time of Romulus Augustulus to his own, had been ruled by barbarian rebels (τύραννοι βάρβαροι) who imitated the precedent set by Theoderic and called themselves ῥῆγες. In reality, since the days of Romulus Augustulus the imperial title (τὸ τῆς βασιλείας ὄνομα) had disappeared from Rome. From the very beginning of his tirade, then, the Byzantine historian stressed that after 476 there was never more than one legitimate *basileus* and that Constantinople and not Rome was his residence. Only the one Emperor at Byzantium could bestow titles such as that of ῥήξ inasmuch as such titles were derived like particles from the imperial power[23].

The principal target of Cinnamus' attack, then, were Western usurpers of the imperial title. Clearly John Cinnamus wrote here as the

---

[21] On John Cinnamus see Hans von Kap-Herr, *Die abendländische Politik Kaiser Manuels*, etc., Diss. Strasburg, 1881, 119—121; Gy. Moravscik, *Byzantino-Turcica*, vol. I (2 nd ed., Deutsche Akademie der Wissenschaften zu Berlin, Institut für griechische und römische Altertumskunde, Berliner Byzantinische Arbeiten 10, Berlin, 1958) 324—329. The work was written during the years 1180—1183.

[22] Johannes Cinnamus, V 7, pp. 218—220 ed. Bonn. See Ferdinand Chalandon, *Jean II Comnène et Manuel I Comnène*, Paris, 1912, p. 556; Ostrogorsky, *loc. cit.* (n. 1 above); Erik Bach, "Imperium Romanum," *Classica et Mediaevalia* 7 (1945) 138—145; Paolo Lamma, *Comneni e Staufer*, vol. I (Roma, 1955) 1—7 (see also vol. II p. 107). Lamma (vol. I p. 3) points out that in reality Duke Vladislaw of Bohemia received the royal title not from Conrad III but from Frederick Barbarossa in 1158.

[23] Johannes Cinnamus, V 7 p. 219, 3: οἷς δὲ μὴ τοῦ τῆς βασιλείας μέτεστιν ὕψους, πόθεν οὗτοι τηλίκας προβεβλήσονται ἀρχάς, αἳ καθάπερ ἤδη ἔφην, οἷόν τινες διαιρέσεις ἐκ τοῦ τῆς βασιλείας καθίενται κράτους; The reference is to II 12 p. 68, 20 Bonn.

spokesman of the Byzantine imperial idea asserted with special vigor by Manuel Comnenus[24]. „Western rulers", Cinnamus continued, „are not content with usurping improperly the majesty of the imperial office and conferring upon themselves the imperial power ... but have in addition the impertinence of maintaining that the imperial office at Byzantium is different from the imperial office at Rome"[25]. With this claim the Western rulers surely touched a raw nerve, for Cinnamus' prose rises at this point to supreme pathos: „As I was reflecting upon this (contention), I often began to weep".

In fact, as will be seen from further analysis of the passage, it was this claim by the Western rulers that had aroused Cinnamus' wrath. In contains the key to an understanding of Cinnamus' remarks; the entire chapter is dedicated to its refutation. It probably took the form of an explicit and formal denial of the Byzantine emperor's right to the Roman title. Implicit denials, for example the address *imperator Constantinopolitanus* or *imperator Grecorum*, had been condoned before by Byzantine emperors and would hardly have provoked Cinnamus' passionate reaction[26]. Because Western rulers had contrasted the imperial office at Byzantium with that at Rome, Cinnamus continued by lamenting what he considered scandalous events at Rome: a man who laid claim to the imperial title had debased himself by running on foot next to a pope seated on a horse and had become his squire, and the pope in turn had called him *imperator*, thereby giving him the same rank as to the emperor at Byzantium. This is the part of this passage which was so brilliantly analyzed by Professor Ostrogorsky. He showed conclusively that Cinnamus knew the Donation of Constantine and used it effectively against the papal claim that the

---

[24] Georg Ostrogorsky, "Die byzantinische Staatenhierarchie," *Seminarium Kondakovianum* 8 (1936) 41—61; *History of the Byzantine State*, New Brunswick, N. J., 1957, p. 341 f.

[25] Johannes Cinnamus, V 7, p. 219, 6: τοῖς δὲ οὐκ ἀπόχρη μόνον, εἰ τοῦ τῆς βασιλείας οὐδὲν προσῆκον ἐπιβατεύουσιν ὕψους, ἰμπέριον ἑαυτοῖς περιτιθέντες κράτος· βούλεται δὲ τοῦτο τὸ ἄκρατον ἑρμηνεύειν· ἀλλ᾽ ἤδη καὶ τὴν ἐν Βυζαντίῳ βασιλείαν ἑτέραν παρὰ τὴν ἐν Ῥώμῃ ἀποφαίνειν τολμῶσιν (I have corrected the punctuation). The Vaticanus gr. 163 reads ἐμπόριον, Ducange and Meineke proposed the emendations ἐμπέριον and ἰμπέριον respectively. Lamma, *Comneni e Staufer*, vol. I p. 5 n. 1 considered the reading of the manuscript "perfettamente giustificata," yet the emendation is guaranteed by Cinnamus' (incorrect) attempt of translating the words: ἰμπέριον... ... κράτος by ἄκρατον where the α privative is apparently supposed to render the Latin negative prefix *in-* or *im-* in *imperium*.

[26] Pope John XIII in 986 had in a letter to Constantinople called Nicephorus Phocas *Grecorum imperator*. This had been deeply resented at Constantinople and Otto I's envoy Liudprand had had to bear the brunt of Byzantine displeasure (*Legatio*, ch. L f., p. 202 Becker, see n. 5 above). Almost two centuries later, in 1142, Conrad III had addressed John Comnenus as *Constantinopolitanus imperator* and in 1145 he had written to Manuel Comnenus as *rex Grecorum* (Otto von Freising, *Gesta Friderici*, I ch. XXV, pp. 37, 30 and 41, 3, ed. 3. by G. Waitz), both times without provoking any violent reaction at Byzantium, cf. Ohnsorge, *Abendland und Byzanz*, 374 f. Such violations of diplomatic protocol could either be ignored at Byzantium, or the record could be set straight in the next official communication placing special emphasis on the Byzantine emperor's right to call himself *imperator Romanorum* (cf. Ohnsorge, *Abendland und Byzanz*, 375 f.). According to Cinnamus, Frederick I went one step further; specifically and formally, in a communication addressed to Manuel, he denied the latter's right to call himself *imperator Romanorum*.

Western „emperor" was obliged to render squire *(strator)* service to the pope[27].

Having mentioned the pope, the Byzantine historian concentrated his further attack on the papacy. It is of crucial importance for a correct interpretation of Cinnamus' thought to realize, however, that his remarks are still directed against the claim of Western rulers that "the imperial office at Byzantium is different from the [imperial office] at Rome". That such was the case is made clear by the first words of the following citation:

> "Unless you [Pope] concede that the imperial
> throne at Byzantium is the throne of Rome, on what
> grounds did you obtain the dignity of Pope? One man
> only made this decision, Constantine, the first Christian
> emperor. How can you gladly accept his one [provision],
> I mean the [bestowal of the papal] throne and of its
> surpassing dignity, and yet reject the other [provision, i. e.
> the principle that the emperor at Byzantium is the Roman
> emperor]? Either you must accept both [provisions] or
> reject even the former [provision]".[28]

Cinnamus' argument, then, is fairly clear. A Western ruler had based his claim to be the true *imperator Romanorum* on the contention that Manuel Comnenus' imperial dignity was not "Roman". Such a contention offended the cardinal principle of Byzantine political thought that the Byzantine emperor was the true and only successor of the Roman emperors and that because of this fact he had the right to universal domination[29]. John Cinnamus obviously either knew that the Pope had adopted the contention advanced by the Western "emperor" or he feared that in the future the pope might be induced to adopt it; in any case he wanted to warn him of the consequences. In Cinnamus' view, to recognize the Western "emperor's" claim would be equivalent to a disavowal of the Donation of Constantine. With such a disavowal the Pope would jeopardize his claim to the "emperor's" squire service as well as to all the other privileges granted to him in that document. Cinnamus was aware that the

---

[27] Ostrogorsky, *loc. cit* (n. 1 above) p. 190 f. There can be no doubt that Ostrogorsky's view is correct. P. 220, 1 Cinnamus states explicitly that it was Constantine who decided to create the dignity of Pope — historically of course a false statement even if the Donation of Constantine were genuine, but clearly a reference to the Donation of Constantine. As will be seen presently, the Donation of Constantine was referred to by Cinnamus not only to reject the papal claim for the *officium stratoris*, but also (and more importantly) to justify the Byzantine emperor's claim to be the true Roman emperor (n. 34 below).

[28] John Cinnamus V 7, p. 219, 20: μὴ γὰρ τὸν ἐν Βυζαντίῳ τῆς βασιλείας θρόνον Ῥώμης θρόνον εἶναι διομολογοῦντί σοι, πόθεν αὐτῷ σοι τὸ Πάπα κεκλήρωται ἀξίωμα; εἷς ἐστιν ᾧ ταῦτα ἔδοξε, Κωνσταντῖνος ὁ πρῶτος ἐν βασιλεῦσι Χριστιανός κτλ. The connection of this with the preceding is clear if the first words (μὴ · · · · διομολογοῦντί σοι) are compared with n. 25 above (ἀλλ' ἤδη καὶ · · · τολμῶσιν).

[29] The bibliography on the Byzantine title βασιλεὺς Ῥωμαίων is immense. It may suffice here to refer to Dölger's many discussions of the subject, especially in *Byzanz und die europäische Staatenwelt*, pp. 79 f., 297 f.

papacy justified its demand of squire service from the Western emperor (and many other prerogatives) by the Donation of Constantine[30]. Of necessity, then, the pope must also accept the proposition clearly expressed in the Donation of Constantine that the imperial power established by Constantine at Byzantium was identical with the Roman imperial power[31].

Cinnamus then formulated two objections that the pope had raised or might raise against Cinnamus' position and in support of the Western ruler's claim that the Byzantine *basileus* was not the Roman emperor. The pope either had said or might say: first, that he had the right to appoint emperors; or, secondly, he had claimed or might claim that he was acting under compulsion[32]. If these (real or imagined) objections of the pope had any connection with the principal Western thesis underlying Cinnamus' remarks, then the first papal objection must mean that because the pope (and only the pope) had the right to appoint emperors, no Byzantine emperor could claim to be Roman emperor, simply because he had not been appointed by the pope. The second objection must imply that the Western ruler had forced the pope to adopt his contention.

Against the first objection Cinnamus declared that the pope had indeed the right to bless and lay his hands upon a new emperor[33] but that he had no power to confer the imperial office. Again Cinnamus argued from the Donation of Constantine, as he had done in the case of the imperial squire service. If the pope could appoint emperors, why then did Pope Sylvester not himself transfer the imperial office from Rome to Constantinople instead of accepting of Constantine the Great's decision against his will[34]? By recognizing the Western "emperor" the pope, as Cinnamus argued, "perhaps does not even assign the same rank to him from whom and through whom and under whom he holds his see [the *basileus* at Constantinople] as to the barbarian, the rebel, the slave [the Western emperor]"[35]. With regard to the pope's second objection, Cinnamus appealed to other documents, namely recent

---

[30] *Constitutum Constantini* § 16: ... tenentes frenum equi ipsius pro reverentia beati Petri stratoris officium illi exhibuimus ...

[31] *Constitutum Constantini* § 18: Unde congruum prospeximus nostrum imperium et regni potestatem orientalibus transferri ac transmutari regionibus et in Byzantiae provintia in optimo loco nostro civitatem aedificari et nostrum illic constitui imperium ...

[32] John Cinnamus, V 7, p. 220, 4: ἀλλ' ἐμοί, φησί, βασιλέας προβεβλῆσθαι ἔξεστιν. p. 220, 16: ἀλλὰ τυραννοῦμαι, φησίν, ἀλλὰ βιάζομαι.

[33] It is not surprising that a Byzantine author recognized the pope's right to consecrate emperors. Basil II, Alexius I and John Comnenus had carried on prolonged negotiations with the papacy on this point. See Ohnsorge, *Zweikaiserproblem*, pp. 69, 87, 88 f., 106 f.

[34] *ibid.*, p. 220, 7: ἐπεὶ εἴ γε ὑμέτερον ἦν βασιλείας μετατιθέναι, τί μὴ τὴν ἐν Ῥώμῃ αὐτοὶ μετετάξατε; ἀλλ' ἑτέρου πράξαντος ἄκων ἠγάπα τοῖς δεδογμένοις ὁ τηνικαῦτα τὴν καθ' ὑμᾶς ἐκκλησίαν λαχών. It is not clear why, according to Cinnamus, Pope Sylvester should have suffered the transfer *unwillingly*. Is this an echo of Pope Sylvester's refusal to wear the imperial diadem (Donation of Constantine § 16)?

[35] *ibid.*, p. 220, 14: κρίνεις τὸν ἐξ οὗ καὶ δι' οὗ καὶ καθ' οὗ σοὶ τοῦ θρόνου μέτεστιν οὐδὲ ταὐτὸν τῷ βαρβάρῳ ἴσως, τῷ τυράννῳ, τῷ δούλῳ. This is an adaptation of *Romans* 11, 36. It is significant that Cinnamus has changed the εἰς αὐτὸν of the biblical text into καθ' οὗ, to mark the superiority of the Byzantine emperor over the pope.

written agreements made between the pope and the Emperor Manuel Comnenus. Cinnamus must have meant that letters of the pope recognized the Emperor Manuel as βασιλεὺς 'Ρωμαίων and that the pope could not withdraw his recognition now[36].

Analysis of John Cinnamus' remarks has shown that the author was repudiating the claim put forward by the Western "emperor" that the Byzantine Emperor was not the Roman Emperor. Cinnamus either knew that the pope had adopted the Western "emperor's" position or feared that this might happen. He rejected the claim largely on the strength of the Donation of Constantine. Two historical questions arise. First, which Western emperor had made this claim and under what circumstances? Secondly, and more important, how was it possible that a document forged in the eighth or early ninth century[37] to buttress the papal position could, in the late twelfth century (and not before), be turned at Byzantium against the West?

With regard to the first question it is clear from the context of Cinnamus' history that only the first two Hohenstaufen rulers, Conrad III (1138—1152) and Frederick I Barbarossa 1152—1190), need to he considered. Conrad III is a most unlikely candidate; not only did he die long before the events narrated in Cinnamus' fifth book took place, but his authority was seriously challenged in Germany and throughout his reign he maintained excellent relations with Byzantium[38]. It must, then, have been Frederick Barbarossa who at some time after 1152 and prior to 1183 (when Cinnamus completed his History) denied Manuel Comnenus the right to call himself *imperator Romanorum*. Experts on the period of Barbarossa will perhaps be able to define these chronological limits more narrowly. Tension between Barbarossa and Manuel was high on so many occasions between 1152 and 1183[39] that it is difficult to decide whether the denial of Manuel's right to the title of Roman emperor occurred prior to the papal schism, during this schism (1159—1177) or after the Peace of Venice (1177) between Barbarossa and Pope Alexander III[40].

---

[36] Compare the ταῦτα διωμολόγεις (p. 220, 18) with the διομολογοῦντί σοι (p. 219, 21). The object of "acknowledgement" is probably the same in both cases, namely the proposition that "the imperial throne at Byzantium is the throne of Rome."

[37] On the controversy over the date of the Donation of Constantine see the recent surveys by Ohnsorge, *Abendland und Byzanz*, pp. 79—81; Wolfgang Gericke, "Wann entstand die Konstantinische Schenkung?" *Zeitschrift der Savigny — Stiftung für Rechtsgeschichte,Kan. Abt.*, 74 (1957) 1—88, esp. 1—3.

[38] Ohnsorge, *Zweikaiserproblem*, pp. 89—97.

[39] Ohnsorge, *Zweikaiserproblem*, pp. 97—116.

[40] The learned Ducange, in a note to his edition of Cinnamus (see Bonn Corpus, p. 366) referred to Rahewinus' statement (in his continuation of Otto von Freising's *Gesta Frederici* to, the effect that Frederick had persuaded Manuel to call himself emperor of New Rome (see the third edition of the *Gesta Frederici* by G. Waitz, IV ch. 86, p. 345). Rahewinus' notice is, however, of doubtful historical value. It may be an excellent paraphrase of German aspirations (see Ohnsorge, *Abendland und Byzanz*, 375) but it cannot possibly be taken at face value. It was one thing for a Byzantine emperor to condone or ignore a Western ruler's *faux pas* of calling the Byzantine emperor *Constantinopolitanus imperator* or *rex Grecorum* and thereby implicitly denying the Byzantine emperor's claim to the Roman empire (n. 26 above). But it is inconceivable that Manuel should in fact have called *himself* emperor of New Rome. Moreover Rahewinus' remark does not help to date:

What about the second problem raised above? Against Frederick's contention that "the imperial office at Byzantium is different from the imperial office at Rome", the Donation of Constantine was for the first time utilized by a Byzantine, the historian John Cinnamus[41]. This document had been compiled three or four centuries earlier in the West to justify the position of the papacy and perhaps had been occasioned by Byzantine attacks upon the papacy[42]. It is surprising, therefore, that it should at any time have been used at Byzantium against the Western empire. The reason that it emerged in the arsenal of Byzantine political polemics during the second half of the twelfth century lies, I suggest, not in any change in the Byzantine empire and its ideology, but in a new phenomenon in Western Europe: the appearance of ihe Hohenstaufen concept of the imperial office, the *staufische Kaisergedanke*. Under the later Carolingian and Saxon dynasties the papacy had established its claim

---

Barbarossa's denial of the title *imperator Romanorum* for Manuel. On the other hand, such a denial by Frederick would fit well into the period after the Peace of Venice (1177). Around 1178 Manuel had written a letter to Frederick in which he had called himself *Romanorum moderator magnificus* (*Annales Stadenses, MGH Scriptores* XVI, p. 349, 11). Frederick, annoyed by this letter, referred to himself in his reply of 1179 not only as *Romanorum imperator* but also pointedly as *Graecorum moderator* and called Manuel *rex Graecorum et imperator*. Further on, Frederick remarked that „not only the Roman empire is ordered by our direction but also the kingdom of Greece should be ruled at our pleasure and governed under our command," and later admonished Manuel to „give due honor to us and the Roman empire and reverential obedience to the Supreme Pontiff..." (Hans von Kap-Herr, *Die abendländische Politik Kaiser Manuels*, etc., Strassburg, 1881, p. 156 f., see also p. 106: Niemals hat meines Wissens vorher ein deutscher Kaiser das griechische Reich so direkt als einen Vasallenstaat in Anspruch genommen"). On this letter see also F. Chalandon, *Jean II Comnène et Manuel I Comnène*, Paris, 1912, p. 599, n. 1; Lamma, *Comneni e Staufer*, II 298 (who declared that in the form in which it is preserved Barbarossa's letter cannot have been sent to Constantinople, „otherwise it would be an act of war.") An explicit denial of Manuel's right to the title *imperator Romanorum* would be consonant with the international atmosphere after Myriokephalon (1176) and the Peace of Venice (1177) but an earlier date is by no means excluded.

[41] Gaudenzi, *loc. cit.* (p. 25 below) p. 76 f. recognized that the Donation of Constantine was ignored during the eleventh century and during the first half of the twelfth century but emerged at Byzantium as a result of „Frederick I's attitude." He also called attention (p. 77 f.) to the fact that on one of the many occasions when Manuel demanded to be crowned by Alexander III (n. 33 above) the Byzantine envoy, the *sebastos* Jordanes, on specific instructions from Manuel, requested ut ... Romani corona imperii a Sede apostolica sibi redderetur quoniam non ad Frederici Alamanni, sed ad suum ius asserit pertinere (Boso's life of Alexander III in *Liber Pontificalis*, ed. L. Duchesne, II, p. 415). Gaudenzi thought that a demand for the return (redderetur) of the crown presupposed the bestowal of the crown by Constantine on Pope Sylvester (Donation of Constantine § 16) and thus indicated a recognition of this document by Byzantium. If this interpretation of the *Liber Ponti-iz alis* is correct, it would confirm my view, obtained by analysis of Cinnamus, that the Byzantines fi rst used the Donation of Constantine under Manuel. The passage has, however, been interpreted to mean simply that by crowning Charlemagne Pope Leo III deprived Byzantium of what belonged to it and that the Byzantine emperor was now reclaiming his property, cf. P. A. Van Den Baar, *Die kirchliche Lehre der Translatio Imperii Romani*, Analecta Gregoriana, vol. 78, Ser. Fac. Hist. Eccl., Section B (n. 12) Rome, 1956, p. 79 and the remarks of Erik Bach, *loc. cit.* (n. 22 above) 142 on the terminology of reconquest and recovery used by Manuel.

[42] This point is argued by Theodor Klauser, *Der Ursprung der bischöflichen Insignien und Ehrenrechte*, 2nd ed., Bonner Akademische Reden 1, Krefeld, 1953, p. 28, but the evidence is not strong.

that papal coronation was a constitutional prerequisite for the imperial title. The reform popes had on several occasions intervened unsuccessfully even in the elections of German kings[43]. Against this papal concept of the imperial office another idea, occasionally and tentatively proposed in the eleventh century and definitely expressed in the early twelfth century, was taking shape. According to this view the pope did not create emperors by coronation but emperors owed their position to their election by the German princes[44]. After the famous scene at the Diet of Besançon (1157) when cardinal Roland of Siena had called the imperial crown a papal fief *(beneficium)*, Frederick I proclaimed in an open letter his anti-papal concept of empire:

> „Inasmuch as our kingdom and empire derives from
> God alone through the election of the princes....,
> whosoever maintains that we have received the imperial
> crown as a fief from the Lord Pope, speaks contrary
> to the divine establishment and the doctrine of Peter
> and will be charged with lying."[45]

This Hohenstaufen concept of the imperial office clashed not only with the papal idea of empire but also with the Byzantine imperial idea and must of necessity have led to a denial on Frederick's part of Manuel's right to call himself Roman emperor, a denial which, as has been seen, underlies Cinnamus' remarks. Against this Hohenstaufen concept the Donation of Constantine could indeed serve as a powerful weapon, and it possessed the additional advantage that it could be wielded by both pope and Byzantine emperor. For all its insistence on papal pregoratives, the Donation of Constantine was based on the recognition that Constantine was the only legitimate Roman emperor and the source of the various privileges assigned to the papacy in that document. Since Constantine undoubtedly had a right to the title of Roman emperor and since in the Donation Constantine had announced his decision to establish the seat of empire *in Byzantiae provintia*, it was clearly implied that Constantine's successors at Byzantium were Roman emperors[46]. Similarly from 800 on popes häd crowned emperors in the West and such imperial coronations by the pope had not been felt in the West to conflict with the Donation of Constantine[47]. It was only when Frederick proclaimed the independence

---

[43] Hermann Bloch, *Die staufischen Kaiserwahlen etc.*, Leipzig und Berlin, 1911, p. 2—5; Ohnsorge, *Zweikaiserproblem*, p. 60 and *passim*.

[44] Bloch, *Die staufischen Kaiserwahlen*, pp. 5—11.

[45] Rahewinus, *Gesta Frederici*, III ch. 11 (ed. 3 by G. Waitz, p. 179).

[46] Donation of Constantine § 18 (n. 31 above).

[47] According to the Donation of Constantine (§ 16) Constantine took the imperial diadem or crown off his own head and decreed that Pope Sylvester and his successors should wear it. As early as 816 the crown brought by Pope Stephen IV to France for the imperial coronation of Louis the Pious was called the crown of Constantine and was described in the same terms as was Constantine's crown in the Donation of Constantine, see Ohnsorge, *Abendland und Byzanz*, p. 82. f. (the article by Max Buchner, *Historisches Jahrbuch der Görresgesellschaft* 53, 1933, p. 143, to which Ohnsorge refers, was not available to me). The assumption underlying this resemblance was that Constantine had empowered the papacy to pass on the crown and to crown emperors.

of the imperial office from the papacy that the Donation of Constantine could be used by the Byzantine emperors as a weapon against their Western rivals as well as a means of rapprochement between Byzantium and the papacy. This, then, seems to be the meaning of Cinnamus' long diatribe : repudiation of the Hohenstaufen concept of the imperial office and of its denial of the Byzantine emperor's claim to be the Roman emperor on the one hand, and on the other an offer of cooperation (even ecclesiastical union?) with the Papacy to combat Frederick's anti-papal idea of empire. It was no accident, then, that the Donation of Constantine was not used at Byzantium against Western emperors prior to the latter half of the twelfth century. In opposition to an upstart power that treated with contempt the most ancient and venerable institutions of the medieval world, the pope in Rome and the emperor in Constantinople, Byzantine rulers and polemicists appealed to a document surrounded with the halo of antiquity, one which derived the distribution of the highest powers, privileges, insignia and honors from the harmonious cooperation of the first Christian emperor with the pope who had baptized him into the Christian faith.

Appendix: Michael Cerularius' Purple Sandals.

I have not discussed in the text an event of Byzantine history in the eleventh century which is generally thought to be connected with the Donation of Constantine. The reason for this omission is partly that the action was not directed against the Western empire, partly that the evidence is inconclusive. The so-called Scylitzes Continuatus, a Byzantine chronicler covering the years 1057 to 1079, records that under Isaac Comnenus (1057—1059) the Patriarch of Constantinople Michael Cerularius "attempted to put on purple-colored sandals, saying that such was the practice of the ancient priesthood and that the archpriest in the new [priesthood] should also use them." (Cedrenus, vol. II, p. 643, 13). A late twelfth century author, Theodore Balsamon, in his commentary on the Nomocanon (*P. G.* 104, 1081 D; *P. G.* 137, 486 D) and in his *Meditata* (P. G. 138, 1029 C), connected the Patriarch's action with the Donation of Constantine and later authors and modern scholars have accepted this connection. See A. Gaudenzi "Il Costituto di Costantino," *Bulletino del Istituto Storico Italiano* 39 (1919), esp. 72—75; Anton Michel, "Schisma und Kaiserhof im Jahre 1054: Michael Psellos," in *L'Eglise et les églises*, vol. I, Chevetogne, 1954, pp. 351—440, esp. p. 374. In fact the earliest source, Scylitzes Continuatus, did not state that Michael Cerularius justified his action by the Donation of Constantine but cited instead a saying of his in which he referred to the "practice of the ancient priesthood." The expression is ambiguous and has been taken to refer to the priesthood of the Old Testament (Michel, *loc. cit.*, p. 374 n. 6). There are, however, several obstacles to such an interpretation; for example, the Old Testament seems to contain no provision concerning the shoes of the priesthood, see Joseph Braun, *Die liturgische Gewandung im Occident und Orient*, etc., Freiburg i. Br., 1907, p. 421. The alternative is to assume that Michael Cerularius had observed, heard or read about the "practice" of wearing purple shoes in the Western Church. Now it is a fact that in 1214 the cardinal legate Pelagius of Albano wore purple sandals at Constantinople, to the great annoyance of Nicholas Mesarites (see August Heisenberg, "Neue Quellen zur Geschichte des lateinischen Kaisertums und der Kirchenunion III," *Sitzungsberichte der Bayerischen Akademie der Wissenschaften*. Philosoph.—philol. und hist. Kl., 1923, no. 3, p. 22, 16 and Georgius Acropolita, ed. Heisenberg, *Hist.*, 17, p. 29, 15), but it is difficult to say whether the papal legates of cardinal rank wore purple sandals as early as the mid-eleventh century. (Karl Ruess, *Die rechtliche Stellung der päpstlichen Legaten bis Bonifaz VIII*, Görres-Gesellschaft zur Pflege der Wissenschaft im Katholischen Deutschland, Sektion für Rechts- und Sozialwissenschaft, 13, Paderborn, 1912, p. 202, knows of no case earlier than Pelagius). If Cardinal Humbert in 1054 wore purple sandals, then this would provide the basis for Michael Cerularius' remark about "the practice of the ancient priesthood." At Byzantium where the privilege of wearing purple boots was an imperial prerogative, the appearance of a member of the Roman clergy wearing purple sandals must have caused considerable furore. Furthermore Michael Cerularius himself reveals with what rapt attention his jaundiced eye had observed the behavior of the papal envoys of 1054: they had entered the imperial palace with cross and (episcopal) sceptre (Michael Cerularius, *Letter № 4 to Peter of Antioch*, ch. 6, *P. G.* 120, 788 A). Anton Michel (*loc. cit.*, p. 406 n. 2), to whom I am indebted for these references, notes further Michael Cerularius' remarks about the rings of Western bishops (*P. G.* 120, 793 A) and continues: "Der Patriarch berichtet wohl als Augenzeuge." Michael Cerularius then may simply have imitated, perhaps on the strength of the 28 th Canon of Chalcedon, a "practice" observed by him in the case of Cardinal Humbert, but without reference to the Donation of Constantine. If this hypothesis proves correct, then it is surely no coincidence that Theodore Balsamon, who wrote under Manuel Comnenus, first connected Michael Cerularius' purple sandals with the Donation of the Constantine, at about the same time that John Cinnamus appealed to the Donation of Constantine against Frederick Barbarossa.

Department of History
University of Michigan
Ann Arbor, Michigan, U.S.A.

ADDITIONAL BIBLIOGRAPHY

The standard work on the Donation of Constantine in the West is Horst Fuhrmann (cited above in Additional Bibliography to no.II). Four years after the publication of my article, Romilly J.H. Jenkins wrote on the fragments of a silver cross acquired by Dumbarton Oaks: "A Cross of the Patriarch Michael Caerularius", Dumbarton Oaks Papers 21, 1967, 233-240. On the basis of the iconography he argued that the cross was commissioned by Michael Caerularius, Patriarch of Constantinople, in 1057 or 1058 and that the most important scene depicted on it (Constantine the Great and Pope Silvester) illustrates the relationship of emperor and pope as envisaged by the author of the Donation. In the appendix to my article (25f.) I had left open the question whether Caerularius' use of the purple boots implied that he claimed for himself the papal prerogatives as laid down in the Donation of Constantine or whether he was simply copying the papal practice, adopted also by papal legates, of wearing purple boots, without any reference to an enabling text. If Jenkins' dating and interpretation of the Dumbarton Oaks cross are correct, then the former alternative is confirmed (as Jenkins remarked p.238 n.14) and the Donation was used for the first time by a Byzantine in the mid-eleventh century, to be exact by a Byzantine patriarch in his relations with his own emperor, not with a Western ruler.

V

A CHRYSOBULL OF THE EMPEROR ANDRONICUS II PALAEOLOGUS IN FAVOR OF THE SEE OF KANINA IN ALBANIA *

Dedicated to the Memory of
Canon William Greenwell,
distinguished Scholar and Collector.

The manuscript treasures of a library are made accessible to the learned public only after they have been catalogued. Such a catalogue has appeared recently for the libraries of the United States and Canada.[1] The results are already beginning to show even in the Byzantine field,[2] and it is to be expected that other finds will follow suit.

The document which will be edited and discussed in this paper owes its discovery to the *Census*. This catalogue [3] describes the *MS. 398* of the Pierpont Morgan Library, of New York City, as follows:

398. Chrysobull of Emperor Andronicus II, in Greek, addressed to the Bishop of Canina. Vellum roll (6815 = A. D. 1307), 157 x 31 cm. Large miniature at top.
Signature of the Emperor in red ink.

So far as I know this is the only mention of our document in literature. The records of the Morgan Library show that it came from the collec-

* The writer wishes to thank, first of all, the authorities of the Pierpont Morgan Library, and Miss Meta Harrsen in particular, for the kind reception which he found there. His work on the manuscript was facilitated in every possible way, and he considers it a great privilege to be allowed to publish it. Professor Henri Grégoire, the editor of this review, inspected the manuscript on various occasions. His advice given unsparingly, both orally and by correspondence, has solved many serious problems; much of what may be good in this paper is due to his suggestions. Finally Professor R. P. Blake, of Harvard University, has aided and encouraged the writer during the preparation of this paper in the most generous way. In particular he is indebted to Professor Blake for reading and correcting his manuscript after its completion.

[1] Seymour de Ricci, *Census of Medieval and Renaissance Manuscripts in the United States and Canada*, 2 vols., New York, 1935-1937.

[2] F. Halkin, " Le mois de janvier du ' Ménologe Impérial ' byzantin," *Analecta Bollandiana*, LVII (1939), 225-236 shows that *Codex 521* of the Walters Art Gallery at Baltimore is identical with the stolen *Codex 33* of the Library of the Patriarchate at Alexandria, and represents the January volume of the *Menologium Anonymum* edited by Latyshev.

[3] Ricci, *Census*, II, p. 1440.

tion of the late Canon William Greenwell, the distinguished English scholar and collector, of Durham Cathedral (1820-1918).[4]

The parchment roll consists of three pieces. The individual pieces have a length of 42, 5, 66, and 53, 5 cm. respectively. The tops of pieces two and three are glued on top of the bottoms of pieces one and two. There are no notes on the back of the manuscript to authenticate the glueings (κολλήματα, " dorsale Klebevermerke ") nor are there notes on the *recto* to record that the document had been registered with the financial bureaux of the capital (" Registriervermerke ").[5] The ink now looks like a greyish brown. The word λόγος (three times as usual, width: 0, 105, 0, 105, and 0, 115 m. respectively), the number of the indiction, the month as well as the tens and units of the *annus mundi* are written in a red ink which looks somewhat faded today. The red ink of the imperial signature is of a darker red. No golden seal is preserved, but there is a hole approximately 3 cm. underneath the signature, and the bottom is folded three times, so that it is probable that originally the silk threads to which the golden seal was attached passed through holes in the folded document.[6] On either margin of the column two marginal lines are drawn with a hard-pointed instrument to bound the text laterally. No traces of ruling are discernible.

The script of the text (see pl. II) is the minuscule of contemporary

[4] On Canon Greenwell, see the memoir in *Archaeologia Aeliana*, 3rd series, XV (1918), pp. 1-21, and the *Dictionary of National Biography*, 1912-1921, p. 226; furthermore *Notes and Queries*, 11th series, I, pp. 227, 277, 291; 12th series, IV, p. 129; CLXI (1931), p. 409. (I am indebted for the references from *Notes and Queries* to the kindness of Miss Ruth S. Granniss, of the Grolier Club, whom I wish to thank in this place.) Greenwell travelled in Italy in 1846 and may have acquired the document on this trip. It is certain, however, that this document lay somewhat beyond the ordinary sphere of interest of this great collector, and this fact may explain why this possession of his never became known to the learned public. The New York art dealer through whose services the Morgan Library bought the *Ms. 398* informed me that the pertinent records of his London office have been destroyed.

[5] On the *Klebevermerke* and *Registriervermerke*, see F. Dölger, *Facsimiles byzantinischer Kaiserurkunden* (Munich, 1931), pp. 6 ff.

[6] In the first and third folding the lower part of the *recto* is folded over its upper part whereas in the second folding the lower part of the *verso* touched its upper part. For a golden seal of Andronicus II attached to a chrysobull see Dölger, *Facsimiles*, p. 66 and plate 65, and Pietro Sella, *Le bolle d'oro dell' archivio vaticano* (Città del Vaticano, 1934), pp. 47 ff. and plate 11.

literary manuscripts. Like other chrysobulls of Andronicus II,[7] the scribe of our document makes an attempt of distinguishing its script from that of contemporary book-hands: the individual letters are particularly neat and rounded, and in the roll the text is arranged in a way which betrays clearly the tradition of the Byzantine chancery. The hand resembles closely that of other chrysobulls of the same Emperor; more particularly a hand that has recently been identified.[8] Yet the hand thus identified is distinctly different from the one which wrote our manuscript.[9]

The most striking part of the document is the miniature which covers the entire first piece of parchment (see plate I). Unfortunately the surface of the parchment, together with the color, has broken away in many places, yet the general impression of the miniature is magnificent. It shows the Emperor Andronicus before the Theotokos against a shining golden background. As one faces the roll, one sees on one's left the Virgin carrying the infant on her right arm. She turns slightly towards the Emperor. From the pleats of the garment it may be inferred that her left arm is raised, but in the present state of preservation it is impossible to say whether she carries anything in her left hand. Her face is brownish, her eyes are blue. Her halo

---

[7] Dölger, *Facsimiles*, pp. 3, 33; idem, " Empfängerausstellung in der byzantinischen Kaiserkanzlei etc.," *Archiv für Urkundenforschung* XV (1938), esp. p. 400. Unlike certain other chrysobulls of this reign, however, this document has a great number of ligatures and raised abbreviations which crowd the space between the lines.

[8] Dölger, *Empfängerausstellung*, esp. pp. 401 ff. According to him this hand, which he calls A, is characterized by the fact that the diacritical points of the ι often are placed to the left of this letter. Furthermore Dölger points to the forms of χ, ω, πρ, of the ἐν in ἐνισταμένης, of κράτος, ἔτους and ἐν ᾧ ὑπεσημήνατο. The Morgan chrysobull shows the same habit with regard to the diacritical points, and the word κράτος is written very much like that of A. I confess that Dölger's identification has not entirely convinced me. Undoubtedly there are similarities, but I wonder whether they cannot be explained by the assumption of the same *scriptorium* within the chancery rather than by an identity of scribes.

[9] To mention but a few of the features that distinguish it from A: The letters of the Morgan document are much more rounded than those of A. They stand vertically on the line, whereas the hand of A slopes towards the right. Certain letter forms (β, ε, λ, φ) are quite different from those of A. Furthermore, the scribe of our chrysobull often shows the queer habit of raising the bottom of the τ above the top of the other letters and of omitting the α, as for instance in δικαιώμ(α)τα (line 25), κτημ(ά)των (line 28), κτήμ(α)τα (lines 35, 42), ἀσωμ(ά)του (line 53) etc.

consists of two concentric circles drawn with purple color on the golden background. She is seen wearing a light blue tunic (ἱμάτιον) which is visible only below the waistline and goes down to her ankles. It falls into delicately shaded pleats, particularly over the right knee. Her head, shoulders and the upper part of her body are covered by a pallium (χλαμύς) of a violet brown. There are faint but distinct traces of purple color at the level of her feet; it is likely, therefore, that she wore purple shoes. She is standing on a *subsellium* of rectangular shape which is carelessly drawn in perspective.

The face of the infant has the same color as that of his mother. His hair is brown. His halo is golden, somewhat darker than the background. It is adorned by a cross drawn in purple color. The child wears a long golden tunic.

The portrait of the Emperor closely resembles that of the Monembasia document (below, pp. 171 f.). He is turning slightly towards the Virgin. His face has disappeared entirely. He has a halo of the same type as that of the Virgin. His crown (στέμμα),[10] of which only the outline is visible, and his ceremonial attire are studded with innumerable jewels of various hues and shapes. His left arm is lifted and in his left hand he carries a purple roll.[11] His right arm and hand are no longer visible, but it is unlikely that the Emperor was carrying a cross. He wears a dark blue tunic (σάκκος) and around his waist he wears the golden λῶρος of which the end is passed over his left arm.[11a] His shoulders are covered with the κατωμαδόν, from which a broad stripe of gold descends to the lowest part of the tunic. The inside of the λῶρος is purple red. Andronicus stands on a purple cushion (σουππέδιον) decorated with the figures of two eagles of which only the talons remain.

The head of the Virgin is flanked by the following inscription (all

[10] On the imperial costume of the time of the Paleologi, see J. Ebersolt, *Les Arts somptuaires de Byzance. Etude sur l'art impérial de Constantinople* (Paris, 1923), pp. 120-129.

[11] It is the ἀκακία, a piece of cloth filled with dust to indicate the humility of the Emperor; it resembles a *codex* (see Heisenberg, *Palaiologenzeit*, 27; Dölger, *BZ*, XXXVII (1937), 485; A. Grabar, *L'Empereur dans l'art byzantin* (Paris, 1936), p. 111, therefore, is definitely wrong when he classifies the miniature of Monembasia as representing an Emperor dedicating his theological works to Christ (Dölger, *Gnomon*, XIV [1938], 209.

[11a] This end of the σάκκος is called ῥωσθέλιον = *rostellum*, see H. Grégoire, " Etymologies byzantino-latines," *Byzantion*, XII (1937), 300 ff.; Dölger, *BZ* XXXVII (1937), 484 (review).

the inscriptions in " epigraphic majuscules " [12]) : $\text{M}\acute{\eta}(\tau\eta)\rho\ \Theta\overline{(\epsilon o)}\nu$ and on the left side of the head there follows: Ἡ Πορφηρῆ (*sic*).[13] At the level of the child's head the inscription runs as follows: $\overline{Ἰ(\eta\sigma o\upsilon)}$ς $\overline{\text{X}(\rho\iota\sigma\tau\acute{o})}$ς. The Emperor's face is surrounded by the words: Ἀνδρόνικος / ἐν Χ(ριστ)ῷ τῷ θ(ε)ῷ / πιστὸς / βασιλεὺς / κ(αὶ) αὐτοκρά/τωρ Ῥωμαί-(ων) / Κομνηνὸς / ὁ / Πα/λαι/ολό/γος.

The entire miniature is surrounded by a purple frame.

I should not think that the authenticity of the chrysobull will be challenged.[14] It has been said above (pp. 168 f.) that the script of the body of the document is closely related to that of contemporary documents. A comparison of the Emperor's signature with that of other chrysobulls shows all the well known characteristics.[15] The *annus mundi* and the indiction coincide, the word κράτος stands alone in the last line of the text immediately before the imperial signature, and the " red words " are written with a distinctly finer pen than the signature. Finally one need only look at chrysobulls which have been recently discovered to be spurious to realize that the Byzantines were not pastmasters in the art of forging imperial documents.

The miniature which adorns our manuscript raises many serious problems. There is only one other genuine chrysobull issued by the Byzantine chancery and adorned with a miniature, the celebrated chrysobull for Monembasia, dated A. D. 1301, which is now preserved in the Byzantine Museum at Athens.[16] Heisenberg had never doubted

[12] On this type of script which was used for instance in the addresses of imperial letters to foreign rulers and in other miniatures, see Dölger, *Facsimiles*, col. 11 and plate IV, no. 6.

[13] The last two letters of the epithet are not absolutely certain, but both Professor Grégoire and the writer are satisfied that no other ending fits the traces.

[14] The criteria for the authenticity of Byzantine imperial documents have been established recently by F. Dölger and others. See the works quoted by G. Rouillard, " La diplomatique byzantine depuis 1905," *Byzantion*, XIII (1938), 628 ff. I wish to acknowledge here my general indebtedness to this article in all questions concerning Byzantine diplomatics.

[15] Facsimiles of Andronicus' signature may be found in many publications, most conveniently in Dölger, *Facsimiles*, plate XII, no. 25. Compare especially the vertical stroke which the Emperor places above his name, also individual letter forms like β, ν, ρ.

[16] The reader will find a beautiful colored reproduction of this miniature in S. P. Lampros, Λεύκωμα Βυζαντινῶν Αὐτοκρατόρων (Athens, 1930), pl. 79. The document and the miniature were discussed by A. Heisenberg, " Aus der

the authenticity of the miniature. Dölger,[17] on the other hand, declared it a later addition, whereas Binon [18] took a non-committal attitude. The present writer believes that Binon's attitude is commendable. We have now, in the chrysobull for Kanina, a new example for a *chrysobullos logos* with a miniature, and it would be a curious coincidence indeed if both at Monembasia and at Kanina somebody would have had the same idea of adding a miniature to a chrysobull. Furthermore we should not forget that, according to Heisenberg,[19] the four imperial miniatures in the *Monacensis* of Georgius Pachymeres are derived from imperial documents. Finally, royal documents both of the French and of the German Chancery of the fourteenth century show a remarkable wealth of artistic decoration and even miniatures.[19a]

What is the purpose of such a miniature on a document issued by

Geschichte und Literatur der Palaiologenzeit," *Sitzungsberichte der Bayer. Akad. der Wiss., Phil.-philol. und histor. Klasse,* 1920, no. 10; F. Dölger, " Ein literarischer und diplomatischer Fälscher des 16. Jahrhunderts: Metropolit Makarios von Monembasia," *Otto Glauning zum 60. Geburtstag. Festgabe aus Wissenschaft und Bibliothek,* I (Leipzig, 1936), 25-35 (proves that the parallel document in the National Library at Athens, likewise adorned with a miniature, is a forgery); and St. Binon, " L'Histoire et la légende de deux chrysobulles d'Andronic II en faveur de Monembasie. Macaire ou Phrantzès ? " *Echos d'Orient,* XXXVII (1938), 274-311.

[17] Dölger, *Metropolit Makarios,* p. 27, note 1: (The document of 1301 is genuine) " bis auf die beiden gleichartigen, je mit dem Bilde des neben Christus stehenden Kaisers versehenen Pergamentstücke, welche beiden Urkunden am Kopf vorgeheftet sind. Solche Miniaturen sind auf keinen Fall zugehörig (vgl. meine Bemerkungen Byz. Zeitsch. 34 [1934], 471); die Pergamentstücke sind vermutlich angebracht worden, während die beiden Urkunden zusammen im Archiv des Metropolitan von Monembasia (bis 1769) aufbewahrt wurden etc."

[18] Binon, *L'Histoire et la légende,* p. 285: " La question reste ouverte de savoir si le document reçut la miniature, à Byzance même, avant qu'il ne parvienne à Monembasie, ou à Monembasie, avant 1750."

[19] Heisenberg, *Palaiologenzeit,* p. 52.

[19a] I owe this information to a kind communication of Professor R. Salomon, of Kenyon College. For the German Chancery, see W. Erben, L. Schmitz-Kallenberg, and O. Redlich, *Urkundenlehre,* pt. I (Munich and Berlin, 1907), 250-252, and for the French, A. Giry, *Manuel de Diplomatique,* nouvelle édition, II (Paris, no date), 504-507. In the fifteenth century artistic decoration appears even in the Papal Chancery, in the so-called *Prunksuppliken* written at Rome, see Schmitz-Kallenberg, *Practica Cancellariae Apostolicae saeculi XV exeuntis* (Munich, 1904), pp. xix-xxii and idem, " Eine Prunksupplik des Kurfürsten Albrecht Achilles," *Hohenzollern Jahrbuch,* IX (1905), 207-209.

the imperial chancery? It represents the Emperor worshipping the Virgin.[20] Heisenberg[21] argued that in the period of the Palaeologi the imperial documents omit the solemn *invocatio* with its trinitarian formula (ἐν ὀνόματι τοῦ πατρὸς καὶ τοῦ υἱοῦ καὶ τοῦ ἁγίου πνεύματος). He suggested that it was replaced, during the Nicaean period, by a portrait of one member of the Trinity, Christ, and he raises the question whether, in times of financial strain, the miniature may also have replaced the golden seal. The Kanina document shows the image of the Virgin, so that there can be no connection with the trinitarian formula. Furthermore, there are traces of some sort of a seal (although not necessarily a golden one) preserved both in the Monembasia document[22] and in that for Kanina (above, p. 168), and we possess a number of golden seals of Andronicus II (above, note 6). It is hard to imagine that even the reduced budget of the Byzantine state would have been unable to finance the thin plates of gold of a seal. The writer would be inclined rather to attribute the appearance of miniatures on imperial chrysobulls to the general artistic revival of the period and to that of portraiture in particular. The Byzantine chancery may have welcomed this new channel of imperial propaganda which, for the Byzantine mind, must have looked like the ancient custom of sending the image of the Emperor to the provinces.[23] It is impossible, however, to explain the differences between the miniature of 1301 and that of 1307: thus the Kanina chrysobull has the Virgin with the child instead of Christ alone and it shows the Emperor on the right of the spectator whereas he had been on the left in the Monembasia document.

The greatest difficulty raised by the miniature is the epithet of the Virgin, ἡ πορφηρῆ. The writer wishes to state candidly that he has not arrived at a satisfactory explanation of it and that, if the sug-

[20] On this theme of the imperial art, see A. Grabar, *L'Empereur dans l'art byzantin etc.*, Paris, 1936, pp. 98-106.

[21] Heisenberg, *Palaiologenzeit*, 54.

[22] Binon, *L'Histoire et la légende*, 305.

[23] In this connection it should be noted that one hour and a half north of Berat, in the Church of St. Nicholas of the village of Pentrochontē, there are frescoes representing Andronicus and other members of his family (A. Alexudes, " Δύο σημειώματα ἐκ χειρογράφων," Δελτίον τῆς ἱστορικῆς καὶ ἐθνολογικῆς ἑταιρείας τῆς Ἑλλάδος, IV (1892), 279 f., note 2) and the same holds true of the monastery of Pojani, on the site of the ancient Apollonia (K. Jireček, " Valona im Mittelalter," in L. von Thalloczy, *Illyrische-Albanische Forschungen*, I (Munich and Leipzig, 1916), p. 174.

174

gestions mentioned below point in the right direction, the credit for this belongs entirely to Professor Henri Grégoire. The epithet as such has not been found anywhere else and the general literature on the iconography of the Virgin [24] does not mention this type at all. A solution of the problem may be sought on two different lines of approach:

(1) The Virgin may be called "the purple one" because of some tradition connecting the Virgin with the purple.

(2) She may be called thus because an image of the Virgin at a place called ἡ Πορφύρα was the object of particular worship at the time of the chrysobull.

Now legend does indeed connect the Virgin with the purple. The *Protevangelium Jacobi* reports that, when the priests decided to have a new curtain made for the temple and assembled for this purpose seven virgins, among them Mary, the lot decided that she should weave "the scarlet and the true purple." [25] She busied herself with the purple when the angel announced the birth of Jesus,[26] and before she visited Elizabeth, she brought the purple and the scarlet back to the temple.[27] The episode of the purple was not forgotten at Byzantium,[28] and it plays a particularly important role in the homilies of

[24] Especially N. P. Kondakov, *Ikonografija Bogomateri*, 2 vols. (Petrograd, 1915). For more recent literature on the subject, see the bibliographical references in V. Lasareff, "Studies in the iconography of the Virgin," *The Art Bulletin*, XX (1938), 26-65.

[25] Ch. Michel, *Evangiles Apocryphes*, vol. I (Paris, 1911), ch. X, p. 20 ff.

[26] *Ibid.*, ch. XI, p. 22.

[27] *Ibid.*, ch. XII, p. 24.

[28] The Virgin is frequently represented as being clad with the purple. I note a few passages: Germanus of Constantinople, *Oratio de ingressu Deiparae*, ch. 7 (*B(ibliotheca) H(agiographica) (G)raeca*, edd. Socii Bollandiani, ed. altera (Brussels, 1909), no. 1103 = Migne, *PG* XCVIII, 300 B): Πορφυρίζονται στολαὶ τῶν κεράτων τοῦ θυσιαστηρίου τῇ ἀλουργοειδεῖ αὐτῆς καὶ παρθενικῇ ἀμφιάσει, cf. also 13, col. 304 D; idem, *In Annuntiationem SS. Deiparae* (= *BHG* 1104), *ibid.*, 321 A: ἡ διὰ πάντων πορφυρίζουσα θεοβάστακτος νεφέλη; 324 B: Τάχα δὲ καὶ ἦν κατέχεις πορφύραν, προμηνύει τὶ βασιλικὸν ἀξίωμα. (The dramatic parts of this homily have been edited critically by G. La Piana, *Le Rappresentazioni Sacre nella letteratura bizantina dalle origini al sec. IX* [Grottaferrata, 1912], pp. 110-123). It is to be noted that the first passage quoted above shows that the purple came to be associated with the Virgin as Queen of Heaven even independently from the episode of the purple; for in the legend the presentation at the temple precedes the weaving of the purple curtain. According to the *Epistola Synodalis ad Theophilum* (ed. L. Duchesne,

the monk James of Coccinobaphus.[29] The Virgin is represented as weaving the sacred veil,[30] but at the same time another connection between the Virgin and the purple makes its appearance: she is called the royal purple (πορφύρα, ἀλουργίς) which prophecies the coming of the King of the Universe[31] and which Christ will put on.[32] The two ideas are confronted very clearly in a passage where the Virgin is represented with the purple cloth and where it is said that " in her own flesh and in herself the Virgin is weaving for the universal King and Lord the purple." [32a] By now the Virgin herself has become the purple of Christ. The difficulty of this explanation of our chrysobull consists in the fact that the miniature itself does not hint in any way at the legend of the purple.

Many epithets of the Virgin, on the other hand, refer to the particular places where an image was located. The Porphyra was a building which formed part of the imperial palace.[33] One of the continua-

---

Roma e l'Oriente, V (1913), 281) the famous image of the Virgin at Lydda showed the purple (see also the anonymous homilies edited by E. von Dobschütz, *Christusbilder. Untersuchungen zur christlichen Legende.* Part II: *Beilagen, Texte und Untersuchungen zur Geschichte der altchristlichen Literatur*, Neue Folge, III (Leipzig, 1899), 220, 241. Finally H. Grégoire, "L'Age héroïque de Byzance," *Mélanges Iorga* (Paris, 1933), p. 392, note 1, called attention to, and translated a passage from a *Life of St. Basil the Younger* († 944, *BHG* 263) where the Virgin appears to Constantine Dukas wearing the purple (πορφυροφορεῖ); see A. Tougard, *De l'histoire profane dans les actes Grecs des Bollandistes*, Paris, 1874), p. 42, and also the γυνὴ πορφυροφοροῦσα, Georgios Mon. (ed. de Boor), II, 655.

[29] Migne, *PG*, CXXVII, 543-700. The date of the author is still uncertain, see Ehrhard in Krumbacher, *Geschichte*, 172.

[30] *PG* CXXVII, 633 A (*BHG* 1153): Ἤδη μὲν οὖν τῆς ἀμιάντου Παρθένου τὴν ἱερὰν ἐργωμένης ἱστουργίαν κτλ., also 669 B (*BHG* 1120). The distribution of the purple also appears on one of the interesting miniatures which adorn two manuscripts of the homilies, see L. Bréhier, "Les Miniatures des ' homélies ' du Moine Jacques et le théâtre religieux à Byzance," *Monuments et Mémoires publiés par l'Académie des Inscriptions et Belles-Lettres*, XXIV (1920), 103, fig. 1.

[31] *Ibid.*, 545 D (= *BHG*, 1126). [32] *Ibid.*, 549 B (= *BHG*, 1126).

[32a] *Ibid.*, 664 B (= *BHG*, 1120): Ἦν οὖν τότε κατιδεῖν τὰ τῆς βασιλικῆς ἀξίας σύμβολα ἐν χερσὶ τὴν βασιλίδα κατέχουσαν, καὶ ὡς τίμια ταῦτα περιπτυσσομένην ἀναθήματα· τῷ δὲ παμβασιλεῖ καὶ Δεσπότῃ τῇ σαρκὶ τὴν ἀλουργίδα ὑπὲρ λόγον ὑφαινομένην ἐν ἑαυτῇ μὴ συνορῶμεν. John of Damascus, *De Imaginibus*, I, 4 (Migne, *Patr. Gr.*, XCIV, 1236 B) = III, 6 (*ibid.*, 1324 A) calls Christ's human nature ἀλουργὶς τοῦ σώματος.

[33] J. Ebersolt, *Le Grand Palais de Constantinople et le Livre des Cérémonies* (Paris, 1910), pp. 148 f.

tors of Theophanes." explains the name by the fact that from old the Empress distributed there, at the time of the Brumalia, the purple to the wives of the officials.[34] Now at the outset the Brumalia, a festival which lasted from November 24 to December 17,[35] had been bitterly opposed by the Church, but at the time of the Macedonian dynasty the Church had accepted it and the Emperor Leo the Wise himself recited during the Brumalia a hymn εἰς τὴν πρεσβείαν τῆς ὑπεραγίας θεοτόκου.[36] There is no indication that the festival itself continued to exist after the time of Constantine Porphyrogenitus. The fact remains that part of the Brumalian ceremonies were performed in the Porphyra and that, to some extent, the festival stood under the protection of the Virgin. Under these circumstances it would be astonishing indeed if there had not been, in the Porphyra, an image of the Theotokos which might be qualified as ἡ πορφυρῆ. It is not impossible even that the distribution of the purple to the ladies of the Court was a reminiscence of that other distribution of the purple to Mary. The ceremonies of the Byzantine court were intended to remind the participant of the earthly life of the Savior.[37] In that case we would have a combination of the two suggested explanations: the Virgin is called ἡ πορφυρῆ because there was an image of hers in the Πορφύρα and the latter building was called thus because the scene performed in it during the Brumalia was a reminiscence of the legend of the Virgin.

It will not be possible to arrive at a clear-cut result until other examples of that epithet are found. Iconographically the Πορφυρῆ is characterized by the fact that she carries the infant on her right arm and that she is standing.[38] She is, therefore, different from the normal type of Hodegetria who holds the child on the left arm and resembles rather the type known as Gorgoepekoos, Vasiotissa, Euergetis, etc.[39]

[34] Theophanes Continuatus, *De Theophilo*, p. 174: . . . πρὸς τὴν Πορφύραν εἰσίν, ἥτις οὕτω λέγεται διὰ τὸ τὴν δέσποιναν ἐκεῖσε ἔκπαλαι διανέμειν τὸ ὀξὺ ταῖς ἀρχοντίσσαις κατὰ τὸν τῶν βρουμαλίων χρόνον.

[35] On the Brumalia, see the excellent dissertation of J. R. Crawford, *De Bruma et Brumalibus festis*, BZ XXIII (1920), 365-396.

[36] Constantinus Porphyrogenitus, *De ceremoniis* II, 18, p. 602 (and the comment of Reiske, pp. 708-710): εὐθὺς ὀνομάζει ὁ βασιλεὺς " εἰς τὴν πρεσβείαν τῆς ὑπεραγίας θεοτόκου."

[37] Heisenberg, *Palaiologenzeit*, p. 83.

[38] The purple boots which the Virgin is wearing on the chrysobull (above, p. 170) must have contributed to the development of the epithet.

[39] Kondakov, *Ikonografija*, II, 267-285. One last suggestion with respect to

Here is the text of the document: [40]

1   † Τοῖς ἐπαινετῶς καὶ ἀρίστως τὰ τῆς αὐτοκρατορίας διέπειν καὶ ἰθύνειν
     ἐθέλουσ(ιν)

2   ἔστι μ(ὲν) προσφυὲς πάνυ καὶ εὐπρεπέστατον πραότητά τε ἔχειν καὶ
     ἐπιείκειαν, ἀληθεί(ας)

3   καὶ δικαιοσύνης διαφερόντως ἀντέχεσθαι καί γε ταύτας ὑπερφιλεῖν καὶ
     τηρεῖν ἀσφαλ(ῶς)

4   ὥστε δὴ καὶ παρ' αὐτῶν κατὰ τὸν ἴσον τρόπον τούτους ἀντιφυλάττεσθαι—
     " φυλακὴ καὶ γὰρ βασιλεῖ,"

5   ὥς που τις φησὶ τῶν σοφῶν, " ἐλεημοσύνη τε καὶ ἀλήθεια καὶ τὸν θρόνον
     αὐτοῦ

6   ἐν δικαιοσύνη κυκλώσουσιν "—ἔτι τὲ περὶ τὸ ὑπήκοον κηδεμονίαν τίθεσθαι
     συνεχῆ

7   καὶ εὐποιΐας δαψιλεῖς καὶ χρηστότητας· ἀλλά τε τούτοις σύστοιχα καὶ
     κατάλληλα, ναὶ μὴν

8   καὶ τὸ τὰς ἐνδεχομένας αἰτήσεις καὶ παρ' εὐγνωμόνων προσαγομένας ἱλαρᾶ

9   τῇ γνώμῃ καὶ φαιδρῷ προσώπῳ προσίεσθαι τάς τε ἀμοιβὰς ἀξιοχρέως ἅμα

10 καὶ δικαίως ἀντιμετρεῖν καὶ τὰς δωρεὰς διανέμειν φιλοτιμότερον, ἐφῶ
     κατὰ

11 τὴν προφητικὴν ἐκείνην ὑποθήκην τὲ καὶ ὑφήγησιν " πάντά γε πράττειν
     ἐμφρόνως

12 καὶ οἰκονομεῖν πρεπωδέστατα." ὃ δὲ τούτων πάντών ἐστι κυριώτερον ἢ
     μᾶλλον

13 εἰπεῖν καὶ ἀναγκαιότατον ὡς καὶ πρὸς τὴν ἀληθινὴν ὄντως ἀπάγον καὶ
     μακαρίαν

our epithet. The type of the Virgin Gorgoepekoos which our miniature resembles to a certain degree expresses the belief that the Virgin if invoked is quick in helping. This " quickness " of the Virgin is often expressed by the word ὀξύς. Thus the famous monastery of Nikolaos Komnenos Maliasenos was dedicated to the Theometer τῆς ὀξείας ἐπισκέψεως (MM IV 330) and a homily of the tenth or eleventh century remarks (Dobschütz, *Christusbilder*, p. 263**) πᾶσι βοηθοῦσα, πᾶσι συνεργοῦσα, πᾶσι τοῖς ἐπικαλουμένοις τὸ ὄνομα αὐτῆς ὀξύτερον ἢ τάχος ἀστραπῆς παροῦσα. Now ὀξύς is also used even in Roman times in the sense of *purpureus* (see J. J. Reiske, *Commentarii ad Constantinum Porphyrogenitum de Ceremoniis Aulae Byzantinae*, p. 228, and above note 34). It is possible that ἡ πορφηρῆ originated as a misunderstanding for ἡ ὀξεῖα?

[40] As to peculiarities of spelling and accentuation, especially of *enclitics*, see Binon, *Histoire et Légende*, p. 305, note 2. I have followed the manuscript. Only the diacritical points which are found on almost every iota and upsilon are omitted and the first letter of proper names is capitalized. Words spelt entirely in capitals stand for " red words."

14 δόξαν τὲ καὶ λαμπρότητα, τὸ ἀκραιφνῶς δηλονότι εὐσεβεῖν τὰ πρὸς τὸν
Θ(εὸ)ν,

15 παρ' οὗ καὶ τὸ ἄρχειν οὕτως αὐτοῖς καὶ βασιλεύειν ἐπιβραβεύεται, καὶ
καθόσον

16 οἷόν τε ὅλῃ ψυχῇ καὶ διανοίᾳ εἰλικρινεῖ καὶ γνώμης εὐθύτητι πάντ' ἐκεῖνα
προθυμεῖσθαι

17 καὶ πράττειν ἐν οἷς Θ(εὸ)ς ἀναμφιλέκτως εὐαρεστεῖται καὶ θεραπευεται,[1]
ὧν οὐχ' ἧττόν

18 ἐστι καὶ τὸ πρὸς σύστασιν ὁμοῦ καὶ βελτίωσιν τῶν τε ἱερῶν φροντιστηρίων
καὶ λοιπῶν

19 θείων οἴκων καὶ εὐαγῶν φροντίζειν ὡς τὸ εἰκὸς καὶ τοῖς τοιούτοις
συναρήγειν

20 κατὰ τὸ ἐγχωροῦν καὶ τῶν προσόντων τούτοις τὴν κτῆσιν ἑδράζειν τὲ
καὶ προσβεβαιοῦν

21 εὐμενέστατα. τοιαῦτα τοίνυν πλεῖστα καὶ τῇ ἡμετέρᾳ εὐσεβεῖ γαληνότητι
ἑκάστοτε

22 Θ(εο)ῦ συνάρσει ἐπιτελούμενα δείκνυται ὥσπερ δὴ κἀπὶ τῷ παρόντι ἔστιν
ἰδεῖν.

23 ἐπεὶ γὰρ καὶ ὁ τῶν Κανίνων θεοφιλέστατος ἐπίσκοπος ἀναφορὰν πρὸς τὴν
βασιλείαν μου

24 ἐποιήσατο ὡς ἡ κατ' αὐτὸν τοιαύτη ἁγιωτάτη ἐκκλησία εἶχε μὲν ἐπὶ τοῖς
προσοῦσιν

25 αὐτῇ κτήμασι καὶ λοιποῖς δικαίοις παλαιγενῆ χρυσόβουλλα καὶ λοιπὰ
δικαιώμ(α)τα,

26 ὑπὸ δὲ τῆς ἐπισυμβάσης ἐκεῖσε πρὸ χρόν(ων) ἀνωμαλίας τὲ καὶ συγχύσεως
τῶν πραγμ(ά)τ(ων)

27 φθάνουσιν ἀπολέσθαι ταῦτα, μόνην δὲ ὅμως τὴν νομὴν καὶ κατοχὴν τῶν
εἰρημένων

28 κτημ(ά)τ(ων) καὶ λοιπῶν δικαίων αὐτῆς κέκτηται, καὶ διὰ τοῦτο
παρεκλήτευσε τυχεῖν χρυσοβούλλου

29 τῆς βασιλείας μου ἐπικυροῦντος καὶ προσεδράζοντος τῇ ὑπ' αὐτὸν τοιαύτῃ
ἁγιωτάτῃ

30 ἐκκλησίᾳ τὴν τῶν αὐτῆς κτημ(ά)των τοιαύτην κατοχὴν καὶ νομὴν ὡς εἰς
τὸ εξῆς[2]

31 ἔχειν ἐπὶ τούτοις ἀσφάλειαν τὴν ἀνήκουσαν, ἤδη καὶ ἡ βασιλεία μου τὴν
τοιαύτην

32 τούτου αἴτησιν προσεδέξατο καὶ ἀποπληροῖ εὐμενῶς· ὅθεν καὶ ἐπιβραβεύει

---

[1] lege θεραπεύεται.　　　　[2] lege ἑξῆς.

PLATE I.
Miniature of *Ms. 398* of the J. P. Morgan Library:
The Madonna, Christ, and the Emperor Andronicus II Palaeologus.

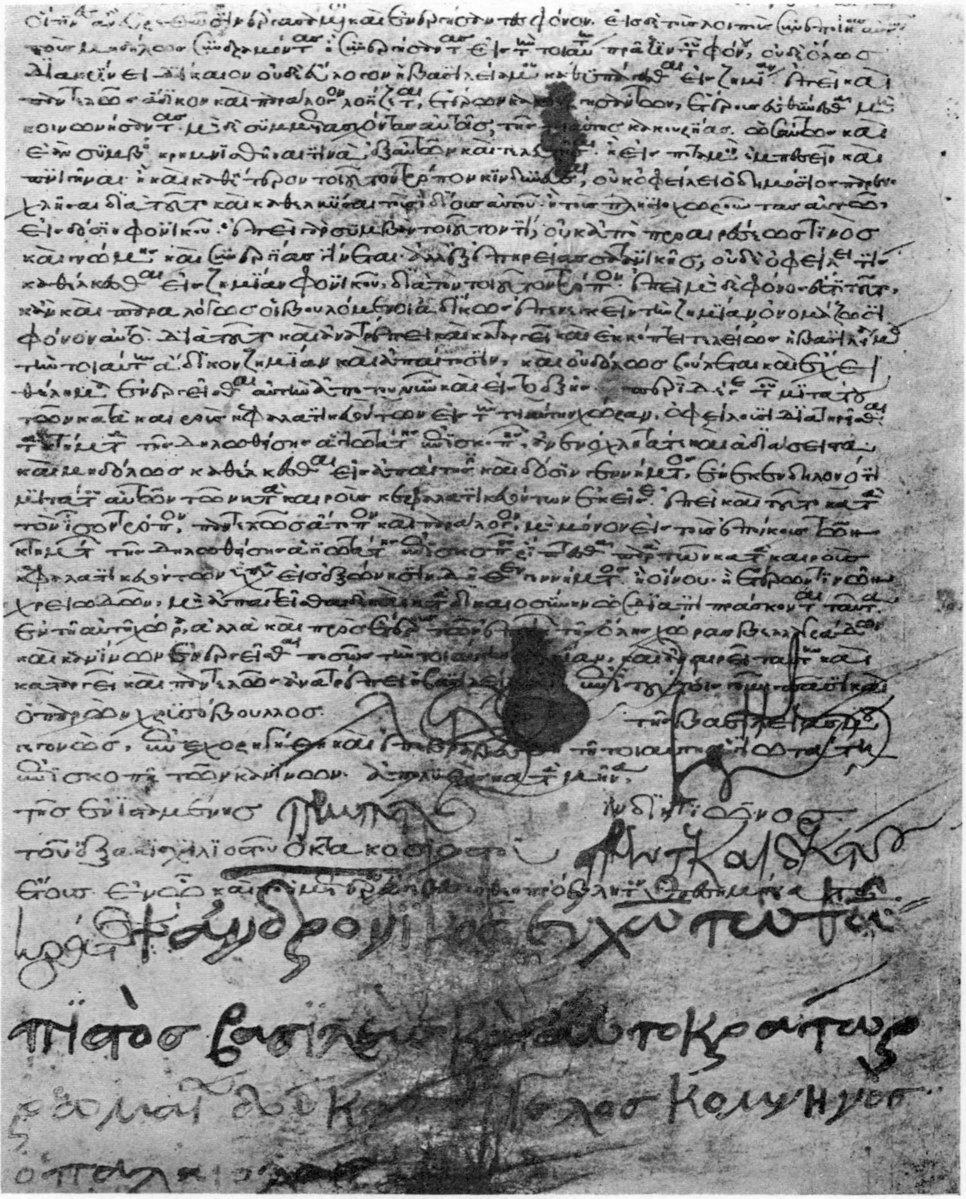

V

PLATE II.

End of *Ms. 398* of the J. P. Morgan Library with the signature of the
Emperor Andronicus II Palaeologus.

33 καὶ ἐπιχορηγεῖ τὸν παρόντα χρυσόβουλλον ΛΟΓΟΝ αὐτῆς

34 δι᾽ οὗ καὶ προστάσσει καὶ διορίζεται κατέχειν καὶ εἰς τὸ ἑξῆς [3] τὴν τοιαύτην

35 ἁγιωτάτην ἐπισκοπὴν ὅσα ἀνέκαθέν τε καὶ μέχρι τοῦ παρόντος κτήμ(α)τα καὶ λοιπὰ

36 δίκαια κεκτημένη ἀδιαστίκτως καὶ ἀναμφιβόλως εὑρίσκεται· περὶ ὧν δὴ

37 καὶ ἀνέφερεν ὁ τοιοῦτος θεοφιλέστατος ἐπίσκοπος ὅτι ἔχουσιν οὕτως κατ᾽ ὄνομα·

38 χωρίον καλούμενον Ἐσωχώριον μετὰ τῆς ἐν αὐτῷ τελουμένης κατέτος πανηγύ–

39 ρεως ἐν τῇ τιμίᾳ γεννήσει τῆς πανυπεράγνου δεσποίνης καὶ θεομήτορος καὶ τῶν λοιπῶν

40 πάντων δικαίων αὐτοῦ· ἐν ᾧ δὴ χωρίῳ καὶ ἡ τοιαύτη ἁγιωτάτη ἐκκλησία ἐνίδρυμ(έν)η

41 εὑρίσκεται· ὡσαύτως εἶχεν ἡ αὐτὴ ἁγιωτάτη ἐπισκοπὴ πέραν τοῦ ἐκεῖσε ποταμοῦ

42 τοῦ ἐπονομαζομένου Σουσίτζης κτήμ(α)τα δύο ἐπιλεγόμ(εν)α Σάρισταν καὶ Μιχάλοβαν·

43 πρὸ χρόνων δὲ ἀπεσπάσθη τὸ πλεῖον μέρος αὐτῶν παρὰ τοῦ πανσεβάστου δομεστίκου τοῦ

44 Πάπυλα ἐκείνου καὶ προσετέθη εἰς τὸν τόπον τὸν περιορισθέντα καὶ ἀποταχθέντα κρατεῖσθαι

45 εἰς κυβέρνησιν τῶν ὀφειλόντων κατοικεῖν εἰς τὸ αὐτὸ κάστρον τῶν Κανίνων· τὸν δὲ ἐπί–

46 λοιπον τόπον τῶν αὐτῶν δύο κτημ(ά)των ὡροστάτησεν ὁμοίως καὶ ἰδιοχώρισεν

47 ὁ δηλωθεὶς πανσέβαστος δομέστικος ὁ Πάπυλας καὶ εἴασε κατέχεσθαι αὖθις παρὰ τῆς

48 τοιαύτης ἁγιωτάτης ἐπισκοπῆς· ὃς δὴ τόπος καὶ κατέχεται ἔκτοτε καὶ μέχρι τουνῦν

49 παρ᾽ αὐτῆς. ἔτι δὲ καὶ μύλωνες πέντε περὶ τὸν αὐτὸν ποταμὸν ὁμοίως κατέχει

50 καὶ χωρίον ἐπιλεγόμενον Κόπρισταν μετὰ τοῦ σύνεγγυς αὐτῷ πακταλίου τοῦ ἐπονομαζομένου

51 Μερτζεβίστης· ἕτερον πακτάλιον καλούμενον τοῦ Τζίκου· γῆν μοδίων χιλίων διακειμένην

52 εἰς τὸν κάμπον τὸν οὕτω πως ἐπονομαζόμενον τοῦ Χρυσηλίου· αὐτούργιον ἐπιλεγόμενον

[3] *lege* ἑξῆς.

180

53 τοῦ Ἀσωμ(ά)του μετὰ τῆς περιοχῆς καὶ τῶν δικαίων αὐτοῦ, ὅπερ
διάκειται πλησίον τοῦ

54 χωρίου τοῦ καλουμένου τῆς Σμοκβίνας, καὶ ἀπὸ τοῦ ἐκεῖσε ποτιστικοῦ
ὕδατος τρίτην

55 μερίδα· χωράφια διακείμ(εν)α ἐν διαφόροις τόποις ἤγουν ἐν τῇ
τοποθεσίᾳ τῇ ἐπιλεγομ(εν)ῃ

56 τῶν Μαρμάρων· ἐν τῷ Μαλομηρίῳ· ἐν τῇ Τραπόμβλῃ· καὶ ἀλλαχοῦ·
εἰς τὸν Αὐλῶνα ἁλυκῆς τηγά—

57 νια τέσσαρα ἀναπομοίραστα καὶ ὀψαρᾶν ἀναπομοίραστον καὶ αὐτὸν·
ὡσαύτως καὶ εἰς τὸ Ἡμίφολον

58 ἁλικῆς τηγάνια ἐννέα ἀναπομοίραστα, περιελθόντα τῇ τοιαύτῃ ἁγιωτάτῃ
ἐπισκοπῇ ἀπὸ

59 προσενέξεως τοῦ πρωτοπαπᾶ τῆς ἐκεῖσε χώρας τοῦ ἐπιλεγομ(έν)ου
Μοναχοῦ· πρὸς τούτοις

60 καὶ ἐντὸς τοῦ ῥηθέντος κάστρου τῶν Κανίνων οἰκήμ(α)τα μετὰ τῆς ἐν
αὐτοῖς εὑρισκομένης παλαιᾶς

61 κινστέρνης ἅτινα προκατείχοντο παρὰ τῆς Φραντζαίνης ἐκείνης, εἶτα
ἐδόθησαν διὰ προστάγμ(α)τος

62 τῆς βασιλείας μου πρὸς τὴν τοιαύτην ἁγιωτάτην ἐπισκοπὴν καὶ κατέχονται
παρ' αὐτῆς

63 καὶ ταῦτα μέχρι τουνῦν ἀδιαστίκτως. ταῦτα γοῦν πάντα τὰ ἀναγεγραμ-
μ(εν)α κτήμ(α)τα καὶ λοιπὰ

64 δίκαια καθέξει καὶ νεμηθήσεται ἡ τοιαύτη ἁγιωτάτη ἐκκλησία τῶν
Κανίνων ἀναφαι—

65 ρέτως καὶ ἀνενοχλήτως τῇ ἐμφανείᾳ τοῦ παρόντος χρυσοβούλλου ΛΟΓΟΥ

66 τῆς βασιλείας μου, καθὼς δηλονότι εὑρίσκεται κατέχουσα καὶ νεμομένη
αὐτὰ ἀνέκαθ(εν)

67 καὶ μέχρι τουνῦν, ὡς ὁ τοιοῦτος θεοφιλέστατος ἐπίσκοπος ἀνέφερε· καὶ
οὐδεὶς ἐπάξει

68 αὐτοῖς χεῖρα πλεονέκτιν καὶ ἅρπαγα ἢ καταδυναστείαν καὶ κατατριβὴν
καὶ ἀδικίαν τινὰ

69 ἀλλ' ἀποτραπήσεται καὶ ἀποπεμφθήσεται πᾶς ὁ τοιοῦτόν τι ἄδικον καὶ
παράλογον πειρασθησό-

70 μενος τούτοις ἐπενεγκεῖν. ἐπεὶ δὲ πρὸς τοῖς ἄλλοις ἀνέφερεν ὁ ῥηθεὶς
θεοφιλέστατος

71 ἐπίσκοπος καὶ ὅτι ὁπόταν συμβῇ ἐνεργηθῆναι φόνον παρά τινος τῶν
παροίκων

72 τῆς κατ' αὐτὸν τοιαύτης ἁγιωτάτης ἐκκλησίας ἢ τινὸς προσγενοῦς τῶν
κληρικῶν αὐτῆς

73 ἀπέρχεται ὁ κατὰ καιροὺς δουκεύων εἰς τὴν ἐκεῖσε χώραν καὶ ἀναλαμβάνει
καὶ δημοσιεύει

74 παντελῶς τὸν ὅλον βίον καὶ τὸ πρᾶγμα τοῦ ἐργασαμένου τὸν τοιοῦτον
φόνον, ἐπάγει δὲ

75 καὶ εἰς τοὺς λοιποὺς συνεποίκους αὐτοῦ ἑτέραν ζημίαν οὐκ ὀλίγην ἕνεκεν
τῆς τοιαύτης ὑποθέσε(ως),

76 καὶ διὰ τοῦτο παρεκλήτευσε τὴν βασιλείαν μου ὁ αὐτὸς θεοφιλέστατος
ἐπίσκοπος ἵνα

77 γένηται διόρθωσις εἰς τοῦτο, παρεκλήτευσε δὲ ὁμοίως καὶ ἵνα διατηρῶνται
καὶ τὰ

78 κτήμ(α)τα τῆς κατ᾽ αὐτὸν τοιαύτης ἁγιωτάτης ἐπισκοπῆς ἀνενόχλητα καὶ
ἀδιάσειστα ἀπὸ

79 ἀπαιτήσεως γεννήμ(α)τος χάριν μιτάτου τῶν κατὰ καιροὺς κεφαλατικευόντων εἰς τὴν ἐκεῖσε

80 χώραν Βελλαγράδων καὶ Κανίνων, ἐπειδὴ ῥίπτουσι μ(ὲν) ὑ(πέρ)π(υ)ρα
αὐτῶν κ(α)τὰ λόγον ἐξωνήσεως

81 ἀπαιτοῦσι δὲ καὶ ἀναλαμβάνουσιν ὑπὲρ αὐτῶν γέννημα οὐ καθὼς πωλεῖται
εἰς τὴν χώραν,

82 ἀλλὰ εἰς τὸ πολλαπλάσιον καὶ ἐκτὸς τοῦ δικαίου, ἔχει θέλημα καὶ διορίζεται καὶ περὶ τούτ(ων)

83 ἡ βασιλεία μου ἵνα ὁπόταν συμβῇ ἐνεργηθῆναι φόνον παρά τινος τῶν
παροίκων τ(ῆς) αὐτῆς

84 ἁγιωτάτης ἐπισκοπῆς ἢ ἑτέρου τινὸς προσγενοῦς τῶν ἐν αὐτῇ κληρικῶν,
εἰ μ(ὲν) εὑρίσκεται

85 οὗτος ἔχων γυναῖκα καὶ παῖδας, ἀπαιτῇ τὸ μέρος τοῦ δημοσίου καὶ
ἀναλαμβάνῃ τὸ ἥμισυ

86 τοῦ κινητοῦ πράγμ(α)τος αὐτοῦ χάριν φονικοῦ, τὸ δὲ ἐπίλοιπον ἥμισυ
κατέχωσιν ἡ γυνὴ καὶ οἱ παῖδες

87 αὐτοῦ ὡς ἂν μὴ τελείως ἐξαπορήσωσ(ιν) οὗτοι καὶ ἐκτριβῶσιν· εἰ δὲ οὐδὲν
εὑρίσκεται

88 ἔχων γυναῖκα καὶ παῖδας αὐτὸς ὁ ἐνεργήσας τὸν φόνον, ὀφείλει τὸ μέρος
τοῦ δημοσίου ἀναλαμ-

89 βαίνειν[4] χάριν φονικοῦ τὸ ὅλον κινητὸν πρᾶγμα αὐτοῦ, τὴν δὲ ὑπό-
στασ(ιν) αὐτοῦ καταλιμπάνειν

90 ἀνενόχλητον κατέχεσθαι ἀδιασείστως παρὰ τοῦ μέρους τῆς δηλωθείσης
ἁγιωτάτης ἐπισκοπῆς·

91 καὶ τὴν τοιαύτην μ(ὲν) διὰ ζημίας παίδευσ(ιν) διορίζεται ἡ βασιλεία
μου ἐνεργεῖσθαι εἰς αὐτ(οὺς) μόνους

---

[4] ι *fortasse postea additum, lege* ἀναλαμβάνειν.

V

182

92 οἵτινες ἂν εὑρεθῶσιν ἐργασάμ(εν)οι καὶ ἐνεργήσαντες φόνον, εἰς δὲ τοὺς
    λοιποὺς συνεποίκους αὐτῶν

93 τοὺς μηδόλως συνδραμόντας ἢ συνεργήσαντας εἰς τὴν τοιαύτην πρᾶξιν τοῦ
    φόνου οὐδὲ ὅλως

94 διακρίνει δίκαιον οὐδὲ εὔλογον ἡ βασιλεία μου καθυπάγεσθαι εἰς ζημίαν
    ἐπεὶ καὶ

95 παντελῶς ἄδικον καὶ παράλογον λογίζεται ἑτέρων κα[κο]υργησάντων
    ἑτέρους εὐθύνεσθαι μὴ

96 κοινωνήσαντας μὴ δὲ συμμετασχόντας αὐτοῖς τῆς τοιαύτης κακουργίας.
    ὡσαύτως καὶ

97 ἐὰν συμβῇ κρημνισθῆναι τινὰ ἐξ αὐτῶν καὶ τελευτῆσαι ἢ εἰς ποταμὸν
    ἐμπεσεῖν καὶ

98 πνιγῆναι ἢ καὶ καθ᾽ ἕτερον τοιοῦτον τρόπον κινδυνεῦσαι, οὐκ ὀφείλει ὁ
    δημόσιος παρενο-

99 χλῆσαι διὰ τοῦτο καὶ καθελκύσαι τοὺς ἰδίους αὐτοῦ ἢ τοὺς πλησιοχωροῦ-
    ντας αὐτῷ

100 εἰς δόσιν φονικοῦ· ἐπεὶ γὰρ συμβὰν τοιοῦτον τί, οὐκ ἀπὸ προαιρέσεως
    τινὸς

101 καὶ γνώμης καὶ συνεργίας γίνεται, ἀλλ᾽ ἐξ ἐπηρείας σατανικῆς, οὐδὲ
    ὀφείλει τίς

102 καθέλκεσθαι εἰς ζημίαν φονικοῦ διὰ τὸν τοιοῦτον πρόπον, ἐπεὶ μὴ δὲ
    φόνος ἔστι τοῦτο

103 κἂν καὶ παραλόγως οἱ βουλόμενοι ἀδίκως ἐπενεγκεῖν τὴν ζημίαν ὀνομάζωσι

104 φόνον αὐτὸ· διὰ τοῦτο καὶ ἀνατρέπει καὶ καταργεῖ καὶ ἐκκόπτει τελείως ἡ
    βασιλεία μου

105 τὴν τοιαύτην ἄδικον ζημίαν καὶ ἀπαίτησιν καὶ οὐδόλως βούλεται καὶ ἔχει

106 θέλημα ἐνεργεῖσθαι αὐτὴν ἀπο⁵ τουνῦν καὶ εἰς τοεξῆς.⁶ περὶ δέ γε τοῦ
    μιτάτου

107 τῶν κατὰ καιροὺς κεφαλατικευόντων εἰς τὴν τοιαύτην χώραν ὀφείλουσι
    διατηρεῖσθαι

108 τὰ κτήμ(α)τα τῆς δηλωθείσης ἁγιωτάτης ἐπισκοπῆς ἀνενόχλητά τε καὶ
    ἀδιάσειστα

109 καὶ μηδόλως καθέλκεσθαι εἰς ἀπαίτησ(ιν) καὶ δόσιν γεννήμ(α)τος, ἕνεκεν
    δηλονότι

110 μιτάτου αὐτῶν τῶν κ(α)τὰ καιροὺς κεφαλατικευόντων ἐκεῖσε, ἐπεὶ καὶ
    τοῦτο κατὰ

111 τὸν ἴσον τρόπον παντελῶς ἄτοπον καὶ παράλογον, μὴ μόνον εἰς τοὺς
    ἐποίκους τῶν

---

⁵ lege ἀπὸ.   ⁶ lege τὸ ἐξῆς.

112 κτημ(ά)τ(ων) τῆς δηλωθείσης ἁγιωτάτης ἐπισκοπῆς ῥίπτεσθαι παρὰ τῶν
    κατὰ καιροὺς

113 κεφαλατικευόντων ὑ(πέρ)π(υ)ρα εἰς ἐξώνησιν δῆθεν γεννήμ(α)τος ἢ
    οἴνου ἢ ἑτέρων τινῶν

114 χρειωδῶν, μὴ ἀπαιτεῖσθαι δὲ καὶ κ(α)τὰ δικαιοσύνην ὡς διαπιπράσκονται
    ταῦτα

115 ἐν τῇ αὐτῇ χώρα, ἀλλὰ καὶ πρὸς ἑτέρους τῶν ἐποίκ(ων) τῆς ὅλης χώρας
    Βελλαγράδων

116 καὶ Κανίνων ἐνεργεῖσθαι ποσῶς τὴν τοιαύτην ἀδικίαν, καὶ ἀναιρεῖ ταύτην
    καὶ

117 καταργεῖ καὶ παντελῶς ἀνατρέπει ἡ βασιλεία μου. Ἐπὶ τούτοις γοῦν
    πᾶσι καὶ

118 ὁ παρὼν χρυσόβουλλος ΛΟΓΟΣ τῆς βασιλείας μου

119 γεγονὼς ἐπεχορηγήθη καὶ ἐπεβραβεύθη τῇ τοιαύτῃ ἁγιωτάτῃ

120 ἐπισκοπῇ τῶν Κανίνων, ἀπολυθεὶς κατὰ μῆνα ΙΟΥΝΙ(ον)

121 τῆς ἐνισταμένης ΠΕΜΠΤ(ης) ἰνδικτιῶνος

122 τοῦ ἑξακισχιλιοστοῦ ὀκτακοσιοστοῦ ΠΕΝΤΕΚΑΙΔΕΚ(α)ΤΟΥ

123 ἔτους, ἐν ᾦ καὶ τὸ ἡμέτερον εὐσεβὲς καὶ θεοπρόβλητον ὑπεσημήνατο

124 κράτος. † ΑΝΔΡΟΝΙΚΟΣ ΕΝ X͞(ριστ)͞]Ω ΤΩ Θ(ε)Ω

125 ΠΙΣΤΟΣ ΒΑΣΙΛΕΥΣ ΚΑΙ ΑΥΤΟΚΡΑΤΩΡ

126 ΡΩΜΑΙ(ων) ΔΟΥΚΑΣ ΑΓΓΕΛΟΣ ΚΟΜΝΗΝΟΣ

127 Ο ΠΑΛΑΙΟΛΟΓΟΣ. †

Summary of Content

(I) *Preface* (lines 1-21). An Emperor should possess mildness
and equity. He should show constant solicitude for his subjects and
he should grant their requests insofar as they are not impossible and
proceed from loyal persons. This is particularly true with respect to
religion, of everything that is concerned with the foundation and
adornment of monasteries and other sacred buildings.

(II) *Narrative* (lines 21-31). The Bishop of Kanina made a
report to the Emperor and set forth that his see had owned ancient
chrysobulls and other documents on its possessions, but that, in consequence of the irregularity and confusion which had there occurred they
were lost. He requested from the Emperor a new chrysobull confirming those possessions.

(III) *Decision* (lines 31-70). The Emperor confirms all previous
possessions of the see and enumerates them as listed in the request:
(1) A village called Esōchōrion together with the annual fair cele-

brated there on the day of the birth of the Virgin Mary (in this village the church of Kanina is situated). (2) Beyond the river Susitzes two properties called Saristan and Michalovan. Years ago the greater part of these properties was detached by the late *domesticus* Papylas and assigned to the land set aside for the inhabitants of the fortress of Kanina. The remainder of the land was set up as an independent unit by Papylas and left with the see. (3) Five mills along the same river. (4) A village called Kopristan with the nearby leasehold called Mertzeviste. (5) Another leasehold called τοῦ Τζίκου. (6) Land measuring one thousand *modii* in a place called Chryselios. (7) A farm called Asomatos, near the village Smokvina, and the third part of the potable water to be found there. (8) Farms located in various places: in the district Marmara, in Malomir, in Trapomble, and elsewhere. (9) In Valona four saltpans, undivided, and a fishing station, likewise undivided. (10) In Hemipholon nine saltpans, undivided, which came to the see from a bequest of the protopapas of the district, Monachos. (11) Buildings within the fortress of Kanina, with the old cistern in them. They had been owned before by the late Phrantzaina and were later given by a *prostagma* of the Emperor to the see.

(IV) *Narrative* (lines 70-82). Furthermore, the bishop of Kanina has reported that if a tenant farmer (πάροικος) of the church of Kanina, or a kinsman of one of its clerics, commits murder, the acting δουκεύων confiscates the entire property of the culprit and even exacts a heavy penalty from his fellow inhabitants (συνέποικοι). The bishop has sought redress from the Emperor. He has also requested that the possessions of the see be exempted from the obligation of furnishing grain for the μιτᾶτον of the acting κεφαλατικεύοντες of the district of Berat and Kanina: they are said to pay for it, but to exact for their hyperpers many times the amount of grain that would correspond to the local price.

(V) *Decision* (lines 82-117). In case of murder committed by a tenant farmer of the see, or a kinsman of one of its clerics, who has a wife and children, the treasury is to take half of his movable property, and the wife and the children are to retain the other half lest they be entirely destitute. If, however, he has no wife and children, the treasury will confiscate his entire movable property, but the see is not to be disturbed in its ownership of the land of the murderer. This penalty is to be exacted exclusively from the murderer himself, but his fellow inhabitants who were not participants in the crime are not to be punished as it would be unjust and absurd to hold somebody responsible for a crime in which he had no part. If somebody happens to fall down from a precipice and die, or to drown, or to perish in a similar way, the government is not to exact the *phonikon* from his relatives or neighbors; this is an accident and not premeditated murder, and it is not a case of murder even though those who want to exact the penalty are absurd enough to call it thus. The see is exempted from furnishing grain for the *mitaton* of the acting κεφαλατι-κεύοντες as it is equally absurd, not only with respect to the inhabitants of the possessions of the see, but also in the case of the other inhabitants of the district of Berat and Kanina, to be requested to sell grain below the local price.

(VI) *Final Protocoll* (lines 117-124). With respects to all the aforesaid points the present chrysobull was granted to the see of Kanina and dispatched in the month of June of the fifth indiction, in the year 6815 (= A. D. 1307).

(VII) *Signature of the Emperor* (lines 124-127).

COMMENTARY [41]

Lines 1-21: For the *prooemia* of Byzantine chrysobulls see F. Dölger, " Die Kaiserurkunde der Byzantiner als Ausdruck ihrer politischen Anschauungen," *Historische Zeitschrift*, CLIX (1939), esp. pp. 242-247.

4-6 φυλακὴ καὶ γὰρ βασιλεῖ . . . ἐλεημοσύνη τε καὶ ἀλήθεια καὶ τὸν θρόνον αὐτοῦ ἐν δικαιοσύνῃ κυκλώσουσιν: Reminiscence of *Proverbs* xx, 28. In Byzantine imperial art the Emperor is sometimes surrounded by the virtues. Cf. Grabar, *L'Empereur*, 31 and plate VI, 1 ('Αλήθεια and Δικαιοσύνη); 119 f. and XXIV, 2 ('Ελεημοσύνη and Δικαιοσύνη).

7 ναὶ: For the double accent here and in lines 87 and 92 (ἀν), see F. Dölger, " Zur Textgestaltung der Lavra-Urkunden und zu ihrer geschichtlichen Auswertung," *BZ* XXXIX (1939), 36 f. and the references (p. 37, note 1).

15 παρ' οὗ καὶ τὸ ἄρχειν οὕτως καὶ βασιλεύειν ἐπιβραβεύεται: Few proems of imperial chrysobulls omit reference to the divine source of the imperial power, see Dölger, *Kaiserurkunde*, pp. 243 sq.

18-19 τῶν τε ἱερῶν φροντιστηρίων καὶ λοιπῶν θείων οἴκων καὶ εὐαγῶν: This passage betrays that at least this proem was written without any considera-

---

[41] The more general problems raised by the document are discussed in the body of the article. This commentary is devoted to problems of detail. I have been unable to identify the following items: Esochorion (line 38), Saristan and Michalovan (line 42, see however the commentary), Kopristan (line 50), Mertzeviste and τοῦ Τζίκου (line 51), Asomatos (line 53), Marmara, Malomerion and Trapomble (line 56); the protopapas Monachos (line 59); and the biblical reminiscence in line 11.

tion of the actual case. The present document grants privileges to the see of Kanina, and a see is neither a φροντιστήριον nor does it belong to the category θεῖοι οἶκοι καὶ εὐαγεῖς (on them see F. Dölger, *Beiträge zur Geschichte der byzantinischen Finanzverwaltung besonders des 10. und 11. Jahrhunderts*, Byzantinisches Archiv, Heft 9, Leipzig, Berlin, 1927, pp. 41 f., note 5).

23 ὁ τῶν Κανίνων θεοφιλέστατος ἐπίσκοπος: Kanina is situated 2½ miles to the South East of Valona, in Southern Albania (or Northern Epirus). The best map of the region (1: 200.000) will be found in Carl Patsch, *Das Sandschak Berat in Albanien*, Schriften der Balkankommission, Antiquarische Abteilung, vol. III (Vienna, 1904). On the history, as well as the political and ecclesiastical geography of Valona and Kanina, see below pp. 189 ff.

23 ἀναφοράν: On this "report" to the Emperor, see K. E. Zachariä von Lingenthal, *Geschichte des griechisch-römischen Rechts*, 3rd ed., Berlin, 1892, p. 356.

24 ἡ τοιαύτη: For ὁ τοιοῦτος = "the above," which occurs regularly in our document, cf. St. B. Psaltes, *Grammatik der byzantinischen Chroniken*, Forschungen zur griechischen und lateinischen Grammatik, Heft 2 (Göttingen, 1913), p. 195.

26 ἀνωμαλίας τε καὶ συγχύσεως: This expression occurs frequently in documents of the Byzantine chancery under Andronicus II, particularly for the period of internecine war between Andronicus II and Andronicus III, but in patriarchal documents it is found even earlier (F. Miklosich and J. Müller, *Acta et Diplomata Graeca Medii Aevi Sacra et Profana* (Vienna, 1860-1890), six vols. = MM, I, 79, 80, 87).

28 παρεκλήτευσε: This verb (here and in lines 76, 77) with the ending -εύω used so frequently in Medieval Greek for the formation of new verbs (Psaltes, *Grammatik*, 316-321) occurs before the reign of Andronicus II (MM, IV, 39, line 12, 1235 A. D.; 256, line 33, 1275 A. D.; 330, line 23, A. D. 1272, etc.), but it is a favorite word of this Emperor and there are few chrysobulls of his where the word does not appear, see *e. g.* MM, IV, 29, line 15, A. D. 1284; V 89, line 21, A. D. 1318, etc.

36 ἀδιαστίκτως: The word occurs here and below line 63. διάστιξις, originally meaning "distinction," appears in various derived meanings in Byzantine documents. As early as the year 1170 A. D. it is used in the sense of a "chapter," "point," or "item" mentioned in a state document: MM III, 36, line 19 κατὰ τὰς ἐγκειμένας αὐτῇ διαστίξεις (Latin text: *secundum extensa ibi capita*); MM IV, 27, line 15 (A. D. 1262): τὰς περιλήψεις καὶ διαστίξεις αὐτῶν; MM III, 100, line 17 (1324 A. D.): πάσας τὰς διαστίξεις καὶ τὰ κεφάλαια. But, in MM IV, 210, line 27 (A. D. 1253): διαστίξεις καὶ διαμάχας; IV, 223, line 33 (A. D. 1260): ὄχλησιν καὶ διάστιξιν; 225, line 24 (A. D. 1242-1250): γεγόνασιν . . . διαστίξεις πολλαὶ περὶ τούτων, it has quite another sense, that of "dispute," "quarrel." The adjective ἀδιάστικτος (adverb ἀδιαστίκτως) in the sense of "without any discussion or objection" seems to occur only in a document issued by the chancery of Constantinople in A. D. 1316, MM I, 61, line 19 where ἀδιαστίκτῳ γνώμῃ should be read instead of ἀδιστάκτῳ γνώμῃ, and in a chrysobull of Andronicus II, A. D. 1292, M. Gudas, Βυζαντιακὰ Ἔγγραφα τῆς ἐν Ἄθῳ ἱερᾶς μονῆς τοῦ Βατοπεδίου, Ἐπετηρὶς Ἑταιρείας Βυζαντινῶν Σπουδῶν IV (1927), 222, line 32 (cf. *ibid.*, p. 231, line 19).

38 χωρίον καλούμενον 'Εσωχώριον: I am unable to identify this village. This is all the more regrettable as, according to line 40, it was in Esochorion (and not in the *kastron* of Kanina itself) that the episcopal church of Kanina was located.

38 μετὰ τῆς ἐν αὐτῷ τελουμένης κατέτος πανηγύρεως ἐν τῇ τιμίᾳ γεννήσει τῆς . . . θεομήτορος: On the birthday of the Theotokos (September 8), an annual fair was held at Esochorion. Such local fairs are mentioned frequently in the documents of the period of the Palaiologoi. MM IV, 107, line 25 (mentions a road and market place used for the fair of St. Panteleemon, A. D. 1274); VV XX (1913), Appendix, p. 13, line 79 (confirming the monastery of Philotheos in the possession of a church dedicated to St. Michael, *σὺν τῇ ἐτησίως ἐκεῖσε τελουμένῃ δημοτελεῖ πανηγύρει κατὰ τὴν ὀγδόην νοεμβρίου*, A. D. 1287); VV XIII (1906), Appendix, pp. 37 f. (gift to the monastery of Zographu of the village of Prevista together with a chapel of St. Christophoros, *σὺν τῇ ἐτησίως γινομένῃ πανηγύρει ἐπὶ τῇ τελετῇ αὐτοῦ*, 1319 A. D.); and VV XX (1913), Appendix, p. 20, line 58 (the monastery of Philotheos is said to own at Saloniki a *τόπος, ἐν ᾧ τελεῖται κατ' ἔτος ἡ πανήγυρις τοῦ ἁγίου μεγαλομάρτυρος Γεωργίου*: finally the most important fair of St. Demetrius at Saloniki (O. Tafrali, *Thessalonique an quatorzième siècle*, Paris, 1912, pp. 117-120). This sudden rise of local annual fairs at various places in the Byzantine Empire reminds us of the fairs flourishing in the Occident, in Serbia (Jireček, C., *Staat und Gesellschaft im mittelalterlichen Serbien* etc., II, Akademie der Wissenschaften zu Wien, Denkschriften, LVI, Heft 3 (1912), p. 65 ff.), in the Champagne, the Po valley, and even England and Germany (R. Kötzschke, *Allgemeine Wirtschaftsgeschichte des Mittelalters*, Jena, 1924, pp. 596 ff.). Was the movement in the Orient due to the same causes as that in the West? On Western analogies it is to be assumed that the bishop of Kanina had considerable revenues from his control over the fair at Esochorion.

42 Σάρισταν καὶ Μιχάλοβαν: These two possessions which are to be said to lie beyond the river *Σουσίτζης* (the modern Susiča, a tributary of the Vjossa) are not found on the maps. But at the place where the river Vlaina flows into the Susiča, to the north east of Kanina and just beyond the Susiča, I find a village called Piskupi. The name may be the last trace of the two possessions *Σάρισταν καὶ Μιχάλοβαν* owned by the see of Kanina.

46 ὡροστάτησεν: Not in the dictionaries. *ὁροστατεῖν* = " to fix boundaries."

51 ff. πακτάλιον: This word is missing in the dictionaries, yet it is clear that it means " leasehold." The word is formed with the suffix *-άλιον* as in the case of many other words derived from the Latin (see Psaltes, *Grammatik*, 279 f.).

52 εἰς τὸν κάμπον . . . τοῦ Χρυσηλίου: It is to be identified with the modern village of Risili to the north east of Valona, which on an older map appended to Count Karaczay, " Geographical Account of Albania," *Journal of the Royal Geographical Society of London*, XII (1842) 45-75 appears as Krisilio. The name reminds one of the family of the Chryselioi, perhaps of the Johannes Chryselios, mayor (*πρωτεύων*) of Dyrrachion, whose daughter Tsar Samuel of Bulgaria married before 989 A. D. (Jireček, Constantin, *Geschichte der Serben*, I (Gotha, 1911) 204 f.; and more recently N. Adontz, " Samuel l'Arménien, roi des Bulgares," *Mémoires de l'Académie Royal de Belgique*, 1938).

52 ff. αὐτούργιον: The αὐτούργιον was land which brought revenues automatically, *i. e.* it did not need new investments every year (Dölger, *Beiträge,* p. 151). For that reason they were particularly valuable possessions for monasteries and churches and the second canon of the Seventh Council of Nicaea forbade that they were leased out. This explains the contrast between αὐτούργιον here and πακτάλιον, line 50.

53 τοῦ 'Ασωμάτου: See Jireček, C., " Das christliche Element in der topographischen Nomenclatur der Balkanländer," *Sitzungsber. der Phil.-Hist. Classe der K. Akad. der Wiss. zu Wien,* CXXXVI (1897) 9 f.

56 εἰς τὸν Αὐλῶνα ἁλυκῆς τηγάνια τέσσαρα: Αὐλών is the port of Valona. What are the ἁλυκῆς τηγάνια? τηγάνιον is, in ordinary Greek, " a small pan." Here, evidently, land is meant. In the modern languages we speak of a " salt-pan," *zoutpan,* or *Salzpfanne,* to signify " a shallow impression near the sea into which sea-water is allowed to flow, where it evaporates leaving a deposit of salt " (*New English Dictionary*). In Greek none of the extant documents concerned with salt works uses τηγάνιον alone, or (as here) in combination with ἁλυκῆς. The occurrence of a place name Τηγάνια in a district where there are saltworks (MM, IV, p. 16; for the topography, cf. A. M. Fontrier, " Le monastère de Lembos près de Smyrne et ses possessions au XIIIᵉ siècle," *Bulletin de Correspondance Hellénique* XVI (1892), 399 and map) may be due to other reasons than the presence of salt-pans. Despite the lack of Greek evidence we may assume that the medieval Greeks used this term just as much as their contemporaries in the Occident used the corresponding term *patella.* See, *e. g.,* W. Hauthaler, *Salzburger Urkundenbuch,* Salzburg, 1910, vol. I, index III, verbo *patella.* The saltworks still exist to the north west of Valona, see Patsch, *Sandschak,* p. 58; M. von Šufflay, *Städte und Burgen Albaniens hauptsächlich während des Mittelalters,* Akad. der Wiss. in Wien, Phil.-Hist. Kl., Denkschriften, LXIII, Abh. 1, Vienna and Leipzig, 1924, pp. 42 f.). In the beginning of the fifteenth century the salt of Valona was exported to Ragusa (C. Jireček, " Die Bedeutung von Ragusa in der Handelsgeschichte des Mittelalters," *Die Feierliche Sitzung der Kaiserlichen Akademie der Wissenschaften am 31. Mai 1899,* Vienna, 1899, p. 171, note 20, and p. 148: " Die Seesalzgewinnung war . . . an der Adria eine der wichtigsten Einnahmequellen aller Küstenstädte von Quarnero bis zum Peloponnes." The same holds true for Venice, see A. Schaube, *Handelsgeschichte der romanischen Völker des Mittelmeergebiets bis zum Ende der Kreuzzüge* (Munich and Berlin, 1906), p. 11 and *passim.*

57 ὀψαρᾶν: This is obviously the accusative of a masculine ὁ ὀψαρᾶς meaning " fishing station." The formation of the word remains puzzling as the ending -ᾶς usually denoted a person (cf. ψωμᾶς = baker, ψαρᾶς = fisher, etc.).*

57 τὸ 'Ημίφολον: Prof. H. Grégoire immediately recognized the identity of that place with Mifoli, on the Vjossa, somewhat more than 15 miles to the North of Valona, and he consequently gave up the explanation he had proposed. " La chanson de Roland et Byzance, etc." *Byzantion* XIV (1939),

---

* [Cf. Γαλατᾶς " le laitier," Μυστρᾶς " le fromager." The case of ὁ Μωρέας or Μωρεάς seems to be similar. Singulars in -ᾶς were used as collectives and frequently became geographical expressions (H. G.)].

301, note 1. The salt pans owned by Kanina must have been situated between the modern Mifoli and the coast of the Valona Lagoon.

87 ff. οὐδὲν εὑρίσκεται ἔχων γυναῖκα: For οὐδὲν instead of οὐ see Psaltes, *Grammatik*, p. 341.

80 Βελλαγράδων: Berat, in Albania.

95 ἄτοπον: The *reductio ad absurdum*, here and line 111, is a favorite type of argumentation in the documents of the period, see MM I, 4 (ἔν τι τῶν ἀτοπωτάτων); 89 (τῶν ἀτόπων ἄν εἴη); etc.

Our chrysobull is concerned with Kanina and it mentions, among the larger places, Berat and Valona. These towns of Southern Albania [42] are, and have been, the natural stepping stones for a conquest of the Near East from Italian soil since Valona lies at a distance of only forty miles from the Italian harbor of Otranto.

Medieval Albania [43] was provided with two large belts of fortresses.[44] The northerly belt started in the West at Durazzo and tried to protect as much of the northern branch of the *Via Egnatia* as could be held against the barbarians. The most important strongholds of the southern line of defense in the fourteenth century were Valona, Kanina, Spinariza, Pirgos and Berat.[45] The medieval fortress of Valona lay to the southwest of modern Valona, near the present harbor; Spinariza at the mouth of the Vjossa; Pirgos near the mouth of the Semeni; and Berat farther inland near the foot of Mt. Tomor.

The fortress of Kanina [46] is located an hour to the southeast of Valona, on a hill which commands an impressive view up to Durazzo

[42] On the geography of Albania, see J. G. von Hahn, *Albanesische Studien*, 2 pts. (Jena, 1854); H. Louis, *Albanien, eine Landeskunde vornehmlich auf Grund eigener Reisen*, Geographische Abhandlungen, Zweite Reihe, Heft 3, Stuttgart, 1927 (with exhaustive bibliography); R. Almagià, *L'Albania* (Rome, 1930).

[43] On the medieval history of Albania, the following works are helpful: M. v. Šufflay, *Städte und Burgen Albaniens hauptsächlich während des Mittelalters*, Akad. der Wiss. in Wien, Phil.-Hist. Kl., Denkschriften, LXIII (1924); L. von Thallóczy, C. Jireček, and M. von Šufflay, *Acta et Diplomata Res Albaniae Mediae Aetatis illustrantia* (= *A. Alb.*), vol. I (Vienna, 1913); and the collection of articles by various authors compiled by L. von Thallóczy, *Illyrisch-Albanische Forschungen*, vol. I (Munich and Leipzig, 1916). Map of Medieval Albania in *A. Alb.*

[44] Šufflay, *Städte und Burgen*, pp. 17 ff., and *passim*.

[45] *Ibid.*, pp. 30-33.

[46] On Kanina, see Hahn, *Albanesische Studien*, p. 72; Šufflay, *Städte und Burgen*, p. 31. For its history, see two articles on Valona, C. Jireček, "Valona im Mittelalter," *Illyrisch-Albanische Forschungen*, pp. 168-187, and W. Miller, "Valona," *Journal of Hellenic Studies*, XXXVII (1917), 184-194.

and Mt. Tomor. It is not impossible that Kanina under the name of Illyricum antedates even the reign of Justinian.[47] The change of name (or if the two names belong to different places: the shift of political importance) must have had a reason and it is tempting to assume that Kanina is a Bulgarian name (formed from the title of the Bulgarian ruler, κάνας or κάννας), "Khan's Town." It is not quite certain whether Kanina was included in the first Bulgarian Empire, but there is much evidence in favor of such an hypothesis. Our chrysobull mentions a τοποθεσία called τὸ Μαλομήριον (line 56), evidently after Khan Malamir.[48] An inscription dating from the reign of Tsar Boris (852-888 A. D.) has been found near the village of Balši, on the middle course of the river Gjanica.[49] Finally a list of archbishops of Bulgaria written in the thirteenth century mentions that, at the time of Tsar Boris (852-889), Kanina lay on the frontier of the Bulgarian domain.[50] Without going into the detail of the

[47] Procopius, *De aedificiis*, IV, 4 mentions among the φρούρια restored by Justinian in *Epirus Nova* that of Illyrin and the *Vat. Gr. 828*, a text of the thirteenth century at the earliest, mentions among the suffragan bishops of Iustiniana Prima in the twentieth place: ὁ Ἰλλυρικοῦ ἤτοι Κανίνων (H. Gelzer, "Ungedruckte und wenig bekannte Bistümerverzeichnisse der orientalischen Kirche," *BZ* I [1892], 257, and II [1893], 50). This latter text shows the general tendency of replacing Slavic by Greek place names (Gelzer, *loc. cit.*, BZ II (1893), 60. Hahn, *Albanesische Studien*, p. 72 found remainders of ancient buildings at Kanina, but see Patsch, *Sandschak Berat*, p. 21.

[48] Malamir reigned from 831 until 836 or 852 (on this controversy, see St. Runciman, *A History of the First Bulgarian Empire* (London, 1930), pp. 292-297.

[49] On this inscription, see V. N. Zlatarski, "Naměreniiat v Albanija nadpis s imeto na bŭlgarskija knjaz Borisa-Michaila," *Slavia*, II (1923), 61-91; H. Grégoire, *Byzantion*, VIII (1933), 663-668; and V. Beshevliev, "Pŭrvo bŭlgarski Nadpisi," etc., (German subtitle: "Die protobulgarischen Inschriften)," *Annuaire de l'Université de Sofia*, Faculté Historico-Philologique, XXX, 1 (1934), no. 47. and pp. 145 ff.

[50] H. Gelzer, "Der Patriarchat von Achrida," Abh. der phil.-hist. Cl. der Königl. Sächs. Gesell. der Wiss., XX, 5 (1902), p. 6: Κλήμης . . . ἐπιτραπεὶς παρὰ Βορίσου βασιλέως Βουλγάρων ἐφορᾶν καὶ τὸ τρίτον μέρος τῆς Βουλγαρικῆς βασιλείας ἤγουν ἀπὸ Θεσσαλονίκης ἄχρις Ἱεριχὼ καὶ Καννίνων ἤτοι Τασηπιάτου. Zachariae von Lingenthal, "Beiträge zur Geschichte der bulgarischen Kirche," *Mémoires de l'Académie Impériale des Sciences de St. Pétersbourg*, VIIᵉ série, VII, 3 (1864), p. 14, note 1, was puzzled by the toponymie Τασηπιάτου. I conjecture that it is identical with Ἰσπατεία which appears in a list of the suffragans of Achrida in the 13th and 14th centuries (Gelzer, *Patriarchat von Achrida*, p. 20: ὁ Ἰσπατείας καὶ Μουζανέλας.

thorny problem of Bulgaria's western frontier in the ninth century,[51] it may be suggested that Kanina at any rate was under Bulgarian control at that period.[51a] We have adduced the evidence in favor of such a view, and there is no evidence against it.

We hear no more of Kanina until the reign of Tsar Samuel. Kanina definitely belonged to his realm, as we learn from a *sigillion* of Basil II dated A. D. 1020: ecclesiastically it stood under the bishop of Glavinitsa who was given 40 clerics and 30 tenant farmers ($\pi\acute{\alpha}\rho o\iota\kappa o\iota$).[52] The toponymic Chryselios mentioned in our document (line 52) is a reminiscence of the family of that name which played such an important role at Durazzo during the rule of Samuel of Bulgaria.[53] It was in the Tmorus mountains, probably in the fortress of Berat, that the last successor of Tsar Samuel, Prusianos, and his brothers surrendered in 1018 to Basil II the "Bulgar-Slayer." [54] This marked the end of Bulgarian domination over Epirus, which now becomes part of the Byzantine Empire. While Basil II left the ecclesiastical geography of Bulgaria unchanged, a list of the episcopal sees from the eleventh century proves that between A. D. 1020 and the compilation of this list Kanina had become independent of Glavinitsa and that its bishop was a direct suffragan of the archbishop of

---

[51] V. N. Zlatarski, "Izvestijata za Bulgaritĕ etc.," *Sbornik za narodni umotovorenija, nauka i knižina*, XXIV (1908), 70-77, to be corrected by Zlatarski, *Slavia*, II (1923), 61-91 (above note 49), where the see of Glavinitsa or Kephalenia is identified with the ruins near the modern village of Balši.

[51a] Whereas in his earlier article Zlatarski (*Izvestiata*, p. 77) ,followed by J. B. Bury, *History of the Eastern Roman Empire* (London, 1911), p. 384, note 5, and Runciman, *First Bulgarian Empire*, p. 104, note 2, and map, made the Western frontier of Bulgaria run along the river Vjossa and leave it *before* it had reached the shore of the Adriatic, he writes in 1927 (*Istorija na pŭrvoto bŭlgarsko tsarstvo*, I, pt. 2 (Sofia, 1927), 26): " (the frontier reaches) the middle course of the river Vjossa, runs along it *to the shore of the Adriatic Sea, along the latter to the mouth of the river Semeni etc.*" In this latter view he would include both Valona and Kanina in the Bulgarian Empire.

[52] Gelzer, *Bistümerverzeichnisse*, BZ II (1893), 42, 50. Complete bibliography on these documents in B. Granić, "Kirchenrechtliche Glossen zu den vom Kaiser Basileios II dem autokephalen Erzbistum von Achrida verliehenen Privilegien," *Byzantion*, XII (1937), 395 ff., note 1.

[53] Nicolas Adontz, "Samuel L'Arménien Roi des Bulgares," Academie Royale de Belgique, Classe des Lettres, *Mémoires*, XXXIX, 1 (1938), esp. pp. 51-63.

[54] Cedrenus, ed. Bonn, II, p. 469: $\tau\acute{o}\tau\epsilon$ $\kappa\alpha\grave{\iota}$ $\Pi\rho o\upsilon\sigma\iota\alpha\nu\grave{o}\varsigma$ $\kappa\alpha\grave{\iota}$ $o\grave{\iota}$ $\tau o\acute{\upsilon}\tau o\upsilon$ $\delta\acute{\upsilon}o$ $\dot{\alpha}\delta\epsilon\lambda\phi o\acute{\iota}$, $o\grave{\iota}$ $\tau o\widehat{\upsilon}$ $B\lambda\alpha\delta\iota\sigma\theta\lambda\acute{\alpha}\beta o\upsilon$ $\pi\alpha\widehat{\iota}\delta\epsilon\varsigma$, $o\grave{\iota}$ $\epsilon\grave{\iota}\varsigma$ $\tau\grave{o}\nu$ $T\mu\widehat{\omega}\rho o\nu$ $\phi\upsilon\gamma\acute{o}\nu\tau\epsilon\varsigma$ . . . $\delta\iota\alpha\kappa\eta\rho\upsilon\kappa\epsilon\acute{\upsilon}o\nu\tau\alpha\iota$ $\pi\rho\grave{o}\varsigma$ $\tau\grave{o}\nu$ $\beta\alpha\sigma\iota\lambda\acute{\epsilon}\alpha$ $\pi\acute{\iota}\sigma\tau\epsilon\iota\varsigma$ $\alpha\grave{\iota}\tau o\widehat{\upsilon}\nu\tau\epsilon\varsigma$.

Bulgaria.[55] This holds true, likewise, for the thirteenth century, when another episcopal list shows the bishop of Kanina to be the ecclesiastical inferior of the Bulgarian archbishop.[56] In 1272 A. D. Michael VIII Palaeologus confirmed the grants of Basil II to their full extent, and expressed the hope that those parts of Basil's conquests which had been lost since—and among them Kanina—would return soon into the fold.[57] Michael's hope came true, Kanina was reconquered, and a *notitia* dating probably after 1370 A. D. lists a bishop of Kanina and Valona.[58]

Valona and its surroundings play an important part during the period of the Comneni when Robert Guiscard and Bohemund attempt to gain footholds in the Balkan peninsula, and these places are mentioned frequently by Anna Comnena.[59] From a document dated 1198 A. D. we learn that at that time Iericho and Kanina were a province (*provincia, θέμα*) of the Byzantine Empire.[60]

After the Latin conquest in 1204 A. D., Michael I Angelos succeeded in establishing a Greek principality called the Despotat of Epirus.[61] Under Michael I Angelos (1204-1214) the Despotat included only the ancient province of *Epirus Vetus* and stretched from Naupactus in the south to Arta and Ioaninna in the north.[62] His brother and

[55] Gelzer, *Bistümerverzeichnisse, BZ*, I (1892), 257, and II (1893), 60.

[56] Gelzer, *Bistümerverzeichnisse, BZ*, I (1892), 257.

[57] V. Beneshevich, *Catalogus Codicum Manuscriptorum Graecorum qui in monasterio Sanctae Catharinae in Monte Sina asservantur*, I (Petrograd, 1911), 542-554. See Dölger, *Regesten*, no. 1992.

[58] Gelzer, *Patriarchat von Achrida*, 20.

[59] These fights between Normans and Byzantines in Epirus form the subject of two sensational publications of Professor H. Grégoire, " La Chanson de Roland et Byzance etc.," *Byzantion*, XIV (1939), 265-316, and " La Chanson de Roland de l'an 1085 etc." *Académie Royale de Belgique, Bulletin de la Classe des Lettres*, 5th series, XXV (1939).

[60] *A. Alb.*, no. 112. A seal of approximately the same period belonged to a strategos of Jericho, cf. H. Grégoire, *loc. cit.*, p. 221, note 1.

[61] There exists no satisfactory account of the Despotat of Epirus. I. A. Romanos, Περὶ τοῦ δεσποτάτου τῆς Ἠπείρου ἱστορικὴ πραγματία (Corcyra, 1895), is very uneven and rather superficial. A. Meliarakes, Ἱστορία τοῦ βασιλείου τῆς Νικαίας καὶ τοῦ Δεσποτάτου τῆς Ἠπείρου (1204-1261), Athens and Leipzig, 1898, deals only with the period of the Latin Kingdom of Constantinople. The best account, therefore, is still that scattered over the pages of Carl Hopf's monstrous but admirable work: *Griechenland im Mittelalter und in der Neuzeit*, in Ersch and Gruber, Allgemeine Encyklopädie der Wissenschaften und Künste, etc., Leipzig, 1867.

[62] Georgius Acropolites, *Historia*, 8, ed. A. Heisenberg, *Georgii Acropolitae*

successor, Theodore I Angelos, expanded the despotat in all directions, and to the north as far as Durazzo.[63] Kanina and its surroundings formed part of the Despotat until in 1258 Michael II Angelos of Epirus betrothed his daughter Helena to King Manfred of Sicily in order to protect himself against the growing power of the Nicaean Empire. His son-in-law received in his wife's dowry the island of Corfu and, among other places on the coast of Epirus, the towns of Velona, Kanina, Berat, and Sphinariza.[64] In the same year King Manfred was in possession of Valona, Berat, and Durazzo,[65] and it is permissible to conjecture that Kanina was occupied by the Hohenstaufen about the same time. Manfred entrusted his Albanian possessions to a loyal servant of the Hohenstaufen, the admiral Philippo Chinardo.[66] King Manfred was thus continuing the aggressive policy of his Norman ancestors against the Byzantine empire.[67] Manfred was not to enjoy his Epirot possessions for a long time: for in the same year or the next (1258/9) Johannes Palaeologus brother of Michael VIII Palaeologos, was despatched to the West, where he conquered most of the Illyrian fortresses, and among them Kanina.[68] Soon,

---

Opera, I (Leipzig, 1903), 14. It should be said that Heisenberg's edition is a model edition both from the philological and the historical point of view, and his indices and genealogical tables have helped the writer considerably in solving many prosopographical problems.

[63] *Ibid.*, 14, p. 25.

[64] *A. Alb.* 245.

[65] MM III, 239 (1258 A. D.): τῆς κυριότητος τῆς πόλεως Δυρραχίου, Βελαγράδου, Αὐλῶνος, Σφηναρίτων λόφων καὶ τῶν ἐπικρατημάτων καὶ θεμάτων τῶν τοιούτων χωρῶν ἔτει πρώτῳ κτλ.

[66] Gregorius Pachymeres, *De Michaele Paleologo*, VI, 32, p. 508 (the *locus classicus* on Kanina). (All Byzantine historians are quoted according to the Bonn edition, except where indicated otherwise.) On Philippo Chinardo, see below p. 199.

[67] Schneider, F., " Eine Quelle für Manfreds Orientpolitik," *Quellen und Forschungen*, XXIV (1932-3), 112-123 has cleared up this point while at the same time exploding the current theory that King Manfred was anxious to make the power of his navy felt in the Eastern Mediterranean. This theory was based on the *Translatio S. Thomae Apostoli*, which mentions a naval expedition to Edessa. Schneider has shown that the *Translatio* is a pious fraud built around a confusion of Edessa in Osroene with Vodena-Edessa in Macedonia, just as in the case of the Palestinian toponymics of " la terre d'Ebire " which had made such an overwhelming impression on the Norman troops of Robert Guiscard and Bohemund (Grégoire, " La Chanson de Roland et Byzance," *Byzantion*, XIV (1939), 265-316).

[68] Gregorius Pachymeres, *De Michaele Paleologo*, II, 11 p. 106 E. Here are

however, the fortune of war turned once more against the Nicaean troops. With the help of his illegitimate son Johannes, ruler of Thessaly, and in alliance with his sons-in-law, King Manfred of Sicily and Prince Guillaume de Villehardouin of Achaea, Michael II Angelos beat the troops of the Palaeologi at Trikoryphos in 1260 A. D., and Nicaea had to make peace. The despot of Epirus recovered the parts of his realm which he had lost to Johannes Palaeologus,[69] and his son-in-law Manfred reoccupied New Epirus.[70] Kanina was now firmly in the hands of the Sicilians, and we cannot fail to sympathize with Georgius Acropolites, who is amazed at the ease with which the inhabitants of the Balkan peninsula adapt themselves to the frequent change of ruler: " such are the inhabitants of the West who submit easily to every dynast; thus they escape destruction and save the majority of their belongings." [71]

In 1266 A. D., Manfred of Sicily lost his life in the battle of Benevento against Charles I of Anjou. The Angevins now laid claim to the Sicilian possessions in Epirus, but Philippo Chinardo, and after his murder (below p. 199) his successor Jacobus de Balignano, held Kanina for a while against the new claimant and against Michael II Angelus, possibly with the intention of preserving it for the legitimate heirs of their late master. Before or in 1273 A. D., however, Balignano handed it over to Charles of Anjou, who appointed him governor, and we have an interesting document, dated 1272 A. D., from the Angevin archives which deals with the grain supply " castri nostri Canine et Avellone." [72]

the reasons for the date suggested for the expedition: Pachymeres notes that Johannes Palaeologos was still only a great domestic (μέγαν ἔτι δομέστικον ὄντα) when he left on the expedition, and we know from Georgius Acropolites (77, pp. 160 ff., Heisenberg) that he was promoted sebastocrator immediately after Michael became Emperor. On the campaign, see Hopf, *Geschichte*, 282 ff.

[69] Pachymeres, *De Mich. Pal.*, I, 32, p. 89. Georgius Acropolites (82, p. 172 Heisenberg) mentions only Arta and Buditza as having gone over to the despot, but he hints that " in this way the affairs of the Romans took a turn for the worse " (οὕτω μὲν ἀρχὴν κακῶν τὰ τῶν 'Ρωμαίων εἴληφε πράγματα).

[70] Pachymeres, *De Mich. Pal.*, II, 26, p. 137 B mentions that " the men of the Sicilian royal power appropriated large parts of the Illyrias and New Epirus," (οἱ ἀπὸ τῆς Σικελικῆς ῥηγικῆς ἐξουσίας πολλὰ τῶν 'Ιλλυριῶν καὶ τῆς νέας 'Ηπείρου προσεσφετερίσαντο).

[71] Ch. 80, p. 167: τοιοῦτοι γάρ εἰσιν οἱ τῶν δυτικῶν οἰκήτορες, ῥᾳδίως πᾶσι τοῖς δυναστεύουσιν ὑποπίπτοντες. ἐντεῦθεν τοὺς ὀλέθρους ἀποφυγγάνουσι καὶ τὰ πλείω τῶν σφετέρων περιουσιῶν διασώζουσι.

[72] *A. Alb.* 295. Jacobus de Baliniano was removed two years later, *ibid.*, 319.

The year 1261 A. D. marks the turning point in the history of the Latin possessions in the Levant. The reconquest of Constantinople by the Nicaean troops was only the beginning of other attempts to restore the Empire of the Comneni. Byzantium could not feel secure as long as the despot of Epirus was hoping to recover the former possessions of his house. Michael II Angelos left to his son Nicephorus, who succeeded him in 1271 A. D., only Old Epirus to the Pindus and to the Acroceraunian Mountains in the North.[73] More dangerous than the Angeli were the Angevins, for Charles I planned nothing more or less than a second Latin conquest of Constantinople. We cannot follow the details of the Angevin-Epirote preparations against the restored Empire of the Palaeologi nor the diplomatic campaigns engineered by Michael VIII against his dangerous opponents.[74] In A. D. 1281 the allied troops, under the command of Hugues de Sully, started out from Kanina to conquer Saloniki, as some members of the expedition thought. The first obstacle on their march was the Byzantine fortress of Berat, to which Sully laid siege. Michael VIII Palaeologus dispatched a strong force under the μέγας δομέστικος Michael Tarchaniotes to help the besieged. At Berat the Angevin troops suffered a complete defeat, and their leader was captured; they retired to Kanina.[75] Even in his autobiography, which Michael Palaeologus must have composed shortly before his death, the old Emperor takes pride in the victory of Berat over his formidable opponent.[76]

This is the last time that Kanina appears in the Byzantine historians before 1307 A. D., the date of our chrysobull. At some time between 1281 and 1307 the Byzantines must have entered the fortress. We know the name of its conqueror, it was Michael Dukas Glabas Tarchaniotes; for in a poem of Manuel Philos dealing with the exploits of this general the following verses occur (287-290) :

> Ἐξ ὧν κατασχὼν τὴν πόλιν Δυρραχίου
> Κροάς τε καὶ Κάννινα καὶ τὰ κυκλόθεν,
> Ὁρμᾷ πρὸς αὐτοὺς τοὺς θρασεῖς πάλαι Βλάχους κτλ.

---

[73] Nicephorus Gregoras, *Historia Byzantina*, IV, 9, p. 110.
[74] Chapman, C., *Michel Paléologue* etc. (Paris, 1926), chs. 8 and 9, 11, 12, 13.
[75] Georgius Pachymeres, *De Mich. Pal.*, VI 32, p. 509.
[76] Editio anonyma, "Imperatoris Palaeologi De Vita Sua Opusculum etc." *Christianskoe Čtenie*, 1885 (November and December), p. 537. For the date of the work, see p. 573.

196

The hero of this poem is to be distinguished carefully from his hononym, the victor of Berat. As the poem proceeds in a biographical fashion, the writer had hoped for some time that an analysis of the poem would yield a close *terminus ad quem* for the conquest of Kanina. Unfortunately, this hope has been disappointed, as will be shown in the Appendix.

It would seem, however, from a passage of the *Istoria del Regno di Romania* by Marino Sanudo Torsello that both Kanina and Durazzo were occupied immediately after the victory of Berat.[77] For Durazzo, however, this information is definitely wrong as Durazzo was still in Angevin hands in 1284.[78] Kroja, on the other hand, the conquest of which is mentioned by the poet even after that of Durazzo, must have fallen before 1282 A. D., as we know of a chrysobull of Michael Palaeologus for the former city (Kroja).[79] Thus it is impossible to date Michael Glabas' conquest of Kanina more accurately than by pointing out that it must have occurred between 1281 and 1294 A. D. (see Appendix).

Our chrysobull of the year 1307 contains certain allusions to the Angevin domination and to the period of reconquest. The ἀνωμαλία καὶ σύγχυσις which occurred at Kanina πρὸ χρόνων (line 26) and caused the loss of the ancient chrysobulls of the see refers, in the well-known Byzantine fashion of understatement, to the Angevin occupation. One feels inclined to assume that the activity of the πανσέβαστος δομέστικος Papylas (lines 43-49) dates back to the same period; he is said to have separated the larger part of Saristan and Michalovan from the possessions of the see and to have assigned it to the future inhabitants of the *castrum* of Kanina. We do not know from other sources that this person participated in the Epirot campaign of Michael Glabas. His activity, however, that

[77] Ed. Hopf, Ch., *Chroniques Gréco-Romanes*, Berlin, 1873, p. 129. Here the capture of the two cities is mentioned immediately after the battle of Berat: *alla fine il detto Castello della Giannina* (read *Canina*, Hopf) *che è in la Vallona, e Duraccio fu restituito all' Imperator de Greci predetto*, and since "the aforesaid Emperor of the Greeks' is Michael Palaeologus, this would imply that Durazzo and Kanina were captured before 1282 A. D.

[78] *A. Alb.* 493, 494.

[79] The chrysobull of Michael Palaeologus for Kroja is mentioned in a similar document of his son Andronicus for the same town, see Thallóczy, *Illyrisch-Albanische Forschungen*, 149 (= *Archiv für slavische Philologie* XXI (1899), 97): *privilegium et mandatum serenissimi imperatoris nostri patris* . . . Dölger, *Regesten*, no. 2058.

is the assignment of land to the future inhabitants of the fortress (οἱ ὀφείλοντες κατοικεῖν εἰς τὸ αὐτὸ κάστρον τῶν Κανίνων) makes it probable that this official was providing for the new Byzantine garrison in the regular way.[80] A person called Papylas held the high rank of μέγας τζαούσιος or Chief of the Secret Police [81] when Michael Palaeologus died in December, 1282, on his last expedition. At that time Papylas was staying at Constantinople. In all likelihood he was an intimate of the co-emperor and heir designate, Andronicus II, for after the death of his father Andronicus dispatched a secret document to Papylas in which he entrusted the safety of the city to him.[82]

Even more interesting than the mention of Papylas is that of Phrantzaina (line 61). We learn that this person had owned houses with a cistern within the *castrum* of Kanina. These houses were given, at a certain moment, by prostagma of Andronicus II, to the see of Kanina, and the see had been in possession of these houses ever since. Is it possible to identify Phrantzaina?

The fact that she owned houses at Kanina would indicate at least that there existed certain family connections with Kanina. This is borne out by an inscription found at Kanina: this inscription mentions a certain Sphrantzes and proves connections between the Phrantzes family and a bishop.[83]

Wherever the family name Phrantzes or Sphrantzes appears in our sources, it has a distinctly Epirot flavor. The first mention occurs after the collapse of Tsar Samuel's possessions in 1018/9: one of Samuel's lieutenants who submits to Basil II is Ἐλίναγος ὁ Φράντζης, governor of Berat.[84] I find no other examples of this name before

---

[80] Thus Johannes Palaeologus had left garrisons in Epirus after the events of 1258, Georgius Pachymeres, *De Mich. Pal.*, II, 12, p. 107: φρουροὺς ἐμβαλὼν καὶ φυλακὰς ἐπιστήσας κτλ.

[81] On this office, see Stein, Ernst, "Untersuchungen zur spätbyzantinischen Verfassungs- und Wirtschaftsgeschichte," *Mitteilungen zur osmanischen Geschichte* II (1923-25), 42.

[82] Georgius Pachymeres, *De Andr. Pal.*, I, 1, p. 13.

[83] Anthimos, bishop of Berat, "Ἐπιγραφαὶ τῆς ἐν Ἠπείρῳ Ἀπολλωνίας," Ἑλληνικὸς Φιλολογικὸς Σύλλογος, Παράρτημα of Vol. XVII (1886), p. 184:

εὐσε]ΒΕCΤΑΤΟΥ ΗΙΕΡΑ(ρχου)
ΥΚΑΤΩCΦΡΑΝΤΖΗΚ

Reprinted in Patsch, *Sandschak Berat*, p. 20. On the meaning of this inscription, see below, note 94.

[84] Cf. Georgius Cedrenus, *Historiarum Compendium*, p. 475, line 3, with the "addition" in B. Prokić, *Die Zusätze in der Handschrift des Johannes*

the middle of the thirteenth century, when we hear of a Sphrantzaina (see below) and of a Gabriel Sphrantzes. In the fourteenth century the name has become frequent. One of the most famous members of the family is the murderer of Syrgiannes.[85]

What do we know of the present Sphrantzaina? Georgius Acropolites [86] mentions a sister-in-law of Michael II Angelos of Epirus. Her name is Maria, her husband had been called Sphrantzes, and she was a widow in 1257. Of her husband nothing is known, but it is easy to establish the pedigree of Maria. Michael II Angelos married once only, and his wife was Theodora, a member of the Petraliphas family. Petrus Aliphas, the ancestor of this family and a native of Alifa near Capua, had entered the Byzantine service before A. D. 1108. His family had distinguished itself under the Comneni,[87] and already in the early days of the Despotat of Epirus the house of Petraliphas was connected with that of the rulers.[88] Maria, the widow of Sphrantzes, therefore, belonged by birth to the family of Petraliphas.

She was a lady of many accomplishments and, after the death of

Skylitzes, codex Vindobonensis hist. graec. LXXIV, Diss. Munich (Munich, 1906), no. 54, p. 34. These "additions" for which we are indebted to the scholarship of the bishop Michael of Diabolis go back either to Skylitzes himself (Grégoire, " Du nouveau sur l'histoire bulgaro-byzantine: Nicétas Pégonitès etc.," *Byzantion,* XII [1937], 290) or to his sources (Prokić, *Zusätze,* 26).

[85] St. Binon, " A propos d'un prostagma inédit d'Andronic III Paléologue," *BZ,* XXXVIII (1938), 385. A poem of Nicephorus Gregoras mentioning a Euphrosyne Sphrantzaina (*Bessarione,* XXXIV (1918), 97) may refer to the wife of the murderer of Syrgiannes (R. Guilland, *Essai sur Nicéphore Grégoras* etc., Paris, 1926, p. 161).

[86] 68, p. 140 (Heisenberg).

[87] Marquis De La Force, " Les conseillers latins du Basileus Alexis Comnène," *Byzantion,* XI (1926), 153-163, especially 158-160 (refuting Ducange). It is not impossible that a fragmentary relief found at Arta represents Petrus Aliphas (see A. K. Orlandos, " Ἡ παρὰ τὴν Ἄρταν Μονὴ τῶν Βλαχερνῶν," Ἀρχεῖον τῶν Βυζαντινῶν Μνημείων τῆς Ἑλλάδος II (1936), 41 and pl. 40), and the tomb of Theodora, wife of Michael II Angelos, has been described recently (idem, " ὁ τάφος τῆς ἁγ. Θεοδώρας," *ibid.,* 105-115). A splendid funerary relief of the *despina* has been found in the tomb (*ibid.,* plates 1 and 4). I abstain from using the information contained in the late *Life of St. Theodora Petraliphaina* (= *BHG* 1736) by the monk Job, as we do not know the sources on which it is based.

[88] Theodorus Angelos (1214-1230) had married the sister of a Petraliphas, Georgius Acropolites, 24, p. 39, Heisenberg.

her first husband (about whom nothing is known), she must still have been a very attractive young widow. In 1256 A. D. the Emperor Theodorus II Lascaris had left a certain Constantine Chabaron in command at the fortress of Albanon, the present Elbassan.[89] Chabaron was a good soldier but an easy prey to female charms (κουφότερος γὰρ οὗτος περὶ τὰ τοιαῦτα τυγχάνων ἦν εἰ καὶ ἄλλως καλὸς ἐτύγχανε στρατιώτης). Maria wrote him love letters and led him into a trap (1257 A. D.); this is the last we hear of the valiant Chabaron. To Michael II of Epirus, however, this capture seemed so important that he rose in open rebellion. This rebellion led to a matrimonial alliance of the Epirot dynasty with Manfred of Hohenstaufen and Prince William of Achaia, but Michael himself gained nothing but that the Angevin supremacy replaced the Nicaean sovereignty.

Maria must have spent uneasy years when the Nicaean troops waged war in Epirus. When Helena, daughter of Michael II Angelos, became engaged to Manfred of Hohenstaufen, the dowry had consisted in various places on the Albanian coast, and among them was Kanina (above, p. 193). Manfred had appointed the admiral Philippo Chinardo governor of his Albanian possessions. After the defeat at Benevento (1266 A. D.), Chinardo held the Sicilian possessions in Albania either for his own account or in the hope that the wife of his dead monarch, Helena, might be freed and claim them as her heritage. Michael II of Epirus, on the other hand, felt that his claims to Manfred's possessions were better: after all, Helena was his own daughter. Chinardo was too powerful to be disposed of by military force. Thus Michael offered Chinardo the hand of his sister-in-law, Maria Sphrantzaina, together with Kanina and Corfu as a dowry. Shortly after the marriage, however, the despot sent assassins to Corfu, and Chinardo was murdered (1266 A. D.).[90] It is not impossible that Maria, Chinardo's wife, was privy to the plot. At any rate, it was rumored later that she ordered Chinardo's

---

[89] *Ibid.*, 66, p. 139. Chabaron's stay at Albanon is mentioned in a letter of Theodorus Laskaris, see *Theodori Ducae Lascaris Epistulae CCXVII*, ed. N. Festa (Florence, 1898), no. CCIII, p. 250.

[90] Georgius Pachymeres, *De Mich. Pal.*, VI, 32, 508. On Philippo Chinardo, see Hopf, *Griechenland*, 298; G. Del Giudice, "La Famiglia di Re Manfredi," *Archivio Storico per le Province Napoletane*, IV (1879), 77 ff., 92-97; and Willy Cohn, "Die Geschichte der sizilischen Flotte unter der Regierung Konrads IV und Manfreds (1250-1266)," *Abhandlungen zur Verkehrs- und Seegeschichte*, IX (1920), 70-104. The valuable book by Domenico Forges Davanzati, *Dissertazione sulla moglie del Re Manfredi e su' loro figliuoli* (Napoli, 1791), was inaccessible to the writer.

chaplain, the later bishop of Kozyla, to perform the funeral rites over the head of the dead admiral which had been placed on a golden platter—a gruesome scene which resembles the story of John the Baptist and Herodias so closely and thereby accuses Maria so clearly of the death of her husband that it must belong to the realm of legend.[91]

Kanina and Corfu had formed the dowry of Maria Sphrantzaina when she married Philippo Chinardo. This fact proves beyond any doubt that she is identical with the Sphrantzaina of our document. Now we understand why the Emperor Andronicus II could dispose of the real estate of Sphrantzaina by prostagma (line 61). Maria Sphrantzaina must have felt uneasy during the years which followed the murder of Philippo Chinardo. This foul deed did not have the desired effect, for the entourage of the deceased admiral resisted the attempts of Michael II Angelos to seize Kanina, and eventually handed it over to Charles I of Anjou.[92] Under these circumstances, Maria can hardly have stayed long at Kanina or, if she did, she must have been virtually a prisoner. However that may be, when the imperial troops entered Kanina for good (between 1281 and 1294 A. D., see above, p. 196) the memory of her behavior towards Constantine Chabaron can hardly have been forgotten,[93] and it is understandable that her possessions were confiscated.[94]

It has been said above (p. 198) that we know, towards the end of

[91] Georgius Pachymeres, *De Andr. Pal.*, I, 14, 44. On Kozyla, see H. Gelzer, "Ungedruckte und wenig bekannte Bistümerverzeichnisse der orientalischen Kirche," *BZ*, II (1893), p. 56; St. Novaković, "Okhridska Archiepikopija etc." *Glas Srpske Kralevske Akademije*, LXXVI (1908), 60 ff.

[92] Georgius Pachymeres, *De Mich. Pal.* VI, 32, 508 ff.

[93] We do not know when this adventurous lady died. It would seem, however, from the term ἐκείνη in our document (line 61) that she was dead in 1307; cf. F. Dölger, "Chronologisches und Prosopographisches zur byzantinischen Geschichte des 13. Jahrhunderts," *BZ*, XXVII (1927), p. 305, note 1: "Der Zusatz ἐκεῖνος ist in den Urkunden bei nichtgeistlichen und nicht-souveränen Personen die Bezeichnung für 'gestorben'."

[94] It would be tempting to interpret the fragmentary inscription found at Kanina (above, note 83) as commemorating the transfer of the houses from the possession of the Sphrantzes family to that of the bishop of Kanina—all the more so as the bishop is mentioned in the genitive whereas the name Sphrantzes appears in the dative. But the fact that Sphrantzaina's possessions were not transferred by herself but by imperial prostagma forbids such an explanation. All that the inscription proves is that at some time there existed relations betwen the Sphrantzes family and the bishop (of Kanina ?).

Michael Palaeologus' reign, a Gabriel Sphrantzes. He had been the Keeper of the Great Seal (παρακοιμώμενος τῆς μεγάλης σφενδόνης) for some time, but had later been deprived of his sight by the ruler.[95] In A. D. 1280 he was ordered to join another victim of the suspicious old Emperor, Johannes Angelos, the youngest son of Michael II Angelos.[96] Now Johannes Angelos is called by Pachymeres the first cousin (αὐτανέψιος) of Gabriel Sphrantzes. Johannes Angelos and Gabriel Sphrantzes, therefore, must have had parents who were brothers and sisters. Since Johannes Angelos was the son of Theodora Petraliphina, the wife of Michael II Angelos, it is clear that Gabriel Sphrantzes was the son of our Sphrantzaina. Her adventurous life, combined with the tragic end of her son, has the romantic flavor of the lives of the great ladies of the Italian Renaissance.

Why did the bishop of Kanina wait at least thirteen years after the reconquest before he asked for a confirmation of his possessions? [97] Epirus, and Kanina in particular, had seen so many political changes in the thirteenth century that the bishop may have decided to wait until the reconquest had been consolidated and he would have other more immediate demands to present to the Emperor. Then he would ask the latter to include in the chrysobull a confirmation of his possessions. However that may be, our chrysobull forms part of the long series of similar documents which confirm the holding of real property after the end of the Latin dominion.[98]

What then was the immediate occasion for our chrysobull? The bishop of Kanina had complained of two points: the first concerned the φονικόν, the second the μιτᾶτον.

The word φονικόν was used in medieval Greek to render the Slavic

[95] Georgius Pachymeres, *De. Mich. Pal.* VI, 25, 493.

[96] Johannes Angelos had been sent to Constantinople in 1261 as a hostage by his father Michael II Angelos (Georgius Pachymeres, *De Mich. Pal.* II, 12, p. 107). The Emperor married him to a lady of the house of the Tornikioi (*ibid.*, p. 108, and III, 27, p. 243). Johannes however, left his wife and lived by himself (*ibid.* VI, 24, 485) until in 1280 he was suspected of aspiring to the Empire. On the orders of the Emperor he was deprived of his eyesight (*ibid.*). After he had been united with his cousin Gabriel Sphrantzes who had suffered the same fate, the unhappy man tried every means to put an end to his miserable life and finally succeeded in doing so (*ibid.* VI, 25, 493).

[97] The citizens of Kroja had asked for a similar document immediately after the reconquest (above, note 79).

[98] G. Rouillard, "Recensements de terres sous les premiers Paléologues," *Byzantion*, XII (1937), pp. 105 ff.

custom of blood vengeance.[99]   Albania has been, and still is, cursed with *vendetta,* and one understands easily that the case envisaged in our chrysobull must have occurred every day in the diocese of Kanina.[100]   This explains the casualness which the Emperor shows in dealing with the facts as presented by the bishop and the complete absence of any but the property punishment for murder.

The Byzantine attitude towards the *vendetta* in its Slavonic and Germanic appearances has been elucidated in a recent article to which the reader may be referred.[101]   The authors of this article quote an unpublished chrysobull of Andronicus II for the Lavra on Mount Athos, dated 1298 A. D., in which the Emperor turns against exactly the same abuses in almost identical language.[102]   The Byzantine officials,[103] both in Epirus and on Mount Athos, apparently were

[99] A. Mirambel, " Blood Vengeance in Southern Greece (Maina) and among the Slavs," to appear in *Byzantion*. On Slavic *vendetta* see F. Miklosich, " Die Blutrache bei den Slaven," *Denkschriften der Kais. Akad. der Wiss. zu Wien*, Phil.-Hist. Cl., XXXVI (1888), 127-209; M. R. Wesnitsch, *Die Blutrache bei den Südslaven* etc., Diss. Munich (Stuttgart, 1898) ; and C. Jireček, " Staat und Gesellschaft im mittelalterlichen Serbien etc.," *Denkschriften der Kais. Akad. der Wiss. in Wien*, LVI, 3 (1912), 12 ff. On Albanian *vendetta* in particular, see Ch. Picard, " L'Ancient Droit Criminel Hellénique et la vendetta albanaise," *Revue de l'histoire des religions*, LXXXI (1920), 260-288. The standard work is Vlavianos, *Zur Lehre von der Blutrache* (1924).

[100] Picard, *Ancien Droit Criminel*, 286: " Plus récemment, les statistiques accusent en général, chez les adultes mâles, 19% de pertes annuelles." The ratio must have been higher in the 14th century, as at the present time many cases which would have led to vengeance in the Middle Ages are settled quasi-judicially.

[101] G. Rouillard, and A. Soloviev, " Τὸ Φονικόν. Une influence slave sur le droit pénal byzantin," Μνημόσυνα Παππούλια (Athens, 1934), pp. 221-232.

[102] Since the above article (note 101) is not easily accessible, I copy this passage in full: Ναὶ μὴν διατηρηθήσεται τὰ τοιαῦτα κτήματα ἀνενόχλητα πάντῃ καὶ ἀδιάσειστα, καὶ ἐξ αὐτοῦ τοῦ φονικοῦ μὲν ὀνομαζομένου, κακῶς δ'ἐπινενοημένου, ἅτε δὴ τοῦ φόνου οὐκ ἐξ ἐπιβουλῆς ἀνθρώπων ἢ ἄλλης τινὸς τοιαύτης ἐπιχειρήσεως, ἀλλὰ κατὰ τρόπον ἕτερον καὶ τυχηρὰν αἰτίαν συμβαίνοντος. Εἰ δέ γε φανερῶς καὶ ὁμολογουμένως εὑρεθείη ἄνθρωπος ἄνθρωπον ἀπεκτονώς, τότε δὴ καὶ μόνον ὀφείλει ἀπαιτεῖν ὁ δημόσιος ἐξ αὐτοῦ μόνου τοῦ φονεύσαντος ἢ καὶ ἑτέρων εἰς τοῦτο συνεργη-σάντων αὐτῷ τὸ ἀνῆκον ὑπὲρ τοῦ τοιούτου φόνου, ἑτέρῳ δέ τινι τῶν μὴ συμπραξάντων μὴ ἐνοχλεῖν ὅλως ὑπὲρ τούτου. According to a suggestion made by the Patriarch Athanasius in 1305 and confirmed by the Emperor in 1306 the family of the victim was to receive part of the murderer's property, Zachariae von Lingenthal, *Ius Graeco-Romanum*, III, 631.

[103] Under the Palaeologi the governor of a theme came to be called δούξ (Stein, *Untersuchungen*, p. 21). For ὁ δουκεύων, see Stein, *ibid.*, p. 28: " es ist

using the institution of the φονικόν for a *Bauernlegen* in the grand
style. They availed themselves rather ingeniously of the local ideas
about the solidarity of the clan to confiscate the property of the
criminal and to fine his kinsmen and neighbors.[104] The Emperor's
injunctions were well-meant but, as so often happened, the *Reichsrecht*
had to yield to the *Volksrecht*. Twelve years later Andronicus II
resigned himself to the fact that in Ioannina the local customs would
prevail over the imperial law (1319 A. D.) : ἔτι ἵνα ὁ μέλλων ἐμπεσεῖν εἰς
φόνον παιδεύηται ὑπὲρ τούτου κατὰ τὴν ἐκεῖσε συνήθειαν.[105]

The last point mentioned in our chrysobull refers to abuses connected
with the μιτᾶτον.[106] The κεφαλατικεύοντες or governors [107] of the country
district of Berat and Kanina (lines 79-80) would ask for grain (γέννημα)[108] for their own provision and they would pay for it (ῥίπτειν

auffallend wie häufig im Spätbyzantinischen Partizipien zur Bezeichnung
amtlicher Funktionen verwendet werden; das Unstäte, 'Repressive' der in
die Brüche gehenden Organisation findet in der Sprache einen unbewussten,
aber vielleicht desto getreueren Ausdruck."

[104] It is interesting that, just as in the case of the *sigillion* of Basil II,
the κληρικοί and the πάροικοι play such an important role in the chrysobull.
The reasons for the bishop's interest in the case of the πάροικοι are obvious,
but it is more difficult to explain the case of the "kinsman of one of the
clerics." It would be plausible that the bishop had wished to protect the
property of his clerics. But why is he interested in the property of the
relatives of his clerics? The only possible explanation is that the clerics
were the heirs of their relatives and that in protecting these latter the
bishop was taking care of property which in the future was to come, more or
less directly, under the control of the see.

[105] MM V, 82.

[106] An almost identical provision occurs in the chrysobull for Ioannina
mentioned above (MM V, 82, 1319 A. D.) : ὡσαύτως οὐδὲ μιτάτον (*sic*) γένηται
εἰς τὰ εἰρημένα κτήματα αὐτῶν, οὐδὲ ζημία τις ἔτερα γένηται εἰς αὐτά, ἀλλὰ διαπω-
λῶσιν αὐτοὶ οἱ κατέχοντες τὰ τοιαῦτα κτήματα τὰ ἐξ αὐτῶν εἰσοδήματα, καθὼς
πωλοῦνται εἰς τὴν χώραν καὶ οὐδὲν ἀναγκάζωνται ὅλως διαπωλεῖν αὐτὰ παρὰ τὴν
συνήθειαν. In the formulae of exemption this ἐξώνησις γεννήματος (line 113)
occurs as ἐκβολὴ γεννημάτων ἐξ ἀγορασίας (MM VI, 3, A. D. 1073) or as ἐξώνησίς
σίτου οἴνου κτλ. (MM VI, 20, A. D. 1079; MM VI, 27, A. D. 1087).

[107] On the history of the term κεφαλατικεύοντες see Stein, *Untersuchungen*,
pp. 21-25, 27, and A. Andréadès, "Deux livres récents sur les finances byzantines," *BZ*, XXVIII (1928), 309.

[108] The passage line 113 (γεννήματος ἢ οἴνου ἢ ἑτέρων τινῶν χρειωδῶν) proves
that γέννημα is used already in the sense of "cereal" or even "grain (wheat)"
in which it occurs in modern Greek, cf. R. M. Dawkins, *Modern Greek in
Asia Minor* etc., p. 591.

ὑπέρπυρα).[109] They required, however, not the amount of grain that would correspond to the normal price in the region, but a multiple of this amount. In accordance with the request of the bishop, the Emperor provides that the possessions of the see of Kanina would no longer be subject to such requests for grain. It may be assumed that in spite of the wording this provision did not mean prohibition of such requests altogether, but constrained the officials to pay the price customary on the free market.

We ignore a large part of the strange odyssey which brought this magnificent monument of the Byzantine Chancery from the Bosporus to the Hudson. It allows us to reconstruct an interesting part of medieval history and to revive the colorful atmosphere of the Epirot court. At all times the Valona region had been coveted by the Latins of the Italian peninsula, the Slavs of the Balkan, and the Greeks: our document shows the region at a period when for the last time it was distinctly under effective Byzantine domination. To Byzantine eyes the Latin occupation of Epirus and the Angevin plans for a Latin reconquest of the restored Byzantine Empire were not more than "irregularity and confusion" and by the valiant campaigns of Tarchaniotes and Glabas the authority of the Roman Emperor was restored in Illyricum.

APPENDIX
Manuel Philes' poem on the protostrator Michael Glabas.[110]

The aesthetic judgment about this banausic compilation cannot be anything

---

[109] 'Ρίπτειν ὑπέρπυρα presents two difficulties. 1. For ῥίπτειν in the sense of "to pay," see MM IV, 153 (1259 A. D.): ἔρριψαν πρὸς αὐτὸν τὸ . . . τίμημα. This meaning may derive from cases where the money was actually thrown, as for instance when it was distributed by the Emperor. 2. ὑπέρπυρον stands here for "money" in general. This term was used at least from the beginning of the twelfth century on for the *nomisma* (F. Dölger, "Zur Textgestaltung der Lavra-Urkunden und zu ihrer geschichtlichen Auswertung," *BZ*, XXXIX (1939), 64 ff.). But by the thirteenth century, and on the Balkan peninsula in particular, the hyperper was nothing but a *monnaie de compte* and the actual coinage had to be specified (C. Jireček, " Die Bedeutung von Ragusa in der Handelsgeschichte des Mittelalters," *Die feierliche Sitzung der Kais. Akademie der Wissenschaften am 31. Mai 1899* (Vienna, 1899), p. 188, note 53, and "Staat und Gesellschaft im mittelalterlichen Serbien II etc.," *Denkschriften der Kais. Akad. der Wiss. zu Wien, Phil.-Hist. Kl.*, LVI, 3 (1912), 62). This explains the use of the word hyperper in the sense of "money."

[110] Text of the poem in E. Miller, *Manuelis Philae Carmina*, II (Paris, 1857), 240-255.

but unfavorable. Yet the historian has to recognize that, unlike most Byzantines, Philes is not afraid of mentioning even the most barbaric-sounding place names and of supplementing our general knowledge of the period in a welcome way. It has been mentioned above that the poem (vv. 288-290) mentions the conquest of Kanina by Michael Glabas. As the poem proceeds in the biographical fashion, one would expect that by analyzing the course of events as related by Philes, and particularly those following the capture of Kanina, it should be possible to find a *terminus ante quem* for this event.[111]

Before starting this analysis, we have to caution the reader against a pitfall. The hero of our poem, Michael Dukas Glabas Tarchaniotes (henceforth called Glabas) is to be distinguished carefully from the victor of Berat, Michael Tarchaniotes (henceforth called Tarchaniotes).[112] It is all the more important and difficult to avoid confusion, as both Tarchaniotes and Glabas have wives who are called Maria (or Martha after their retirement from the world) and founded monasteries, that both men were important generals under the two first Palaeologi, and at a certain time both seem to have been μέγας δομέστικος.[113] In spite of these truly amazing coincidences, the distinction ought to be upheld, chiefly because (1) Tarchaniotes is said to have died in 1284 A. D. whereas Glabas lived much longer,[114] and (2) when Glabas makes

---

[111] Such an analysis was given by the Russian scholar Kh. Loparev in a monograph entitled: *Vizantiski poet Manuil Fil k istorii Bolgarii v XIII-XIV veke* (St. Petersburg, 1891). See K. Krumbacher, *Geschichte der byzantinischen Literatur* etc., in Iwan von Müller, *Handbuch der klassischen Altertumwissenschaft*, IX, 1, second edition (Munich, 1897), p. 780; and the announcement in *BZ*, I (1892), 169. Of this work only 160 copies were printed, and it was inaccessible to the writer. It is possible, however, to get a general idea of the work from C. Jireček, " Das christliche Element in der topographischen Nomenclatur der Balkanländer," *Sitzungsberichte der Akad. der Wiss. zu Wien, Phil.-Hist. Cl.*, CXXXVI, no. XI (1897), 77-85.

[112] The career of Tarchaniotes had been examined by M. Treu, *Maximi monachi Planudis epistulae*, Programm des Königlichen Friedrichs-Gymnasium zu Breslau, 1886, p. 236. E. Martini, " Manuelis Philae Carmina Inedita," *Atti della R. Accademia di Archeologia, Lettere e Belle Arti*, XX (Supplemento), Naples 1900, examined the descent and career of Glabas and distinguished him from Tarchaniotes. Recently this view has been taken up again and confirmed by one of the best experts of Byzantine prosopography, V. Laurent, " Kyra Martha. Essai de topographie et de prosopographie byzantine," *Echos d'Orient*, XXXVIII (1939), 296-329, esp. 297-305.

[113] Laurent, *Kyra Martha*, 301.

[114] Georgius Pachymeres, *De Andr. Pal.*, I, 27, p. 72, states that Tarchaniotes was smitten by the disease (τέλος δὲ καὶ αὐτὸς ὁ στρατηγὸς πρωτοβεστιάριος νόσου γέγονε παρανάλωμα) and this is confirmed by a letter of Planudes according to which Tarchaniotes was dead in 1295 A. D. (Treu, *Maximi monachi Planudis epistulae*, pp. 97, 251). Glabas lived much longer (Martini, *Manuelis Philae Carmina Inedita*, p. 65).

his first appearance in the *History* of Georgius Pachymeres he appears with a *cursus honorum* altogether different from that of Tarchaniotes.[115]

Turning to our poem, we shall conveniently take up the thread of the narrative with the mention of the Bulgarian ruler Constantine (vv. 92, 165) who ruled from 1258-1277.[116] Sventislav (v. 166) is the despot James Svetslaw whom Constantine's wife, Maria, murdered after she had first adopted him as a son (1277 A. D.).[117] Lachanas (vv. 168, 222, 241) is the famous swineherd Ivailo, nicknamed "the kitchen-gardener," who managed to marry Queen Maria, widow of Constantine, in 1278 A. D.[118] The poet further reports that Glabas removed the Queen of the Bulgarians with the young "kinglet" from Trnovo and brought them to Constantinople; this refers to the action of the inhabitants of Trnovo of handing over Queen Maria and her son Michael to the Byzantine troops, and to their coming to Constantinople.[119] The next engagement with Lachanas (v. 259) refers to the events of the year 1280 when he laid siege to Trnovo with Tartar help.[120] The "flight of the satrap" (vv. 260-262) very probably is an allusion to the escape of the Byzantine *protégé*, Johannes Asen III, from Trnovo in 1280, which raised Michael Palaeologus' anger to such a high degree.[121]

Thus the analysis of Philes' verses has led us safely to the year 1280 A. D. Glabas now leaves for the West to fight the "Italians" (vv. 282 ff.), and there follow the verses about the capture of Durazzo, Kroja and Kanina quoted above (p. 195). One would expect that, simply by analyzing in the above way the data which follow Glabas' conquest in Epirus, it should be easy to date the Epirot occurrences. Unfortunately, however, these data are difficult to interpret.

Glabas is said to start out against the Vlachs and the sebastocrator Theodore, whose territory he occupies (vv. 290-293). His victories at Dreanobiskos and Astron were witnessed by a lady of imperial origin, by an

---

[115] Tarchaniotes: Georgius Pachymeres, *De Mich. Pal.*, IV, 19, p. 295 (μέγας πριμικήριος); VI, 20, p. 469 (μέγας δομέστικος, later πρωτοβεστιάριος); *De Andr. Pal.*, I, 25, p. 68 (πρωτοβεστιάριος). Glabas: *De Andr. Pal.*, I, 1, p. 12 (μέγας παπίας, later πιγκέρνης, finally μέγας κονοσταῦλος).

[116] The chief sources for the period are Georgius Pachymeres and Nicephorus Gregoras. The best modern treatments of this period of Bulgarian history are C. J. Jireček, *Geschichte der Bulgaren* (Prague, 1876), pp. 269-284, and W. Miller, "The Balkan States," *Cambridge Medieval History*, IV (New York, 1927), esp. pp. 525-531.

[117] Georgius Pachymeres, *De Mich. Pal.* VI, 2, p. 430. Cf. Jireček, *Bulgaren*, pp. 275 ff.; Miller, *Balkan States*, p. 528.

[118] On Lachanas, see Georgios Pachymeres, *De Mich. Pal.*, VI, 3-7, pp. 431-446; Jireček, *Bulgaren*, p. 276 f.; Miller, *Balkan States*, p. 529.

[119] Georgius Pachymeres, *De Mich. Pal.* VI, 8, pp. 446 ff.; Nicephorus Gregoras, V, 4, p. 132.

[120] Georgius Pachymeres, *De Mich. Pal.* VI, 19, pp. 466 ff.

[121] *Ibid.*, VI, 9, pp. 448 ff.

unthinking baby, and by a man who was prosperous before a battle (vv. 294-300).[122]

Now we know that Tarchaniotes, Glabas' homonym, waged war against Johannes of Thessaly and his son Michael in 1284. During this campaign disease killed a large part of the Byzantine army and the general himself, while their opponent's energetic son, Michael, was kidnapped by the intrigues of Nicephorus of Epirus and his wife Anna.[123] The sebastocrator Theodore of Manuel Philes is identical with Johannes of Thessaly mentioned by Pachymeres; for he is likewise called Theodore by the Chronicle of Morea and Marin Sanudo Torsello. Since, however, Glabas' campaign is not necessarily identical with that of Tarchaniotes, and since all we know about Johannes of Thessaly is that he died before 1294 A. D.,[124] the campaign of Glabas cannot be dated with any degree of certainty except that it must have occurred before the latter year. For Philes' further remarks about the lady of imperial origin, her baby and husband, the writer does not find a satisfactory explanation.

After this irksome interlude, the poem can be checked again with our historians. The war against Koteanitzes (vv. 301-319) is mentioned by Pachymeres for the year 1298 (he calls Glabas " that man of God," τὸν τοῦ θεοῦ ἄνθρωπον ἐκεῖνον),[125] and the struggle with Terteres (vv. 320 ff.) must have preceded the year 1294 when this Bulgarian ruler fled to the Tatars.[126] The last mention of Lachanas (v. 322) must refer to the Pseudo-Lachanas who made his appearance in 1294.[127] The Smilos of v. 323 is the Bulgarian prince who was supported by the Tatars [128] and Glabas' victories mentioned in vv. 326 ff. refer to the Byzantine campaigns against the Bulgarian Tsar Theodore Sventslav (1295-1322).[129]

HARVARD UNIVERSITY

---

[122] Vv. 296-299:

> Ἐχρῆν γὰρ αὐτοῦ μαρτυρεῖσθαι τὰς νίκας
> παρὰ γυναικὸς εὐπρεποῦς βασιλίδος
> καὶ παρὰ παιδὸς μὴ φρονοῦντος ὡς βρέφους,
> εἶτα παρ' ἀνδρὸς εὐτυχοῦς πρὸ τῆς μάχης κτλ.

[123] Georgius Pachymeres, *De Andr. Pal.* I, 25-27, pp. 67-72.

[124] *Ibid.*, III, 4, p. 201: ἐκποδὼν γεγονότος καὶ τοῦ σεβαστοκράτορος Ἰωάννου; for the date see the note of Possin, pp. 785-787.

[125] *Ibid.*, III, 30, pp. 271 ff. Here the dates show a noticeable gap in the career of Glabas. It may be assumed that the events of the intervening years were not to the credit of Philes' hero. On the other hand, the affair of Koteanitzes does not appear in the chronological order in Philes as the events mentioned afterwards in the poem precede it chronologically. It may be that Glabas fought against Koteanitzes even before 1298 as Koteanitzes escaped from the monastery in which he was virtually a prisoner (*De Mich. Pal.* VI, 22, p. 474; 27, p. 499; *De Andr. Pal.* I, 24, pp. 66 ff.) in 1283 A. D.

[126] *Ibid.*, III, 26, p. 264. [127] *Ibid.*, II, 30, p. 188. [128] *Ibid.*, III, 26, p. 266.

[129] *Ibid.*, V, 28, pp. 445-448; VII, 18, p. 601. See Jireček, *Bulgaren*, p. 286 and *Christliches Element*, p. 79.

V

207a

ADDITIONAL BIBLIOGRAPHY

André Mirambel,"Blood Vengeance (Maina)in Southern Greece and among the Slavs",Byzantion 16, 1942-43 (published 1944),381-392;Peter Charanis, "The Phonikon and Other Byzantine Taxes",Speculum 20,1945,331-333;Franz Dölger,"Die Entwicklung der Byzantinischen Kaisertitulatur und die Datierung von Kaiserdarstellungen in der byzantinischen Klein- kunst",Studies presented to D.M. Robinson II,1953, 985-1005,esp.1003 (reprinted in Dölger's Byzanti- nische Diplomatik,Ettal,1956,130-151,esp.150;cf. also 37 and n.165);Franz Dölger, Regesten der Kaiserurkunden des Oströmischen Reiches von 565- 1453,part 4,Munich and Berlin,1960,nos.2304 and 2305 (p.49);Franz Dölger and Johannes Karayanno- pulos,Byzantinische Urkundenlehre,Munich,1968,30. R.W.Southern,Western Society and the Church in the Middle Ages,Penguin Books,1970,240,portrays Canon William Greenwell,who discovered the chry- sobull here edited,as a survival into the twentieth century of the type of personality characteristic of the Benedictine monasteries in the Middle Ages.

ICONS AND ICONOCLAST CONTROVERSY

HYPATIUS OF EPHESUS

A NOTE ON IMAGE WORSHIP IN THE SIXTH CENTURY *

In a recent article Professor Norman H. Baynes discussed the evidence for opposition to religious art prior to the outbreak of the Iconoclastic Controversy.[1] In the course of his illuminating article, he called attention to an important fragment of patristic literature which was first published in recent years and which but for Professor Baynes might have remained unnoticed. It is an excerpt taken from the Miscellaneous Enquiries (Συμμικτὰ Ζητήματα) by Hypatius of Ephesus, who was archbishop of this most important see from 531 to about 538 and in addition one of Justinian's most trusted theological advisers.[2] Professor Baynes used the text to illustrate the fact that prior to the Iconoclastic Controversy "any general cult of the icons in such extreme forms as later appears in the apologies of the iconodules would seem dangerous and a wrongful use of a practice which was tolerated only in the interest of the weaker members of the church." (p. 95). The text, however, is

* Professor Ernst Kantorowicz, of the Institute for Advanced Study, has kindly read the typescript of this article and discussed it with the writer. He has made several important suggestions for which I wish to thank him in this place. The author is also grateful to Professor A. D. Nock for several helpful suggestions. The article was written while the author was a fellow of the John Simon Guggenheim Memorial Foundation and a member of the Institute for Advanced Study.

[1] Baynes, Norman H., "The Icons before Iconoclasm," Harvard Theological Review XLIV (1951), 93–106, esp. 93–95.

[2] Ed. Diekamp, Franz, "Analecta Patristica etc.," in Orientalia Christiana Analecta CXVII (1938), pp. 127–129 (text), pp. 118–120 (commentary). The edition is based on Paris. gr. 1115, ff. 254ᵛ–255ᵛ, written A.D. 1276. The ms. is interesting from the paleographical point of view. It contains a collection of dogmatic florilegia. In the colophon the thirteenth century scribe states that it was copied from a codex "found in the old library of the Holy Church of the Older Rome, which codex was itself written in the year 6267" (=759 A.D.). On this ms. see Melioranski, B. M., Georgii Kiprianin i Ioann Ierusalimlianin etc., in Zapiski istoriko — filologicheskago fakulteta imperatorskago S.-Peterburgskago universiteta LIX (1901), pp. 78ff. and Schermann, Theodor, Die Geschichte der dogmatischen Florilegien etc., Texte und Untersuchungen, N.F. XIII (1904), 6–10, with the corrections made by Fr. Diekamp in his review of Schermann's book (Theologische Revue IV [1905], 445–450) and in Diekamp's edition of the Doctrina Patrum (Münster i. W., 1907), p. xx. In his review (col. 449) Diekamp cautions us, rightly, against accepting the evidence of the colophon at face value. Yet for the part of the ms. which interests us here only extraordinary circumstances, such as provenance from an outlying region, could account for the fact that a thirteenth century ms. preserves a passage in favor of image worship which had escaped all the iconophile writers during the one hundred and twenty-odd years of the Iconoclastic Controversy. In P.G. CIX 499–516 (=P.G. XCVI 1347–1362) an *Invectiva contra Haereticos* was edited from this codex, see (Combefis'?) *prolusio*.

also important from other points of view. Since it is difficult Greek and since the trend of Hypatius' thought, though entirely logical, may not be clear at first sight, it is advisable to submit here a translation of the document, accompanied by explanatory notes. The writer gratefully acknowledges that he owes much to Diekamp and Baynes for an understanding of the document.

"Hypatius archbishop of Ephesus, from the Miscellaneous Enquiries addressed to Julian bishop of Atramytium, Book One, Chapter Five, concerning the objects in sacred buildings.[3]

You say that those who set up in the sanctuaries what is revered and worshipped, in the form of paintings and carvings alike, are once again disturbing divine tradition.[4] And you say that you understand clearly that the Sayings [of the Bible][5] prohibit this, that is, they prohibit not only to make [carvings] but even ordain that they be destroyed[6] once they are coming or have come into existence.

We must examine why the Sayings state this, and at the same time consider for what purpose the sacred objects[7] are moulded in the way in which they [actually] are. For inasmuch as certain people believed that, as Holy Scripture says, "the divine nature is like gold or silver or stone or the imprint of the art of man,"[8] and improvised in accordance with their view material gods and "worshipped what he had created, instead of the Creator,"[9] it is said: "Tear down their altars"[10] and "cut down,"[11] and "the carved images of their gods you must burn up,"[12] and "watch your souls well (since you knew no likeness on the day when the Lord spoke to you at Mount Horeb out of the fire), that you do not act perniciously by carving an image for yourselves."[13] For no existing thing is like or identical or the same as the good and divine Trinity which transcends all existing things and is the creator and cause of all existing things, for it is said

[3] περὶ τῶν ἐν τοῖς ἁγίοις οἴκοις. The term "church" is not used at all in our fragment. Instead we find everywhere, except in the title, τὰ ἱερά, which I translate "sanctuaries." Are the ἅγιοι οἶκοι churches, or sacred buildings of a more general or more specialized character? The term occurs, in the sense of "church building," in a fragment attributed, perhaps wrongly, to St. Epiphanius, see Georg Ostrogorsky, Studien zur Geschichte des byzantinischen Bilderstreites, Breslau, 1929, pp. 67 ff. (frg. III 6, p. 68).

[4] παρακινεῖν δὲ αὖθις φῆς τὴν θείαν παράδοσιν τοὺς ὁμοίως τὰ σεπτὰ καὶ προσκυνητὰ γραφαῖς ἢ γλυφαῖς ἐπὶ τῶν ἱερῶν ἀνατιθέντας. Julian says that this is done "once again" (αὖθις) because it had been done a first time by the pagans.

[5] Ex. 20:4–5 and similar passages. [In my translation, I have used as basis for the rendering of biblical passages the Chicago translation, but adjusted it where the Septuagint differs from the Hebrew or where Hypatius, who is quoting from memory, differs from the text of the Greek Bible. The biblical passages have been identified by Diekamp.]

[6] Reading καθαιρεῖν (for καθαίρειν). Cf. Diekamp p. 118 ". . . die vorhandenen zu zerstören befehle."

[7] Here τὰ ἱερά does not mean "sanctuaries" but "sacred objects." Cf. note 3.

[8] Acts 17:29.

[9] Romans 17:25.

[10] Deut. 7:5.

[11] Deut. 7:25.

[12] Deut. 7:25.

[13] Deut. 4:15–16.

"who is like thee?",[14] and we hear the divines sing "who will be likened to Thee?"[15] But since this is so, you say: We allow the paintings to be worshipped in the sanctuaries but we who often prohibit carvings in wood and stone do not allow this [sculpture] either to be sinless [i.e. like paintings] except on the doors.[16] Yet, oh beloved and holy man,[17] we own and record that, whatever the divine essence be, it is not like, or identical with, or the same as any of the existing things. We ordain that the unspeakable and incomprehensible love of God for us men and the sacred patterns set by the Saints be celebrated in holy writings [18] since so far as we are concerned we take no pleasure at all in sculpture or painting. But we permit simpler people, as they are less perfect, to learn by way of initiation about such things by [the sense of] sight which is more appropriate to their natural development, especially as we find that, often and in many respects, even old and new divine commandments lower themselves to the level of weaker people and their souls for the sake of their salvation.[19] Indeed even the holy priest Moses, who issued these laws on God's prompting, sets up, in the Holiest of Holies, golden images of the Cherubim in beaten work.[20] And in many other instances we see

[14] Ps. 70:19 (Sept.).
[15] Ps. 82:2 (Sept.).
[16] This is a difficult and important sentence: ἀλλὰ τούτων οὕτως ἐχόντων φῇς· προσκυνητὰς ἐπὶ τῶν ἱερῶν ἐῶμεν εἶναι γραφάς, ἐπὶ ξύλου δὲ καὶ λίθου πολλάκις οἱ τὰ τῆς γλυφῆς ἀπαγορεύοντες οὐδὲ τοῦτο ἀπλημμελὲς ἐῶμεν, ἀλλ' ἐπὶ θυραῖς. Diekamp, p. 118 comments: "Das . . . Fragment . . . handelt . . . von den heiligen Gemälden und Skulpturen in den Gotteshäusern. Der Bischof Julian hatte das Bedenken, das Anbringen solcher Bildwerke [I suppose Diekamp means: of sacred paintings and sculptures] in den Kirchen sei gegen die Überlieferung und gegen die heilige Schrift. . . . Höchstens auf den Türvorhängen will er Malereien zulassen, nicht auf Holz oder Stein, auch keine Skulpturen." According to Baynes, p. 94, Julian "will allow representations (γραφάς) in the churches but none on wood or stone and no sculpture. These γραφαί may be on the door-curtains (ἐπὶ θυραῖς: I suppose this is how the words must be translated), but no more is permissible." But clearly Julian distinguished paintings (γραφαί) from carvings (τὰ τῆς γλυφῆς). He does not prohibit the paintings, although his approval seems somewhat grudging (ἐῶμεν); he merely objects to those who set up "what is revered and worshipped in the form of paintings and carvings equally" (above note 4). The ἐπὶ θυραῖς must therefore refer to sculptural decoration of the doors, not to doorcurtains. The οὐδὲ τοῦτο I take to mean that Julian permits paintings, but he will not in addition approve of carved works.
[17] The ms. reads ὀφείλη καὶ ἡ ἱερὰ κεφαλή. Diekamp proposes ὦ θεῖα καὶ ἱερὰ κεφαλή which seems unnecessarily violent. I suggest: ὦ φίλη καὶ ἱερὰ κεφαλή.
[18] The text is corrupt. The ms. reads: τὴν ἄρρητον δὲ καὶ ἀπερίληπτον εἰς ἡμᾶς τοῦ Θεοῦ φιλανθρωπίαν καὶ τοὺς ἱεροὺς τῶν ἁγίων εἰκόνας ἐν γράμμασι μὲν ἡμεῖς ἱεροῖς ἀνευφημεῖσθαι διατυποῦμεν κτλ. Diekamp emends τοὺς ἱερούς into τὰς ἱεράς. Professor Kantorowicz calls my attention to the use of εἰκών in the sense of "example" or "pattern." In fact, Liddell and Scott, verbo εἰκών, refers to [Timaeus Locrus] De Anima Mundi et Naturae, ed. C. F. Hermann, 99D where the demiurge creates mortal beings ἵν' ᾖ τέλεος ποτὶ τὰν εἰκόνα παντελῶς ἀπειργασμένος (sc. ὁ κόσμος) and where εἰκών is used in the sense of "archetype" or "pattern." Baynes (p. 94) takes the γράμματα ἱερά to be "sacred representations." But Hypatius uses γραφαί in the sense of "paintings" and γράμμα in the sense of "writing."
[19] A difficult phrase: καὶ αὐτὰς πολλάκις καὶ ἐν πολλοῖς τὰς θείας παλαιάς τε καὶ νέας διατάξεις εὑρόντες τοῖς ἀσθενέσι τὰς ψυχὰς ὑπὲρ σωτηρίας αὐτῶν συγκατακλινομένας. (I have translated the last word in the light of κατακλίνεται p. 128:19 = Diekamp.) Yet the sense is clear from the illustrations which follow in the text.
[20] Exodus 25:18. Should we write τορευτὰς (for τορνευτὰς)?

the divine wisdom in saving love of men sometimes remit the strictness for those souls which still need guidance. And for this reason it is said that even magi were led to Christ by a star of heaven at the time of His earthly birth.[21] [Scripture] leads Israel away from sacrifices to the idols but allows them to make these [sacrifices] to God.[22] And it names a certain "Queen of the Heavens"[23] although there exists no other king except Him who truly is king of kings in heaven and on earth. But it also mentions stars and uses pagan Greek language [as well as concepts],[24] calling some of them Pleiad and Bear and Orion,[25] but it does not lower itself to any of the myths and stories told about them by the Greeks, since it knows well and sings the praise of Him who "numbers the multitude of the stars and gives names to all of them."[26] It teaches those who cannot otherwise learn them, the same stars with the help of the nomenclature which they know and use. For these reasons we, too, allow even material adornment in the sanctuaries, not because we believe that God considers gold and silver and silken vestments and gem-studded vessels venerable and sacred but because we permit each order of the faithful to be guided and led up to the divine being in a manner appropriate to it [the order] because we think that some people are guided even by these [gold, silver, etc.] towards the intelligible beauty and from the abundant light in the sanctuaries to the intelligible and immaterial light.[27]

And yet some who have pondered about the higher life have held that "in every place" spiritual worship should be offered to God and that holy souls are the temples of God.[28] For the Sayings are said to speak thus:[29] "I want the men in every place to offer prayer lifting to heaven hands that are holy,"[30] and "Bless the Lord in every place of his dominion,"[31] and it is said: "The heavens are my throne, and the earth is my footstool,"[32] and "What house can you build for me?

[21] Matthew 2:9.
[22] Exodus 34:13; Leviticus 1–7. The ms. reads: τὸν δὲ Ἰσραὴλ ἀπάγει μὲν θυσιῶν εἰδώλων, ἐνδίδωσι δὲ ταύτας τῷ θεῷ θύειν. I see no reason to emend, with Diekamp, ταύτας to ταῦτα. It refers to θυσιῶν.
[23] Jeremiah 51:17 (Sept.).
[24] συνεξελληνίζουσα τῇ φωνῇ. There is, of course, here the ambiguity of the word "Hellen" which means "Greek" as well as "pagan."
[25] Job 9:9; 38:31.
[26] Ps. 146:4 (Sept.).
[27] ὥς τινων καὶ ἀπὸ τούτων ἐπὶ τὴν νοητὴν εὐπρέπειαν χειραγωγουμένων καὶ ἀπὸ τοῦ κατὰ τὰ ἱερὰ πολλοῦ φωτὸς ἐπὶ τὸ νοητὸν καὶ ἄϋλον φῶς. I have discussed the meaning of the last sentence at some length with Professor Kantorowicz. It represents, as it were, the application of what precedes. Just as Scripture had made certain concessions to the uneducated, so the clergy ("we") has permitted the adornment of the Churches with all kinds of beautiful objects.
[28] καίτοιγέ τισι τῶν τὴν ὑψηλοτέραν ζωὴν φιλοσοφησάντων καὶ ἐν παντὶ τόπῳ τὴν ἐν πνεύματι λατρείαν θεῷ προσάγειν ἔδοξε καὶ ναοὺς εἶναι θεοῦ τὰς ὁσίας ψυχάς. This is a reference to the famous argument, repeated by many theologians since the days of Clement of Alexandria and Origen, that the only true image of Christ is the virtuous (just, pious, etc.) soul. I intend to deal with it in a larger context. For the moment I merely refer to the stimulating article by Florovsky, George, "Origen, Eusebius, and the Iconoclastic Controversy," Church History XIX (1950) 3–22, esp. p. 17 f.
[29] φησιν εἰρηκέναι τὰ λόγια. Should we emend into φασιν, i.e. those τινες "who have pondered about the higher life"?
[30] I Tim. 2:8.
[31] Psalms 102:22 (Sept.).
[32] Isaiah 66:1.

says the Lord," [33] and "Was it not my hand that made it all?" [34] and the Highest "does not live in temples built by human hands," [35] and "For whom shall I have regard if not for the one who is gentle and quiet and who trembles at my word?" [36] and "He who loves me will observe my teaching, and I shall love him, and I and my Father will come and live with him." [37] For Paul says to the Saints: "You are God's temple, and God's spirit makes its home in you." [38]

We do not, then, disturb the divine [commandments] with regard to the sanctuaries but we stretch out our hand in a more suitable way to those who are still rather imperfect, yet we do not leave them untaught as to the more perfect [knowledge] but we want even them to know that the divine being is not at all identical or the same or similar to any of the existing things."

The translation and the notes have, I trust, made clear both the trend of the thought and the intention of the author. Julian of Atramytium had been concerned about the use and worship of religious images, presumably in his diocese. His objections had been based on the Old Testament prohibitions of art (Ex. 20:5, etc.). Julian had, however, not questioned the use and worship of religious *paintings* at all. He had approved, though perhaps somewhat grudgingly, both their use and the practise of prostration (προσκύνησις) before painted images (cf. note 16). Julian had objected, however, to religious *sculpture*. Hypatius, in replying to these scruples of his suffragan, examines the reason for the Old Testament prohibitions, as well as the reasons for the legitimacy of Christian sculpture. The Old Testament prohibitions were meant for people who believed in the similarity or identity of cult-statues on the one hand and the Divine on the other. The Christians of the sixth century are no longer in danger of accepting such a view. Therefore Hypatius will permit the use of religious sculpture for the uneducated although he himself, as a learned theologian, maintains that the true praise of God and of the Saints must continue to be performed by the written word. For the benefit of the uneducated, Hypatius even thinks that acts of worship before sacred paintings and sculptures [39] will serve a useful pedagogical purpose. He then passes in review a number of instances where the Bible itself records concessions to the uneducated. Hypatius declares himself in full agreement with those

[33] Isaiah 66:1.
[34] Acts 7:49.
[35] Acts 17:24.
[36] Isaiah 66:2.
[37] John 14:23.
[38] I Cor. 3:16.
[39] There may be some doubt whether Hypatius authorizes the *worship* (not only the use) of religious *sculpture*. Yet when he anticipates the objection of "some who have pondered about the higher life," he makes them proponents of "spiritual *worship*." The target of their protest, therefore, are all other (non-spiritual) kinds of worship.

182

who recognize only acts of spiritual worship performed by holy souls. Yet he feels that his concession will not vitiate this requirement as long as the clergy constantly emphasizes to the simpler people Hypatius' oft-repeated principle as to the total difference of material objects and divine being.

If my interpretation of the fragment has merits, a number of interesting conclusions follow:

(1) Baynes is, of course, quite correct when he emphasizes the hesitations which both Julian and Hypatius show in their attitude towards religious images. It also is true that neither Julian nor Hypatius allow more than pedagogical functions for the images. In particular, not a word is said about any miraculous power residing in them.

(2) There is, at least on the part of Julian, a much greater hesitancy towards religious sculpture than towards Christian paintings. This is interesting, in view of the almost complete absence of religious sculpture in the Byzantine Church after the restoration of images.

(3) But it is at least as interesting that neither Julian nor Hypatius as much as raise the question of the legitimacy not only of using but even of *worshipping* religious *paintings*. In all probability, individual acts of worship had occurred much earlier without objection from the clergy. Yet this is, to the best of my knowledge, the earliest [40] clear evidence of official approval, on the part of two members of the higher clergy, one of them even prominent.[41] If from Julian's and Hypatius' attitude towards painted images inferences may be drawn as to the

[40] I know of only one earlier text: certain craftsmen in fifth century Rome seem to have attributed an apotropaic effect to images of Symeon the Older Stylite (+459/60), and the historian who reports this feature *may* share this feeling (Theodoret, hist. rel. 25, PG 82, 1473 A, cf. Holl, Karl, ."Der Anteil der Styliten am Aufkommen der Bilderverehrung," in Gesammelte Aufsätze zur Kirchengeschichte II, Tübingen, 1928, 390). Yet this case is quite different from that at Atramytium: (1) the Roman images of Symeon are set up in craftshops not in churches; and (2) no ritual act of worship (prostration) is reported. Basil's letter 360 (PG 32, 1100B) is probably spurious; cf. Elliger, Walter, Die Stellung der alten Christen zu den Bildern etc., in Studien über christliche Denkmäler XX (1930) p. 61. Bréhier, Louis, La Querelle des Images, Paris, 1904, p. 7f. cites no other approval of image worship prior to the seventh century.

[41] Holl, loc. cit., 388: "Angesichts der Schärfe, mit der das Christentum sich ursprünglich gegen die Idole und ihre Verehrung wendete, bleibt es immer überraschend, wie ungehindert und fast unbeachtet sich später der heidnische Brauch in der Kirche selbst festsetzen konnte. Nur gegen den ersten noch harmlosen Schritt in dieser Richtung, gegen die aufkommende Sitte, Bilder in den Kirchen auzubringen, hat sich im 4. Jahrhundert ein gewisser Protest erhoben. Der schlimmere, zweite Schritt, die Herübernahme der heidnischen Auffassung und Verehrung des Bildes, ist ohne solchen Widerspruch erfolgt. . . . Syrien und Kleinasien sind, sofern nicht alles trügt, in unserem Fall die Länder gewesen, wo der Gang der Dinge sich entschied."

feelings of the high clergy in the capital of the Empire, new light is shed on the appearance of images, one generation later, on the columns separating the sanctuary from the choir in Justinian's newly rebuilt Church of St. Sophia — of images of Christ among the angels, of Christ among the prophets, of Christ among the apostles, and of the Virgin Mary.[42]

(4) Hypatius, however, does not stop at religious paintings but sanctions likewise the use and worship (cf. note 39) of religious sculpture towards which the Byzantine Church always had felt, and continued to feel, greater scruples than towards the painted icons.

The reader of Hypatius' remarks will inevitably be reminded of a kindred document from the West which dates not quite a century after the new fragment and which has always played a large rôle in discussions of attitudes towards religious art: the letter of Pope Gregory the Great to Serenus, bishop of Marseille.[43] Serenus had broken the images of some Saints to prevent people from worshipping them. Pope Gregory writes that he would have praised his correspondent if he had merely prohibited their worship but now blames him for having broken them.[44] Like Hypatius, Gregory recognizes that the images have a pedagogical function, especially for pagans.[45] Yet how fundamental is the difference between the archbishop of Ephesus and his suffragan on the one hand, and the Roman Pope, two generations later, and the bishop of Marseille on the other! In the first place, Serenus had taken immediate action and broken the images while Julian was much more cautious and consulted his superior before he acted. Are we dealing here just with two different individual temperaments? Or is Serenus' behavior char-

---

[42] Paulus Silentiarius, Description of the Temple of Holy Wisdom, verses 668ff., ed. Friedländer, Paul, Leipzig and Berlin, 1912, p. 246f. and 287–289. The poem dates of the year 563. The columns, it seems, were not part of a regular iconostasis, but the prominent position of the icons, on a part of the church which clearly was the forerunner of the later iconostases, recommended them to the special attention of the congregation.

[43] Gregorius Magnus, Epistolae, XI, 10, ed. L. M. Hartmann, in Monumenta Germaniae Historica, Epistolarum Tomus II (Berlin, 1899) pp. 269ff. The letter dates from October 600. For comment, see Koch, Hugo, Die altchristliche Bilderfrage, in Forschungen zur Religion und Literatur des Alten und Neuen Testaments XXVII (1917), p. 77ff. (where other texts from the same author about religious images are cited). It is difficult to say whether Serenus had "broken" sculptures or paintings, but the former is perhaps more likely.

[44] Loc. cit.: *Et quidem quia eas adorari vetuisses, omnino laudavimus; fregisse vero reprehendimus.*

[45] Loc. cit.: *Aliud est enim picturam adorare, aliud per picturae historia, quid sit adorandum, addiscere. Nam quod legentibus scriptura, hoc idiotis praestat pictura cernentibus, quia in ipsa ignorantes vident quod sequi debeant, in ipsa legunt qui litteras nesciunt; unde praecipue gentibus pro lectione pictura est.*

acteristic for the energetic Western missionary to the heathens while
Julian's is typical for the bishop of a region where Hellenic Christianity
had been the established religion since times immemorial? Or, finally,
is the trend towards image worship much stronger in the diocese of
Atramytium so that Julian has to assure himself of support before
taking action? Possibly all these factors have to be taken into account
together to explain the different behavior of Julian and Serenus. But
Hypatius and Gregory take as different an attitude as Julian and
Serenus. Hypatius had permitted acts of worship before the images;
Gregory explicitly prohibits them. More important even, Hypatius had
approved of Christian images as means of spiritual, perhaps even
mystical, pedagogy which would guide men towards "the intelligible and
immaterial light." Gregory, on the other hand, sees in the images pedagogical devices through which a pagan could learn to worship the Christian God rather than his heathen gods and in which he could find patterns of conduct — in a word, devices for practical and moral instruction. A comparison of the two documents demonstrates clearly a funda-
mentally different attitude towards the images between East and West.
Yet both in the Ephesian and the Roman documents we see at work
the powerful force of popular piety which, in the East at any rate,
was to impose concession after concession upon the theologians,[46] until
in the eighth and ninth centuries the Iconoclastic Controversy probed
all the theological and philosophical depths of the issue.

[46] Holl, loc. cit., p. 389: "Erst in zweiter Linie ist die Theologie an diesem
Prozess [i.e. the development of image worship] beteiligt. Sie hat nicht geschoben,
aber — was vielleicht ebenso wichtig war — das Gefühl für das, was vorging, ab-
geschwächt und das sich behauptende Heidentum mit ihren Prinzipien gedeckt."

INSTITUTE FOR ADVANCED STUDY,
PRINCETON, NEW JERSEY, AND
HOBART COLLEGE, GENEVA, NEW YORK.

ADDITIONAL BIBLIOGRAPHY

Important comments on Hypatius'letter by Ernst
Kitzinger,"The Cult of Images in the Age before
Iconoclasm",Dumbarton Oaks Papers 8,1954,83-150,
esp.94f.,131,138 (reprinted in his The Art of Byz-
antium and the Medieval West.Selected Studies,
Indiana University Press,1976).Jean Gouillard,
"Hypatius d'Ephèse ou du Pseudo-Denys à Théodore
Studite",Revue des Etudes Byzantines 19,1961,63-
75,discovered a citation from Hypatius' letter in a
letter of Theodore the Studite (ninth century).This
quotation enabled first Gouillard and later S.Gero
("Hypatius of Ephesus on the Cult of Images",in
Christianity,Judaism and Other Greco-Roman Cults:
Studies for Morton Smith at Sixty,Leiden,1975,208-
216)to improve the text translated by me in a
number of important passages and to arrive at a
moresatisfactory interpretation.See also Ihor Šev-
čenko,"Hagiography of the Iconoclastic Period",
Anthony Bryer and Judith Herrin,editors,Iconoclasm.
Papers given at the Ninth Spring Symposium of
Byzantine Studies,University of Birmingham,March
1975,Birmingham,1977,113-131,esp.120 and n.49.

VII

AN ASCETIC SECT OF
ICONOCLASTS IN SEVENTH CENTURY ARMENIA*

PRIOR to the outbreak of the Iconoclastic Controversy in the Byzantine Empire, *individual* manifestations of hostility to religious images had been frequent and sometimes violent. To my knowledge, however, it was only in Armenia that in the last years of the sixth century and then in the seventh century Iconoclasm became one of the central tenets of a sectarian *movement* which separated itself from the Armenian Church. The documentary evidence concerning this movement has been translated and interpreted in a number of publications.[1]

One important document is a treatise attributed, rightly or wrongly, to a monk Vrt'anes K'ert'ogh who was prominent in the ecclesiastical affairs of Armenia in the early seventh century.[2] The treatise is interesting as one of the earliest apologies for Christian images, but sheds only a very dim light upon the Iconoclastic Movement, its leadership and its motivation. We learn that the author knew of people who objected to the use of paintings and (other?) images in the churches. Their Iconoclasm was based on the prohibitions of idol worship in the Old Testament, as well as on the view that paints are vile.[3] They worshiped the Cross.[4] They claimed that the Armenian King Pap (369-374), who was possessed by demons, had introduced images into the Church.[5] The first Iconoclasts were Thaddaeus and Isaiah who together with others

* Much of the research for this paper was done during the academic year 1951-1952 when the writer held a John Simon Guggenheim Memorial Fellowship and was a member of the Institute for Advanced Study. In my forthcoming book on *The Patriarch Nicephorus of Constantinople* I attempt to show that the Armenian Iconoclasts influenced the thought of Byzantine Iconoclasm in the ninth century. Unfortunately, I do not read Armenian, and I am keenly aware of the danger involved in using translations. I have, however, received help from two scholars, Professors Arthur Jeffery and Bernhard Geiger, both of Columbia University. They have had the great kindness of checking many Armenian passages for my benefit, as well as correcting my translation of John Mayragometsi's letter (below note 12). Without their help I could never have ventured into the Armenian field. I also wish to thank Professor Ernst Kitzinger, of Dumbarton Oaks, and Professor Michael Cherniavsky, of Wesleyan University, who made most useful suggestions.

[1] The Armenian documents have been referred to by students of Armenian history such as Ter Mkrttschian and Conybeare. To my knowledge, the first to make the material available to western scholars, though in somewhat fragmentary and perhaps not entirely reliable form, was P. Polykarp Samuel, "Die Abhandlung 'Gegen die Bilderstürmer' von Vrt'anes K'ert'ogh," *Wiener Zeitschrift für die Kunde des Morgenlandes*, XXVI (1912), 275-293. More recently it has been translated afresh by S. Der Nersessian, "Une Apologie des images du septième siècle," *Byzantion*, XVII (1944-1945), 58-87. See also her article, "Image Worship in Armenia and Its Opponents," *Armenian Quarterly*, I (1946), 67-81; and N. H. Baynes, "The Icons Before Iconoclasm," *Harvard Theological Review*, XLIV (1951), 93-106.

[2] German translation by Samuel, *loc. cit.* French translation by Miss Der Nersessian, *Byzantion* XVII (1944-1945), 58-59 (all references to Miss Der Nersessian's articles are meant to refer to the first of her publications mentioned in note 1 unless indicated otherwise).

[3] "... les partisans des études obscures ... introduisent des hérésies dans l'Eglise. Il ne faut pas, disent-ils, avoir des peintures et des images dans les églises; et ils apportent en témoignage des paroles de l'Ancien Testament qui ont été dites au sujet de l'idôlatrie denoncée par les prophètes" (Der Nersessian, p. 59). "Quant à ceux qui disent que les pigments sont vils ..." (p. 68, see pp. 64f.).

[4] "... vous honorez la croix ..." (Der Nersessian, p. 61).

[5] "Il était écrit que Pap introduisit les images dans les églises. Or tout le monde sait que vous mentez" (Der Nersessian, p. 67). On King Pap, see Der Nersessian, p. 67, n. 34; Ernst Stein, *Geschichte des Spätrömischen Reiches*, I, Vienna 1928, 288f. and W. Ensslin, Pauly-Wissowa, *RE*, XXXVI, 3, 1949, 923f.

seduced many people.[6] Furthermore, and this is a most interesting point which will concern us later, the Iconoclasts "give themselves the name saint."[7] Finally, in a passage contained in the Venice manuscript but omitted in the Jerusalem codex of the treatise, the Iconoclasts are represented as claiming that the images "are made by human hands and are not worthy of us."[8]

Before utilizing the information contained in the treatise, it will be advisable to survey a second and more important source on the Movement. The *History of the Albanians* by Moses of Kaghankatuik[9] (tenth century), Part Two, Chapter XLVI consists of two parts: (1) Moses' account of the circumstances which prompted Bishop David of Med-Koghmn (province of Artsakh, then part of Caucasian Albania[10]) to ask the Armenian theologian John Mayragometsi[11] for a written statement on the origins of Iconoclasm, and (2) John Mayragometsi's reply to David's enquiry. The chapter runs as follows:[12]

[6] "Aucun d'eux [Armenian kings and clergy] ne fit rien concernant les images et les peintures des églises, mais seulement l'impie et l'égaré Thaddée et Isaie et leur compagnons qui entraînèrent à leur suite un grand nombre de personnes, tels vous-mêmes" (Der Nersessian, pp. 67f.). Miss Der Nersessian (p. 73) interprets the *tels vous-mêmes* as referring to the rank and file of the movement and not to its leaders. Yet an earlier passage of the treatise: "N'avez-vous pas vu ces écrits, ô ami, qui vous opposez aux commandements de Dieu? Je dis ami, non pas à cause de l'orthodoxie de votre foi, mais à cause de ce que nous entendîmes de notre Seigneur; ami pour lequel il vint" (p. 63) make it probable that the author of the treatise addressed in his apology of image worship no particular person or group of persons but the Iconoclastic Movement personified.

[7] "Mais vous, enorgueillis par le démon, vous appelez saintes vos propres personnes" (Der Nersessian, p. 69, see also her comments pp. 85f., n. 131). Samuel, *loc. cit.*, p. 293 translates: "Da ihr . . . euch für gerecht ausgebt . . ." which would be much less interesting. Professors Arthur Jeffery and Bernhard Geiger, have had the great kindness to check this passage against the Armenian originals. Professor Jeffery supplied the translation given in the text and remarks in a letter: "I imagine the writer's thought is that they have no right to any such name as is implied by *sovrb* = saint, but moved by the Devil they apply this exalted name to themselves."

[8] "O hommes méchants, d'une méchanceté sans bornes, qui tantôt accusez les pigments, tantôt les images et les peintures, disant qu'elles sont faites de main d'homme et ne sont pas dignes de nous" (Der Nersessian, p. 68). Professor Jeffery kindly called my attention to the fact that the words "et ne sont pas dignes de nous" are omitted in the Jerusalem manuscript. They look genuine, however, and the omission is probably due to the repetition of "hand of man" in the text.

[9] On the author, see Manuk Abegian, *Istoriia Drevnearmanskoi Literatury*, I, Erevan 1948, 390f. and 521 (bibliography): his *History of the Albanians* is "neither a history, nor a chronicle, but in some way a compilation in which the material is arranged in chronological order."

[10] On the location of Mec-Koghmn (or Mec-Koghmankh), see the work of H. Hübschmann, "Die altarmenischen Ortsnamen," *Indogermanische Forschungen*, XVI (1904), 351, with the invaluable map. It lay on the River Terter, a Southern tributary of the River Cyrus or Kur, in the province of Rostak, in the plain of Chlakh, see K. Patkan'ian, *Istoria Moiseia Kagankatvatsi pisatelia X vieka*, St. Petersburg 1861, pp. 165f. (Part Two, ch. XXIX), cf. also p. 169. (Of this rare book I used the copy owned by the Yale University Library on a most generous Interlibrary Loan.)

[11] On John Mayragometsi, see Der Nersessian, *Byzantion*, XVII (1944-1945), 72f. and Gérard Garitte, *La Narratio de Rebus Armeniae. Edition Critique et Commentaire*, Corpus Scriptorum Christianorum Orientalium, Subsidia 4, Louvain 1952, 273-348 and *passim*. I became acquainted with this excellent work, which is basic for the ecclesiastical history of Armenia, only after I had finished with the research for this paper. John Mayragometsi reached a Biblical age, or, to put it in the terms used by the *Narratio*, which is hostile to him, he died ἐν γήρει σαπρῷ (§ 142). He was a grown man in 628, for the catholicus Komitas (610/11-628) wanted to make him his successor (§118). He died, according to a Georgian source of the ninth century (Garitte, *La Narratio*, 16f.), in 684 (*ibid.*, 346).

[12] The reader will find partial translations of this document in the works of Samuel (above note 1) and Der Nersessian in *Byzantion*, XVII (1944-1945), 71-72. For my purposes they were insufficient as they omit passages of importance. Another partial translation can now be found in Garitte, *Narratio*, pp. 247f. My own translation was made from the Russian rendering of Patkan'ian (above note 10), but checked by Professors Jeffery and Geiger against the Armenian original (in the Tiflis edition, 1913).

AN ASCETIC SECT OF ICONOCLASTS IN VII CENTURY ARMENIA

Translation from Moses of Kaghankatuik, History of the Albanians,
Tiflis 1913, II, 46, pp. 302-305

David bishop of Mec-Koghmn [province of Artsakh, then part of Caucasian Albania] enquires about the opinion of John Mayragometsi concerning images and icons.

At that time when in Albania Ukhtanes was still catholicus, and after him Iliazar,[13] and when many rebellions and heresies arose in various places between learned men and ignorant men, and wars and strife between Greeks and Armenians, and the country of the Albanians remained untroubled by those [things], at that time the news reached them [the Albanians]: many do not accept the images, some[14] do not take baptism, do not bless the salt, do not put on the crown at weddings, on the grounds that the priesthood had ceased to exist in the land.[15] For this reason David, bishop of Mec-Koghmn, enquired in writing from the Armenian vardapet [= theologian] John [Mayragometsi] concerning the causes of these events. And he, well versed in this matter, gave him the following answer:[16]

[LETTER FROM JOHN MAYRAGOMETSI TO BISHOP DAVID OF MEC-KOGHMN]

"This sect was seen after the time of the apostles, and Iconoclasm appeared at first in Greece. For this reason there was called together a great council at Caesarea, and the order was given to paint icons in the house of the Lord. As a consequence the artists bragged that they were higher than all the ecclesiastical artists. They said: Our art is light [enlightening], both young and old generally read [the scriptures], but few read the Holy Books understandingly. Thereupon there arose disorders, and once again a council was called together. They considered the matter, did justice to the scribes, and placed them higher than the painters.

"And from this time until Moses catholicus of the Armenians [Moses II, 574-604],[17] this schismatic sect did not appear. When the Armenian patriarchate was split, there were violent

---

13 Miss Der Nersessian (p. 71) gives as the dates of the catholicus Ukhtanes 670-689 and as those of Iliazar 682-688. These dates seem too low. Among the few certain dates in Albanian history are those of the ruler Dzhevanshir, the hero of Moses of Kaghankatuik or rather of one of his sources. In Part Two, ch. XXIX (Patkan'ian, p. 144), Moses identifies the twentieth year of the Sassanid Yazdegard III (who came to the throne in 632 but never ruled) with the thirty-first year of the Hegira ("of the universal victories of the Agarenes"), i.e. the year 652, and with the fifteenth year of Dzhevanshir's rule. Accordingly Dzhevanshir came to the throne in 637 or 638. In Part II, ch. XXVIII (Patkan'ian, p. 162) it is said that he ruled 33 years, i.e. until 670 or 671. Patkan'ian (pp. 342 and 344) gives his dates as 636-670. Moses further makes it clear (Part Two, ch. XXXII, Patkan'ian, p. 173) that the Albanian catholicus Iliazar succeeded Ukhtanes while Dzhevanshir was still alive, i.e. in 671 or earlier. I suppose that Miss Der Nersessian's dates are based on the list of Albanian catholici given in Part III, ch. XXIII (Patkan'ian, pp. 279-283). It mentions Ter Abbas (ca. 551-595) and the names of the later catholici together with the number of years during which they held office. If one follows these indications, one arrives roughly at 671-683 for Ukhtanes and 683-689 for Iliazar. M. Brosset, Additions et Eclaircissements à l'histoire de la Géorgie etc. (St. Petersburg 1851) 483f. arrives, on the basis of the list of Albanian catholici, at 669-681 for Ukhtanes and 681-687 (or somewhat later) for Iliazar. However, this entire list is full of contradictions and may have been corrupted by copyists (Patkan'ian, p. 352). At any rate, the chronological data in the body of Moses' narrative, and especially the equations with the Sassanid and Mohammedan eras, seem more trustworthy than the chronological list of catholici.

14 According to Professors Jeffery and Geiger, "the many and some obviously refer to the same people" (letter of May 12, 1952).

15 "On earth" would be "a remotely possible translation," but Professor Geiger points out that the same word occurs later in the chapter in the sense of "land."

16 Terminus post quem for David's enquiry: accession of the Albanian catholicus Iliazar (see above note 13) who is mentioned in John Mayragometsi's reply. Terminus ante: the mission of Bishop Israel of Mec-Koghmn, David's successor, to the "Huns" in the sixty-second year of the Hegira (Part II, ch. XXXIX, Patkan'ian, p. 190), i.e. 684 (which is also the date of John Mayragometsi's death, above note 11). Cf. Der Nersessian, p. 72. On the date of the hearing before John Mayragometsi, see Der Nersessian, p. 73.

17 The dates for the Armenian catholici given in the text are taken from the work of Garitte (above note 11). See also the list by Fr. Tournebize, "Arménie," Dictionnaire d'Histoire et de Géographie Ecclésiastiques, IV, 371-377. The reader should be warned, however, that the chronology of the Armenian catholici for our period is confusing.

struggles between Moses and Theodore Bishop of Karin [= Theodosiupolis = Erzerum, in Byzantine Armenia] who was called the chief of the philosophers. And the Orthodox [the followers of Moses] condemned the Greek sects. Moses assembled the vardapets of his region and ordered them not to hold communion in any way with the Greeks who obeyed the Council of Chalcedon, for their acts are false,[18] and not to accept from them books, icons or relics. Then Theodore ordered the Armenian bishops of his region to assemble in the city of Karin and said: We must choose a catholicus, and they brought in a certain stylite John, ordained him and followed the Chalcedonian faith. None of them became zealous for the orthodox [= anti-Chalcedonian] faith, except the blessed Yenovs[19] who left them and came to the catholicus Moses who received him joyfully. Moses resided as catholicus at Dvin, and the Greeks [the Armenians in favor of Chalcedon], adapted [themselves to having] the residence of the Catholicus John in Avan [a village west of Dvin] [so that John and Moses might be] near each other. Among them [the pro-Chalcedonian and anti-Chalcedonian clergies] there arose violent disagreements because there [in Persian Armenia] the ordinations of John [the catholicus of Byzantine Armenia] were not recognized. Then a priest, Yesu by name, Thadeos, and Grigor, being of Moses' party, left Dvin and proceeded to the region of Sotkh [in Siunik] and settled in the desert, for they were monks. They began to teach: 'Scratch off the icons painted in the churches. Do not hold communion with the secular priests.' There arose unrest in the region, and the report reached the catholicus Moses. He wrote them right away that they should immediately come to him. They did not obey his order, departed from there and settled with you in the region of Artsakh [south of the River Cyrus or Kur, then part of Caucasian Albania]. The catholicus consulted his learned men: How do you explain this action of [those] people? They [the learned men] adduced as its cause the errors of the Greeks. Then they [the learned men] wrote a letter that nobody should dare to treat with contempt an image in a church.

"At the death of the catholicus Moses and during the reign of Chosroes [II, 592-628] in Armenia, the country became united. Abraham [I, 607-610] was set up as catholicus, a just and select man who at first by curses annulled the Council of Chalcedon but later was already ordained [?]. The Iconoclasts, however, who had gone to Albania [i.e. to Artsakh] disturbed your country. Then the prince of Gardman [a canton of Uti] arrested the three men whose names were recorded above [Yesu, Thadeos, Grigor] and gave orders to bring them in chains to Armenia. When they appeared before us [John Mayragometsi] we asked them: For what reason do you not accept the image of the God Incarnate? They answered: 'This is outside the commandments, and this is the doing of the idol worshipers who worship all things created. We do not worship the icons because we have for this no commandment in the sacred books.' Then we demonstrated to them the decorations of Moses' tent, the various carvings in the temple of Solomon: 'and such was also represented by images in our churches.' Having said this and something like it, we corrected their errors."

Moses' account and John Mayragometsi's letter seem fairly clear and consistent. Bishop David of Mec-Koghmn had been worried about the spread of a sectarian movement in his diocese which at his time belonged to the principality of Caucasian Albania. One of the principal characteristics of this movement was its hostility towards religious images. Knowing that the Armenian theologian John Mayragometsi, many years earlier, had been concerned with this same movement, Bishop David sent a letter to John Mayragometsi enquiring about the origins of the sect. Moses preserves the reply of John Mayragometsi. In it John Mayragometsi links the Armeno-Albanian

---

[18] The words "for their acts are false" are taken from Patkan'ian's Russian translation. In the Tiflis edition of the Armenian original they are represented by three dots.

[19] I was unable to identify this person.

movement with certain church councils held at Caesarea. It reappeared (John Mayragometsi implies: much later) at the time of the Armenian catholicus Moses when a counter-catholicus, the stylite John, was elected by the bishops of Byzantine Armenia among whom the most prominent was Theodore of Theodosiupolis. The counter-catholicus John moved his residence from Theodosiupolis eastward to the village of Avan so that now the catholicus Moses who resided at Dvin was separated from his rival only by a few miles of territory. The rivalry was especially explosive because John's ordinations were not recognized in Persian Armenia. At that point three monks, Yesu, Thadeos, and Grigor, left Dvin and their catholicus Moses and settled to the South in the desert of Siunikh. They urged their followers to obliterate the icons and to abstain from communion with the secular clergy. Summoned by the catholicus Moses to Dvin they moved northward to the province of Artsakh.[20] Later Armenia was again united and the Armenian church received a single catholicus Abraham. The sectarian movement on the other hand continued to gain ground in Albania. Its three leaders were finally arrested by a prince of Gardman and brought to Armenia. There they were interrogated by John Mayragometsi who in his letter flatters himself of having corrected their errors.

The first paragraph of John Mayragometsi's letter is almost certainly legendary,[21] but the rest can be checked with the help of other sources. The election of the counter-catholicus John in Byzantine Armenia is mentioned in a number of texts. The *Narratio de Rebus Armeniae*, the Armenian original of which dates from about A.D. 700, records this event among the results of the cession by Chosroes II of all Armenia west of Dvin to the Emperor Maurice in 591.[22] This strengthening of Byzantine political influence in Armenia was followed immediately, so the *Narratio* tells us, by theological disputes between the Byzantine (Chalcedonian) and Armenian (anti-Chalcedonian) churches. In the course of these disagreements Maurice summoned the Armenian catholicus Moses and his theologians to Constantinople.[23] Moses as well as

---

[20] Artsakh was a border province between Armenia and Albania which after 387, and throughout Persian and Arab times, remained a part of Albania, see J. Marquardt, *Eranšahr etc.*, Abhandlungen der Kgl. Gesellschaft der Wissenschaften zu Göttingen, Phil.-Hist. Kl., N.F. III, 2 (1901), 119; Hübschmann, *Die altarmenischen Ortsnamen*, 266; Josef Markwart, *Die Entstehung der armenischen Bistümer*, Orientalia Christiana, XXVII, 2 (1932), 219. In view of this, it is likely that the Iconoclasts who, according to John Mayragometsi, "had gone to Albania," never crossed the river Cyrus or Kur but stayed in Artsakh. John Mayragometsi's phrase "who had gone to Albania" simply is a repetition of his earlier statement that the Iconoclasts "settled with you in the region of Artsakh." This would also explain Bishop David's concern since his diocese was located in Artsakh (above note 10).

[21] Miss Der Nersessian, p. 71 and n. 51, correctly characterized it thus. In view of the ancient ecclesiastical connections of Armenia with Caesarea and, on the other hand, the christological differences between Byzantines and Armenians, a church council held at Caesarea was the obvious means of discrediting the movement in the eyes of Armenians. John Mayragometsi all but admits the weakness of his story in the sentence: "And from this time until Moses catholicus of the Armenians this schismatic sect did not appear."

[22] On the Byzantino-Persian border in Armenia after 591, see H. Gelzer, *Georgii Cyprii Descriptio Orbis Romani*, Leipzig 1890, l-lxi; H. Hübschmann, *Die altarmenischen Ortsnamen* (who also enters the new borderline on his invaluable map); Dölger, *Regesten*, no. 104; Ernst Honigmann, *Die Ostgrenze des byzantinischen Reiches*, Bruxelles 1935, 29-37 (see also his fourth map); *Cambridge Medieval History*, II, 280 and Map 18; Garitte, *Narratio*, 236.

[23] Maurice's attempt to win Armenia over to the side of Chalcedonian orthodoxy was undoubtedly connected with his concern for Armenia as a reservoir of military manpower (on this see Ernst Stein, *Studien zur Geschichte des byzantinischen Reiches etc.*, Stuttgart 1919, 117, 127-129, and *passim*).

the bishops of Persian Armenia and of the province of Aspurakan refused to cross the River Azat (now the Garni-čai) along which the Byzantino-Persian frontier had run since 591. The bishops of Taron and of Byzantine Armenia, on the other hand, complied and signed a sworn document, presumably accepting the Council of Chalcedon. When these bishops returned from Constantinople to Armenia, they were not accepted by the catholicus Moses and the bishops of Persian Armenia. They elected a counter-catholicus John from Kogovit (in the province of Airarat, in the region of Bagaran). For fourteen years, until the death of Maurice, the catholicus Moses and the counter-catholicus John quarreled with each other over the two natures in Christ and over the Council of Chalcedon. After Maurice's death Chosroes II recaptured Armenia when Abraham became catholicus.[24] The election of the counter-catholicus John is also mentioned by Sebeos,[25] by an anonymous historian of Albania who wrote before the tenth century[26] and by the historian Johannes Catholicus.[27]

None of these sources mentions the Bishop Theodore of Theodosiupolis and the role he played in Armenian ecclesiastical history after 591.[28] But in all other respects they support or supplement the story of the Armenian schism as told by John Mayragometsi. The *Narratio* indicates the reason for the schism between John and Moses: the change in the political situation due to the events of the year 591 and the ensuing christological quarrels. Sebeos and Johannes Catholicus further confirm that the counter-catholicus John moved his residence from Theodosiupolis to Avan, a fact which is further corroborated by the ruins of a magnificent Church of the Virgin built by John at Avan.[29] Unfortunately, none of these sources allows us to date either the

---

[24] The above is a summary of the account given in the *Narratio de Rebus Armeniae*, ed. Garitte, §§93-110. This critical edition makes all earlier publications of this text completely obsolete and misleading. On the date of the document, see Garitte, 398. The election of the counter-catholicus John is mentioned as follows: [the bishops of Byzantine Armenia returning from Constantinople] ἐποίησαν δὲ ἑαυτοῖς καθολικὸν τὸν Ἰωάννην ἀπὸ τοῦ Κοκοτβὰν Πακρὰν τῆς χώρας (§107). The reader will now find a fuller collection of sources for the counter-catholicus John in Garitte, *Narratio*, 246-251, 263-265.

[25] Sebeos, *Histoire d'Héraclius*, transl. by F. Macler, Paris 1904, 36: "Le siège patriarcal fut partagé entre deux catholicos, l'un nommé Moise, l'autre Jean; le premier pour l'Arménie persane, le second pour l'Arménie grecque. Jean admettait les Grecs à sa communion, mais Moise ne voulut avoir aucun rapport avec eux."

[26] The Armenian catholicus Anania (Mokatsi?, 943-946) visited Albania and studied there a (now lost) manuscript containing a *History of the Albanians* different from that of Moses Kaghankatuik. From this he quotes verbatim and reports that John was elected in the nineteenth year of the Armenian catholicus Abraham. (I know Anania's quotations, published in the Armenian periodical *Ararat*, 1896-1897, only from the paraphrase of Agop Manandian, *Beiträge zur albanischen Geschichte*, Diss. Jena, Leipzig 1897, pp. 20, 30.)

[27] Jean VI Catholicus, transl. by Saint-Martin, 61f.: "Après cela [council of Dvin, see note 30] par l'ordre de l'empereur Maurice, un nommé Jean, du bourg de Pagaran, dans la province de Houeg, fut créé patriarche de la partie de l'Arménie que était soumise aux Grecs. On lui donna pour résidence la petite ville d'Avan, où il fit bâtir une superbe église, qu'il orna partout magnifiquement pour être le lieu de sa résidence. . . . Jean était un homme vrai et juste, vertueux dans ses moeurs. Il n'était pas uni avec ceux qui admettaient la doctrine du concile de Chalcédoine; mais il éleva un trône rival du trône patriarcal, rompit l'unité du patriarcat, et le divisa en deux parties qui, par la suite, furent opposées." This notice is in sharp conflict with John Mayragometsi's and Sebeos' (above note 25) statements that the bishops who had elected the counter-catholicus and the counter-catholicus John himself were pro-Chalcedonian. It must be erroneous in this respect.

[28] In fact, this bishop is otherwise unknown in the ecclesiastical annals and does not appear in Lequien.

[29] Sebeos, transl. Macler, p. 62. At the time of the Persian campaign, the anti-catholicus John withdrew from Avan to Karin and was captured there by the Persians. He died in 610-611 in Persian captivity at

election of the counter-catholicus John or his move to Avan with accuracy. All that can be said with confidence is that both events must have taken place at some time after 591, when Chosroes II ceded much of Persian Armenia to Byzantium, and before 607/8 when he recaptured it.[30] When John Mayragometsi states that "at the death of the catholicus Moses and during the reign of Chosroes the country became united," this refers to the Persian campaign shortly prior to 607/8 when Chosroes II drove the Byzantines once more out of Armenia.

Except for the legendary data on the origins of Iconoclasm, John Mayragometsi's information has proved reliable wherever we could check it. We shall accordingly be disposed to trust his narrative of the secession of the monks Yesu, Thadeos and Grigor[31] for which we have only the somewhat vague support of Vrt'anes K'ert'ogh. Here too John Mayragometsi is inherently plausible. The three monks must have watched for a while the quarrels between the anti-Chalcedonian clergy of the catholicus Moses at Dvin and the pro-Chalcedonian clergy of the counter-catholicus John at Avan. They felt that at the bottom of these theological and hierarchical disputes lay secular and political interests: the desire of the clergy in Byzantine Armenia to come to terms with the Emperor Maurice and the corresponding wish of Moses and his clergy to remain loyal to their Persian overlords. Much like the founders of the

---

Hamadan (the ancient Ecbatana) and his body was buried in the Church of Avan which he had built (Sebeos, pp. 36, 63; Jean VI Catholicus, p. 63). Church of the Virgin at Avan: Joseph Strzygowski, *Die Baukunst der Armenier und Europa*, I, Vienna 1918, 89 (with illustrations) and N. M. Tokarskii, *Arkhitektura Drevnei Armenii*, Erevan 1946, 79 (with photograph of West wall restored in 1941, plate 25). At the time of his stay in Avan, Strzygowski was told of a Greek inscription of three lines, and Tokarskii states that an inscription with the name of the counter-catholicus John was found when the church was restored in 1941. I do not know whether this inscription has been published since.

[30] Here are the disappointing chronological data of our sources, apart from John Mayragometsi: *Narratio de rebus Armeniae*: after the treaty of 591, after the catholicus Moses II refused to cross the Azat, after a journey of Armenian bishops to Constantinople and after their return to Armenia fourteen years prior to the death of Maurice (above n. 24); Frédéric Macler, *Histoire d'Heraclius par l'évêque Sebeos*, Paris 1894, 36: after an imperial edict of ca. 590 (Dölger, *Regesten*, no. 93) to the effect that the doctrine of Chalcedon should be preached in all the churches of Armenia; J. Saint-Martin, *Histoire d'Arménie par le patriarche Jean VI*, Paris 1841, p. 61: after a council of Dvin under Abraham anathematizing Kiuron of Georgia; Moses of Kaghankatuik, *History of the Albanians*, Part II, ch. XLVIII (Patkan'ian, p. 219): at the time of the Armenian catholicus Moses. The Armenian catholicus Anania quoting from the lost *History of Albania* (above note 26): John was elected in the nineteenth year of the Armenian catholicus Abraham. John cannot have been elected, as the *Narratio* claims, fourteen years before the death of Maurice (†602) because the election must have taken place after 591 (cf. Garitte, p. 254). On the other hand, the chronological data of John VI Catholicus and of Anania's source are vitiated by the fact that Abraham (607-615) seems to have become catholicus long after Maurice's death (602). If one could assume that these two sources meant the catholicus Moses (574-604) and not Abraham, then the nineteenth year of Moses (593) would be very satisfactory. All that can be said with certainty is that considerable time must have elapsed between the treaty of 591 and John's move to Avan, to allow for the journey of the bishops from Byzantine Armenia to Constantinople (above p. 156) and back.

[31] It is easy to see why the secessionists went first to the province of Siunik. Moses of Kaghankatuik tells in a later chapter (Part II, ch. XLVIII, Patkan'ian, p. 219) how "when the patriarchal throne [of Armenia] was divided [between the catholicus Moses and the counter-catholicus John] the rulers of Siunik made themselves independent and obeyed neither of the two" and how Siunik placed itself under the ecclesiastical jurisdiction of the Albanians until the time of the Armenian catholicus Abraham when the Armenian schism was healed. It was natural for the secessionists to seek refuge in a province where the secular and ecclesiastical authorities shared their condemnation of both the Armenian catholicus and the counter-catholicus—although the secessionists were more radical in their condemnation than the people of Siunik and combined it with an iconoclastic doctrine.

monastic movement in fourth century Egypt and elsewhere, these men became disgusted with the worldliness of the secular clergy and withdrew to the wilderness. They even preached against communion with the secular clergy. The story of their secession as told by John Mayragometsi is entirely understandable against the background of the political situation of Armenia and there is no evidence for any theological or doctrinal differences on the part of the secessionists.[32]

We are, therefore, indebted to John Mayragometsi for a satisfactory account of the secession. He does not explain, however, the Iconoclasm of the secessionists. How did Yesu, Thadeos, and Grigor come to reject religious images? Here we must return to a hint given in the treatise attributed to Vrt'anes K'ert'ogh. There it was said that the Iconoclasts "give themselves the name saint" and in another passage which is probably genuine (above p. 152 and note 8)—that the icons "are not worthy of us." It would seem likely that the Iconoclasm of the secessionists and their belief in their own saintliness were not unconnected. Indeed, several fathers of the Early Church, and especially Clement and Origen of Alexandria, had opposed to the pagan ἀγάλματα the true image of Christ as represented by the virtuous (just, pious, etc.) soul. A text from the fourth decade of the sixth century proves that this was still a well-known argument against Christian religious images in the sixth century.[33] This piece of evidence dates from the period immediately preceding the astounding intensification of the belief in the miraculous powers of religious images, and consequently of their worship, during the later part of Justinian's reign. This ancient argument against religious images is met again in seventh century Armenia. Three pious monks, Yesu, Thadeos, and Grigor are disgusted with the clergy which, in their opinion, is more concerned with winning the good graces of secular rulers and with hierarchical quarrels than with the salvation of souls. Consequently they not only settle in the desert and refuse to hold communion with the secular clergy, but preach the need for spiritual reform. The point to which they attached the greatest importance seems to have been the concept of sanctity. While the secular clergy emphasized the role of the religious images as sacred objects (*res sacrae*), the secessionists considered them "not worthy of us (i.e. Christians)." True sanctity, so they taught, following such fathers as

---

[32] Miss Der Nersessian connects the secessionists with various christological positions. In *Byzantion* XVII (1944-1945), 85-87, n. 130, she concludes: "Les iconoclastes arméniens se rattachaient probablement aux Julianistes et ils semblent avoir aussi conservé certaines croyances des Manichéens." In *Armenian Quarterly*, I (1946), 71, n. 16a, she connects them with the Armenian Χατζιντζάριοι or "servants of the Cross" who "believed that there were two persons in Christ, one of whom had suffered on the Cross while the other had watched his suffering." It is not impossible that as time went on the secessionist movement came to deviate on points of christology from the Armenian Church (which was Monophysite, probably Julianist, see Erward Ter-Minassiantz, *Die armenische Kirche in ihren Beziehungen zu den syrischen Kirchen*, Texte und Untersuchungen, N.F. XI, 4 (1904), p. vi and *passim*). But it is inconceivable that such could have been the case at the time of the secession or even one generation later. Otherwise Vrt'anes K'ert'ogh and John Mayragometsi would have mentioned and criticized its christological aberrations.

[33] I have collected some of the pertinent material in my forthcoming book (see note *). For the moment see *Harvard Theological Review*, XLV (1952), 180, n. 28 and *Dumbarton Oaks Papers*, VII (1953) 35-66, esp. 50f. The sixth century text mentioned above is a decision of the Archbishop of Ephesus Hypatius (531-538) who summarizes an objection against religious images in the following words: "And yet some who have pondered about the higher life have held that in every place spiritual worship should be offered to God and that holy souls are the temples of God."

Clement and Origen, lay not in sacred objects at all, but in Christian ascetics who cultivated the Christian virtues, who themselves became the true images of Christ and who could "give themselves the name saint."[34] Thus the treatise of Vrt'anes K'ert'ogh allows us to answer a question which the letter of John Mayragometsi had left open.

The early secessionists then did not differ from the Armenian Church on questions of christology or dogma. Their schismatic refusal to hold communion with the secular clergy, however, contained the germ of heresy. It is noteworthy that while John Mayragometsi himself mentions that Yesu and his companions, in the early days of their secession, preached against the icons and against communion with the secular clergy, Moses Kaghankatuik, in his introductory remarks, mentions that the Iconoclasts of the time of Bishop David of Mec-Koghmn, a generation or more later, "do not take baptism, do not bless the salt, do not put on the crown at weddings, on the grounds that the priesthood has ceased to exist in the land." These features cannot have existed at the beginning of Yesu's preaching, in fact not even at the time of the arrest of Yesu and his followers, as neither Vrt'anes K'ert'ogh in his treatise, nor John Mayragometsi in his letter, speak of anything except Iconoclasm. Vrt'anes and John Mayragometsi could hardly have failed to record as heretical a position as the rejection of baptism. On the other hand, these features, and especially the rejection of the sacrament of baptism, were the natural corollary of the Iconoclasts' refusal to hold communion with the secular clergy and their conviction of the holiness of their own persons. As the first generation of schismatics, some of whom may have been ordained priests like Yesu himself, died, it must have become increasingly difficult and finally even impossible to get a priest ordained, a couple married or a child baptized. Furthermore, the Iconoclasts considered their own persons holy, from which they may later have drawn the consequence that the sacraments were unnecessary. They thus seem to have slipped from schism into heresy. These remarks may be of interest to the historians of Paulicianism: the doctrine of the Iconoclasts at the time of Bishop David resembles that of the Paulicians more closely than that of Yesu and his followers a generation earlier. In fact we know that the Iconoclasts were ousted from Albania by the Albanian catholicus and allied themselves with the Paulician Movement.[35] In Armenia, however, the Iconoclasts

---

[34] This emphasis on personal sanctity was a common feature of Mesopotamian and Armenian monasticism and was not characteristic of sectarian movements only. On Mesopotamian monasticism, see A. Vööbius, *Les Messaliens et les réformes de Barçauma*, Contributions of Baltic University, LXV, Pinneberg, Germany 1947. On Armenian monasticism, see the Armenian catholicus John of Otzun, *Contra Paulicianos* (quoted in Fred. C. Conybeare, *The Key of Truth*, Cambridge 1898, p. 154): "Sui autem nominis sordes inferre ausi sunt [the Paulicians] iis, qui caelestia bona per spem arripiunt, *electis ex hominibus atque divina habitatione dignis inventis*, qui super terram caelestem vitam agere aggrediuntur. Contra hos audacter evomere praesumunt impietatis suae bilem, atque insanientes, ex mali spiritus blasphemia, Sculpticolas eos vocant."

[35] John of Otzun, *Contra Paulicianos* (written in 717) which I quote in the translation of Fred. C. Conybeare, *op. cit.*, 152-154: "In primis, incestuosae Paulicianorum gregis sordescentes reliquiae obiurgationem sane sustinuerunt a Nersete catholico, sed minime resipiscentes, post illius obitum aufugientes, alicubi in quibusdam regionis nostrae finibus latitarunt. Ad quos Iconomachi quidam ab Alvanorum catholicis repraehensi advenientes adhaeserunt." Steven Runciman (*The Medieval Manichee*, Cambridge 1947, 34) claims that John of Otzun is here referring to the Armenian catholicus Nerses III (641-661), not to Nerses II (548-557). Henri Grégoire, "Pour l'histoire des églises pauliciennes," *Miscellanea Guillaume de Jerphanion*, II, Rome 1947, 511, n. 1, accepted Runciman's thesis. Miss Der Nersessian kindly let me read the typescript of an unpublished lecture entitled "Iconoclastic Movements in Armenia" in which she gives new evidence

remained in existence down to the eve of the Iconoclastic Controversy in the Byzantine Empire and they influenced the thought of the Byzantine Iconoclastic Movement in the ninth century.[36]

In conclusion we can formulate our results as follows:

(1) The earliest known Iconoclasts in Armenia seceded from the Armenian Church not because of christological differences but in protest against what they considered an undue involvement of the Armenian hierarchy in the power struggle between Byzantium and Persia over Armenia and a corresponding neglect of its spiritual duties.

(2) The principal objection of the Armenian Iconoclasts to religious images was based on the ancient idea that sanctity belonged to persons not to things. The Iconoclasts saw in the religious images unlawful rivals of the Christian ascetic.[37] Unlike the Iconoclastic movement in the Byzantine Empire, Armenian Iconoclasm, therefore, developed in ascetic circles.

(3) Because the Armenian movement was the result of a double protest against the secular clergy and against holy images, it developed into a sectarian movement which soon came to reject the sacraments and which made no attempt to capture the Church. In that respect, too, it differed from the Iconoclastic movement in the Byzantine Empire.

for her view that John of Otzun was thinking of the catholicus Nerses II. It is to be hoped that Professor Der Nersessian will soon publish her interesting paper.

[36] The reader will find the evidence for the last statement in my forthcoming book (above note *). I have examined the views of the Iconoclasts of the ninth century in my article "The Iconoclastic Council of St. Sophia (815) and Its Horos," *Dumbarton Oaks Papers*, VII (1953), 35-66.

[37] It is unfortunate, though understandable, that the movement founded by Yesu, Thadeos and Grigor has been considered primarily in the light of its hostility to images. Vrt'anes K'ert'ogh and John Mavragometsi show indeed that this feature impressed the contemporaries of the secessionists above all others. In reality, this was only a corollary of their extreme emphasis on asceticism, a fact which I have tried to emphasize in the title of this paper.

ADDITIONAL BIBLIOGRAPHY

Moses of Kaghantuik's History of the Albanians (cf. pp.152-158) is now available in an English translation of the Armenian original by C.J.F. Dowsett, The History of the Caucasian Albanians by Movsēs Dasxurançi, School of Oriental and African Studies, University of London, London Oriental Series 8, 1961; the passage translated on p.153 of my article will be found on p.173f. of Dowsett's volume (as Book II, ch.47). On the problem of a relationship between Armenian Iconoclasts and Paulicians see Nina G. Garsoïan, The Paulician Heresy. A Study of the Origin and Development of Paulicianism in Armenia and the Eastern Provinces of the Byzantine Empire, The Hague and Paris, 1967, 133f.; between Byzantine Iconoclasts and Paulicianism: Nina G. Garsoïan, "Byzantine Heresy. A Reinterpretation", Dumbarton Oaks Papers 25, 1971, 85-113, esp.99-104; Paul Lemerle, "L'Histoire des Pauliciens d'Asie Mineure d'après les sources greques", Centre de Recherche d'Histoire et Civilisation Byzantines, Travaux et Mémoires 5, 1971, 131; Leslie Barnard, "The Paulicians and Iconoclasm", Iconoclasm. Papers Given at the Ninth Spring Symposium of Byzantine Studies, University of Birmingham, March 1975, Birmingham, 1977, 75-84.

VIII

THE ICONOCLASTIC COUNCIL OF ST. SOPHIA (815)
AND ITS DEFINITION (*HOROS*)

THE purpose oɪ ɯɪs paper is to present a fresh appraisal of the Second Iconoclastic Period. So far as I can see, modern scholarship is in complete agreement in its views on the Iconoclastic Controversy in the ninth century. The Russian historian F. I. Uspenski called the iconoclasm of the Second Period "already spiritually exhausted." According to Ostrogorsky, the iconoclasts of the ninth century "lacked the intellectual freshness which had been characteristic of Iconoclasm in the eighth century." "The new Iconoclasm produced no new ideas. It resigned itself to repeating the old theses of its teachers" which were now "formulated more vaguely, diluted, and robbed of their previous vigor." Elsewhere Ostrogorsky even attributes to the Iconoclastic Council of 815 senile impotence, "epigonenhafte Impotenz." These views, propounded by the man who had made the most profound and brilliant study of the Second Iconoclastic Period and who was furthermore one of the very few who had had access to some of the unpublished manuscript material dealing especially with the Second Period, were pretty generally acclaimed and underlie the more popular books on the Iconoclastic Controversy. To Martin "in these later stages of the controversy the philosophical and theological arguments were subsidiary to the appeal to authority." [1] And if everybody is agreed that there was very little originality on the iconoclastic side during the Second Period, it stands to reason that scholars often do not have a very high opinion of the orthodox writers of the Second Period who undertake the refutation of the supposedly traditional iconoclastic arguments.

In the course of my work on the Patriarch Nicephorus of Constantinople,[2] I have come to the conclusion that the current view cannot stand the test of critical examination. I shall attempt to show in this paper that the iconoclasm of the Council of St. Sophia, far from being the weak replica of the First Period, far from being tainted with "senile impotence" and with "the exclusive reliance on authority," is on the contrary the philosophical climax of the entire Controversy. During this period the attention of both sides, iconoclasts and iconophiles, centers around one fundamental problem: the nature of the true religious image. Here was the most basic aspect of the entire problem that had hardly been touched upon during the eighth century. So long as it was not taken up, discussed, and settled in one sense or the other, the Controversy was concerned with relatively superficial aspects of the problem. It was only in the ninth century that iconoclasts and iconophiles came to grips with the real issue, and the theo-

38

logians of the ninth century show real originality in the way in which they probe its depth.

Little need be said here about the life of the man to whom we are indebted for what we know about the position of the iconoclasts of 815 and who devoted his entire adult life and his writings to a militant refutation of iconoclasm: the Patriarch Nicephorus. He was born at Constantinople during the reign of the famous iconoclastic Emperor, Constantine V. His father, an Imperial Secretary, was an ardent image-worshipper and was exiled by the Emperor because of his religious convictions. Thus iconoclasm was the great issue that overshadowed Nicephorus' life from the days of his childhood. The young man received a most careful education, and when he was grown up received an appointment in the Imperial Secretariate. In this capacity, he was the subordinate of Tarasius, whose successor he was to be on the patriarchal throne. Young Nicephorus attended the Seventh Ecumenical Council of 787 where he probably acted as mandator, i.e., as a spokesman for the palace. Several years after the Council Nicephorus retired from the court, founded a monastery on the other side of the Straits, and devoted himself to ascetic exercises. Later on the Patriarch Tarasius appointed him director of one of the Church's largest charitable institutions in Constantinople, and in 806 he became Patriarch of Constantinople, thanks largely to pressure exercised on the clergy by the Emperor Nicephorus. During his patriarchate, Nicephorus clashed on various occasions with the monastic party led by Theodore Abbot of Studios. However, when in 813 Leo V the Armenian ascended the imperial throne and soon began to favor iconoclasm, Nicephorus and the monastic party put up a common front against this new outbreak of the heresy. Nicephorus was deposed and exiled to the monastery which he had founded. The exiled Patriarch decided to continue his fight by turning to the literary field.[3] From the new outbreak of the Controversy shortly before 815 to his death in 828 Nicephorus wrote a large number of treatises, all of which attack specific documents written or adduced by the iconoclasts in favor of their views. It is unnecessary to draw up the impressive list of his theological works which were directed against the arguments of Constantine V, against certain patristic texts quoted by the iconoclasts such as those of Eusebius, Epiphanius, Macarius, and so forth. These texts have been published by cardinals Mai and Pitra. Here we are interested exclusively in an unpublished treatise by Nicephorus which is the climax of his literary activity, as well as the most complete treatment of the issues involved.

This last and most important work by Nicephorus had a very long title: "Criticism and Refutation of the unlawful, undefined and truly spurious

Definition set forth by men who seceded from the Catholic and Apostolic Church and adhered to a foreign way of thinking, to the destruction of the saving dispensation granted by God the Word." The very title of the work gives a hint of its content; for at least since the days of Irenaeus [4] works of an anti-heretical nature had gone under the title of Ἔλεγχος καὶ Ἀνατροπή, *Detectio et Eversio*, "Criticism and Refutation." In the case of Nicephorus the heresy which he combatted was of course iconoclasm. So far as I know, only two manuscripts, both at Paris, the *Graecus* 1250 (B) and the *Coislinianus* 93 (C), contain this treatise. In 1939 these two manuscripts, as well as manuscripts of other treatises by Nicephorus, were examined at the Bibliothèque Nationale by one of the oldest and most learned friends of Dumbarton Oaks, my late teacher, Professor R. P. Blake. According to Professor Blake, somebody in the ninth century made a two-volume edition of Nicephorus' theological works. The Ἔλεγχος καὶ Ἀνατροπή appeared in the second tome. The Paris manuscripts *Graecus* 1250 and *Coisl.* 93 derive from that second volume and date, according to Professor Blake, from the thirteenth and fifteenth centuries, respectively — although another excellent paleographer was inclined to assign them to the fourteenth and twelfth centuries.[5] I have copied the entire treatise from *Paris. Gr.* 1250 and collated parts of *Coisl.* 93. The treatise as a whole is still unedited, though the Benedictine Banduri had planned a publication in the early 1700's, Serruys another early in our century, and a young Russian scholar, J. D. Andreev, a third in the 1920's.[6] However, the treatise quotes at length from the *Definition* of the Iconoclastic Council of 815, and these quotations were edited in our own century first by D. Serruys and later in a brilliant book by Ostrogorsky.[7] This method of picking the heretical raisins and leaving the orthodox cake was of course entirely unfair to Nicephorus' treatise. What is more, the raisin-pickers overlooked a great deal, roughly one half, of the heretical material and consequently arrived at half-baked and even erroneous conclusions.[8]

Let me explain what I have in mind by examining for a moment the structure of the unpublished treatise. It clearly falls into two major parts, and the raisin-pickers have concentrated their attention exclusively upon the first part. In this first part the author quotes large sections of the *Definition* issued by the Iconoclastic Council of 815 and refutes it sentence by sentence. The second and longer part of the treatise is the refutation of a florilegium of patristic quotations compiled by the iconoclastic bishops of 815. That such a florilegium was compiled is clear from the *Scriptor Incertus de Leone Armeno*,[9] as well as from indications in Nicephorus' treatise. The treatise makes it clear, furthermore, that in it the patristic quotations collected by the iconoclasts appear in the order in which they were attached to the *Definition* of 815 and that none of the quotations is omitted. It is this patristic florilegium attached to the *Definition* of 815 that has been neglected by previous students of Nicephorus and which will allow us to draw certain conclusions which the text of the *Definition* alone would hardly justify.[10]

We must now consider for a moment the treatise to which we are indebted for our quotations. It is clear first of all that it was not completed prior to the murder of Leo the Armenian on Christmas Day 820.[11] It was written therefore when the Patriarch was in exile. There is some uncertainty about the conditions under which it was written. Later in the century, Photius referred in one of his letters to the relative freedom that Nicephorus had enjoyed in his exile under Leo V, especially to the fact that he had free access to books.[12] This is borne out by the Ἔλεγχος καὶ Ἀνατροπή, where Nicephorus not only quotes from a great number of patristic texts but on occasion even is able to consult several manuscripts of the same work and to derive from them variant readings.[13] In another passage, however, he abstains from pronouncing on the genuineness of a quotation on the grounds that he had been unable to obtain a manuscript of the work in question. He gives as his reason the fact that he was "already locked up in a very safe prison, was in no way granted freedom, certainly not to set foot outside, but not even to send out word." [14] In view of this somewhat conflicting evidence, we must assume that at times he was more severely guarded than at others. We may imagine the exiled Patriarch residing in the monastery which he himself had founded and dedicated to St. Theodore not far from Chalcedon. There he must have lived, sometimes in complete isolation, at other times in relative comfort, always pondering the great issue of iconoclasm which had overshadowed his life and especially his entire tenure of the patriarchal office.

What was the content of that famous *Definition* of 815 which the first part of the Ἔλεγχος καὶ Ἀνατροπή was meant to "criticize and overthrow"? It praised the Isaurian Emperors and the Iconoclastic Council of 754 for its fight against religious images and reënacted its canonical legislation. The Council of 754, so the bishops of 815 said, gave a long period of peace to the Church until it was ruined by the womanly simplicity of the Empress Irene and the Council of 787. Then the Lord took pity upon the world sunk into a flood of sin and sent it a second Noah (the Emperor Leo V). The Iconophiles, following the heresies condemned by the six ecumenical councils, either circumscribed the divine nature together with the human nature by painting the image of Christ, or separated the two. The bishops of 815 concluded by condemning the worship of the spurious images, invalidated the decisions of 787, accepted those of 754, and declared the making of images to be devoid of worship and useless — while at the same time, in a spirit of compromise, expressly abstaining from calling them idols.

Such is the content of the famous *Definition* of 815. While a new edition of this *Definition* is needed,[15] it is clear that a new study of the first part of Nicephorus' treatise will not add much to our knowledge of the *Definition*. If one looks only at the *Definition*, one will have to admit that it is an exceedingly tame and disappointing document. The iconoclastic bishops say as little as possible on their own authority: they summarize and approve the iconoclastic *Definition* of 754, they summarize and reject the orthodox *Definition* of 787. Into their summaries they insert skillfully a review of the principal arguments used against religious images by the earlier iconoclasts. Only certain epithets give an inkling of what we shall recognize as the Council's main thesis: the Saints are called "sharers in the form [of Christ]" (frg. 9 τοὺς συμμόρφους αὐτοῦ ἁγίους), the icons are called "soulless" (frg. 13 ἀψύχοις εἰκόσι). Only once in the *Definition* does the Council of St. Sophia speak on its own authority, a fact which is clear even stylistically from the use of the first person plural:

Embracing the straight doctrine we banish from the Catholic Church the invalid production, presumptuously proclaimed [by the Seventh Ecumenical Council of 787] of the spurious images (τῶν ψευδωνύμων εἰκόνων).[16]

These epithets and this pronouncement — I repeat that it is the only one where the iconoclastic bishops speak in their own name — contains only one real objection to religious images: they are called "spurious." To a ninth-century Byzantine who studied only the *Definition* (and not the florilegium) of 815, this charge of the spuriousness of pictorial images can have meant only one thing: a repetition of a famous argument used earlier by Constantine V and by the Council of Hiereia that a pictorial image of Christ was "spurious" and that the true image was the bread and wine of the Eucharist.[17] It will be seen presently that this was not at all the real doctrine of the Council of 815, yet there can be no doubt that in their *Definition* the bishops of the Council of St. Sophia take cover behind the shield of conciliar authority. It should be added that while they do not hesitate to revile their opponents in a general way, they hesitate to drive them into theological despair: the argument of idol-worship is officially disclaimed by the Council, and the famous dilemma of Constantine V — Monophysitism or Nestorianism — is presented without naming these heresies.[18] In a word, the *Definition* was expressed *fortiter in modo, fortiter in re theologica, sed suaviter in re ecclesiastica*. There can be no doubt that the iconoclastic bishops of 815 thought that by relying in their *Definition* on conciliar authority and by abstaining from charging their opponents with specific heresies, they might have an easier time in winning them over to their side.

Let us now examine with some care the patristic florilegium refuted in the second part of Nicephorus' treatise. It quoted a passage from each of the following sources: [19]

> *Apostolic Constitutions* (frg. 17)
>
> Asterius of Amaseia, Homilia I: *De Divite et Lazaro* (=P.G. XL, 168 B) (frg. 18)
>
> A certain Leontius (frg. 19)
>
> Theodotus of Galatia (frg. 20)
>
> Basil of Seleucia (frg. 21)
>
> Amphilochius of Iconium, *Encomium on St. Basil* (=*Oriens Christianus* XXXI [1934] 68 sq.) (frg. 22)
>
> Basil the Great, *First Homily on the Creation of Man in the Image of God* (=P.G. XLIV, 273A–B) (frg. 23)
>
> Gregory of Nyssa (frg. 24)
>
> Gregory Nazianzen (frg. 25)
>
> John Chrysostom, *In Romanum Martyrem* (=P.G. L, 616) (frg. 26)
>
> John Chrysostom, *Homily on Abraham* (frg. 27)
>
> John Chrysostom, *On the Gaoler* (frg. 28)
>
> A letter by the ascete Nilus to Olympiodorus (*P.G.* LXXIX, 577) (frg. 29)
>
> A great number of passages attributed to Epiphanius (frgs. 30A–D)

In our analysis of this florilegium we are interested primarily in the following questions: What objections to religious images are the patristic quotations contained therein supposed to convey to the reader? And do these objections tally with those expressed (or at least alluded to) in the *Definition* itself? To facilitate an answer to these questions, it will be advisable to reduce the patristic material of the florilegium in order to be able to recognize its purpose. Now if we wish to penetrate to the core of iconoclastic thought in 815, it will obviously be advisable to study most carefully those quotations of the florilegium that had not been used before by the Council of Hiereia. I shall henceforth designate such passages as "new passages." If anywhere, the motivation and tendencies of iconoclastic thought in 815 should appear in these "new passages," i.e., in our fragments 17, 18, 19, 21, 23, 24, 26, 27, 29, 30 B, 30 C, 30 D.[20] Of these "new" quotations, the passages from the *Apostolic Constitutions* (frg. 17), from John Chrysostom's *De Abraham* (frg. 27), from Nilus' letter to Olympiodorus (frg. 29), and from Epiphanius' letters to the Emperor Theodosius (frg. 30 C) and to Johannes of Aelia (frg. 30 D), do not seem to contain any idea that was not already contained in the passages used by the Council of Hiereia. Of the other "new passages," the most important and most elaborate was undoubtedly that taken from Epiphanius' *Treatise against Those Who Are Engaged in Making, after the Fashion of Idols, Images in the Likeness of Christ, the Mother of God, Martyrs, Angels and Prophets* (frg. 30 B). Here is the claim that images of the saints do not honor but rather dishonor them. Here, as in the *Definition* itself, the images are called "spurious" (ψευδώνυμοι). Here is the request to set up the Apostles' commandments as their images through the virtues (οὐκοῦν εἰκόνας αὐτῶν [i.e., τῶν Ἀποστόλων] τὰς αὐτῶν ἐντολὰς δι' ἀρετῶν στήσωμεν) — which I understand to mean that, to portray the Apostles, one has to acquire their virtues·and obey their commands. And we also have here the assertion that the Apostles never commanded anybody to look at their images in memory of their form (ἰδέα). Pictorial representations of Christ and the saints are "spurious" images (ψευδώνυμοι εἰκόνες), in reality they are not images at all, according to Epiphanius. Why not? Because, according to 1 John 3:2, as quoted by Epiphanius, "when He appears, we are to be like Him," and, according to Romans 8:29 (the wording of which Epiphanius changed slightly to suit his purposes), the saints "would share in the shape of the Son of God." If that was so, i.e., if the saints were somehow like Christ, then a pictorial representation of saints was possible only if it was possible for Christ. Was it possible for Christ? Obviously not, for he is incomprehensible and uncircumscribable, otherwise he would not be like the Father and would be unable to give life to the dead. Christ, Epiphanius says, can be worshipped only "in the spirit and in truth," and any pictorial representation of him is a "pseudonymous image," a "spurious" image. The same must be said of the saints, whose true image is not a pictorial portrait but the imitation of their virtues.

So much about the passage from Epiphanius. The remaining "new passages" underline the thesis of Epiphanius' treatise (and of the Council of St. Sophia) that pictorial representations of Christ and the saints are not true images. The quotation from Asterius of Amaseia (frg. 18) forbids pictorial representations of Jesus Christ and ordains the listener "to carry Christ in his soul and to carry the incorporeal Word about in his mind (νοητῶς)." The passage from Leontius (frg. 19) points out that painters rightly disagree regarding the image (εἰκών) of Christ because it was different at different stages of his life and that the likeness (ὁμοιωσίδιον) can be acquired only in the heart. The passage from Basil of Seleucia (frg. 21) states that the only way of commemorating the saints is by reading about them, not by "the evil art of these figures." In interpreting Genesis 1:26 on the creation of Man in the image and likeness of God, Basil the Great (frg. 23) is said to make a distinction between "image" and "likeness." A painter's "image" is "lying vain and idle," whereas creation in God's "likeness" gave Man the power of becoming like God. The purport of this quotation was to show that St. Basil did not have a very high opinion of Man's creation in the "image" of God but saw the dignity of Man in the power given to him by divine grace to make himself resemble God through his own efforts — a view in harmony with the iconoclastic contention that the true representation of Christ and of the saints was the virtuous man. The quotation from Gregory of Nyssa (frg. 24) emphasizes the supra-corporeal nature of Christ. The sentences from John Chrysostom's *In Romanum Martyrem* (frg. 26) insist that Christ cannot be perceived by the senses and that he is concerned exclusively with human *souls* and their salvation.

The "line" indicated by the "new passages" is, therefore, clear: pictures of Christ and of the saints are "spurious," and their only true image is the virtuous Christian worshipping God in his heart.[21]

Now the reader will recall that the one contention made in the *Definition* of St. Sophia on the authority of the Council itself was that pictorial images are "spurious." It is certainly no mere accident that the entire patristic florilegium is an elaboration of that thesis.[22] It now is clear, also, that the point about the spuriousness of pictorial images made in the *Definition* was not a replica of the earlier thesis of Constantine V and of the Council of Blachernae that the only true image of Christ was the bread and wine of the Eucharist. Theologically, that doctrine, making of the Eucharist an image of Christ rather than his body itself, was dangerous ground which had given an altogether too easy weapon to the iconophiles. The doctrine of the spuriousness of pictorial images means something entirely different to the Council of St. Sophia from what it had meant to the Council of Hiereia — although the term remains the same: the true image of Christ is no longer the Eucharist but Man endowed with the Christian virtues.[23]

If the interpretation of the Council of St. Sophia as given here has any merits, then the iconoclasts of the Second Period were indeed not merely repeating the arguments of their predecessors of Hiereia. The bishops of St. Sophia are concentrating as explicitly as possible on what had been by implication, as Ostrogorsky had seen,[24] the central problem of the Controversy since the days of Constantine V: the nature of the true image. To Constantine V the true image had to be consubstantial with the original: καὶ εἰ καλῶς, ὁμόουσιον αὐτὴν [τὴν εἰκόνα] εἶναι τοῦ εἰκονιζομένου.[25] For the Council of St.

Sophia, the "true image" of Christ and the saints was not any kind of pictorial representation. The only true image was, in the language of the quotation from Basil the Great (frg. 23), Man who "with permission of God, made himself resemble God." Here was an iconoclastic doctrine that, philosophically speaking, was immeasurably more profound than that of the earlier period, although by implication it was still based on the same premise. This premise was that the image had to be consubstantial with the original. The Christological arguments first advanced by Constantine V and then taken up by the Council of Hiereia were more basic from a theological point of view; they connected the image controversy with the earlier Christological disputes. But they applied exclusively to the image of Christ. Constantine V once had said, in one of his programmatic speeches, that if he could convince his listeners that the image of Christ was inadmissible, it would be easy for him to repeat the operation for other religious images.[26] Actually, the case for iconoclasm was more easily made in the case of the image of Christ than for that of the saints — though it is very far from my purpose to belittle the ingenuity of Constantine's formulation of the Christological argument. It was after all obvious to every Christian that Christ was more than an ordinary human being, and the pictorial representation of Christ was therefore theologically at least questionable. But such a way of thinking was not applicable to the saints. To invalidate pictorial representations of Christ *and* saints, it was necessary to strike much deeper, to develop a philosophy of religious representation, and this is precisely what the Council of St. Sophia did. True, the Council availed itself of a doctrine implied and even of the terminology used in the works of Constantine V. To this extent, therefore, it is true that the spirit of Constantine V triumphed in 815. But the Council of St. Sophia spelled out in detail the implications of Constantine's philosophy of religious representation, of course without specifically referring to it. A religious personality, Christ or a saint, could be represented only by something consubstantial with this personality. From this it followed that the pictorial image of a religious personality, Christ or saint, was not a true representation but "spurious" and therefore inadmissible.

So far we have deduced the meaning of the Council of St. Sophia from its *Definition* and from its patristic florilegium, without paying attention to Nicephorus' refutation. In fact, our interpretation is confirmed when we turn to the Ἔλεγχος καὶ Ἀνατροπή. The very title of the treatise is illuminating:

Criticism and Refutation of the unlawful, undefined and truly spurious *Definition* set forth by men who seceded from the Catholic and Apostolic Church and adhered to a foreign way of thinking, to the destruction of the saving dispensation granted by God the Word.[27]

Every word of this title is chosen with deliberation. I have commented before (p. 39) on the implications of the words "Criticism and Refutation." It is also obvious what is meant with the charge that the iconoclasts were destroying the "saving dispensation granted by God the Word." This is the traditional claim of the iconophiles that the iconoclasts, by rejecting Christ's image, were denying the Incarnation. But how are we to interpret the contention that the *Definition* of the Council of St. Sophia is "unlawful, undefined and truly spurious"? Is this mere rhetoric, or do we have here basic contentions of the militant Patriarch? It would seem to me that these three adjectives sum up Nicephorus' main objections to the *Definition* of 815. The *Definition* is ἄθεσμος or unlawful: the meaning of this charge is explained particularly at the beginning of the treatise. The *Definition* is unlawful, first, because the bishops assembled at St. Sophia had signed a written promise "on the altar of God and in the face of God and the angels and the entire congregation of the Church" not to assemble in holy synods (B 175a). Nicephorus secondly considers the *Definition* "lawless" because, as he says in the text of the treatise, it raised a dogmatic issue, but Rome and the patriarchs were not represented at the Council (B 175b). The charge of "lawlessness" against the *Definition* thus has the very specific meaning that no local synod at Constantinople could nullify the decision of an Ecumenical Council. The typically Byzantine pun that the *Definition* is "ill-defined" (ἀόριστος) has an equally precise meaning. In the body of the treatise, Nicephorus criticizes the iconoclasts for being entirely negative, for rejecting the iconophile position without offering anything of their own:

But they define nothing. They demolish and reject the other view. . . But they neither affirmed nor constructed anything of their own, for they had nothing to affirm . . . and the lie is undefined and unsubstantial, and they could not stop it. Their *Definition* has only the power of denial and negation but possesses in no way at all a principle of affirmation. Therefore it may not even be called a *Definition* if definitions properly so called proceed from affirmations and from assertions and reveal what the subject is rather than what it is not. For a definition is a brief saying revealing the essence of the subject . . .[28]

From this excerpt it is clear that Nicephorus called the *Definition* "undefined" because it merely rejected that of the Seventh Ecumenical Council without saying anything positive of its own. Now we remember that there is indeed some reason for this criticism. Most of the *Definition* of 815 was taken up with the rejection of the *Definition* of Nicaea and the reaffirmation of that of the Council of Hiereia. We noted, however, one significant exception: the *one* thing that the Council of Blachernae does on its own authority is that it calls the images "spurious." Is it not significant that Nicephorus applies to the iconoclastic *Definition* of 815 the very epithet "truly spurious" which his opponents had fastened upon pictorial images? Does this not indicate that Nicephorus considered this iconoclastic thesis, i.e., that pictorial images were not "true" images, one of the most important lines of attack used by his opponents, comparable in its importance only with the Christological implications of the iconoclastic position? Is it not as if Nicephorus wanted to say in his title: "You call religious images 'spurious.' I tell you, and I shall demonstrate to you in the body of my treatise, that they are true images. What is 'really spurious' is your own *Definition*." In view of the occurrence of the epithet in the title of the treatise, where every word, as we have seen, is heavy with meaning, this does not seem to me an unwarranted inference. In fact, most of the treatise is devoted to a rejection of two lines of argumentation: the one based on Christological doctrine, and the other based on the new doctrine of the true image. At first sight it might seem that the refutation of the Christological doctrine takes up much more space than that of the doctrine of the true image. Strictly speaking, the refutation of the spuriousness of pictorial images takes up only three folios out of a total of one hundred and sixty (in manuscript B), while Nicephorus returns to the issue of Christology repeatedly and at great length. But after all it should be kept in mind that the *Definition* itself dealt with the spuriousness of pictorial images in exactly one word and that the real burden of the charge was elaborated upon in the florilegium of patristic quotations. In reality, then, the entire second part of Nicephorus' treatise — or ninety-five out of a total of one hundred and sixty folios — is devoted to the refutation of the doctrine of the true image. Nicephorus' refutation thus seems to bear out the thesis of this paper concerning the real meaning of the iconoclastic Council of St. Sophia.

One last remark before we conclude our discussion of the iconoclastic side and turn our attention to the iconophiles. It remains puzzling that the iconoclasts of 815 relegated the positive side of their contention to the florilegium and only hinted at it in the *Definition*. One may speculate why this was done. In the first place, it was good strategy to "define" as little as possible, and since the object of the *Definition* was negative — the rejection of religious images — there was no need to make the positive side of the iconoclastic views a part of the formal *Definition*. But secondly, there simply was no conciliar authority for the positive side of the doctrine of the true image, and the iconoclasts of St. Sophia thought — probably rightly — that in order to prevail it was expedient not to advance, in the formal *Definition*, beyond the positions covered by the authority of the Council of Hiereia.

If, then, the distinction between false and true images is the major new attack of the iconoclasts of the ninth century, the question arises: How did Nicephorus meet it? Nicephorus begins by stating that to call Christ's pictorial image false (ψευδής) is equivalent to saying that every image of Christ is false: "But there never could be the absurd argument which would deny that a thing endowed with real existence and naturally capable of representation by image could not be delineated in one particular way but admit that it could be represented in some other way." [29] If the iconoclasts were right, then neither Man in general nor the priest in particular would be in the image of Christ.

The only trouble with this counter-argument is that the argument which it calls "absurd" is precisely the thesis of the iconoclasts — and you do not refute an argument by calling it names. As if he realized the insufficiency of his effort, Nicephorus therefore goes on with his refutation. An image is a likeness (ὁμοίωμα), and as such it belongs to the logical category of relation. The similarity between thing represented and representation binds them together in form though they differ in nature. Consequently, where there is similarity, the two things that resemble each other come into being together and are destroyed together.[30] If you have the portrait of an emperor and if the emperor is a true emperor, then his image will be a true image; but if he is a false emperor, then his portrait will be false. In fact, the image of a false thing is not an image at all, like centaurs and goat-stags. Now in evaluating this counter-argument of Nicephorus, *difficile est saturam non scribere*, so full is it of the most elementary logical blunders. It just is not true that there can be no falseness of the image without falseness of the original: the process of pictorial representation can certainly "distort" the truth contained in the original. And if Aristotle had said in the *Categories* [31] that correlatives come into existence simultaneously and that they cancel each other, he of course did not mean that they depended upon each other in their *existence* but merely in their *relation*. Neither Aristotle nor his Byzantine commentators would have said, as Nicephorus claims, that if an image of Christ was false Christ himself was false, or did not exist, but merely that in this case Christ was no longer the original for *this particular kind of image*. But whatever the validity of Nicephorus' counter-arguments, we are here interested primarily in the fact that he applies to the problem of religious images a concept of Aristotelian logic, i.e., the category of relation.

The application of Aristotelian philosophy to the problem of images does not stop here. To disprove the spuriousness of the religious images, Nicephorus further relies on the Aristotelian doctrine of causation. Nicephorus knows five meanings of the word "cause," of which three agree with Aristotle's own: the efficient, the material, and the final cause. But in the place of Aristotle's formal cause there appear the instrumental and the exemplary cause.[32] For his present argument Nicephorus uses exclusively the exemplary cause. The exemplary cause of Christ's pictorial image is Christ himself or his form, and the iconoclasts by calling the images "spurious" destroy the corporeal form or pattern itself after which the image is modeled.[33]

The question naturally arises: How does Nicephorus deal with the positive side of the iconoclastic argument, i.e., with the contention that the true image of the saints is the reproduction of their virtues? So far as I can see, he deals with it only twice, namely, in connection with the quotations from Theodotus of Galatia (frg. 20) and from Amphilochius of Iconium (frg. 22). If the virtues of the saints can be reproduced, so Nicephorus says in discussing the first quotation, this should all the more be true of their bodies. The virtues are activities exercised by the bodies of the saints. Their bodies are therefore active, productive, causes, and prior, while the virtues are passive, receptive, effects, and secondary. The virtues of the saints reveal their capabilities, but their form (ἰδέα) reveals *the saints themselves* and is therefore more worthy of honor.[34] This defense, which is again couched in the language of the schools, would emphasize the physical over the spiritual aspects of the religious personality, but the point should perhaps not be pressed unduly since this was hardly Nicephorus' intention. Similarly, in refuting the passage from Amphilochius of Iconium, Nicephorus points out that the bodies of the saints bear witness to the condition of their souls and are the instruments of their sainthood. He adds that the sense of sight is the foremost and most impressive of the senses[35] — a statement for which again there was ample precedent in Aristotle and in the philosophy of the Byzantine schools. On the whole, one must admit that Nicephorus' refutation of the principal iconoclastic thesis is not convincing. His treatise is learned and applies to a theological problem concepts of Aristotelian logic and physics. It is incisive and decisive where the genuiness and interpretation of a Biblical or patristic passage is concerned. Yet neither the argument from the category of relation, nor that from causation, nor that from the relationship of body and virtues seems a valid answer to the iconoclastic argument of the spuriousness of pictorial images.

We must now return to the general problem to which this paper is devoted and try to summarize our conclusions. Was the Second Period of Iconoclasm really one of "spiritual exhaustion," of "senile impotence," of mere reliance on authority, of slavish imitation of the First Period? We have seen how this misinterpretation of the evidence arose. It is due to the simple fact that in order to be conciliatory and to make the best use of conciliar authority the Council of St. Sophia, in its *Definition*, did indeed to a large extent simply repeat and approve what had been said by the Council of Hiereia. But we know now that the real thesis of the Council was developed in the florilegium, and that during the Second Period of Iconoclasm the emphasis lay elsewhere than before. True, somewhere or other, in the *Definition* or in the florilegium, every single one of the old arguments used by the earlier iconoclasts is repeated. This is particularly true of the famous Christological argument. True also that the new "line" of 815, in its formulation, "The pictorial image is spurious," reminds one of Constantine V and of the Council of Hiereia with their doctrine of the Eucharist as the only true image of Christ. The difference lies, however, in the new *positive* meaning implied by this term and made explicit in the patristic florilegium: for the Council of St. Sophia the only true image of Christ and of the saints is Man endowed with the Christian virtues. It is on this point that the Council of St. Sophia places the emphasis, and the final judgment on the Council and, with it, on the iconoclasm of the ninth century, must be based on the answer to the question: How original was that position itself? Here everything depends on what one calls "original." If we mean by it a position never taken by anybody before, we must state categorically that it was not original at all. For Origen, in the third Christian century, the problem of a Christian art had hardly existed, yet he had justified the Christian opposition to pagan cult images, in a passage to which Jean Daniélou and Professor Florovsky have recently called attention, by exactly the same argument as that used by the iconoclasts in 815:

[Our] cult-statues and fitting offerings to God are not fabricated by uneducated craftsmen but are rendered clear and formed within us by the Word of God: the virtues, which are imitations of "the first born of all creation" (Col. I 15) in Whom are the patterns of justice, prudence, courage, wisdom, piety and of the other virtues. Therefore cult-statues are in all those who, in accordance with the Divine Word, furnish for themselves justice and courage and wisdom and piety and the furnishings of the other virtues. . . And in each of those who, to the best of their ability, imitate Him even in this respect there is the cult-statue "in the likeness of the Creator" (Col. III 10) which they furnish by contemplating God with a pure heart when they have become imitators of God (Ephes. V 1). And in short, all Christians attempt to erect the aforesaid altars and the cult-statues mentioned before, not those that are without soul and without perception and that let greedy demons reside in objects without soul, but those that receive the Spirit of God, coming to rest upon the aforementioned cult-statues of virtue and upon him who is "in the likeness of the Creator" as Its own [kindred]; thus the Spirit of Christ will also settle upon "those who share in His shape" (τοῖς, ἵν' οὕτως ὀνομάσω, συμμόρφοις, cf. Rom. VIII 29), to use that expression. . .[36]

From the Alexandrian School the view of the virtuous human soul as the image of Christ was taken up by the Fathers of the Church, notably by Gregory of Nyssa, however with the difference that the pagan statue, which for Origen had been *replaced* by the true Christian man, now appears merely as a literary simile.[37]

An examination of the *Definition* (including the florilegium) of St. Sophia, thus, seems to point toward a connection of the iconoclasts of 815 with Origenism.[38] This brings to mind a recent study of iconoclasm by Professor Florovsky to which the present writer is greatly indebted. In it Professor Florovsky inferred, from the use of Eusebius' *Letter to the Empress Constantia* by the iconoclasts in the eighth century and from its unquestionably Origenist flavor, that the inspiration of iconoclasm was Origenist.[39] We now have an incomparably broader basis for Florovsky's thesis: the decisions of the Council of St. Sophia in 815 are steeped in the thought and argumentation with which we are familiar from the passage quoted from Origen. Let us not forget, however, that among certain iconoclasts, notably with the Emperor Constantine V, there are clear indications of Monophysite tendencies.[40] Let us remember also that the notion of the virtuous man as the true image of the deity was older than Origen, who took it from Clement of Alexandria and shared it with his pagan contemporaries Plotinus and Porphyry.[41] Both the Origenist and the Monophysite labels of iconoclasm, therefore, seem somewhat narrow, and its true nature can perhaps be seen best if we consider what Origenism, Monophysitism, and iconoclasm have in common: they put undue emphasis (from the orthodox point of view) on the divine aspect of Christ at the expense of his humanity. Origenism, Monophysitism, and iconoclasm, thus, are — and this was again suggested by Florovsky — manifestations of that strand of Hellenic mentality to which the concept of "Christ crucified" seemed "foolishness" (I Corinthians 1:23) and which made piety a concern for the inner man.

The main thesis of the Council of St. Sophia, then, was not "original," in the sense that it had never been stated before — though it certainly had not been stated in this way by the iconoclasts of the First Period. But I am afraid that if originality is defined so strictly there will be very little originality left. In the history of thought, originality does not lie only in the first formulation of a thesis. There can be real originality where a thesis first proclaimed more or less incidentally by others is made the foundation stone for the solution of a new set of problems. This is what happened in the Second Period of Iconoclasm with the doctrine of the true Christian cult-statues formulated by Origen. The iconoclasts of the Second Period are certainly not indebted to the First Period for their principal thesis. True to

Hellenic tradition, the iconoclasts of the Second Period use Origen's doctrine of the true Christian cult-statue as a basis for an elaborate attack on Christian religious images. Here was real originality,[42] just as there had been originality in Constantine V's connecting the image problem with Christology. Originality may be claimed not only for the iconoclastic but also for the iconophile side, which, in order to meet the new "line," relied on Aristotelian philosophy. The spiritual force of iconoclasm was therefore far from spent in the ninth century. In fact, the full depth of the attack on religious images was not probed prior to the Council of St. Sophia. The opposition to the pictorial images of the saints, for example, could be put on the same footing as that to images of Christ only after the problem of the nature of religious images as such had been raised. This fresh and vigorous attack, as is frequent in the history of thought and particularly of religious thought, produced an original and learned, if not altogether convincing and final, defense on the part of the image-worshippers, and particularly the literary masterpieces of Theodore of Studios and of Nicephorus of Constantinople.

HOBART AND WILLIAM SMITH COLLEGES
Geneva, New York

NOTES

1. F. I. Uspenski, as quoted by A. A. Vasiliev, *Histoire de l'empire byzantin*, I (Paris, 1932) 380; Georg Ostrogorsky, *Studien zur Geschichte des byzantinischen Bilderstreites*, Historische Untersuchungen 5 (Breslau, 1929) p. 56; also *Geschichte des byzantinischen Staates*, Byzantinisches Handbuch, in Handbuch der Altertumswissenschaft XII, 1, 2 (Munich, 1940) p. 141; Edward James Martin, *A History of the Iconoclastic Controversy* (London, 1930) 190; Emile Amann, *L'Epoque carolingienne*, Histoire de l'Eglise 6 (Paris, 1947) 230: "Jean [Hylilas] se fit ouvrir les bibliothèques et les chartriers tant des couvents que des églises: il n'y trouva que les actes du concile de Hiéria; depuis trois quarts de siècle la critique des iconoclastes n'avait pas fait de progrès." In the last resort, all these statements go back to the iconophile *Scriptor Incertus de Leone Armeno*, P.G. CVIII, 1025 A–B, who asserts that the committee charged by the Emperor Leo V to compile a florilegium of iconoclastic quotations did not make progress until they found the florilegium attached to the *Definition* of the Iconoclastic Council of Hiereia (754) and looked up the passages quoted there. Although, in this paper, I shall have to disagree repeatedly with findings of Ostrogorsky, I want to record here my indebtedness to his publications, without which my work would have been impossible.

2. I hope to complete, in the near future, a biography of this author, as well as an edition of his unpublished main work, the Ἔλεγχος καὶ Ἀνατροπή.

3. The biographical data are based on Ignatius Diaconus' *Vita Nicephori* written within one generation after the death of the saint and published by Carl de Boor in the appendix to his edition of Nicephorus' *Opuscula Historica* (Leipzig, 1880) 130–217.

4. The full title of Irenaeus' *Contra Haereses* was Ἐλέγχου καὶ Ἀνατροπῆς τῆς ψευδωνύμου γνώσεως βιβλία πέντε; cf. the edition by W. Wigan Harvey, I, 1.

5. R. P. Blake, "Note sur l'activité littéraire de Nicéphore Iᵉʳ Patriarche de Constantinople," *Byzantion* XIV (1939) 1–15; Paul Maas, "Die ikonoklastische Episode in dem Brief

des Epiphanius an Johannes," *B.Z.* XXX (1929–30) 279–286, esp. 279. Maas's ninth-century archetype is possibly identical with the edition in two volumes the existence of which was proved by Blake. Robert Devreesse, who does not cite Blake's paper, assigns *Coisl.* 93 to the eleventh or twelfth century (*Le Fonds Coislin*, Paris, 1945).

6. On Banduri's projected edition see his *Conspectus* (most conveniently in *P.G.* C, 17–38). On Andreev's project, Ostrogorsky, *Studien*, 47.

7. Daniel Serruys, "Les Actes du concile iconoclaste de l'an 815," Ecole Française de Rome, *Mélanges d'archéologie et d'histoire* XXIII (1903) 345–351; and Ostrogorsky, *Studien*, 48–51.

8. In this article, as I must sadly confess, I have myself sinned in the same way as others before me. I can only plead that the paper is based on a careful transcript and study of the entire treatise.

9. *Scriptor Incertus de Leone Armeno*: see above, note 1. A. Ehrhard (in Karl Krumbacher, *Geschichte der byzantinischen Literatur* etc., Handbuch der klassischen Altertumswissenschaft IX, 1 [2d ed., Munich, 1897] p. 68) thought that the florilegium was lost. Banduri as well as Serruys recognized that the florilegium was preserved. Ostrogorsky, *Studien*, 58 f.: "Auf die eigentlichen Bestimmungen des Konzils folgt eine Kette von solchen Zeugnissen aus den Kirchenvätern. . . Auf die Wiedergabe all dieser Zeugnisse glaubte ich verzichten zu können. . ." By omitting the florilegium, Ostrogorsky came to an erroneous appraisal of the Council of St. Sophia, as we shall see.

10. First part of Nicephorus' treatise: B fols. 173a–235b and C fols. 1a–66a. Second part: B fols. 235b–332a and C fols. 66a–158b. In B fol. 237a, immediately preceding the first quotation of the iconoclastic florilegium, we find the following line: ἀρχὴ τῆς τῶν χρήσεων ἀνατροπῆς; while C fol. 66b has in the margin: ἀρχὴ τῶν χρήσεων. The formulae introducing each quotation of the florilegium are printed in the Appendix and will show that Nicephorus is quoting *all* the quotations in the order in which they appeared in the florilegium.

11. Nicephorus, Ἔλεγχος καὶ Ἀνατροπή, on Leo V: εἰς οἷον τέλος τὰ ἐπικεχειρημένα ἐκβέβηκε, τὸ θυσιαστήριον μέγα κεκράξεται, ὃ καὶ ζῶν κακῶς καθαιρῶν ἐβεβήλου καὶ ἀναιρούμενος ἐνδίκως τῷ λύθρῳ τῶν ἐναγῶν αἱμάτων πλέον ἔχρανέ τε καὶ κατεμόλυνεν, ἄξια ὄντως τὰ ἐπίχειρα τῆς εἰς Χριστὸν ὕβρεως δεξάμενος ὁ ἀλιτήριος (B fol. 174a, C missing). Again Nicephorus says (C fol. 35a–b, lost in B), in answering frg. 11 of the *Definition* (see Appendix) and after characterizing Leo V in harsh terms as a persecutor: καὶ ὧδε [i.e., as follows] ὡς ἀληθῶς εἰπεῖν εὔκαιρον· εἰ μὴ Κύριος Σαβαὼθ διὰ σπλάγχνα ἐλέους καὶ οἰκτιρμῶν αὐτοῦ ἐπέβλεψεν ἐξ οὐρανοῦ ἁγίου κατοικητηρίου αὐτοῦ καὶ κατηλέησεν καὶ ἐβοήθησεν ἡμῖν καὶ τὸν ἐπαναστάντα τῇ ἐκκλησίᾳ σάλον καὶ κλύδωνα παραδόξως κατηύνασεν καὶ τῇ καταιγίδι τῆς ἀποστασίας καὶ δυσσεβείας ἐπιτάξας εἰς αὔραν γαληνιῶσαν ἔστησεν καὶ τῶν συμφορῶν τούτων τὸν αἴτιον, τὴν πάντων τῶν κακῶν ποριμωτάτην φύσιν, ψήφοις θεοκρίτοις μετελθὼν ὧν ἦν ἄξιος ἐκπόδων ἐποιήσατο, οὐδὲν ἐκώλυεν τοὺς κατὰ τήνδε τὴν ἀρχὴν ἅπαντας μεγίστῳ καὶ ἐξαισίῳ περιπεσόντας ναυαγίῳ εἰς βυθὸν ἀπιστίας κατολισθεῖν. These are allusions to the murder of Leo V in the Palace Chapel of St. Stephen on the morning of Christmas 820 (see J. B. Bury, *A History of the Eastern Roman Empire* [London, 1912] 52 f.) and to the tolerant religious policy of Michael II.

12. Photius, *Epistulae*, I 16 (*P.G.* CII, 768 B).

13. I quote an instance primarily *editorum Gregorii Nysseni in usum*. The Council of St. Sophia quoted a passage from Gregory of Nyssa, without further identification, as follows: μηκέτι τὴν σωματώδη καὶ δουλικὴν μορφὴν ἐν τῇ σεαυτοῦ πίστει ἀνατυπώσῃ, ἀλλὰ τὸν ἐν τῇ δόξῃ τοῦ Πατρὸς ὄντα καὶ ἐν μορφῇ Θεοῦ ὑπάρχοντα καὶ Θεὸν ὄντα Λόγον, τοῦτον προσκύνει, καὶ μὴ τὴν τοῦ δούλου μορφήν (B 278a, C 107b). Nicephorus remarks (B 279b, C 109b): γινώσκειν δὲ χρὴ ὡς ἕν τισι τῶν ἀντιγράφων φέρεται· τὸν ἐν τῇ δόξῃ τοῦ Πατρὸς ὄντα καὶ Θεὸν ὄντα, τοῦτον προσκύνει λαβόντα τὴν τοῦ δούλου μορφήν.

14. In discussing the authenticity of an *Encomium on Basil* attributed by the Council of 815 to Amphilochius of Iconium (frg. 22), Nicephorus says: ἡμῖν γὰρ οὐκ ἐξεγένετο, καίτοι πολλὰ καμοῦσιν, ὅτι μὴ ἑνὶ μόνῳ ἀντιγράφῳ, καὶ τούτῳ νεογράφῳ, περιτυχεῖν ἐν φρουραῖς ἀσφαλεστάταις ἤδη ἐγκαθειργμένοις καὶ μηδαμοῦ ἐλευθεριάζειν συγκεχωρημένοις, οὐ μὴν οὐδὲ πόδα προτείνειν πώποτε (B 275a, C 105a).

15. In the Appendix the reader will find a new edition of the *Definition* of 815. I had

54

originally thought to reprint that of Ostrogorsky. Soon, however, I convinced myself that in certain respects Serruys' edition was better than that of Ostrogorsky. Ostrogorsky's fragments 5, 6, and 7, which he was so proud (*Studien*, p. 48) to have added to those collected by Serruys, are in reality quotations by Nicephorus from the Council of Hiereia (754). This is made quite clear by the trend of Nicephorus' argument (which it would take too long to sketch here). The fragments 5, 6, and 7 are even printed among the Acts of the Seventh Council of Nicaea (787), (frg. 5 Ostrogorsky = Mansi XIII 324 D–E, 328C; frg. 6 Ostrogorsky = Mansi XIII 221C; frg. 7 Ostrogorsky = Mansi XIII 225D, 229A, D–E). Serruys seems to have realized this: "C'est ainsi qu'il [Nicephorus] reproduit en partie les actes de 754" (p. 346). Ostrogorsky's error was due, partly, to insufficient study of Nicephorus' presentation, partly to the fact that frg. 5 is written in B, and frg. 7 in both manuscripts, in the way in which fragments from the Council of 815 are normally presented in these manuscripts. Frg. 6 is marked in neither manuscript as belonging to the Council of St. Sophia. For these reasons it was impossible simply to repeat Ostrogorsky's edition. On the other hand, I could not use Serruys' text since Ostrogorsky had correctly added two fragments (frgs. 4 and 11 my numbering = frgs. 3 and 13 Ostrogorsky). Also I, myself, was able to add two fragments (frgs. 1 and 12) which had escaped both Serruys and Ostrogorsky because they are only Nicephorus' paraphrases (not verbatim quotations) from lost passages from the *Definition* of 815. I also have corrected a few minutiae. I have no illusion that in a task where such outstanding scholars have erred I shall be able to present the final text. That will have to wait until after the critical edition of Nicephorus' treatise is completed. All quotations, in this paper, from the *Definition* (including the florilegium) of 815 will be numbered according to my own edition to be found in the Appendix, but, to make comparisons easier, the reader will find in the Appendix a concordance of the three editions.

16. Frg. 14.

17. Constantine V, Πεῦσις II, frg. 21 (Ostrogorsky p. 10) καὶ εἰκών ἐστι τοῦ σώματος αὐτοῦ καὶ ὁ ἄρτος ὃν λαμβάνομεν, μορφάζων τὴν σάρκα αὐτοῦ, ὡς εἰς τύπον τοῦ σώματος ἐκείνου γενόμενος. Council of Hiereia: Mansi XIII, 261E–264C, quoted by Ostrogorsky pp. 21 f.

18. Frgs. 12–13.

19. Each of these quotations raises problems of attribution, of meaning, and so forth, into which we cannot go at the present time. To give but one example: the passage attributed in the florilegium to Basil (frg. 23) may actually be Gregory of Nyssa's; see E. v. Ivánka, "Die Autorschaft der Homilien . . . " *B.Z.* XXXVI (1936) 46–57. To make communication easier, I shall in this paper speak of "passages from Basil" or "from Gregory" or use the phrase "Basil or Gregory says" where precision would require clumsy formulae such as "passages attributed by the Council of St. Sophia to Basil or to Gregory" or "the Council of St. Sophia attributed to Basil or Gregory the saying . . ." I should like to state here, however, that such formulae should not be construed to imply any opinion regarding authenticity or real meaning. In other words, at the moment we are not interested in the views of Church Fathers such as Basil or Gregory on pictorial images but in an analysis of the view on pictorial images which the Council of St. Sophia attributed, rightly or wrongly, to the Fathers cited.

20. The "old passages," i.e., those already quoted at Hiereia, are our fragments 20 (= Mansi XIII 309E where it is attributed to Theodotus of Ancyra); 22 (= Mansi XIII 301 D where the fragment appears in much shorter form); 25 (= Mansi XIII 297A); 28 (= Mansi XIII 300A); 30 A (= Mansi XIII 292 D–E). Frg. 18 (Asterius of Amaseia) was quoted in 787 (Mansi XIII 305B) but by the Orthodox, not by the iconoclasts. Incidentally, several of the prize pieces of the Council of Hiereia were omitted by the bishops of the Council of St. Sophia. In the first place, no Biblical passage appears in the florilegium as such — though two are quoted in a text attributed to Epiphanius. Secondly, Eusebius' famous *Letter to the Augusta Constantia* was omitted from the florilegium — a fact specifically emphasized by Nicephorus. There were other less important cases of exclusion.

21. A subsidiary (and connected) theme that occurs in many of our passages (20, 21, 22, 28) are declarations in favor of the written and spoken word (over what is perceived by the eyes) which is apt to produce, in the listeners' souls, the true image of Christ. I plan

to deal with this theme, which implies a preference of the sense of hearing over that of sight, in a different context.

22.   We see now that the other "epithets" contained in the *Definition* itself (above, p. 41) are also connected with the central thesis of the florilegium. If the *Definition* had called the saints "sharers in the form of Christ" (τοὺς συμμόρφους αὐτοῦ ἁγίους), we see here the influence of Epiphanius (frg. 30B, referring to Rom. VIII 29) and his theory of the virtuous man as Christ's image. If the *Definition* had called pictorial images soulless (ἄψυχος), just like frg. 28 of the florilegium, the reader is reminded of true images that are not "soulless" but are in fact the souls of the Just. Furthermore, we can now understand why the "old passages" (above, note 20) were taken over from the florilegium of Hiereia: frgs. 20, 22, and 25 were indeed precious supports for the central thesis of 815, while frg. 30A was probably taken over simply because it was iconoclastic and was attributed to the same witness as the most important piece in the entire dossier of 815 (frg. 30B). The last reasons probably account also for the inclusion of frgs. 30C and 30D, which are unconnected with the central thesis of 815. What motives prompted the inclusion of frgs. 17, 27, and 29, I am unable to say.

23.   The Council of Hiereia had expressed, in one of its anathemas, what was to become the central thesis of the Council of St. Sophia, Mansi XIII 345C: εἴ τις τὰς τῶν ἀπάντων ἁγίων ἰδέας ἐν εἰκόσιν ἀψύχοις καὶ ἀναύδοις ἐξ ὑλικῶν χρωμάτων ἀναστηλοῦν ἐπιτηδεύοι μηδεμίαν ὄνησιν φερούσας, ... καὶ οὐχὶ δὴ μᾶλλον τὰς τούτων ἀρετὰς διὰ τῶν ἐν γραφαῖς περὶ αὐτῶν δηλουμένων οἷόν τινας ἐμψύχους εἰκόνας ἐν ἑαυτῷ ἀναζωγραφεῖ καὶ πρὸς τὸν ὅμοιον αὐτοῖς ἐκ τούτου διεγείρεται ζῆλον, καθὼς οἱ ἔνθεοι ἡμῶν ἔφησαν πατέρες, ἀνάθεμα. Yet the emphasis, in 754, lay on the Christological issues.

24.   Ostrogorsky, *Studien*, 40–45.

25.   Frg. 2 (*ibid.*, p. 8).

26.   Frg. 24 (*ibid.*, p. 11).

27.   B 173b (lost in C): Ἔλεγχος καὶ ἀνατροπὴ τοῦ ἀθέσμου καὶ ἀορίστου καὶ ὄντως ψευδωνύμου ὅρου τοῦ ἐκτεθέντος παρὰ τῶν ἀποστατησάντων τῆς καθολικῆς καὶ ἀποστολικῆς ἐκκλησίας καὶ ἀλλοτρίῳ προσθεμένων φρονήματι ἐπ' ἀναιρέσει τῆς τοῦ Θεοῦ Λόγου σωτηρίου οἰκονομίας.

28.   C 56b–57a (B lost): ἀλλ' ὁρίζονται μὲν οὐδέν, τὸ ἀλλότριον δὲ ἀνασκευάσαντες καὶ ἀποπεμψάμενοι . . . ἴδιον ἔθεντο παντελῶς οὐδὲν οὐδὲ κατεσκεύασαν· οὐ γὰρ εἶχον ὃ θήσουσιν . . . τὸ γὰρ ψεῦδος ἀόριστον καὶ ἀνύπαρκτον καὶ οὐκ ἔχον ὅποι ποτὲ στήσεται. δύναμιν γοῦν ἀποφάσεως καὶ στερήσεως ὁ κατ' αὐτοὺς ὅρος μόνον περιέχει, θέσεως δὲ οὐδαμῶς ὅλως λόγον κέκτηται ὥστε κινδυνεύειν μηδὲ ὅρον ὀνομάζεσθαι, εἴπερ οἱ κυρίως ὅροι ἐκ τῶν θέσεων μᾶλλον καὶ καταφατικῶν λόγων προΐασιν καὶ τὸ τί εἶναι ἀλλ' οὐ τὸ τί μὴ εἶναι τὸ ὑποκείμενον δηλοῦντες· ὅρος γάρ ἐστιν λόγος σύντομος δηλωτικὸς τῆς οὐσίας τοῦ ὑποκειμένου πράγματος . . .

29.   B 223a, C 50a: ἀλλ' οὐδ' ἄν τις ἀναφανείη ποτὲ ἀποκληρωτικὸς λόγος ὃς ἐπὶ τῶν ἀληθῶς ὄντων καὶ εἰκονίζεσθαι πεφυκότων τὸ μὲν οὕτω γράφεσθαι κωλύσειεν, ἑτέρως δὲ εἰκονίζεσθαι συγχωρήσειεν.

30.   B 223b, C 50b: ἐντεῦθεν λοιπὸν ἐφ' ὧν τὰ ὅμοια πρόκειται, τῷ κοινῇ μετέχειν τῆς σχέσεως συνεισάγεσθαι ὡς τὰ πολλὰ καὶ συναναιρεῖσθαι κατὰ τὸ εἶδος τοῦ λόγου το⋅ύτου συμβήσεται·

31.   Aristotle, *Categories*, 7b 15–19.

32.   B 224b, C 51b: τὸ αἴτιον τῶν πολλαχῶς λεγομένων οἱ περὶ τὰ τοιαῦτα ἐσχολακότες φασίν· ποιητικόν τε γὰρ εἶναι καὶ ὀργανικὸν παραδειγματικόν τε αὖ καὶ ὑλικὸν καὶ ἔτι πρὸς τούτοις τελικόν. Note that Aristotle himself, in *Physics* II 3, 1946 b 26, uses εἶδος and παράδειγμα as synonyms to designate the formal cause (τὸ εἶδος καὶ τὸ παράδειγμα, τοῦτο δ'ἐστὶν ὁ λόγος ὁ τοῦ τί ἦν εἶναι). Yet the separate mention of the exemplary cause together with the instrumental cause in Nicephorus ought to make it possible to define more closely the handbook of Aristotelian philosophy used by Nicephorus in this and his other writings.

33.   B 224b–225a, C 51b–52a: ἐπεὶ οὖν καὶ ἡ τοῦ Σωτῆρος ἡμῶν Ἰησοῦ (om B) Χριστοῦ εἰκὼν τεχνητή τέ (om B) ἐστι καὶ χειρόκμητος, ἵνα τἆλλα παρῶμεν νῦν, παραδειγματικὸν αἴτιον οὐχ ἕτερόν τι ἢ αὐτὸν τὸν Χριστὸν κέκτηται ἤτοι τὸ κατ' αὐτὸν εἶδος. οἱ τοίνυν τοῦ ψεύδους καθηγεμόνες διὰ τῆς φωνῆς ταύτης [i.e., ψευδώνυμος'] λυμαίνονται τῷ τοῦ αἰτίου λόγῳ, ταὐτὸν δὲ εἰπεῖν ἀναιροῦσι τὸ σωματικὸν εἶδος αὐτὸ καθ' ὃ ἡ τοιαύτη γραφὴ διακεχάρακται. τούτου δὲ τί ἂν γένοιτο εἰς τὴν τοῦ Λόγου σάρκωσιν δυσφημότερον;

56

34. B 261b, C 91b: εἰ γὰρ αἱ ἀρεταὶ τῶν ἀγίων οἱονεὶ (οἷον C) εἰκόνες ἔμψυχοι διὰ τῶν γεγραμμένων δείκνυνται, τὰ κατορθοῦντα τὰς ἀρετὰς σώματα πόσῳ δικαιότερον κατὰ τὰς ἰδέας (εἰδέας C) αὐτῶν εἰκονίζεσθαι; ὅσῳ καὶ σῶμα πράξεως ἀναγκαιότερόν τε καὶ τιμιώτερον ὡς τὰ μὲν ἐνεργοῦντα τὰ δὲ ἐνεργούμενα, καὶ τὰ μὲν ἀποτελοῦντα τὰ δὲ ἀποτελούμενα, καὶ αἴτια καὶ πρῶτα αἰτιατῶν καὶ δευτέρων τῶν (om B) ἔργων ὄντων. εἰ γοῦν μὴ ταῦτα οὕτως ἔχοι, καὶ οἶκος καὶ ναῦς καὶ κλίνη τοῦ κατασκευάσαντος οἰκοδόμου καὶ τέκτονος τιμιωτέρα. καὶ αἱ μὲν ἀρεταὶ οἷα πράξεις (πράξις C) τυγχάνουσαι περὶ τὰ σώματα τὸ ἐπιεικὲς καὶ πρακτικὸν αὐτῶν παραδηλοῦσιν, αἱ ἰδέαι (εἰδέαι C) δὲ αὐτὰ τὰ σώματα ἤγουν αὐτοὺς τοὺς ἁγίους ἡμῖν ἐμφανίζουσιν ὁποῖοί τε ὄντες ἐτύγχανον καὶ ὅπως εὐανδρίας εἶχον καὶ γενναιότητος.

35. B 273a–274a, C 102b–103b: ταῦτα (ταύτῃ B) δὴ καὶ τὰ σώματα οἷς ὡς ὀργάνοις χρησάμενοι τῶν ψυχῶν τὸ γενναῖον καὶ ἀήττητον παράστημα ἐπεδείξαντο [i.e., οἱ ἅγιοι]· οὐ γὰρ ἄν τις εἴποι ὡς σωμάτων δίχα διήθλησαν . . . εἰ γοῦν τῶν ἁγίων τὰς πράξεις ἀποσεμνύνειν προῄρησο, ἐτίμησας ἄν καὶ τὰ σώματα . . . ἔτι καὶ τὰ τούτων ἐκτυπώματα διὰ χρωμάτων τε καὶ ὡς ἑτέρως γραφόμενα . . . οὐ γὰρ ἀκοῆς ὄψις δευτέρα ἢ ἀσθενεστέρα οὐδὲ ἀμυδρότερον τῶν οἰκείων αἰσθητῶν ἀντιλαμβάνεται . . . ἴσμεν γὰρ δήπου ἅπαντες ὅτι γε ὄψις τῶν αἰσθητηρίων τὸ τιμιώτατον καὶ ἀναγκαιότατον τρανέστερόν τε καὶ ὀξυωπέστερον (τρανεστέραν τε καὶ ὀξυωπεστέραν?) τῶν ὑποπιπτόντων αἰσθήσει σχοίη ἄν τὴν ἀντίληψιν (τῶν ὑποπιπτόντων . . . ἀντίληψιν om B)· καὶ γὰρ τὸ ἀκουστὸν ὑπὸ τοῦ ὁρατοῦ πέφυκε φθάνεσθαι, καὶ θᾶττον ἐφελκύσεται τῶν ἄλλων ἡ ὅρασις ὅσῳ καὶ μᾶλλον τὸ ἐπαγωγὸν ἔχει. On the hierarchy of the senses, see above, note 21.

36. Origen, *Contra Celsum* VIII 17–18 (ed. Kötschau, vol. II, pp. 234 ff.). ἀγάλματα δὲ καὶ πρέποντα θεῷ ἀναθήματα, οὐχ ὑπὸ βαναύσων τεχνιτῶν κατεσκευασμένα ἀλλ' ὑπὸ λόγου θεοῦ τρανούμενα καὶ μορφούμενα ἐν ἡμῖν, αἱ ἀρεταί, μιμήματα τυγχάνουσι τοῦ πρωτοτόκου "πάσης κτίσεως," ἐν ᾧ ἐστι δικαιοσύνης καὶ σωφροσύνης καὶ ἀνδρείας καὶ σοφίας καὶ εὐσεβείας καὶ τῶν λοιπῶν ἀρετῶν παραδείγματα. ἐν πᾶσιν οὖν ἐστι, τοῖς κατὰ τὸν θεῖον λόγον σωφροσύνην ἑαυτοῖς κατασκευάσασι καὶ δικαιοσύνην καὶ ἀνδρείαν καὶ σοφίαν καὶ εὐσέβειαν καὶ τῶν λοιπῶν ἀρετῶν τὰ κατασκευάσματα, ἀγάλματα . . . καὶ ἐν ἑκάστῳ δὲ τῶν κατὰ δύναμιν ἐκεῖνον καὶ ἐν τούτῳ μιμησαμένοις ἐστὶν ἄγαλμα τὸ "κατ' εἰκόνα τοῦ κτίσαντος," ὅπερ κατασκευάζουσι τῷ ἐνορᾶν θεῷ καθαρᾷ καρδίᾳ, "μιμηταὶ" γενόμενοι "τοῦ θεοῦ." καὶ ἀπαξαπλῶς πάντες Χριστιανοὶ ὁποίους εἴπομεν βωμοὺς καὶ ὁποῖα παρεστήσαμεν ἀγάλματα πειρῶνται ἱδρύεσθαι, οὐκ ἄψυχα καὶ ἀναίσθητα οὐδὲ δαιμόνων λίχνων ἐφεδρευόντων τοῖς ἀψύχοις δεκτικὰ ἀλλὰ πνεύματος θεοῦ, τοῖς εἰρημένοις ἀγάλμασι τῆς ἀρετῆς καὶ τῷ "κατ' εἰκόνα τοῦ κτίσαντος" ὡς οἰκείοις ἐπιδημοῦντος· οὕτω δὲ καὶ τὸ πνεῦμα τοῦ Χριστοῦ τοῖς, ἵν' οὕτως ὀνομάσω, συμμόρφοις ἐφιζάνει. Note that even the quotation from Rom. VIII 29 (above, note 22) occurs in Origen. See Jean Daniélou, *Origène* (Paris, 1948) 48, and George Florovsky, "Origen, Eusebius and the Iconoclastic Controversy," *Church History* XIX (1950) 3–22, esp. 17.

37. Gregory of Nyssa, *De perfectione*, ed. W. Jaeger (Leiden, 1952) p. 177 f. = *P.G.* XLVI, 256 A–B: εἰ δένδρῳ τις ἢ πέτρᾳ προσηγορίαν ἀνθρώπου χαρίσαιτο, ἆρα ἄνθρωπος ἔσται διὰ τὴν κλῆσιν ἢ τὸ φυτὸν ἢ ὁ λίθος; οὐκ ἔστι ταῦτα, ἀλλὰ χρὴ πρῶτον εἶναι ἄνθρωπον, εἶθ' οὕτως ὀνομασθῆναι τῇ προσηγορίᾳ τῆς φύσεως. οὐδὲ γὰρ ἐπὶ τῶν ὁμοιωμάτων αἱ κλήσεις τὸ κύριον ἔχουσι, ὡς εἴ τις ἄνθρωπον λέγοι τὸν ἀνδριάντα ἢ ἵππον τὸ μίμημα, ἀλλ' εἰ μέλλοι τι κυρίως καὶ ἀψευδῶς ὀνομάζεσθαι, ἀληθῆ δείξει πάντως τὴν προσηγορίαν ἡ φύσις. ἡ δὲ ἀναδεξαμένη τὴν μίμησιν ὕλη, ὅπερ ἄν οὖσα τύχῃ, τοῦτο καὶ ὀνομάζεται, χαλκὸς ἢ λίθος ἢ τι τοιοῦτον ἕτερον ᾧ ἐπέβαλεν ἡ τέχνη τὸ εἶδος πρὸς τὸ δοκοῦν σχηματίσασα. (This text was referred to by Professor Werner Jaeger, of Harvard University, in the discussion following the reading of my paper.)

38. One quotation of the florilegium of 815, that attributed to Leontius (frg. 19), even seems to imply that Christ looked different at different times. This was indeed a characteristic doctrine of Origen (see E. von Dobschütz, *Christusbilder*, Texte und Untersuchungen zur Geschichte der altchristlichen Literatur, N.F. III [1899] 105 °) which was connected with his theology of the Incarnation. See also Erik Peterson, "Einige Bemerkungen zum Hamburger Papyrus — Fragment der Acta Pauli," *Vigiliae Christianae* II (1949) 142–162, esp. 157 ff. The Persian tradition where the infant Jesus appeared to each of the Magi as being of his own age before he appeared to the three of them together as a baby thirteen days old (see L. Olschki, "The Wise Men of the East in Oriental Traditions," *University of California Publications in Semitic Philology* XI [1951] 375–395, esp. 381–386) is a somewhat special case.

39.   For Florovsky's study, see above, note 36. Page 12: ". . . do we have here one of the original sources of the Iconoclastic inspiration, at least in its later theological form? Should we not explain the obvious popularity of the Iconoclastic bias among the learned bishops and clergy . . . on the basis of their Origenist leaning?"

40.   Ostrogorsky, *Studien*, 24–29.

41.   Clement of Alexandria, *Strom.*, VII 5 (vol. III, pp. 21 f. Stählin): εἴη δ'ἂν οὗτος ὁ γνωστικὸς ὁ πολλοῦ ἄξιος ὁ τίμιος τῷ θεῷ, ἐν ᾧ ὁ θεὸς ἐνίδρευται, τουτέστιν ἡ περὶ τοῦ θεοῦ γνῶσις καθιέρωται. ἐνταῦθα καὶ τὸ ἀπεικόνισμα εὕροιμεν ἄν, τὸ θεῖον καὶ ἅγιον ἄγαλμα, ἐν τῇ δικαίᾳ ψυχῇ, ὅταν μακαρία μὲν αὐτὴ τυγχάνῃ, ἅτε προκεκαθαρμένη, μακάρια δὲ διαπραττομένη ἔργα. ἐνταῦθα καὶ τὸ ἐνίδρυτον καὶ ἐνιδρυόμενον, τὸ μὲν ἐπὶ τῶν ἤδη γνωστικῶν, τὸ δὲ ἐπὶ τῶν οἵων τε γενέσθαι, κἂν μηδέπω ὦσιν ἄξιοι ἀναδέξασθαι ἐπιστήμην θεοῦ. πᾶν γὰρ τὸ μέλλον πιστεύειν πιστὸν ἤδη τῷ θεῷ καὶ καθιδρυμένον εἰς τιμὴν ἄγαλμα ἐνάρετον, ἀνακείμενον θεῷ. Plotinus, *Enneades*, I, VI, 9 (ed. R. Volkmann, vol. I, p. 95): πῶς ἂν οὖν ἴδοις ψυχὴν ἀγαθὴν οἷον τὸ κάλλος ἔχει; ἄναγε ἐπὶ σαυτὸν καὶ ἰδέ· κἂν μήπω σαυτὸν ἴδῃς καλόν, οἷα ποιητὴς ἀγάλματος, ὃ δεῖ καλὸν γενέσθαι, τὸ μὲν ἀφαιρεῖ, τὸ δὲ ἀπέξεσε, τὸ δὲ λεῖον, τὸ δὲ καθαρὸν ἐποίησεν, ἕως ἔδειξε καλὸν ἐπὶ τῷ ἀγάλματι πρόσωπον, οὕτω καὶ σὺ ἀφαίρει ὅσα περιττὰ καὶ ἀπεύθυνε ὅσα σκολιά, ὅσα σκοτεινὰ καθαίρων ἐργάζου εἶναι λαμπρὰ καὶ μὴ παύσῃ τεκταίνων τὸ σὸν ἄγαλμα, ἕως ἂν ἐκλάμψῃ σοι τῆς ἀρετῆς ἡ θεοειδὴς ἀγλαΐα, ἕως ἂν ἴδῃς σωφροσύνην ἐν ἁγνῷ βεβῶσαν βάθρῳ (quoted by Daniélou, *Origène*, 49). For Porphyry, see E. Norden, *Agnostos Theos*, ed. 2 (Berlin and Leipzig, 1913) 345 (quoting a text from Hierocles which seems to be based on Porphyry).

42.   The question arises: Did the doctrine of the Council of St. Sophia prevail down to the end of official iconoclasm in 843? There are some indications that this was not so. If this doctrine was accepted and if therefore the saintly soul was the true image of Christ, then the iconoclasts of St. Sophia and their followers should not have objected to the cult of the saints. Yet an important hagiographical text, which has received far too little attention, the *Vita St. Theophanis* by Methodius Patriarch of Constantinople (ed. V. V. Latyshev, *Zapiski Rossiiskoi Akademii Nauk*, VIIIᵉ série, XIII, 4, Petrograd, 1918), which was written under Theophilus (*ibid.*, p. ix), contains a lengthy and highly interesting dissertation on the effective inter-cession of the saints (chs. XXIX–XXXII, pp. 32–35) and the explicit information that it is directed against *contemporary* opponents (ch. XXXII, p. 34, line 18: αἰσχυνέσθωσαν ἐντεῦθεν οἱ τὰς πρεσβείας τῶν ἁγίων οὐκ ἐκδεχόμενοι κτλ.). It is probable, therefore, that just as under Constantine V (Ostrogorsky, *Studien*, 29–40), at least some iconoclasts under Theophilus objected not only to the images but also to the cult of the saints. Now V. Grumel, "Recherches récentes sur l'iconoclasme," *Echos d'Orient* XXIX (1930) 99, shows that a third Iconoclastic Council was held at Blachernae under Theophilus and that it once again (above, p. 41) called the Eucharist the true image of Christ. It is possible that under Theophilus official iconoclasm abandoned the position of the Council of St. Sophia (815) and returned to the views of Constantine V, even accepting, unlike the Council of Hiereia (754), his hostility to the cult of the saints.

APPENDIX

DECRETUM CONCILII ICONOMACHI SUB LEONE V ARMENO CONSTANTINOPOLI IN ECCLESIA
SANCTAE SOPHIAE HABITI, CUM FLORILEGIO IN CALCE DECRETI ADIECTO.

Libri:
B = *Paris. Graecus* 1250, saec. XIII (XIV?), fols. 173a–332a.
C = *Paris. Coislinianus* 93, saec. XV (XII?), fols. 1a–159a.°

Editiones Impressae:
Serr = D. Serruys, "Les Actes du concile iconoclaste de l'an 815," Ecole Française de
Rome, *Mélanges d'archéologie et d'histoire*, XXIII (1903) 345–351.
Ostr = Georg Ostrogorsky, *Studien zur Geschichte des byzantinischen Bilderstreites*,
Historische Untersuchungen 5 (Breslau, 1925) 48–51.

1. (B 176a–b). (ἐν τούτῳ γοῦν τῷ δοκοῦντι Ὅρῳ εὐθὺς μὲν καὶ ἐκ προοιμίων τὴν ἀσέβειαν
οὐ παρρησιάζονται, κατασχηματίζονται δὲ τὴν εὐσέβειαν καὶ καταχρωννύουσί πως τοὺς ἑαυτῶν λόγους
ἐπειδὴ τοῦτο φίλον καὶ σύνηθες τοῖς αἱρετίζουσιν· οὕτω γὰρ καὶ Ἀρειανοῖς καὶ Εὐνομιανοῖς καὶ ἄλλοις
αἱρεσιώταις γινόμενον ἔγνωμεν· οὓς μιμούμενοι ὥσπερ δὴ κοινωνοῦντες τῇ ἐκείνων κακοδοξίᾳ καὶ αὐτοὶ
ἐπ᾽ ἀλλοτρίοις καλοῖς ἐγκαλλωπίζονται· τὸ γὰρ φυσικὸν τῆς ἀληθείας κάλλος οὐκ ἔχοντες ὀθνείαις
τισὶ καὶ ξέναις σοφιζόμενοι χρῶνται μορφαῖς. . . . μετὰ γὰρ δὴ ταῦτα . . . τὰ τῆς γνώμης
παραγυμνοῦσι κνήματα. . .). om Serr Ostr

2. (B 176b–177a). (ἄγουσι τοιγαροῦν εἰς μέσους τὸν Λέοντα ἐκεῖνον . . . τὸν ἐκ τῶν
Ἰσαύρων τῶν δυσωνύμων ὁρμώμενον . . . , ἔτι μὴν καὶ τὸν ἐκείνου υἱὸν Κωνσταντῖνον. . . . περὶ μὲν
οὖν τούτων εἰκαιομυθοῦντες γράφουσι τοιαῦτα ὅτι) οὗτοι [1] τὴν εὐσέβειαν τῆς ὀρθοδόξου πίστεως
ἀσφάλειαν βίου ἡγησάμενοι τὴν τιμὴν τοῦ δι᾽ ὃν τὸ βασιλεύειν ἔλαβον ἐζήτησαν καὶ πολυάνθρωπον
πνευματικῶν πατέρων [2] καὶ θεοφιλῶν ἐπισκόπων ἀθροίσαντες σύνοδον

> [1] auctor est Nicephorus verbum οὗτοι de Leone III et Constantino V dictum
> esse, sed cum concilium in Hiereia (754) multos annos post excessum Leonis III
> (+ 741) habitum sit, puto synodum Sanctae Sophiae (815) revera de Constantino
> V et Leone IV locutam esse (vide frg. 16).
> [2] πατέρων om Ostr

3. (B 178a, C 15b) τὴν ἀκέφαλον καὶ ἀπαράδοτον, μᾶλλον δὲ εἰπεῖν ἄχρηστον ποίησιν καὶ
προσκύνησιν τῶν εἰκόνων κατέκριναν, τὴν ἐν πνεύματι καὶ ἀληθείᾳ λατρείαν [1] προτιμήσαντες,
> [1] Ev. Joh. IV 23.

4. (B 183a, C 6b) ὡς θεοῖς προσεληλυθέναι ταῖς εἰκόσιν αὐτοὺς ἀποφαινόμενοι. om Serr

5. (B 184a, C 7a, 11b) ἥτις σύνοδος κυρώσασα καὶ βεβαιώσασα τῶν ἁγίων πατέρων τὰ
θεόκλυτα δόγματα καὶ ταῖς ἁγίαις οἰκουμενικαῖς ἓξ [1] συνόδοις ἐπακολουθήσασα εὐαγεστάτους κανόνας
ἐξέθετο.
> [1] ἓξ ante οἰκουμενικαῖς coll C 7a, sed recto 11b.

> ° Codex C non est ex B descriptus, ut docebat Ostrogorsky, *Studien*, 47 (vide
> R. P. Blake, *Byzantion* XIV [1939] 14 adn. 1) sed ambo ex archetypo litteris
> uncialibus scripto fluxerunt (Paul Maas, *B.Z.* XXX [1929–30] 279).

6. (B 194a, C 19b) διὸ καὶ ἀκύμαντος οὐκ ἐν ὀλίγοις ἔτεσιν ἡ ἐκκλησία τοῦ Θεοῦ μεμένηκεν, εἰρηνικώτερον τὸ ὑπήκοον φυλαττομένη,[1]

[1] φυλαττόμενον libri: corr Serr

7. (B 196a, C 21b–22a) ἕως ἂν τὸ βασιλεύειν ἐξ ἀνδρῶν εἰς γυναῖκα μετέπεσε καὶ τῇ γυναικείᾳ ἀφελότητι ἡ ἐκκλησία τοῦ Θεοῦ ἐπημαίνετο [1]· ἀπερίσκεπτον γὰρ ἄθροισμα συναγείρασα ἀμαθεστάτοις ἐπισκόποις ἐπακολουθήσασα,

[1] ἐπημαίνετο libri: ἐποιμαίνετο Ostr

8. (B 206a, C 17a) τὸν ἀκατάληπτον Ὑιὸν καὶ Λόγον τοῦ Θεοῦ κατὰ τὴν σάρκωσιν δι᾽ ἀτίμου [1] ὕλης ζωγραφεῖν ἐδόγματισε,

[1] δι᾽ ἀτίμου Ostr: διὰ ἀτίμου libri (alterum ἀ- fort del C) Serr fort recto.

9. (B 207b–208a, C 62b–33a sic!) τήν τε παναγίαν Θεοτόκον καὶ τοὺς συμμόρφους αὐτοῦ [1] ἁγίους νεκραῖς χαρακτήρων ὄψεσιν ἀναστηλοῦν καὶ προσκυνεῖσθαι ἀπαραφυλάκτως ἐξέθετο, εἰς αὐτὸ τὸ καίριον δόγμα τῆς ἐκκλησίας προσκόψασα. καὶ τὴν λατρευτικὴν ἡμῶν προσκύνησιν ἐπιθολώσασα τὰ τῷ Θεῷ πρέποντα τῇ ἀψύχῳ ὕλῃ τῶν εἰκόνων προσάγεσθαι κατὰ τὸ δοκοῦν ἐβεβαίωσεν

[1] αὐτοῦ libri: αὐτῶν coniecit A. M. Desrousseaux apud Serr, sed vide Rom. VIII 29.

10. (B 208b, C 34a) καὶ ταύτας ἀφρόνως θείας χάριτος ἐμπλέους [1] εἰπεῖν κατετόλμησε, κηρῶν τε ἀφὰς καὶ θυμιαμάτων εὐωδίας ⟨προσενεγκοῦσα⟩ [2] σὺν προσκυνήσει βιαίᾳ τοὺς ἀφελεῖς [3] ἀπεπλάνησε

[1] ἐμπλέους libri: ἔμπλεως?
[2] προσενεγκοῦσα addidi: προσφέρουσα add Serr Ostr. vide frg. 15 προσενέγξεις.
[3] ἀσφάλεις C

11. (C 35a) εἰ μὴ Κύριος †ἡμῖν, (λέγοντες), συγκεκρότηκε† καὶ ναυαγοῦντα κόσμον. . . .[1] κατακλυσμὸν ἁμαρτίας ἠλέησε καὶ δεύτερον Νῶε τοῖς Χριστιανοῖς ἐχαρίσατο, ὃς καὶ τὴν καταιγίδα τῆς αἱρέσεως σὺν τῷ κέντρῳ τοῦ διαβόλου ἀμβλῦναι ἐσπούδασε. om Serr

[1] lacunam ante κατακλυσμὸν statui, quam ex refutatione Nicephori (supra, p. 53, adn. 11) supplere ausus non sum.

12. (B 210a, C 36a) (ἀλλὰ γὰρ τοῦ τηλικούτου βυθοῦ τῆς πλάνης ἀνατετραμμένου καὶ ἀνακεκαλυμμένου τινὰς ἐν μέσῳ φευκτὰς καὶ ἀπηχεστάτας φωνὰς κειμένας παραδραμόντες αὐτοὶ ἐπὶ τὰ ἐπόμενα ἄπιμεν· μετὰ γὰρ δὴ ταῦτα καὶ ἕπεσθαι αὐτοὺς καὶ ἀποδέχεσθαι τὰς ἱερὰς συνόδους καταφρυάττονται, προσεκτέον δὲ ὅτι ἐνταῦθα ὥσπερ ἐν καταλόγῳ τὰς ἐξ συνόδους ἀπαριθμούμενοι οὗτοι τῆς νῦν αὐτοὺς μαιευσαμένης ἑταιρικῆς φατρίας μνήμην οὐδόλως πεποίηνται . . .) om Serr Ostr

13. (B 210a–b, C 36a–b) (ἐν γοῦν τῷ καταλόγῳ τῶν συνόδων ἃς κατέκριναν αὗται [1] αἱρέσεις προάγοντες τοιάδε τινὰ προσεπιφέρουσιν·) ἀλλὰ ταύτας πάλιν τὰς αἱρέσεις οἱ ταῖς ἀψύχοις εἰκόσι τὴν προσκύνησιν δόντες [2] ἀφορμὴν τῆς πρὶν αὐτῶν ἀτοπίας ἐχαρίσαντο,[3] ἢ συμπεριγράφοντες τῇ εἰκόνι τὸν ἀπερίγραφον, ἢ τὴν σάρκα ἐκ τῆς θεότητος κατατέμνοντες, κακῷ τὸ κακὸν διορθούμενοι· ἀτόπημα γὰρ περιφεύγοντες ἀτοπήματι περιπίπτουσι.

[1] αὗται B: αὐταὶ C
[2] δόσαντες C
[3] nonne corruptum?

14. (B 222a, C 49a–b) ὅθεν ἡμεῖς τὸ ἰθὺ τοῦ [1] δόγματος ἐγκολπωσάμενοι τὴν αὐθαδῶς δογματισθεῖσαν ἄκυρον ποίησιν τῶν ψευδωνύμων εἰκόνων τῆς καθολικῆς ἐκκλησίας ἐξοστρακίζομεν,

[1] τὸ ἰθὺ τοῦ C: τοιούτου B

60

15. (B 225a–b, C 52a–b) οὐ κρίσει ἀκρίτῳ φερόμενοι, ἀλλὰ κρίσιν δικαίαν κατὰ τὴν ἀκρίτως ὑπὸ Ταρασσίου [1] ἐκφωνηθεῖσαν τῶν εἰκόνων προσκύνησιν ὁρίζοντες [2] ἀνατρέπομεν καὶ τὸν αὐτοῦ σύλλογον ἀθετοῦμεν ὡς ὑπερβάλλουσαν τιμὴν τοῖς χρώμασι χαρισάμενον, κατὰ τὸ πρόσθεν [3] εἰρημένον,[4] κηρῶν τε καὶ λύχνων ἀφάς, θυμιαμάτων προσενέ⟨γ⟩ξεις, ὡς ἔπος εἰπεῖν σέβασμα λατρείας.[5]

[1] Ταρασσίου C: Ταρασίου B
[2] lacunam post ὁρίζοντες statuit Ostr, sed ad ἀνατρέπομεν pertinet obiectum τὴν
. . . ποίησιν τῶν ψευδωνύμων εἰκόνων (frg. 14)
[3] cf. frg. 10
[4] κατὰ . . . εἰρημένον om Serr
[5] σεβασμαλατρείας libri Ostr: σέβασμα ⟨τὰ πάντα⟩ λατρείας Serr. intelligo reverentiam (σέβασμα = σέβασις) adorationis, sed displicet clausula.

16. (B 226b, C 53a) τὴν δὲ εὐαγῆ σύνοδον τὴν συγκροτηθεῖσαν ἐν Βλαχέρναις ἐν τῷ ναῷ τῆς παναχράντου Παρθένου ἐπὶ τῶν πάλαι εὐσεβῶν βασιλέων Κωνσταντίνου καὶ Λέοντος ἀσπασίως ἀποδεχόμενοι ὡς ἐκ πατρικῶν δογμάτων ὀχυρωθεῖσαν ἀκαινοτομητὰ τὰ ἐν αὐτῇ ἐμφερόμενα φυλάττοντες ἀπροσκύνητόν τε καὶ ἄχρηστον τὴν τῶν εἰκόνων ποίησιν ὁρίζομεν, εἴδωλα δὲ ταύτας εἰπεῖν φεισάμενοι· ἔστι γὰρ καὶ [1] κακοῦ πρὸς κακὸν ἡ διάκρισις.

[1] και sscr C, om libri infra (B 234a, C 64a).

⟨ΧΡΗΣΕΙΣ⟩ [1]
[1] ΧΡΗCΕΙC addidi ex B 237a: ἀρχὴ τῆς τῶν χρήσεων ἀνατροπῆς, C 66b (in marg): ἀρχὴ τῶν χρήσεων.

17. (B 236b, C 66b–67a) (πρωτίστην καὶ κρατίστην κατὰ εἰδώλων προτιθέασι χρῆσιν, ὡς ἐξ ἀποστολικῶν καταρχόμενοι διατάξεων, φάσκοντες ὅτι ἀρχῆθεν αὐτῶν τῶν ἀποστόλων ἐστὶν ἡ διάταξις πρὸς τὸν τῇ ποικιλίᾳ καὶ βαφῇ τῶν χρωμάτων χρώμενον αὕτη [1].) Τοίνυν ἔσο τὸν [2] δάκτυλον ῥυθμίζων [3] ἐπὶ τῇ τοῦ σταυροῦ γραφῇ. φεῦγε τὸν ἄκοσμον κόσμον ἵνα μὴ τὸν τῆς παρακοῆς ἐνδύσῃ δερματινὸν χιτῶνα.[4]

[1] αὕτη scripsi: αὐτῇ libri
[2] ἔσο τὸν B: ἔσονται C
[3] ῥυθμίζοντες (corr) C
[4] Gen. III 21.

18. (B 241b, C 71b) (δεύτερον γὰρ παράγουσιν Ἀστέριον ἐπίσκοπον Ἀμασείας ἐπιγραφόμενον ἐν τῷ πεποιημένῳ αὐτῷ Εἰς τὸν πλούσιον καὶ τὸν Λάζαρον λόγῳ φάσκοντα οὕτως·) Μὴ γράφε τὸν Χριστόν· ἀρκεῖ γὰρ αὐτῷ ἡ μία τῆς ἐνσωματώσεως ταπεινοφροσύνη ἣν αὐθαιρέτως δι' ἡμᾶς κατεδέξατο· ἐπὶ δὲ τῆς ψυχῆς σου βαστάζων νοητῶς τὸν ἀσώματον Λόγον περίφερε. P.G. XL 168 B.

19. (B 246a–b, C 76b) (προάγουσι γὰρ μετὰ ταῦτα Λεοντίου τινὸς λόγον περιέχοντα οὕτως [1].) Ἐν δὲ τῷ [2] προσεύχεσθαι αὐτὸν ἐγένετο τὸ εἶδος τοῦ προσώπου αὐτοῦ ὡς ὁ ἥλιος καὶ ὁ ἱματισμὸς αὐτοῦ λαμπρῶς ἐξαστράπτων.[3] οἷς ἐπιφέρει [4] λέγων· καλῶς οἱ χρωματόγραφοι ζωγράφοι μίαν εἰκόνα τοῦ Κυρίου γράφειν οὐ μεμαθήκασιν. ποίαν γὰρ εἰκόνα ἰσχύουσι γράψαι; τὴν ἐν τῷ βαπτίσματι ἣν ὁ Ἰορδάνης ἰδὼν ἔφριξεν; ἀλλὰ τὴν ἐν τῷ ὄρει ἣν οὐχ ὑπήνεγκαν κατανοῆσαι Πέτρος καὶ Ἰάκωβος καὶ Ἰωάννης; ἀλλὰ τὴν ἐν τῷ σταυρῷ ἣν ὁ ἥλιος κατανοήσας ἐσκοτίσθη; ἀλλὰ τὴν ἐν τῷ τάφῳ ἣν κατανοῆσαι αἱ κάτω δυνάμεις ἔφριξαν; ἀλλὰ τὴν ἐν τῇ ἀναστάσει ἣν ὅτε [5] οἱ μαθηταὶ θεασάμενοι οὐ συνῆκαν; ἐκπλήττει με σφόδρα εἰς ἕκαστος τῶν [6] λεγόντων ὅτι ἐγὼ τὸ ὁμοιωσίδιον [7] τοῦ Κυρίου κέκτημαι. θέλεις τὸ ὁμοιωσίδιον [7] αὐτοῦ κτήσασθαι; [8] ἐν τῇ ψυχῇ σου αὐτὸ κτῆσαι· εἰκόνι γὰρ ἀμήχανον γραφῆναι τὸν Κύριον.

[1] Λεοντίου Νεαπόλεως τῆς Κύπρου in marg C
[2] τῷ B: τὸ C
[3] Ev. Luc. IX 28.
[4] ἐπιφέρει C: ἐπιφέροι ? B

[5] ὅτε non intelligo
[6] τῶν B: om C
[7] ὁμοιωσίδιον: ὁμοιωσείδιον B ὁμοιωσίδην C
[8] κτίσασθαι C

20. (B 254b, C 84b) (ἐντεῦθεν ἐφ' ἑτέραν χρῆσιν οἱ τῆς Ἰουδαϊκῆς μοίρας ἵενται Θεοδότου τοῦ ἐκ Γαλατίας ἐπιγραφομένην τοὔνομα ἔχουσαν ὧδε· [1]) Τὰς τῶν ἁγίων ἰδέας [2] οὐκ ἐν εἰκόσιν ἐξ ὑλικῶν [3] χρωμάτων διαμορφοῦν παρειλήφαμεν, ἀλλὰ τὰς τούτων ἀρετὰς διὰ τῶν ἐν γραφαῖς περὶ αὐτῶν δηλουμένων οἷόν τινας ἐμψύχους εἰκόνας ἀναμάττεσθαι δεδιδάγμεθα, ἐκ τούτου πρὸς τὸν ὅμοιον αὐτοῖς διεγειρόμενοι ζῆλον. ἐπεὶ εἰπάτωσαν οἱ τὰς τοιάσδε ἀναστηλοῦντες μορφὰς ποίας ἄρα ἐκ τούτων [4] καταπολαύοιεν ὠφελείας· ἢ ἐν ποίᾳ διὰ τῆς τούτων ἀναμνήσεως ἀνάγονται [5] πνευματικῇ θεωρίᾳ· ἀλλ' εὔδηλον ὡς ματαία ἡ τοιαύτη ἐπίνοια καὶ διαβολικῆς μεθοδείας εὕρημα. Vide Mansi XIII 309 E.

[1] Θεοδότου ἐπισκόπου Ἀγκύρας in marg C
[2] εἰδέας C
[3] ἐξ ὑλικῶν: ἐκ ξυλικῶν C
[4] ἐκ τούτων sscr C
[5] ἀνάγονται B

21. (B 266a, C 96a) (προστιθέασι γὰρ τοῖς προλαβοῦσι Βασίλειόν τινα Σελευκείας ἀρχιερέα παραπλασάμενοι τὰ αὐτὰ τοῖς τοῦ πεποιημένου Θεοδότου κατὰ τῶν ἁγίων κενοφωνοῦντα. ἔχει δὲ τὰ προφερόμενα ὧδε· [1]). Τοὺς ἐν ἀρετῇ γοῦν βεβιωκότας οὐ διὰ τῆς ἐν χρώμασι τεχνουργικῆς ἐπιστήμης τιμᾶν δεῖ, ὅπερ ἐστὶν ἑλληνικῆς μυθοποιΐας ἀνάπλασμα, ἀλλὰ διὰ τῆς γραφικῆς θεωρίας τούτους εἰς ἀνάμνησιν ἕλκειν καὶ μιμεῖσθαι τὸν ζῆλον. τίς [2] γὰρ ἂν γένοιτο τοῖς ἀνθρώποις ἐκ τῆς τῶν τοιῶνδε μορφωμάτων κακοτεχνίας εὐεργεσία, ἢ τί ἔχοι θεοφιλές τε καὶ τίμιον ἡ τῶν ἀψύχων ὁμοιωμάτων περιεργία;

[1] Βασιλείου ἐπισκόπου Σελευκείας in marg C
[2] τῆς C

22. (B 267b, C 97a–b) (μετὰ δὴ ταῦτα παρατιθέασιν Ἀμφιλοχίου τοῦ ἐξ Ἰκονίου λόγους ἐκ τοῦ πεποιημένου αὐτῷ Ἐγκωμίου εἰς τὸν μέγαν Βασίλειον, ἐν οἷς τὰ [1] τοιαῦτα λέγεται [2].) Οἱ ἅγιοι οὐ προσδέονται τῶν διὰ γραμμάτων ἡμῶν ἐγκωμίων, ἐγγεγραμμένοι ἤδη τῷ βιβλίῳ τῶν ζώντων, ὧν ἡ δικαιοσύνη παρὰ τῷ [3] Θεῷ πεφύλακται. ἡμεῖς δὲ χρῄζομεν τῶν διὰ μέλανος γραμμάτων ὅπως ὁ νοῦς ἡμῶν διαγράφῃ τὴν τούτων μνήμην εἰς κοινὴν ὠφέλειαν καὶ ὦμεν ἀκροαταὶ τούτων, ὅταν διὰ τῆς ἀναγνώσεως τῇ ἀκοῇ παραπέμπωμεν [4]· ὡς γὰρ ἐκ μεγάλου θησαυροῦ πρὸς οἰκονομίαν τὰς εὐεργεσίας λαμβάνομεν καὶ πληροῦμεν ἡμῶν τὰ ὑστερήματα ταῖς τούτων πολιτείαις (οὐ γὰρ πληροῦται ἀκοὴ δι' ἐπιθυμίας ἔχουσα ἀκοῦσαι τὴν τούτων τελείωσιν). ἀλλ' οὐ χρώμασι τοῖς πίναξι τὰ σαρκικὰ αὐτῶν πρόσωπα ἐπιμελὲς ἡμῖν ἐκτυποῦν ὅτι οὐ χρῄζομεν τούτων, ἀλλὰ τὴν τούτων ἄθλησιν ἐκμιμούμενοι καὶ τὰς ἀγαθὰς πράξεις δευτεροῦμεν καὶ τὴν πρὸς Θεὸν ἀγάπην διαγράφομεν καί ἐσμεν μιμηταὶ τῶν ἀγαθῶν πράξεων αὐτῶν, ἐντιθέντες τῇ γραφῇ τὰς τούτων μνήμας μετὰ θάνατον πρὸς τοὺς ἀκούοντας ὅπως γνῶσι τὴν ἐν κόσμῳ αὐτῶν ἀναστροφήν.

Graece non extant, sed Syriace habes, vide K. V. Zetterstéen, "Eine Homilie des Amphilochius von Iconium über Basilius von Cäsarea," *Oriens Christianus* XXXI (1934) 68 sq. Vide Mansi XIII 301D.

[1] τὰ om C
[2] Ἀμφιλοχίου ἐπισκόπου τοῦ Ἰκονίου ἐκ τοῦ ἐγκωμίου τοῦ εἰς τὸν ἅγιον Βασίλειον in marg C
[3] τῷ om B
[4] παραπέμπομεν C

23. (B 275a, C 105b) (ἑξῆς δὲ παραφέρουσι φωνὰς τοῦ μεγάλου ὥς φασι Βασιλείου ἐκ τοῦ περὶ τῆς τοῦ ἀνθρώπου γενέσεως Εἰς τὸ κατ' εἰκόνα λόγου πρώτου διαγορευούσας [1] τοιάδε [2].) Εἰ μὴ τὴν τοῦ γενέσθαι καθ' ὁμοίωσιν δύναμιν ἡμῖν ἐχαρίσατο, οὐκ ἂν τῇ ἑαυτῶν ἐξουσίᾳ τὴν πρὸς Θεὸν ὁμοίωσιν ἐδεξάμεθα· νῦν δὲ δυνάμει ἡμᾶς ἐποίησεν ὁμοιωτικοὺς Θεῷ, δύναμιν δὲ δοὺς πρὸς τὸ ὁμοιοῦσθαι Θεῷ ἀφῆκεν ἡμᾶς ἐργάτας εἶναι τῆς πρὸς Θεὸν ὁμοιώσεως ἵνα τέλειος ᾖ [3] τῆς ἐργασίας ὁ

μισθός, ἵνα μὴ ὥσπερ εἰκόνες ὦμεν παρὰ ζωγράφου γενόμεναι εἰκῇ καὶ μάτην κείμεναι· ὅταν γὰρ ἀκριβῶς μεμορφωμένην εἰκόνα ἴδῃς τῇ ποικιλίᾳ τῶν χρωμάτων, οὐ τὴν εἰκόνα ἐπαινεῖς, ἀλλὰ τὸν ζωγράφον θαυμάζεις.[4]

P.G. XLIV, 273 A–B.

    [1] διαγορεύσας C
    [2] τοῦ μεγάλου Βασιλείου ἐκ τῆς Ἑξαημέρου in marg C
    [3] τέλιος εἰ C
    [4] θαυμάζῃς B

24. (Β 277b–278a, C 107b–108a) (ἑπόμενα τούτοις τὸν ἱερὸν Γρηγόριον τὸν Νυσσαέων[1] ἱεράρχην παρακομίζουσιν ὡς οἴονται διδάσκοντα οὕτως[2].) Μηκέτι τὴν σωματώδη καὶ δουλικὴν μορφὴν ἐν τῇ σεαυτοῦ πίστει ἀνατυπώσῃ, ἀλλὰ τὸν ἐν τῇ δόξῃ τοῦ Πατρὸς ὄντα καὶ ἐν μορφῇ Θεοῦ ὑπάρχοντα καὶ Θεὸν ὄντα Λόγον, τοῦτον προσκύνει, καὶ μὴ τὴν τοῦ δούλου μορφήν.

    [1] νυσαέων C
    [2] Γρηγορίου ἐπισκόπου Νύσης in marg C

25. (Β 282b, C 112b) (ἐπὶ δὲ τὰ ἑπόμενα πρόϊμεν ἐν οἷς ἔκκειται τοῦ θεηγόρου Γρηγορίου ἐκ τῶν Ἐπῶν αὐτοῦ ῥῆσις ἔχουσα τόνδε τὸν τρόπον[1].) Ὕβρις πίστιν ἔχειν χρώμασι, μὴ ἐν καρδίᾳ. ἡ μὲν γὰρ ἐν χρώμασιν εὐχερῶς ἐκπλύνεται, ἡ δὲ ἐν τῷ βάθει τοῦ νοός, ἐκείνη μοι προσφιλής[2].).
Carmina Moralia 31, 39 sq. (P.G. XXXVII 913), vide Mansi XIII 297 A–B.

    [1] Γρηγορίου τοῦ Θεολόγου ἐκ τῶν Ἐπῶν in marg C
    [2] προσφιλεῖς C

26. (Β 284b, C 114a–b) (ἐντεῦθεν ἐπ' ἄλλην ματαιοπονίαν μεταρρυθμίζονται φάσκοντες·) Ἰωάννης δὲ ὁ Χρυσόστομος ἐν τῷ εἰς Ῥωμανὸν τὸν μάρτυρα.[1] Μὴ γὰρ τοίχοις ὁ Χριστὸς περιγράφεται, μὴ γὰρ ὀφθαλμοῖς ὁ ἡμέτερος δεσπότης ὁρᾶται. ὁ ἐμὸς δεσπότης, μᾶλλον δὲ ὁ τῶν ὅλων δεσπότης Χριστὸς οὐρανὸν οἰκεῖ καὶ κόσμον ἡνιοχεῖ, καὶ θυσία τούτῳ ψυχὴ πρὸς αὐτὸν ἀνανεύουσα, καὶ μία τούτῳ τροφὴ τῶν πιστευόντων ἡ σωτηρία.
Vide P.G. L, 616.

    [1] τοῦ Χρυσοστόμου ἐκ τοῦ μάρτυρος Ῥωμανοῦ ἐγκωμίου in marg C

27. (Β 286b, C 116b) (τοῖς προηγουμένοις τὰ ἑπόμενα καὶ παρ' αὐτοῖς ἐκτεθέντα τοιαῦτα·) Καὶ πάλιν ὁ αὐτός, (φασίν), ἐν τῷ λόγῳ αὐτοῦ τῷ Εἰς τὸν Ἀβραὰμ φάσκει·[1] οἱ δὲ τρεῖς ἄγγελοι ὅτι ἦλθον πρὸς τὸν Ἀβραὰμ καὶ ταῦτα ἐποίησαν ὑπὸ Ἑλλήνων ἀκόντων μαρτυροῦνται. οἱ γὰρ τὴν τῶν[2] Παλαιστινῶν οἰκοῦντες γῆν καὶ εἰκόνας γράφοντες τῶν[3] σεβασμάτων αὐτῶν τρεῖς γράφουσιν ἀγγέλους καὶ τὸν Ἀβραάμ, μετ' αὐτῶν[4] καὶ τὴν Σάρραν καὶ μόσχον καὶ ἄλευρον καὶ πάντα ὅσα λέγει ἡ Γραφὴ διὰ μέλανος λέγουσιν ἐκεῖνοι δι' ἀγαλμάτων. ταῦτα δὲ εἴρηται ἵνα οὐ τοῖς πιστοῖς δι' ἑλληνικῶν γίνηται ἡ πίστις· ἡμεῖς γὰρ παρὰ τῶν ἔξωθεν οὐ δεχόμεθα τὰς ἀποδείξεις.

    [1] τοῦ αὐτοῦ ἐκ τοῦ εἰς τὸν Ἀβραὰμ λόγου in marg C
    [2] τῶν om B
    [3] τῶν om C
    [4] verba τρεῖς. . . . αὐτῶν om, in marg add (sed ἀγγέλους) C

28. (Β 290b, C 118a) (ἔτι φασὶν ὅτι·) Εἶθ' οὕτως καὶ ἐν ἑτέρῳ λόγῳ τῷ Εἰς τὸν δεσμοφύλακα ἐπιγραφομένῳ λέγει·[1] εἰ γὰρ εἰκόνα τις ἄψυχον ἀναθεὶς παιδὸς ἢ φίλου ἢ συγγενοῦς νομίζει παρεῖναι ἐκεῖνον τὸν ἀπελθόντα καὶ διὰ τῆς εἰκόνος αὐτὸν φαντάζεται τῆς ἀψύχου, πολλῷ μᾶλλον ἡμεῖς διὰ τῶν γραφῶν τῆς τῶν ἁγίων ἀπολαύομεν παρουσίας, οὐχὶ τῶν σωμάτων αὐτῶν τὰς εἰκόνας ἔχοντες ἀλλὰ τῶν ψυχῶν· τὰ γὰρ παρ' αὐτῶν εἰρημένα τῶν ψυχῶν αὐτῶν εἰκόνες εἰσίν.
Vide Mansi XIII 300A.

    [1] τοῦ αὐτοῦ ἐκ τοῦ εἰς τὸν δεσμοφύλακα in marg C

29. (B 293b–294b, C 121a–b) (κατοκνήσειέ τις τάχα τοῖς προσαπαντῶσιν ἑξῆς
ἐπιβάλλειν. . . . ἔχει δὲ τὰ παρὰ τῶν ὑπεναντίων[1] ῥαδιουργηθέντα οὕτως[2]) Νείλου ἀσκητοῦ
πρὸς Ὀλυμπιόδωρον ἔπαρχον.[3] νηπιῶδες καὶ βρεφοπρεπὲς ἡ τοιαύτη ἐρώτησις. περὶ πλανήσεως τῶν
ὀφθαλμῶν τοῦτο γινόμενον, ἀνδρὸς δὲ φρονίμου τοῦτο μακρὰν ἀπέχει· ἐν γὰρ τῷ ἱερατείῳ κατὰ τὸ
πρόσταγμα τῆς ἐκκλησιαστικῆς παραδόσεως σταυρὸν ἐγχαράξας ἀρκέσθητι, δι' οὗ σταυροῦ ἐσώθη
πᾶν τὸ ἀνθρώπινον γένος, καὶ τὸ λοιπὸν τοῦ οἴκου λεύκανον.
Vide P.G. LXXIX, 577 D.

[1] ἐναντίων C
[2] Νείλου ἀσκητοῦ ἐκ τῆς ἐπιστολῆς πρὸς Ὀλυμπιόδωρον ἔπαρχον in marg C
[3] verba Νείλου . . . ἔπαρχον om C

30.[1] (B 295b, C 122b–123a) (καὶ τελευταίας τῆς ἐπιτεχνηθείσης[2] αὐτοῖς τερατείας οἰονεὶ
σφραγῖδα ἐπιτιθέντες συμπλάσσουσι χρήσεις, εἰς μὲν Ἐπιφάνιον τὸν θεοφόρον τὸν τῆς Κυπρίων κατὰ
τὴν ἱερωσύνην ἐξηγησάμενον ψευδῶς καὶ ἀλλοκότως ἀναφέροντες. . .)

[1] Hic invenies locos Epiphanio adscriptos sicut a concilio in ecclesia Sanctae
Sophiae anno 815 habito adlati sunt. saepius autem difficillimum erat discernere
utrum Nicephorus disiecta membra Epiphanii prompserit e Definitione concilii
an ex ipsis operibus Epiphanio adscriptis, quae se praesto habuisse saepe asserit.
ubi verba facit Nicephorus de opere quod Κατὰ τῶν ἐπιτηδευόντων κτλ. inscribitur
(infra frg. 30 B), se adferre dicit, ut videtur, ab Iconomachis omissa
(Hollii frga. 12–15, Ostrogorskii frga. 15–18). de locis ex Epistula ad Theodosium
ipsa a Nicephoro excerptis, vide infra ad frg. 30 C adn. 1. editiones criticas frag-
mentorum contra imagines Epiphanio adscriptorum habes a Carolo Holl (Gesammelte Aufsätze zur Kirchengeschichte II, Tübingen, 1928, 356–363) et Georgio
Ostrogorsky (Studien, 67–75) confectas.
[2] ἐπιτεχνήσεις C

A. (B 296a, C 123b) (προχειρίζονται οὖν ὡς δῆθεν Ἐπιφανίου Διαθήκην πρὸς τοὺς τῆς
ἐκκλησίας τῆς αὐτοῦ[1] τετυπωμένην, ὧδέ πως ἔχουσαν·[2]) Προσέχετε ἑαυτοῖς καὶ κρατεῖτε τὰς
παραδόσεις ἃς παρελάβετε. μὴ ἐκκλίνητε δεξιὰ ἢ ἀριστερά. οἷς ἐπιφέρει· καὶ ἐν τούτῳ μνήμην ἔχετε,
τέκνα ἀγαπητά, τοῦ μὴ ἀναφέρειν εἰκόνας ἐπ' ἐκκλησίας μήτε ἐν τοῖς κοιμητηρίοις τῶν ἁγίων, ἀλλὰ
διὰ μνήμης ἔχετε τὸν Θεὸν ἐν ταῖς καρδίαις ὑμῶν, ἀλλ' οὔτε κατ' οἶκον κοινόν· οὐκ ἔξεστι γὰρ
Χριστιανῷ δι' ὀφθαλμῶν μετεωρίζεσθαι καὶ ῥεμβασμῷ τοῦ νοός.

[1] τῆς αὐτοῦ: αὐτοῦ C
[2] Ἐπιφανίδου in marg C

B. (B 298b, C 125b) (τούτοις ἕτερον αὐτῷ ἐφαρμόζουσι λόγον οὗ ἡ ἐπιγραφή) Κατὰ τῶν
ἐπιτηδευόντων εἰδωλικῷ θεσμῷ εἰκόνας εἰς ἀφομοίωσιν Χριστοῦ καὶ τῆς Θεοτόκου, μαρτύρων καὶ
ἀγγέλων καὶ προφητῶν. (B 299a, C 126a) (γράφει δὲ ἑξῆς ὁ τούτων διδάσκαλος ταῦτα·) ἴδωμεν
τοὺς κατὰ τὸ θέλημα τοῦ Θεοῦ πολιτευσαμένους πατριάρχας καὶ προφήτας καὶ μιμησώμεθα αὐτοὺς
ἵνα ὄντως καθολικῆς καὶ ἀποστολικῆς ἐκκλησίας υἱοὶ ὀνομασθῶμεν· εἰδόσιν οὖν νόμον λαλῶ. (B 299b,
C 126b) (φησίν) εἰπάτωσαν δὲ καὶ οἱ ἀδήλως τρέχοντες τίς τῶν ἁγίων πατέρων χειροποίητον
προσεκύνησεν ἢ τίς τοῖς ἰδίοις σέβειν παρέδωκεν. τίς τῶν ἁγίων καταλιπὼν τὸν ἀνεκλιπῆ[1] πλοῦτον,
τὴν εἰς Θεὸν ἐλπίδα ἐν γνώσει, ἑαυτὸν[2] ζωγραφήσας προσκυνεῖσθαι ἐκέλευσεν; ὁ ἡγούμενος[3] τῶν[4]
ἐν πίστει Ἀβραὰμ[5] οὐχὶ φεύγων τὰ νεκρὰ φίλος ζῶντος Θεοῦ ἐκλήθη; ἢ Μωσῆς οὐχὶ φεύγων τὴν
τοιαύτην πλάνην ἠρνήσατο τὴν παροῦσαν ἀπόλαυσιν; (B 302b, C 129b) (ἐπισυνάπτει τοιαῦτα·)
ἀλλ' ἐρεῖς μοι ὅτι οἱ πατέρες εἴδωλα ἐθνῶν ἐβδελύξαντο, ἡμεῖς δὲ τὰς εἰκόνας τῶν ἁγίων ποιοῦμεν
εἰς μνημόσυνον αὐτῶν καὶ εἰς τιμὴν ἐκείνων ταῦτα προσκυνοῦμεν. καὶ πάντως γὰρ ταύτῃ τῇ ὑποθέσει
ἐτόλμησάν τινες ὑμῶν ἔνδον τοῦ ἁγίου οἴκου τὸν τοῖχον κονιάσαντες χρώμασι διηλλαγμένοις εἰκόνας
ἀνατυπώσαντες Πέτρου καὶ Ἰωάννου καὶ Παύλου ὡς ὁρῶ κατὰ τὴν ἐπιγραφὴν ἑκάστης[6] τῶν ψευδωνύμων

εἰκόνων ὑπὸ τῆς μωρίας τοῦ ζωγράφου κατὰ τὸν νοῦν αὐτοῦ τυπωθεῖσαν. καὶ πρῶτον μὲν οἱ νομίζοντες ἐν τούτῳ τιμᾶν τοὺς ἀποστόλους μαθέτωσαν ὅτι ἀντὶ τῆς τιμῆς πλέον αὐτοὺς ἀτιμάζουσι. Παῦλος γὰρ τὸν ψευδώνυμον ἱερέα ἐνυβρίσας [7] τοῖχον κεκονιαμένον ἀπεφήνατο.[8] οὐκοῦν εἰκόνας αὐτῶν τὰς αὐτῶν ἐντολὰς δι' ἀρετῶν στήσωμεν. ἀλλ' ἐρεῖς ὅτι εἰς ὑπόμνησιν τῆς ἰδέας αὐτῶν τὰς εἰκόνας αὐτῶν [9] θεωροῦμεν. καὶ ποῦ γάρ σοι ταῦτα προενετείλαντο; προῃτιασάμεθα γὰρ τοὺς τοιούτους ὅτι ἀγνοίᾳ φερόμενοι κοπιῶσιν εἰκῇ. (Β 304a, C 131a) (διὸ ἐπὶ τοῖς προκειμένοις εὐθὺς μετοιχόμεθα· φάσκει γὰρ οὑτωσί·) οἴδαμεν γάρ, φησίν Ἰωάννης,[10] ὅτι [11] ὅταν φανερωθῇ ὅμοιοι αὐτῷ ἐσόμεθα, καὶ Παῦλος [12] δὲ [13] τοὺς ἁγίους συμμόρφους τοῦ Υἱοῦ τοῦ Θεοῦ ἐκήρυξεν. (Β 305a, C 132a) (ὁ δὲ τῆς ἀποστατικῆς παρανοίας εἰσηγητὴς τοῖς προηγουμένοις παρατίθεται ταῦτα·) πῶς οὖν τοὺς ἐν δόξῃ μέλλοντας φαιδρύνεσθαι ἁγίους ἐν ἀδόξῳ καὶ νεκρῷ καὶ ἀλάλῳ θέλεις ὁρᾶν, τοῦ Κυρίου λέγοντος περὶ αὐτῶν· ἔσονται γάρ, φησίν, ὡς ἄγγελοι Θεοῦ.[14] (Β 307a, C 134a) (ἀλλ' ἐπὶ τὰ λοιπὰ τοῦ ἄφρονος μέτειμι ἔνθα φράζει·) πῶς δὲ καὶ ἀγγέλους πνεύματα ὑπάρχοντας καὶ ἀεὶ ζῶντας ἐν νεκροῖς γράφων προσκυνεῖς, τοῦ προφήτου [15] λέγοντος· ὁ ποιῶν τοὺς ἀγγέλους αὐτοῦ πνεύματα [16] καὶ τοὺς λειτουργοὺς αὐτοῦ πυρὸς φλόγα. (Β 307b, C 134b–135a) (καὶ λέγει·) ἤκουσα δὲ ὅτι καὶ τὸν ἀκατάληπτον Υἱὸν τοῦ Θεοῦ τινες γράφειν ἐπαγγέλλονται, ὃ φρῖξαί ἐστι τὸ ἀκοῦσαι καὶ τὸ πιστεῦσαι βλάσφημον. (Β 213a, C 140b) (ἑξῆς δ' ἂν εἴη τὰ ὑπερτεθέντα τῆς χρήσεως τούτοις ἐπισυνάπτειν, ἐν οἷς ἰουδαΐζων φάσκει τοιάδε·) ποῦ γάρ σοι διέταξε ἐλθὼν ἐπὶ τῆς [17] γῆς ποιῆσαι ὅμοιον αὐτοῦ καὶ προσκυνεῖν ἢ ὁρᾶν; αὕτη ἡ διάταξις τοῦ πονηροῦ, δῆλον ἵνα καταφρονήσῃς Θεοῦ. (Β 314a, C 141b) (ἀκόλουθον ἐν οἷς ταῦτα παρεγγυᾶται ὁ κενὸς οὗτος διδάσκαλος ὑποτιθέμενος.[18]) δεῖ οὖν αὐτῷ ζῶντι προσκυνεῖν, ὡς εἶπεν, ἐν πνεύματι καὶ ἀληθείᾳ.[19] (Β 315b, C 143a) (τοῖς δὲ ἑξῆς προκειμένοις τῆς παρούσης χρήσεως καὶ ἐπιβάλλειν αἰσχρὸν καὶ σιωπᾶν οὐκ ἀνεκτόν. ἔχει γὰρ οὕτως·) μὴ οὖν ἡ γάγγραινα νομὴν ἕξει [20] ὁ Θεὸς γὰρ ἐν πάσῃ τῇ παλαιᾷ καὶ καινῇ ταῦτα ἀναιρεῖ ἀκριβῶς λέγων· [21] Κύριον τὸν Θεόν σου προσκυνήσεις καὶ αὐτῷ μόνῳ λατρεύσεις, λέγων· ζῶ ἐγώ, λέγει Κύριος, καὶ ἐμοὶ κάμψει πᾶν γόνυ.[22] οὐ δυνάμεθα οὖν δυσὶ κυρίοις δουλεύειν,[23] ζῶντι καὶ νεκρῷ· ἐπικατάρατος γάρ, φησίν, ὃς κτίσμα παρὰ τὸν κτίσαντα προσκυνήσει·[24] πάντα γὰρ ταῦτα περιέχει αὐτὸς καὶ οὐ περιέχεται ὑπό τινος.

[1] ἀνελλιπῆ Β ἀνεκλιπὴ C
[2] αὐτὸν C
[3] ἡγούμενον C
[4] τὸν C
[5] αβρααν C
[6] ἑκάστην Β
[7] ἐνυβριάσας ? C
[8] Act. XXIII 3.
[9] τὰς εἰκόνας αὐτῶν om C
[10] I Joh. III 2.
[11] ὅτι om B
[12] Rom. VIII 29.

[13] δὲ om B
[14] Ev. Marci XII 25.
[15] Ps. CIII 4.
[16] πνεῦμα C
[17] τῆς om B
[18] ὑποτίθεται Β
[19] Ev. Joh. IV 34.
[20] ἕξη C cf. II Tim. 2:17
[21] Ev. Matth. IV 10.
[22] Rom. XIV 11.
[23] Ev. Matth. VI 24.
[24] Rom. I 25.

C. (Β 316a, C 143b) (ἐπακολουθεῖ γὰρ ἐκ τῆς πρὸς Θεοδόσιον τὸν βασιλέα Ἐπιφανίου δῆθεν ἐπιστολῆς χρῆσις. . . .) [1] (Β 324b, C 152a) (ἐντεῦθεν ἐπὶ τὰς λοιπὰς τῶν ἐν τῷ ὅρῳ αὐτῶν προσκειμένας χρήσεις ἐπισκεψόμενοι ἄπιμεν ἐν αἷς γράφεται τοιάδε·) τίς ἤκουσε τοιαῦτα πώποτε; τίς τῶν παλαιῶν πατέρων Χριστοῦ εἰκόνα ζωγραφήσας ἐν ἐκκλησίᾳ ἢ ἐν οἴκῳ ἰδίῳ κατέθετο; τίς ἐν βήλοις θυρῶν τῶν ἀρχαίων ἐπισκόπων Χριστὸν ἀτιμάσας ἐζωγράφησεν; τίς τὸν Ἀβραὰμ καὶ Ἰσαὰκ καὶ Ἰακὼβ Μωσέα τε καὶ τοὺς λοιποὺς προφήτας καὶ πατριάρχας, ἢ Πέτρον ἢ Ἀνδρέαν ἢ Ἰάκωβον ἢ Ἰωάννην ἢ Παῦλον ἢ τοὺς λοιποὺς ἀποστόλους ἐν βήλοις ἢ ἐν τοίχοις ζωγραφήσας οὕτως παρεδειγμάτισε καὶ ἐθριάμβευσεν; (Β 326a–b, C 153b–154a) (τοῖς προγεγραμμένοις συντάττουσι ταῦτα·) οὐχ ὁρᾷς, θεοφιλέστατε βασιλεῦ, τὸ ἔργον οὐ πρέπον Θεῷ; διὸ παρακαλῶ, βασιλεῦ θεοσεβέστατε καὶ μισοπόνηρε, πᾶσαν [2] πλάνην ἐλέγχων τῷ ἐν σοὶ ζήλῳ Θεοῦ ἐν ἀληθείᾳ διὰ στερεᾶς σου νομοθεσίας μετὰ προστίμου ὁριζομένης εἰ δυνατόν — πιστεύω δὲ ὅτι ἐὰν θέλῃς [3] ἐν Θεῷ δύνασαι — ὅπως τὰ βῆλα ὅπου ἂν [4] εὑρεθῇ ἔχοντα ψευδῶς μὲν ὅμως δὲ ἢ ἀποστόλων ἢ προφητῶν ζωγραφίας ἢ αὐτοῦ τοῦ Κυρίου καὶ Χριστοῦ, ταῦτα πάντα συλλεγέντα ἀπὸ ἐκκλησιῶν ἢ βαπτιστηρίων ἢ οἰκιῶν ἢ μαρτυρίων εἰς ταφὴν πτωχῶν προχωρήσει,[5] τὰ δὲ ἐν τοίχοις διὰ χρωμάτων λευκανθῆναι· τὰ δὲ ἐν μουσαρίῳ προληφθέντα γραφῆναι, ἐπειδὴ δὲ [6] δυσχερές ἐστι τὸ τοιοῦτον ἀνασκεύασμα, ἐν τῇ δοθείσῃ σοι ὑπὸ τοῦ [7] Θεοῦ σοφίᾳ εἰδέναι πῶς προστάξεις. εἰ μὲν δυνατὸν ταῦτα ἀνασκευασθῆναι, εὖ ἂν ἔχοι· εἰ δὲ ἀδύνατον, ἀρκεσθῆναι τοῖς προγεγονόσι,[8] καὶ μηκέτι τινὰ ζωγραφεῖν οὕτως· καὶ γὰρ οἱ ἡμέτεροι πατέρες οὐδὲν ἄλλο ἔγραφον, εἰ μὴ τὸ σημεῖον, τοῦ Χριστοῦ τὸν σταυρόν, ἐν ταῖς ἑαυτῶν [9] θύραις καὶ πανταχοῦ.

[1] Hic adfert Nicephorus et alia fragmenta epistulae Epiphanii ad Theodosium (Holl, frga. 19, 20, 21, 28, 31; Ostrogorsky, frga. 22, 28–30). quae autem non ex 'florilegio' concilii anno 815 habiti, sed ex epistula ipsa prompsisse testatur: ἀλλὰ τί δεῖ πλειόνων πόνων ἢ πολλὰ κάμνειν καὶ πράγματα ἑαυτοῖς παρέχειν, ἐξὸν τοῖς κατὰ τὴν ἐπιστολὴν γεγραμμένοις ἀκριβέστερον ἐπιβαλόντας ἐκεῖθεν ἑλεῖν ὅστις ποτὲ ἦν ὁ ταύτης πατήρ (B 322b, C 150a–b). deinde (B 324b, C 152a) ad 'florilegium' his verbis redit: ἐντεῦθεν ἐπὶ τὰς λοιπὰς τῶν ἐν τῷ ὅρῳ αὐτῶν προσκειμένας χρήσεις ἐπισκεψόμενοι ἄπιμεν.
[2] πᾶσαν bis scr C
[3] θέλεις C
[4] ἐὰν C
[5] προχωρήσεις C
[6] δὲ om C
[7] τοῦ om C
[8] ex προγεγραμμένοις corr C
[9] αὐτῶν B

D. (B 327a–328a, C 154–155a) (λοιπὴ γὰρ καὶ τελευταία τῶν παρ' αὐτοῖς παρενηνεγμένων παρομαρτεῖ χρήσεων ἥτις [1] ὡς Ἐπιφανίου πεπλαστούργηται πρὸς Ἰωάννην τὸν Αἰλίας [2] ἐπίσκοπον ἐπιγεγραμμένη ἐπιστολὴ ἀπαγγέλλουσα [3] τοιαῦτα·) Ὁ δὲ Θεὸς τῆς εἰρήνης ποιήσει μεθ' ἡμῶν κατὰ τὴν αὐτοῦ φιλανθρωπίαν εἰς τὸ συντριβῆναι τὸν Σατανᾶν ὑπὸ τοὺς πόδας ἡμῶν τῶν Χριστιανῶν καὶ ἀποδιωχθῆναι πᾶσαν πρόφασιν πονηρὰν εἰς τὸ μὴ σχισθῆναι [4] τὸν σύνδεσμον ἐξ ἡμῶν τῆς τοῦ Χριστοῦ ἀννποκρίτου ἀγάπης καὶ εἰρήνης καὶ ὀρθῆς πίστεως καὶ ἀληθείας. ἐπειδὴ δὲ ἤκουσα ὅτι τινὲς ἐγόγγυσαν καθ' ἡμῶν ὅτι ἐν τῷ διαβαίνειν ἡμᾶς ἐπὶ τὸν ἅγιον τόπον τῆς Βεθὴλ τοῦ συναγελασθῆναι [5] τῇ σῇ τιμιότητι ὡς ἤλθομεν εἰς τὴν κώμην τὴν λεγομένην Ἀναυθὰ θεασάμενοι λύχνον καιόμενον καὶ ἐρωτήσαντες ἔγνωμεν ἐκκλησίαν εἶναι ἐν τῷ τόπῳ. εἰσερχόμενοι δὲ τοῦ εὐχὴν ἐπιτελέσαι εὕρομεν βῆλον ἐν τῇ θύρᾳ βαπτὸν ἐν ᾧ ἐξωγράφητο ἀνδροείκελόν τι εἰδωλοειδές· ὃ ἔλεγον τάχα ὅτι Χριστοῦ ἦν τὸ ἐκτύπωμα ἢ ἑνὸς τῶν ἁγίων· οὐ γὰρ μέμνημαι. ἐγὼ θεασάμενος καὶ εἰδὼς ὅτι μύσος ἐστὶν ἐν ἐκκλησίᾳ τοιαῦτα [6] εἶναι διέρρηξα αὐτὸ καὶ συνεβούλευσα ἀμφιάσαι ἐν αὐτῷ πένητα τελευτήσαντα. οἱ δὲ γογγύσαντες ἔλεγον ἔδει αὐτὸν ἀλλάξαι ἐκ τῶν ἰδίων τὸ βῆλον πρὶν ἢ αὐτὸ [7] σχίσῃ.[8] καίτοι γε ἐμοῦ ὑποσχομένου ὅτι ἀντ' αὐτοῦ ἀποστελῶ [9] ἕτερον, ἐβράδυνα δὲ τοῦ ἀποστεῖλαι διὰ τὸ ἀναγκαῖόν με ζητεῖν· προσεδόκων γὰρ ἀπὸ Κύπρου ἀποστέλλεσθαί μοι. νῦν οὖν ὅπερ εὗρον ἀπέστειλα. καταξίωσον οὖν κελεῦσαι τῷ πρεσβυτέρῳ τῆς παροικίας δέξασθαι παρὰ τοῦ ἀναγνώστου [10] τὸ ἀπεσταλμένον. καὶ παρακαλῶ, πρόσταξον ἵνα μὴ τοιαῦτα ἁπλοῦται ἐν ταῖς ἐκκλησίαις· πρέπει γὰρ τῇ σῇ τιμιότητι περὶ πάντων φροντίζειν καὶ ἀκριβολογεῖν [11] περὶ τῶν συμφερόντων τῇ τοῦ Θεοῦ ἐκκλησίᾳ καὶ τοῖς λαοῖς.[12]

[1] εἴτις C
[2] Ἀιλείας C
[3] ἀπαγγέλουσα B
[4] σχεσθῆναι B
[5] συναγελασθεῖναι C
[6] ταῦτα B
[7] αὐτὸς B αὐτῷ C
[8] σχίσει B

[9] ἀποστέλλω C

[10] ἀναγνώσ C

[11] ἀκριβεῖ λόγον C

[12] Docet V. Grumel (*Echos d'Orient* XXIX, 1930, 98) Theodorum Studitam, in opere quod inscribitur Ἔλεγχος καὶ ἀνατροπὴ τῶν ἀσεβῶν ποιημάτων Ἰωάννου, Ἰγνατίου, Σεργίου καὶ Στεφάνου τῶν νέων Χριστομάχων. . . . , ὁμοῦ τε καὶ τῆς ἀσεβοῦς ὑπογραφῆς (*P.G.* XCIX, 435) subscriptionem episcoporum iconomachorum anni 815 servavisse (*ibid.*, 465 A–B). sed si ita est, videri non potest cur Theodorus subscriptionem concilii una cum opusculis iconomachis refutaverit. veri similius puto poetas illos subscriptionem a se compositam, subscriptionem ipsius concilii fortasse imitantem, in calce opusculorum suorum addiddisse. sed cum res incerta esset, textum subscriptionis hic adiungendum esse putavi: Ὑπογραφή. Τῇ ἀποστολικῇ καὶ πατρικῇ διδασκαλίᾳ ἑπόμενος καὶ τῇ τῆς ἐκκλησίας θεσμοθεσίᾳ πειθόμενος τάς τε ἁγίας καὶ οἰκουμενικὰς ἓξ συνόδους ἀποδεχόμενος καὶ τὴν ἐν Βλαχέρναις κροτηθεῖσαν σύνοδον καὶ τὴν ταύτης ἐπικυρωτικὴν ἀθροισθεῖσαν καὶ τοῖς ὑπ' αὐταῖς ἐκτεθεῖσιν ὀρθοδόξοις δόγμασιν ἑπόμενος καὶ ἐμμένων τούς τε παρ' αὐτῶν ἀποβληθέντας ἀποβαλλόμενος καὶ τοὺς ὑπ' αὐτῶν δεχθέντας (δειχθέντας Migne) ἀποδεχόμενος πᾶσαν εἰκονικὴν ποίησίν τε καὶ προσκύνησιν ἀθετῶν, τὸν δὲ ὑπὸ Ταρασίου σύλλογον ἀποβαλλόμενος καὶ τοὺς μὴ οὕτως ἔχοντας ἀναθεματίζων ὑπέγραψα ἰδιοχείρως.

CONSPECTUS EDITIONUM

Ed. Serruys	Ed. Ostrogorsky (fragmenta numerantur secundum Ostr.)	Ed. Alexander (fragmenta numerantur secundum editionem meam)
vacat	vacat	1
habet	1	2
habet	2	3
vacat	3	4
habet	4	5
vacat	5	vacat [1]
vacat	6	vacat [1]
vacat	7	vacat [1]
habet	8	6
habet	9	7
habet	10	8
habet	11	9
habet	12	10
vacat	13	11
vacat	vacat	12
habet	14	13
habet	15	14
habet	16	15
habet	17	16
vacat	vacat	17–30 (florilegium)

[1] Vide supra p. 53 f., adn. 15.

ADDITIONAL BIBLIOGRAPHY

Milton V.Anastos,"The Ethical Theory of Images formulated by
the Iconoclasts in 754 and 815",Dumbarton Oaks Papers 8, 151-
160,and "The Argument for Iconoclasm as presented by the Iconoclastic Council of 754",Late Classical and Mediaeval Studies in
honor of Albert Mathias Friend,Jr.,Princeton,New Jersey,1955,
177-188,criticized my evaluation of the Second Iconoclasm. I
replied in my book on The Patriarch Nicephorus (cited in Preface),137-140 and 237f. Later I attempted to reconstruct the procedures adopted by the Iconoclasts in compiling the florilegium of
patristic quotations appended to the Definition of 1815 in a separate article (here no.IX). The fragments of Definition and florilegium have been republished,with revisions, by Herman Hennephof,
Textus Byzantini ad Iconomachiam Pertinentes, Leiden,1969,79-
84. On the Patriarch Nicephorus' works as evidence for a rebirth
of Aristotelian philosophy at Byzantium see Paul Lemerle,Le premier humanisme byzantin.Notes sur l'enseignement et culture a
Byzance des origines au Xe siècle,Paris,1971,129-135.

IX

CHURCH COUNCILS AND PATRISTIC AUTHORITY

THE ICONOCLASTIC COUNCILS OF HIEREIA (754) and ST. SOPHIA (815)

DURING the Iconoclastic Controversy considerable attention was paid in the Byzantine Empire to the views of the Church Fathers concerning religious images. Ecclesiastical councils in particular relied heavily on patristic authority. In recent years publications of new texts as well as scholarly investigations of known documents have shed light on the attitude of councils, both iconophile and iconoclastic, towards the writings of the Fathers. On the following pages an attempt will be made to define on the basis of some of the new evidence the relation of two iconoclastic councils towards patristic authority and to describe the handling of patristic manuscripts by these councils and by their drafting committees. My hope is that Professor Werner Jaeger, who has collected in Harvard's Institute of Classical Studies and elucidated in his editions and monographs the manuscript tradition of several Church Fathers, will be interested in a similar search and study of patristic manuscripts undertaken by churchmen of the eighth and ninth centuries.

Shortly after Easter 815 an ecclesiastical council assembled at St. Sophia in Constantinople to reconsider the problem of religious images. It was presided over by Theodotus, Patriarch of Constantinople, and speedily discharged its business in three meetings. At its last session a Decree condemning religious images and their worship and also including a *florilegium* of patristic quotations was read, approved by the members and signed by the Emperor.[1] This document revealed a high degree of dependence upon a similar Decree issued by the earlier iconoclastic Council of Hiereia (754). The Decree of Hiereia had been divided into four parts: a "doctrine" containing the conciliar decision against images, a biblico-patristic *florilegium* supporting Iconoclasm, disciplinary canons, and a set of anathemas.[2] The Decree of St. Sophia explicitly approved and accepted the decisions of the earlier council.[3] Moreover, the principal arguments advanced or implied by the Decree of St. Sophia were derived from that of Hiereia. Indeed, both councils objected to images of Christ on christological grounds and to images of

494

Christ and of Saints as unable to render the essential holiness of the prototypes.[4] The dependence of the Council of St. Sophia on the earlier council was not limited to the realm of ideas. It also extended to the armor of patristic authorities and the later Council took over several quotations from its eighth-century predecessor.[5]

There can be no doubt that the later iconoclastic council relied heavily in thought and patristic apparatus on the work done in the eighth century, yet a close examination of its Decree shows that the person or more probably the committee responsible for its drafting had recourse to other documents in addition to the Decree of Hiereia. In the first place, for several quotations contained in the patristic *florilegium* of St. Sophia the drafting committee supplied more adequate information concerning the title of the works from which they were taken. Thus a passage quoted in the Decree of Hiereia from St. John Chrysostom without identification of the particular work of this prolific writer was attributed in the Decree of St. Sophia to this author's *On the Gaoler*.[6] Similarly, a quotation assigned in the Decree of Hiereia to Epiphanius of Cyprus without further identification reappears in the *florilegium* of St. Sophia as a citation from that author's *Testament*.[7] Moreover, it is likely that the identification of Amphilochius of Iconium's *Enkomion on Basil the Great*, from which both councils quoted, was due to the drafting committee of the ninth century.[8]

This Committee furthermore not infrequently expanded the text of patristic excerpts taken over from the earlier *florilegium*. Thus a much more generous extract from Amphilochius of Iconium's *Enkomion on Basil*, just mentioned, appeared in the *florilegium* of St. Sophia.[9] The same is true of the excerpt from St. John Chrysostom's *On the Gaoler*.[10] One may conclude, therefore, that the drafting committee, for all its dependence on the *florilegium* of Hiereia, relied on additional sources of information and derived from them the more precise attributions as well as the expanded text of some quotations. These additional sources must have been either manuscripts of the patristic works quoted or *florilegia* other than that contained in the Decree of Hiereia. Is it possible, therefore, to discover more precisely the mode of operation and sources used by the drafters active at Constantinople in 814/5?

To answer this question it will be useful to consider two puzzling sentences from the "doctrine" of Hiereia, that is, from that part of the Decree in which the Council was formulating its own views on religious images. These sentences contained in the dogmatic pronouncement of 754 echo the text of two patristic quotations absent from the Decree of Hiereia but incorporated into that of St. Sophia (815). For the first of these sentences agreement in content and wording with a phrase attributed by the Decree of St. Sophia to Epiphanius of Cyprus was first noticed by Professor George Ostrogorsky.[11] It escaped his attention, however, that a similar relationship existed between the sentence immediately following in the "doctrine" of Hiereia and a fragment attributed by the Council of St. Sophia to a dubious work of St. John Chrysostom on Abraham. According to this quotation, the pagan inhabitants of Palestine in the patriarchal period made "images" of the three angels, Abraham, Sarah, the calf and the "fine meal" (*Genesis* 18). Chrysostom (?) protests that he is relating this incident not with the intention of producing faith among the believers through the testimony of pagans: "for we [Christians] do not accept proofs from those outside [the Church]." The same sentence occurs almost *verbatim* in the "doctrine" of Hiereia where it is used as an argument against pictorial representations of the Virgin Mary and the Saints.[12] Professor Ostrogorsky, aware only of the first occurrence and concerned primarily with the writings attributed to St. Epiphanius, suggested that the passage attributed in the *florilegium* of St. Sophia to Epiphanius was a forgery perpetrated in iconoclastic circles in the period between the two iconoclastic councils. This hypothesis, though based not only on the passage from the Council of Hiereia but on a thorough examination of other iconoclastic quotations attributed to St. Epiphanius, was re-examined and rejected by prominent scholars.[13] In the light of a second instance of borrowing, this time from St. John Chrysostom's (?) *On Abraham*, it would be necessary if one wished to maintain Professor Ostrogorsky's hypothesis to postulate a forger or an atelier of forgers fathering iconoclastic statements not only on St. Epiphanius but also on St. John Chrysostom. Such an assumption, though by no means impossible, should be accepted only after other attempts to explain have failed. Is it not more natural to assume that the patristic passages cited in the Decree of St. Sophia were known at the Council of Hiereia and that in an age respectful of ecclesiastical authority the members of that Council were prone to prefer to their own words formulations derived (or thought to be derived) from patristic authority?

This tendency can be demonstrated in one instance where there is no doubt as to the authenticity of the authority. In an early passage of the Decree of Hiereia the Iconoclasts mention that after Jesus Christ, the Apostles and the Early Church had purged the world of idol-worship, it was re-introduced by the Devil. They express this thought in a fairly literal quotation from Gregory of Nyssa's *Enkomion on his*

Brother Basil, where Gregory had spoken of Arianism as a new form of idol-worship.[14] Nothing in the context of this dogmatic pronouncement indicates that this was a patristic quotation.[15] It was appropriated by the Iconoclasts because Gregory was recognized as an authority in matters theological. No scruples were felt about misapplying to image worship what Gregory had said of Arianism. In another instance, there is verbal agreement between a passage quoted from Theodotus of Ancyra (or Galatia) by both iconoclastic councils and an anathema pronounced by the Council of Hiereia.[16] Thus these "hidden quotations", that is, passages quoted from patristic authorities (Gregory, Theodotus) by the Council of Hiereia as if they were the Council's own formulations, suggest that other "hidden quotations", such as those from Epiphanius and from Chrysostom *On Abraham*, also were known to be quotations and indeed considered genuine by the Council of Hiereia.

Thus, internal evidence furnished by the Decrees of Hiereia and St. Sophia permits several conclusions. The Council of Hiereia, of whose deliberations only the Decree survives, expressed several of its dogmatic pronouncements in the language of patristic texts not quoted in the *florilegium* of this Council's Decree (Epiphanius, John Chrysostom *On Abraham*, Gregory of Nyssa, Theodotus). It may be inferred that the Decree derived its knowledge of these quotations not directly from the authors to which they were attributed but from an iconoclastic *florilegium*. This inference will be presently corroborated by external evidence. So far as the Council of St. Sophia is concerned, it has been shown that its drafting committee obtained from a source yet to be defined the title of some of the works excerpted by the Iconoclasts, that it presented more generous fragments of other texts, and that it quoted with indication of title the patristic passages, parts of which had appeared as "hidden quotations" in the Decree of Hiereia. For the Council of St. Sophia, as for the earlier assembly, external evidence will supplement the conclusions gathered from a study of its Decree and help to define the source or sources of the new data supplied in that document.

With regard to the Council of Hiereia it is well known that it relied heavily on the writings of the Emperor Constantine V. In the present context a *florilegium* of patristic quotations compiled by the Emperor is of particular importance. The Patriarch Nicephorus read and refuted this *florilegium* in the ninth century and mentioned that it contained among other texts the same quotation from Gregory of Nyssa's *Enkomion on his Brother Basil* which was cited as a "hidden quotation" in the Decree of Hiereia.[17] In view of the general influence exerted by the Emperor Constantine V upon the Council of Hiereia it is virtually certain that any passage included in his *florilegium*, such as the excerpt from Gregory of Nyssa's *Enkomion on Basil*, was read and considered at Hiereia. Indeed the Council of Hiereia, in some of its early sessions whose records are lost, examined and discussed the patristic evidence relating to images and their worship. This was the general practice of church councils in the seventh and eighth centuries. Moreover, at the Council of Nicaea two repentant Iconoclasts who had attended the Council of Hiereia asserted that at Hiereia passages from Nilus' *Letter to Olympiodorus* and from an apocryphal work on the wanderings of the Apostles had been read.[18] There must have been other patristic passages read before the Council of Hiereia. The compilers of the Decree of Hiereia, of course, attended the meetings of the Council, had access to the records of these meetings as well as to Constantine's *florilegium* and could easily cite in the form of "hidden quotations" patristic passages contained in these documents or incorporate them into the *florilegium* which formed part of the Decree. As a consequence, to members of the Council of Hiereia and to the compilers of its Decree, the "doctrine" of this Council must have sounded like a potpourri of patristic quotations read and debated at earlier sessions.

For the later iconoclastic Council of St. Sophia the internal evidence of the Decree is likewise supplemented by references in narrative sources. The composition of the drafting committee whose existence and activities have been inferred from a comparison of the *florilegia* of St. Sophia and Hiereia is known. It was appointed by the Emperor Leo V, was presided over by an ambitious young abbot and lector, John the Grammarian, who later was to become Patriarch of Constantinople (834-843) under the Emperor Theophilus, and had among its members a bishop, two senators and two monks.[19] The operations of this Imperial Committee are described in an historical work by the *Scriptor Incertus de Leone Armeno*. This account reports how the Emperor Leo V empowered John the Grammarian and his associates "to collect from all quarters the ancient manuscripts preserved in monasteries and churches". Thereupon the Imperial Committee gathered a large number of manuscripts and searched through them. The author then continues: πλὴν οὐδὲν εὕρισκον οἱ ἄφρονες ὧνπερ αὐτοὶ κακούργως ἐπεζήτουν, ἕως οὗ μετὰ χεῖρας ἔλαβον τῷ συνοδικῷ [τὸ συνοδικὸν] Κωνσταντίνου τοῦ Ἰσαύρου τοῦ καὶ Καβαλλίνου καὶ ἐκ τούτου τὰς ἀρχὰς λαβόντες ἤρξαντο καὶ ἐν τοῖς βιβλίοις εὑρίσκειν τὰς χρήσεις ἅσπερ αὐτοὶ ἀφρόνως καὶ ἀνοήτως προέφερον, σημάδια βάλλοντες εἰς τοὺς τόπους

498

ἔνθα εὕρισκον, βουλόμενοι πεῖσαι τὸν ἄφρονα λαὸν ὅτι 'Εν παλαιοῖς βιβλίοις εὕρομεν τοῦ μὴ προσκυνεῖσθαι τὰς εἰκόνας.[20]

The passage mentions a document which aided the Imperial Committee in locating quotations in "ancient manuscripts" but unfortunately this reference is ambiguous: τὸ συνοδικὸν Κωνσταντίνου τοῦ 'Ισαύρου τοῦ καὶ Καβαλλίνου.[21] The context makes it clear that the author opposed Constantine V's religious policies, an attitude which is also indicated by his use of the Emperor's nickname ("Horsey"). The author is speaking as a partisan and consequently refers to the document in question not by its official title but by a sarcastic characterization. Technically and officially, a document either emanated from a church council or from an emperor but not from both. The mention of a hybrid such as the "synodical document of Constantine" is obviously part of the sarcasm of the passage. Two interpretations are possible. Either the document was one of the writings of Constantine V, more particularly his *florilegium*; in that case the writer is implying that the Emperor was usurping the functions of a church council. Alternatively, the *Scriptor Incertus* may refer to the *Acta* of Hiereia, more particularly to those sections now lost in which the conciliar discussions of patristic authorities were recorded; if this is the meaning, the writer by connecting the conciliar *Acta* with the name of the ruling emperor is criticizing the Council, as did many orthodox writers, for its subservience to Constantine V.

Although it must be admitted that *synodikon* is an unusual term for the *Acta* of a church council,[22] the second of the alternatives is more probable.[23] In the first place a hagiographic text of the early ninth century, the *Life of St. Stephen the Younger* written in 806 by a disciple of Stephen, speaks of the Decree of Hiereia alternately as emanating from the Council or from the Emperors Constantine and Leo.[24] Secondly, during the months when the Imperial Committee was investigating the manuscripts, the Patriarch Nicephorus, aware of the threatening explosion and in all probability of the objectives pursued by the Imperial Committee, forbade members of the clergy to engage in discussions over the Emperor Constantine's opinions and over patristic passages collected by that Emperor. But he was still hopeful that a compromise could be found and therefore suggested that a new enquiry into image worship could be undertaken and even a new ecumenical council summoned "if certain conciliar books have been found".[25] The "conciliar books" were the *Acta* of Hiereia. In all probability, therefore, the Imperial Committee made use of the *Acta* of Hiereia rather than of Constantine's *florilegium*.

IX

The Imperial Committee improved upon the Patriarch's suggestion by using the newly found *Acta* of Hiereia as a guide to the manuscripts of the patristic texts from which the Council had quoted. This procedure was useful from three points of view. In the first place, as the Patriarch Nicephorus at a time when he still expected a peaceful argument had suggested, this was a convenient way of re-opening the issue of religious images without openly disavowing the Council of Nicaea (787) — and Leo V like the Patriarch Nicephorus may have hoped in 813/4 that he would not be driven to this disavowal. The Decree read and approved at the final session of Hiereia had been officially repudiated at Nicaea in 787, but the patristic authorities adduced and debated during the early sessions of the Council of Hiereia and recorded in the *Acta* could properly be re-examined without fear of the objection: *res iudicata est*. It could be argued by Leo V and his advisers that the Empress Irene and the Patriarch Tarasius had submitted to the Council of Nicaea only part of the evidence issued by the Council of Hiereia (the Decree) and that a new enquiry and decision should be based on a complete survey of patristic utterances. Secondly, at the Council of Nicaea the iconoclastic Council of Hiereia had been severely taken to task for not producing manuscripts of the authorities quoted and for having read the quotations from "tablets" prepared *ad hoc*.[26] The passage from the *Scriptor Incertus* shows that iconoclastic circles in the ninth century took this criticism to heart and that Leo V had charged his Imperial Committee with the task of producing ancient and authoritative manuscripts containing the *ipsissima verba* of the Fathers quoted at Hiereia. Thus the Imperial Committee was searching less for new patristic quotations than for the manuscript evidence of the passages already read at Hiereia. Finally, the procedure adopted by the Imperial Committee allowed for a second display of the full patristic evidence in favor of Iconoclasm. It is true that most of this material was derived from the *Acta* of Hiereia, yet these *Acta* had been relegated by Canon 9 of the Second Nicaenum to the collection of heretical books in the Patriarchal Library and were therefore inaccessible to all but a few members of the clergy. Thus the mode of operation developed by the Imperial Committee from a suggestion originally made by the iconophile Patriarch Nicephorus was bound to be of considerable advantage to the iconoclastic cause.

There remains only one problem raised by the passage from the *Scriptor Incertus*: precisely what help did the Imperial Committee derive from the *synodikon* of Constantine V? In other words, what is the meaning of the phrase used by the *Scriptor Incertus*: ἐκ τούτου τὰς ἀρχὰς λαβόντες? Ever since Combefis' (?) translation in the seventeenth century this was interpreted to mean that the Imperial Committee "started out" or "took its departure" from the *synodikon*.[27] This interpretation rests on the assumption that originally the Imperial Committee wished to proceed without the help of earlier iconoclastic *florilegia* but did not possess sufficient learning; therefore it resigned itself to borrow quotations from the Iconoclasts of the eighth century. The sequence of the passage in the *Scriptor Incertus* shows that this assumption misconstrues the objectives of the Imperial Committee. Its purpose was not so much to find new patristic texts (although it may not have rejected new evidence) but to discover ancient patristic manuscripts for the authors quoted in earlier documents. "They wished to persuade the senseless rabble by saying: We have found it declared in ancient manuscripts that images should not be worshipped." As has been stated, one of the reasons for this procedure was the criticism leveled against the Council of Hiereia that it had not produced the manuscript evidence.[28] The passage from the *Scriptor Incertus* shows that iconoclastic circles in the ninth century took this criticism seriously and that the Emperor Leo V had charged the Imperial Committee with the task of supplying ancient and authoritative manuscripts containing the patristic quotations which had been read from "tablets" at Hiereia.

In the light of these considerations it will be possible to give a more satisfactory interpretation to the phrase: ἐκ τούτου τὰς ἀρχὰς λαβόντες. At the beginning, the Imperial Committee must have been guided in its search among the manuscripts by the Decree of Hiereia — the only iconoclastic document easily accessible in the ninth century because of its incorporation into the *Acta* of the Second Nicaenum. Even a modern scholar armed with printed editions and bibliographical tools would find it difficult to locate the manuscript evidence for all the "hidden" and "open" patristic quotations and allusions contained in that document. The Imperial Committee faced with this difficulty therefore consulted the *synodikon*. What did it obtain from it? The anwser to that question is: τὰς ἀρχάς, which should be translated: the *incipits*. The *incipit* or in Greek ἀρχή was a frequent and reliable way of identifying a work of literature.[29] Like the *Acta* of the Second Nicaenum Constantine's *synodikon*, whether this Emperor's *florilegium* or the full *Acta* of Hiereia, must have identified the works quoted by means of their *incipits*. It is easy to see why the work of the Imperial Committee proceeded swiftly and expeditiously once the provenance of the quotations had been clarified.[30]

The results of this paper may be summarized as follows:

(1) Of the *Acta* of Hiereia only the final Decree (ὄρος) survives.

(2) This Decree of Hiereia contains a brief biblico-patristic *florilegium* but even other parts of the Decree, such as the "doctrine" and "anathemas" in which the Council formulated its own teachings, frequently borrow both their ideas and their expression from patristic texts.

(3) Some of these "hidden quotations" were not incorporated into the *florilegium* issued by the Council of Hiereia. They had been read, however, and discussed during the early sessions of the Council. Many of them had first appeared in the *florilegium* compiled by the Emperor Constantine V.

(4) At the Seventh Ecumenical Council of Nicaea, the Decree of Hiereia was read in an open meeting and refuted in a document prepared by the Patriarch Tarasius. The Council of Nicaea, furthermore, criticized the Council of Hiereia for not having produced manuscripts of the patristic passages read during its sessions.

(5) In the early ninth century, manuscripts of Constantine's writings and of the full text of the *Acta* of Hiereia were difficult to procure but copies survived in the Patriarchal Library at Constantinople where they were preserved among the heretical books. The Decree of Hiereia alone was easily available because it was quoted among the *Acta* of the Seventh Ecumenical Council.

(6) In 814 the Emperor Leo V contemplated a revival of Iconoclasm. He instructed a committee presided over by John the Grammarian to prepare for a new discussion of image worship by empowering this committee to bring to Constantinople manuscripts of the Church Fathers which belonged to ecclesiastical libraries and by instructing it to find in these manuscripts passages which supported the iconoclastic views.

(7) The Imperial Committee experienced considerable difficulty in its attempt at finding the manuscript evidence on the basis of the Decree of Hiereia and of the patristic manuscripts gathered at Constantinople. Then an earlier iconoclastic *florilegium*, called συνοδικόν by the *Scriptor Incertus* (either the Emperor Constantine V's *florilegium* or more probably the full *Acta* of Hiereia) was discovered, perhaps in the Patriarchal Library. The Patriarch Nicephorus, still hopeful of a peaceful solution, suggested that the newly discovered manuscript could form the basis for a new enquiry into image worship. The Emperor Leo and his advisers, reacting to the criticisms raised at Nicaea against the Council of Hiereia, decided to base the new enquiry on manuscripts of

502

the patristic texts favoring Iconoclasm rather than on the earlier *florilegium*. The recently discovered συνοδικόν, by supplying the *incipits* of the patristic works to be quoted, guided the Imperial Committee through the labyrinth of patristic manuscripts. It enabled the Imperial Committee to find many patristic quotations that had not appeared in the Decree of Hiereia, to improve on the identification of some passages quoted in the earlier document and in some instances to supply fuller excerpts than the Decree of Hiereia had done.

(8) The patristic quotations selected by the Imperial Committee were read at the first session of the Council of St. Sophia, presumably from the ancient patristic manuscripts collected.

(9) With minor additions and subtractions the patristic *florilegium* attached to the Decree of the Council of St. Sophia represents the results of the labors performed by the Imperial Committee.

NOTES

1. For information on the Council of St. Sophia see Paul J. Alexander, *The Patriarch Nicephorus of Constantinople. Ecclesiastical Policy and Image Worship in the Byzantine Empire* (Oxford, 1958), 136–140 (cited below as Alexander, *Patriarch Nicephorus*). The Decree of St. Sophia was first reconstructed from the Patriarch Nicephorus' unpublished *Refutatio et Eversio* by D. Serruys (École française de Rome, *Mélanges d'archéologie et d'histoire*, XXIII, 1903, 345–351), and later by G. Ostrogorsky (*Studien zur Geschichtes des byzantinischen Bilderstreites*, Breslau, 1929, 48–51). I re-edited this text with some minor corrections and added the patristic *florilegium*. Cf. "The Iconoclastic Council of St. Sophia (815) and Its Definition (*Horos*)", *Dumbarton Oaks Papers* VII (1953), 35–66, esp. 58–66 (henceforth cited as Alexander, *Iconoclastic Council*). In the following the Decree of St. Sophia will be cited from my edition. Several of the connections to be discussed in this paper became clearer to me after these publications were printed. In such cases I have stated my new views without specifically pointing out the differences from my earlier opinions.

2. The Decree of Hiereia with its appendices including a patristic *florilegium* was quoted *in extenso* and refuted, probably by the Patriarch Tarasius, in a work read at the Seventh Ecumenical Council of Nicaea (787). It will be cited from the *Acta* of the Council of Nicaea, I. D. Mansi, *Sacrorum Conciliorum Nova et Amplissima Collectio* etc., XIII (Florence, 1767), 208C–356D. For an analysis of the Decree of Hiereia, see M. Anastos, "The Argument for Iconoclasm as presented by the Iconoclastic Council of 754", *Late Classical and Medieval Studies in Honor of Albert Mathias Friend, Jr.* (Princeton, 1955), 177–188. On the four parts of the Decree of Hiereia: Alexander, *Patriarch Nicephorus*, 237, also 138. Except for the Decree and its appendages, the *Acta* of Hiereia are lost. Most copies must have been deposited at the Patriarchal Library in Constantinople according to Canon 9 of the Seventh Ecumenical Council (Mansi XIII 430 A–B).

3. Decree of St. Sophia, frgs. 2–6, 16.
4. Alexander, *Patriarch Nicephorus*, 138–140.
5. Alexander, *Iconoclastic Council*, p. 54 n. 20.
6. Decree of Hiereia (Mansi XIII 300 A): Ἰωάννης δὲ ὁ Χρυσόστομος διδάσκει οὕτως. Decree of St. Sophia (frg. 28): . . . ἐν ἑτέρῳ λόγῳ τῷ ᾿Εἰς τὸν δεσμοφύλακα ἐπιγραφομένῳ λέγει. Nicephorus makes it clear that this rubric is not his own but that of the bishops assembled at St. Sophia, cf. the ἔτι φασὶν ὅτι in my edition of frg. 28.
7. Decree of Hiereia (Mansi XIII 292 D): λέγει οὖν ὁ ἐν σημειοφόροις περιβόητος ᾿Επιφάνιος ὁ Κύπρου. Decree of St. Sophia, frg. 30 A, about which Nicephorus remarks: προχειρίζονται οὖν ὡς δῆθεν ᾿Επιφανίου Διαθήκην πρὸς τοὺς τῆς ἐκκλησίας τῆς αὐτοῦ τετυπωμένην . . . Nicephorus clearly does not accept the attribution which is that of the Iconoclasts (cf. ὡς δῆθεν).
8. Decree of Hiereia (Mansi XIII 301 D): ᾿Αμφιλόχιος ὁ τοῦ ᾿Ικονίου φησίν. Decree of St. Sophia (frg. 22): . . . παρατιθέασιν ᾿Αμφιλοχίου τοῦ ἐξ ᾿Ικονίου λόγους ἐκ τοῦ πεποιημένου αὐτῷ ᾿Εγκωμίου εἰς τὸν μέγαν Βασίλειον. To judge merely from Nicephorus' wording the identification of Amphilochius' work might be due either to the drafting committee or to himself. However, in view of the instances discussed in the two preceding notes the former alternative is more probable.
9. Decree of Hiereia (Mansi XIII 301 D): οὐ γὰρ τοῖς πίναξι τὰ σαρκικὰ πρόσωπα τῶν ἁγίων διὰ χρωμάτων ἐπιμελὲς ἡμῖν ἐντυποῦν, ὅτι ἐχρήζομεν τούτων, ἀλλὰ τὴν πολιτείαν αὐτῶν δι᾿ ἀρετῆς ἐκμιμεῖσθαι. Decree of St. Sophia (frg. 22): Οἱ ἅγιοι οὐ προσδέονται τῶν διὰ γραμμάτων ἡμῶν ἐγκωμίων, ἐγγεγραμμένοι ἤδη τῷ βιβλίῳ τῶν ζώντων, ὧν ἡ δικαιοσύνη παρὰ τῷ θεῷ πεφύλακται. ἡμεῖς δὲ χρήζομεν τῶν διὰ μέλανος γραμμάτων ὅπως ὁ νοῦς ἡμῶν διαγράφῃ τὴν τούτων μνήμην εἰς κοινὴν ὠφέλειαν καὶ ὦμεν ἀκροαταὶ τούτων, ὅταν διὰ τῆς ἀναγνώσεως τῇ ἀκοῇ παραπέμπωμεν. ὡς γὰρ ἐκ μεγάλου θησαυροῦ πρὸς οἰκονομίαν τὰς εὐεργεσίας λαμβάνομεν καὶ πληροῦμεν ἡμῶν τὰ ὑστερήματα ταῖς τούτων πολιτείαις (οὐ γὰρ πληροῦται ἀκοὴ δι᾿ ἐπιθυμίας ἔχουσα ἀκοῦσαι τὴν τούτων τελείωσιν). ἀλλ᾿ οὐ χρώμασι τοῖς πίναξι τὰ σαρκικὰ αὐτῶν πρόσωπα ἐπιμελὲς ἡμῖν ἐκτυποῦν ὅτι οὐ χρήζομεν τούτων, ἀλλὰ τὴν τούτων ἄθλησιν ἐκμιμούμενοι καὶ τὰς ἀγαθὰς πράξεις δευτεροῦμεν καὶ τὴν πρὸς θεὸν ἀγάπην διαγράφομεν καί ἐσμεν μιμηταὶ τῶν ἀγαθῶν πράξεων αὐτῶν, ἐντιθέντες τῇ γραφῇ τὰς τούτων μνήμας μετὰ θάνατον πρὸς τοὺς ἀκούοντας ὅπως γνῶσι τὴν ἐν κόσμῳ αὐτῶν ἀναστροφήν.
10. Decree of Hiereia (Mansi XIII 300 A): ἡμεῖς διὰ τῶν γραφῶν τῆς τῶν ἁγίων ἀπολαύομεν παρουσίας, οὐχὶ τῶν σωμάτων αὐτῶν, ἀλλὰ τῶν ψυχῶν τὰς εἰκόνας ἔχοντες· τὰ γὰρ παρ᾿ αὐτῶν εἰρημένα τῶν ψυχῶν αὐτῶν εἰκόνες εἰσί. Decree of St. Sophia (frg. 28): εἰ γὰρ εἰκόνα τις ἄψυχον ἀναθεὶς παιδὸς ἢ φίλου ἢ συγγενοῦς νομίζει παρεῖναι ἐκεῖνον τὸν ἀπελθόντα καὶ διὰ τῆς εἰκόνος αὐτὸν φαντάζεται τῆς ἀψύχου, πολλῷ μᾶλλον ἡμεῖς διὰ τῶν γραφῶν τῆς τῶν ἁγίων ἀπολαύομεν παρουσίας, οὐχὶ τῶν σωμάτων αὐτῶν τὰς εἰκόνας ἔχοντες ἀλλὰ τῶν ψυχῶν· τὰ γὰρ παρ᾿ αὐτῶν εἰρημένα τῶν ψυχῶν αὐτῶν εἰκόνες εἰσίν.
11. Decree of Hiereia (Mansi XIII 277 D): οὐ θεμιτὸν γὰρ τοῖς ἐλπίδα ἀναστάσεως κεκτημένοις Χριστιανοῖς . . . τοὺς τοιαύτῃ μέλλοντας δόξῃ φαιδρύνεσθαι ἁγίους ἐν ἀδόξῳ καὶ νεκρᾷ ὕλῃ καθυβρίζειν. Decree of St. Sophia (frg. 30 B, Epiphanius): πῶς οὖν τοὺς ἐν δόξῃ μέλλοντας φαιδρύνεσθαι ἁγίους ἐν ἀδόξῳ καὶ νεκρῷ καὶ ἀλάλῳ θέλεις ὁρᾶν; cf. Ostrogorsky, *Studien* etc., 100.
12. Decree of Hiereia (Mansi XIII 277 D): ἡμεῖς γὰρ παρὰ τῶν ἀλλοτρίων οὐ δεχόμεθα τὰς ἀποδείξεις . . . Decree of St. Sophia (frg. 27, John Chrysostom?): ταῦτα δὲ εἴρηται ἵνα οὐ τοῖς πιστοῖς δι᾿ ᾿Ελληνικῶν γίνηται ἡ πίστις· ἡμεῖς παρὰ τῶν ἔξωθεν οὐ δεχόμεθα τὰς ἀποδείξεις.

13. Of the reviews of Ostrogorsky's work (listed in Alexander, *Patriarch Nicephorus*, 277) that of F. Dölger is most important for present purposes: *Göttingische Gelehrte Anzeigen*, 1929, 353–372, esp. 367–370. Dölger suggests that the Seventh Ecumenical Council may have deleted the iconoclastic quotations attributed in the Decree of Hiereia to Epiphanius (except the *Testament*).

14. Mansi XIII 221 C: Πάλιν δὲ ταύτης . . . κλήσει ἐπονομαζόμενον is a quotation from Gregory of Nyssa's *Enkomion on Basil* (*P.G* XLVI, 796 B–C).

15. This fact was noticed, however, by the Patriarch Tarasius in his refutation read at the Seventh Council of Nicaea, cf. Mansi XIII 221 B: κεκλοφότες πατρικὰς φωνὰς ὡς οἰκείας προτίθενται.

16. Quotation from Theodotus of Ancyra in Decree of Hiereia: Mansi XIII 309 E–312 A. Anathema of the same council: Mansi XIII 345 C–D. Quotation from Theododotus of Galatia in Decree of St. Sophia (frg. 20). This relation between quotation and anathema was discovered by M. Anastos, "The Ethical Theory of Images formulated by the Iconoclasts in 754 and 815", *Dumbarton Oaks Papers*, VIII (1954), 150–160, esp. 155, 160. Ostrogorsky, *Studien*, 100 had pointed out a similar case: the language of the earlier Council's first anathema agrees with a fragment from Epiphanius' *Dogmatic Epistle* (frg. 3 Ostrogorsky).

17. Above n. 14. Cf. Nicephorus, *Contra Eusebium et Epiphanidem*, LXIII (J. B. Pitra, *Spicilegium Solesmense*, Paris, 1852, I 472f.). In the same section (p. 476) Nicephorus mentions that Constantine's *florilegium* contained one excerpt from Cyril of Alexandria's *Commentaries on the Prophet Isaiah*. I know of no other reference by Iconoclasts to this work and in spite of much searching have been unable to connect any of its passages with the Decree of Hiereia. The information on the content of Constantine's *florilegium* is discussed in Ostrogorsky, *Studien*, 13 n. 4 and Alexander, *Patriarch Nicephorus*, 174f. and 175 n. 1.

18. For the general practice, see P. van den Ven, "La patristique et l'hagiographie au concile de Nicée", *Byzantion*, XXV–XXVI–XXVII (1955–56–57), 325–362 (does not consider the iconoclastic councils). At Nicaea Gregory Bishop of Neocaesarea and Theodosius of Amorium declared that a passage from Nilus' *Letter to Olympiodorus* and another from the apocryphal περίοδοι τῶν ἁγίων ἀποστόλων had been read at Hiereia (Mansi XIII 37 A–C and 173 D). Neither passage appears in the *florilegium* of the Decree of Hiereia.

19. The information on this imperial drafting committee is collected in Alexander, *Patriarch Nicephorus*, 126f.; on John the Grammarian, 235f.

20. *P.G.* CVIII 1025 A–B.

21. The only manuscript of the *Scriptor Incertus*, Paris. Gr. 1711, saec. XI, seems to read τῷ συνοδικῷ which was emended by Goar (?) into τὸ συνοδικόν. In view of what C. de Boor, in his edition of Theophanes (Leipzig. 1885, vol. II, 380f.) says about abbreviations and ligatures in this manuscript, a misreading or corruption of a case ending is not surprising. At any rate the τούτου, which follows, excludes readings such as τὴν συνοδικήν or τὰ συνοδικά.

22. Thus Photius in his *Bibliotheca* regularly refers to manuscripts of conciliar *Acta* as πρακτικόν or πρακτικά, cf. *Bibliotheca*, codd. 16–20 (ed. I. Bekker, p. 4f.), Robert Devreesse, *Introduction à l'étude des manuscrits grecs* (Paris, 1954), 70, also the passage from the Patriarch Nicephorus cited below n. 25. But see A. Michel, vo. "Synodikon", *Lexikon für Theologie und Kirche*, IX (Freiburg i. Br., 1937): Synodikon kann einen einzelnen Synodalakt oder eine Sammlung von solchen bezeichnen.

23. For the purposes of this enquiry it is immaterial whether Constantine's *florilegium* or the *Acta* of Hiereia are meant by the *Scriptor Incertus*. In view of the Emperor Constantine's influence upon the Council of Hiereia, it is virtually certain that any passage cited in Constantine's patristic *florilegium* was considered at Hiereia and consequently mentioned in the *Acta*.

24. *P.G.* C, 1124 A–B. In this passage Constantine himself refers to the Decree as τὸν τῆς ὀρθοδόξου ἡμῶν συνόδου ὅρον (but note the ἡμῶν: the Council was the Emperor's, the Decree was the Council's) while his emissary Kallistos transmits the message as concerning τῶν βασιλέων τὸν ὅρον.

25. Nicephorus, *Apologeticus Minor*, 9 (*P.G.* C, 845 A–B). In Nicephorus' view no clerical person (ἐκκλησιαστικὸς ἄνθρωπος) can be permitted to discuss the Emperor Constantine's views on religious images or the quotations collected by him. He continues: ἐὰν δὲ ἐκ τούτων τῶν χρήσεων τινὰ βιβλία πρακτικὰ εὑρέθησαν περὶ εἰκόνων τι διαγορεύοντα, διὰ τὴν εἰς τὸν εὐσεβέστατον βασιλέα ἡμῶν πληροφορίαν δέχεσθαι ταῦτα [ταύτην cod.] τὴν Ἐκκλησίαν καὶ ἐπιλύεσθαι [sc. καλῶς ἔχειν δοκεῖ]. The βιβλία πρακτικά are clearly the *Acta* of Hiereia which Nicephorus seems to realize have been discovered (cf. εὑρέθησαν), presumably in the Patriarchal Library. On this passage see Alexander, *Patriarch Nicephorus*, 163–165, 182.

26. Gregory of Neocaesarea and Theodosius of Amorion declared at Nicaea that at Hiereia patristic passages, particularly a quotation from Nilus' *Letter to Olympiodorus*, were read from tablets (πιττάκια) not from the manuscripts (βίβλοι, Mansi XIII 37 B–D). The same bishops stated in connection with a passage from the apocryphal περίοδοι τῶν ἀγίων ἀποστόλων that at Hiereia no manuscript of patristic texts was brought before the Council and that "lying tablets" only were produced. See Mansi XIII, 173 D: βίβλος ἐν μέσῳ ἡμῶν ἢ σύγγραμμα πατρικὸν οὐκ ἐφάνη, εἰ μὴ τὰ ψευδοπιττάκια προεκόμιζον . . . The bishops of Neocaesarea and Amorion had attended the Council of Hiereia.

27. *P.G.* CVIII 1026 B: donec in manus venit synodus sub Constantino Isauro et Caballino habita ex qua occasione accepta coeperunt in libris auctoritates invenire etc.

28. Note 26 above.

29. The Seventh Ecumenical Council of Nicaea was in the habit of identifying the works from which it quoted by their ἀρχή, cf. for example, Mansi XIII 21 A (Ἐκ τοῦ μαρτυρίου τοῦ ἀγίου Ἀναστασίου τοῦ Πέρσου οὗ ἡ ἀρχή); 21 C (Ἐκ τῶν θαυμάτων τοῦ ἀγίου μάρτυρος Ἀναστασίου· ὧν ἡ ἀρχή); 37 E (Ἐκ τῶν κινηθέντων δογμάτων . . . ὧν ἡ ἀρχή). Cf. Devreesse, *Introduction*, 78, 181.

30. The *Scriptor Incertus* may have oversimplified the events. It is improbable that theologians of John the Grammarian's caliber should have been unable to discover any (cf. οὐδὲν) patristic quotations without the help of the *synodikon*. It may also be that the Imperial Committee obtained more from the *synodikon* than the *incipits*. It must have learned from this text of the existence of many "hidden quotations" in the "doctrine" of Hiereia.

ADDITIONAL BIBLIOGRAPHY

On the meanings of the term <u>synodikon</u> see Jean
Gouillard,"Le synodikon de l'Orthodoxie",Centre
de Recherche d'Histoire et Civilisation Byzantines,
<u>Travaux et Mémoires</u> 2,1967,3-6.

X

RELIGIOUS PERSECUTION AND RESISTANCE IN THE BYZANTINE EMPIRE OF THE EIGHTH AND NINTH CENTURIES: METHODS AND JUSTIFICATIONS*

In the history of the Byzantine church the eighth and ninth centuries were a period of frequent, probing, and vigorous debate on a variety of issues. In keeping with the inveterate Byzantine tendency to theological controversy, even problems that to modern eyes may not seem to touch on the fundamentals of faith — the questions of the use and worship of pictorial images of biblical personages or scenes, of Emperor Constantine VI's (780–797) divorce from his first wife and second marriage, or of Emperor Michael III's (842–867) deposition of Patriarch Ignatius and appointment of Photius — were apt to develop into basic theological issues and to lead to acts of violence on one side and of resistance on the other. By way of introduction to the subject matter of this paper, I shall begin with a discussion of three episodes illustrating the consequences resulting from the implementation of specific religious policies.

1. The Problems

During the reign of the great persecutor of religious images and of Iconophiles, the Byzantine emperor Constantine V (741–775), there lived in Cilicia an iconophile monk, George. One of his associates named Theosebes, after he had escaped to Syria which was then in Arab hands, described some of George's experiences. The most dramatic episode in his life was his appearance, shortly prior to 754, before a local council summoned and presided over by an iconoclastic bishop Cosmas. On this occasion Cosmas and George held a lengthy disputation on image worship in the course of which the following exchange took place:

Cosmas said: "Indeed, you acted impiously, therefore this wrath (persecution) descended upon you. Therefore our pious Emperor, great among emperors, knowing the will of God, ordained as follows. He ordered those who worship them (icons), because they set themselves directly against our (imperial) power, to be 'utterly laid waste' (ἐρημίᾳ ἐρημωθῆναι, Is. 60.12) and to be despoiled because their hope is vain." The old man (George) said: "So the words of the Holy Spirit spoken by the prophet Daniel will be fulfilled: His power shall be great and strong and destroy a saintly people and those who do not obey 'he will utterly lay waste' (ἐρημίᾳ αὐτοὺς ἐρημώσει, Daniel 8.24 and Is. 60.12), but the people will become foolish and perish." Cosmas: "You blasphemed against the Emperor and should be executed according to imperial law."[1]

* In an abbreviated form, this paper was presented at the Second International Colloquium in Ecclesiastical History held at Oxford, England, 22-29 September 1974. I am indebted for

Two points are worth noting in this episode. The author has both persecutor and victim speak in language borrowed from the prophet Isaiah, with the result that the persecution decreed by Emperor Constantine V appears as the fulfillment of Old Testament prophecy. Furthermore, the iconoclastic bishop Cosmas explicitly justifies his threat of execution by the claim that George, in relating the emperor's order to Isaiah's prophecy, violated the provisions of Roman law on "blasphemy" against the imperial person.

Half a century later, the chronicler Theophanes recorded and commented on a series of measures regarding two heretical groups: the Paulicians and the Athinganoi. In 811/2 the pious emperor Michael I (811–813), acting on the advice of the patriarch of Constantinople, Nicephorus, and others, decreed the death penalty against them, but was later induced to countermand this measure "by other evil-minded advisers." According to Theophanes, the opponents of the death penalty based their objection on the consideration that execution deprived the victims of the possibility of repentance. Furthermore, they denied that churchmen had the right of imposing the death penalty on persons deemed impious. The chronicler vigorously rejects this argumentation as being contrary to Scripture. He points to St. Peter's role in the deaths of Ananias and Sapphira (Acts 5) who, according to him, had uttered "a mere lie" and to St. Paul's remark "that those who do such things deserve to die" (Rom. 1.32). In fact, Theophanes notes with satisfaction that under Michael I "not a few" of the heretics were executed, obviously before the revocation of the original decree reached the authorities charged with its implementation. It will be seen later that the "evil-minded advisers" opposing the death penalty were the monks of the Constantinopolitan monastery of Studios led by their famous abbot Theodore (759–826).[2]

Theophanes' account is valuable because it gives details on a memorable debate over the question whether there were limitations to the punitive power of state and church. The case is somewhat atypical as the state, here represented by the pious but ineffective emperor Michael I, acts merely as the umpire in an essentially ecclesiastical conflict. Neither side has the slightest sympathy for the doctrines of the victims. The proponents of the death penalty rest their case on references to actions of St. Peter and an opinion of St. Paul while its opponents refuse to deprive even a heretic of his opportunity for repentance.

---

helpful observations and criticism to several members of that gathering, especially to the Very Rev. Dr. Henry Chadwick, dean of Christ Church, Oxford, and to two anonymous readers of my article.

[1] B. M. Melioranski, *Georgii Kipriianin i Ioann Ierusalimlianin* etc., Zapiski Istoriko-Filologicheskago Fakulteta Imp. S.-Peterburgskago Universiteta 59 (St. Petersburg, 1901), p. xxiv. On the identification of the orthodox disputant George in this disputation with a certain George of Cyprus mentioned in iconophile sources, see pp. 72–74.

[2] Theophanes, *Chronographia*, ed. C. de Boor, 1 (Leipzig, 1883), pp. 494, l. 33–495, l. 15. Cf. V. Grumel, *Les regestes des actes des patriarches de Constantinople*, 1, fasc. 2 (Chalcedon, 1936), no. 384.

A final example will be drawn from that inexhaustible treasure house, the correspondence of Theodore of Studios. In 815 the Emperor Leo V had embarked on a new persecution of religious images and their worshippers. Theodore was exiled and in one of his letters written in 819 he described in detail his behavior during meetings with the iconoclastic bishop of Chonae (in Phrygia) and with an "exarch," a title that in this instance designates a powerful imperial official who combined in his hands the administration of five of the "themes" of Asia Minor.[3] Theodore writes to his favorite disciple (and future successor as abbot), Naucratius, that when he met the bishop, he bent his knee, kissed him, accepted a drink but did not eat with him, in spite of the fact that the bishop "had entreated him earnestly to do so and had whispered fraudulent words." This was the yardstick ($\mu\acute{\epsilon}\tau\rho\sigma\nu$), Theodore writes, that he applied. Later he had been summoned by the exarch. This official again raised "the matter" ($\acute{\upsilon}\pi\acute{o}\vartheta\epsilon\sigma\iota\varsigma$), presumably the demand that Theodore eat with him or another Iconoclast by claiming that it was an insignificant concession ($o\dot{\upsilon}\delta\acute{\epsilon}\nu$ $\dot{\epsilon}\sigma\tau\iota$ . . . $\kappa\alpha\grave{\iota}$ $\sigma\mu\iota\kappa\rho\acute{o}\nu$), but Theodore replied that it was a matter of the highest importance. Having reached an impasse, the two men then decided to talk of other things. The exarch mentioned that he might mitigate the harshness of Theodore's exile and they then discussed the affairs of the five "themes" administered by the exarch and mentioned the emperor. Again, Theodore accepted a drink, which he was careful to mark thrice with the sign of the cross. Gradually, the exarch steered the conversation to the subject of icons and the two men "shot at each other with citations," clearly from Scripture and the Church Fathers for and against religious images. Theodore writes that he was on his guard as the discussion involved the emperor, perhaps in a way similar to the conversation between Bishop Cosmas and the monk George (p. 238 above). No agreement was reached, but Theodore explains his objective during the exchange: "to abandon my (previous) dissembling ($\acute{\upsilon}\pi\acute{o}\kappa\rho\iota\sigma\iota\varsigma$) and to show a different countenance as is appropriate towards an impious official." He concludes by saying that as a consequence of his behavior he is now strictly guarded and kept incommunicado.

This third episode is revealing inasmuch as it shows both sides exploring the limits of persuasion and resistance. The bishop and exarch test Theodore's attitude and attempt, through social courtesies and promises, to win over the inconophile abbot by gradual procedures: by inducing him to associate with them in ever more intimate fashion, as long as feasible without raising the issue of the images. Theodore, on the other hand, is anxious not

---

[3] Theodore of Studios, *Letters* 2.63 (PG 99:1281D–1284C). Cf. J. B. Bury, *A History of the Eastern Roman Empire from the Fall of Irene to the Accession of Basil I (A.D. 802–867)* (London, 1912), pp. 10, n. 4; 221 f. All further references to Theodore's works are to vol. 99 of Migne's *Patrologia Graeca*, except for those of the letters edited by I. Cozza (-Luzi) in *Nova Patrum Bibliotheca*, vol. 8, pt. 1 (Rome, 1871) (henceforth abbreviated: ed. CL and cited by number and page).

to provoke a conflict with ecclesiastical and particularly with imperial power. He goes as far as he deems permissible in his dealings with the bishop: gestures of respect, of Christian love, of politeness, but somewhat surprisingly he draws the line at eating with the iconoclastic bishop. He exhibits extreme caution in his conversation with the exarch, in order not to be charged with "blasphemy" against the throne, at the same time unflinching firmness in religious matters, hence his insistence that the matter of eating with men whom he considers heretics is of utmost importance, as well as his fervent defense of the icons.

The episodes just discussed raise a number of questions. What means were used and considered permissible by the persecutors of the eighth and ninth centuries? How did they justify the use of coercion in attempting to win the assent of their victims? What procedures were employed by the resisters and in what terms did they see the conflict?

A survey of some of the relevant literature, of necessity partial and incomplete, will make it clear that the three scenes discussed hitherto may serve as an introduction to the problems faced by religious persecutors and resisters during the eighth and ninth centuries. For the first half of the eighth century the historian depends largely upon the chronicles of a later age: in addition to that of Theophanes, already mentioned (p. 239 above) and completed between 810 and 814, principally the *Breviarium* of Patriarch Nicephorus (†829) based partially on sources common to both chronicles.[4] Strictly contemporary sources are rare, primarily because from 650 to 750 foreign invasions and internal upheavals were unfavorable to literary production. Beginning in the middle of the eighth century literary activity begins to develop, with the result that for the ninth century in particular the historian disposes of a wide variety of extensive and detailed writings of high quality. Among them, saints' lives and other hagiographic documents, as well as the works of Theodore of Studios, are the most informative, but works of theological polemics, biblical commentaries and other types of literature also are helpful. Furthermore the treatise of Peter of Sicily (and documents probably dependent upon it), now available in an excellent edition, is of special value because alone of other sources to be mentioned, it is written from the point of view of the persecuting authorities.[5] It is worth stressing again that the following observations do not aim at completeness of documentation or of issues. Examples will be chosen primarily from the persecutions of Iconophiles, anti-Moechians (i.e., opponents of Emperor Constantine VI's second "adulterous" marriage) and Paulicians and are meant to illustrate some of the problems raised by religious persecutions and resistance during the eighth and ninth centuries.

---

[4] *Nicephori . . . Opuscula Historica*, ed. C. de Boor (Leipzig, 1880), pp. 3–77.

[5] Ch. Astruc and others, "Les Sources grecques pour l'histoire des Pauliciens d'Asie Mineure," Centre de Recherche d'Histoire et Civilisation Byzantines, *Travaux et Mémoires* 4 (1970), 1–227.

2. MEASURES OF PERSECUTION

Theophanes mentions attempts in 721/2 on the part of Emperor Leo III (717–741) to bring about the conversion of Jews and "Montanists."[6] Under the year 725/6 he records mass unrest at Constantinople over the iconoclastic doctrines favored by the emperor and the punishment of many persons, especially men from noble families and men of learning, by mutilation, whipping, exile or fines, and for 728/9 (or the following year) he and Nicephorus note the first punishments and mutilations of image worshippers.[7] For the reasons just indicated, information on the persecution of image worshippers is more copious for the reign of Leo III's son and successor, the emperor Constantine V. It is indicative, however, of the unsatisfactory character of the sources even for this reign that one iconophile martyr of the period, the monk Andreas Kalybites, publicly flogged to death in 760/1 in the hippodrome of the Constantinopolitan quarter of Mangana after he had censured the emperor for his Iconoclasm and compared him to two earlier persecuting emperors, Julian and Valens, is known to posterity only from a brief entry in Theophanes' chronicle.[8] He found no biographer and his name does not even appear in the liturgical book containing short notices of the saints commemorated in services at the capital, the *Synaxarium Ecclesiae Constantinopolitanae*. Another iconophile martyr of the reign of Constantine V, St. Stephen the Younger (†764), did become the subject of an important saint's life by the deacon Stephen, frequently to be drawn upon in this paper, but it is significant that this work was composed as late as 808, more than a generation after the death of the saint.[9]

Late though they are, the sources allow a fairly detailed reconstruction of the means employed by Constantine V in the implementation of his policies and of the decisions of the iconoclastic council of Hiereia-Blachernae (754).

---

[6] Theophanes, p. 401, l. 21. See Andrew Sharf, "The Jews, the Montanists and the Emperor Leo III," *Byzantinische Zeitschrift* 59 (1966), 37–46, and *Byzantine Jewry from Justinian to the Fourth Crusade* (New York, 1971), pp. 61–67.

[7] Theophanes, pp. 405, l. 5; 409, l. 19; cf. Nicephorus, p. 58, l. 25.

[8] Theophanes, p. 432, l. 16. Another reference to the same earlier persecutors, Julian and Valens, in the *Life of St. Stephen the Younger, BHG* 1666, PG 100:1172A. — Saints' lives will henceforth be referred to by their numbers in F. Halkin, *Bibliotheca Hagiographica Graeca* (=*BHG*), 3rd ed., Subsidia Hagiographica 8a (Brussels, 1957). The *Auctarium* of this reference work (Subsidia Hagiographica 47 [Brussels, 1969]) will be designated as follows: *BHG*ᵃ. — The *Synaxarium Ecclesiae Constantinopolitanae*, ed. H. Delehaye (Brussels, 1902), col. 62 f., further records the executions at Constantinople under Leo III of a bishop Hypatius and a priest Andrew, both from Lydia.

[9] It is surprising that the *Life of St. Philaretus* (*BHG* 1511z, ed. M.-H. Fourmy and M. Leroy, "La Vie de S. Philarète," *Byzantion* 9 [1934], 85–170), composed by his grandson Nicetas in 821/2, makes no allusion to the Iconoclastic Controversy. The saint died in 792 and was a contemporary of Leo III's and Constantine V's persecutions and of the Seventh Ecumenical Council, yet none of these events is mentioned. The explanation of the author's silence is probably related to the political situation under Michael II when Nicetas wrote the biography of his grandfather and when the Emperor discouraged discussion of the issue.

The emperor took personal charge of iconoclastic propaganda by composing thirteen short addresses on the subject which he delivered in the course of two weeks and subsequently published.[10] The chroniclers also describe a scene in the main Hippodrome at Constantinople where on 21 August 765 Constantine forced monks to parade, each leading a nun by the hand.[11] On one occasion, during the celebration of the festival called the Brumalia, he supposedly had all relatives and friends of monks beaten and banished from the capital.[12] According to the *Life of St. Stephen the Younger*, the Emperor "declared war upon the monastic garb, called it the garb of darkness . . . and called those wearing this garb (the monks) Unmentionables (ἀμνημόνευτοι) and idol worshippers."[13] He gave orders that his subjects shave their beards, probably so that the monks, who were likely to resist this break with their tradition, would be distinguishable from the rest of the population and thus could be put under additional pressure to conform.[14] To isolate them further he obtained from a public gathering a solemn oath that those present would not worship icons, would not receive communion from a monk or even greet him, but rather would curse him and throw stones at him.[15] He infiltrated his agents into monasteries and stirred up popular feeling against monks.[16] The persecution of monks was carried out with particular cruelty by Michael Lachanodrakon, commander of the Thracesian "theme" in Western Asia Minor. He had monasteries destroyed, beards of monks shaved or singed off, their noses slit.[17] Thirty-eight monks of the monastery of Pelekete in Bithynia were buried alive, others given the choice, in a public scene at Ephesus, either of marrying nuns or of being blinded and exiled to Cyprus.[18] Theodore of Studios further implies that under Constantine V men were forbidden or prevented from entering monasteries.[19] Theosteric-

---

[10] *Life of St. Nicetas of Medikion*, *BHG* 1341, Acta Sanctorum April. 1, pp. xxii–xxxii, esp. ch. 29, p. xxiv. Fragments of Constantine's pamphlets ed. H. Hennephof, *Textus Byzantinos ad Iconomachiam pertinentes* etc. (Leiden, 1969), pp. 52–57.

[11] Theophanes, p. 437, l. 26; Nicephorus, p. 74, l. 1.

[12] *Life of St. Stephen the Younger*, col. 1169D.

[13] *Life of St. Stephen the Younger*, col. 1112A. The term "Unmentionable" occurs frequently as the equivalent of "monk" in words attributed by the hagiographer to Iconoclasts, e.g. cols. 1133A, 1136B, 1140A, 1156B, D, etc. Also *Life of St. Nicetas of Medikion*, ch. 29, p. xxiv, and Theophanes, p. 443, l. 1, but according to the chronicler the word was used for any pious person. De Boor suggests, in his index to Theophanes (2:728), the meaning: *cuius mentio non fit in ecclesia, excommunicatus.*

[14] *Life of St. Stephen the Younger*, col. 1133C: "μέχρι τῆς δορᾶς τῆς ὄψεως τὴν σίμωσιν ποιεῖσθαι τῆς γενειάδος." In Migne the words τὴν σίμωσιν ποιεῖσθαι are translated by *radere* 'to shave,' but the expression is not clear. Cf. Nicephorus, p. 72, ll. 3 f.: "κομῆται . . . ἀντὶ κεκαρμένων."

[15] *Life of St. Stephen the Younger*, col. 1112B. Cf. Franz Dölger, *Regesten der Kaiserurkunden* etc. (Munich and Berlin, 1924 ff.), no. 324.

[16] See the incident involving George Synkletus, *Life of St. Stephen the Younger*, col. 1132D ff.

[17] *Life of St. Stephen the Younger*, col. 1165A; Theophanes, pp. 445, ll. 3 and 28.

[18] *Life of St. Stephen the Younger*, col. 1165A, B.

[19] Theodore of Studios, *Laudatio Platonis*, *BHG* 1553, ch. 21, PG 99:824B.

tus, author of a *Life of St. Nicetas of Medikion*, characterizes the objective of
Constantine's policy in the following way: "Ever since he became emperor,
his entire purpose and desire was to wipe out the entire monastic garb."[20]
When the emperor received the news that because of Michael Lachanodrakon's persecution no monk was left in the Thracesian "theme," he wrote to
him: "I found you a man after my heart, you are carrying out my every
wish."[21] One of the critical moments in St. Stephen's career occurred in a
debate with the emperor when he trampled on a coin carrying the imperial
portraits. Constantine could only with great difficulty restrain his entourage
from hurling the saint down headlong from the sun parlor in which the
confrontation took place.[22]

During the interval of almost thirty years between the Seventh Ecumenical
Council of Nicaea (787) and the new outbreak of Iconoclasm (815), the
sources make no mention of a persecution of Iconoclasts. One might be
tempted to surmise that during this period or later during the Second
Iconoclasm (715–843) lives of iconoclastic saints were in fact composed but
were destroyed after the restoration of orthodoxy in 843. Yet on reflection it
seems highly unlikely that if the post-Nicene governments had launched a
persecution of Iconoclasts, the rich iconophile literature of the ninth century
should not have preserved a single refutation of the claims of such supposed
iconoclastic confessors or martyrs. Moreover, an attitude of forgiveness towards Iconoclasts is entirely in keeping with the decisions and spirit of the
leadership and majority of the Seventh Council.

While the post-Nicene emperors thus seem to have considered it impolitic
to use coercion against Iconoclasts, they had no such hesitations in their
relations with other groups. In 795 Emperor Constantine VI (780–797) di-
vorced his wife and married one of her ladies-in-waiting, Theodote, a cousin
of Theodore, the abbot of Sakkudion (near Prusa), later of Studios in
Constantinople. Theodore's biographer narrates how the young emperor
tried to win over Theodore and his adherents, for example by sending them
gold. He even decided to visit the warm springs of Prusa, in the vicinity of
Theodore's monastery, in the hope that the abbot would avail himself of the
vicinity of the court to pay his respects to the emperor.[23] But the monks of
Sakkudion did not take the hint. Several years later, in his funeral oration
for his mother, Theodore told of the subsequent harsh treatment meted out
by the emperor to him and his monks. They were expelled from their
monastery, beaten and exiled to Thessalonica.[24] The monks were recalled
after Empress Irene (797–802) blinded and deposed her son and Patriarch

---

[20] *Life of St. Nicetas of Medikion*, ch. 29, p. xxiv; cf. Theophanes, p. 443, l. 7.
[21] Theophanes, p. 446, l. 12. Cf. Dölger, *Regesten*, no. 332 (A.D. 771).
[22] *Life of St. Stephen the Younger*, col. 1160A. One of Constantine V's gold coins carries indeed
the portrait of his father on the obverse and his own and his son Leo's portraits on the reverse,
cf. André Grabar, *L'Iconoclasme byzantin, Dossier Archéologique* (Paris, 1957), p. 116 and fig. 27.
[23] *Life of St. Theodore of Studios* (by the monk Michael), *BHG* 1754, PG 99:253B.
[24] Theodore of Studios, *Laudatio funebris in matrem*, *BHG* 2422, PG 99:893–896.

Tarasius was even forced to apologize for his tolerant attitude towards the adulterous union. In 808 the controversy flared up anew, over the restoration to the priesthood of Joseph of Kathara who had officiated at Constantine's second wedding. On this occasion, it involved a larger circle of persons and was once more accompanied by violence. A number of abbots and even two bishops sided with Theodore, were exiled and suffered for their cause until after the accession of Michael I in 811 a reconciliation of the two warring factions was arranged.[25]

During the same interval between Seventh Council and Second Iconoclasm there occurred an even more violent though brief persecution of three other religious groups: Paulicians, Athinganoi and Jews. Upon the request of Patriarch Nicephorus of Constantinople, Emperor Michael I imposed in 811/2 the death penalty upon them. The passage from Theophanes' chronicle mentioned at the beginning of this paper (p. 239, above) shows that a considerable number of executions of Paulicians took place as a consequence of the emperor's decree, but it was eventually withdrawn because of the objections of the Studite party. Peter of Sicily recounts, in his treatise against the Paulicians, how in accordance with the imperial decree Paulicians were executed in the Armeniac "theme."[26] Undoubtedly, the decision to persecute the Paulicians was related, on the one hand, to Byzantium's defeats during the war against the Bulgars and, on the other hand, to the highly effective missionary work carried out by the Paulician movement under one of its greatest "teachers," Sergios.

Persecution of the Iconophiles resumed during the reign of Leo V (813–820), was interrupted under his successor Michael II (820–829) and was renewed by Theophilus (829–842). Theodore of Studios never tires of repeating that Patriarch Nicephorus, several archbishops, bishops, priests, monks and nuns were exiled, jailed, tortured or even executed and churches destroyed or confiscated.[27] Theodore's descriptions of the persecution can be corroborated by many saints' lives. The experience of one of the abbots, St. Nicetas of Medikion, may serve to illustrate the fate of Iconophiles under Leo V. Several abbots, including St. Nicetas, were summoned to Constantinople and subjected to flattery and then to threats. When they did not yield, they were sent to separate jails. In prison St. Nicetas was visited by emissaries of the emperor and harassed. After several days the emperor

---

[25] On the Moechian Controversy, see Paul J. Alexander, *The Patriarch Nicephorus of Constantinople. Ecclesiastical Policy and Image Worship in the Byzantine Empire* (Oxford, 1958), pp. 82–101.

[26] Peter of Sicily, ed. Astruc, § 175 ff., p. 65; cf. Nina G. Garsoïan, *The Paulician Heresy* (The Hague, 1967), p. 124, and Paul Lemerle, "L'Histoire des Pauliciens d'Asie Mineure d'après les sources grecques," Centre de Recherche d'Histoire et Civilisation Byzantines, *Travaux et Mémoires* 5 (1973), 81 f. As to the implementation of Michael I's decree with regard to the Athinganoi, it is probable that a portion of the sect transferred, or was transferred, to the western provinces; see Joshua Starr, "An Eastern Christian Sect: The Athinganoi," *Harvard Theological Review* 29 (1936), 93–106, esp. pp. 94, 97.

[27] For example, Theodore of Studios, *Letters* 2.12 (to Pope Paschal), col. 1152D.

banished him to Asia Minor and St. Nicetas was forced to walk, in the company of a guard, at great speed for seven days in bitter winter weather until he reached his destination. The other abbots were given similar treatment. After only five days, when St. Nicetas showed no sign of yielding, the emperor recalled him and had him jailed again at Constantinople. He and his colleagues were then handed over to the notorious John (Morocharzanios), the future iconoclastic patriarch, and subjected by him to punishment and harassment "such as not even the pagans inflicted upon the martyrs." The hagiographer describes St. Nicetas's sufferings in jail in somber colors. When all proved unsuccessful, the authorities promised the abbots release from prison and safe return to their monasteries if they would just once take communion from the iconoclastic patriarch Theodotus (815–821). The other abbots agreed, visited St. Nicetas in his prison and argued as follows: "what they require of us is nothing, let us make a small concession (οἰκονομίσωμεν μικρόν) lest we lose all." Under this prodding, St. Nicetas finally gave in, against his will, not, so the hagiographer adds, because he wanted to escape from the harassment but "because he respected the appeal of the fathers (abbots)." The abbots then went to "the so-called Chapels," adorned as before with images, and took communion from Theodotus who said: "Anathema to those who do not worship the image of Christ." St. Nicetas was to regret his hour of weakness to the end of his life.[28]

When the Iconoclastic Controversy came to an end in 843, the government of Empress Theodora did not adopt, towards the iconoclastic clergy, the tolerant attitude taken in 787 by Irene, but under pressure from the monastic party carried out a thorough purge of the clergy. This is the more remarkable as because of the surviving strength of iconoclastic sentiment among the laity the government proceeded in a most circumspect and gradual fashion in the matter of the restoration of religious images.[29] Beyond the purge of the clergy, there is no evidence that after the "restoration of orthodoxy" the victorious Iconophiles embarked on a persecution of their opponents.

3. MEANS OF RESISTANCE

How did the victims react to persecution? The defensive measures adopted by the various groups ran the gamut from passive resistance to

---

[28] *Life of St. Nicetas of Medikion*, chs. 38–41, pp. xxv f. The Patriarch Theodotus's saying is surprising. Was he totally insincere? Or did he interpret "the image of Christ" to mean, as Emperor Constantine V had done before him, the Eucharist?

[29] V. Grumel, "La Politique religieuse du patriarche saint Méthode," *Echos d'Orient* 34 (1935), 389–401; F. Dvornik, "The Patriarch Photius and Iconoclasm," *Dumbarton Oaks Papers* 7 (1953), 68–97, esp. p. 82; Grabar, *L'Iconoclasme byzantin*, pp. 208–214. I do not know the source of Jean Gouillard's statement ("Le synodikon de l'orthodoxie," Centre de Recherche d'Histoire et Civilisation Byzantines, *Travaux et Mémoires* 2 [1967], 127 f.) that between two and three thousand members of the clergy lost their positions. The text that he cites (*Life of Methodius*, *BHG* 1278, PG 100:1257AB) does not say so.

military secession and to the use of armed force. Thus after Constantine VI's second marriage to Theodote the abbot Theodore and his adherents failed to appear at the emperor's court (p. 244 above) and after the restoration of Joseph to the priesthood they avoided for two years communion with him and with other members of the clergy who officiated with him.[30] Theodore was also aware of large numbers of people who sympathized with him secretly although they did not dare formally to join him in his passive resistance.[31] When Emperor Leo V began to implement his iconoclastic policies and many Iconophiles were banished or jailed, the confessors were received hospitably in homes, supplied with food and other necessities and otherwise comforted by members of the clergy as well as by laymen, despite imperial prohibitions and the danger of harassment or punishment by agents of the government. A large number of Theodore's letters contain expressions of gratitude to good Samaritans of this kind.[32]

The banishment of the ecclesiastical leadership and the breaking up of monastic communities were intended to isolate members of the iconophile resistance movement. It was one of the principal achievements of Theodore that he organized a Studite community-in-exile which towards the end of his life expanded into a church-in-exile. The principal surviving monument of this organization is Theodore's massive correspondence. During his exiles in the Moechian Controversy and especially after the second outbreak of Iconoclasm he wrote letters not only to the dispersed members of his own monastery but also to monks and abbots of other institutions, to bishops, archbishops and patriarchs (including the pope), to imperial officials and other laymen. Other clerical victims of the persecution such as the "Graptoi" brothers, Theodore and Theophanes, Michael Syncellus and the future Patriarch Methodius also maintained a wide correspondence.[33] In Theodore of Studios's case, the vast network of his communications was made possible as well as supplemented by an elaborate and where possible regular courier service. Indeed, Theodore's messengers often transmitted information and advice that the abbot did not wish to write down.[34] During the Moechian Controversy he even set up a system of ciphers in which the twenty-four letters of the Greek alphabet signified the more important members of the

[30] Theodore of Studios, *Letters* 1.21, col. 972C; 1.24, col. 984A.

[31] Theodore of Studios, *Letters* 1.48, col. 1081A.

[32] For example, Theodore of Studios, *Letters*, ed. CL, nos. 31, p. 25; 72, p. 58 f.; 129, p. 114 f.; 182, p. 155 f.

[33] *Life of St. Michael Syncellus, BHG* 1296, ed. Th. N. Schmit, *Kahrie-dzhami,* Izvestiia Russkago Arkheologicheskago Instituta v Konstantinopolie 11 (1906), 227–259, esp. pp. 237, l. 25; 239, l. 6; 243, l. 29; 246, l. 36 ff. (text of a letter by Michael to the "Graptoi" brothers), see p. 232, l. 8 (letters to orthodox Sicilian monks); p. 247, l. 27 (letters of Methodius). For a stimulating and thorough historical analysis of a section of this fascinating saint's life, see Vittorio Peri, "Leone III e il 'Filioque.' Echi del Caso nell' Agiografia Greca," *Rivista di Storia della Chiesa in Italia* 25 (1971), 3–58.

[34] Theodore of Studios, *Letters*, ed. CL, no. 104, p. 93.

Studite community and the three obsolete letters (digamma, etc.) certain deviant Studite monks as well as Patriarch Nicephorus and the emperor of the same name, a system that Theodore continued to use during the icono-clastic period.[35] Theodore realized that these communications were apt to endanger both messenger and recipient (he was indifferent to his own danger) but considered it his duty to speak out for the truth during a persecution. In his eyes the principal function of the correspondence was to preserve the cohesion of the scattered Studite community — "the letters are like diaries in that they tie us together in love," he wrote — just as St. Paul's letters had served to join the early Christian churches in the Roman Em-pire.[36] Above all, according to him, the persecuted Christian had an obliga-tion to speak freely (παρρησιάζεσθαι) and to teach others in a period of persecution.[37] He advised disciples such as the monk Naucratius, who suc-ceeded him as abbot, "to correspond, visit, support, exhort, comfort, awak-en, teach and encourage" and expressed his determination "to write to all the fathers in exile," in spite of an imperial order to be silent.[38] He em-phasized the duty of speaking freely during a persecution, without however provoking martyrdom:

> For if the Lord's enemies (the Iconoclasts) who have the support of Caesar speak freely their impiety, lead astray the people of God and set every church on fire, what shall we suffer who have the King of all men (as our helper) if we do not even secretly speak to our companions? . . . And yet we have been told to avoid temptation. So we must choose the mean, as the saying goes.[39]

When the murder of Emperor Leo V and the accession of Michael brought the persecution to a halt, Theodore noted with satisfaction that "the door of free speech (παρρησία)" had been opened.[40]

In addition to the correspondence maintained by Theodore of Studios and others, several members of the ecclesiastical resistance, including Theo-dore himself and Patriarch Nicephorus, wrote learned works of theological polemics refuting the theses of the Iconoclasts, others composed saints' lives celebrating heroic members of their own group. Iconophile circles were also responsible for less pretentious literary works directed against their perse-cutors. Thus the chronicler Theophanes knows of an exchange between Patriarch Germanos and Emperor Leo III in which the patriarch referred to a prophecy according to which the images would be destroyed "under Conon." Leo then informed the patriarch that Conon was his given name.[41]

---

[35] Theodore of Studios, *Letters* 1.41, col. 1057 ff. This letter must have been written prior to 814 as Theodore's uncle Plato (ὁ πατὴρ ἡμῶν) is mentioned together with the living Studites.

[36] Theodore of Studios, *Letters* 2.39, col. 1233C; cf. 2.208, col. 1629A.

[37] Theodore of Studios, *Letters* 2.2, col. 1120B; 2.46, col. 1249C.

[38] Theodore of Studios, *Letters*, ed. CL, no. 46, p. 39; cf. nos. 48, p. 41; 109, p. 98.

[39] Theodore of Studios, *Letters*, ed. CL, no. 63, p. 52 f. Cf. 2.44, col. 1248B (one should not provoke martyrdom as St. Gordios did).

[40] Theodore of Studios, *Letters* 2.90, col. 1340A.

[41] Theophanes, p. 407, l. 17. On the diffusion of the name Conon and on this name's possible

Of this prophecy it is impossible to say whether or when it circulated in written form, but a century later there is evidence that Iconophiles, allegedly the future patriarch Methodius, published successively three pamphlets predicting, more or less correctly, the date of death for Emperors Leo V, Michael II and Theophilus.[42]

Among the topics most frequently discussed in Theodore's correspondence were the permissible limits of association with Iconoclasts, the attitude to be taken towards persons who transgressed these limits and cooperated with the persecutors and above all the subject of martyrdom. The incident of Theodore's meeting with the bishop of Chonae related at the beginning of this paper (p. 240)   shows that Theodore was, for example, willing to accept a drink from Iconoclasts but refused to eat with them. He had followed this practice with regard to his earlier opponents at the time of the Moechian Controversy and had further laid down the rule not to share a meal with persons who had eaten with Moechians. He based these precepts, which he continued to apply during the Iconoclastic Controversy, on 1 Cor. 5.11 or Ps. 140(141).5, but on the other hand warned against overzealous enquiries as this would be an act of self-appointed censorship (ἐθελόγνωμον) and produce complete isolation.[43] Similarly, St. Michael Syncellus and his companions while in jail at Constantinople under Leo V went on a hunger strike and refused to eat the "ascetics' diet" of dates and figs sent them by the emperor, referring to the passage from the Psalms (140.5) also cited by Theodore.[44] The latter exhorted one of his lay correspondents to observe three rules: not to accept a blessing from a heretic, not to sing psalms or eat bread with him. In a reply to another layman, however, he implies that while strict practice (ἀκρίβεια) forbade association with heretics by eating, drinking and (other kinds of) sharing, exceptions might be made in dangerous situations.[45] With regard to the taking of communion, Theodore advises that the only question to be considered is the orthodoxy and innocence of the celebrant himself. If one were to investigate in addition the credentials of the bishop who had ordained the priest in question, "the gift of the priesthood, by virtue of which we have the right to be called Christians, would cease to

---

implication for the problem of Leo III's origin see ch. 2 ("Leo — alias Conon") of Stephen Gero, *Byzantine Iconoclasm during the Reign of Leo III with Particular Attention to the Oriental Sources*, Corpus Scriptorum Christianorum Orientalium 346, Subsidia Tomus 41 (Louvain, 1973), pp. 13–24.

[42] *Life of Euthymius of Sardis, BHG*ᵃ 2145, unpublished; cf. Jean Gouillard, "Une oeuvre inédite du patriarche Méthode: la Vie d'Euthyme de Sardes," *Byzantinische Zeitschrift* 53 (1960), 38. Compare also the passage in the *Life of Sts. David, Symeon and George, BHG* 494 *Analecta Bollandiana* 18 (1899), 211–259, §16, where one of the Saints comforts his audience by referring to a local saying, twelve days prior to Leo V's murder: "αἱ . . . τῶν χοίρων φωναὶ [read φοναὶ] περὶ τὰς καλάνδας." D. Michailidis has shown (*Analecta Bollandiana* 89 [1971], 147) that pigs were customarily slaughtered on Christmas eve.

[43] Theodore of Studios, *Letters* 1.49, col. 1089B; 2.119, col. 1393A; cf. 2.32, col. 1205A.

[44] *Life of St. Michael Syncellus*, p. 236, l. 22.

[45] Theodore of Studios, *Letters* 2.172, col. 1541B; 2.174, col. 1544D.

such an extent that we should lapse back into pagan worship."[46] Priests ordained overseas, at Rome, at Naples, in "Longibardia" and Sicily are to be accepted.[47]

In the matter of association with heretics, the practice of the Iconophiles was not uniform and some of them were considerably more rigorous than Theodore. For example, during the persecution of Leo V St. Peter of Atroa admonished his monks not to join Iconoclasts in eating, drinking, praying, and singing of psalms, and even forbade them to greet them, "for he who greets them partakes in their fruitless works."[48] St. Peter practiced what he preached, for, according to his biographer, when one day on a road leading from Lydia to Phrygia he saw from afar two bishops, he made himself invisible, "for he did not wish to be seen by the bishops because the heresy of the lawless Iconoclasts was then prevailing." It is noteworthy that both the saint and the hagiographer, the monk Sabas, take it for granted that during the reign of Leo V bishops are Iconoclasts.[49] On a later occasion, St. Peter and his brother Paul were imprisoned in a chapel controlled by iconoclastic clergy. When the time came for the two brothers to say their morning devotions, they passed their guards unseen, prayed in the open air and then returned to the chapel. The hagiographer explains their behavior by referring to one of the apostolic canons: "a pious man must not enter or pray in the church of the impious."[50]

Theodore of Studios's letters are full of advice on the treatment of persons, especially of clergy, who under the pressure of the persecutors had made concessions to the Iconoclasts and later wished to be forgiven by the Iconophiles. What for example was to be done with an abbot who had accepted the decisions of the iconoclastic council of St. Sophia (815) in writing but with mental reservations (ὑποκριτικὴ ὑπογραφή) and later claimed, as did others, that he had done so in order to protect a church building and the images therein from destruction? In this case the abbot referred for support of his views to an otherwise unknown report (ἀναφορά) of the ex-patriarch Nicephorus. Under what conditions and penalties was a priest who had done the same thing to be reinstated in his priestly functions?[51] Should a plea from a priest that he had been forced to accept communion from an Iconoclast be accepted? And did "compulsion" in the taking of communion, if that was indeed a valid excuse, require that the recipient's jaw was forcefully held open? Were beatings, threats, torture, or mere fear legitimate excuses? What type of repentance was required in cases

---

[46] Theodore of Studios, *Letters* 1.53, col. 1105C.

[47] Theodore of Studios, *Letters* 2.215, col. 1645D f.

[48] *Life of St. Peter of Atroa*, *BHG* 2364, ed. V. Laurent, Subsidia Hagiographica 29 (Brussels, 1956), pp. 65–225, esp. ch. 14.20, p. 103; cf. ch. 83.28, p. 219.

[49] *Life of St. Peter of Atroa*, ch. 19.11, p. 110 f.

[50] *Life of St. Peter of Atroa*, ch. 26.33, p. 127.

[51] Theodore of Studios, *Letters* 2.106, col. 1365A; 2.6, col. 1128A.

where concessions were made to Iconoclasm and for what length of time? What penalties were to be imposed?[52]

Theodore deals with these and other practical matters in many of his letters, but he invariably insists that his replies be considered advisory and that the final and authoritative disposal of these cases was to be reserved for a future church council which, he fervently hoped, would liquidate the Iconoclastic Controversy.[53] Nevertheless, since the ex-patriarch Nicephorus in his exile abstained from all public activity, Theodore's authority, during the last years of his life, far transcended the Studite community. He was consulted widely by members of the persecuted church. Thus during the reign of Michael II St. Peter of Atroa visited Theodore at a time when his miracles were questioned by his detractors, told him about his life as an ascetic and his creed and received from him a letter certifying his holiness and threatening his critics with anathema.[54] The author of the *Vita Retractata* of this saint knows even of a second meeting of the two abbots in the course of which Theodore "advised" his colleague to regroup his monks scattered by the persecution of Leo V in new communities (κατὰ συστήματα).[55]

Theodore's activity as a "doctor of souls" did not go unchallenged. A monk, also called Theodore, issued an "encyclical letter" in which he criticized the practice of the persecuted clergy of imposing penalties on penitent bishops, priests and monks who had sided with the Iconoclasts. He charged that these activities had produced unseemly rivalries and jealousies, to such an extent that the competing clergy failed to recognize each other's decisions. The monk Theodore even suggested that pardons had been granted for cash and urged that there was no difference between Iconoclasm and Manichaeanism, a thesis that if accepted would have had the consequence that a return from Iconoclasm to orthodoxy would be extremely onerous. The abbot of Studios replied to these allegations that Patriarch Nicephorus had, for the duration of the persecution, "allowed all those so inclined to treat the illnesses as they happened and as best they could."[56] It was undoubtedly because of Theodore's genius in organizing and directing first the Studite community-in-exile and gradually large sections of the Byzantine church in general that he was one of only two monastic leaders of

---

[52] Theodore of Studios, *Letters* 2.32, col. 1205A; 2.49, col. 1257B. Especially full details in 2.215, cols. 1645–1653.

[53] Theodore of Studios, *Letters* 2.152, col. 1472D f., note the formula: οὐχ ὁριστικῶς ἀλλὰ συμβουλευτικῶς. St. Peter of Atroa considered his decisions more definitive, cf. *Life of St. Peter of Atroa*, ch. 28, p. 130 f. and the editor's note 3 on p. 130.

[54] *Life of St. Peter of Atroa*, ch. 37 f.; pp. 144–148.

[55] *Vita Retractata of St. Peter of Atroa*, *BHG* 2365, ed. V. Laurent, Subsidia Hagiographica 31 (Brussels, 1958), ch. 41 bis and p. 42 f.

[56] Theodore of Studios, *Letters* 2.162, cols. 1504–1516. The charge of venality: col. 1505B (λημμάτων ἡττώμενοι πόρους ἐπινοοῦντες). The author of the *Life of St. Stephen the Younger*, col. 1084B, also called the Iconoclasm of Leo III a Manichaean heresy.

a past generation who was commemorated in the original *synodikon* celebrating the return to orthodoxy in 843.[57]

No theme recurs more frequently in Theodore's letters than the call to constancy (ἔνστασις), confession (ὁμολογία) and martyrdom (μαρτυρία). In some letters the loss of blood under punishment seems to differentiate the martyr from the confessor, yet most of the time Theodore does not seem to make a clear-cut distinction between these terms. Thus he speaks of Empress Irene after the Seventh Ecumenical Council as "having shown herself as a martyr without bloodshed," just as Theosterictus, author of the *Life of St. Nicetas of Medikion*, mentions Irene's "act of constancy on behalf of the truth" in reference to her dismissal of the iconoclastic garrison at Constantinople and speaks of his hero as "a confessor or bloodless martyr."[58] Theodore never tires of exhorting his correspondents to continue their resistance to the Iconoclasts. Just as, in his opinion, it is illegitimate to provoke martyrdom as St. Gordios had done long ago, so he admonishes his disciples to spurn the example of "the lukewarm brethren" and to join instead the ranks of "the fervent."[59] Martyrdom, in the sense of being whipped, while not required from those who have "fallen," i.e., who made concessions to the Iconoclasts, demonstrates the forgiveness of their sin.[60] Theodore constantly reminds his flock of those of his monks who had suffered for their iconophile convictions and admonishes his correspondents to follow their example. Among the Studite martyrs he praises with special frequency and intensity the monk Thaddaeus who was beaten to death by the persecutors. He had been of Bulgarian origin, a freedman of Theodore and a person without education.[61]

The most desperate and violent form of resistance was adopted by the group exposed to the most severe type of religious persecution, the Paulicians. According to the most recent studies, elements of this group, which probably was of Armenian origin, had in the course of the eighth century left Byzantine territory, settled on the other side of the Arab frontier and later returned to the Empire.[62] At the end of the eighth and early ninth centuries the Paulicians won many converts and on certain occasions played a role in the internal politics of the Empire and especially in its capital. Because of their success, the government of Michael I decreed, as noted at

[57] Ed. Jean Gouillard, "Le Synodikon de l'orthodoxie," Centre de Recherche d'Histoire et Civilisation Byzantines, *Travaux et Mémoires* 2 (1967), 1–316, esp. line 127, p. 53, and p. 144. The other earlier monastic leader was "Isaac the miracle worker" whom Gouillard proposes to identify with St. Theophanes (the chronicler).

[58] Theodore of Studios, *Letters*, ed. CL, no. 108, p. 96 f.; *Laudatio Platonis*, ch. 24, col. 828B; *Life of St. Nicetas of Medikion*, chs. 30, p. xxiv, and 47, p. xxvii.

[59] Theodore of Studios, *Letters* 2.44, col. 1248B; ed. CL, no. 107, p. 96.

[60] Theodore of Studios, *Letters* 2.45, col. 1249A.

[61] Cf. Alexander, *Patriarch Nicephorus*, p. 101, n. 1. Add *Synaxarium Ecclesiae Constantinopolitanae*, col. 353, l. 51, *BHG*[a] 2415e; Theodore of Studios, *Letters* 2.5, col. 1124C; ed. CL, nos. 112, 113, 114 (p. 102), 116, 120, 121, 124.

[62] Garsoïan, *Paulician Heresy*, pp. 112–125; Lemerle, "L'Histoire des Pauliciens," p. 49 f.

the beginning of this paper (p. 239 above) the death penalty against them and a number of executions took place. Peter of Sicily recounts that in the Armeniac "theme," i.e., in northeastern Asia Minor, the bishop of Neocaesarea and the "exarch," in this case probably a monastic official, "executed [those Paulicians] whom they discovered because they deserved death and led [others] to perdition."[63] The result of this cruel persecution, unparalleled in the Empire's treatment of other heretical groups, was dramatic. A Paulician militia called the *Astatoi* (a term of uncertain meaning) was formed, the bishop and the exarch were slain and the *Astatoi* fled beyond the Arab frontier where they found refuge in the territory of the emir of Melitene, Amr b. Abdallah. This violent reaction took place prior to 834/5. Reinforced by new emigrants during the following decades the Paulicians built an organization closely resembling a state and repeatedly raided the eastern provinces of the Empire. Eventually it took the emperor Basil I (867–886) a series of hard-fought campaigns until he succeeded in 878 to capture the Paulician capital of Tefrik.[64] The Paulician reaction to their fierce persecution by the Byzantine authorities was the most extreme employed by a persecuted group during the eighth and ninth centuries. Both the persecution of the Paulicians and their response will be reconsidered in the discussion of the arguments advanced by persecutors and resisters in defense of their activities.

4. JUSTIFICATIONS OF PERSECUTION

Before commenting on the ways in which the persecutors of the eighth and ninth centuries justified their measures a few preliminary remarks are in order. In the first place, I shall be concerned with some of the justifications adduced by the persecutors, not with the historical reasons for the persecutions, which is another topic. Then, a great difficulty in this discussion is the fact that, except for the treatises against the Paulicians, the surviving literature reflects the point of view of the anti-Moechians and the Iconophiles. To a large extent, therefore, any study of the argumentation used by the persecutors must be based on sources emanating from their victims. This is true even of the vocabulary of persecution beginning with the word itself (διωγμός). Indeed, it is highly unlikely that the Moechians, the Iconoclasts or any other persecutors thought or spoke of themselves as "persecuting" their opponents. Instead they saw themselves as defending the truth, restoring the unity of the church divided by dissension, implementing imperial or ecclesiastical law, safeguarding the prerogatives of the imperial office, etc. The entire terminology of persecution derives from the views and experience of the victims and any inference as to the intentions of the persecutors is therefore hazardous. Finally it is obvious that especially in the persecution of Iconophiles and Paulicians questions of doctrine were of

---

[63] Peter of Sicily, ed. Astruc, § 176, p. 65.
[64] Garsoïan, *Paulician Heresy*, p. 119 f.; Lemerle, "L'Histoire des Pauliciens," pp. 71–108.

paramount importance. However, I shall not be concerned here with doctrinal matters but with the arguments advanced by the group in power for taking the crucial step from doctrinal debate and polemic to measures of coercion.

Such escalation had by no means gone unchallenged in the history of the Church. Thus probably in the late fourth century an unknown revisor, perhaps an Arian or an Apollinarian, interpolated into Ignatius of Antioch's *Epistle to the Philadelphians* a passage to the effect that the addressees should hate and admonish those who hate God (i.e., heretics) and call them to repentance, but should not beat or persecute (διώκειν) them.[65] A century and a half later, the secular historian Agathias, when commenting on the paganism of the Alamanni and contrasting it with the Christianity of the Franks, expressed the opinion that the Alamanni deserved to be pitied rather than being treated harshly (χαλεπαίνεσθαι, i.e., persecuted). Agathias even generalized his statement by adding that it applied to "all those who fell short of the truth," a formulation that includes Christian heretics.[66] It may be doubted whether such tolerant attitudes survived into the eighth and ninth centuries. The fourth-century interpolator of Ignatius of Antioch's *Epistle to the Philadelphians* had made it clear, by citing 1 Thess. 4.5, that he rejected persecutions of Christian heretics of the kind that had occurred in his own experience during the Arian Controversy, on the grounds that they represented a repetition of the pagan persecutions of Christians. In the eighth and ninth centuries the persecutions of the early church were only a dim memory. Thus Theodore of Studios, so far as I know, never cited Pseudo-Ignatius and the tradition represented by him as a general argument against persecution, except on one occasion when he used it to justify his opposition to the death penalty imposed upon the Paulicians.[67]

Yet although the voices opposing persecution of heretics had fallen silent by the eighth and ninth centuries, historical circumstances often prevented authorities from enforcing their religious convictions. Each of the "Isaurian" emperors of the eighth century, for example, waited several years before launching a persecution of the Iconophiles, just as Empress Irene did not take steps to restore image worship during the first four years of her reign. As already noted (p. 244 above), there is no evidence of persecutions of Iconoclasts in the interval between the Seventh Ecumenical Council and the Second Iconoclasm. The new outbreak of the controversy was initiated by

---

[65] Ed. J. B. Lightfoot, *Apostolic Fathers*, vol. II, 3, p. 206 f., cited by Theodore of Studios, *Letters* 2.155, col. 1485A. On the date of the interpolation, see Wilhelm von Christ, Wilhelm Schmid and Otto Stählin, *Geschichte der griechischen Literatur*, 6th ed., Zweiter Teil, Zweite Hälfte (Munich, 1924), p. 1227 f.

[66] Agathias, ed. Rudolf Keydell, 1.7.3., p. 18, l. 13. The first part of the passage contains echoes of Plato's *Republic*, Book I, 336e–337a. See Averil Cameron, *Agathias* (Oxford, 1970), pp. 94, 110.

[67] See note 65 above.

Emperor Leo V almost immediately after the Bulgar attack on the Empire, which had brought him to the throne and had ended with the death of the Bulgar ruler Krum. Michael II did not persecute the Iconophiles and under his son Theophilus the persecutions did not begin until he had been on the throne for several years.[68] The pattern is clear: while, as will be seen, the political and religious establishments considered the transition from a more or less non-violent propagation of their religious views to acts of coercion and persecution as little more than a continuation of missionary activity by additional means, most emperors, especially those belonging to new dynasties (Leo III, Michael II) or those whose throne was initially shaky (Constantine V, Irene), delayed measures of religious persecution until they had consolidated their power over state and church. The one apparent exception, Leo V, confirms the pattern, for the population of the capital in particular related the Bulgar victories over Byzantine armies with the iconophile policies of his immediate predecessor and a vigorous return to Iconoclasm seemed the best means of securing their allegiance.

What then were the grounds for persecution adduced by the persecutors of the eighth and ninth centuries? For the Iconoclast and Moechian controversies there exist, as noted before (p. 253 above), no narrative sources emanating from the persecutors. The campaign against the Paulicians was given, at least partially, a biblical foundation (p. 254 above). Furthermore, the (historically false) connection of the Paulicians of the ninth century with the Manichaeans, which emerges as early as the chronicle of Theophanes and later underlies Peter of Sicily's account of the genesis of the sect, was designed to legitimize the application of the severe century-old legislation against the Manichaeans to the new sect.[69] It was an instance of the general tendency on the part of an established church to brand a new group as heretical by relating it to an earlier heresy. The motivation is especially clear in the text of Peter of Sicily where the narrative of the executions of "Manichaeans" follows immediately upon the mention and explanation of the supposed change of the sect's name from Manichaeans to Paulicians.[70] Here, however, Peter supplies in addition an argument for persecution of which it is not certain whether it was advanced by the persecuting government or whether it is Peter's own. He writes that these executions occurred in accordance with a saying of Jesus at the conclusion of the Parable of the Pounds which he cites, somewhat freely, as follows: "those who do not want

---

[68] On the difficult problem of chronology regarding the initial date of Theophilus's persecution, see V. Laurent in his edition of the *Life of St. Peter of Atroa*, on ch. 63, p. 186 and n. 2.

[69] Theophanes, p. 488, l. 22: "τῶν δὲ Μανιχαίων, τῶν νῦν Παυλικιάνων καλουμένων." Cf. the title of Peter of Sicily's treatise: . . . τῶν Μανιχαίων, τῶν καὶ Παυλικιάνων λεγομένων . . .; Garsoïan, *Paulician Heresy*, pp. 201–205 and passim; also "Byzantine Heresy: A Reinterpretation," *Dumbarton Oaks Papers* 25 (1971), 87–113, esp. p. 94 f.; and Lemerle, "L'Histoire des Pauliciens," p. 124 and passim.

[70] Peter of Sicily, ed. Astruc, § 86 f., p. 37 f. Peter does not state clearly which persecuting emperors he has in mind.

me to reign (βασιλεῦσαι) over them, bring them before me and slay them"
(Luke 19.27).[71] The argument, which exploits the messianic connotations of
Byzantine imperial titulature (βασιλεύς), is interesting inasmuch as it is both
biblical and political, the latter in the sense that the Paulicians are implicitly
charged with opposition against the Byzantine emperor, just as the king in
the parable calls those who did not want him to reign over them his enemies.
The dialogue between Bishop Cosmas and the monk George, cited at the
beginning of this paper (p. 238) above), shows that a political allegation of a
similar nature served also as a justification for the persecution of the
Iconophiles.

The charge of political insubordination on the part of the Paulicians was
undoubtedly reinforced by the consideration that by the second half of the
ninth century they had indeed repudiated the authority of the Byzantine
emperor and established themselves in Arab territory. In addition the persecutors of the Paulicians reassured their consciences with the consideration
that the Manichaean heresy, from which in their opinion Paulicianism descended, "was persecuted by all peoples because it was incurable and full of
all kinds of disgusting features."[72] Perhaps under Emperor Theophilus, an
iconophile abbot, Macarius of Pelekete, himself jailed because of his
iconophile conviction, refused the request of Paulician prisoners about to be
executed to recite the funeral prayers, by saying:

> Light and darkness have nothing in common, therefore you are dying a death
> worthy of your impiety. And your punishment will not end at this point, but after
> your execution chastisement without end awaits you.[73]

It is one of the attractive aspects of Theodore of Studios's personality that
under Michael I he and his adherents opposed the execution of the Paulicians with the argument that the death penalty would deprive them of their
opportunity to repent (p. 239 above). Many years later, Theodore de-
fended this position against one of the few iconophile bishops, Theophilus
of Ephesus, who called advocacy of the death penalty for the Paulicians "the
greatest and noblest deed." Against the cruel fanaticism of men like
Macarius and Theophilus, Theodore cited biblical and patristic evidence and
concluded that while it was permissible for emperors to wage war against
Scythians (i.e., Bulgars) and Arabs because they were slaughtering Christians, heretics under the control of the Byzantine emperor (οἱ ὑπὸ χεῖρα
αἱρετικοί), as was still the case with the Paulicians under Michael II when
Theodore's letter was written, should be taught but not punished. At the end
of his letter to Theophilus of Ephesus Theodore cites words that he had
once said, presumably in connection with the problem of the death penalty

---

[71] Peter of Sicily, ed. Astruc, § 87, p. 39, l. 7.
[72] Peter of Sicily, ed. Astruc, § 33, p. 19, l. 12.
[73] *Life of St. Macarius of Pelekete, BHG* 1003, *Analecta Bollandiana* 16(1897), 142–163, esp. p.
159, l. 8; cf. Lemerle, "L'Histoire des Pauliciens," p. 83.

for Paulicians, to Patriarch Nicephorus and which the latter had approved: "The Church does not punish with the sword."[74]

The arguments of the Iconoclasts in support of their persecution of the Iconophiles are described by the latter as predominantly political in nature. This is clear in an early document, the *Nuthesia,* discussed earlier (p. 238 above), where the persecuting bishop accused the Iconophiles of "setting themselves directly against our (imperial) power" and the monk George in particular of blasphemy against the emperor and concludes that he (George) "should be executed according to imperial laws." Theophanes gives as the reason advanced for the execution of Andreas Kalybites under Constantine V that Andreas had "refuted his impiety [i.e., Iconoclasm] and had called him a second Valens and Julian."[75] He also says that one of the charges against St. Stephen the Younger was that he admonished many persons "to look down on imperial honors and money gifts."[76] A related accusation was that St. Stephen persuaded many persons to enter monasteries at a time when Emperor Constantine V was exerting great pressure on monastic institutions (pp. 242–244 above). The successful recruitment of monks by St. Stephen was therefore considered an act of political sabotage. Supposedly association with and admiration for St. Stephen was one of Constantine V's allegations against a number of high officials, which resulted in their decapitation or blinding.[77] According to Methodius, the chronicler and saint Theophanes was accused of undoing the work of Leo V's henchmen who had by means of coercion (θλίβειν) converted many to Iconoclasm. Theophanes had later persuaded them to return to orthodoxy.[78] Leo V also is said to have construed an all-night vigil held by Patriarch Nicephorus at St. Sophia at the beginning of the Second Iconoclasm as an attempt of the patriarch to stir up disturbance and revolution and an act of opposition against the emperor's policy of religious peace.[79]

Even more revealing is another incident reported in the *Life of the Patriarch Nicephorus.* He had refused to debate the issue of religious images with the emperor's iconoclastic advisors unless every one of the emperor's subjects was allowed to follow his own inclination (ἡ ἑκάστου ῥοπή), prisoners were released, exiles allowed to return and the persecution (μάστιξ) halted. Thereupon Leo's entourage urged the emperor to reject the patriarch's conditions with the following argument:

[74] Theodore of Studios, *Letters* 2.155, coll. 1481C–1485D.
[75] Theophanes, p. 432, l. 18.
[76] Theophanes, p. 437, l. 6; cf. Nicephorus, p. 72, l. 14.
[77] Theophanes, p. 438, l. 6.
[78] *Life of Theophanes,* BHG 1787z, ed. B. Latyshev, Mémoires de l'Académie de Russie, 8th series, 13, pt. 4 (1918), 1–40, esp. 30, 26.
[79] *Life of St. Nicephorus,* BHG 1335, ed. C. de Boor, *Nicephori . . . opuscula historica* (Leipzig, 1880), pp. 139–217, esp. p. 167, l. 19 f.: Leo V, afraid of νεωτερισμός, holds the Patriarch responsible for ταραχή and claims that he, the Emperor, is working for εἰρήνη; cf. p. 169,23ff. The Patriarch in his turn accuses the Emperor of turning βαθεῖα εἰρήνη into στάσεις, p. 168, l. 8.

If every one's inclination (ἡ ἑκάστου ῥοπή) were allowed to turn in whichever direction he wished and those condemned to exile were allowed to return and every one could choose his own way of thinking (αἵρεσις, heresy?) without compulsion, we (the court) should promptly be left naked and alone. For everybody's opinion would quickly follow him (the Patriarch) and our (side) lose all support."[80]

The passage is interesting because at least for one fleeting moment a patriarch of Constantinople supposedly discussed with the emperor's entourage the possibility of allowing freedom of religious conscience — or at least the hagiographer imagined that a discussion of this sort might have taken place. What is more germane to the present purpose, however, is that in the eyes of the court the right to persecute heretics was an indispensable component of imperial power and any relaxation of the persecution of Iconophiles, therefore, a dangerous weakening of the emperor's prerogatives.

During the second period of Iconoclasm and after the Restoration of Orthodoxy the Iconophiles tended to emphasize more and more that the Iconoclasts justified their persecution in terms of imperial power. In the *Life of St. Nicetas of Medikion*, for example, the iconophile bishop Peter of Nicaea is made to say to Leo V that even if the emperor allied himself with the so-called Manichaeans (i.e., Paulicians), the most pernicious heretics, they would win because they had the support of the emperor. To this the hagiographer added a personal observation: "for where power is combined with impiety, truth is defeated and justice tyrannized and crushed."[81]

The risk of basing a discussion of arguments advanced by Iconoclasts in support of their persecution of the Iconophiles on sources emanating from their victims cannot be overstressed. On the other hand, two considerations make it probable that the picture derived from Iconophile sources is not seriously distorted. In the first place, it has been shown, on the basis of surviving evidence drawn from spokesmen of the persecuting authorities, that the political argumentation predominates in the persecution of the Paulicians. More importantly, it would be surprising if the Iconophiles who on the doctrinal level preserved much of iconoclastic literature and theory, in order to refute it, should have ignored nonpolitical justifications for the persecution if such had been put forward in consistent and powerful fashion. It does seem, then, that the Iconoclasts based their measures of persecution principally on the authority of the emperor to decide in matters of doctrine and to implement his decision by coercive measures. The persecutors frequently cited biblical and patristic authority in favor of their doctrinal position and in general they attempted to justify their attitudes towards Iconophile or Paulician teachings in religious terms. Yet except in the case of the death penalty they never resorted to religious arguments in

---

[80] *Life of St. Nicephorus*, p. 191, l. 19–192, l. 1 and 192, l. 24–193, l. 2.
[81] *Life of St. Nicetas of Medikion*, ch. 33, p. xxiv.

support of the emperor's right or duty of persecuting religious dissidents. They considered it inherent in the imperial office.

5. JUSTIFICATIONS OF RESISTANCE

Iconophiles were aware of the claims of the imperial power over the church and made their rejection an important part of their resistance. If it is true that information on the justifications for persecution comes largely from Iconophiles, this is so because they cited them in order to refute them and to account for their resistance to imperial demands. Thus many biographies of iconophile saints contain as one of their purple passages a dialogue between an iconoclastic emperor and the saint (or with several saintly persons) in which the emperor asserts his control of the church and the saint rejects it. In the *Life of St. Nicetas of Medikion*, for example, Emperor Leo V claims the right to act as a mediator (μεσίτης) between iconoclast and iconophile clergy and Theodore of Studios replies as follows:

> Do not undo the status of the church, for the Apostle spoke thus: "And he gave some to be apostles, and some prophets, and some evangelists, and some pastors and teachers, for the perfecting of the saints" (Eph. 4.11), but he did not speak of emperors. To you, Emperor, has been entrusted the body politic and the army. Take care of them and leave the church to its shepherds and teachers according to the Apostle. If you do not agree to this — even if an angel from Heaven should give us a message about a deviation from our faith we shall not listen to him, and certainly not to you.[82]

The author of this saint's life even states that Iconoclasm differed from all earlier heresies in that it was launched not by bishops or priests but by an emperor, a view that is not far off the truth if he is thinking of Emperor Leo V and the Second Iconoclasm.[83] In a similar vein Theodore of Studios concluded a description of the persecution under Leo V — the destruction of altars and of sacred vessels, the burning of vestments and manuscripts, the investigation of individuals and households, the recriminations among members of the clergy and the rewards offered for betrayal, beatings, jailings, exile and execution of resisters — with the remark: "There is one law only — the will of Caesar."[84]

The principal ground, however, adduced by the victims of persecution was the contention that they were acting on behalf of truth or justice or that they were defending God, Christ, the Virgin Mary and the saints against their detractors. In a letter to his uncle Plato written during the Moechian Controversy Theodore wrote that he was suffering "because of the law of God."[85] When in 808 he was asked to hold communion with the priest

---

[82] *Life of St. Nicetas of Medikion*, ch. 33, p. xxiv. Similar passage in *Life of St. Nicephorus*, p. 188, l. 12.

[83] *Life of St. Nicetas of Medikion*, ch. 27, p. xxiii.

[84] Theodore of Studios, *Letters* 2.16, cols. 1165D–1168B.

[85] Theodore of Studios, *Letters* 1.3, col. 916A.

Joseph who had officiated at the second marriage of Constantine VI, he claimed that "a commandment of God and the canons of the Fathers" forbade compliance.[86] In a letter of uncertain date he speaks of his brother, Archbishop Joseph of Thessalonica, as being exiled for the third time "on behalf of God's truth" and in another letter he calls the Iconoclasts "persecutors of the truth and rebels (ἀντάρται) against Christ."[87] Indeed, the notion of resistance for the sake of Christ is ubiquitous during the Iconoclastic Controversy inasmuch as the Iconophiles equate attacks on Christ's image with a persecution of Christ himself.[88]

The resisters often refer to biblical passages for support. Both Theodore of Studios and the author of the *Life of St. Peter of Atroa* invoke one of the Beatitudes from the Sermon on the Mount: "Blessed are those who are persecuted for righteousness' sake, for theirs is the kingdom of heaven" (Mt. 5.10) and to a Studite monk who had sinned with women Theodore praises "the beatitude of persecution."[89] Elsewhere Theodore cites in letters to monastic correspondents Jesus' exhortation to the twelve apostles to "confess me before men" (Mt. 10.32) as an encouragement to join the ranks of the confessors of the Iconophile cause.[90] In the same letter he declares that a written promise not to assemble signed by some of the monks conflicts with Jesus' injunction, "him that cometh to me I will in no wise cast out" (Jo. 6.37), a favorite quotation which Theodore used in a variety of contexts.[91] In another letter he cites the *Second Letter to Timothy* (3.12) to the effect that persecution is the result of a pious Christian life.[92]

The resisters also appeal regularly to the example of earlier martyrs and confessors, either in general terms or by references to specific personalities. Only a few examples can be given here. St. Stephen the Younger is of course frequently compared to the first martyr Stephen (Acts 6 f.), as is Patriarch Nicephorus by his biographer.[93] When St. Stephen was dragged by Constantine V's henchmen through the streets of the capital and paid his last respects to a chapel of the martyr Theodore as he was passing it, one of the executioners shouted: "Behold, the Unmentionable wishes to die like a martyr."[94] The example of the Maccabees is invoked in the *Life of St. Michael Syncellus* and by Theodore of Studios (together with that of John the Bap-

---

[86] Theodore of Studios, *Letters* 1.21, col. 969D.

[87] Theodore of Studios, *Letters*, ed. CL, nos. 1, p. 1; 127, p. 113.

[88] Theodore of Studios, *Letters* 2.2, col. 1120B: ὁ Χριστὸς διώκεται διὰ τῆς εἰκόνος αὐτοῦ.

[89] Theodore of Studios, *Letters*, ed. CL, no. 183, p. 156; 2.105, col. 1364A–B; cf. *Life of St. Peter of Atroa*, ch. 83.34, p. 219.

[90] Theodore of Studios, *Letters* 2.2, col. 1121B.

[91] For example, also as an argument against handing over refugees to the Bulgars, Theophanes, p. 498, l. ·3.

[92] Theodore of Studios, *Letters*, ed. CL, no. 98, p. 86.

[93] *Life of St. Stephen the Younger*, col. 1124B; *Life of St. Nicephorus*, p. 204, l. 8.

[94] *Life of St. Stephen the Younger*, col. 1176C.

tist).⁹⁵ Theodore reminds his correspondents constantly of earlier martyrs, for example of the Ten Martyrs of Crete, of Cyprian of Antioch and Justina, the Forty Martyrs of Sebaste and of Sabas and Theodosius (under Anastasius I).⁹⁶ He consoles an iconophile abbess, who had complained that bishops, priests and abbots had joined the ranks of the Iconoclasts, by observing that even in earlier generations few men and women had obtained the crown of martyrdom. Upon hearing the news that Pope Paschal had spoken out in favor of the images he remarks: "let the blood of the martyrs irrigate the church."⁹⁷ The biographer of St. Macarius of Pelekete even attempts a quasi-philosophical argument to prove that the martyrs of the Iconoclastic Controversy such as St. Macarius were the equals of the early Christian martyrs:

> [The martyrdom of Macarius] is inferior in one respect only, namely that time in that case [the early martyrs] came first and in this case [Macarius] came second. But it [time] contributes nothing to holy men, is potentially indifferent and is responsible neither for vice nor for virtue. The [free] choice of the sufferers, on the other hand, demonstrates by their labors their equality or even superiority [over the early martyrs], for goodness is achieved not through [priority of] time but by the free choice and zeal of the will.⁹⁸

The comparison of the iconophile confessors with earlier martyrs served to assure them that their resistance to persecution was no less meritorious than that of previous sufferers for religion's sake. Theodore of Studios affirms, apparently in reaction against persons who expressed doubts concerning the importance of the issue of religious images, that the resister was "a true martyr and that he did in no way fall behind those who suffered martyrdom from the hands of pagans or Jews."⁹⁹ But Theodore connects the persecution of Iconophiles even more directly with earlier divisions in the church, going as far back as the situation prior to the Seventh Council. In a letter to a perfume dealer he writes:

> Do you see what is happening, my friend? Fire is, as it were, setting the church of God on fire, a fire fed by previous fuel. We were devoured by the flame of adultery (μοιχεία), consumed by the flash of the adulterous wedding ceremony (μοιχοζευξία). . . . I should add, not inappropriately, earlier happenings concern-

⁹⁵ *Life of St. Michael Syncellus*, p. 247, l. 14; Theodore of Studios, *Letters* 2.21, col. 1185A.
⁹⁶ Theodore of Studios, *Letters*, ed. CL, no. 108, p. 97; 2.63, col. 1281C and ed. CL, no. 49, p. 42; 2.59, col. 1273C; 2.2, col. 1120D.
⁹⁷ Theodore of Studios, *Letters*, ed. CL, no. 71, p. 58; 2.63, col. 1281B. Cf. 2.21, col. 1181B; 2.62, col. 1280B. In 2.63, col. 1281B Theodore also rejoices over the pope's intervention as an indication that the Iconoclasts "cut themselves off from the body of Christ." Similarly, Tarasius in 784 was hesitant to accept the patriarchal office because both eastern Christians (i.e., those under Arab rule) and the West were separated from the Byzantine church, Theophanes, p. 459, ll. 18–24.
⁹⁸ *Life of St. Macarius of Pelekete*, p. 156, ll. 9–15.
⁹⁹ Theodore of Studios, *Letters* 2.21, col. 1185A.

ing and caused by the Simoniacs. . . . And then in addition the (measures taken) because of and against the Paulicians, for the law of the church does not use the sword or the whip against anybody, for, says [Scripture], "all who take the sword will perish by the sword" (Mt. 26.52).[100]

Here Theodore sees in Iconoclasm and persecution a divine punishment for earlier sins: the lax attitude of the clergy towards the second marriage of Constantine VI in 795 and towards the restoration in 808 of the priest Joseph who had performed the ceremony, towards those who prior to the Seventh Ecumenical Council had bought ecclesiastical office, and the cooperation of the clergy in the execution of Paulicians.[101]

6. CONCLUSION: EFFECTIVENESS OF PERSECUTION AND RESISTANCE

Byzantine literature of the eighth and ninth centuries presents religious persecution as a frequent occurrence, almost a normal fact of life. Monks and nuns suffered most intensely while the overwhelming majority of the secular clergy and laity either joined the ranks of the persecutors or gave at most secret support to the victims. In some instances, Byzantine rulers prepared for persecution by issuing propaganda pamphlets and holding public meetings in which the religious issue was discussed. The means used by the persecuting emperors ranged from promises of rewards for collaborators to harassment of all sorts, banishment, imprisonment and corporal punishment, all designed to break down the resistance of the victims at a gradual or rapid pace. The death penalty was not imposed on heretics, except intermittently on groups such as the Paulicians considered particularly nefarious. Impressive intellectual efforts were often made by the persecutors to justify the theological positions espoused by them, but the reasons given for measures of persecution as such strike one as perfunctory, contrived and predominantly political rather than religious: individuals singled out for punishment are charged with disobedience to the emperor and to imperial law.

The resisters, too, resorted to the written word to defend their cause and composed both learned refutations of their opponents' theses and pamphlets of a popular kind. Because of the persecution, they were not often in a position to assemble in larger groups. Their leaders compensated for this disadvantage by organizing a more or less clandestine network of communications through which they reminded each other of the right and duty of free religious expression (παρρησία), even at the risk of suffering punishment or martyrdom. In this way the iconophile resistance movement, for example, grew into an underground church, a development that confronted its leaders with the problem of striking a reasonable balance between the

---

[100] Theodore of Studios, *Letters*, ed. CL, no. 23, p. 20 f.; cf. also 2.55, col. 1269B; ed. CL, no. 124, p. 111.

[101] On these developments, see Alexander, *Patriarch Nicephorus*, pp. 80–101.

need for unity within the resistance movement, on the one hand, and for regional and local flexibility to make authoritative decisions in individual cases on the other. In fact, the leadership was faced daily with quarrels and rivalries difficult to arbitrate in a climate of isolation and fear, as well as with the problems of those who had weakened under duress and later repented. In its resistance the Paulician heresy is again exceptional as the extraordinary fierceness of persecution resulted in military secession of the Paulicians and the establishment of a state hostile to Byzantium. In response to the political argument for persecution the resisters contested the right of the emperor to decide on matters of church doctrine and discipline. They justified their resistance by means of biblical citations, by the example of earlier martyrs, by their conviction of defending religious truth and by seeing the persecution as divine punishment for sins committed during former religious crises.

The material discussed in this paper has implications for the question of the effectiveness of religious persecution and resistance, although it should be stressed that they derive from a body of evidence narrowly defined in time and place and that they should not be generalized without wider research. The sources show that for the victims there was little hope that a persecution once begun might end while the emperor who had initiated it sat on his throne. He had burned his bridges and was likely to intensify the persecution as time went on. On the other hand, there was every reason to expect that with the accession of a new ruler, of a prince belonging to the same dynasty and particularly of a successful usurper, the persecution would be interrupted for a considerable period of time so that the new emperor could consolidate his power, or would even be halted altogether. In the case of the Iconoclastic and Moechian Controversies the persecutors lost in the end, not however without leaving the imprint of their views on Byzantine church and civilization (witness, for example, the introduction or intensification of ecclesiastical control over religious art).[102] The Iconophiles, on the other hand, who did not persecute the Iconoclasts (or did so only minimally), ultimately won. The persecutors were more successful in their treatment of the Paulicians whom they exterminated individually by executions and collectively by warfare, but at a very high price to themselves in lives and money. It should be remembered, moreover, that Paulicians and Paulicianism survived in northern Greece and Bulgaria and there exercized a profound influence on the Bogomil movement and indirectly on the Albigensians and related heretical groups in Western Eruope. The conclusion, encouraging though hardly original and based on severely limited evidence, seems inescapable that religious persecution did not pay.

The rights of the Byzantine autocrat in the church were numerous and his influence over its personnel, institutions and on occasion even its teachings powerful. They could produce fierce repression of religious dissidents. Yet

---

[102] Grabar, *L'Iconoclasme byzantin*, pp. 214–261, esp. pp. 259–261.

the high price to be paid for it, coupled with its normal restriction, in the event of widespread and determined resistance, to one reign, demonstrate once again that the so-called Caesaropapism, that is the notion that the Byzantine emperor was supreme in and over the church, was subject to severe limitations.[103]

UNIVERSITY OF CALIFORNIA, BERKELEY

[103] On the characterization of church-state relations at Byzantium as Caesaropapism see, for example, Ernest Barker, *Social and Political Thought in Byzantium* (Oxford, 1957), pp. 7–10; Wilhelm Ensslin, *Cambridge Medieval History*, vol. 4, part 2 (Cambridge, 1967), p. 12 f.; Emil Hermann, ibid., p. 105 and n. 1 (bibliography); Steven Runciman, ibid., p. 374; Francis Dvornik, *Early Christian and Byzantine Political Philosophy*, 2, Dumbarton Oaks Studies 9 (Washington, D.C., 1966), p. 837 f. and n. 409 (bibliography).

BYZANTINE APOCALYPTIC

XI

ПСЕВДО-МЕФОДИЙ И ЭФИОПИЯ

Я считаю за честь и удовольствие участвовать в этом юбилейном сборнике, посвященном восьмидесятилетию Нестора русских византинистов, профессору М. Я. Сюзюмову. Мне хочется выразить свою благодарность и признательность выдающемуся ученому за многочисленные книги и статьи, в которых на протяжении чрезвычайно плодотворной деятельности, длящейся уже более полувека, он сумел осветить многие проблемы истории, как общественно-экономические, так и интеллектуальные.

* * *

Во второй половине VII в. неизвестный человек перевел апокалипсис, ошибочно приписываемый отцу церкви Мефодию, с древнесирийского языка на греческий [1]. Древнесирийский оригинал был открыт в прошлом столетии венгерским востоковедом М. Кмоско, но остался не опубликованным поныне [2]. Эта статья основана, главным образом, на греческой версии, которая в общем точно передает древнесирийский текст.

Греческий текст состоит из трех частей. Первая содержит весьма причудливую псевдоисторию мира от изгнания Адама и Евы из рая до турко-аварского нападения на Римскую, т. е. Византийскую, империю. Автор, вероятно, имеет в виду персидско-аварскую осаду Константинополя в 626 г., в которой принимали участие некоторые турецкие племена. Вторая часть написана как пророчество о нашествии измаилитов, что есть, без сомнения, ссылка на арабское вторжения на Ближний Восток в течение четвертого и пятого десятилетий VII в. Третья, эсхатологическая, часть предвещает великую победу греческого царя над врагами, его отречение от власти в Иерусалиме, явление антихриста и уничтожение последнего Иисусом Христом во время Второго Пришествия [3].

Цель этого странного документа полемична. Несколько раз автор цитирует Псалом (далее — Пс.) 67 : 32 (Септуагинт (далее — Септ.) — XX): aithiopia prophtasei cheira autes to theo, т. е.

«Эфиопия первая протянет руку к Богу» [4]. Однако автор подчеркивает, что, делая эту ссылку на Эфиопию, псалмописец подразумевал Римскую (Византийскую) империю, которая произошла, согласно Псевдо-Мефодию, «от семени Эфиопии»:

«Ибо благословенный Давид глазами духа предвидел, что Хузифа, дочь Фола, поднимет Римскую Империю, и предвещал так: «Эфиопия первая протянет руку к Богу» (Пс. 67 : 32). Некоторые люди верили, что святой Давид это сказал, намекая на царство эфиопов. Однако те, что придерживались этого мнения, заблуждались» [5].

Мысль, выраженная в этом отрывке, является ключом к пониманию всего произведения. Она объясняет первую, псевдоисторическую часть, ибо автор излагает взгляд, согласно которому правители Византийской империи, происшедшие от Бизаса (Byzas), основателя Византии, являлись с материнской стороны наследниками царя Эфиопии Фола [6]. На этом отрывке также базируется сцена на горе Голгофе, где последний римский император сдает свою власть Богу. Эта сцена является кульминацией третьей эсхатологической части, так как автор считает этот акт, рассматриваемый в духе своего своеобразного толкования (Пс. 67 : 32) и в свете своих пара-исторических рассуждений, исполнением пророчества псалмописца [7].

Таким образом, автор написал свой труд в оправдание тому толкованию Пс. 67 : 32, которое рассматривало этот библейский отрывок как пророчество, а также с целью указать на то, что эфиопское царство непременно сыграет важную роль в событиях, непосредственно предшествующих Второму Пришествию, и, следовательно, простоит до конца мира. Псевдо-Мефодий противопоставил свою «Византийскую интерпретацию» этой «Эфиопской интерпретации» — по Пс. 67 : 32, не Эфиопия, а Византия простоит до самых последних дней мира [8]. В остальном Псевдо-Мефодий соглашался со своими безымянными предшественниками в том, что Пс. 67 : 32 повествует о конце мира и должен быть истолкован эсхатологически.

Каково происхождение той точки зрения, которую Псевдо-Мефодий разделял со своими предшественниками? Ясно, что хронологический приоритет принадлежит «Эфиопской интерпретации», так как Псевдо-Мефодий развил свою «Византийскую интерпретацию» в противодействие ей. Представляется целесообразным искать начало этих толкований в литературе Эфиопии, где убеждение в существовании Эфиопии до конца мира должно быть выражено наиболее отчетливо.

Почти сорок лет тому назад А. Васильев привлек внимание к одному из главнейших произведений эфиопской литературы — «Кебра Нагаст», или «Книге о славе царей» [9]. Книга эта приняла свою настоящую форму в первой половине XIV в. (или немного раньше), во времена, когда новая династия, якобы происшедшая от царя Соломона, захватила власть [10]. Васильев был, главным образом, заинтересован отголосками в ней политического и военного сотрудничества двух христианских властителей — византийского императора Юстина I (518—527) и Аксимского (Axum) царя Калеба, или Элесбаса (Kaleb or Elesboas), против иудействующего царя Иемена, Дхуновеса (Dhu — Nowas).

В дальнейшем станет ясно, однако, что книга «Кебра Нагаст» интересна не только историей византийско-эфиопских политических отношений, но также некоторыми идеологическими течениями, преобладавшими в поздней античности. Труд этот представляет собой собрание исторических и легендарных сведений, относящихся к древней истории эфиопского народа, и считался национальным талисманом вплоть до XIX в. [11] Он состоит из трех независимых частей: из повествования о посещении Царицей Юга Царя Соломона, о рождении их сына Давида и похищении им из Иерусалима Скинии (Tabernacle), доставленной в Эфиопию; из описания позднего периода царствования Соломона; из длинной вереницы библейских и других пророчеств и их толкований. Все три части объединены общей целью — стремлением доказать происхождение эфиопской династии, которая начала царствовать с 1270 г., от Давида или Соломона [12]. Все отрывки, приведенные в этой статье, находятся в первой части книги «Кебра Нагаст».

Первая часть написана в форме дискуссий, якобы состоявшихся между тремястами восемнадцатью отцами церкви, собравшимися на Первый Вселенский Собор в Никее. Епископы определили славу царей, что и послужило заглавием всей книги — «Сион, скиния закона Божьего» [13]. Некий Домитий, или Тимофей (Domitius, или Timotheus), патриарх Рима, т. е. Константинополя, вычитал из рукописи, будто бы найденной «в церкви св. Софии», историю Царицы Юга, Соломона и их сына Давида [14]. Основным эпизодом в этом повествовании является похищение Скинии (Tabernacle) принцем Давидом и перевоз ее в Эфиопию. Когда потеря обнаруживается, население Иерусалима вместе с царем Соломоном погружаются в плач и жалобы. Так говорит Соломон:

«С этого мгновения наша слава ушла от нас, и наше царство было унесено к чужим людям... Отныне и впредь закон, мудрость и прозрение будут даны им. И мой отец Давид предрекал о них, говоря: „Эфиопия преклонится перед Ним, и Его враги будут глотать пыль" (Пс. 71 : 9 — Септ.). И в другом псалме он сказал: „Эфиопия протянет свои руки к Богу, и Он примет ее с честью, и цари земные восхвалят Бога" (Пс. 67 : 32 — Септ.) [15].

Таким образом, «Кебра Нагаст» толкует Пс. 67 : 32 как предсказание славы и мощи Эфиопии, т. е. сходно с тем, как он истолковывается предшественниками Псевдо-Мефодия. Однако ввиду того, что их интерпретация очевидна и буквальна, т. е. могла возникнуть независимо в нескольких местах, это сходство недостаточно для того, чтобы прочно связать предшественников Псевдо-Мефодия с «Кебра Нагаст». Это можно было бы утверждать, если было бы доказано, что уже книга «Кебра Нагаст» видела в этой библейской цитате предсказание того, что Эфиопия простоит до конца мира, как это сделали предшественники Псевдо-Мефодия.

Хотя эсхатологическое значение не высказано в первой цитате Пс. 67:32, приведенной в «Кебра Нагаст», вторая цитата из той же строки не оставляет никакого сомнения в том, что автор придал ей это значение. Это объясняет, что цари Рима (Константинополя) оставались ортодоксальными (т. е., с точки зрения эфиопского автора, монофиситными) в течение ста тридцати лет после Константина (или до Собора в Халкедоне), но они были сбиты с праведного пути ересью Нестория, Ария и Ябасо (Ибаса?), в то время как Эфиопия оставалась ортодоксальной (монофиситной) [16]. По словам отцов церкви из Никеи,

«цари Эфиопии прославились и возвеличились через Сион, т. е. Скинию. И цари Рима также возвеличились благодаря гвоздям «с Креста», которые Елена вставила в уздечку, ставшую покорительницей врагов в руках Римских царей».

Итак, оба царства обладают своими особыми талисманами, которые обеспечивают их величие и непобедимость. Далее отцы спрашивают:

«Как долго может покорительница врага, уздечка с гвоздями Креста, оставаться у Римского царя, а колесница, содержащая Сион, у царя Эфиопии?».

Григорий (Чудотворец, которого на протяжении всей книги «Кебра Нагаст» путают с Григорием Просветителем) отвечает, что царь Рима извратил веру — еще один намек на Собор в Халкедоне, что для монофиситного автора означало принятие несторианства:

«И Бог отнимет покорительницу врага, уздечку, у царя, который не соблюдает веру, и персы пойдут на него войной и победят его... И царь Персии, имя которого Гареневос (Иреней?) (Harênêwôs — Irenaeus?), покорит (унизит?) его и утащит вместе с конем; и по воле Бога конь этот, на котором покорительница врага, будет возбужден (или: спасется от смятения) и войдет в море и погибнет в нем. Но гвозди будут сиять в море до тех пор, пока Христос не придет вновь в великой славе на облаке с небес и не принесет с собой силу».

Эфиопия же, с другой стороны, останется ортодоксальной (монофиситной) до конца мира и сохранить свой талисман, Скинию. И, наконец, Григория спрашивают: «Будет ли уничтожена вера народа Эфиопии во время пришествия антихриста?». Он отвечает:

«Конечно, нет. Не предсказал ли Давид, что «Эфиопия протянет руки к Богу» (Пс. 67:32). И эти его слова означают, что эфиопы не извратят веру и не изменят ей...» [17].

Вторая цитата, Пс. 67:32, из «Кебра Нагаст» доказывает, что автор знал и принимал эсхатологическое толкование этой строки. Так же, как предшественники Псевдо-Мефодия, автор этой книги видел в библейском отрывке пророчество о том, что Эфиопия простоит до конца мира.

Ни Псевдо-Мефодий, ни его предшественники не читали «Кебра Нагаст» в той форме, в которой она известна в наше время, так как она стала такой не раньше чем к концу XIII в. Но, по общему мнению, книга могла впитать в себя традиции, распространенные в Сирии, Палестине, Аравии и Египте в течение первых четырех столетий христианской эры, и поэтому кажется вероятным, что самый ранний вариант текста был составлен, может быть, коптским священником в VI в. [18] Во всяком случае, отрывок, содержащий вторую цитату (Пс. 67 : 32), был написан до победы арабов у Кадисии (Qadisiyya) в 636 г., потому что трудно себе представить, что после этого события автор предсказал бы победу персов, а не арабов над Византией [19]. Так как пророчество Григория о персидской победе над Византией и его «Эфиопская интерпретация» (Пс. 67 : 32) дополняют друг друга, то кажется вероятным, что это толкование тоже предшествовало арабским нашествиям и имеет свое начало не позже чем в VI в., возможно, под влиянием аксумитных (Axumite) походов в Иемен, предпринятых во время Юстина I для защиты христиан в том районе [20].

Каким-то образом «Эфиопская интерпретация» попала, с одной стороны, в руки автора книги «Кебра Нагаст», с другой — предшественников Псевдо-Мефодия и через их посредство — к нему самому. Автор «Кебра Нагаст» и предшественники его приняли ее, но Псевдо-Мефодий ее отверг (expressis verbis) и заменил своей «Византийской интерпретацией». Почти за век до того, как Псевдо-Мефодий написал свое произведение, связи между Сирским христианским миром и Эфиопией были прекращены сначала из-за персидской оккупации и Иемена (между 570 и 575 гг.), а позднее из-за арабского нашествия на Ближний Восток. Итак, стало тщетным для христиан в оккупированных районах ожидать помощи против арабов от царя Эфиопии. Псевдо-Мефодий сделал реалистические выводы из создавшейся ситуации, отверг «Эфиопскую интерпретацию» Пс. 67 : 32, которая была традиционной в предыдущем веке, и создал свой апокалипсис, чтобы доказать, что Византийской империи было предназначено исполнить пророчество псалмописца об Эфиопии. В процессе его написания выражение уверенности духовенства VI в. в защите со стороны тогда еще сильного властителя Эфиопии было превращено в пророчество о византийском освобождении церквей Ближнего Востока от победоносных мусульман [21].

ПРИМЕЧАНИЯ

[1] Греческий текст, под ред. В. Истрина: Откровение Мефодия Патарского и Апокрифические Видения Даниила в византийской и славяно-русской литературах. — Чтения в Императорском Обществе Истории и Древностей Российских при Московском Университете 1897 г., № 181 (Исследование) и 183 (Тексты), вместе с другими греческими, латинскими и славянскими версиями. (Если не указано иначе, ссылки будут сделаны на № 183 — Тексты). Латинская версия с ценным вступлением и комментарием: *Ernst Sackur*. Sibyllinische Texte und Forschungen. Hallea. S., 1898 (reprint Torino, 1963), S. 3—96. Cf.: F. Halkin. Bibliotheca Hagiographica Graeca, 3rd ed., Subsidia Hagiographica 8a, 8b, 8c. Brussels, 1957, No. 2036.

[2] *M. Kmosko*. Das Rätsel des Pseudo-Methodios. — Byz., v. 6, 1931, p. 273—296 (see also v. 5, 1929—1930, p. 422—424). Дальнейшую информацию о древнеси-

рийском тексте, сохраненном в cod. Vat. Syrus 58 XVI в., см. в моих двух статьях: Medieval Apocalypses as Historical Sources. — AHR, v. 73, 1968, p. 997—1018; Byzantium and the Migration of Literary Motifs: The Legend of the Last Roman Emperor. — Medievalia et Humanistica, n. s., v. 2, 1971, p. 47—68.

³ Часть первая: ред. Истрин, стр. 5—26 (гл. I — VI).

Часть вторая: там же, стр. 26—39 (гл. VIII—X).

Часть третья: там же, стр. 40—50 (гл. XI—XII).

⁴ Ред. Истрин, стр. 22, 16; 23, 4; 24,12; 46, 5 (apparatus). Славянская версия (стр. 99, 21 Истрин) и латинский перевод (p. 94, 3 Sackur) доказывают, что последний из этих отрывков был частью подлинного греческого текста, см.: Истрин, стр. 63 (№ 181 — Исследование).

⁵ Ed. Istrin, p. 22, 13—18: tines oun oethesan hoti dia ten ton aithiopon basileian ainittomenos ho hagios Dabid tauta eireken. all'epseusthesan ten aletheian hoi tauta noesantes. Древнесирийский оригинал, более подробный в этом месте, говорит о безымянных предшественниках Псевдо-Мефодия (tines в греческом тексте) как о «многих собратиях духовенства» (codex Vaticanus Syrus 58, fol. 126 recto).

⁶ См. особенно гл. VI, стр. 20—22 у Истрина. Отрывок, приведенный в предыдущей сноске, находится в конце этой главы и следует непосредственно за кратким изложением воображаемой родословной.

⁷ В конце сцены отречения автор замечает: «Итак, исполнилось пророчество Давида: в последние свои дни Эфиопия первая протянет свою руку к Богу». P. 46, 5 (apparatus) Istrin, см. сн. 4.

⁸ Подобное верование в непобедимость Римской империи и в ее существование до конца времени было выражено на столетие раньше: Cosmas Indicopleustes, Christian Topography, II 75, ed. W. Wolska-Conus, v. 1, p. 390. Этому тезису тоже предшествовал обзор разрушения прежних империй по образцу книги Даниила, но тут нет ссылки на Пс. 67:32.

⁹ A. Vasiliev. Justin I (518—527) and Abyssinia. — BZ, Bd. 33, 1933, S. 67—77, bes. S. 73 f. См. также: eiusdem. Justin The First. — Dumbarton Oaks Studies, v. 1. Cambridge, Mass., 1950, p. 299—301.

¹⁰ Есть два перевода этого произведения, один на немецком языке: C. Bezold. — ABAW, Bd. 23, 1909, другой на английском: E. A. W. Budge. The Queen of Sheba and Her Only Son Menyelek (I). Oxford, L., 1932. Впредь я полагаюсь, главным образом, на английский перевод, хотя я также сверил нужные мне места с немецким. О дате этого произведения см.: Bezold, S. XXXIV (до конца XIII в.) и Budge, p. XVI (между 1314 и 1344 гг.). Ср. также: Walter Krebs. Zur Rolle der Bundeslade in Äthiopien. — Das Altetum, Bd. 16, 1970, S. 228—237.

¹¹ См. письмо принца Каза (Kasa) (впоследствии царь Иван IV) Эфиопии к графу Гренвиллю (Granville) от 10-го августа 1872 г., цитируемое Budge, p. XV and XXXIV f.: «Кебра Нагаст» «содержит в себе закон всей Эфиопии и имена властителей, церквей и провинций. Я молюсь о том, чтобы вы узнали, у кого эта книга, и прислали ее мне, ибо люди в моей стране не подчиняются моим приказам без нее».

¹² Касательно цели и главных разделов этой книги см.: Bezold, S. XXXIX f. Первая часть состоит из гл. 1—63, 84—95 и 113 до конца.

¹³ Ch. I, p. I, Budge. Относительно роли Скинии в Абиссинии см.: E. Ullendorff. Hebrais-Jewish Elements in Abyssinian (Monophysite) Christianity. — «Journal of Semitic Studies», v. 1, 1956, esp. p. 233 f.

¹⁴ Ch. 21, p. 16 Budge.

¹⁵ Ch. 50, p. 74 Budge.

¹⁶ Ch. 93, p. 164 Budge.

¹⁷ Ch. 13, p. 221 f. Budge.

¹⁸ Budge p. XVI; cf.: Bezold, S. XL.

¹⁹ Обратите внимание на отрывок о победе персидского царя Гереневоса (Harênêwôs) над царем Рима, цитируемый на стр. 24. Этот хронологический вывод основан на внутренних доказательствах и не зависит от противоречивого вопроса относительно достоверности и правдивости концовки, приделанной к «Кебра Нагаст» (p. 228, Budge; S. 138, Bezold), согласно которой эфиопский

текст был переведен с арабского, опирающегося на коптский оригинал. Для обсуждения концовки см.: *Bezold*, S. XXXIV f. и *Budge*. p. XXXVIII f.

[20] Касательно абиссинских военных интервенций в Иемене и истории Эфиопии в общем см. в дополнение к трудам Васильева (сн. 9) также следующее: *C. Rossini*. Storia d'Etiopia I. Bergamo, 1928; *G. Lanczkowski*. Äthiopia. — Jahrbuch für Antike und Christentum, Bd. 1, 1958, S. 134—153 (обзор с библиографией) и прежде всего: *N. Pigulevskaja*. Byzanz auf dem Wege nach Indien. — BBA, Bd. 36, 1969, bes. S. 175—271 (полный пересмотр данных).

[21] Автор считает своим приятным долгом поблагодарить госпожу Н. Вейкман за перевод этой статьи на русский язык и своего коллегу, профессора Н. В. Рязановского, за полезные советы.

ADDITIONAL BIBLIOGRAPHY

A thorough treatment of the Ethiopic Kebra Nagast , its date, purposes and Weltanschauung will now be found in Irfan Shahîd's stimulating article,"The Kebra Nagast in the Light of Recent Research",Le Muséon 89,1976,133-178 (see especially Appendix II,pp.174-176).Like myself, Shahîd believes that it contains early (possibly sixth century) features.He calls attention to the author's reliance on Ps.68(67):31 and considers Pseudo-Methodius' work a "counterblast" directed against the "Ethiopian interpretation" of the Psalmist's verse.(Professor Shahîd's remarks about my work were based on my article of 1971 (no.XII below),which should be supplemented by the present article (no.IX).All future work on Pseudo-Methodius will now be facilitated by the first truly critical edition of the Greek versions by Anastasios Lolos,Die Apokalypse des Ps.-Methodius,Beiträge zur Klassischen Philologie 83,Meisenheim am Glan,1976.So far as the Greek text of Pseudo-Methodius is concerned,it will replace the rare and inconvenient edition by V.M.Istrin (Moscow, 1897) frequently referred to in my articles.

ENGLISH SUMMARY

A complex,obscure and influential apocalypse attributed
falsely to the church father Methodius was composed in
the second half of the seventh century.The key to this document is the author's interpretation of a biblical verse
which he cites repeatedly,Ps.67:32 (Sept.):"Ethiopia
will first stretch out her hand to God".According to the
author's involved and pseudo-historical speculations,
this passage refers to the end of time,when it will be fulfilled by a Last Roman (i.e. Byzantine)Emperor.He makes
it clear,however,that his "Byzantine interpretation" of
the passage was not universally accepted and that "some
persons" expected it to be fulfilled by the kingdom of Eth-
iopia.This "Ethiopian interpretation" of Ps.67:32 is indeed found in a work of Ethiopian literature,the Kebra
Nagast or Book of the Glory of Kings.It received its final
form in the fourteenth century but embodied traditions
and materials of the pre-Islamic period. Pseudo-
Methodius wrote his apocalypse in Mesopotamia not long
after the Arab conquest in reaction against the "Ethiopian
interpretation",presumably because by his time political
and military reliance on the ruler of Ethiopia had become
futile and he thus transferred his hopes for deliverance
from the Arab yoke to the powerful emperor on the Bosporus.

XII

Byzantium and the Migration of Literary Works and Motifs
THE LEGEND OF THE LAST ROMAN EMPEROR*

THE BYZANTINE EMPIRE, during the more than one thousand years of its existence, was not only the storehouse of classical Greek literature; it was also "the great clearing house of East and West," in folk literature as well as in other branches.[1] Bulgarians, Russians, Armenians, and Georgians received their first literary stimuli from Byzantium, so much so that the early written monuments of these and other peoples are largely translations from Byzantine Greek originals. Furthermore, a considerable number of Byzantine literary works were translated in the Middle Ages into Latin and had a profound influence on the development of literature in western and central Europe.[2] All this is well known, but it is not always stressed sufficiently that Byzantium functioned not only as a literary donor but also frequently as the recipient of literary gifts. This process has so far been studied in its more general aspects only for one field of literature, hagiography, but influences of Syriac, Arabic, Armenian, Coptic, and even Far Eastern literatures upon that of Byzantium are also important in other genres.[3] Particularly interesting are the migrations of works which originated in the Far East and thence travelled via various intermediate stages including Byzantium to western or Slavic Europe. A case in point is the Indian story about Buddha extant in Greek in the guise of the *Romance of Barlaam and Joasaph* as well as in a Latin transla-

*Several friends and colleagues have read an earlier draft of this paper and made valuable comments, especially Professors Fred Amory, Wolfgang Sauer, and Stephen J. Tonsor. Furthermore, I presented it orally to the Collegium Orientologicum at the University of California, Berkeley, and received many suggestions from various colleagues. I take this opportunity to express my sincere gratitude for all this help. I also wish to thank Mr. Stephen Benin, a graduate student in the Department of History at Berkeley, for checking my references, as well as two readers for *Medievalia et Humanistica* for good advice.

tion of the early eleventh century; or the Indian tale of the two jackals Calila and Dimna translated into Greek in the eleventh century and into various Slavic languages, at the latest, in the early thirteenth; or finally the Hebrew story of the wise Achikar which surfaced at Byzantium in the form of a *Life of Aesop* and thence reached the Slavs.[4] What constitutes the peculiar interest of these and of other instances of long-distance literary migration is not only the appeal of these works to the many cultures into whose languages they were translated, but also the fact that, once many philological and historical labors are completed, it should become possible to define more precisely the process of migration and to ascertain the reasons for their spread. In most cases, however, no such precision is as yet attainable, simply because the scholarly problems are too difficult and the work has just begun.

There is, however, one case of literary borrowing for which the process can be studied in some detail and certain conclusions reached: the legend or expectation of a Last Roman Emperor. The story of its spread is by no means typical, but it may serve to illustrate one type of appeal that facilitated long-distance migration: an appeal to religio-political ideology. This legend is not limited to one particular literary work but is a motif that appears in a variety of forms. Normally it emerges in contexts dealing with Christian expectations concerning the end of the world. At some point, during the course of events leading to the end, there emerges a Last Roman Emperor who defeats the national or religious enemy, journeys to Jerusalem, and resides there for a number of years. At the end of this period he hands over the insignia of his office to God. That act is usually followed immediately by a manifestation of Antichrist, who then seduces vast numbers of people but is finally liquidated by Jesus Christ at his Second Coming. The characteristic features of the legend, therefore, are a war of liberation and an imperial abdication.

What is the origin of this story? It will be advisable to begin at the end to define the circumstances under which this legend was first studied by modern scholars. This happened in nineteenth-century Germany.

The historical development of Germany and of much of Europe in the nineteenth century was determined by two series of events: the Napoleonic wars at the beginning of the century and the foundation of the German Empire towards its end. These happenings, separated though they were by a span of seven decades, were of course related.

Byzantium and the Migration of Literary Works and Motifs

The Bismarckian unification of the many German states under the authority of the Prussian dynasty owed a great deal to the nationalist feelings aroused or at least released by the foreign invasions. As a result not only political tracts, but also the philosophy, literature, and historiography of nineteenth-century Germany were permeated by the hope for a united effort of the German principalities and peoples against foreign domination and influence.

In Germany these hopes and dreams reinforced apocalyptic expectations of a restored empire current in eighteenth-century Europe. Characteristically, the legends of the medieval Empire had originated in the Late Middle Ages after the Great Interregnum, when the Empire was little more than an empty title and a nostalgic dream, and when sovereignty in Germany was parcelled out among a host of secular and ecclesiastical princes. In this political atmosphere the popular longing for peace, for freedom from oppression by local dynasts, and for the strengthening of the imperial power produced sagas such as that of Mount Kyffhäuser.[5] A Bavarian chronicle of the early fourteenth century, for example, spoke of an Emperor, buried but not dead, who would return with great military power. By 1434 this legend had gradually crystalized around an Emperor Frederick who was expected to await his reappearance in a castle on Mount Kyffhäuser.[6] After the Napoleonic wars had removed the last vestiges of German unity and demonstrated German impotence, the Romantic movement reinvigorated the medieval legends.

In the second decade of the nineteenth century Friedrick Rückert published his famous and influential poem "Barbarossa." Here, the sleeping Emperor with his fiery beard was described sitting in a subterranean castle to which he had descended, taking with him the Empire's glory. There he will sit, on an ivory chair at a marble table, as long as the ravens fly around Mount Kyffhäuser. But one day he will return to restore the Empire to its former splendor:

> Er hat hinabgenommen
> Des Reiches Herrlichkeit
> Und wird einst wiederkommen
> Mit ihr, zu seiner Zeit.

The popular dream of freedom from foreign influences and interventions, and of national unification affected not only poets and publicists but also the world of scholarship and historiography. Characteristic in this respect is one of the outstanding and influential German works on medieval history, Wilhelm von Giesebrecht's *Geschichte der deut-schen Kaiserzeit*, of which the first volume was published in 1855. The preface to the first edition of the work is permeated by an awareness of the depth and intensity of national feeling; it stresses the author's "patriotic purpose" and expresses his fervent desire to provide for the best among the young, as he puts it, "the torch illuminating a brighter future for the German nation."[7] It is instructive to compare the preface of 1855 with that of the fourth edition of 1873. In the interval between the two editions Denmark and Austria had been defeated in battle, the Prussian and allied armies had laid siege to Paris, overthrown Napoleon III, and imposed a burdensome peace upon France. Above all, King William of Prussia had been proclaimed German Emperor at Versailles in January, 1871. This was heady wine indeed for German patriots, and Giesebrecht's preface of 1873 shows its effects very clearly. It speaks of "the most miraculous change of circumstances . . . which we have witnessed in wonder" and expresses the hope that a time "when the resurrected names of Emperor and Empire exert their magical power on millions of people" will generate an interest in the subject of medieval German history.[8]

The events of the 'sixties and 'seventies served not only as the justification for the historical study of the medieval Empire, but also seemed the fulfillment of medieval prophecies and oracles about its revival. Indeed, after these prophecies seemed validated on the battlefields of Europe and in the Hall of Mirrors at Versailles, the study of medieval oracular literature became an academically respectable, even a passionate, scholarly concern in Bismarckian Germany. It is, therefore, no accident that in 1871 the *Historische Zeitschrift*, founded and directed by Heinrich von Sybel, who had played an active role in Prussian politics and was later commissioned by Bismarck to write the official history of the foundation of the Empire, published Georg Voigt's important and influential article on "Die deutsche Kaisersage." In it the author defined his topic, somewhat narrowly, as "the legend of the old Emperor who would not die, who would some day return in order to refound the empire."

In the same *annus mirabilis* of 1871 there appeared a study informed by a different and independent spirit, the Roman Catholic theologian Johann Joseph Ignaz von Döllinger's essay entitled "Der Weissagungsglaube und das Prophetentum in der Christlichen Zeit."[9] In this article Döllinger did not join the chorus of nationalistic wonderment and intoxication over recent successes, nor did he, like his German contemporaries, focus primarily on German prophecies. He cast his net wider, both geographically and typologically, distinguishing four types of medieval prophecy (purely religious, dynastic, national, and cosmopolitan) and emphasized in particular the religious and ecclesiastical component in medieval prophecy. German predictions are touched on only occasionally, and Döllinger discusses instead materials ranging from Portugal to England and from Byzantium to papal Rome. In fact, one gains the impression that with this profound essay Döllinger intended to provide a counterfoil to the prevalent exploitation of medieval prophecies for nationalist purposes. The net effect of the essay on the reader is the realization that medieval prophecy had its roots in early Christianity; was by no means a monopoly of the German nation; was very frequently inspired by political motivations; and miscarried as often as it succeeded in predicting later events. Characteristically, Döllinger concluded with a citation from Isaiah 55:8–9: "My thoughts are not your thoughts, neither are your ways my ways, says the Lord," and remarked that this Biblical verse must have occurred to many a reader of his essay. One cannot escape the conclusion that this sceptical and broadminded study of medieval prophecy by a prominent and pious Roman Catholic churchman was meant to serve as a warning against the prevailing spirit of excitement over the military and political successes of the German nation. Döllinger seems to have felt that the excessive impressionability evidenced by German scholars with regard to recent developments required a learned refutation. Indirectly, therefore, even Döllinger's sober and wide-ranging article offers powerful testimony to the widespread and intense fascination of German intellectuals with the legends surrounding the medieval empire.

In the years that followed the proclamation at Versailles German historians, philologists, and theologians vied with each other in attempting to elucidate the origin and development of the legends about the German Emperors. They were patriots as well as scholars, and occasionally interpreted medieval developments in the light of political programmes of the nineteenth century. It should be recognized, however, that, probably under the influence of Döllinger's cosmopolitan approach, they were to a large extent free of another possible bias. With remarkable objectivity they traced the genesis of German imperial ideology to its roots in cultures far distant from either medieval or modern Germany in time, place, and cultural tradition. Indeed, it is no exaggeration to say that they rejoiced in discovering Biblical, classical, or Oriental foundations to the imperial legends, and considered that such "exotic" origins strengthened and authenticated German expectations of imperial splendor, rather than providing an embarrassment for the German patriot.

The first scholar to connect explicitly the German imperial legends of the Middle Ages with foreign sources [10] was a Lutheran theologian at the University of Erlangen, Gerhard von Zezschwitz, in a book published in 1877 and indicating in its subtitle his claim that he had discovered Byzantine sources for the legends concerning the medieval German Emperors.[11] Zezschwitz's point of departure was a play, the *Ludus de Antichristo*, written in the days of Frederick Barbarossa and embodying the far-reaching imperial claims of that period. He published this text from a twelfth-century manuscript and related the ideas contained therein to the realities and claims prevalent in twelfth-century Germany. In this play the stage is set in Jerusalem and shows the Temple and seven royal thrones: those of the kings of Jerusalem, of the Synagogue, the Roman Emperor, and of the German, French, Greek, and Babylonian kings. The Roman Emperor demands that the French king recognize his universal sovereignty. The latter refuses, is defeated in battle, and finally acknowledges the Emperor's authority. The other kings follow suit, with one exception: the king of Babylon, as the spokesman for polytheism, decides to destroy Christianity and to attack it at its place of origin, Jerusalem. The Roman Emperor comes to the aid of the king of Jerusalem, defeats the king of Babylon in war, and enters the Temple. There he takes off his crown and offers it to God at the altar. This is followed by the entry of the Antichrist into the Temple, the establishment of his reign, and his final destruction.

Zezschwitz provided his edition of this play with a series of "introductory treatises." The first of these, significantly entitled "The New and the Old Empire," demonstrates, both by this heading and its content, how closely related in Zezschwitz's view the medieval play and its subject matter were to the electrifying events of the Bismarckian era. He explained that it illustrated in lively colors the theory of universal monarchy as it had been entertained at the court of Frederick Barbarossa, and in its most extreme form by the Emperor's chancellor Reinald von Dassel.[12] He then investigated in depth the political and religious ideas underlying this play and succeeded in relating them to the historical realities of Barbarossa's Germany and to the vast body of historical and legendary materials surrounding the medieval Empire. There was, however, one pivotal feature of the play which he was unable to explain in terms of the German tradition: the voluntary abdication of the Last Roman Emperor in the Temple at Jerusalem, followed by the entry of the Antichrist.[13] It is true that he found this trait in a treatise of the mid-tenth century by Adso, later abbot of Moustier-en-Der, in the diocese of Chalons-sur-Marne. In his *Epistola . . . de Ortu et Tempore Antichristi* Adso had mentioned a tradition according to which a last king of the Franks would journey to Jerusalem and would lay down scepter and crown on the Mount of Olives. Here too this act of abdication was followed by the coming of the Antichrist.[14] Clearly this was the same tradition of a ruler's abdication at Jerusalem as in the *Ludus de Antichristo*. Yet Zezschwitz pointed out that in the West this tradition was attested only in these two documents of the tenth and twelfth centuries respectively, as well as in a few texts dependent upon them, and that the act of abdication in particular was not derived from Adso's usual ninth-century source, Haymo of Halberstadt's Commentary on *Second Thessalonians*. Zezschwitz was thus driven to look beyond the Western tradition for the source of the notion, expressed by Adso and the *Ludus*, that a ruler would lay down his crown at Jerusalem.

He found this source in a Greek Apocalypse attributed to the "martyr" Methodius.[15] True, here the act of abdication at Jerusalem followed upon the Antichrist's first appearance, but it was clearly in all other respects the tradition underlying Adso and the *Ludus*.[16] Zezschwitz had thus discovered a new dimension for the Western legends about the Emperors and he therefore dedicated to the *Apocalypse* attributed to Methodius a lengthy and detailed section of his book.[17] His results were partly invalidated or refined by later research, but there can be no doubt that it was Zezschwitz who gave the new "orientation" to the further investigation of the Legend of the Last Emperor.

This dependence of all later work on that of Zezschwitz can be demonstrated in detail. The connecting link was a review of Zezschwitz's book by the great German classicist and orientalist Alfred von Gutschmid.[18] Zezschwitz's book and Gutschmid's review then provided the impetus for a series of further publications on the German imperial legends and their sources in ancient apocalyptic legends. In 1895 and 1896, respectively, when all Germany was celebrating the twenty-fifth anniversary of the Empire's founding, two important works on the subject appeared: the historian Franz Kamper's *Kaiser-*

prophetien und Kaisersagen im Mittelalter [19] and the theologian Wilhelm Bousset's book *Der Antichrist in der Überlieferung des Judentums, des Neuen Testaments und der Alten Kirche.* Three years later was published Ernst Sackur's *Sibyllinische Texte und Forschungen* (1898). All of them show the impact of Zezschwitz's and Gutschmid's work in that they combine a study of the ancient apocalyptic tradition, as represented for example by Pseudo-Methodius' work, with that of German political legends. Wilhelm Bousset quoted the concluding sentence of Gutschmid's review in the preface of his book. Sackur in turn stated in his foreword that he found Gutschmid's remarks the best that had been written on Pseudo-Methodius and that he owed to him the idea of preparing a critical edition of the Latin text. Work on the subject continued with reduced intensity into the twentieth century, but these remarks must suffice to illustrate the close connection between German scholarly work on the legends concerning medieval Emperors and their origins in Early Christian and Byzantine apocalypses on the one hand and the emergence of German nationalism and the unification of the country on the other.

What was this *Apocalypse* of Pseudo-Methodius, which the German scholars of the nineteenth century, to their surprise, found had exerted a strong influence on the German legends concerning their medieval Emperors? The Greek text is a strange, indeed an enigmatic, document.[20] According to the Greek title, the author was Methodius, bishop of Patara, and the book deals with the kingdoms of the barbarians and the Last Times. The first part of the work (chaps. I–VII) is written in the past tense and contains an extremely fanciful history of the world from Adam to the Moslem invasions. It is based to some extent on the Bible, but the Biblical account is generously "improved" by apocryphal additions and combined with a legend about the founding of Byzantium by the hero Byzas, allegedly the second husband of Alexander the Great's mother, the Ethiopian princess Chuseth. In this part (chap. VII) the author quotes prominently II Thessalonians 2:1–8 and interprets the difficult phrase: "only he who now restrains it [the mystery of lawlessness] will do so until he is out of the way" to refer to the Roman or the Byzantine Empire. It followed from this interpretation that the Empire, destined to restrain the Antichrist, would last to the end of time. He also cited for the same purpose I Corinthians 15:24: "Then comes the end when he delivers the kingdom to God the Father." [21] This same objective of proving that the Byzantine Empire will endure to the last days is also evident in the interpretation which the author gives to Psalms 68:31: "let Ethiopia hasten to stretch out her hands unto God," for the author states that in accordance with the parahistorical genealogies developed by him the Byzantine Emperor is the descendant of an Ethiopian princess, and it is therefore a Byzantine Emperor, as the legitimate heir of Ethiopian royalty, who will "stretch out his hands to God." [22] In this interpretation of the psalm the author reveals his purpose in writing the "historical" section and indeed the entire *Apocalypse*: to prove that the Byzantine Empire would last to the end of time and consequently be victorious over all its enemies, the Moslems included.

In the second part (chaps. VII–X), written in the future tense, the apocalyptist "prophesies" the Arab invasions and describes at great length and in lurid detail their destructiveness and cruelty. The third section of the work (chaps. XI and XII) is eschatological and therefore most interesting in the present context. Pseudo-Methodius predicts that at the time when the Moslems are at the height of their power, an Emperor of the Greeks and Romans will arise against them. He will, in the words of the psalmist (78:65), be "awakened as one out of sleep and like a man drinking wine," whom men had considered dead and worthless. He will defeat the Moslems, drive them back into Arabia, and free the lands of the Empire that they had occupied. The Emperor will then proceed to Jerusalem, where he will reside for one year-week and a half (ten and a half years). The Antichrist will be born. Then the Emperor will ascend Golgotha, will take off his diadem, and depose it on the Cross. He will stretch out his hands to heaven and hand over his imperial power to God. Then the Antichrist will seduce many people, but in the end he will be slain by Jesus Christ at the Second Coming.

This very brief summary hardly gives an adequate impression of the strangeness of the document, and it is impossible in the present context to discuss all the many problems which it poses. Here it must suffice to say that the Greek text was written in the seventh or early eighth century, after Syria and Mesopotamia had been occupied by the Arabs, and is therefore half a millennium later than the church father Methodius to whom it was attributed.[23] The earlier parts of the *Apocalypse*, therefore, consist largely of *vaticinia post eventum*. It is also clear that the work, though strange, fanciful, and legendary, is inspired by the Byzantine ideology of empire which it makes the pivot of an impressive and coherent parahistorical construction culminating in the abdication scene on Golgotha — a point that Zezschwitz, once again, was the first scholar to emphasize.[24] In the first place, the transfer of imperial authority from the Last Roman Emperor to God at the end of time reflects the Byzantine idea that the Emperor is God's vice-regent on earth.[25] From this basic concept it followed logically that successful completion of the divine mandate by the defeat of all non-Christian powers by the Last Roman Emperor meant the end of the mandatory's power, i.e., abdication. Secondly, the role of the Cross in the act of abdication is closely bound up with the Byzantine notion, already known to Eusebius, that God had bestowed universal power on the first Christian Emperor Constantine the Great by a vision of the Cross.[26] Finally, the abdication of the Last Roman Emperor on Golgotha is the visual representation and dramatization of Pseudo-Methodius' interpretation of II Thessalonians 2; I Corinthians 15:24; and Psalms 68:31. In this scene, the restraining influence, i.e., the Empire, is shown to be "out of the way" because by the act of abdication the Empire comes to an end. In this scene, also, it is imagined that Christ, represented by his mandatory the Emperor, "delivers the kingdom to God the Father." Finally, in this act of abdication, Ethiopia, i.e., the Byzantine Emperor descended from the Ethiopian princess Chuseth, quite literally is seen "to stretch out her hands to God." In turn this interpretation of Psalms 68:31 presupposes the entire series of parahistorical genealogies in the first part of the *Apocalypse*, for only if the Byzantine Emperor is descended from the Ethiopian rulers can it be maintained that he personifies the "Ethiopia" of the psalmist. It thus becomes clear that in this *Apocalypse* the abdication scene on Golgotha is deeply rooted in the eschatological, theological, and ideological conceptions of Byzantine Christianity. The scene is clearly an invention based on the three Biblical passages mentioned above, as is the parahistorical construction which buttresses it, but it is an invention which expresses in visual imagery the Byzantine theory of imperial power and Byzantine eschatological expectations.

Is the author of the Greek text responsible for this invention? This raises the question of the originality of the Greek text, and in this connection an important discovery was made about a generation ago. A Hungarian Orientalist, the late Michael Kmosko, proved not only that the Greek text was derived from an original written in the Syriac language, but that this critical text actually survives in a Vatican manuscript of the sixteenth century.[27] Kmosko had the intention of studying the Syriac text in detail but unfortunately was not able to carry out his project. I have, however, transcribed and translated the manuscript, and there can be no doubt, for a variety of philological reasons, that the Syriac text is the original and the Greek text its translation.

By and large, the content of the Syriac is very similar to that of its Greek, Latin, and other translations. Like the Greek text, the Syriac original is attributed to Methodius, who is here called "bishop of Olympus and martyr." Its subject matter is defined as "the succession of kings and concerning the end of times." In the Syriac document the revelation properly speaking is introduced by a preamble according to which Methodius "asked God to learn concerning the generations and concerning the kingdoms, how they were handed down from Adam and until today." God then sent to Methodius "one from among his hosts," i.e., an angel, who showed him all the generations and kingdoms. From the point of view of literary history the most interesting detail in this preamble, all of which is missing in the Greek and all other translations, is the statement that the angel's revelation took place on "the mountain of Shenāgar." [28] This remark makes it highly probable, if not certain, that the text was composed in Mesopotamia, to be exact near Tour Shiggar, or Djabal Sindjar, a mountain range about one hundred miles west of modern Mosul on the slopes of which had been situated the ancient city of Singara. So far as the time of composition is concerned, there are rather clear indications that it cannot have been written prior to A.D. 644 or later than 678. [29]

As in the Greek translation, the first part of the Syriac apocalypse is "historical" and reaches from Adam to the Moslem invasions of "Rome," that is of the Byzantine Empire. Here again there is the Biblical story generously expanded by fanciful data from Oriental history and legend; for example the marriage of the hero Byzas with the princess Chuseth, mother of Alexander the Great, as well as the citations from II Thessalonians 2 and Psalm 68. This parahistorical part is followed, again as in the Greek text, by "prophecies" of the Arab invasions and the terrible destruction and suffering inflicted by the enemy. In the third, or eschatological, section of the Syriac text, this mood of despair gives way to one of hope and triumph. Just as the Moslems are at the height of their power and proclaim blasphemously that "there is no deliverer for the Christians," Pseudo-Methodius predicts that a king of the Greeks will defeat them and drive them back into the desert. This king will then proceed to Jerusalem, will deposit his diadem on the Holy Cross, will stretch out his hands to heaven, and surrender his kingship to God. [30]

In general layout, then, the Syriac original resembles closely the Greek translation. There exist, however, a great many differences in detail, such as the preamble omitted in the Greek version. Some of these differences shed light on obscurities in the translation; others, as is usually the case with newly discovered texts, pose new problems. A most revealing feature is the reference, in the parahistorical section of the Syriac text, to Psalms 68:31: "Let Ethiopia stretch out her hands unto God." Here the author attacks "many brethren of the clergy" who, not unnaturally, assumed that the psalmist meant the kingdom of Ethiopia. Not so, says the author, "the kingdom of Greece" was meant, because its ruler was descended from the Ethiopian princess Chuseth.[31] The first conclusion to follow from this passage in which the author calls his unknown opponents "brethren of the clergy" is that he himself must have been a member of the clergy, a priest, or a monk.

The passage allows a further inference. Why should Methodius' opponents, who were priests in Mesopotamia in the seventh century, have expected the Ethiopian kingdom to last until the end of time and the Ethiopian king to play so important a role in the eschatological events? In the distant past there had indeed been strong religious ties between Syriac-speaking Christianity and Ethiopia, and Syrian missionaries had played an important role in the Christianization of Ethiopia. Furthermore, for a short period in the first half of the sixth century Ethiopia had intervened militarily in the affairs of southern Arabia and even played a role in Mediterranean diplomacy. But in 570 the Persian conquest of Yemen had put an end to Ethiopia's role.[32] The only reason why in the seventh century Pseudo-Methodius' opponents could be so concerned to find a Biblical guarantee for the permanence of the Ethiopian kingdom was that Ethiopia was the only country in the world where Monophysitism was the official religion and the ruler himself a Monophysite.

There is one further inference to be drawn from Pseudo-Methodius' statement that "many brethren of the clergy" interpreted Psalms 68:31 to refer to the ruler of Ethiopia. For Mesopotamian Christians under Moslem rule, to rely in the seventh century for liberation upon the Monophysite monarch of Ethiopia was tantamount to saying that the time of delivery lay in the indefinite future and to permitting an interim accommodation with the conquerors. This, indeed, was the policy pursued by the Monophysite religious leader in that area, Marutha, the metropolitan bishop of Tagrit, who opened the gates of the

Byzantium and the Migration of Literary Works and Motifs

citadel of his city to the Moslems. His example was followed by many Christian individuals and communities. So successful was this policy that Marutha's biographer, his successor Denha of Tagrit (649–59), was able to describe in dithyrambic terms the security, prosperity, good ecclesiastical organization, and charitable activities of the Jacobite Church in Mesopotamia and its submission to the Arab authorities.[33] This description was approximately contemporaneous with the composition of the Syriac *Apocalypse* of Pseudo-Methodius. However, in contrast to his ecclesiastical superior Denha, the anonymous author of the *Apocalypse* paints in the darkest colors the ravages of the invaders and speaks with great bitterness of collaborators and apostates:

> . . . a multitude of members of the clergy will deny the true faith of the Christians and the Holy Cross and the mysteries of power [the sacraments], and without compulsion and blows and harsh words they will deny Christ and will agree with the unbelievers. . . . They will separate themselves from the congregation of the Christians of their own accord. . . . their false words will find credence. And they will listen concerning something that was said to them and they will comply.[34]

Thus all the aspects of Pseudo-Methodius' pamphlet fit together: his terrifying picture of the Moslems' treatment of the Christian population in Mesopotamia, his bitter complaints over priests and laymen collaborating with the conquerors, his rejection of the "Ethiopian" interpretation of Psalms 68:31 as defeatist, or even treacherous, and finally his insistence on a "Byzantine" interpretation of the verse of the Psalmist and his reliance on help from the Byzantine emperor. Pseudo-Methodius' tract thus was a politico-religious manifesto, rejecting any kind of defeatism or collaboration with the Moslems, warning against reliance on the weak and distant ruler of Ethiopia as a will-o'-the-wisp, calling for war to the finish against the conquerors, and preaching that salvation from the Moslem yoke could come from only one source, the most powerful Christian monarch of the time, the *basileus* at Byzantium. In the end this hope of the author was to be disappointed, for Mesopotamia has remained under Moslem rule to the present day, but in the seventh century this outcome was by no means a foregone conclusion. Byzantine rulers had for centuries acted, and were to continue to act, as protectors of Christians everywhere, even of anti-Chalcedonians under foreign rule. There was thus nothing quixotic in Pseudo-Methodius' political doctrine.

It will now be convenient to retrace the course of this enquiry which has led from Bismarckian Germany to seventh-century Mesopotamia. The legend of the Last Roman Emperor is first attested in the Syriac *Apocalypse* of Pseudo-Methodius, composed in northern Mesopotamia during the third quarter of the seventh century. It is impossible to say with certainty whether this first evidence represents at the same time the historical origin of the legend.[35] At any rate, it appears here as the visualization and culmination of an elaborate substructure of parahistory and Biblical exegesis designed to demonstrate the military superiority of the Byzantine Empire over all past, present, and future enemies and, as a result, the certainty of its survival to the end of time. Zezschwitz was therefore right in concluding that the *Apocalypse* of Pseudo-Methodius, such as he knew it, was based on Byzantine imperial ideology, but wrong in assuming that it must therefore have originated in the Byzantine Empire. This pointed formulation of Byzantine imperial claims was conceived, not on the soil of the Empire, but in an area not far removed from its eastern frontier that had only for relatively short periods formed part of the Roman or Byzantine Empires but which contained sizable Christian minorities looking to the Empire for protection and guidance.

It is not difficult to see why this Jacobite priest's call for resistance to the finish against the Moslem invaders of his country and reliance on the might of the Byzantine Emperor was quickly translated from Syriac into Byzantine Greek. In order to make his message palatable to his Mesopotamian coreligionaries the author of necessity ignored the doctrinal differences that separated his church from that of Byzantium. He gave a coherent, if fanciful and extreme, formulation to Byzantine confidence in the Empire's military superiority over all foreign peoples and in its universal Christian mission: the Byzantine Emperor, by virtue of his possession of the relic of the True Cross on which the Savior had suffered, would conquer all his enemies to the end of time and would then be able to hand over his Empire, made safe for Christ's kingdom and cleansed of its Moslem invaders, to God the Father. Pseudo-Methodius' Syriac tract expressed what every Byzantine recognized as the Byzantine ideology of Emperor and Empire. It buttressed with scriptural arguments and an elaborate parahistorical construction the Byzantine claim to a protectorate over Christians everywhere. Nobody can say in whose travel bag this powerful document of politico-religious irredentism crossed the Arab-Byzantine frontier, but it is easy to see why it appealed strongly to

Byzantium and the Migration of Literary Works and Motifs

the Byzantine public and was translated into Greek soon after its composition in the Syriac language.

And why was it translated into Latin, and why did it exert an influence on the Latin Middle Ages? The Latin manuscripts of Pseudo-Methodius' *Apocalypse* make it certain that the monk Peter did his translation during the late seventh or in the eighth century. He was probably of Eastern extraction and wrote in a monastery in Merovingian Gaul.³⁶ In his *praefaciuncula* he writes that he performed his labor of love for his brethren in his monastery "because they [Pseudo-Methodius' predictions] have been rather aptly prophesied for our time . . . so that by means of the happenings which we observe with our own eyes we may give credence to what has been predicted by our fathers."³⁷ Perhaps Peter was alarmed by the Moslem advance through Spain into Gaul that took place at the beginning of the eighth century and considered Pseudo-Methodius' apocalypse a tract for his times inasmuch as it seemed to describe in lively colors the destructiveness of the Arab invasion and held out a hope for delivery. However this may be, it was the monk Peter's Latin translation that first introduced into the Western political consciousness the notion of a "king of the Greeks or Romans" who would defeat the Moslems and surrender his empire to God.³⁸

The later destiny of this motif in the West is well known and need only be summarized here. Directly or indirectly, the impact of Pseudo-Methodius' prediction of a Last Emperor is noticeable in the *Letter . . . on the Origin and Time of the Antichrist* composed in the middle of the tenth century by the monk Adso. As stated before (p. 53), Adso himself informs us that for this one particular feature he is departing from his normal source and is relying on another tradition. It is precisely the passage prophesying the coming of the Frankish king who would restore the Roman Empire and lay down scepter and crown on the Mount of Olives at Jerusalem. As Zezschwitz pointed out a century ago, Adso was here following the apocalypse of Pseudo-Methodius.³⁹ The only important innovation was that a prophecy originally referring to a Byzantine ruler was rewritten to fit a Frankish king.

This tradition about a future restorer of the Roman Empire who would defeat the Moslems, surrender his crown at Jerusalem, and usher in the reign of Antichrist was to play a powerful role in later German developments. Peter Munz has shown recently that "in the period immediately preceding the First Crusade, more and more people began to identify the final emperor's journey to Jerusalem with a crusade for the reconquest of the Holy Sepulchre." He also has pointed out that in the early twelfth century, "by the time Frederick [Barbarossa] was a young man Antichrist speculation was the universal topic of conversation."[40] At least once in Frederick's lifetime, probably at his coronation in 1152, the *Ludus de Antichristo* was performed in his presence. At a climactic point in the play, at the very end of the first part, the Emperor, after having defeated in battle the last of his enemies, the king of Babylon, enters the Temple at Jerusalem, takes the crown from his head, holds it as well as his scepter and the other insignia before the altar and chants:

> Receive what I offer, for with a kindly heart
> I resign the insignia to Thee, King of Kings
> Through Whom kings rule, Who alone mayst be called
> Emperor and Who art the ruler of all men.[41]

In the second half of the thirteenth century and later, these notions about the Last Emperor, ultimately of Eastern provenance, coalesced with legends concerning the return of Barbarossa's grandson Frederick II from death.[42] By the fifteenth century it was believed that Frederick II was living on in Mount Kyffhäuser, and early in the next century there is evidence that Frederick Barbarossa began to replace his grandson as the hero of the legend.[43] In this final form the motif of the Last Emperor exercised, as we have seen at the beginning of this paper, a profound effect on German literature and historiography in the nineteenth century.[44]

Thus the religio-political manifesto of a Monophysite churchman in Mesopotamia, alarmed by the Moslem occupation of his country, was, as it travelled westward, translated and transformed into a powerful and influential formulation of Byzantine imperial ideology and eschatology, then into an expression of Western hopes for an imperial restoration after a long period of Moslem threats, subsequently into an assertion of the medieval German Empire's claim to hegemony over Christendom, and finally into the gradual realization by German scholars of the nineteenth century that the roots of their nation's imperial legends lay to a considerable degree in Biblical and Oriental traditions.

NOTES

1. Franz Dölger, "Byzantine Literature," in J. M. Hussey, ed., *The Cambridge Medieval History*, vol. IV, part II (Cambridge, 1967), p. 263.

Byzantium and the Migration of Literary Works and Motifs

2. See, for example, for patristic literature: A. Sigmund, *Die Überlieferung der Griechischen Christlichen Literatur in der Lateinischen Kirche bis zum 12. Jahrhundert* (Munich, 1949).

3. On hagiography, see Paul Peeters, *Orient et Byzance: Le Tréfonds Oriental de l'hagiographie byzantine*, Subsidia Hagiographica 26 (Brussels, 1950). This remarkable book touches on many instances of translations outside the hagiographical genre in the strict sense and raises many general problems concerning intercultural literary borrowings.

4. Dölger, p. 242.

5. Albrecht Timm, *Der Kyffhäuser im deutschen Geschichtsbild*, Historisch-Politische Hefte der Ranke-Gesellschaft, III (Göttingen, n.d. [1960–61?]). The author offers a useful collection and discussion of materials that I have used in the text. Recently F. Graus, "Die Herrschersagen des Mittelalters," *Archiv für Kulturgeschichte*, LI (1969), 65–93, esp. 80–82, made some interesting comments on the typology of royal legends in the Middle Ages, including that of Mount Kyffhäuser. After this paper had been submitted for publication, an anonymous reader for *Medievalia et Humanistica* called my attention to a recent book, Peter Munz' *Frederick Barbarossa: A Study in Medieval Politics* (London, 1969). The first and last chapters of this book contain an interesting discussion of the Kyffhäuser legend, of which I have made grateful use in the revision of this paper.

6. Georg Voigt, "Die deutsche Kaisersage," *Historische Zeitschrift*, 26 (1871), 131–87, esp. 161.

7. Wilhelm von Giesebrecht, *Geschichte der deutschen Kaiserzeit*, 5th ed. (Leipzig, 1881). The preface of 1855 is here reprinted, pp. v–xvi.

8. Giesebrecht, pp. xvii–xx.

9. Now most conveniently accessible in Döllinger's *Kleinere Schriften* (Stuttgart, 1890), pp. 451–557. At the time when he wrote this article, Döllinger was already deeply involved in his conflict with the Papacy over the issue of papal infallibility; see S. J. Tonsor, "Döllinger," *New Catholic Encyclopedia*, IV (New York, etc., 1967), 959 f. By letter Professor Tonsor calls my attention to the lively political and religious interest in Russia, Greece, and the Near East prevailing at Munich during the nineteenth century and suggests that Döllinger and other Munich savants may have hoped seriously to reverse at long last the tide of Islam.

10. In 1871 Döllinger (*op. cit.*; in *Kleinere Schriften*, esp. p. 497 ff.) had discussed Pseudo-Methodius' *Apocalypse* in some detail, but so far as I can see, he did not establish any connection with German imperial legends. As early as 1857 Adolf von Gutschmid, whose later publications were to make decisive contributions to the investigation of the genesis of the German imperial legends (see p. 65 and n. 18), had become acquainted with this *Apocalypse* through the casual use made of it by Franz C. Movers in his *History of the Phoenicians*. In his review of one volume of this work, Gutschmid inserted a lengthy footnote (now reprinted in his *Kleine Schriften*, II (Leipzig, 1890), 1–19, esp. 14–17, n. 1) on Pseudo-Methodius which ranged far beyond the purposes for which Movers had cited this text. He called the *Apocalypse* of Pseudo-Methodius "ein in mehrfacher Hinsicht interessantes und in einer gewissen Beziehung auch historisch wichtiges Doku-

ment," pointed out the medieval popularity of the Latin translation in the West, and urged a critical edition. These references to the historical importance of the text are vague, but the suggestion may not be far-fetched that he had guessed its connections with the legends about the medieval rulers of Germany.

11. Gerhard von Zezschwitz, *Vom Römischen Kaisertum Deutscher Nation: Ein mittelalterliches Drama, nebst Untersuchungen über die byzantinischen Quellen der deutschen Kaisersage* (Leipzig, 1877). At the end of the book (pp. 213–41) the author edits the Latin text of what he calls "das Drama vom Römischen Kaisertum Deutscher Nation und vom Antichristen" from the only manuscript of the twelfth century, formerly at Tegernsee. This Latin play was later published, under the more appropriate title of *Ludus de Antichristo* and with many improvements by Wilhelm Meyer, in *Sitzungsberichte der Kgl. Bayerischen Akademie der Wissenschaften, Philosophisch-Philologische und Historische Klasse* (1882), Heft 1, 17–40. There are several later editions, as well as an English translation by J. Wright, *The Play of Antichrist* (Toronto, 1967). See also Zezschwitz's popular lecture "Der Kaisertraum des Mittelalters in seinen religiösen Motiven" (Leipzig, 1877).

12. It is noteworthy that, in spite of all his enthusiasm for the achievement of German unity in 1871, Zezschwitz expresses some reservations with regard to these far-reaching claims of universal monarchy. He states that in the twelfth century the older notion of the Emperor's protectorate (*Schirmherrschaft*) over Christendom was steadily transformed into the idea of universal monarchy (p. 20) and calls this change "the most serious political mistake perpetrated by the imperial government" (p. 23). He even believes that the author of the *Ludus* viewed these claims with some irony (p. 22).

13. Zezschwitz, *Vom Römischen Kaisertum*, p. 37 and passim.

14. The *Epistola* is available in a critical edition by Ernst Sackur, *Sibyllinische Texte und Forschungen* (Halle a.d.S., 1898; now reprinted Turin, 1963), 97–113. See p. 110: "*Quidam vero doctores nostri dicunt, quod unus ex regibus Francorum Romanum imperium ex integro tenebit, qui in novissimo tempore erit. et ipse erit maximus et omnium regum ultimus. qui postquam regnum feliciter gubernaverit, ad ultimum Ierosolimam veniet et in monte Oliveti sceptrum et coronam suam deponet. hic erit finis et consummatio Romanorum christianorumque imperii. statimque secundum predictam Pauli apostoli sententiam* [II Thess. 2:3]. *Antichristum dicunt mox affuturum. . . .*" See Zezschwitz, *Vom Römischen Kaisertum*, pp. 18 and 37 ff. and the English translation of the *Epistola* by J. Wright (n. 11 above), pp. 100–10. The composition of Adso's work may be connected with popular beliefs concerning the year 1000.

15. Zezschwitz, *Vom Römischen Kaisertum*, pp. 43–84 and passim. He, as well as the other older scholars, could use only a most unsatisfactory edition in the anonymous publication *Monumenta S. Patrum Orthodoxographa*, 2nd ed. (Basel, 1569), 93 ff. The Latin translation was edited, after Zezschwitz's publication, by Sackur, *Sibyllinische Texte*, pp. 57–69, and the Greek version by V. M. Istrin, in *Chteniia Obshchestvia Istorii i Drevnostei Rossiisskiikh pri Moskovskom Universitete*, 193 (1897), pp. 4–50.

Byzantium and the Migration of Literary Works and Motifs

16. Sackur, *Sibyllinische Texte*, p. 93: "Et cum apparuerit filius perditionis, ascendit rex Romanorum sursum in Golgotha . . . et expandit manus suas in caelum et tradit regnum christianorum Deo et patri et adsumetur crux in caelum simul cum coronam regis . . ."

17. Zezschwitz, *Vom Römischen Kaisertum*, p. 43: "Aber eben von diesem Punkte aus eröffnet sich für jeden, der die einschlagenden morgenländischen Traditionen kennt, eine ganz neue Fernsicht." Pseudo-Methodius' *Apocalypse* is discussed on pp. 43–84.

18. The review is reprinted in Gutschmid's *Kleine Schriften*, V (Leipzig, 1894), 495–506.

19. A second edition of Kampers' book was entitled *Die Deutsche Kaiseridee in Prophetie und Sage* (Munich, 1896). Kampers continued to publish a great deal on this and related subjects, e.g., *Vom Werdegang der Abendländischen Kaisermystik* (Leipzig and Berlin, 1924).

20. There still exists no critical edition of the Greek text, but Istrin's edition (see n. 15, above) prints the Greek text from a Vatican manuscript of the sixteenth century and records the variants of several others. Sackur's edition of the Latin translation (n. 15, above) is frequently useful where the Greek text is in doubt, especially where the question of interpolations arises. The summary in the text is based on Istrin's edition.

21. Pseudo-Methodius' interpretation of II Thess. 2 and I Cor. 15:24, pp. 23–25 Istrin.

22. Pseudo-Methodius' interpretation of Psalms 68:31, p. 22 Istrin.

23. See, for example, G. Moravcsik, *Byzantino-Turcica*, 2nd ed., vol. I, Berliner Byzantinistische Arbeiten, X (1958), 426. For some remarks about the purpose of this work see my article "Medieval Apocalypses as Historical Sources," *American Historical Review*, LXXIII (1968) 997–1018.

24. *Vom Römischen Kaisertum*, p. 50 and passim.

25. On the Byzantine view of God as the source of imperial power see, for example, W. Ensslin, in *Cambridge Medieval History*, IV, Part II (Cambridge, 1967), p. 6 f.

26. Zezschwitz, *Vom Römischen Kaisertum*, p. 50.

27. "Das Rätsel des Pseudo-Methodius," *Byzantion*, VI (1931), 273–96; see also V (1929–30), 422–24. The manuscript referred to in the text is the *cod. Vat. Syrus* 58, fol. 118–36. Sackur, *Sibyllinische Texte*, pp. 53–55, had shown from internal evidence that the author of the Greek text had been a Syrian, but had been of the opinion that this Syrian author had written in the Greek language (p. 55).

28. *Cod. Vat. Syrus*, fol. 118 verso: "And the Lord sent to him [Methodius] one from among his hosts to the mountain of Shenāgar and he showed him all the generations. . . ."

29. *Terminus post*: allusion to an Arab navy, which was created between 644 and 649. *Terminus ante*: no reference to the Arab civil war (661–65) and particularly to the unsuccessful Arab siege of Constantinople (674–78). The author's silence on the latter event is all the more remarkable inasmuch as in connection with his general thesis that the Byzantine Empire is superior to all its enemies and will last to the end of the world he mentions several Roman-Byzantine victories down to the Persian-Avar siege

of Constantinople in 626, but fails to mention the Arab failure before Constantinople in 678.

30. *Cod. Vat. Syrus* 58, fol. 135 recto: "And immediately the Son of Perdition [= Antichrist] is revealed. Then the king of the Greeks will go up and stand on Golgotha and the Holy Cross will be set in that place in which it was set up when it carried the Christ. And the king of the Greeks will place his diadem on top of the Holy Cross, and will stretch out his two hands to heaven and will hand over the kingship to God the Father."

31. *Cod. Vat. Syrus* 58, fol. 126 recto: "However, many brethren of the clergy suppose that the blessed David spoke this word [Psalms 68:31] concerning the kingdom of the Ethiopians. And those who thought this erred concerning this, for it is the kingdom of Greece which is from the seed of Chuseth. . . ."

32. On the history of Ethiopia to the seventh century see Carlo Conti Rossini, *Storia d'Etiopia*, I (Bergamo,1928). On religious developments in particular: G. Lanczkowski, "Aethiopia," *Jahrbuch für Antike und Christentum*, I (1958), 134–53, esp. 143–45 (with bibliography).

33. Denha of Tagrit, *Biography of Marutha*, ed. and trans. F. Nau, *Patrologia Orientalis*, III (Paris, 1909), pp. 81–83: "Quand je considère tous les biens que possèdent maintenant les fils de Tagrit (la ville) bénite, c'est à dire: leur foi orthodoxe, leur zèle pour elle et l'accomplissement des bonnes oeuvres qui lui conviennent; leurs offices spirituels et la célébration des divins mystères: le bel ordre des clercs; les rangs disciplinés des prêtres qui sont à leur tête, le beau maintien et la belle tenue des diacres au milieu d'eux dans le sanctuaire; leur station autour l'autel; le service des sous-diacres, des lecteurs et des chantres; les continuelles, louangeuses et loua-bles psalmodies de l'esprit et d'intelligence; et tout le clergé, et les beaux vêtements qui les ornent ainsi que toute l'église et l'autel; le voile (du calice), les tentures, les patènes, les calices, les encensoirs, les tabernacles et leurs richesses avec le reste des ornements sacrés; de plus leur exultation et leur joie dans les fêtes du Seigneur et les mémoires des saints qu'ils fêtent et célèbrent joyeusement et ardemment avec attention et sans négligence; en même temps que leur amour et leur soumission les uns vers les autres et surtout envers leurs chefs et leurs gouverneurs ecclésiastiques et séculiers (litéralement: dans l'Eglise et dans la ville et le monde); quand je vois ce consentiment et cette adhésion unanime au bien, je comprends que notre saint père a été pour eux la racine, la cause et le fondement de tout cela. . . . (il fut cause) aussi qu'avec amour (les habitants de Tagrit) honorèrent les Pères, les reçurent avec joie, participèrent à leurs honneurs et à leurs bénédictions, s'occupèrent des besoins des solitaires et des moines et de la construction des églises, des monastères et des saints couvents; répandirent des aumônes sur les pauvres; délivrèrent les captifs et les prisonniers. . . . En un mot Tagrit grandit tellement et acquit un si bon renom et une (telle) efflorescence de biens à son époque. . . ."

34. *Cod Vat. Syrus* 58, fol. 131 recto.

35. Wilhelm Bousset, *Der Antichrist . . .* (Göttingen, 1895), p. 82, was of the opinion that probably the voluntary surrender by a Last Roman Emperor of his empire to God is implied in an apocalypse preserved in Latin

and attributed variously to St. Ephraem or St. Isidore. The relevant passage reads as follows: ". . . iam regnum Romanorum tollitur de medio, et Christianorum imperium traditur Deo et Patri; et tunc venit consummatio, cum coeperit consummari Romanorum regnum . . ." (ed. C. P. Caspari, *Briefe, Abhandlungen und Predigten aus den zwei letzten Jahrhunderten des kirchlichen Altertums und dem Anfang des Mittelalters* [Christiania, 1890], pp. 208–20, esp. 213 f.). In all probability the work dates from the late fourth century. The passage has indeed many similarities with the *Apocalypse* of Pseudo-Methodius. In particular it contains the same references to II Thess. 2:7 and I Cor. 15:24 and is immediately followed by a reference to the appearance of the Antichrist. It is noteworthy, however, that it lacks the most characteristic Biblical citation of Pseudo-Methodius, Psalms 68:31, and fails to mention the Last Roman Emperor as agent of the surrender, which is put in the passive voice (*traditur*). The most natural interpretation of the passage of Pseudo-Ephraem, therefore, is that the author is here simply following I Cor. 15:24 and thinking of Christ himself as surrendering the kingdom to God. In other words, Pseudo-Ephraem seems to be lacking precisely that element which is important in the present context, the figure of the Last Roman Emperor. Pseudo-Ephraem's work originated, however, within the Syrian church (Johannes Dräseke, "Zu der eschatologischen Predigt Pseudo-Ephräms," *Zeitschrift für Wissenschaftliche Theologie*, XXXV (1892), 177–84), and very probably represents a stage of Christian eschatology from which the legend of the Last Roman Emperor developed organically. Sackur, *Sibyllinische Texte*, 164–70, also was of the opinion that the legend of the *Last Roman Emperor* surrendering his power at Jerusalem originated in the fourth century. It is indeed mentioned in the Latin translation of the apocalypse attributed to the Tiburtine Sibyl (Sackur, p. 186, lines 7 ff.), but not in the Greek version of the same text (see my *Oracle of Baalbek*, Dumbarton Oaks Studies X [Washington, D.C. 1967], p. 116). Consequently it is unlikely to have formed part of the original (Theodosian) version of the Sibyl's apocalypse (*Oracle of Baalbek*, p. 136). Its presence in the Latin translation probably represents a borrowing from Pseudo-Methodius.

36. Sackur, *Sibyllinische Texte*, p. 55 f. Four of the Latin manuscripts are no later than the eighth century.

37. Ibid., p. 59 f.: ". . . quoniam nostris sunt aptius prophetata temporibus. . . . ut iam per ipsa que nostris cernimus oculis vera esset credamus ea quae praedicta sunt a patribus nostris."

38. Ibid., p. 89 f.: ". . . et exiliet super eos rex Gregorum siue Romanorum in furore magna et expergiscitur tamquam homo a somno vini, quem extimabant homines tamquam mortuum esse et in nihilo utilem profecisse. hic exiet super eos a mare Aethiopiae et mittit gladium et desolationem in Ethribum. . . ." P. 93: ". . . ascendit rex Romanorum sursum in Golgotha, in quo confixum est lignum sanctae crucis . . . et tollit rex coronam de capite suo et ponet eam super crucem, et expandit manus suas in caelum et tradit regnum christianorum Deo et patri. . . ."

39. See notes 15 and 17, above.

40. Peter Munz, *Frederick Barbarossa*, p. 376.

41. *Ludus de Antichristo*, ed. K. Langosch, *Geistliche Spiele* (Berlin, 1957),

p. 206: "Imperator cum suis intret templum et, postquam ibi adoraverit, tollens coronam de capite et tenens eam cum sceptro et imperio ante altare cantet:

> Suscipe, quod offero!   nam corde benigno
> Tibi regi regum   imperium resigno
> Per quem reges regnant,   qui solus imperator
> Dici potes et es   cunctorum gubernator."

Cf. Munz, *Frederick Barbarossa*, p. 377.

42. Munz, *Frederick Barbarossa*, p. 8 f. See, for example, in the mid-fourteenth century the chronicler John of Winterthur's sceptical report on rumors concerning a return of Frederick II from the dead: "Post resumptum imperium iustius et gloriosius gubernatum quam ante cum exercitu copioso transfretabit et in monte Oliveti vel apud arborem aridam imperium resignabit" (ed. F. Baethgen and C. Brun, in *Monumenta Germaniae Historica, Scriptores Rerum Germanicarum*, N.S. 3 [Berlin, 1924], p. 280 f., *sub anno* 1348).

43. Munz, p. 14.

44. See also Munz, esp. pp. 19–21.

ADDITIONAL REMARKS

On pp.58,60,62 above and in other articles (for example no.XIII,1006) I expressed the opinion that Pseudo-Methodius was a Monophysite.The basis for my view was a sentence from the Syriac original which I translated as follows (p.66 n.31):"However, many brethren of the clergy suppose that the blessed David spoke this word (Ps.68:31) concerning the kingdom of the Ethiopians".My reasoning was that in the seventh century when Pseudo-Methodius composed his apocalypse,Ethiopia no longer played a role in the international politics of the Near East, and that the author's political reliance on the Ethiopian ruler was therefore explicable on the ground that Ethiopia was then the only country where Monophysitism was the official religion.However, my translation was inaccurate:the verb rendered above by the present tense ("suppose") appears in the Syriac original in the "perfect" (<u>asberu</u>),the form

of the historical narrative.The author,therefore,
means not that contemporary members of the Mesopotamian clergy placed their hope on the Ethiopian
ruler,but that members of the Mesopotamian clergy
had done so in the past. This statement is not surprising as ecclesiastical relations between the Syrian
churches and Ethiopia had long been close and as in
the sixth century Ethiopia had collaborated militarily with Byzantium in the Red Sea region.The sentence mentioned above,in its revised translation
("supposed"),therefore neither requires nor allows
any inference as to Pseudo-Methodius' christological orientation or ecclesiastical affiliation. Walter
E.Kaegi,Jr. has assembled in useful fashion the
earliest evidence for Byzantine comments on the
Arab conquests:"Initial Byzantine Reactions to the
Arab Conquest",Church History 38,1969,1-11,and
included a discussion of Pseudo-Methodius (5-8).

XIII

Medieval Apocalypses as Historical Sources

T HE apocalypses contained in the Old and New Testaments, especially the Books of Daniel and of Revelation, as well as the many extant extracanonical apocalypses have been examined intensively by generations of scholars, most of them theologians.[1] The historian can learn much from such studies, yet their authors frequently concern themselves with historical matters only to the extent of explaining the historical allusions and prophecies *ex eventu* contained in these texts. The reverse problem—whether these ancient apocalypses may contain historical information not known from other historical sources—is rarely raised by modern scholarship, presumably because for the Jewish and early Christian periods when the best-known apocalypses were written, documentary and narrative sources provide fairly ample evidence. There is, consequently, little incentive to resort to such de-

* A professor at the University of Michigan, Mr. Alexander is the author of *The Patriarch Nicephorus of Constantinople: Ecclesiastical Policy and Image Worship in the Byzantine Empire* (Oxford, Eng., 1958). He delivered an earlier version of this paper at the annual dinner of the Mediaeval Academy of America, New York City, December 28, 1966. The research on which this paper is based was carried out primarily in Rome, under fellowships from the John Simon Guggenheim Memorial Foundation, the Social Science Research Council, the Ford Foundation, and the Fulbright Organization, and a Summer Faculty Research Fellowship and several research grants from the Horace Rackham School of Graduate Studies at the University of Michigan.

[1] For Daniel, see, e.g., Otto Eissfeldt, *The History of the Formation of the Old Testament: An Introduction including the Apocrypha and Pseudepigrapha, and also the Works of a Similar Type from Qumran* (Oxford, Eng., 1965), 512–29 (with full bibliography); on apocalypses outside the canon, see Emil Schürer, *Geschichte des Jüdischen Volkes im Zeitalter Jesu Christi* (4th ed., 4 vols., Leipzig, 1901–1909), III, 258–370; on Revelation, see A. H. McNeile, *An Introduction to the Study of the New Testament* (2d ed., Oxford, Eng., 1953), 260–65.

liberately obscure texts as apocalypses. It is surprising, however, that apocalypses have not been used as historical sources for late ancient and early medieval times for which the documentation is less satisfactory and where every scrap of information must be used for the reconstruction of events. May not apocalyptic texts fill some of the gaps left by more conventional historical sources?

In all apocalypses, by the very nature of the genre, historical fact and eschatological prophecy intertwine. To separate the two, a historian must begin by asking a number of questions: Can he ascertain the date and place of composition of apocalyptic texts? Were they more or less evenly distributed in time and place, or were some occasions and localities especially favorable for the production of such writings? In what circles did they originate, and to what audiences were they addressed? For what purpose or purposes were apocalypses written, rewritten, copied, excerpted, and translated? What conventions did the writers follow? To what extent can apocalypses be used by the historian to corroborate historical facts contained in other, especially narrative, sources? What do they reveal concerning the reactions of individuals and groups to historical events, their judgments on the course of history, and their hopes and fears for the future? Only after disposing of such preliminary questions can the historian undertake with confidence the task of extracting from apocalyptic texts information unknown from other sources or of reaching, with the help of these texts, historical conclusions for which the evidence of the narrative sources is insufficient.

This paper will illustrate these problems by referring to a particular body of historical apocalypses, all of which are pseudonymous.[2] They claim to be the words of an ancient worthy either of classical myth (for instance a sibyl), or of the Biblical record (the prophet Daniel), or of the patristic tradition (Methodius); the true authors, however, are normally unknown. The texts were composed in what was, or had once been, Byzantine territory. They survive, or existed at one time, in the Greek language. All deal with Byzantine wars against the enemies of the Empire, notably against Persians and Arabs. In date of composition they extend from the early sixth to the ninth century. Here is the list: the Oracle of Baalbek, a prophecy of a Christian sibyl written in Greek prose at Baalbek in Phoenicia in the first years of the sixth century;[3] Syriac Apocalypse of Pseudo-Methodius, com-

---

[2] I call apocalypses "historical" if they recapitulate historical events in the guise of prophecy (prophecies *ex eventu*), and I distinguish them from other apocalypses concerned primarily or exclusively with religious topics such as the afterlife.

[3] The text is unedited. I am publishing the *editio princeps* under the title *The Oracle of Baalbek, The Tiburtine Sibyl in Greek Dress*, "Dumbarton Oaks Studies," X (Washington, D. C., 1967). Wherever in this paper the Oracle of Baalbek is referred to, the documentation

posed in the Syriac language in the seventh century;[4] First Greek Version of Pseudo-Methodius' Apocalypse;[5] Second Greek Version of Pseudo-Methodius' Apocalypse;[6] First Greek Vision of Daniel, of the ninth century;[7] Second Greek Vision of Daniel, also composed in the ninth century;[8] Old Church Slavonic Vision of Daniel, the translation of a lost Greek original that was composed in the ninth century.[9]

Discussion of this corpus of apocalypses may well begin with the problem of dating. The answer to this problem seems at first simple enough. Every apocalypse must have been written not long after the latest event to which it alludes. The sibyl in the Oracle of Baalbek, for instance, refers in detail to the defeats suffered by the Byzantine armies at the hands of the Persians under Emperor Anastasius I in 502 and 503, but says nothing of the military recovery of the period following the year 504, of the truce concluded in 505, or of the peace treaty of 506. It follows that in its present form the text was composed between 502 and 506, and this date is confirmed by further internal evidence.

The question next arises: how does one recognize the latest historical element referred to in an apocalypse? Usually it precedes immediately a passage in which the author shifts from history to eschatology. Thus in the Old Church Slavonic Vision of Daniel the author gives a long list of Byzantine emperors. The last recognizable figure is Michael II of Amorion (820–829). His reign is followed immediately by a series of eschatological emperors, for instance, a tetrarchy of two Eastern and two Western rulers—

---

will be found in my book. Latin versions of this work have been known for a long time; see Ernst Sackur, *Sibyllinische Texte und Forschungen* (Halle, 1898; reprint, Turin, 1963), esp. 177–87.

[4] It is unpublished and occurs in *codex Vaticanus Syrus* 58, fols. 118–36, of the sixteenth century; see Michael Kmosko, "Das Rätsel des Pseudo-Methodius," *Byzantion*, VI (No. 1, 1931), 273–96, and description of the Vatican manuscript in St. E. and J. S. Assemani, *Bibliothecae Apostolicae Vaticanae Manuscriptorum Catalogus* (3 vols., Rome, 1756–59) II, 342.

[5] *Otkrovenie Mefodiia Patarskago i Apokrificheskiia Videnia Daniela v Vizantiiski i Slaviano-Russkoi Literaturakh* [Revelation of Methodius of Patara and Apocryphal Visions of Daniel in Byzantine and Slavo-Russian Literature], ed. V. M. Istrin, in the series *Chteniia v Imperatorskom Obshchestvie Istorii i Drevnostei Rossiiskikh pri Moskovskom Universitetie*, Nos. 191 and 193 (Moscow, 1897). Istrin's work is divided into two parts, each with a separate pagination: *Izsledovanie* [Research] and *Teksty* [Texts]. The First Greek Version of Pseudo-Methodius' Apocalypse is printed in *Teksty*, 5–50.

[6] The variants of the Second Version from the First are noted by Istrin in the *apparatus criticus* to his edition of the First Version.

[7] *Anecdota Graeca-Byzantina*, ed. Afanasii Vassiliev (Moscow, 1893), 33–38.

[8] *Ibid.*, 38–43.

[9] This text has been printed three times, first by P. S. Srechkovic, *Zbornik Popa Dragolia*, Srpska Kralievska Akademija, *Spomenik*, V (1890), 10–11 (from a manuscript, now lost, once No. 466 [632] of the Belgrade National Library, thirteenth century); then by Istrin, *Otkrovenie*, *Teksty*, 156–58 (from *codex Athos Chilandar* 24, twelfth or thirteenth century); again by P. A. Lavrov, *Apokrificheskie Teksty* [Apocryphal Texts], *Sbornik Otdeleniia Russkago Iazyka i Slovesnosti Imp. Akad. Nauk*, LXVII, No. 3 (St. Petersburg, 1899), 1–5 (from the Chilandar manuscript, with variants of the Belgrade codex noted in the *apparatus criticus*, but unfortunately without the beginning which is missing in the Chilandar manuscript).

a feature to which no historical reality corresponded in the ninth century.[10] Consequently the list was composed under Michael II, for, if its author had lived under a later emperor, he would not have missed the opportunity of recording the reign of Michael's successors to authenticate his prophecies.

Sometimes the latest historical event is less easy to distinguish from genuine predictions. The Greek versions of Pseudo-Methodius' Apocalypse mention the Muslim invasion of Africa but not of Spain. Consequently scholars have concluded that the Apocalypse must be later than the beginning of the Arab raids against the province of Africa in 670 and earlier than the conquest of Spain in 711.[11] The difficulty, however, is that in other sections of his book Pseudo-Methodius also refers to Muslim raids against Sicily and Greece,[12] and these did not occur until much later than any scholar would allow for the composition of the work. Pseudo-Methodius clearly lived in the seventh century, was observing the rapid and irresistible advance of the Arab armed forces, and prophesied, on the analogy of past Arab progress, that even geographic areas that had not yet been exposed to Muslim attacks would soon succumb to the infidels. It will not do to interpret every apocalyptic prophecy as a *vaticinium ex eventu* and to base the date of apocalyptic documents on such an assumption. In interpreting an apocalypse the historian should never lose sight of the possibility that the author may have been an intelligent observer of current affairs and have at-

---

[10] I translate as literally as possible: ". . . And the horns that I saw are the Roman emperors. They will arise in the last days. The first [emperor] will lift his hand against the son, and afterward he will rule five years. Woe to Thee, Babylon of the Seven Hills [Constantinople], that in Thee the Amazon will rule. A second horn [or, scepter] will arise, another emperor from the Gothic race who has the number 812 [?], and his imperial power will be strong and powerful. In his days there will go forth a strong people and it will struggle with him. And that people will flee from his face, and afterward that people will return, for he [the angel] said: finally that emperor will weaken and become powerless and will give up his soul miserably. Then another horn [or, scepter] will arise from his seed. He will be short lived above all others. Another horn [or, scepter] will arise, his name will be angelic, and he will hold his [i.e., his predecessor's] throne. A fifth horn will arise and go forth seven years. And afterward there will arise another horn [or, scepter] from the first imperial letter. And while he occupies the throne, another horn [or, scepter] [will arise]. And they will blaspheme against the Highest [God]. And because of this blasphemy he will perish miserably and they will lead him to the *Kynēgion*." The Byzantine emperors or empresses here referred to are Irene (797–802), who blinded her son Constantine VI; Nicephorus (802–811), killed on a campaign against the Bulgars; his son Stauracius (July 26–October 2, 811); Michael I (811–813); Leo V (813–820); Michael II (820–829), founder of the Amorian dynasty, a moderate iconoclast. The text probably also refers to Michael's son Theophilus who became coemperor in 821. All the emperors that follow in the text are the product of eschatological fantasy. The writer predicts that Michael II will be led to the *lovec* (literally, "hunter"), but this does not make sense. I interpret it as a literal translation of the Greek word *kynēgos* or *kynēgion*, meaning "hunter" or "hunt," respectively. These were also the designations of quarters of the city of Constantinople. In the *Kynēgion*, in particular, criminals were frequently executed (Raymond Janin, *Constantinople Byzantine* [2d ed., Paris, 1964], 376–77). Thus the author seems to predict a violent end for Michael II. In reality, Michael died a natural death, from a disease of the kidney, another indication that the author wrote under Michael II.

[11] First Greek Version of Pseudo-Methodius' Apocalypse, *Otkrovenie,* ed. Istrin, *Teksty,* 42, 8 (Africa); see Sackur, *Sibyllinische Texte,* 45–46.

[12] First Greek Version of Pseudo-Methodius' Apocalypse, *Otkrovenie,* ed. Istrin, *Teksty,* 29, 2–4; 42, 8.

tempted genuine prophecies of future happenings based on his appraisal of the direction in which events were moving.[13]

Another notorious difficulty in dating an apocalypse is the essential instability of numerals in apocalyptic texts. This is illustrated in crude and drastic fashion in the text tradition of the Oracle of Baalbek. The fourth-century source of the text predicted that the city of Byzantium, refounded by Constantine the Great at the beginning of the century, would cease to rule the Empire before sixty years had elapsed. A sixth-century editor at Heliopolis in Phoenicia, obviously perplexed that Constantinople was still the imperial capital, adjusted this figure to "thrice sixty years," and a medieval successor, active in or before the twelfth century, observing that even the "thrice sixty years" had elapsed and that Constantinople was tenaciously clinging to its imperial position, played it safe and resolutely changed the numerals into "thrice six hundred years." Undoubtedly, he would, had he lived long enough, have noted with satisfaction the captures of the city on the Bosporus by the Latin crusaders in 1204, by the Ottoman Turks in 1453, and by the Allied armies at the end of World War I.

Less transparent is another case of tampering with an apocalyptic time span. Pseudo-Methodius prophesied that Arab domination would end after the lapse of a certain number of "year-weeks" or intervals of seven years. This was the unit of time popular among apocalyptic writers because it was employed in the classical prototype, the canonical Book of Daniel (9:24). The number of year-weeks is given as "ten" in the only extant manuscript of the Syriac original of Pseudo-Methodius, as "seven" in some Greek manuscripts, and as "seventeen" in others.[14] Since Muslim rule in Mesopotamia ended neither after seven year-weeks, that is around 689, nor after ten year-weeks (around 710), nor indeed after the lapse of seventeen of these units (around 751), this is clearly a genuine prophecy that was not fulfilled. If it were not for the "numbers game" played by the copyists and editors of apocalypses, such an unfulfilled prophecy would furnish a valuable *terminus ante quem* for the composition of the original text. In fact, the more one studies apocalyptic writings, the more one comes to distrust numerals

---

[13] When a series of events is mentioned in an apocalypse, it is sometimes difficult to decide whether the latest event, or events, in the series is historical. Thus it will be seen below that the Old Church Slavonic Vision of Daniel speaks of an unsuccessful Arab siege of Enna in Sicily, which must have taken place in 827 or 828. Now it is true that Enna did not fall to the Muslims until 859, but one wonders whether the mention of the Arab failure before Enna reflects historical fact or wishful thinking. In the latter case, the text was written while the siege was going on; in the former, at some time after the event.

[14] Syriac original of Apocalypse of Pseudo-Methodius, in *codex Vaticanus Syrus* 58, fol. 122 verso: "And after those ten weeks of years they [the Arabs] also will be overpowered and subjected to the Kingdom of Rome. . . ." First Greek Version of Apocalypse of Pseudo-Methodius, *Otkrovenie*, ed. Istrin, *Teksty*, 15, 10: seventeen weeks according to some manuscripts, seven weeks of years according to others.

indicating a time span even in cases where the surviving manuscript evidence does not point to the existence of textual variants.[15] The lapse of time and the course of historical events practically forced every copyist of apocalyptic numerals to turn editor if he had any respect for the prophetic merits of the author whose prophecies he was copying.

The emergence of apocalyptic texts, and especially their cumulation, at particular moments in history may interest the historian because it may serve as a kind of barometer for the measuring of eschatological pressures at a given time in history.[16] For example, no less than three apocalyptic writings were composed about A.D. 500: the Oracle of Baalbek; a "Seventh Vision of Daniel" preserved in Armenian only but derived from a lost Byzantine original;[17] and a "Very Brief Chronicle" referred to in the *Theosophy of Tübingen*.[18] Why did apocalyptic texts pile up at that particular time? The last of the three documents gives an answer. It stated specifically that the world would end six thousand years after its creation,[19] that is, either in 501 or 507–508 according to the chronological era used. Because certain millenarian circles around A.D. 500 expected the end of the world to occur momentarily, a considerable number of apocalypses were produced. This is not to say that apocalypses always or even regularly owed their composition to calculations of the end of the world, but the example may illustrate the general proposition that the mere fact of the emergence or of the copying of apocalyptic texts at any particular time may be a matter of historical interest.

As important for the historian as the date of an apocalyptic text is its place of composition. For while it is possible, or even likely, that an author writing in the area where particular historical events took place may have preserved reliable information on these happenings, it is, prima facie, less likely that such data may be found in a source written at the other end of the Empire. To events mentioned in an apocalypse the historian will therefore attach much greater weight if they took place in the vicinity of the

[15] I am not referring here to the well-known tendency of all scribes of miscopying numerals by inadvertence. In apocalytic texts, numerals are exposed to the additional danger of deliberate changes.

[16] On the famous question whether or not there was a general expectation in Western Europe that the world would end in the year 1000, see Alexander A. Vasiliev, "Medieval Ideas of the End of the World," *Byzantion*, XVI (No. 2, 1942–43), 462–502, esp. 478–87.

[17] Most convenient translation into French by Frédéric Macler in *Revue de l'histoire des religions*, XXXIII (No. 6, 1896), 290–309.

[18] *Fragmente Griechischer Theosophien*, ed. Hartmut Erbse, "Hamburger Arbeiten zur Altertumswissenschaft," No. 4 (Hamburg, 1941).

[19] *Ibid.*, 2–3, 167, 15–20; see also Hilarianus, *De Cursu Temporum*, ed. Karl Frick, in *Chronica Minora* (Leipzig, 1893), 170–71, who wrote his treatise in A.D. 397 and expected the world to end after 101 years, that is, in 498. (Professor John Eadie of the University of Michigan furnished this information.) The passage shows that the expectation of the world ending around A.D. 500 existed at least a century prior to that year and was based primarily on chiliastic calculations and combinations, rather than on particular historical events in the late fifth or early sixth century.

author's place of residence rather than if they happened in an area beyond the reach of his sources of information. An apocalyptic description of political, economic, or religious conditions couched in general terms, moreover, becomes meaningful to the historian only if he can identify the areas about which the author is writing. Such descriptions are particularly notable in the Syriac and Greek texts of the Apocalypse of Pseudo-Methodius. It is therefore important to realize that the Syriac original was composed in Mesopotamia, as I hope to show elsewhere, rather than in Syria, as other students of the document thought probable.[20]

Frequently, therefore, it becomes imperative to identify the places and regions mentioned in a particular apocalyptic text, and this may also be a difficult or indeed a hopeless task. It would be important, for example, to identify some of the localities mentioned in the Second Greek Version of Pseudo-Methodius' Apocalypse. It is true that the author writes of Asia Minor, of Caesarea, and of the Maeander. He means presumably Asia Minor, Caesarea in Cappadocia, and the River Maeander. But where were the localities called Gephyra and Chortoranon (or Chartokoran or Chartokoranon, the spellings of other manuscripts) situated where an unnamed emperor would fight battles against the Arabs?[21] It would be interesting to clarify this problem, for the author seems here to preserve information on armed conflicts between Byzantines and Arabs that are not mentioned in the narrative sources of either side. Almost as difficult are certain place names mentioned in the Second Greek Vision of Daniel. It refers to two localities, Mariana and Elinia. Now the Old Church Slavonic Vision of Daniel, which, as mentioned before, derives from a lost Greek original, contains a passage mentioning these two localities, but in lieu of the mysterious toponym Elinia it reads "Enna," which when written in Greek uncial script invited corruption into something akin to Elinia.[22] Now Enna is the famous natural, steep, wind-swept fortress at the geographic center of Sicily. The other lo-

---

[20] Sackur, *Sibyllinische Texte*, 53–55, who in 1898 was unaware of the Syriac text, considered either an Alexandrian or a Syrian origin, tended toward the latter alternative, but also realized the influence of Babylonian and Persian influences on the author. I have developed my reasons for the Mesopotamian origin of the text in a paper delivered before the Twenty-seventh International Congress of Orientalists in Ann Arbor, Michigan, in August 1967.

[21] The passage relevant in the present context will be found in *Otkrovenie*, ed. Istrin, *Teksty*, 41, in the *apparatus criticus*.

[22] Greek text, *Anecdota Graeca-Byzantina*, ed. Vassiliev, 39, 13: "And afterward the sons of Ismael [i.e., the Arabs] will be struck by fear and will cry out with a loud voice and will flee to Mariana. And afterward the sons of Ismael will once again attack the territory of Elinia." The corresponding passage in the Old Church Slavonic Vision of Daniel (*Apokrifischeskie Teksty*, ed. Lavrov, 3, 4) reads: "And the Ismaelites will go forth into the extremity of the island and will take many prisoners until they will come to a place called Mariianii, and the rebel will install them in that place. And they will come to a place called Ienna, and they will come to its aid, and they will not capture it." Clearly in the Greek text a copyist misread the first uncial letter *ny* in the place name Enna for *lambda* plus *iota*, so that "Enna" was corrupted into "Elinia."

cality mentioned in the text, Mariana, cannot be identified, but it, too, must be situated in Sicily.[23] In addition, the Old Church Slavonic Vision of Daniel shows that two meaningless words in the First Greek Vision of Daniel are a corruption of the celebrated suburb of Syracuse, Achradina.[24] My point here is not so much that the Old Church Slavonic translation has preserved some Sicilian place names better than the Greek tradition, but rather that in the latter all Sicilian place names without exception have been corrupted beyond recognition. Without the Old Church Slavonic text not even the most ingenious historian could suspect that the Greek Visions of Daniel refer to Sicily. With the help of these identifications of place names in the Old Church Slavonic text, however, the Greek Visions of Daniel, as well as the Old Church Slavonic document itself, emerge as precious new sources for the history of the Muslim conquest of the island.[25]

Even this, however, is merely an instance of the miscopying of place names common in all classical or medieval texts. To such corruptions by scribal error should be added another kind of instability in nomenclature that was specific to apocalyptic texts. They were living texts, and each copyist was tempted to adapt geographical, as well as chronological, data to his own historical experience. A striking example occurs in the Old Church Slavonic Vision of Daniel dealing with the Arab invasion of Sicily. One of its manuscripts, of the thirteenth century, exhibits the disconcerting habit of adding to several Sicilian toponyms, without any kind of syntactical link, the name of a Slavic river or town. So far I have identified Dunaia (the Danube), Sredec (the modern Sofia), Pernik, Velbuzhd, and Strumica (all southwest of Sofia). The other localities mentioned (Glavinica, Mraky,

---

[23] In spite of much searching in works on the historical geography of Sicily, I have been unable to clear up this point. Place names ending with -ianum or -iana, so frequent on the Italian mainland and usually reflecting the previous existence of a Roman *fundus*, were much more frequent in Sicily before the Arab conquest than they are now. (See Adolf Holm in a review of Giovanni Flechia's *Nomi Locali del Napolitano derivati da gentilizi Italici*, in *Atti della reale accademia delle scienze di Torino*, X [No. 1, 1874], in *Bursian's Jahresbericht für die Fortschritte der Classischen Altertumswissenschaft*, IV [No. 2, 1877], 83–84.) One thinks naturally of the modern town of Marianopoli, west of Enna. It was founded in the nineteenth century, but its name may possibly derive from a village named after an (unattested) *fundus Marianus*.

[24] First Greek Vision of Daniel, *Anecdota Graeca-Byzantina*, ed. Vassiliev, 36, 21: καὶ τουτον κρατήσαντες ἀπάξουσιν αὐτὸν μέχρι δίνης κἀκει χρίσουσιν αὐτὸν εἰς βασιλέα κτλ. The corresponding passage in the Old Church Slavonic Vision of Daniel runs in translation (*Apokrificheskie Teksty*, ed. Lavrov, 3, 20): "and they will lead him to Askrodun [variant, Akrodun] and forthwith they will anoint him emperor."

[25] Because the references to Sicilian place names in the Old Church Slavonic and Greek Visions of Daniel have not been recognized before, these texts have escaped the attention of historians of the Arab conquest of Sicily. Several years ago I called these texts to the attention of a historian of art, Signora Angela Daneu Lattanzi, who used them in her *Lineamenti di Storia della Miniatura in Sicilia* (Florence, 1965), 12–13. I plan to utilize these texts more fully in a separate study of the Muslim invasion of Sicily. In this paper only a few of the more obvious conclusions will be developed.

and Khlimy) presumably were also located in Bulgaria.[26] It is easy to imagine what happened. As the Slavonic text was copied and recopied, a scribe, either the individual whose copy is preserved or one of his predecessors, imagined that what was in fact a *vaticinium ex eventu* of the Muslim conquest of Sicily was a genuine prophecy and that this prophecy had found its fulfillment in events occurring in his native Bulgaria.[27] He marked this fulfillment in his manuscript by inserting, perhaps in form of marginal glosses, the Slavic names of the places where the fulfillment supposedly occurred. One shudders to think what was bound to happen in the process of further copying of the Slavonic text. Sooner or later the familiar Slavonic toponyms would inevitably displace the less familiar Sicilian place names, and the Old Church Slavonic Vision of Daniel would thus be deprived of much of its relevance to the historian.

It is not enough, of course, to know when and where a particular apocalypse was composed. The historian can evaluate the detailed information that it contains only if he also understands the purposes of the apocalyptic writer and the methods he employed. Only then can the historian discount the specific bias of the text.

Most apocalypses were written to provide comfort in time of tribulation, particularly during grave military crises. Such consolation may be material or otherworldly. Thus the Oracle of Baalbek was composed to announce that the disasters of the Persian War under Anastasius would be followed by the Second Coming of Christ. The First Greek Version of Pseudo-Methodius' Apocalypse in turn prophesied that the Arab domination of the Near East would be ended by a Roman or Byzantine emperor who would drive the Muslims back into the desert and impose upon them a yoke a hundred times heavier than had been that of Muslims over Christians.[28] Similarly the Greek Visions of Daniel knew of a last emperor of Rome who would defeat the Arabs in a great battle. Such references to military victories over a national enemy were meant to be expressions of hope and encouragement, especially if mentioned at the end of a long series of military disasters, and it would be an egregious error to interpret them as *vaticinia post eventum*.

Hopes for the redress of economic and fiscal evils, especially those caused by war, also played a role in some of the apocalypses. The First Greek Version of the Apocalypse of Pseudo-Methodius, for example, predicted that after the end of Arab domination prisoners made by the defeated enemy

---

[26] The Balkan place names mentioned above in the text are inserted into the Belgrade manuscript of the Old Church Slavonic Vision of Daniel. (See the *apparatus criticus, Apokrificheskie Teksty,* ed. Lavrov, 2–3.)

[27] I have so far been unsuccessful in ascertaining which invasion of Bulgaria by which people the scribe had in mind.

[28] *Otkrovenie,* ed. Istrin, *Teksty,* 41, 1; 42, 1.

would return to their native places and recover their property.[29] Similarly, the Oracle of Baalbek knew of a messianic ruler who "will grant an exemption from paying a public tax and will restore all the people of the entire East and of Palestine."

This consolatory function of apocalyptic literature may on occasion be accompanied by another that may be as close to the heart of the writer. The Syriac and Greek Apocalypses of Pseudo-Methodius, for example, had, in addition, a polemical purpose. The author argued explicitly against anonymous opponents who interpreted Psalm 68:31 ("Ethiopia shall haste to stretch out her hands unto God") as indicating that liberation from the Muslim yoke would come from the ruler of Ethiopia.[30] Against their thesis the author established, with a wealth of Biblical and historical (or pseudohistorical) documentation, his own conviction that the Near East would be saved by a Byzantine ruler. This is all the more remarkable as the author of the Syriac original was a Monophysite.[31] Consequently, if doctrinal considerations had been all-important to him, he, like his opponents, should have relied for aid on the Monophysite ruler of Ethiopia rather than on the Chalcedonian monarch at Byzantium. Sectarian attitudes and polemics did indeed play a role in the sibyl's apocalypse of the early sixth century, but in the later texts doctrinal positions (Monophysitism, Monotheletism, Iconoclasm) were ignored. This may be due to either or both of two reasons. It may have been felt, in the circles to which the apocalyptic writers belonged and for whom they wrote, that sectarian differences separating the Christians should be ignored in face of the common Muslim danger. Alternately, these circles may have had little interest in theological controversy.

With regard to the procedures and methods employed by apocalyptic writers, mention has already been made of the tendency of apocalyptists to tamper with numerals and place names whenever the course of history seemed to prove that a prophecy had not been fulfilled during the period stipulated in the original text or had been fulfilled near the editor's place of residence. But this is only a particular application of a general principle governing the procedures of apocalyptic writers. Whenever later events seemed to fulfill an apocalyptic prophecy, the text of the apocalypse tended to be brought in harmony with its alleged fulfillment. Some of these changes

---

[29] *Ibid.*, 42, 8.

[30] For the Greek text, see *ibid.*, 22, 16: "some persons (*tines*) supposed that Saint David, in saying this [Psalm 68:31], hinted at the kingdom of the Ethiopians. But those who thought so were in error. . . ." The Syriac original (*codex Vaticanus Syrus* 58, fol. 126 recto) is more explicit: "However, many brethren of the clergy suppose that the blessed David spoke this word [Psalm 68:31] concerning the kingdom of the Cushites. And those who think so err. . . ."

[31] The author's unnamed opponents must have been Monophysites as they pinned their hopes of liberation from Muslim domination on the only Monophysite ruler, the king of Ethiopia. Therefore the author, too, was a Monophysite as he referred to his opponents as "brethren of the clergy." (See note 30, above.)

were drastic. At some time prior to the twelfth century it must have proved embarrassing that in the seventh century the First Greek Version of the Apocalypse of Pseudo-Methodius had prophesied a final Byzantine victory over "Turks and Avars,"[32] for by the eleventh century a number of Turkish peoples (Pechenegs, Seljuks, and so forth) were harassing the Empire most effectively. But this situation was remedied easily enough, for when the book was translated for the first time into Old Church Slavonic, a particular Turkish tribe, the Ugurs, had been substituted for the Turks, and this Turkish people had indeed disappeared in the mid-Byzantine period.[33] Thus did a later editor safeguard the prophetic prestige of Pseudo-Methodius.

Yet even the Greek text of this apocalypse had adjusted certain prophecies of the Syriac original to the course of events. The Syriac text knew of an archetypal invasion of Israel by Midianites at the time of the Hebrew Judges and mentioned their four leaders in accordance with the Old Testament, Oreb and Zeêb, Zebel and Zalmunna (Judg. 8). Several manuscripts of the Greek translation, however, call these four Midianite leaders "sons of Umayya,"[34] obviously because the translator believed that Pseudo-Methodius' prophecy had found its fulfillment at the time of the Umayyad rulers of Damascus. Another instance of an older prophecy being adapted to later events occurs in the Oracle of Baalbek. Here a fragment originally referring to the activities of a Roman general at Hierapolis near the Euphrates under the Emperor Constantius II was in later versions lifted bodily from its fourth-century context and relocated in the reign of Theodosius II in the fifth century, presumably because the later author held that this "prophecy" had found its fulfillment during the Persian Wars under the later Emperor.

These examples may serve as illustrations for a type of *aggiornamento* wherein a later editor brought details of earlier prophecies into harmony with the course of history by tampering with the text. In other cases the text of an earlier apocalypse was brought up to date by the insertion of a larger or smaller body of historical events that occurred in the intervening years. The original Greek text of the Oracle of Baalbek, for example, had reached down to the reign of Theodosius the Great, but, when the text was re-edited in the early sixth century, the later editor inserted a brief chronicle of the period from Theodosius to Anastasius, that is, of roughly one century, couched *more apocalyptico* in the future tense.

The preceding remarks about the dating, geographic provenance, pur-

---

[32] *Otkrovenie*, ed. Istrin, *Teksty*, 26, 1.
[33] *Ibid.*, 92, 25.
[34] *Ibid.*, 14, 3, and *apparatus criticus*.

poses, and methods of apocalyptic writers naturally lead to the consideration of the historical information contained in apocalyptic texts. Without exception they recorded historical events in the guise of prophecy and thus confirmed data known from other sources. Thus the Oracle of Baalbek, as stated before, included a brief chronicle of the fifth century, especially of the invasion of Asia Minor by Persians and Isaurians and of the Balkan Peninsula by the Huns during the fifth century. The First Greek Version of Pseudo-Methodius' Apocalypse furnished some details on the Arab invasion of the Fertile Crescent, in particular on the Arab victory over the Byzantine armies in the Battle of the River Jarmuk in 636, and spoke in general terms about the Arab conquest of Sassanid Persia.[35] The Greek and Old Church Slavonic Visions of Daniel in turn concerned the Muslim advance in Sicily at the beginning of the ninth century.[36]

At least as interesting as corroborative evidence of this kind were the reactions to historical events expressed by apocalyptic writers, their judgments on the course of history, and their expectations for the future. In the early years of the sixth century the Oracle of Baalbek despaired of the cities destroyed by Isaurian raiders at the beginning of the preceding century ever being restored or of the city of Rome recovering its imperial position after the sack by the Vandals in 455. In the author's opinion the reign of Leo I marked the beginning of the end for the Roman Empire. Where the author attempted to give an explanation for the disasters of the fifth century, such as the depredations by Huns and Vandals, he expressed a simple kind of moralism by stating, for example, that such events were due to Roman treachery or greed or that emperors who espoused heretical positions lost their throne. According to the Greek Versions of Pseudo-Methodius' Apocalypse, the Roman Empire would last to the end of time because it possessed a powerful talisman, the relic of the true Cross on which Jesus was crucified and which bestowed victory upon its owner over all his enemies. The author explained the Muslim victories over the Byzantine armies not, as was apparently done in certain Christian circles in Mesopotamia whose faith was shaken by the military successes of the infidels, as acts of divine partiality for the Arabs, but by Christian iniquity and sinfulness. The Arabs would be God's tool for the punishment of the Christians, but after a period of 49 (or 70 or 119) years of their rule over Christians they would become overconfident, would publicly deny God's ability to deliver his flock, and would, because of this blasphemy, be defeated and subdued by a Christian

---

[35] On the Battle of the Jarmuk, see *ibid.*, 26, 11 (the author localizes the battle at the nearby town of Gabaon), and Kmosko, "Das Rätsel des Pseudo-Methodius," 286.

[36] See pages 1003–1004, above.

emperor.[37] These naïve views about the irreversibility of the historical process, these moralist explanations of historical events as divine retribution for human sin, and this somewhat mechanistic pattern of military success breeding excessive self-confidence and blasphemy are features familiar from certain books of the Old Testament, for instance from Judges, and are faint echoes from Jewish prophecy and apocalyptic, the ultimate source of Eastern as well as Western Christian apocalyptic thought.

It is to be expected that in addition to confirming historical facts known from other sources and expressing their judgments and evaluations of historical events and situations, apocalyptic writers should on occasion mention historical information not discussed elsewhere. In this connection it is vital to grasp clearly the reason why apocalyptic writers normally prefaced their genuine prophecies of the future with *vaticinia ex eventu* referring to events of the past. The motive for this practice was invariably a desire to establish their prophetic authority and thus win credence for their genuine predictions. It follows that the historical information contained in *vaticinia ex eventu* cannot be of their own invention or knowingly incorrect, for they obviously would defeat their own purpose if they attempted to validate their prophecies by invented or consciously false data about the past.[38]

One example of new information occurred in the Oracle of Baalbek. Here the sibyl spoke of Constantine the Great rebuilding the city of Byzantium and predicted that the name of this city would be altered to Eudocopolis-Constantinopolis. To the best of my knowledge this double name for the new capital is unattested elsewhere, and as it stands this information cannot be correct. Eudocopolis was obviously a dynastic name and must have referred to Theodosius II's Empress Eudocia (who died in 460). It is impossible that Constantine the Great should have named his new city after a fifth-century empress. Yet it is quite plausible that a part of the city enclosed behind the new land and sea walls erected during the reign of Theodosius II should have been named after the Empress. These grandiose walls, which to the present day demonstrate the past might of the new capital on the Bosporus, protected a territory much larger than had the Constantinian walls of the preceding century.[39] The sea walls were built by a

---

[37] *Otkrovenie*, ed. Istrin, *Teksty*, 23, 7 (Cross as talisman of Empire); see also *ibid.*, 15, 13; 27, 9 (Muslim successes not due to God's favor for Muslims but to Christian lawlessness); *ibid.*, 37–39 (Arab overconfidence and blasphemy).

[38] This does not imply, of course, that historical information contained in *vaticinia ex eventu* is always objectively correct. It merely indicates that such information has the same claim to serious consideration by the historian as do facts reported in the conventional sources such as histories, chronicles, letters, and so forth. Like data contained in other sources, it may turn out to be mistaken, biased, or confused.

[39] Raymond Janin, *Constantinople Byzantine* (2d ed., Paris, 1964), 32.

favorite of the Empress Eudocia, the city prefect (later also praetorian prefect of the East) Cyrus.[40] In fact, the Empress Eudocia played an important role in the history of later Roman urbanism. No less than three cities in Asia Minor were named Eudocias after her, and upon her retirement to Jerusalem in 443 she built a new southern wall for the sacred city.[41] It was a custom in antiquity to give a new quarter of a city a dynastic name. Thus it is indeed probable that the Oracle of Baalbek preserved a faint memory of the Empress Eudocia's concern for the enlargement, protection, and beautification of the imperial capital.

The greatest amount of novel historical information, however, was contained in the Visions of Daniel and especially in the Old Church Slavonic text. As I have already pointed out, this document gave, among other things, an account of a Muslim invasion of Sicily; in fact, it referred to the first years of the Muslim attack on the island, the period from 827 to 829.[42] It is no exaggeration to say that this event can claim its place in world history, for it resulted eventually not only in the Arab conquest of the entire island but also in the Muslim occupation of considerable parts of southern Italy and in the confrontation of Western and Arab civilizations in these areas. It will therefore be worthwhile to recapitulate the present state of knowledge concerning this event and then to discuss the contribution made by the Old Church Slavonic Vision of Daniel.

Our knowledge of the invasion has come from two Arab historians, Ibn-al-Athir (who died in 1233) and Nuwairi (who died in 1332); from one Byzantine historical source of the tenth century, the so-called Continuator of Theophanes; and from two Latin chronicles written in Naples and Salerno during the ninth and tenth centuries, respectively.[43] The principal modern authorities are the great Sicilian historian Michele Amari, the late Alexander A. Vasiliev, and J. B. Bury, none of whom used the Old Church

[40] J. B. Bury, *History of the Later Roman Empire* (reprint, 2 vols., New York, 1958), I, 72; Ernest Stein, *Histoire du Bas-Empire* (2 vols., Paris, 1949–59), I, 294.

[41] On cities in Asia Minor named after Eudocia, see A. H. M. Jones, *The Cities of the Roman Provinces* (Oxford, Eng., 1937), 69, 109, 137, 144; on the southern wall at Jerusalem, see Hughes Vincent and Félix Abel, *Jérusalem* (2 vols., Paris, 1914–26), II, 910–11.

[42] The principal reason for this statement is that the text mentioned a "rebel" facilitating the Arab seizure of the town of Mariana (see note 22, above). The "rebel" cannot be anyone but Euphemius who was assassinated during the Arab siege of Enna in 828–829. (Michele Amari, *Storia dei Musulmani di Sicilia* [2d ed., 3 vols., Catania, 1933–39], I, 411–12; J. B. Bury, *History of the Eastern Roman Empire* [London, 1912], 302; Alexander A. Vasiliev, *Byzance et les Arabes* [2 vols., Brussels, 1935–50], I, 83–84.)

[43] Italian translation of the principal Arabic sources by Michele Amari, *Bibliotheca Arabo-Sicula* (2 vols. and Appendix, Turin, 1880–89), I, 364–68; II, 113–17 (French tr. by Vasiliev, *Byzance et les Arabes*, I, 356–59, 379–81); Theophanes Continuatus in *Corpus Scriptorum Historiae Byzantinae* (49 vols., Bonn, 1828–78), 81–82; *Chronicon Salernitanum*, ed. Ulla Westerbergh, "Studia Latina Stockholmiensia," No. 3 (Stockholm, 1956), 59; an earlier edition of the same text was that published in *Monumenta Germaniae Historica, Scriptores*, ed. G. H. Pertz (32 vols., Hanover, 1826–1934), III, 498; Johannes Diaconus Neapolitanus, *Monumenta Germaniae Historica, Scriptores Rerum Langobardicarum* (Hanover, 1878), 429.

Slavonic Vision of Daniel.[44] They agreed that the Arab invasion of Sicily was the consequence of a Sicilian revolt against the Byzantine Emperor Michael II, but they differed about the chronology of this event. Amari was of the opinion that the Sicilian revolt began as early as 821 when Michael II was threatened by an even more dangerous rebellion in Asia Minor, that of Thomas the Slav. Around five years later, or about 826 according to Amari, the Emperor appointed a new governor of Sicily called either Constantine or Photinus who in turn entrusted a naval command to Euphemius. Amari thus postulated two stages in the Sicilian revolt, interrupted by an interval during which the island recognized the government of Michael II: one period beginning in 821 in which Euphemius played no role, and another starting in 826 in which he was the key figure. Later tradition telescoped these two stages into one.

Vasiliev rejected this view of Amari's as "fantastic," Bury held that Amari's proofs were insufficient, and both accordingly dated the beginning of the Sicilian revolt in 826–827. In that year, Euphemius, one of the Byzantine turmarchs or commanders stationed in Sicilian waters, was in danger of being arrested by the governor of the island on personal orders from the Emperor. He decided to revolt. The reason for the imperial order was not given in the Arabic sources, but the Greek and Latin historians told a romantic tale according to which Euphemius had married a nun, against her will and in violation of canonical and secular legislation. Neither Amari nor Vasiliev was satisfied that this story provided an adequate explanation for Euphemius' revolt and suspected that political considerations were the true reason for it.[45] Neither scholar nor anyone else, however, could specify what these political considerations might have been.

At any rate, Euphemius and some of his colleagues of the imperial navy seized Syracuse by a *coup de main* and defeated the governor in battle. The latter fled to Catania, but was captured and executed, and Euphemius was proclaimed emperor. In this capacity he rewarded some of his followers with administrative appointments. In particular he named a new governor of

---

[44] Amari, *Storia*, I, esp. 367–417; Vasiliev, *Byzance et les Arabes*, I, 61–88; Bury, *History of the Eastern Roman Empire*, 294–308, 478–80; see also Adolf Holm, *Geschichte Siziliens* (3 vols., Leipzig, 1870–98), III, 327–33; Agostino Rossi, "Delle Cause della Sollevazione di Eufemio contro la Dominazione Bizantina in Sicilia," *Rendiconti della Reale Accademia dei Lincei, Classe di Scienze Morali Storiche Filologiche*, Ser. V, XIII (1904), 198–233; L. M. Hartmann, *Geschichte Italiens im Mittelalter* (4 vols., Gotha, 1897–1915), III, Pt. 1, 161–93; Biagio Pace, *Arte e Civiltà della Sicilia Antica* (4 vols., Rome, 1935–49), IV, 126–34. The work of Amari remains fundamental.

[45] See Amari, *Storia*, I, 378; Vasiliev, *Byzance et les Arabes*, I, 71: "Il va de soi qu'il ne faut pas chercher la cause du soulèvement d'Euphémios dans son mariage romanesque. La politique, on s'en doute, primait ici . . ."; Bury, *Eastern Roman Empire*, 479, is aware that Amari and Vasiliev "think it likely that in his action in regard to Euphemius Michael was influenced by political reasons and used the matrimonial delinquency as a pretext," but does not press the matter further.

1012

Sicily to whom the Arabic sources refer as Balata. Balata, however, played false and declared against Euphemius as the Arabic sources say, or for the Emperor Michael as the modern authors put it.[46] He assembled a large army, defeated Euphemius in battle, and forced him to leave Syracuse. Euphemius and a part of the navy then crossed the Sicilian Channel, which separates Sicily from North Africa, and asked the Aghlabid ruler of Kairouan to come to his aid. In consequence an Arab fleet landed in Mazara, at the western extremity of Sicily, on June 17, 827, and marched upon Syracuse. At Syracuse the Arabs failed after a long siege, mainly because of a famine and plague that harassed them. Their land army withdrew. One part of it, accompanied by Euphemius and his partisans, marched upon Enna and began the siege of that fortress. In the course of this siege, in 828–829, Euphemius was killed, according to the Arab chronicler, but one Greek source placed his assassination slightly earlier while the siege of Syracuse was still in progress. On this occasion the Arabs did not succeed in capturing Enna; in fact, the city successfully resisted a great number of Arab assaults until it was finally taken in 859. The last stages in the Arab conquest of Sicily were the fall of Syracuse in 878 and that of Taormina in 902.

Such in brief is the story of the Arab conquest of Sicily as it emerges from the narrative sources. The new data supplied by the Old Church Slavonic Vision of Daniel must now be fitted into this framework. It told the Sicilian story, in the form of a prophecy, in six acts, which may be summarized as follows:

Act I: The Byzantine Emperor sent messengers to the western provinces. They arrived at Syracuse, and the Emperor was insulted.

Act II: A rebellion occurred at Syracuse, and the rebels were killed.

Act III: Disorders erupted at Syracuse; two rebels arose and fought at Achradina.

Act IV: From Syracuse came a pregnant woman; her brother died, and she gave birth to a child and grieved.

Act V: The Arabs landed at the extremity of Sicily, ravaged the island, arrived at Mariana, and the rebel established them in that city.

[46] Ibn-al-Athir (Amari, *Biblioteca*, I, 365): "il quale (Balatah) spiccossi da Eufemio e rivoltossi contro di lui"; Nuwairi (*ibid.*, II, 114): "Costui (Balatah) si spiccò [poscia] da Eufemio e [apertamente] gli si ribellò. . . ." Amari's remark (*Storia*, I, 380) to the effect that Balata and his cousin declared for Michael II is nothing but an inference, as are Vasiliev's (*Byzance et les Arabes*, I, 69) and Bury's (*Eastern Roman Empire*, 297) statements that Balata espoused the cause of Michael.

Act VI: From Mariana the Arabs marched upon Enna, but reinforcements were sent, and they did not take the city.[47]

The author was here trying to tell the story of the first Arab invasion of Sicily in 827–828. Not all the elements of his story can be identified,[48] but many of them can be explained without too much difficulty. In Act III the battle between the two rebels at Achradina, the famous suburb of Syracuse known to all readers of Thucydides, must be that between Euphemius and his disloyal governor Balata. In fact, the Slavonic text, in speaking of "two rebels," corrected the modern historians on a detail of some importance: the second of the Sicilian rebels, Balata, did not fight Euphemius because he adhered to the Emperor Michael as the modern historians hold, but because he, like Euphemius, repudiated Michael's authority and wished to gain control of Sicily for himself.[49] The Arab landing on the extremity of Sicily in Act V is that of June 17, 827, when the forces of the Aghlabid ruler of Kairouan disembarked at Mazara at the westernmost tip of the island. The rebel who helped the Arabs to capture the Sicilian city of Mariana can be none other than Euphemius.

Thus most, though not all, of the events narrated by the apocalyptic writer under Acts III–VI can be accounted for, and in this portion of his

[47] In the following translation from the Old Church Slavonic Vision of Daniel I have added numerals to mark the six "acts" mentioned in the text above: "[I] And he (the Emperor) will send envoys [or, to the forces and] to the western lands which in a similar fashion [?] are faithful to themselves [?, to him ?]. And when they [the envoys] will have reached the western lands, the [inhabitants] of the so-called Rebel City (τύραννος πόλις), having rebelled, will sally forth and begin to insult him. [II] And afterward men who are in that place will arise, and they will kill them with the sword. [III] And they will arise against each other and will fight each other. And there will arise two rebels (τύραννοι), the first from the east of that city and the other from the west. And they will encounter each other in a place called Akrodunii [or, Krodunii] and will slay each other, so that the sea will be mixed with their blood. [IV] And a woman who is with child will come from the territory of that city where there stood in those days a sign [?]. And she will see her brother lying dead [or, after having become a mother] and will beat her breast, and she will give birth to her child and grief will overcome [or, her son will embrace] her for a long time. [V] And the Ismaelites will go forth into the extremity of the island and will take many prisoners until they will come to a place called Mariianii, and the rebel will install them in that place. [VI] And they will come to a place called Ienna, and they will come to her aid, and they will not capture her." Throughout this passage I have translated the verb *mąchiti* and the noun *mąchitel* by "to rebel" and "the rebel," respectively. These words, which often mean "to torture" and "torturer," are also used to render the Greek words *tyrannein* and *tyrannos*, which in Byzantine Greek normally mean "to rebel" and "the rebel." The term Rebel City (*tyrannos polis* or *polis tyrannou*) is also used in the Greek Visions of Daniel (Vassiliev, *Anecdota Graeca-Byzantina*, 36, 15, 19; 39, 15, 19). Inasmuch as the Old Church Slavonic text later mentions an "island" as well as a number of Sicilian place names (Achradina, Enna), the Rebel City must be Syracuse.

[48] Thus I am at a loss to explain the remarks in Act IV on the pregnant woman from Syracuse, her brother, and her child. Naturally, one thinks of the nun whom Euphemius married, and the accounts about her mention that she and her brother had a child. Yet it is doubtful that the author is here alluding to her, for none of the other sources mention her brother's death. The identification with Euphemius' wife, moreover, does not explain the author's remark about the "sign" in the city of Syracuse.

[49] See note 46, above.

1014

"prophecy" the writer confirmed the data already known from the Arab, Greek, and Latin sources.[50] But what of Acts I and II? Here the apocalyptist wrote of the Emperor sending messengers to the western provinces, of their arrival at Syracuse, of the Emperor being insulted by the Syracusans, of the outbreak of a rebellion at Syracuse, and of the rebels being put to death. The question is unavoidable: why did he record all these Syracusan events before launching into the story of Euphemius and of the Arab invasion of Sicily? He wrote rather clumsily, but there can be no doubt that he was trying to give a continuous account of the Arab invasion of Sicily and to reproduce the causal connection between events. As pointed out above, modern scholars have been dissatisfied with the only reason adduced in the narrative sources for Euphemius' rebellion—his marriage to a nun—and both Amari and Vasiliev suspected a political motivation. The Old Church Slavonic Apocalypse, in its awkward way, seems to point to the events reported in Acts I and II as being the true cause of Euphemius' revolt. According to it, the Emperor Michael II sent emissaries to Syracuse, as well as to the other parts of his western dominions, he was insulted at Syracuse, and an unsuccessful local revolt followed. The Slavonic apocalypse did not specify, unfortunately, the content of the message sent by the Emperor to the people of Syracuse, but since it led to a revolution against the imperial authority, the Emperor must have made certain demands. Perhaps he asked for recruits for his armies, for military supplies, for new taxes, or for any combination of these items.[51] At any rate it is legitimate to infer from the Slavonic document that the principal cause of the abortive Syracusan revolt, of the later rebellion of Euphemius, and of the Arab invasion of the island were not the trite marital troubles of Euphemius but a demand by the Emperor addressed to the citizens of Syracuse that the latter deemed unacceptable.

This is a significant contribution made by the Slavonic text, but its interest does not end here. Two further features are noteworthy. In the first place messengers were dispatched not only to Syracuse but to all of the Emperor's western dominions. These included certainly the rest of Sicily

[50] Three new details were added to the story of the Arab invasion of 827–828. The Slavonic text localizes the battle between Euphemius and Balata at Achradina. The Arabs captured the Sicilian town of Mariana (location unknown, see note 23, above) with the help of Euphemius and besieged Enna unsuccessfully.

[51] One other possibility comes to mind. It is known from a letter of Theodore of Studios (Bk. *II*, No. 190, in Migne, *Patrologiae Cursus Completus. Series Graeco-Latina* [166 vols., Paris, 1857–66], 99, 1577 D–1581 A) that there was considerable iconoclastic agitation in Sicily, and this letter is probably to be dated in the reign of Michael II. It is, however, highly unlikely that Michael, who in the eastern provinces where iconoclasm was still strong followed a conciliatory policy toward the iconophiles (Bury, *Eastern Roman Empire*, 110–13), should have officially promoted iconoclastic policies in Sicily where iconoclasm had never flourished before. The iconoclastic agitation of which Theodore complains is likely to have been undertaken on the private initiative of Byzantine officials, rather than as a result of an official communication from the Emperor.

and the Byzantine portions of southern Italy. Presumably the messengers transmitted demands similar to those sent to Syracuse. No such demands were, on the other hand, recorded for the core lands of the Empire, notably for Asia Minor. One suspects that the reason for this omission was that these core lands were undergoing a crisis of some sort and that the messengers had been sent to the western provinces to solicit aid for the eastern regions. Secondly, according to both Vasiliev and Bury, as stated above, Euphemius' revolt broke out in 826 and was followed in the next year by the Arab invasion. Amari, on the other hand, had conjectured that the Sicilian revolt began in 821, five years earlier, and his chronology now receives support from the Old Church Slavonic Vision of Daniel. He had based his opinion on several arguments. In the first place, the earlier date seemed more plausible on grounds of general probability, for by 821 the upstart Emperor Michael II, who owed his throne to the murder of his predecessor, was faced with a dangerous revolt in Asia Minor, that of Thomas the Slav, but Thomas' revolt was suppressed by 823.[52] Furthermore, the Latin chronicle of the bishops of Naples by John the Deacon written in the first half of the ninth century mentioned the revolt of "the Syracusans belonging to the party of a certain Euthimius [Euphemius]" immediately following Michael's accession in 820, and the Byzantine chronicle of Symeon Magister of the tenth century stated in so many words that the Arab conquest of Sicily began "when Michael was busy with the rebel Thomas."[53] Now, according to the Old Church Slavonic Vision of Daniel, the two rebels, that is, Euphemius and Balata, "arose" in Act III only. Their rebellion, however, was preceded in Acts I and II by an earlier revolt at Syracuse at the end of which the rebels were executed. According to this new Slavonic source, therefore, the Sicilian rebellion began before Euphemius assumed its leadership. John the Deacon and Symeon Magister were therefore correct in stating that the Sicilian revolt began soon after the accession of Michael II in 820, say in 821, and Amari's brilliant conjecture of two stages in the development of this revolt is thus confirmed by evidence unavailable to him.

Indeed, the demands made, according to the Old Church Slavonic Vision of Daniel, by the government of Michael through the messengers upon the citizens of Syracuse and upon the inhabitants of the other western provinces, rather than upon his subjects in Asia Minor, are more plausible while

---

[52] On the revolt of Thomas the Slav, see Bury, *Eastern Roman Empire*, 84–110, 462–64; Franjo Barišić, "Deux versions sur Thomas chef de l'insurrection de 821–823," *Zbornik Radova Vizantološkog Instituta*, VI (1960), 145–69; Paul Lemerle, "Thomas le Slave," *Travaux et Mémoires*, I (1965), 254–97.

[53] John the Deacon, *Gesta Episcoporum Neapolitanorum, Monumenta Germaniae Historica, Scriptores Rerum Langobardicarum* (Hanover, 1878), 429–30; Symeon Magister, 621–22, in Theophanes Continuatus, Bonn ed.

Michael was still fighting for his throne against Thomas the Slav. Thomas had rallied around him the partisans of religious images who had been persecuted by Leo V and parts of the population of Asia Minor which was heavily burdened with taxes. Thus the movement headed by Thomas had both a religious and a social character. In addition Thomas had at the beginning of his revolt succeeded in obtaining control of the tax revenue of Asia Minor.[54] It is entirely credible that in this grave crisis the Emperor Michael, who had himself reached the throne by usurpation and by the murder of his predecessor, should have asked the western parts of his realm, among them the city of Syracuse, to make extraordinary contributions of a military or fiscal kind for the suppression of Thomas' revolt.

If one accepts, then, the chronology for the Sicilian revolt first suggested by Amari and now supported by the Old Church Slavonic Vision of Daniel, one recognizes that there existed an essential connection between Thomas' revolt in Asia Minor and the Syracusan rebellion. In order to overcome the usurper Thomas who threatened the core lands of the Empire in Asia Minor and had seized most of their fiscal revenue, the upstart Emperor Michael II was forced to demand special contributions from the hitherto loyal provinces in the west. In a similar way, about a century earlier, the Byzantine Emperor Leo III, shortly after the Arab siege of his capital (717–718) and during the period of Muslim occupation of large parts of Asia Minor, had been driven to increase taxes and to insist on a more rigorous collection, with the ultimate result that Byzantium lost control of most of the Italian mainland.[55] Michael's action, about a hundred years later, led to the emergence of two sets of Sicilian rebels. The names of the earlier rebels are, unfortunately, unknown. The later leaders of the rebellion in its second stage were Euphemius and Balata.

Thus at the beginning of Michael's reign rebellion was ubiquitous. Michael had rebelled against his imperial master Leo V and had become emperor by murdering him. Thomas the Slav, whose friendship and association with the murdered Leo were long standing, had rallied behind him Asiatic circles loyal to the memory of Michael's victim. The first anonymous set of Sicilian rebels must have felt that the duel for power between Michael and Thomas in Asia Minor offered especially favorable circumstances for the

[54] Genesius, Bonn ed., 32; Theophanes Continuatus, Bonn ed., Bk. II, Chap. xi, 53.

[55] Pope Gregory II refused to pay the increased taxes on the properties of the Roman Church. His refusal in turn led later in the eighth century to the famous series of events culminating in the Frankish conquest of Italy and the foundation of the Papal State. (See the stimulating article by François Masai, "La politique des Isauriens et la naissance de l'Europe," *Byzantion*, XXXIII [No. 1, 1963], 191–221, esp. 191–99.) Both in the eighth and ninth centuries, then, the Byzantine government, in order to save the Asiatic core lands of the Empire, made exorbitant demands on the western provinces, with the result that it lost control of the Italian mainland in the eighth and of Sicily in the ninth century.

secession of Sicily. Thus in the years 821–823, if my reconstruction of the events based on the Old Church Slavonic Vision of Daniel is correct, at least two sets of rebels—Thomas the Slav and his associates on the one hand, the unnamed Sicilian rebels on the other—were competing with Michael II for power, and it was anything but a foregone conclusion who would ultimately be victorious. In the end Michael preserved his throne but at the price of losing Sicily to the Muslims whose aid had been invoked by one of the later Sicilian usurpers, Euphemius.

In attempting to summarize what has been learned about the historical value of medieval apocalypses it may be prudent to begin with the shortcomings peculiar to this type of source. In the first place, the dating of an apocalypse is not always an easy task because even specific factual details mentioned in an apocalypse may not be *vaticinia ex eventu* but genuine prophecies. Furthermore, numerals indicating time spans, which might otherwise offer clues for dating the document, are frequently altered by later editors. Secondly, it is often difficult to define the geographic region referred to in a particular apocalypse, not only because, as in all other medieval texts, outlandish place names have a tendency to be miscopied inadvertently but because a copyist of apocalypses is apt to change them deliberately, on the assumption that an earlier prophecy found its fulfillment in events occurring in his own neighborhood long after the original text was composed. A third possible pitfall in the historical interpretation of medieval apocalypses concerns the purpose for which a particular text is written. Detailed prophecies closely tied to this purpose, as, for example, of ultimate victories over the national enemy, may represent wishful thinking rather than historical fact. Finally, apocalypses are living texts and are subject to editorial tampering of all sorts in order to bring ancient prophecies in harmony with later events. To these four types of difficulties should be added the deliberate obscurity of apocalyptic documents, yet because the apocalyptist must strive to have his allusions understood by his contemporaries, it is rare indeed that the modern historian is unable to crack the apocalyptic code.

Once the obstacles to a historical interpretation and exploitation of apocalypses are removed, these texts may yield a rich crop of information of all kinds. Almost without exception they corroborate evidence already known from other, especially narrative, sources. Their authors express in concrete language the reactions of contemporaries to historical events, their usually primitive philosophies of history, their despair over the military situation or over the economic plight of the circles to which they belong or for which they write, and, above all, their expectations for a brighter future.

1018

Sometimes apocalypses contain valuable new factual details, such as the name Eudocopolis for the part of the imperial capital enclosed within the new city walls during the first half of the fifth century. The accumulation of apocalypses at particular periods, for example around the year 500, permits inferences as to the intensity of eschatological expectations and thus provides a barometer of eschatological pressures at different moments in history. Finally, some apocalypses such as the Old Church Slavonic Vision of Daniel permit new inferences as to the causes and chronology of important developments in world history, in this case on the Muslim invasion of Sicily in the first half of the ninth century. Medieval apocalypses, then, are chronicles written in the future tense and deserve close attention on the part of historians of the Middle Ages.

ADDITIONAL BIBLIOGRAPHY

I have returned to several of the problems discussed in this article in later publications, esp. nos.XIV and XVI. Of the paper mentioned on p.1003 n.20 only an extract was published in the Proceedings of the 27th International Congress of Orientalists, Ann Arbor, Mich., 13-19 August 1967, Wiesbaden, 1971, 106f. Since the publication of my article Riccardo Maisano provided the editio princeps of a Greek apocalypse closely related to the Greek Visions of Daniel: L'Apocalisse Apocrifa di Leone di Constantinopoli, Naples, 1975. According to the editor, the nucleus of this text was composed during the first decade of the ninth century. Less close are the contacts with the Greek Visions of Daniel exhibited by a Syriac apocalypse of uncertain provenance recently edited and translated by Hans Schmoldt, Die Schrift "vom Jungen Daniel" und""Daniels Letzte Vision". Herausgabe und Interpretation Zweier Apokalyptischer Texte, Diss., Hamburg, 1972. However, the editor makes many helpful comments on the Greek texts attributed to Daniel, as does Lennart Rydén in his excellent new edition of a well-known text: "The Andreas Salos Apocalypse. Greek Text, Translation, and Commentary,"Dumbarton Oaks Papers 28, 1974, 197-261.

XIV

LES DÉBUTS DES CONQUÊTES ARABES EN SICILE ET LA TRADITION APOCALYPTIQUE BYZANTINO - SLAVE [1]

En 827 une armée arabe venant de l'Afrique du Nord aghlabide débarqua en Sicile, remporta une victoire sur les forces byzantines envoyées à sa rencontre, assiégea vainement les grandes forteresses de Syracuse et d'Enna et finit en 828 par se retirer à l'ouest de l'île. Des garnisons musulmanes ne se maintenaient qu'à Mineo à l'est et à Mazara à l'ouest de la Sicile. Quelques coûteuses que fussent ces opérations pour les envahisseurs et bien que les villes occupées par eux ne fussent pas parmi les centres les plus importants de la Sicile, ces conquêtes de 827/8 devinrent les bases militaires pour l'établissement d'un émirat quasi-autonome à Palerme en 831 et pour la conquête arabe de l'île entière au cours du neuvième siècle. De plus, c'étaient les Arabes de Sicile qui à partir de 840 commencèrent l'invasion de l'Italie méridionale. Ces événements, et de plus l'établissement en Crète d'un autre état musulman en 825, eurent des effets profonds sur la situation politique, militaire, économique et culturelle du monde méditerranéen et même européen, du moins pendant les deux siècles suivants. Les débuts des conquêtes arabes en Sicile font donc partie d'un chapitre important de l'histoire mediévale et il vaut la peine d'étudier de nouveau les

[1] Une première version de cet article fut présentée oralement en 1966 à deux reprises, dans une conférence faite à Palerme, sur l'invitation du doyen, le professeur Bruno Lavagnini, et à l'Université d'Oxford. J'ai profité des conseils qu'on m'a donnés à ces occasions. Plusieurs collègues ont eu la bonté de m'aider: le professeur Albert Lord de l'Université d'Harvard; le professeur Ladislav Matejka de l'Université de Michigan; les professeurs Ariel Bloch, Gerard E. Caspary, Jonas C. Greenfield, Erich S. Gruen et F. J. Whitfield, de l'Université de Californie à Berkeley. Je tiens aussi à remercier M. Lavagnini et ses collègues à Palerme de l'accueil si bienveillant qu'ils ont eu la bonté de me donner et qui a rendu mon séjour en Sicile un des plus intéressants et agréables. Monsieur le professeur G. Cusimano m'a fait l'honneur de publier mon article dans le « Bollettino ». Je l'offre en hommage à la beauté de la Sicile, à l'intérêt de ses monuments et à la fascination de son histoire.

sources et les problèmes historiques de l'invasion de 827/8 qui ont formé le sujet de maintes publications, dont plusieurs de la plume des maîtres de notre science [2].

Les sources grecques, latines et arabes sur la campagne de 827 et ses préliminaires sont extrêmement riches. Comme on l'a bien remarqué, elles ne se contredisent guère, mais chaque auteur, très naturellement, insiste sur les phases de. l'invasion qui intéressent le plus ses lecteurs et est disposé à abréger et même à omettre d'autres aspects des événements [3]. Ainsi la tradition byzantine s'occupe surtout des préliminaires de l'invasion, c'est-à-dire de la révolte du tourmarque byzantin Euphémius qui demanda au monarque aghlabide de Qayrawān, Ziyādat Allāh Ier (817-833), d'intervenir en Sicile, mais ne dit grand-chose ni sur les délibérations à Qayrawān ni sur les opérations militaires en Sicile. La tradition arabe, par contre, est très brève sur la révolte d'Euphémius, mais très riche en détails sur les décisions politiques prises à Qayrawān et sur le cours de l'invasion même. La tradition latine ou italienne, enfin, ne dit rien des événements dans l'état aghlabide, mais contient certains renseignements sur la révolte d'Euphémius. Il s'agira, dans cet article, non de refaire en détail et de façon systématique l'analyse de ces sources nombreuses, tâche qui en général a été menée à bonne fin par d'illustres historiens, mais de poser quelques-uns des problèmes historiques qui, à mon avis, n'ont pas encore été résolus d'une manière convaincante et d'essayer d'y trouver des solutions à l'aide et de sources historiques négligées jusqu'ici et d'interprétations nouvelles et approfondies de textes bien connus.

Parmi les problèmes qu'on se propose d'examiner dans cet article, est celui des causes de la révolte sicilienne contre le gouvernement byzantin, révolte qui déclencha l'attaque arabe sur la Sicile. A ce sujet

---

[2] M. AMARI, *Storia dei Musulmani di Sicilia*, seconde éd., 3 volumes, Catania, 1933-1939 [cité ci-après: *Storia*], I, p. 367-417; A. A. VASILIEV, *Byzance et les Arabes*, 2 volumes, Bruxelles, 1935-1968 [cité: *Byzance*], I, p. 61-88; J. B. BURY, *A History of the Eastern Roman Empire*, London, 1912 [cité: *History*], p. 294-308, 478-480. Autres ouvrages d'Amari d'une importance capitale pour notre sujet: sa *Biblioteca Arabo-Sicula* contenant les textes arabes (Leipzig, 1857), la traduction italienne de ces textes (Torino et Roma, 1880) que je citerai toujours dans l'édition in folio, et sa *Carte comparée de la Sicile moderne avec la Sicile du douzième siècle*, Paris, 1859 (en collaboration avec A. H. DUFOUR) [cité: *Carte comparée*]. Voir aussi A. HOLM, *Geschichte Siziliens im Alterthum*, 3 volumes, Leipzig, 1870-1898 [cité: *Geschichte*], III, p. 327-333; A. ROSSI, *Delle cause della sollevazione di Eufemio* etc., dans « Rendiconti della Reale Accademia dei Lincei », Classe di Scienze morali, storiche e filologiche, ser. V, XIII, 1904, p. 198-233 [cité: *Delle cause*]; L. M. HARTMANN, *Geschichte Italiens im Mittelalter*, 4 volumes, Gotha, 1897-1915, III, part 1, p. 161-193; B. PACE, *Arte e civiltà della Sicilia antica*, 4 volumes, Roma, 1935-1949 [cité: *Arte e civiltà*], IV, p. 126-134. J'ai fait quelques remarques à ce sujet dans l'article: *Medieval Apocalypses as Historical Sources*, dans « American Historical Review », LXXIII, 1968, p. 997-1018.

[3] PACE, *Arte e civiltà*, IV, p. 128 s.

deux thèses s'opposent. Le grand historien sicilien Michele Amari, dont la *Storia dei Musulmani di Sicilia* reste toujours l'ouvrage classique et fondamental, était d'avis que les raisons de la révolte étaient d'ordre politique [4]. Amari fut suivi dans son interprétation par plusieurs historiens postérieurs [5]. Du reste, ni Amari ni Vasiliev n'ont précisé quel aurait été le but politique des rebelles syracusains, mais il me semble que, d'après eux, Euphémius et ses alliés politiques auraient voulu s'emparer du pouvoir du moins à Syracuse, peut-être aussi en Sicile, et rendre leur territoire indépendant de l'empereur de Byzance. De l'autre côté, en 1904, Agostino Rossi dédia à ce problème un long mémoire dans lequel il examina d'une manière minutieuse et critique la théorie d'Amari et les textes sur lesquels elle s'appuyait. Le résultat de cette étude fut que tous les textes, grecs aussi bien que latins et arabes, ou bien ne disent rien à ce sujet ou ne mentionnent que des raisons personnelles pour la révolte d'Euphémius [6].

Deuxièmement, il y a le problème de la chronologie des événements en Sicile. Tout le monde est d'accord que l'invasion arabe a commencé en 827. Reste à savoir quand a eu lieu la révolte sicilienne qui mena à l'invasion arabe. Amari a remarqué que le chroniqueur napolitain Jean le Diacre, son collègue byzantin Syméon Magister et l'historien arabe Nuwayrī pensaient à l'année 821 comme date initiale de la révolte sicilienne, tandis que les autres sources la placent en 826. De cette observation Amari s'est avancé à une hypothèse aussi compliquée qu'ingénieuse. Selon lui, la sécession sicilienne se serait developpée en deux phases abrégées en un seul événement par la plupart des sources. Dans une première période, qui aurait duré de 821 à 825, les commandants militaires de la Sicile se seraient soulevés contre le gouvernement de l'empereur Michel II. Euphémius n'aurait joué dans cette affaire qu'un rôle subalterne ou n'y aurait pas figuré du tout. La se-

---

[4] AMARI, *Storia*, I, p. 378: « Politico del tutto fu dunque il movimento d'Eufemio, come il dicono i due più antichi scrittori, italiano e bizantino, Giovanni diacono e Simone maestro ».

[5] VASILIEV, *Byzance*, I, p. 71: « Il va de soi qu'il ne faut pas chercher la cause du soulèvement d'Euphémius dans son mariage romanesque. La politique, on s'en doute, primait ici: Euphémius, profitant de la révolte de Thomas et surtout du succès des armes musulmanes en Crète, a dû préparer dès les années 822-827 [3?] une révolte pour son propre compte ». Plus loin (p. 84-86) Vasiliev donne un résumé de la thèse de F. GABOTTO, *Eufemio e il movimento separatista nell'Italia bizantina*, Torino, 1890, selon laquelle Euphémius aurait aspiré à rendre l'Italie et la Sicile indépendantes, de former un « Impero romano italiano ». En d'autres mots, Euphémius aurait été un proto-Cavour. Vasiliev rejette cette thèse. D'après lui, J. B. BURY, *The Naval Policy of the Roman Empire*, dans *Centenario della nascita di Michele Amari*, II, Palermo, 1910, p. 26 s., s'est rallié complètement à l'opinion de Vasiliev contre Gabotto. Malheureusement, je n'ai pu me procurer le livre de Gabotto ni l'article de Bury dans *Centenario... Amari*.

[6] ROSSI, *Delle cause*.

conde période du soulèvement, qui aurait commencé en 826, aurait été déclenchée par le gouverneur byzantin de la Sicile, qui aurait voulu frapper les chefs militaires de la Sicile dans la personne d'Euphémius [7]. Cette hypothèse d'Amari a été qualifiée de « fantaisiste » par Vasiliev et il n'est pas possible de la mettre d'accord avec la chronologie pro posée par Bury [8].

Enfin, il y a la question topographique de la route prise par l'armée arabe en 827. Il n'y a pas de doute que les envahisseurs débarquèrent à Mazara à l'extrémité occidentale de l'île et de là se dirigèrent vers Syracuse à l'est. Mais tout le reste est sujet à caution. La marche des troupes arabes, commandées par le cadi Asad ibn al-Furāt, d'un bout de l'île à l'autre, est décrite, comme on s'y attend, par les chroniqueurs arabes, Ibn al-Atīr (m. 1233) et Nuwayrī (m. 1332), avec le plus grand détail par le dernier. Signalons, en passant, qu'il y a un lien bien étroit entre ces deux chroniqueurs, soit qu'ils se fussent servis d'une source commune, soit que Nuwayrī ait fait des extraits du texte d'Ibn al-Atīr et de certaines autres chroniques perdues [9]. D'après Nuwayrī, la bataille dècisive eut lieu dans une prairie ayant le même nom que le général byzantin grec vaincu par les Arabes, Balāṭa. Toujours d'après Nuwayrī, l'armée arabe s'est dirigée ensuite vers une église d'Euphémie située sur le bord de la mer. De là elle partit vers l'église d'al-M. s.l. qīn (ou al-Š. l. qīn). Nuwayrī fait aussi mention d'un endroit qu'il appelle Qal'at (« la forteresse ») al-K.rāt, où les habitants auraient rassemblé les richesses de l'île. Amari s'est efforcé à identifier les localités mentionnées dans la tradition arabe. Pour la plaine de Balāṭa, champ de bataille entre troupes arabes et siciliennes, Amari finit par choisir, entre plusieurs localités de ce nom ou à peu près, le village de Balata situé entre les fleuves Pietralonga et Frattina à l'ouest de la ville moderne de Corleone [10]. Ensuite Amari propose de corriger le nom de l'église d'Euphémie, où les troupes arabes se seraient dirigées, d'après Nuwayrī, après la bataille, en Finzia, la Phintia classique, située à l'embouchure du fleuve Salso non loin de la ville actuelle de Licata sur la côte méridionale de la Sicile [11]. Quant à l'église de al-M. s.l. qīn,

---

[7] AMARI, Storia, I, p. 378-380.

[8] VASILIEV, Byzance, I, p. 66; BURY, History, p. 296.

[9] Amari semble avoir changé d'opinion à ce sujet. Dans sa Storia, I, p. 373, il est d'avis que les deux chroniqueurs ont copié une source perdue du onzième siècle, mais plus tard dans la Tavola analitica delle fonti arabiche etc., qui précède la traduction italienne de sa Biblioteca Arabo-Sicula et qui est réimprimée en tête de la seconde édition de la Storia, il affirme (Storia, I, p. 83) que Nuwayrī a copié non seulement Ibn al-Atīr, mais aussi certaines chroniques perdues.

[10] AMARI, Storia, I, p. 369 s., n. 2.

[11] AMARI, Storia, I, p. 399, n. 1.

Amari la situe, non sans quelque hésitation, au promontoire appelé aujourd'hui Pietra di San Nicola et par les Arabes Marsà aš-Šalūq, qui se trouve entre Licata et Terranova (Gela), toujours sur la côte méridionale de l'île [12]. A cet endroit l'armée d'Asad aurait quitté la route côtière et aurait marché en direction nord-est à travers les montagnes vers Syracuse, en traversant les sites des villes modernes de Biscari, Chiaramonte et Palazzolo Acreide. Le seul point d'appui de cette thèse est l'identification proposée par Amari pour la forteresse appelée Qal'at al-K.rāt avec la cité classique d'Acrae située non loin de Palazzolo Acreide moderne [13]. Ces identifications topographiques furent répétées, non sans hésitation à ce qu'il paraît, par Vasiliev [14]. Bury, suivant une indication d'Amari, plaçait le champ de bataille, Balāṭa, dans la plaine côtière qui s'étend de Mazara vers le sud-est, au Capo Granitola, et acceptait provisoirement l'identification de Qal'at al-K.rāt avec Acrae, mais il ne s'est pas prononcé sur la situation des deux églises mentionnées par Nuwayrī. Malgré ses doutes, il répétait la thèse d'Amari que l'armée arabe marchait le long de la côte méridionale [15]. Plusieurs érudits, tel Vincenzo Epifanio, ont fait la critique des identifications d'Amari et en ont proposé d'autres, sans réussir cependant à convaincre les arabisants [16].

Pour résoudre ces problèmes qui ont exercé les esprits de tant d'historiens, il ne s'agira pas ici de refaire l'analyse systématique des sources. Evidemment, il y aurait de quoi ajouter, par ci et par là, quelques précisions aux résultats obtenus par nos prédécesseurs, mais il est fort douteux que la reprise d'un tel travail puisse donner des résultats essentiellement supérieurs à ceux d'un Amari, d'un Vasiliev ou d'un Bury. On se propose, plutôt, d'étudier certaines sources historiques non encore utilisées pour l'examen des débuts des conquêtes arabes en Sicile et de les comparer aux textes bien connus sur lesquels elles pourront jeter de nouvelles lumières.

La plus importante de ces sources négligées jusqu'ici est une apo-

---

[12] AMARI, *Storia*, I, p. 399 s., n. 1.
[13] AMARI, *Storia*, I, p. 400 s., n. 1.
[14] VASILIEV, *Byzance*, I, p. 76 s.
[15] BURY, *History*, p. 299 s.
[16] V. EPIFANIO, *La Rocca del Kratas e la prima invasione dei musulmani in Sicilia*, Palermo, 1904. Cf. les remarques négatives dans l'édition française de VASILIEV, *Byzance*, I, p. 77 s., n. 2, et dans la seconde édition d'AMARI (par C. A. NALLINO), *Storia*, I, p. 400 s., n. 1. Signalons encore l'ouvrage de I. SCATURRO, *Storia della città di Sciacca* etc., 2 volumes, Napoli, 1924-1926, qui croyait que les deux églises d'Euphémie et de Marsà aš-Šalūq, aussi bien que la forteresse d'al-K.rāt, devaient être non loin de Syracuse (I, p. 136), sans du reste donner des preuves suffisantes pour sa thèse. L'éditeur de l'ouvrage d'Amari, le professeur C. A. Nallino, lui-même spécialiste en études arabes, admet le bien-fondé de la critique des vues d'Amari à ce sujet, mais déclare ne pas pouvoir accepter les thèses positives d'Epifanio (*Storia*, I, p. 400 s., n. 1 à la fin).

calypse attribuée au prophète Daniel [17]. Elle nous est conservée en vieux-slavon, mais est sans doute traduite d'un original grec (byzantin) perdu [18]. Le titre de cette apocalypse dans le manuscrit du monastère de Chilandar au Mont-Athos est le suivant: « Vision du prophète Daniel sur les empereurs et les derniers jours et la fin de l'âge ». Au commencement de ce texte, l'ange Gabriel montre à Daniel une vision de quatre animaux semblable à celle du livre canonique de Daniel et ensuite lui en donne l'interprétation. Il s'agirait d'une suite d'empereurs. On reconnaît facilement les empereurs byzantins, de Léon III « l'Isaurien » (717-741) à Michel II l'Amorien (820-829) [19]. Suivent quelques lignes de fantaisies eschatologiques et puis le passage suivant:

Et il [20] va expédier aussi aux régions occidentales des envoyés proprement fidèles à lui. Et quand ils arrivent dans les régions occidentales, les gens de la ville appelée Ville Rebelle [21], qui se sont révoltés [22], sortent et

---

[17] Le texte vieux-slavon a été publié à trois reprises. D'abord, par le professeur SRECHKOVICH, Zbornik Popa Dragolia, dans « Srpska Kralievska Akademia, Spomenik », V, 1890, p. 10-11, d'après un manuscrit, aujourd'hui perdu, du treizième siècle, le n° 466 (632) de la Bibliothèque Nationale de Belgrade. Deuxièmement, le texte vieux-slavon a été édité par V. M. ISTRIN, Otkrovenie Mefodiia Patarskago i Apokrificheskiia Videnia Daniila v Vizantiiski i Slaviano-Russkoi Literaturakh, dans « Chtenia v Imperatorskom Obshchestvie Istorii i Drevnostei Rossisskikh pro Moskovskom Universitete », CXCI et CXCIII, 1897, spécialement Teksty (vol. CXCIII), p. 156-158, d'après le codex Athos, Chilandar 24, du douzième ou treizième siècle. Enfin, la Vision a été publiée par P. A. LAVROV, Apokrificheskie Teksty, dans « Sbornik Otdeleniia Russkago Iazyka i Slovenosti Imp. Akademii Nauk », LXVII, n° 3, 1899, p. 1-5, d'après le manuscrit de Chilandar, avec les leçons du manuscrit de Belgrade dans l'apparatus. On se servira ici principalement de la dernière des ces publications.

[18] Voir l'étude de ce document par V. M. ISTRIN (note 17), vol. CXCI, p. 260-268.

[19] Signalons deux exemples. Le règne de Léon III est décrit de la manière suivante: « Le premier animal, la forme duquel est comme un lion, est l'empire Isaurien. Il surgit contre l'autel (allusion à l'iconoclasme de Léon III) et le détruit. Il tient l'empire vigoureusement et fortement pendant vingt-deux années (inexact)... Il chasse un prêtre de son trône (le patriarche Germain Ier, 715-730) ». Le règne de Michel II d'Amorion, auquel fut associé dès 821 son fils Théophile, est mentionné comme suit: « Surgit un autre sceptre de la première lettre impériale (Amorion). Et pendant qu'il occupe le trône, il y a un autre sceptre (Théophile). Et ils commencent à blasphémer contre le Plus Haut (iconoclasme). Et à cause de leur blasphème il périt misérablement ».

[20] Il s'agit évidemment du dernier empereur historique mentionné avant l'alinéa eschatologique, c'est-à-dire Michel II.

[21] Manuscrit de Chilandar: tyinaridi, manuscrit de Belgrade: turinidy. Sans doute le traducteur trouvait dans l'original les mots πόλις τυραννίς, cf. la Vision Grecque de Daniel attribuée à St. Jean Chrysostome, ed. A. VASILIEV, dans Anecdota Graeca-Byzantina, Moscou, 1893, p. 36, l. 15: τὴν καλουμένην Τυραννίδα πόλιν. Le mot τύραννος, en grec byzantin, signifie souvent « rebelle », voir par exemple G. W. H. LAMPE, A Greek Patristic Lexicon, Oxford, 1968, sub verbo. Dans le manuscrit de Belgrade plusieurs mots sont suivis du nom d'une localité de la péninsule des Balkans. Ainsi turinidy est suivi de srědca (= Sardica, Sofia), « l'ouest de la ville » de ωt glavinice, le « signe » de u perinika (= près de Pernik), « l'île » de dunaja (le Danube), marijanii de i na mraky et jennie de velĭbluda. Évidemment, un copiste ou scholiaste a voulu appliquer la prophécie à certains événements de l'histoire balkanique, qui malheureusement m'échappent.

[22] mučeštei. Le mot mučitel sert en vieux-slavon pour traduire le grec τύραννος. Voir la première traduction en vieux-slavon de l'apocalypse du PSEUDO-MÉTHODE (ed

commencent à commettre des actes injustes [23]. Et ensuite ceux qui se trouvent dans cet endroit surgiront et se détruiront par le glaive. Et ils surgissent l'un contre l'autre et se livrent des batailles l'un à l'autre. Et deux rebelles vont surgir, le premier de l'est de cette ville, l'autre de l'ouest. Et ils vont se rencontrer à un endroit appelé Akrodounii [24]. Et ils se détruiront l'un l'autre de sorte que la mer soit mêlée de leur sang. Et une femme enceinte (?) [25] arrive du territoire de cette ville (à l'endroit) où un signe (ou: monument funèbre) [26] se trouvait dans ces jours, et elle voit son frère étant mort. Et elle se frappe la poitrine et met au monde un enfant [27]. Et le deuil l'assaillit pour beaucoup de temps. Et les Ismaélites (Arabes) envahissent l'extrémité de cette île et prennent beaucoup de butin. Et ainsi ils arrivent à un endroit appelé Marianii, et le rebelle les établit dans cet endroit. Et ils arrivent à un endroit appelé Ienna, et on vient à son secours et ils ne la prennent pas.

Signalons d'abord que les événements décrits dans cet alinéa se rapportent à la Sicile. On parle bien de l'invasion arabe (ismaélite) d'une île. Au moins deux localités siciliennes se reconnaissent immédiatement, Achradine (*Akrodounii*) et Enna (*Ienna*). La première est bien le quartier de Syracuse situé sur terre ferme en face et à l'ouest de l'île d'Ortygie et bien connu des auteurs anciens, tels Cicéron et Tite-Live. Enna est elle aussi une ville ancienne appelée « nombril de la Sicile » par Cicéron [28] et située sur un rocher de grande hauteur au coeur même de l'île. Une troisième ville, *Marianii*, est difficile à identifier (voir plus loin), mais doit également être placée en Sicile. On constate ensuite que les événements auxquels fait allusion l'auteur de l'apocalypse se sont déroulés sous le règne de Michel II (820-829). L'empereur qui dépêcha ses envoyés à l'ouest doit être le dernier monarque historique mentionné dans ce qui précède.

La fin de l'alinéa traduit ci-dessus montre qu'il s'agit de l'invasion

---

ISTRIN, dans « Otkrovenie Mefodiia », CXCIII, p. 87, l. 16): *mučitele i vojevody*, qui traduit le τύραννοι ἀρχιστρατηγοί du texte grec (éd. ISTRIN, p. 14, l. 3 dans l'apparatus; voir le commentaire d'ISTRIN, CXCI, p. 34). Puisque le verbe *mučiti* signifie « torturer », le nom *mučitel* rend assez bien τύραννος au sens de « tyran », mais est une traduction fautive et mécanique pour le sens de « rebelle ».

[23] Manuscrit de Chilandar: *wbii*, manuscrit de Belgrade: *obidy*.

[24] Manuscrit de Chilandar: *akrodounii*, manuscrit de Belgrade: *krodounii*.

[25] Selon Istrin le manuscrit de Chilandar a *brěna*, selon Lavrov *brěža*, et le manuscrit de Belgrade *brěžda*. Il faut lire sans doute *brěmenina = onerata*.

[26] *stoja vĭ dnī wni znamenije*. Le mot *znamenije* est probablement une traduction littérale du grec σῆμα, qui signifie « signe », mais aussi « monument funèbre ». C'est un second exemple du caractère mécanique de la traduction en vieux-slavon, voir n. 22.

[27] C'est la leçon du manuscrit de Belgrade. Le manuscrit de Chilandar omet *poroditi*.

[28] CICÉRON, *Seconde action contre Verrès*, IV, 48, 106. La mention d'Achradine dans le texte slave est intéressante, car M. AMARI (*Storia*, I, p. 402 et *Biblioteca Arabo-Sicula*, traduction italienne, Appendice, p. 1, n. 11) pensait que ce quartier de Syracuse avait été détruit ou abandonné longtemps avant la conquête arabe. Le texte vieux-slavon prouve que le nom de ce quartier existait encore au neuvième siècle.

arabe de la Sicile décrite dans les sources grecques, latines et arabes bien connues. L'invasion arabe de « l'extrémité de l'île », dont parle l'apocalypse, doit être le débarquement de l'expédition navale d'Asad le 17 juin 827 à Mazara, qui se trouve en effet sur la côte occidentale de l'île [29]. On devra donc rapprocher le reste de cet alinéa des autres sources pour essayer de trouver des solutions aux problèmes historiques formulés ci-dessus [30].

D'abord, la question des raisons de la rébellion de la Sicile contre le gouvernement à Byzance. Ces raisons étaient-elles d'ordre purement personnel (la mariage du tourmarque Euphémius à une religieuse et ses conséquences) ou y avait-il des raisons politiques? Dans l'apocalypse l'arrivée des Arabes à Mazara est précédée de l'épisode des deux rebelles qui se livrent une bataille sanglante à Achradine. Qui sont-ils? Ibn al-Aṯīr rapporte qu'Euphémius, après avoir été proclamé roi [31], préposa au gouvernement d'une région de la Sicile un homme appelé Balāṭa. Mais Balāṭa se révolta contre Euphémius et lui fit la guerre. Euphémius

---

[29] IBN AL-AṮĪR, traduction italienne d'AMARI, p. 93: « Mandò seco lui Zîâdat 'Allâh un esercito, del mese di rabî‘ primo dell'anno dugento dodici (31 maggio a 29 giugno 827). Arrivati alla città di Mazara, in Sicilia etc. ». Voir NUWAYRĪ, trad. AMARI, p. 174. « Salpò l'armata dalla città di Susa, il sabato quindici del mese di rabî‘ primo dell'anno dugentododici (14 giugno 827)... Arrivato a Mazara il martedì, 'Asad fece sbarcar dalle navi i cavalli etc. ». Pour les textes arabes je citerai normalement la traduction italienne d'Amari, plutôt que la traduction française de Vasiliev, parce que dans cette dernière il y a trop de coupures.

[30] Je ne sais expliquer les deux phrases au sujet de la femme enceinte, son frère et son enfant. Il doit s'agir ici d'un détail inconnu des autres textes.

[31] Quelle était la position d'Euphémius? Les chroniqueurs arabes disent: ḫūṭiba fīmī bi-malikin, c'est-à-dire, Euphémius fut adressé comme (proclamé) roi ou empereur (ed. AMARI, Biblioteca Arabo-Sicula [texte arabe], Leipzig, 1857, p. 222, l. 2 = IBN AL-AṮĪR et p. 427, l. 8 = NUWAYRĪ). D'après la Continuation de THÉOPHANE (éd. Bonn, p. 82, l. 13) c'est l'émir aghlabide qui aurait proclamé Euphémius βασιλεὺς 'Ρωμαίων après que celui-ci eut promis de lui soumettre la Sicile et de lui payer de hauts tributs. B. PACE, Arte e civiltà, IV, p. 131, n. 1, a fait une communication très intéressante à ce sujet. Selon lui, l'archéologue sicilien A. Salinas aurait acquis un sceau de plomb avec la légende: ΕΥΦΗΜΙVΣ ΡΕΞ, un mélange de lettres grecques et latines. Malheureusement le sceau a disparu, mais son existence est garantie par l'autorité de ces deux érudits. Comme l'a observé très bien le professeur Pace, le titre de rex prouve qu'Euphémius ne visait pas à l'usurpation du trône de Byzance, mais au gouvernement autonome de la Sicile. Ajoutons les renseignements des chroniqueurs arabes d'après lesquels, pendant le séjour de l'armée d'Asad à l'église de al-Maslaqīn et lors des négociations du cadi avec les patriciens syracusains, Euphémius leur a conseillé de tenir ferme (trad. AMARI, p. 93 et 174, voir la note 92 ci-dessous) — par amour de ses coreligionnaires, dit Nuwayrī. Euphémius voulait donc empêcher la soumission de Syracuse aux Arabes, évidemment parce qu'il avait l'intention de se rendre maître de la ville à son propre compte. De plus, il était prêt à payer tribut à l'émir de Qayrawān. Il paraît donc qu'Euphémius eût l'intention de s'installer comme maître au moins d'une partie de la Sicile, qui comprenait la ville de Syracuse, avec le titre de rex, de payer tribut à Qayrawān et à se gérer en monarque autonome envers le basileus à Byzance. Il doit avoir cru avoir le consentement des Arabes à un arrangement de ce genre, mais pendant que l'armée d'Asad approchait Syracuse, il semble s'être aperçu que ses alliés étaient en train de le tromper et de saisir Syracuse pour eux-mêmes. Le but de son message aux patriciens byzantins était donc de sauvegarder son accord avec l'émir de Qayrawān.

fut battu, Balāṭa saisit la ville de Syracuse, et Euphémius avec ses partisans se rendit en Afrique pour demander secours à Ziyādat Allāh [32]. Nuwayrī a un récit très semblable, mais ajoute un détail: au cours de la bataille dans laquelle Balāṭa battit Euphémius, furent tués mille soldats de ce dernier [33]. Evidemment, les deux rebelles mentionnés dans l'apocalypse ne sont nuls autres qu'Euphémius et Balāṭa [34]. L'apocalypse ajoute un détail précieux aux données des sources arabes: la bataille entre les deux rebelles eut lieu à Achradine.

Il est évident que les données de l'apocalypse sur l'invasion arabe de la Sicile et sur la rébellion d'Euphémius s'accordent, on ne peut mieux, avec les indications des sources arabes et qu'elles les complètent sous plusieurs rapports. Ceci nous donne le droit de supposer que le commencement de l'alinéa, lui aussi, nous donne un récit fidèle des événements antérieurs à la révolte d'Euphémius. L'apocalypse décrit une situation révolutionnaire dans la « ville appelée Ville Rebelle ». Quelle est cette ville? Le texte dit un peu plus loin que les deux rebelles, c'est-à-dire Euphémius et Balāṭa, surgissent de l'est et de l'ouest « de cette ville » [35] et se livrent bataille à Achradine. Ici il n'y a pas de doute qu'il s'agit du territoire de Syracuse, puisque les deux rebelles partent de différents quartiers de « cette ville » et se recontrent à Achradine. Mais évidemment « cette ville » est aussi identique avec la seule ville mentionnée auparavant, la « Ville Rebelle ». Il s'ensuit donc que l'auteur parle d'une rébellion à Syracuse et que la « Ville Rebelle » est nulle autre que Syracuse. Le texte apocalyptique nous apprend donc qu'il y avait une rébellion et des désordres internes à Syracuse avant l'entrée en scène d'Euphémius.

Mais l'apocalypse nous dit davantage. D'après elle, la rébellion de Syracuse et les dissensions auraient éclaté après l'arrivée de certains envoyés de l'empereur (Michel II). *Post hoc, ergo propter hoc* — du moins dans le style apocalyptique, quoique l'apocalypse ne le dise pas expressément. A Syracuse les envoyés de l'empereur doivent avoir fait ou demandé quelque chose qui fut mal reçu des habitants. Il s'agirait

---

[32] IBN AL-AṮĪR, trad. AMARI, p. 93.

[33] NUWAYRĪ, trad. AMARI, p. 174.

[34] Les auteurs modernes supposent que Balāṭa, en se révoltant contre Euphémius, qui lui avait donné son poste, se déclarait partisan de l'empereur Michel II, ainsi AMARI, *Storia*, I, p. 380: (Balāṭa et son cousin le gouverneur de Palerme, Michel) « gridarono il nome di Michele il Balbo ». De même VASILIEV, *Byzance*, I, p. 69, et BURY, *History*, p. 297. C'est là une hypothèse pure et simple qui n'a pas de fondement dans les sources. En effet, l'apocalypse en vieux-slavon prouve que Balāṭa se révolta à son propre compte, puisque le texte parle de deux rebelles. Signalons, de plus, qu'au onzième siècle le *Riyāḍ an-nufūs*, dans la biographie d'Asad, citant un auteur antérieur, Sulaymān ibn Salīm, appelle Balāṭa « roi de Sicile » (éd. AMARI, p. 184, l. 11: *malik Ṣiqilliyah*).

[35] ѺТ ТОГА ГРАДА.

donc de deviner quels furent les actions ou demandes des envoyés qui avaient pour suite la rébellion syracusaine. On pense d'abord à des mesures ayant rapport à la querelle des images. Mais Michel II, quoique lui-même de persuasion iconoclaste, mit fin à la persécution des iconophiles entreprise par son prédecesseur Leon V et en général tâchait d'établir un *modus vivendi* avec eux. Il est donc très invraisemblable qu'il se soit proposé d'introduire des mesures iconoclastes dans une région périphérique de son empire.

Reste la possibilité de demandes fiscales ou militaires faites par le gouvernement à la cité de Syracuse. L'apocalypse en vieux-slavon ne nous permet ni de confirmer ni de réfuter cette hypothèse. Pourtant il y a d'autres textes qui nous mettent en état de la démontrer. Plusieurs chroniqueurs byzantins rapportent une anecdote au sujet de la révolte sicilienne sous Michel II. La chronique dite du Pseudo-Syméon, par exemple, raconte qu'au cours de la révolte de Thomas le Slave la Crète, la Sicile et les Iles Cycladiques furent conquises « par les Africains et les Arabes ». L'empereur aurait appelé le *magister* Irénée et lui aurait dit: Je vous félicite, *magister*, que la Sicile soit en tumulte. Alors Irénée aurait répondu: Ceci, Sire, n'est pas affaire de félicitations, et aurait récité à un des courtisans les vers suivants:

Le commencement des maux va frapper le pays
Quand va régner sur Babylone
Un dragon entièrement bègue et bien avide d'or [36].

Aucune des chroniques qui contiennent ces trois vers ne souffle mot qu'ils n'étaient que le commencement d'un long poème. Cependant, dans une communication faite au IIIᵉ Congrès International des Etudes Byzantines à Athènes feu le professeur S. G. Mercati notait que le poème entier se trouvait dans le *Codex Vaticanus Graecus 1257*, folios

---

[36] PSEUDO-SYMÉON, éd. I. BEKKER, Corpus de Bonn, 1838 (après la *Continuation de Théophane*), p. 621 s.: Ἐν τούτοις τοῦ Μιχαὴλ ἐνασχολουμένου Κρήτη καὶ Σικελία καὶ αἱ Κυκλάδες νῆσοι τῆς τῶν Ῥωμαίων ἀρχῆς ἐξ Ἀφρικῶν τε καὶ Ἀράβων περιηρέθησαν, λαβόντος ἀρχὴν ἄρτι πρῶτον διὰ τὰς τοῦ λαοῦ ἁμαρτίας καὶ τὴν τῶν κρατούντων δυσσέβειαν. τῶν δὲ πραγμάτων οὕτως ἐχόντων προσκαλεῖται ὁ βασιλεὺς Εἰρηναῖον τὸν μάγιστρον καὶ φησὶ πρὸς αὐτόν "συγχαίρω σοι, μάγιστρε, ὅτι ἡ Σικελία ἐμούλτευσεν." ὁ δὲ ἔφη "τοῦτο ξένον χαρᾶς ἐστι, δέσποτα." καὶ στραφεὶς πρός τινα τῶν μεγάλων ἔφη
ἀρχὴ κακῶν γε πεσεῖται τῇ χθονί,
ὅταν κατάρξῃ τῆς Βαβυλῶνος δράκων
δύσγλωσσος ἄρδην καὶ φιλόχρυσος λίαν.
Sur cette chronique, voir G. MORAVCSIK, *Byzantina-Turcica*, seconde éd., Berlin, 1958, I, p. 500 s. Les vers sont cités aussi par le CONTINUATEUR DE THÉOPHANE, p. 84; SCYLITZES-CÉDRÉNUS, éd. Bonn, II, p. 99, et ZONARAS, éd. Dindorf, III, p. 400, mais l'anecdote d'Irénée se trouve seulement dans le Pseudo-Syméon.

36 ss., qui date du dixième siècle [37]. Il s'agit d'un poème de cent-quatre-vingt-une lignes en vers dodécasyllabiques attribué dans le titre au « philosophe Bryson » [38]. Malheureusement, le texte du poème dans le manuscrit de la Vaticane est très corrompu et, de plus, l'auteur écrit dans un style tellement ampoulé et intentionnellement obscur que le sens en est très difficile à extraire. Pourtant, non seulement la chronique du Pseudo-Syméon, mais aussi le titre du poème dans le manuscrit (« Les événements en Occident ») et certaines gloses marginales laissent entrevoir que le poète envisageait la ville de Syracuse et l'époque de la révolte de Thomas le Slave en Orient (821-823) [39]. Heureusement, il n'est pas nécessaire, par rapport à notre problème, de faire l'analyse détaillée du poème entier, car déjà le quatrième vers, qui suit immédiatement les lignes dans la chronique du Pseudo-Syméon sur Michel II citées plus haut, nous intéresse ici: « Il (c'est-à-dire Michel II) va secouer les îles (en demandant) des fardeaux (ou vexations) plus grands » [40]. Ce vers du « philosophe Bryson » tend à renforcer notre hypothèse, fondée sur l'apocalypse en vieux-slavon, que les demandes présentées par les envoyés de Michel II à la ville de Syracuse étaient du moins partiellement d'ordre fiscal [41].

Ainsi l'apocalypse en vieux-slavon nous a mis en état de trancher la première question que nous nous sommes posée, celle des causes de la rébellion sicilienne. Nous aiderait-elle aussi à résoudre le second problème, celui de la chronologie des événements en Sicile? Partons, encore une fois, de la partie du texte qui est la plus facile à mettre d'accord avec les autres sources historiques: « les Ismaélites envahissent l'extrémité de cette île ». Il s'agit bien, comme nous l'avons vu, du débarquement de l'expédition aghlabide commandée par Asad à Mazara le 17 juin 827. Cette phrase est précédée par l'épisode de la femme

---

[37] Résumé de cette communication dans le *IIIe Congrès International des Etudes Byzantines*, Athènes, 1932, pp. 111-113. Le titre de la communication du professeur Mercati: *Sur une poesie inédite dont on connaît seulement les trois premiers vers relatés par le Pseudosiméon et par d'autres chroniqueurs au sujet de la révolte d'Euphémius*. La cote du manuscrit y paraît sous le numero 1234, mais c'est là une faute d'impression.

[38] Le titre: Λόγοι Βρύσονος φιλοσόφου διὰ ἰαμβῶν περὶ τῶν ἐσχάτων ἡμερῶν καὶ τί τὰ συμβησόμενα εἰς τὴν Δύσιν.

[39] Par exemple, en marge de la première colonne du poème on lit les scolies suivantes: ὁ θωμᾶς, ἡ πό(λις) συράκουσα, ἡ τυραννεῖς (sic), etc.

[40] *Cod. Vat. Gr. 1257*, f. 36 recto: Νίσους (lege: νήσους) δονήσει μηζῶσει δαχθηδῶσει (lege: μείζοσι δ'ἀχθηδόσι).

[41] Bryson fait mention des îles au pluriel. Evidemment, il s'agit non seulement de la Sicile, mais aussi d'autres îles, peut-être de la Crète et des îles de la mer Egéenne. Ceci correspond au texte vieux-slavon, d'après lequel l'empereur dépêche ses envoyés « aussi » (en slave: *i*) aux régions occidentales. Il les envoyait donc aussi autre part, eux ou d'autres envoyés.

enceinte, son frère et son enfant que je ne peux expliquer. Plus haut encore il y a l'entrée en scène des deux rebelles et leur bataille à Achradine. On vient de voir qu'il s'agit du conflit entre Euphémius et Balāṭa, qu'il faut placer au plus tard au commencement de l'année 827, puisque la fuite d'Euphémius en Afrique et les délibérations à Qayrawān se sont déroulées après la bataille d'Achradine et avant l'arrivée des Arabes en Sicile. Signalons aussi que ces événements intermédiaires, tels que la proclamation d'Euphémius comme roi et la nomination de Balāṭa à son poste par Euphémius, sont entièrement omis dans le texte vieux-slavon. Ce texte, d'autre part, ne laisse aucun doute que cette entrée en scène d'Euphémius et de Balāṭa (vĭstaneta) ne marque pas dans l'apocalypse le commencement des troubles à Syracuse. Elle est précédée d'une période plus ou moins longue de conflits entre factions rivales et de désordres civils à Syracuse. D'après le texte vieux-slavon, il paraît que par suite des demandes du gouvernement de Michel II la population de Syracuse ait été divisée en deux groupes au moins. Un premier groupe se révolta contre le gouvernement et commit des actes injustes. Mais le texte montre aussi qu'une partie des habitants restait loyale au gouvernement de Constantinople et était prête à combattre les insurgés les armes à la main. On ne saurait préciser, d'après le texte vieux-slavon seul, combien de temps a duré cette période de désordres à Syracuse avant l'entrée en scène d'Euphémius et de Balāṭa. Mais il est clair qu'ici aussi l'auteur de l'apocalypse présente un rapport très abrégé et simplifié de ce conflit armé entre factions à Syracuse. Sans doute, c'est pendant cette période qu'Euphémius fut nommé tourmarque et se distingua comme commandeur d'un escadron qui fit des descentes sur le territoire aghlabide[42]. Ainsi Euphémius arriva à être connu en Sicile comme homme énergique et habile. Au cours des conflits de partis à Syracuse, il réussit à se faire chef de faction. La chronique de Naples, par exemple, parle de « la faction d'un certain Euthimius (sic) », et c'est probablement pendant cette période que les insurgés tuèrent « Grigoras patricius »[43].

---

[42] Ibn al-Aṯīr, trad. Amari, p. 93: « Il re dei Rûm, [sedente] in Constantinopoli, avea preposto alla Sicilia, l'anno dugento undici (13 apr. 826 - 1 apr. 827), un patrizio per nome Costantino; il quale, arrivato nell'isola, diè il comando dei soldati d'armata ad un rûmî per nome Fîmî (Eufemio), uomo di proposito e valoroso. Questi fece una scorreria nell'Africa [propria]; prese dei mercatanti in quelle costiere; le saccheggiò e vi si mantenne alquanto ». Voir Nuwayrī, trad. Amari, p. 174. D'après Bury, History, p. 479 s., et la nomination d'Euphémius et son mariage à la religieuse auraient eu lieu au printemps de l'année 826. En tout cas, c'est là la date la plus basse pour ces événements; ils pourraient aussi se placer plus tôt.

[43] Johannes Diaconus, Gestorum Episcoporum Neapolitanorum Pars Altera, ed. G. Waitz, Monumenta Germaniae Historica, Scriptores Rerum Langobardicarum et Italicarum, Hannover, 1878, ch. 54, p. 429, l. 18: « Tum illi (certains conspirateurs à Con-

Le texte vieux-slavon vérifie donc de la manière la plus formelle l'hypothèse d'Amari, d'après laquelle la révolte sicilienne se serait déroulée en deux phases: le texte slave ne dit rien sur une participation d'Euphémius dans la période initiale du mouvement. Peut-être y jouait-il un rôle subalterne, mais il se peut aussi que dans cette première phase il s'occupait entièrement de ses activités navales. Ce n'est que dans la seconde phase qu'Euphémius devint protagoniste de la révolte sicilienne. Une partie de la tradition a confondu ces deux phases de l'insurrection et en a fait une. Amari avait raison aussi de supposer que dans la première période de la révolte sicilienne le motif principal était d'ordre politique. On a vu, en effet, qu'il s'agissait, du moins en partie, de la résistance syracusaine aux demandes fiscales de Constantinople. Dans la seconde phase, de l'autre côté, il se peut que les problèmes matrimoniaux d'Euphémius aient joué un rôle, sinon prépondérant, du moins secondaire.

Les théories d'Amari concernant les raisons et les deux phases de la révolution sicilienne ayant été confirmées par le texte vieux-slavon, il convient de rétablir la branche de la tradition qui a conservé les traces de la verité. C'est, d'abord, la chronique napolitaine qui fait commencer la révolte syracusaine immédiatement après le meurtre de Léon V et l'avènement de Michel II (voir n. 43). Puis, il y a la chronique, déjà citée, du Pseudo-Syméon. Pour le règne de Michel II le chroniqueur décrit, au chapitre 2, la révolte de Thomas le Slave qui dura trois ans (821-823). Puis, au chapitre 3, il parle de la perte de la Crète, de la Sicile et des Cyclades « pendant que Michel s'occupait de ces affaires », c'est-à-dire de la révolte de Thomas [44]. En d'autres mots, le procès historique qui allait aboutir à la perte de la Sicile aurait du moins commencé dès avant 823.

Mais du moins aussi importante que ces textes, confirmés dorénavant par le texte vieux-slavon, est une considération générale proposée par Amari [45]. C'est la probabilité que le soulèvement eut lieu en Sicile pendant que la capitale de Constantinople fut menacée par les armées et flottes de Thomas le Slave. Ainsi, pendant le siège de la capitale sous

---

stantinople)... eundem Leonem (l'empereur byzantin Léon V)... gladio percusserunt. Et statim excussum de carcere Michahelium Syracusani cuiusdam Euthymii factione rebellantes, Grigoram patricium interfecerunt ». On notera que cette chronique fait mention de la *Euthymii factio* au début même de l'insurrection.

[44] Voir n. 36.

[45] AMARI, *Storia*, I, 378. Il croit pouvoir tirer un argument en faveur de sa thèse chronologique de Nuwayrī. L'année de l'hégire donnée par cet auteur s'accorderait avec l'année 821. Je ne comprends pas cet argument puisque Nuwayrī (trad. AMARI, p. 174) donne l'an de l'hégire 201 (30 juillet 816 - 19 juillet 817), qui est trop haut en tout cas.

Léon III, un siècle auparavant, Sergius, stratège de la Sicile, avait fait proclamer empereur un certain Tibère (717/8)[46]. A l'aide du texte vieux-slavon et du poème inédit attribué à Bryson on peut maintenant renforcer cet argument d'ordre général. On a vu que les envoyés de Michel II demandèrent des impôts nouveaux ou plus élevés qu'auparavant aux habitants de Syracuse; qu'ils furent dépêchés non seulement en Sicile mais aussi en d'autres régions de l'Occident (texte slavon), spécialement aux îles autres que la Sicile (Bryson); et que c'est cette demande qui en premier lieu avait déclenché l'insurrection à Syracuse. Il semble bien qu'à ce moment le gouvernement central se soit trouvé dans une situation fiscale des plus gênantes. Aucune période du règne de Michel II n'est plus adaptée à de telles mesures fiscales que celle de l'insurrection de Thomas le Slave. Pour le gouvernement de Michel II c'était la crise suprême. Thomas contrôlait presque toute l'Asie Mineure et les armées et les flottes qui y étaient stationnées, plus tard aussi la Thrace. Il avait obtenu le secours politique et militaire du calife al-Ma'mūn. Il avait les sympathies du parti iconophile et peut-être des Pauliciens et on a même voulu voir dans sa rébellion un mouvement de protestation sociale. De plus, Thomas posait en vengeur de Léon V que Michel II, usurpateur, avait fait assassiner[47]. Or parmi les difficultés de ce dernier il y avait le manque de revenus publics, car Thomas avait « fait saisir tous les receveurs d'impôts publics et par écrit réservait pour lui-même les revenus coutumiers »[48]. Le gouvernement de Michel II devait donc être dans la plus grande pénurie, puisque les impôts des provinces les plus riches de l'empire allaient dans les coffres du rebelle. Rien de plus naturel donc, mais aussi rien de plus dangereux, que de faire payer aux provinces de l'Occident, qui n'étaient pas touchées par la révolte de Thomas, les frais de la guerre civile en Orient ainsi que ceux de la répression de la révolte. Ainsi, en 726, l'empereur Léon III avait augmenté les taxes et exigé une per-

---

[46] AMARI, *Storia*, I, 342.

[47] Sur la révolte de Thomas, voir VASILIEV, *Byzance*, I, p. 22-40; BURY, *History*, p. 84-110; F. BARISIC, *Deux Versions sur Thomas* etc., dans «Zbornik Radova Vizantološkog Instituta », VI, 1960, p. 145-169; P. LEMERLE, *Thomas le Slave*, dans « Centre de recherche d'histoire et civilisation byzantines. Travaux et Mémoires », I, 1965, p. 254-297; M. Ia. SIUZIUMOV, dans *Istoriia Vizantii*, II, Moscou, 1967, p. 72-74.

[48] GÉNÉSIUS, ed. Bonn, p. 32, l. 12: οὗτος (Thomas) οὖν κατασχὼν τοὺς τῶν δημοσίων φόρων πάντας ἀπαιτητὰς ἐγγράφως τὰς νενομισμένας ἀπεκληροῦτο εἰσπράξεις κτλ. Le CONTINUATER DE THÉOPHANE (ch. 11, p. 53) dit, plutôt, que Thomas se réconcilia (εἰς ἑαυτὸν εἰσποιησάμενος) les receveurs d'impôts. En dépit de cette différence légère, il semble que les deux chroniqueurs se fussent servis ici d'une source commune, ou de la monographie perdue de Serge le Confesseur sur le règne de Michel II ou du poème, également perdu, d'Ignace le Diacre sur la révolte de Thomas; voir BARISIC (n. 47), p. 167 du résumé français.

ception plus exacte des impôts existants pour pouvoir réorganiser son armée contre le péril arabe. Cette mesure avait eu pour conséquence la sécession de l'Italie inspirée par la papauté et son revirement de Byzance aux souverains francs que l'on sait [49]. Une seconde fois, au neuvième siècle, à cause du danger où se trouvait l'Asie Mineure au cours de la révolte de Thomas aidé par le calife, des demandes fiscales extraordinaires furent faites au reste de l'empire. Cette fois-ci, le résultat était la sécession de Syracuse d'abord, puis d'autres parties de la Sicile et en fin de compte la conquête de l'île par les Musulmans d'Afrique. Inutile de dire que ces considérations d'ordre général pourraient servir d'appui et pour une date haute de la révolte sicilienne, soit 821, et pour la date basse de 826. Pourtant, si elles sont combinées avec les textes de la chronique de Naples, du Pseudo-Syméon, de l'apocalypse en vieux-slavon et du poème de Bryson, on conviendra qu'elles s'accordent à merveille avec l'hypothèse chronologique d'Amari, d'après laquelle les désordres à Syracuse auraient commencé pendant la révolte de Thomas en Asie Mineure.

Abordons maintenant le troisième problème, celui de la route prise par le corps expéditionnaire commandé par Asad en Sicile, et voyons si une troisième fois l'apocalypse en vieux-slavon pourra nous être utile. Commençons par quelques remarques sur la méthode à suivre. Parmi les grands historiens de l'invasion arabe de la Sicile Amari a été le seul à étudier à fond les questions topographiques. Il s'est laissé guider principalement par la ressemblance de certains noms de lieux mentionnés dans la tradition arabe à la nomenclature classique, médiévale et moderne de l'île. Dans cette matière, Vasiliev et Bury se sont fiés, plus ou moins, à l'autorité de l'historien sicilien qui connaissait si bien la topographie de son pays natal. Pourtant, plus récemment, on a mis en question la validité de cette méthode et de ses résultats, à juste titre comme on va le voir. Dans les remarques qui suivent on essaiera d'utiliser l'ensemble des données topographiques, militaires et historiques pour identifier la situation des villes mentionnées dans les chroniques arabes. La ressemblance des noms n'y jouera qu'un rôle secondaire. De cette manière on espère arriver à des conclusions sûres et convaincantes.

On se souvient que la tradition musulmane donne les étapes suivantes de l'avance arabe en Sicile: Mazara — Plaine de Balāṭa (bataille) — Eglise d'Euphémie — Eglise de al-Maslaqīn — Syracuse (siège). De plus, les sources arabes font mention de la forteresse de al-K.rāt [50]. Les sources grecques et latines ne disent rien au sujet de la marche des Arabes en Sicile. L'apocalypse en vieux-slavon, traduite ci-dessus, fait mention de l'invasion arabe de l'extrémité de l'île — c'est évidemment le débarquement à Mazara —, de la prise d'une ville appelée Marianii, enfin d'un assaut sur Ienna, c'est-à-dire sur la ville d'Enna au centre de la Sicile.

La seule chose qui soit sûre, c'est que les Arabes aient marché de Mazara à l'ouest de l'île vers Syracuse à l'est. Tout le reste pose des problèmes. Quant à la bataille contre les forces de Balāṭa, Amari pensait qu'elle eut lieu au village de Balata à l'ouest de Corleone. Mais Amari lui-même avait aussi mis en ligne de compte le promontoire de Granitola, six lieues au sud-est de Mazara, appelé Ra's al-Balāṭ par Idrīsī [51]. En effet, le mot arabe balāṭ a la signification de « dalle, pavé », mais aussi en dialecte sicilien de « pierre vivante et polie avant d'être séparée de la montagne » [52]. Les localités appelées balata sont extrêmement nombreuses en Sicile, puisque des pierres polies, naturellement, se trouvent un peu partout. Par exemple, en plus des Balata mentionnées par Amari, il y a, environ trois kilomètres et demi à vol d'oiseau au nord du fameux temple dorique de Ségeste, non moins de trois endroits de ce nom: Contrada (district) Balata, Borgo Balata Inici et Borgo Borruso Balata [53].

Malheureusement, hors la nomenclature topographique, il est difficile de trouver des critères solides pour choisir entre les endroits siciliens appelés Balata et le problème ne semble donc pas susceptible de solution [54]. On se demande, pourtant, s'il n'y aurait pas dans le voisinage

---

[50] La liste complète se trouve chez NUWAYRĪ, trad. AMARI, p. 174. Ibn al-Atīr fait mention seulement de Mazara, Qal'at al-K.rāt et Syracuse.

[51] AMARI, Storia, I, p. 396, n. 2.

[52] AMARI, Storia, I, p. 396, n. 2: [balâtah] « in oggi nel dialetto dell'isola significa 'pietra di lastrico', e altresì 'pietra viva e liscia, non tolta per anco dal monte' ». Le mot est dérivé du latin platea et grec πλατεῖα, « rue large », parce que de telles rues étaient normalement pavées; voir G. B. PELLEGRINI, Terminologia geografica araba in Sicilia, dans « Annali dell'Istituto Orientale di Napoli », Sezione Linguistica, III, 1961, p. 124.

[53] A consulter le carte de l'Italie 1:100.000, de l'Istituto Geografico Militare (1948), revue en 1955, folio 257: Castelvetrano. Il y a en plus un Ballata (sic) onze kilomètres et demi au nord-ouest de Ségeste.

[54] AMARI, Storia, I, p. 396, n. 2, a insisté, très justement, que l'armée arabe est partie de Mazara en ordre de bataille (NUWAYRĪ, p. 428, l. 10: ta'biya) et en a tiré la conclusion que la Plaine de Balāṭa ne devait pas être loin de Mazara. Pourtant, cette conclusion ne s'impose pas, car autant du moins que l'armée sicilienne était intacte, il fallait bien que l'armée arabe marchât en ordre de bataille. En tout cas, le Balata qu'Amari finit par choisir, à l'ouest de Corleone, est à plus de cinquante kilomètres de Mazara à vol d'oiseau. D'autre part, Amari a raison: on ignore le point de départ de l'armée de Balāṭa. On pourrait penser à tirer un argument du fait qu'Asad ne nomma Abū Zakī commandant (ista'mala 'alà) de son principal point d'appui, le port de Mazara,

d'une des Balata siciliennes d'autres souvenirs topographiques de la grande bataille entre les soldats d'Asad d'une part et l'armée grecque de Balāta de l'autre. En ce cas, il serait permis, en bonne méthode, de supposer que ce voisinage ne peut être accidentel. Or il y a un nom de lieu de ce genre, bien que, à ce que je sache, on ne s'en soit jamais servi pour identifier la bataille de Balāṭa: Calatafimi. La ville est située au sud-est des ruines du fameux temple dorique de Ségeste, donc moins de quatre kilomètres des Balata mentionnées ci-dessus. Presque tout le monde est d'accord que ce nom arabe veut dire « la forteresse d'Euphémius » [55]. Evidemment donc, il y avait aux yeux des envahisseurs un lien qui attachait Euphémius à ce site. Aurait-il possédé des terres dans les environs de l'ancienne Ségeste? C'est possible, mais de telles possessions seules, à défaut d'un service rendu par Euphémius à l'armée arabe, n'auraient eu aucune importance pour les fondateurs arabes de la ville. Mais quelle contribution précise Euphémius aurat-il rendue à ses alliés arabes? On sait, de par le texte vieux-slavon, qu'il leur a procuré la ville de Marianii. De plus, il est probable qu'on devait le manque d'opposition militaire, lors du débarquement de Mazara, à certaines ententes qu'avait l'ancien officier de marine (tourmarque) Euphémius avec les autorités ou les habitants du port. Il se peut qu'Euphémius ait aidé les conquérants arabes en maintes autres occasions, quoique la tradition arabe ait fait de son mieux pour réduire sa contribution au minimum. Elle insiste qu'avant la bataille de Balāṭa Asad demanda à Euphémius de ne pas prendre part au combat, évidemment parce qu'il se méfiait de lui et de ses compagnons grecs [56]. Il est difficile de dire si cette tradition arabe est correcte, car plus tard, quand la conquête arabe de l'île avait réussi, les conquérants, très naturellement, étaient

---

qu'après sa victoire (NUWAYRĪ, trad. AMARI, p. 174). S'il n'y avait pas laissé de garnison en sortant de Mazara, cela pourrait signifier que son armée restait près de la ville et qu'il comptait pouvoir la défendre lui-même contre un coup de main. Mais Nuwayrī dit seulement qu'Asad nomma un commandant après la bataille. Probablement, il y avait laissé une garnison avant de sortir et après la bataille de Balāṭa nomma un de ses meilleurs officiers commandant pour assurer ses communications.

[55] AMARI, *Biblioteca Arabo-Sicula*, trad. italienne, p. 23; HOLM, *Geschichte*, III, p. 511; G. B. PELLEGRINI, *Terminologia geografica araba* (n. 52), p. 183. La seule exception que j'aie trouvée est l'opinion de Pietro Longo, citée par Giacomo Giacomazzi, sans indication de titre et de date, dans son oeuvre de vulgarisation (guide) sur Calatafimi, Palermo, 1961, p. 9, d'après laquelle le nom dériverait de Diocles Phimes qui, d'après Cicéron (*Seconde action contre Verrès*, III, 40.93), avait pris à bail des terres dans le territoire de Ségeste. Mais pourquoi les Arabes auraient-ils perpétué la mémoire d'un cultivateur du temps de la République Romaine mort neuf siècles auparavant, d'autant plus que pendant ces neuf siècles le nom de Phimès n'apparaît nulle part dans la nomenclature topographique du territoire de Ségeste?

[56] Ce détail se trouve déjà dans le premier récit arabe qui nous soit parvenu, le *Riyāḍ an-nufūs* du onzième siècle, et n'y est attribué à aucune source précise: « Narrasi che 'Asad abbia detto a Eufemio, il cristiano, ambasciatore [dei sollevati di

disposés à ignorer la contribution d'Euphémius et de ses amis grecs et de s'attribuer exclusivement le mérite des conquêtes. En tout cas, le nom de la ville de Calatafimi, où mille ans plus tard Garibaldi et ses Mille devaient battre l'armée du roi Bourbon de Naples, prouve formellement que dans les premières années de la conquête arabe on était prêt à admettre les services d'Euphémius et même à lui rendre l'honneur de nommer une ville nouvelle d'après lui. Ainsi la présence de trois localités nommées Balata dans la proximité de « la forteresse d'Euphémius » (Calatafimi) prouve que la grande bataille fut livrée non loin de cette ville et de l'ancienne Ségeste, mais le nom de Calatafimi dans le voisinage du champ de bataille démontre aussi qu'Euphémius doit avoir apporté une contribution des plus importantes à la victoire arabe [57].

Ce résultat permet une seconde conclusion. Si le nom de Calatafimi est l'écho des activités d'Euphémius à l'occasion de la victoire arabe de Balāṭa, il s'ensuit que le champ de bataille n'était pas loin du site de cette ville, donc une des localités appelées Balata au nord de Ségeste. Il se peut, comme Nuwayrī semble vouloir le dire, que le pré ou la plaine où eut lieu la bataille fut appelée plus tard par les habitants de langue arabe « Plaine de Balāṭa » d'après le général vaincu [58]. Mais il est plus probable que c'est là une façon d'embellir l'histoire et qu'en vérité la Contrada Balata, comme les autres endroits en Sicile de ce nom, doit son appellation à ses pierres polies. En tout cas, on sera justifié dorénavant d'appeler le conflit décisif entre l'armée d'Asad et celle de Balāṭa la bataille de Ségeste.

Passons à l'étape suivante de la marche des Arabes, l'église d'Euphémie. L'identification proposée par Amari avec Licata moderne sur la côte méridionale de l'île n'est pas convaincante. Elle est basée sur une correction du texte de Nuwayrī. Le chroniqueur arabe dit qu'après la bataille de Balāṭa « le cadi Asad marchait vers l'église qui se trouvait sur la côte et s'appelait de [Sainte] Euphémie » [59]. Amari proposait de

---

Sicilia?]: Scostate da noi, non abbiamo bisogno d'aiuto vostro... » (trad. AMARI, p. 78). Voir aussi IBN AL-AṬĪR, trad. AMARI, p. 93: « ... i Musulmani avvertirono Eufemio e i suoi seguaci di metterci in disparte », et NUWAYRĪ, trad. AMARI, p. 174: « ma fece ('Asad) trarre in disparte Eufemio coi suoi seguaci ricusando l'aiuto loro ».

[57] Du reste L. M. HARTMANN, *Geschichte Italiens im Mittelalter*, III, part 1, Gotha, 1908, p. 176, à déjà soupçonné que les contributions d'Euphémius aux evahisseurs doivent avoir été bien plus grandes que ne l'admet la tradition arabe.

[58] NUWAYRĪ, texte arabe, éd. AMARI, p. 428, l. 10: 'Asad marchait à la rencontre de Balāṭa « qui était dans un pré appelé d'après lui (*wa huwa bimarğin yansubu ilayhi*) ». Un cas parallèle: la ville de Caltavuturo, au sud-est de Termini Imerese, doit son nom actuel à un officier arabe Abū aṭ-Ṭawr qui y fut tué avec toute son armée en 881; voir AMARI, *Storia*, I, p. 562.

[59] Trad. AMARI, p. 174: « Il cadì 'Asad intanto, lasciato il comando di Mazara ad 'Abû Zakî 'al Kinânî, marciò verso una chiesa che giacea su la costiera e s'addimandava di [Santa] Eufemia ».

corriger « Euphémie » en « Finzia ». Or un texte, qui avait échappé à Amari, prouve qu'il y avait en réalité une église Sainte-Euphémie en Sicile bâtie à la fin du huitième siècle, bien qu'on ignore son site[60]. On se gardera donc de suivre Amari et de corriger le texte de Nuwayrī, ce qui veut dire qu'à ce moment il n'y a pas moyen de placer l'église sicilienne Sainte-Euphémie.

Ensuite, Nuwayrī fait mention de l'église de al-M.s.l.qīn, ou de al-Š.l.qīn d'après un autre manuscrit. Amari, non sans quelque hésitation, propose de la situer à Marsà aš-Salūq, dont fait mention Idrīsī comme étant située à huit lieues arabes à l'est de l'embouchure du fleuve Salso, l'ancien Refugium Gelae, la Falconara moderne[61]. Il est vrai qu'il y a quelque ressemblance entre les noms, mais Amari nous dit très justement dans sa traduction d'Idrīsī que *šalūq* veut dire « scirocco » et il rejette une identification de Marsà aš-Salūq avec Sciacca parce que le nom de cette ville est arabe, donc postérieur à l'invasion musulmane. Pour la même raison al-M.s.l.qīn ne peut être identique avec Marsà aš-Salūq. En effet, on va voir que tous les autres noms topographiques mentionnés par Nuwayrī pour les événements siciliens des années 827/8 sont pré-arabes. Pour cette raison, il faut renoncer à vouloir identifier l'église de al-M.s.l.qin avec le Marsà aš-Salūq d'Idrīsī et de la placer à Falconara, comme le proposait Amari. Les hypothèses d'Amari sur cette église et sur celle Sainte-Euphémie étant donc écartées, il faut aussi conclure qu'il ne reste plus la moindre preuve de sa thèse que les Arabes auraient marché de Mazara à Syracuse le long de la côte méridionale de la Sicile.

Reste la forteresse de al-K.rāt. Ibn al-Atīr en dit que l'armée d'Asad arriva à cette forteresse et qu'une grande quantité de personnes

[60] VASILIEV, *Byzance*, I, p. 76, n. 3; BURY, *History*, p. 299, n. 2. Il s'agit de l'histoire des reliques de Ste. Euphémie, composée entre 796 et 806 par Constantin, évêque de Tios Ce texte vient d'être republié par F. HALKIN, *Euphémie de Chalcédoine*, dans « Subsidia Hagiographica », XLI, 1965, p. 81-106, surtout p. 104: ὡς καὶ τὴν χεῖρα τὴν ἁγίαν, δι' ἧς τὸν τόμον ἐδέξατο, ἀπὸ Νικήτα πατρικίου, τὸ ἐπίκλην Μονομάχου, ἐν τῇ Σικελῶν νήσῳ τῇ μάρτυρι ναὸν δειμαμένου, ἀναθέσθαι φασίν. Le patrice Nicétas Monomaque est très probablement identique, comme l'a récemment démontré Mademoiselle D. PAPACHRYSSANTOU, *Un Confesseur du second iconoclasme. La vie du patrice Nicétas (m. 836)*, dans « Centre de recherche d'histoire et civilisation byzantines. Travaux et Mémoires », III, 1968, p. 309-351, surtout p. 316 s., avec le patrice Nicétas qui fut nommé stratège de la Sicile en 796 ou 797. Malheureusement, l'extrait de sa biographie dans le *Synaxaire Constantinopolitain* ne parle pas de sa fondation de l'église Sainte-Euphémie en Sicile et dans le seul manuscrit de cette oeuvre hagiographique, éditée par Mademoiselle Papachryssantou, manquent les chapitres concernant la carrière laïque de Nicétas, où aurait dû être mentionnée la fondation de l'église sicilienne. Je tiens à remercier Mademoiselle Papachryssantou qui a bien voulu répondre à mes questions avant la publication de son article.

[61] AMARI, *Storia*, I, p. 399 s., n. 1. Voir IDRĪSĪ, trad. AMARI, p. 31. Dans DUFOUR et AMARI, *Carte comparée*, p. 32, Amari met un point d'interrogation après son identification et marque Kanīset el-M.s.lqīn comme étant de position inconnue.

s'y étaient réunies [62]. Nuwayrī, d'après la traduction Amari, nous informe que lorsque les Arabes étaient en marche vers l'église de al-M.s.l.qīn, une délégation de patriciens syracusains se présenta pour entamer des négociations. En même temps, la population de l'île se serait réunie dans la forteresse d' al-K.rāt où l'on rassemblait toutes les richesses du pays. Le cadi Asad se serait aperçu que les Syracusains le trompaient pour gagner du temps, pour renforcer la forteresse (d' al-K.rāt) et pour y enfermer tout l'or, l'argent et les provisions (al-miyar) qui se trouvaient dans le faubourg et dans les églises. C'est pourquoi Asad aurait ouvert les hostilités contre Syracuse [63].

Dans sa *Storia*, Amari proposait, en 1854, que la forteresse de al-K.rāt était l'ancienne Acrae, l'actuelle Palazzolo Acreide, située quarante-trois kilomètres à l'ouest de Syracuse [64]. Encore une fois, plusieurs historiens postérieurs ont suivi Amari [65]. Pourtant, cette identification se heurte à des difficultés qui ressortissent du texte même de Nuwayrī. Regardons de plus près le texte arabe. Nuwayrī nous dit que, lorsque les patriciens de Syracuse vinrent rencontrer Asad pendant sa marche vers l'église de al-M.s.l.qīn, le peuple de l'île (*ahl al-ğazīrah*) se réunit dans la forteresse de al-K.rāt (*qal'at al-K.rāt*) et y assembla toutes les possessions de l'île (*ğamīc amwāl al-ğazīrah*). Plus loin, il parle de tout l'or, argent et provisions du faubourg et des églises. Le peuple, les possessions et les provisions de quelle île? Amari ne s'est pas prononcé à ce sujet, mais il paraît avoir été d'avis que Nuwayrī parlait de la Sicile entière [66]. Vasiliev et Bury ont pensé plutôt à Syracuse [67]. Le texte arabe ne laisse aucun doute que la seconde opinion est correcte. En effet, cela aurait été la folie suprême, et d'ailleurs tout à fait impraticable du point de vue de la politique intérieure des cités siciliennes, que de concentrer les habitants, possessions et provisions des villes

---

[62] Trad. AMARI, p. 93: « I Musulmani... arrivati ad una rocca detta Qal'at 'al-Kurrāt nella quale s'era raccolta gran gente etc. ».

[63] Trad. AMARI, p. 174: Asad « mosse poi verso la chiesa 'Al-Maslaqîn. Allora gli si appresentò una brigata di patrizii Siracusani, i quali per frode ed inganno gli domandarono l' 'amàn [mentre] la gente dell'isola si adunava nella rocca di 'Al K.rāt, nella quale si raccoglieano [altresì] tutte le ricchezze del paese... il cadì 'Asad, sostato parecchi giorni, si accorse che costoro lo raggiravano e menavanlo per le lunghe a fin di rafforzare il castello e di racchiudervi tutto l'oro, l'argento e le vittuaglie che erano sparsi nel borgo e nelle chiese. Avanzossi dunque; denunziò le ostilità etc. ». La traduction française de VASILIEV, *Byzance*, I, p. 381, est à peu près la même, sauf qu'au lieu de « rafforzare il castello » on y lit: « réparer *leur* forteresse ». On verra plus loin que c'est là une différence importante.

[64] AMARI, *Storia*, I, p. 400 s. et n. 1.

[65] VASILIEV, *Byzance*, I, p. 77; BURY, *History*, p. 299.

[66] AMARI, *Storia*, I, p. 399 s.: « Quanti Siciliani non perdettero l'animo al primo disastro, avean raccolto ad Acri, credo io, le poche armi che rimaneano nell'isola etc. »; voir aussi p. 402.

[67] VASILIEV, *Byzance*, I, p. 78 et BURY, *History*, p. 299.

autres que Syracuse, disons de Palerme ou de Messine, villes qui n'étaient pas encore menacées par l'avance musulmane, dans une même forteresse. Nuwayrī nous raconte plus loin qu'Asad s'aperçut qu'ils, c'est-à-dire les Syracusains qu'Euphémius venait d'encourager de résister aux Arabes, le trompaient « afin de préparer leur fort (*ḥiṣnahum*) et d'y faire entrer tout ce qui se trouvait dans le faubourg (*ar-rabaḍ*) et dans les églises ». Un peu plus bas, il raconte que les Syracusains trompèrent Asad « jusqu'à ce qu'ils eussent réparé leur forteresse (*ḥiṣnahum*) et y eussent porté tout l'or, l'argent et les provisions qui se trouvaient dans le faubourg et dans les églises ». Le fort (*ḥiṣn*) des Syracusains est évidemment identique avec « la forteresse d' al-K.rāt » (*qal'at al-K.rāt*) mentionnée plus haut par Nuwayrī. Mais puisque, selon Nuwayrī, al-K.rāt est *leur* forteresse et que c'est les Syracusains qui y portent leurs objets de valeur, il s'ensuit que l'île dont parle Nuwayrī ne peut être la Sicile entière. Il s'agit, plutôt, de l'île d'Ortygie, le quartier le plus ancien de la ville de Syracuse. C'était encore en 877 le quartier principal de la ville et tous les autres quartiers en formaient les faubourgs[68]. Mais il en découle aussi que la forteresse de al-K.rāt, la forteresse des Syracusains, « leur fort », comme dit Nuwayrī, ne pouvait être à 43 kilomètres de l'île d'Ortygie et de son faubourg qu'elle devait protéger, surtout si l'on y déposait, comme le dit Nuwayrī, toutes les provisions qui se trouvaient dans le faubourg, car elles n'auraient servi à rien en cas de siège si elles étaient enfermées dans une forteresse à grande distance de Syracuse et dont les Arabes pouvaient à tout moment couper les communications. Elle devait être beaucoup plus proche et l'identificaiton de al-K.rāt avec l'ancienne Acrae, proposée par Amari est donc inadmissible. Il semble qu'Amari lui-même ait commencé à douter de sa solution, car quatre ans après la publication de sa *Storia* il proposa, il est vrai avec deux points d'interrogation et sans donner ses raisons, de situer al-K.rāt ou à Acrae ou bien à Carrano près de Syracuse[69].

Avant de proposer une identification positive de al-K.rāt, il faut insister que la conclusion à laquelle nous venons d'arriver n'a rien à faire avec les ressemblances de noms grecs et arabes, ressemblances qui ont égaré tant de nos illustres prédécesseurs. La constatation qu' al-K.rāt devait être située près de l'île d'Ortygie ressort simplement d'une lecture attentive d'Ibn al-Aṯīr et de Nuwayrī.

Essayons maintenant d'identifier positivement le nom de la for-

---

[68] AMARI, *Storia*, I, p. 536.
[69] DUFOUR et AMARI, *Carte comparée*, p. 32. Ici Amari appelle la forteresse K.rrāth ou K.rrāt.

teresse d' al-K.rāt. Il ne se trouve que dans les chroniques ayant trait à l'invasion arabe de 827: Ibn al-Aṯīr, Nuwayrī et Ibn Ḥaldūn. Ni Amari ni aucun de ses successeurs n'ont réussi à trouver de nom topographique sicilien qui lui corresponde, à l'exception d'Acrae, qui est impossible comme on vient de le voir. S'agirait-il peut-être non d'un nom propre mais de la description d'une localité? Amari lui-même a insisté que les indications topographiques pour la campagne de 827 doivent être pré-arabes. Cherchons donc des mots grecs dont les caractères arabes pourraient être la traduction ou transcription. Deux possibilités se présentent: τὸ κάστρον (ou équivalent) τοῦ κέρατος ou τῶν κεράτων. La graphie des mots arabes chez Nuwayrī correspond exactement à ces mots grecs. Or le mot κέρας signifie litéralement « la corne (d'un animal) », puis toutes choses ayant la forme d'une corne, specialement le bras d'un fleuve, un promontoire ou un isthme, ou une baie ou un golfe d'une mer [71]. Il faudra donc chercher un ou plusieurs isthmes ou golfes non loin de l'île d'Ortygie [72]. Quant aux isthmes on pourrait penser à la section sud-est de l'ancien quartier d'Achradine, le long du Corso Umberto actuel, peut-être aussi à la partie nord-ouest d'Ortygie même où se trouve maintenant le Bureau de Poste. Si l'on traduit κέρας par baie, on songe naturellement aux deux ports de Syracuse, le Porto Grande et le Porto Piccolo modernes. Pour choisir entre ces deux alternatives — fortifications des isthmes ou fortifications des deux ports de Syracuse? — on peut signaler qu'il y avait des fortifications des ports de Syracuse et avant et après le siège de 827/8. Procope de Césarée écrit qu'en 550/1 l'empereur Justinien dépêcha une flotte commandée par l'ex-*praefectus augustalis* d'Egypte Libérius en Sicile pour délivrer l'île des forces du roi ostrogoth Totila. En ce moment la ville de Syracuse était assiégée par les Goths. Libérius et toute sa flotte, dit Procope, réussirent à entrer au port et à pénétrer au dedans des murailles. Il y avait donc à Syracuse, en 550/1 du moins,

---

[70] Autres graphies du même nom dans Ibn al-Aṯīr: al-K.rāb, al-K.rāt; dans Ibn Ḥaldūn, qui suit de près le texte de Nuwayrī: al-K.rrāt, al-K.rād.

[71] Voir les lexiques; puis OBERHUMMER, *sub verbo* Keras, dans PAULY-WISSOWA-KROLL, *Realenzyklopädie der Klassischen Altertumswissenschaft*: « sowohl für Landvorsprünge als für Meeresbuchten gebraucht »; et C. MÜLLER, *Geographi Graeci Minores*, I, Paris, 1882, p. 10: « κέρας vocabulum plerumque de montium verticibus vel de promontoriis in mare excurrentibus usurpat; nonnumquam vero etiam fluviorum ostia tamquam Oceani cornua, nec non maris sinus tortuose in terram penetrantes eadem voce describuntur ». Le κέρας le plus fameux au Moyen-Age était la Corne d'Or à Constantinople.

[72] Voir les cartes de Syracuse ancienne, par exemple dans HOLM, *Geschichte*, II, carte XIII, ou dans *Westermann's Atlas zur Weltgeschichte*, Teil I: *Vorzeit und Altertum*, Berlin etc., 1956, n. 17, II. Carte de Syracuse moderne dans *Guida d'Italia* del Touring Club Italiano, *Sicilia*, Milano, 1968, après la p. 608.

un port muni de fortifications [73]. Trois siècles plus tard, en 877/8, au cours du siège final par les Arabes qui aboutit à la conquête de la ville, les Arabes parvinrent à dominer sur mer et à bloquer l'importation de vivres dans la ville assiégée « après avoir détruit les murs entourant les deux ports qu'on appelle ' bracelets ' » [74]. Le moine Théodose, témoin oculaire de la prise de la ville, parle clairement de murs qui entouraient et le Porto Grande et le Porto Piccolo. Les paroles dont il se sert: τὰ ἀμφὶ τοῖν λιμένοιν τοιχία correspondent mot par mot à la formule arabe: qal'at al-K.rāt, en grec: τὸ κάστρον τῶν κεράτων, en français: la forteresse des baies ou ports, où τὰ τοιχία est l'équivalent de qal'at et τοῖν λιμένοιν de al-K.rāt [75]. Il n'est pas aisé de préciser où au juste se trouvaient ces fortifications. A première vue, il semble qu'Amari ait raison et qu'il puisse s'agir ici non de murailles entourant le parcours entier des deux ports, mais seulement de fortifications de l'entrée septentrionale du Porto Piccolo et de l'embouchure méridionale du Porto Grande [76]. Mais la désignation courante de ces fortifications en 877/8: bracelets (βραχιόλια) laisse entrevoir qu'elles doivent avoir été circulaires (ou presque) et avoir entouré les deux ports comme un bracelet d'or encercle un bras de femme [77]. En tout cas, les murailles entourant les deux ports doivent avoir compris non seulement les ports

---

[73] *Guerres*, VII. 40. 13: ... ἔς τε τὸν λιμένα κατῆρε καὶ παντὶ τῷ στόλῳ ἐντὸς τοῦ περιβόλου ἐγένετο. HOLM, *Geschichte*, III, p. 498, croit qu'il s'agit du Petit Port. Dans la période classique, le Porto Piccolo seul était fortifié; voir K. LEHMANN-HARTLEBEN, *Die antiken Hafenanlagen des Mittelmeeres* etc., dans « Klio », XIV, 1923, p. 84 s.

[74] THÉODOSE LE MOINE ET GRAMMAIRIEN, *Lettre à l'archidiacre Léon sur la prise de Syracuse*, éd. C. O. ZURETTI, dans *Centenario della nascita di Michele Amari*, I, Palerme, 1910, p. 167. ἐθαλασσοκράτουν γὰρ οἱ πολέμιοι τὰ ἀμφὶ τοῖν λιμένοιν τοιχία, ἃ δὴ βραχιόλια ὀνομάζουσιν, ἐδαφίσαντες. Sur l'auteur, voir les remarques de VASILIEV, *Byzance*, II, p. 71 s., n. 6, et l'article de B. LAVAGNINI, *Siracusa occupata dagli Arabi e l'epistola di Teodosio Monaco*, dans « Byzantion », XXIX-XXX, 1959-1960, p. 267-279.

[75] Il est possible qu'en 827/8 un seul des deux ports était fortifié et que les fortifications de l'autre ne furent érigées qu'après ce premier et avant le second siège arabe. En ce cas al-K.rāt serait l'equivalent de τοῦ κέρατος.

[76] AMARI, *Storia*, I, p. 539.

[77] THÉODOSE LE MOINE, éd. ZURETTI, p. 168: ... ἀρτὶ τοῦ πρὸς θάλασσαν πύργου τοῦ ἐν αὐτῷ μεγάλῳ λιμένι, ἵνα δὴ τὸ δέξιον κέρας τῆς πόλεως ἐτετάχατο... κατασεισθέντος καὶ πεπτωκότος κτλ. Amari cite ce passage dans une traduction latine moderne et, dans une note que je trouve quelque peu obscure (*Storia*, I, p. 536, n. 3), semble vouloir dire que τὸ δέξιον κέρας est l'isthme nord-est de l'île d'Ortygie. Cependant, on notera que le verbe ἐτετάχατο est au pluriel (du plusqueparfait) et que le sujet (τὸ δέξιον κέρας) a donc le sens d'un pluriel. Je traduis donc: « la tour du côté de la mer dans le Grand Port, à l'endroit où l'aile droite (de la garnison ou milice) de la ville avait été placée, fut ébranlée et était tombée »; τὸ δέξιον κέρας est donc ici une partie des défenseurs de la ville et non une indication topographique. Ajoutons, d'ailleurs, que la forme assez rare ἐτετάχατο se trouve du moins deux fois dans le texte de Thucydide (V 6.5 et VII 4.6), la seconde fois précisément avec un sujet au singulier mais au sens d'un pluriel, au cours du récit du siège athénien de Syracuse, que devait bien étudier un grammairien tel que Théodose qui résidait à Syracuse: τοῖτον γὰρ μέρος τῶν ἱππέων τοῖς Συρακουσίοις.... ἐπὶ τῇ ἐν τῷ Ὀλυμπιείῳ πολίχνῃ ἐτετάχατο.

eux-mêmes, mais aussi une certaine partie de la superficie de la terre ferme pour qu'en 827/8 les habitants de l'île d'Ortygie et du faubourg (Achradine?) aient pu y déposer leurs possessions, comme le dit Nuwayrī.

En identifiant le forteresse d' al-K.rāt avec les fortifications de l'un ou des deux ports de la ville de Syracuse nous avons fini l'analyse des données topographiques dans la tradition arabe [78]. Approchons maintenant le texte vieux-slavon de ce point de vue. Il nous dit que l'armée arabe s'est rendue à deux autres localités: Marianii et Ienna. Quant à la seconde, Ienna, c'est certainement la ville d'Enna, la vieille cité située sur son rocher au « nombril de la Sicile », comme disait Cicéron [79]. Mais la mention d'Enna pose un problème chronologique. La tradition arabe ignore une attaque sur Enna avant le siège de Syracuse en 827. En revanche, elle en parle longuement après la retraite de Syracuse de l'armée arabe dans l'année suivante [80]. L'apocalypse en vieux-slavon envisagerait-elle ce siège d'Enna en 828? En ce cas, l'auteur aurait négligé complètement le long siège dramatique de Syracuse. C'est très invraisemblable, surtout chez un auteur qui dans ce qui précède s'était montré si fortement préoccupé des affaires de Syracuse. D'autre part, une tentative arabe sur Enna avant le siège de Syracuse est éminemment plausible. Balāṭa, le général grec vaincu dans la bataille de Ségeste contre les Arabes, s'était refugié d'abord à Enna [81] et sans doute il y avait conduit les restes de son armée. Il est naturel que les Arabes aient suivi le général et l'armée battus. En tout cas, il est probable que l'apocalypse en vieux-slavon nous a conservé une allusion à une première tentative arabe de prendre cette puissante forteresse. Il est fort probable qu'en 827 la tentative arabe de saisir cette grande forteresse presqu'imprenable d'Enna n'était pas très sérieuse, qu'on s'est vite aperçu de la difficulté de l'entreprise et a préféré de concentrer l'effort militaire sur la ville beaucoup plus riche de Syracuse. Enna ne devait

---

[78] Cette identification explique un autre détail curieux. Les chroniqueurs arabes ne disent rien du sort de la forteresse d'al-K.rāt. Si elle était loin de Syracuse, comme le pensait Amari (à Acrae), on s'attendrait à une remarque renseignant le lecteur si oui ou non elle tomba dans le mains des Arabes en 827/8. Or il n'y en a pas. Mais puisqu'il s'agit tout simplement des fortifications principales de l'un ou des deux ports de Syracuse, le récit de chroniqueurs arabes sur l'incapacité de l'armée arabe de prendre la ville de Syracuse suffisait.

[79] CICÉRON, Deuxième action contre Verrès, IV 48. 106.

[80] AMARI, Storia, I, p. 411-416; VASILIEV, Byzance, I, p. 83-87; BURY, History, p. 302 s.

[81] NUWAYRĪ, trad. AMARI, p. 174: « Balaṭah riparò in Castrogiovanni (= Enna); ma, temendo [ancora], passò in terra di Calabria; dov'egli fu ucciso ». Peut-être l'approche de l'armée arabe vers Enna était justement ce qui épouvantait Balāṭa et le fit fuir en Calabre.

tomber dans les mains des Arabes qu'après maints assauts postérieurs en 859.

Mais avant de mettre le siège à Enna, l'armée arabe, à l'aide d'Euphémius, s'est emparée en 827 de la ville de Marianii mentionnée dans l'apocalypse en vieux-slavon. Elle doit avoir été sur la route des envahisseurs entre Ségeste et Enna. Ce nom de ville apparaît aussi dans un texte grec très proche de l'original grec perdu de l'apocalypse en vieux-slavon [82], mais il n'est pas mentionné ailleurs, à ce que je sache. Pourtant, si l'on jette un coup d'oeil sur la carte de la Sicile, on trouvera, trente-cinq kilomètres environ à l'ouest d'Enna, la ville actuelle de Marianopoli [83]. Elle ne fut fondée qu'au dix-huitième siècle [84], mais c'était le site de l'ancien Mytistratum, muni de grandes fortifications naturelles, le Monte Castellaccio, et occupé et détruit par les Romains au cours de la Première Guerre Punique en 258 avant J.-C. [85]. Au premier siècle de notre ère cette ville existait de nouveau, car Pline l'Ancien la connaît parmi les cités stipendiaires [86]. Or le *Liber de viris illustribus urbis Romae* attribué (faussement) à Sextus Aurelius Victor nous dit qu'en 100 avant J.-C., date du sixième consulat de Caius Marius, le tribun de la plèbe Lucius Appuleius Saturninus, allié de Marius, « assigna la Sicile, l'Achaïe et la Macédonie à de nouveaux colons et employa l'or acquis par fraude ou par crime par (Q. Servilius) Caepio (cos. 106 avant J.-C.) pour l'achat de terres ». Les historiens de la République Romaine ne sont pas d'accord si ce projet a jamais été exécuté [88], mais l'existence d'une ville appelée Marianii

---

[82] Apocalypse grecque de DANIEL, éd. A. VASILIEV, dans *Anecdota Graeco-Byzantina*, Moscou, 1893, p. 39: καὶ μετὰ ταῦτα ἐκπλήξουσιν καὶ ὀλολύξουσιν υἱοὶ Ἰσμαὴλ ἀποφεύγοντες εἰς Μαριανά. καὶ μετὰ ταῦτα ἐπελεύσονται πάλιν οἱ υἱοὶ Ἰσμαὴλ εἰς τὴν γῆν τῆς Ἐλινίας (lege: Ἔννας) οἱ μὲν κλητοί, οἱ δὲ ἄκλητοι εἰς πόλιν Τυράννου. La parenté entre les textes vieux-slavon et grec saute aux yeux. Ils parlent tous les deux des Arabes en Sicile et des mêmes localités: Mariana, Enna, la Ville du Rebelle (= Syracuse).

[83] Voir, par exemple, la carte dans la *Guida d'Italia* del Touring Club Italiano, *Sicilia*, Milano, 1968, après la p. 288.

[84] Guide de la Sicile (cité dans la note précédente), p. 339: « fondata a metà del '700 dal barone Della Scala con coloni epiroti ». Je n'ai pas réussi à trouver une discussion plus détaillée de la ville moderne et de son histoire.

[85] HOLM, *Geschichte*, III, p. 17, 348.

[86] PLINE, *Histoire Naturelle*, III, 91. Consulter K. ZIEGLER, *sub verbo* Mytistraton, dans PAULY-WISSOWA-KROLL, *Realenzyklopädie der Klassischen Altertumswissenschaft*.

[87] [SEXTUS AURELIUS VICTOR], *Liber de viris illustribus urbis Romae*, éd. F. PICHLMAYR, Leipzig, 1911, 73, 5, p. 65: « Saturninus... tribunus plebis refectus Siciliam, Achaiam, Macedoniam novis colonis destinavit; et aurum dolo an scelere Caepionis partum ad emptionem agrorum convertit ».

[88] H. LAST, dans *Cambridge Ancient History*, IX, p. 169; E. BADIAN, *Foreign Clientelae (264-70 B. C.)*, Oxford, 1958, p. 203-208; H. H. SCULLARD, *From the Gracchi to Nero*, New York, 1959, p. 60, 392; J. VAN OOTEGHEM, *Caius Marius*, dans « Bibliothèque de la Faculté des Lettres de Namur », XXXV, 1964, p. 241 s.; Th. F. CARNEY,

(Marianum? Mariana?) au neuvième siècle après J.-C. laisse entrevoir la possibilité qu'au début du premier siècle avant J.-C. Saturninus, chef des *populares*, a reconstruit la vieille cité de Mytistratum en *colonia Mariana*, pour l'honneur de son associé politique, consul pour la sixième fois en 100 avant J.-C.

Nous venons de voir qu'en 827 l'armée arabe s'est dirigée des environs de Ségeste à Enna et puis à Syracuse. Répétons que ce sont là des étapes sûres et, en bonne méthode, n'insistons pas trop à ce moment sur l'identification quelque peu hypothéthique de Marianii avec Marianopoli. Assurément, l'armée arabe a marché le long d'une des routes de la Sicile qui nous sont connues des sources géographiques anciennes et médiévales [89]. Ces sources, qui datent du troisième au neuvième siècle, font connaître quatre anciennes routes romaines qui nous intéressent ici. Une première voie, la *via Valeria* ou *Pompeia* passe, comme le dit l'*Itinerarium Antonini* du troisième siècle, *per maritima loca* de Drepana sur la côte occidentale de l'île à Aquae Segestanae, deux kilomètres environ au nord-est des ruines de Ségeste, puis à Palerme, Tyndaris et Messine sur la côte septentrionale. Une seconde route partait de Lilybée, la Marsale actuelle, puis semble avoir traversé la partie occidentale de l'intérieur en passant par les sites des villes modernes de Salemi, Vita, Calatafimi, et gagnait la route côtière à l'ancienne Hykkara, au nord-ouest de Carini actuelle [90]. Une troisième route partait de Thermae à l'embouchure du fleuve Himera sur la côte du nord et puis allait à Enna, Agyrium, Centuripe, Etna et Catane. Enfin, une quatrième route longeait la côte orientale de la Sicile de Messine à Catane et Syracuse. L'armée d'Asad doit donc avoir marché de Mazara à Ségeste ou bien le long de la route côtière à l'ouest de l'île jusqu'à Drepana, la Trapani moderne, puis sur la *via Valeria* à Ségeste, ou bien de Mazara à Lilybée et puis par la route de l'intérieur de Lilybée à Ségeste. Non loin de cette ville est intervenue la grande bataille entre Arabes et Grecs. Après le combat, l'armée arabe doit avoir gagné la

A Biography of C. Marius, dans « Proceedings of the African Classical Association », Supplement n⁰ 1, Assen, 1969, p. 41, n. 197.

[89] Sur le réseau des routes siciliennes, voir HOLM, *Geschichte*, III, p. 260-263, 481-489; V. M. SCRAMUZZA, dans T. FRANK, *An Economic Survey of Ancient Rome*, III, Baltimore, 1937, 291-293; PACE, *Arte e Civiltà*, I, p. 464-483; G. UGGERI, *La Sicilia nella « Tabula Peutingeriana*, dans « Vichiana », VI, 1969, p. 11-55. On trouvera les routes mentionnées dans le texte marquées de façon assez claire sur la carte de l'Italie ancienne (n⁰ 8) dans *Murray's Classical Atlas for Schools*, éd. G. B. GRUNDY, seconde édition. Pour plus de détails sur la géographie ancienne de la Sicile, mais sans indication des routes, voir la carte de la Sicile dans le troisième volume de l'ouvrage de Holm.

[90] La seconde de ces routes se lit très clairement dans l'*Itinerarium Antonini*, mais ne se retrouve que d'une manière très confuse dans le géographe anonyme de Ravenne et dans Guido; voir HOLM, *Geschichte*, III, p. 484.

côte septentrionale et s'être dirigée le long de cette côte, pour une partie du moins de la route de Ségeste à Thermae, la Termini Imerese moderne. A cet endroit elle doit avoir pris la route de l'intérieur qui la menait par Enna à Catane et puis le long de la côte orientale à Syracuse. C'est pendant la marche à travers l'intérieur de l'île qu'a eu lieu la prise de Marianii facilitée par Euphémius, comme le dit le texte vieux-slavon, car nous venons de voir qu'il s'agit probablement de la Marianopoli moderne. C'est aussi pendant cette marche à travers l'intérieur qu'Asad a essayé en vain de s'emparer d'Enna.

Le cours de cette marche nous aide aussi à serrer d'un peu plus prés la situation des deux églises Sainte-Euphémie et de al-Maslaqīn (ou de al-Š.l.qīn), où l'armée arabe, au dire de Nuwayrī, s'est dirigée après la bataille de Ségeste. Nuwayrī nous renseigne que la première de ces églises se trouvait au bord de la mer. D'autre part, on vient de voir que l'armée n'a marché au bord de la mer que pendant deux phases de son avance après la bataille de Ségeste: le long de la côte septentrionale entre Aquae Segestanae et Thermae (ou du moins pour une partie de cette marche) et encore sur la côte orientale entre Catane et Syracuse. C'est donc là qu'il faut chercher les deux églises, mais il est difficile de choisir entre ces possibilités. Il me semble plus probable que l'église de al-Maslaqīn, où les patriciens de Syracuse vinrent rencontrer Asad pour se soumettre, se trouve assez près de Syracuse, plutôt que sur la côte septentrionale, si loin de la ville, lorsqu'on ne pouvait pas même être sûr que les Arabes avaient l'intention de l'attaquer. Mais ce n'est là qu'un argument de probabilité et il ne faudra pas écarter la possibilité que les Syracusains aient préféré négocier avec les envahisseurs quand ces derniers se trouvaient encore sur la côte du nord, à grande distance de leur cité.

La discussion des trois problèmes posés au commencement de cet article étant terminée, on notera que les débuts des conquêtes arabes en Sicile se présentent, selon nous, sous un jour assez différent de celui qu'on trouve dans les ouvrages classiques sur ce sujet. Il sera donc utile de résumer le cours des événements tels qu'ils se dégagent de l'analyse qui précède et de mettre en relief les conclusions que nous croyons pouvoir ajouter à celles de nos prédecesseurs aussi bien que celles qui s'écartent des leurs. La sécession sicilienne a commencé pendant la révolte de Thomas le Slave en Asie Mineure (821-823). A cet égard l'hypothèse brillante d'Amari a été confirmée par l'apocalypse en vieux-slavon. Le gouvernement central, étant à court d'argent parce que les forces de Thomas s'étaient approprié la plupart des revenus de l'Asie Mineure et voyant la capitale même de l'empire menacée par les armes et les flottes des insurgés, décida d'augmenter la recette d'impôts dans les provinces fidèles à l'empereur Michel II, notamment en Sicile. C'est encore le texte vieux-slavon et un poème inédit grec attribué au philosophe Bryson qui nous renseignent à ce sujet. L'empereur dépêcha des envoyés aux régions occidentales de l'empire. Quand ils arrivèrent à Syracuse pour présenter leurs demandes fiscales, des conflits armés éclatèrent dans la ville. Une partie des habitants restait fidèle au gouvernement, mais d'autres groupes s'opposaient au paiement des impôts nouveaux ou même préconisaient la rupture. On ne sait au juste quel fut le résultat de ces désordres internes à Syracuse et si, dans cette première période, le mouvement s'est répandu au reste de la Sicile. Il est même possible, comme le croyait Amari, que cette première sécession fut suivie d'une période pendant laquelle Syracuse s'est soumise de nouveau au gouvernement de Constantinople [91].

En tout cas, ce doit être au cours de cette première période que le tourmarque sicilien Euphémius s'est distingué par ses incursions navales des côtes de l'état aghlabide en Afrique du Nord. Il doit avoir réussi à gagner les sympathies de plusieurs autres officiers de marine siciliens et s'être créé une position importante de chef de faction, comme le dit la chronique de Naples, dans la politique interne de Syracuse. A un moment donné, le gouvernement de Michel II à Constantinople donna l'ordre au stratège de la Sicile de faire le procès à Euphémius pour avoir épousé une religieuse et de le punir, le cas échéant. Il n'y a aucun doute, comme l'a déjà observé Amari, que dans la personne d'Euphémius le gouvernement impérial a voulu frapper les éléments de loyauté suspecte en Sicile, qui avaient pris part à l'émeute syracusaine au temps de la révolte de Thomas. La réaction d'Euphémius aux ordres de l'empereur fut de continuer ou de ranimer cette émeute On est en 825 ou 826. Le tourmarque avec ses compagnons d'armes s'empara de la ville de Syracuse, y livra bataille et vainquit les forces loyalistes et fit exécuter leur commandant. Puis, il se fit proclamer *rex*, comme on sait par un sceau de plomb qui appartenait jadis au professeur Salinas. En qualité de *rex*, Euphémius nomma gouverneur d'une certaine région de la Sicile un de ses partisans, ques les sources arabes appellent Balāṭa. Ce dernier, cependant, se révolta contre Euphémius, non, comme on l'a cru, pour se ranger du côté de Michel II, mais parce qu'il briguait lui-même la position suprême en Sicile. Les deux rebelles, Euphémius et Balāṭa, se disputèrent le pouvoir les armes à la main et une bataille sanglante fut livrée — on le sait de par l'apocalypse en vieux-slavon — à Achradine. Euphémius fut battu et s'infuit en

[91] AMARI, *Storia*, I, 378.

Afrique pour demander du secours militaire à lémir de Qayrawān.

Notre discussion n'a révélé rien de nouveau sur les négociations à Qayrawān, sauf qu'Euphémius paraît avoir obtenu de Ziyādat Allāh, ou avoir cru obtenir de lui, la promesse qu'après une conquête arabe une partie de la Sicile comprenant le territoire de Syracuse et peut-être davantage ne serait pas occupée par · les Arabes, mais serait gouvernée de façon plus ou moins autonome par lui-même en qualité de *rex*. Il n'y a pas d'autre moyen de comprendre le conseil donné par Euphémius à la ville de Syracuse avant le commencement du siège en 827 de tenir ferme et d'autre part les négociations d'Euphémius l'année suivante avec les habitants d'Enna pendant le siège de cette forteresse [92]. En général, il est évident que les services rendus par le « roi » Euphémius à l'entreprise d'Asad furent bien plus importants que ne le laissent entrevoir la tradition arabe et les historiens modernes (sauf L.M. Hartmann). Après les succès décisifs des Arabes en Sicile dans la deuxième moitié du neuvième siècle, les conquérants se trouvaient gênés par la mémoire de leur collaborateur grec. En réalité, c'est Euphémius, ancien tourmarque de la marine sicilienne, qui doit avoir empêché toute résistance lors du débarquement du corps expéditionnaire d'Asad à Mazara le 17 juin 827. D'ailleurs, le nom arabe de Calatafimi (« forteresse d'Euphémius ») prouve que lors de la bataille ᾽entre les forces arabes d'Asad et les troupes grecques de Balāṭa à (ou non loin de) Ségeste Euphémius et ses partisans ont joué un rôle de première importance. Enfin, tandis qu'en 827 à Syracuse Euphémius a voulu empêcher la prise arabe de la ville et qu'à Enna en 828 il a payé de sa vie la tentative de faire tomber cette forteresse entre les mains des Arabes, c'est Euphémius, selon l'apocalypse en vieux-slavon, qui leur a procuré la ville de Marianii.

Quant à la route suivie par les envahisseurs en 827, il n'y a pas le moindre fondement dans nos sources en faveur de la thèse d'Amari que l'armée d'Asad aurait marché de Mazara le long de la côte méri-

---

[92] Comparer le récit de NUWAYRĪ sur le siège arabe de Syracuse en 827/8, trad. AMARI, p 174: « Al sentir ciò (c'est-à-dire l'offerte des Syracusains de se rendre) destossi nell'animo d'Eufemio la carità di [patria che lo portava a favorire] gli Infedeli (les Chrétiens de Syracuse); perlocchè mandò a dir loro che tenessero fermo... » avec celui de IBN AL-AṮĪR sur le siège d'Enna en 828, trad. AMARI, p. 94: Les Arabes « mossero contro la città di Castrogiovanni (= Enna), accompagnati da Eufemio. Allora i cittadini, usciti per abboccarsi con costui, gli si prostrarono dinanzi e gli assentirono di riconoscerlo re del paese ». Voir aussi NUWAYRĪ, trad. AMARI, p. 175. Devant Syracuse Euphémius tâcha d'empêcher la conquête arabe, devant Enna il est leur collaborateur fidèle. Donc ou bien Enna ne faisait pas partie du territoire promis à Qayrawān à Euphémius comme appartenant à son futur royaume, ou les Arabes avaient promis, après leur échec devant Syracuse, d'honorer à Enna la promesse de l'émir qu'ils avaient voulu violer à Syracuse et de lui livrer Enna s'ils pouvaient s'en emparer.

dionale de l'île. Au contraire, elle s'est dirigée de Mazara à Ségeste. C'est dans les environs des ruines de cette ville ancienne, et non à l'ouest de Corleone ou au sud-est de Mazara comme le croyait Amari, qu'a eu lieu la fameuse bataille entre Arabes et Grecs que les sources arabes placent dans la plaine de Balāṭa. De Ségeste l'armée arabe a continué vers Thermae sur ou près de la côte septentrionale. Là elle a pris l'ancienne voie romaine pour Catane qui traversait l'intérieur de l'île en direction sud-est. Au cours de cette phase de la marche, Euphémius réussit à livrer à ses amis arabes la ville de Marianii mentionnée dans l'apocalypse en vieux-slavon, probablement au site de l'ancienne ville de Mytistraton et de Marianopoli moderne. En passant près de la ville d'Enna, on tenta un premier coup sur cette forteresse, mais les forces d'Asad n'étaient préparées d'aucune façon pour le siège d'une position aussi formidable, et d'ailleurs des renforcements arrivèrent pour la secourir, comme nous dit l'apocalypse. Impossible de préciser où se trouvaient les deux églises mentionnées par Nuwayrī comme étapes de la marche, l'église Sainte-Euphémie érigée par le patrice Nicétas à la fin du huitième siècle et celle de al-M.s.l.qīn, mais on devrait les chercher sur la côte orientale de l'île entre Catane et Syracuse ou, moins probablement, sur la côte septentrionale entre Ségeste et Termini Imerese. Enfin, la forteresse de al-K.rāt mentionnée par Ibn al-Aṯīr et Nuwayrī, où les habitants de Syracuse avaient déposé leurs possessions précieuses et leurs provisions, n'est pas l'ancienne Acrae, le Palazzolo Acreide actuel, comme le voulait Amari. Il s'agit, plutôt, da la traduction-transcription arabe des mots: τὸ κάστρον τῶν κεράτων (ou: τοῦ κέρατος), en d'autres mots des fortifications d'un ou des deux ports de Syracuse qu'un demi-siècle plus tard, lors du siège final arabe de Syracuse, le moine Théodose allait appeler τὰ ἀμφὶ τοῖν λιμένοιν τοιχία et le peuple « bracelets » (βραχιόλια).

Quels furent les résultats de la grande campagne aghlabide de 827/8 en Sicile? Les protagonistes sont tous morts pendant qu'elle suivait son cours. Balāṭa fut exécuté en Calabre, sans doute par des agents du gouvernement impérial. Euphémius fut tué dans un guet-apens non loin d'Enna par des habitants de cette ville en 828. Le vieux cadi Asad, septuagénaire né à Ḥarrān en Iraq en 759/60, était mort au cours du siège de Syracuse, de l'épidémie qui y ravageait le camp arabe, et encore au douzième siècle on montrait son tombeau aux voyageurs sur la route de Catane à Enna [93]. L'armée arabe ne réussit pas à s'emparer de Syracuse et battit la retraite. Elle saisit la ville de Mineo, à l'inté-

---

[93] Harawī, trad. Amari, Appendice, p. 1.

rieur de l'île, au nord-ouest de Syracuse, mais elle souffrit un second échec devant Enna et ne se maintint pas longtemps à Agrigente. On ne saurait dire ce qui devint de leur base de Marianii ou de leur fondation de Calatafimi. Deux années après le débarquement à Mazara, seuls ce port et Mineo restaient dans les mains des Arabes. Mais des renforcements furent envoyés en Sicile par les Arabes d'un peu partout, d'Espagne, de la Crète et de Qayrawān, et au cours du neuvième siècle presque toute la Sicile et une partie de l'Italie méridionale tombèrent dans les mains des Musulmans. Ainsi les débuts des conquêtes arabes en Sicile ouvrirent un chapitre nouveau de l'histoire politique et culturelle de l'Europe méridionale.

University of California, Berkeley

ADDITIONAL BIBLIOGRAPHY

I have attempted an historical interpretation of the Balkan place names in the Belgrade ms. no.466(632) of the Old Church Slavonic Vision of Daniel (p.1004f. and nn.25-26) in no.XVI below.

XV

HISTORIENS BYZANTINS ET CROYANCES ESCHATOLOGIQUES*

Dans la communication que j'ai l'honneur de présenter au Congrès il s'agira de l'influence de certaines croyances eschatologiques sur l'historiographie byzantine. Les textes primaires qui contiennent ces croyances, aussi bien que ces croyances elles-mêmes et leur développement historique, ont formé le sujet d'un livre remarquable, quoique déjà ancien, celui de Wilhelm Bousset sur la légende de l'Antéchrist.[1] Ces textes primaires appartiennent à une quantité de genres littéraires — rappelons seulement les homélies grecques et syriaques sur l'Antéchrist attribuées à tort ou à raison à St. Ephrem; les apocalypses dites de Pseudo-Jean, de Pierre, d'Ezra; les poèmes apologétiques de Commodien; enfin les Oracles Sibyllins. Ils s'échelonnent du moins du troisième siècle (voir le traité d'Hippolyte sur l'Antéchrist) à travers le moyen-âge byzantin (on pense surtout à la prophécie de la Sibylle Tiburtine; aux Visions de Daniel et au Pseudo-Méthode) jusqu'aux derniers siècles de Byzance et même à la période de la domination turque. Bousset a démontré que ces textes si variés étaient basés sur une tradition qu'il croyait, peut-être à tort, être orale, mais certainement datant de l'époque paléochretinne, sinon juive. Cette tradition eschatologique est distincte de celle du livre canonique de la Révélation de S. Jean en ce qu'elle regarde l'empire romain non pas comme une puissance antichrétienne mais au contraire comme une garantie contre l'arrivée de l'Antéchrist. Ces textes s'ingénuent à décrire en détails minutieux les événements des temps finals. Il y a, premièrement, certains signes et omina qui annonçaient l'arrivée de l'Antéchrist. Puis on s'occupe du ou des noms

---

*Cette communication forme les prémices d'un projet de travail sur les textes et idées politico-eschatologiques des Byzantins. Elle a été écrite au cours de l'année académique 1960-1 que j'ai pu passer en Europe grâce à des bourses d'études du Social Science Research Council, du Committee on the Behavorial Science Fund (Ford Foundation) et de la Rackham School for Graduate Studies de l'Université de Michigan. Je tiens à remercier ces organisations de leur assistance généreuse.

[1] *Wilhelm Bousset*, The Antichrist Legend etc. (London, 1896).

de l'Antéchrist et Satan, de la tribu juive à laquelle il appartient, de sa physiognomie. On parle de ses victoires militaires sur les armées de certains royaumes, de ses méfaits dans le Temple de Jérusalem encore existant ou reconstruit par l'Antéchrist, de ses miracles, de ses messagers et serviteurs. Il va régner sur le monde entier envahi par toutes sortes de maux tels que sécheresses ou famines et le signe de sa domination doit être un sceau en forme de serpent. Elie et Enoch lui doivent faire opposition, il les tue, les journées sont raccourcies par la clémence divine, enfin l'Antéchrist lui-même est vaincu par une intervention divine et le royaume des cieux est établi.

Etant donné que dans cette communication nous nous intéressons tout particulièrement à l'influence de ces croyances sur les historiens byzantins qui s'occupent naturellement d'empereurs et dynasties, de guerres contre des ennemis étrangers de l'empire tels que les Perses, Arabes, Bulgares, Turcs, de guerres civiles, de crises économiques et de cataclysmes naturels, il importe de préciser un peu davantage ce que les textes eschatologiques étudiés par Bousset disent sur les événements «contrôlables» qui devaient avoir lieu dans les temps finals. Tout d'abord il y aurait des combats violents, au sein des familles et des nations et entre amis. Trois grands rois, ceux d'Egypte, de Lybie et d'Ethiopie, seraient conquis. L'Antéchrist, en tant que monarque cosmique, séduirait les peuples parce qu'il prétendrait posséder toutes les vertus; naturellement ce ne sera qu'hypocrisie. Plus tard il ôterait son masque et il y aurait des famines effroyables dues à de longues périodes de sécheresse, mais en d'autres versions les temps de l'Antéchrist seraient précédés de récoltes prodigieuses. Mais l'événement «contrôlable» le plus remarquable des temps finals devait être la fin de l'empire — Romain d'abord, Byzantin ensuite. Ce motif se trouve déjà dans la Seconde Epitre aux Thessaloniciens où l'empire est considéré comme une puissance qui retarde la fin. Des textes plus tardifs parlent ou bien d'une division de l'empire en dix parties ou de sa dissolution ou d'un transfert du pouvoir impérial par le dernier empereur à Dieu le Père. Comme l'a dit très bien feu M. Bousset, »c'est précisément dans cette version pro-romaine que la légende de l'Antéchrist a exercé une influence politique« et il aurait pu ajouter: influence historiographique.[2]

Passons donc à l'influence de la tradition eschatologique sur l'historiographie byzantine et remarquons d'abord qu'elle a pu servir aux besoins des groupes d'opposition. Dans un livre récent et dans plusieurs articles, le professeur Berthold Rubin a démontré que l'historien Procope de Césarée s'était servi de cette tradition eschatologique pour exprimer, surtout dans son *Histoire Secrète* que Rubin appelle «l'apocalypse» de Procope, l'opposition farouche de la classe sénatoriale à la politique militaire, étrangère

---

[2] II Thess. 6—7. Voir *Bousset*, Antichrist.

et économique de Justinien. Pour Procope l'empereur Justinien était le »prince des démons«, c'est à dire l'Antéchrist. Il était un démon qui, avec sa femme Theodora, avait l'intention d'exterminer les races humaines le plus vite possible. Au cours de ses guerres il aurait tué un milliard de personnes, au moins cinq millions rien qu'en Afrique. Aux guerres de Justinien il convient d'ajouter, dit Procope, les dégâts causés par les tremblements de terre, les inondations, les épidémies. De plus M. Rubin a étudié à fond la manière dont les successeurs de Procope se sont servis de la même légende de l'Antéchrist pour faire la critique des successeurs de Justinien sur le trône impérial. En bref, dans les cadres de cette application de la tradition eschatologique par un groupe politique d'opposition, l'Empereur byzantin est identifié avec l'Antéchrist ou avec un des ses ministres, précurseurs, etc. Voici l'intérêt politique de la légende sur laquelle il serait vain de parler de plus longue haleine après tout ce qu'en a écrit M. Rubin.[3]

Mais l'historiographie byzantine a aussi subi l'influence de cette tradition eschatologique d'une manière différente. Ici je fais allusion à ce qu'on pourrait appeler, pour le distinguer de l'intérêt politique étudié par M. Rubin, à l'intérêt eschatologique des historiens byzantins. On connaît bien l'angoisse des Byzantins qui se sentaient toujours tout près d'un abîme et s'attendaient à une fin du monde plus au moins prochaine. Les gens voulaient savoir à Byzance si cette fin arriverait sous l'empereur régnant ou bien combien de générations les séparaient de l'acte final. Rien de plus naturel donc que d'étudier les temps passés et surtout le passé récent pour voir si les événements «contrôlables» décrits dans les oeuvres apocalyptiques étaient en train de se réaliser. Y avait-il déjà les querelles interfamiliales, civiles, internationales prédites pour les temps finals? Où en était-on vis-à-vis des rois et armées étrangères? Les empereurs byzantins de la dynastie régnante possédaient-ils la physiognomie et les qualités morales requises pour l'Antéchrist et ses serviteurs? Les conditions du ravitaillement ressemblaient-elles ou à la famine ou à la prosperité prédites alternativement pour le règne de l'Antéchrist? Et surtout la domination byzantine sur le monde méditerranéen était-elle solide ou faible de sorte qu'on dût s'attendre à sa dissolution prochaine et à la naissance de l'Antéchrist? Et si ces questions étaient naturelles pour qui connaissait la tradition eschatologique byzantine, qui était mieux justifié de les poser et d'y répondre que les historiens et chroniqueurs de Byzance qui s'occupaient normalement de guerres, dynasties, princes, conditions économiques, cataclysmes etc.?

---

[3] B. *Rubin*, Das Zeitalter Justinians, vol I (Berlin, 1960), pp. 204—244 et notes, surtout note 546, pp. 441—454. En plus du même auteur: Der Fürst der Dämonen etc., dans B. Z, 44 (1951) 469—481; Prokopios von Kaisareia, dans *Pauly-Wissowa-Kroll-Mittelhaus*, Realencyclopädie 45, 273—599, spéc. p. 334; Der Antichrist und die „Apocalypse" des Prokopios von Kaisareia, dans Zeitschrift der Deutschen Morgenländischen Gesellschaft 110 (1960) 55—63.

Il n'est donc point surprenant qu'expressément ou tacitement l'historiographie byzantine ait confronté les événements réels de l'histoire avec les prédictions eschatologiques.

Donnons quelques exemples de cet intérêt que les historiens et chroniqueurs byzantins portaient à l'eschatologie. C'est que toute (ou presque toute) la chronographie byzantine postule un parallélisme entre la création du monde en sept jours et sa durée future. Puisque d'après le psalmiste «devant Dieu une journée est comme mille ans»[4], il s'ensuit que l'Incarnation, c'est à dire la création du nouvel Adam, eut lieu pendant le sixième millénaire du monde et que la durée totale de ce monde sera de sept millénaires. On trouve cette thèse fondamentale par exemple dans les chronographies de Malalas et de Leo Grammaticus et dans les *Patria Constantinopoleos*, mais elle est beaucoup plus ancienne et se trouvait au plus tard au commencement du troisième siècle dans la chronographie de Sextus Julius Africanus[5], et toute la chronographie byzantine en a subi l'influence.

Mais le calcul des sept mille ans dépendant de la date initiale de l'ère mondiale, on n'était jamais très sûr de la date précise. L'oeuvre historique de Théophylacte Simocatta, qui vivait sous Héraclius, est d'un intérêt particulier de notre point de vue. Au commencement de son ouvrage Théophylacte fait mention d'un songe de l'empereur Tibère II. Tibère avait vu un ange qui lui avait apporté un message de la part de la Sainte Trinité. Voici le texte du message divin: «Les temps tyranniques de l'impiété n'arriveront pas tant que tu seras empereur».[6] L'impiété ainsi retardée pour une génération, c'est évidemment le règne de l'Antéchrist. La source apocalyptique de Théophylacte supposait donc qu'aux temps de l'empereur Tibère on s'inquiétait d'une fin du monde imminente. Encore plus intéressant est un autre passage du même auteur. Il s'agit d'une prophécie attribuée au roi perse Chosroès II au moment où en 591 il avait dû s'enfuir en territoire byzantin. Le roi avait prédit au général byzantin Jean Mystakon que pendant le cinquième cercle hebdomadaire, c'est à dire de 619 (591 + 28) à 626 (591 + 35), les Byzantins allaient réduire la Perse en esclavage. Après cela, dit l'historien, «arrivera pour les hommes la journée sans soir et se fera la fin du pouvoir (byzantin) à laquelle on s'attend quand tout ce qui est sujet à corruption sera dissolu et quand commencera la vie meilleure.»[7] Cette prophécie,

---

[4] Ps. 89 (90) 4 = II Pierre 3, 8.

[5] Malalas X p. 228 s.; XVIII p. 428 ed Bonn (à noter que, sauf indication contraire, tous les textes historiques seront cités d'après l'édition de Bonn); Leon Grammaticus p. 14; Patria II 77 p. 190; III 40 p. 232 ed. *Preger*; H. *Gelzer*, Sextus Julius Africanus und die byzantinische Chronographie, vol. I (Leipzig, 1880) 24—26; Reallexikon für Antike und Christentum, verbo „Chronologie."

[6] I 2 § 1—2 p. 43 ed. *de Boor*. Théopylacte raconte ce rêve d'après le rapport d' autrui (λόγος δὲ κτλ.).

[7] V 15 p. 216 s. ed. *de Boor* (prophécie attribuée au roi Chosroès II).

que pour certaines raisons je daterais du commencement des campagnes d'Héraclius contre la Perse et avant leur conclusion triomphale en 627/8, envisageait la fin du monde et la dissolution de l'empire romain au bout de sept années tout au plus. Il est vrai que Théophylacte lui-même qualifie cette prophécie de »vanité affairée« (πολυάσχολος ματαιότης) — n'oublions pas qu'il écrivait son *Histoire* après que les sept années de la prophécie se fussent écoulées — mais il va sans dire que son auteur anonyme l'avait prise au sérieux. On retiendra que dans la première moitié du septième siècle il y avait à Byzance des milieux qui croyaient que l'état romain ou byzantin avait été suffisament affaibli pour faire place, suivant la tradition mentionnée dans la seconde Epître aux Thessaloniciens, au règne de l'Antéchrist.

Prenons un autre exemple, d'une époque sensiblement postérieure, l'oeuvre historique de Léon le Diacre. Dans un mémoire concernant les idees mediévales sur la fin du monde, M. Vasiliev écrivait naguère que cet historien, tout pessimiste qu'il était, ne s'attendait pas à une fin prochaine du monde.[8] A vrai dire on ne connaît pas bien la pensée personnelle de Léon à ce sujet, mais il est tout à fait remarquable que dans la préface de son oeuvre, donc dans un endroit «sanctifié» par une tradition remontant à l'historiographie de la Grèce ancienne, l'auteur parle non seulement des événements »monstrueux et étranges et nouveaux« de son temps, de phénomènes météorologiques, de tremblements de terre et de guerres, mais il cite expressément ce qu'il appelle »l'opinion de bien des gens que la vie humaine venait de changer et que la seconde venue du Sauveur et Dieu à laquelle on s'attendait était imminente.«[9] Si en lisant l'oeuvre de Léon le Diacre et surtout ses remarques sur les cataclysmes naturels et les désordres politiques et sociaux au dixième siècle on se souvient de cette vue d'ensemble exprimée dans la préface, on verra que l'oeuvre de cet historien est tout imprégnée des idées contemporaines sur la fin du monde.

Il y a bien d'autres exemples de cette influence de la tradition eschatologique sur l'historiographie byzantine. Pendant l'épidémie qui ravageait Constantinople sous Justinien Ier en 557, aux dires d'Agathias, on colportait la prophécie que le monde entier serait détruit bientôt.[10] A l'occasion de la révolte de Euphémius et de la perte de la plus grande partie de la Sicile aux Arabes, le magistre Irénée, d'après le pseudo-Syméon, aurait cité un »vieil oracle« en vers qui rattachait le «commencement du mal» au règne

---

[8] Medieval ideas of the End of the World: West and East, dans Byzantion 16, 1942-3, 462—502. Voir p. 488: „in the long list of various disasters that fell upon the empire at that time, none was interpreted by Leo as foreboding the final world catastrophe."

[9] Leo Diaconus I 1, p. 4, 15.

[10] Agathias V 5, p. 287, 11.

6

d'un dragon «avide d'or et bègue» sur Babylone.[11] Cette notice du pseudo-Syméon et des autres chroniqueurs remonte à une source historique du neuvième ou dixième siècle, peut-être à cette histoire perdue de Serge le Confesseur dont Photius nous a laissé un sommaire et dont M. Barišić a parlé dans un récent article sur la révolte de Thomas le Slave.[12] Que cet oracle cité par la source du pseudo-Syméon au neuvième ou dixième siècle ait en fait été ancien ou de fabrication récente, il est évident que la source perdue du pseudo-Syméon se servait du langage de la tradition eschatologique et qu'elle y avait vu une prédiction des événements du neuvième siècle.

Les exemples cités jusqu'ici ont été pris dans les textes historiques et on pourrait y ajouter sans difficulté. Il vaut mieux faire le dépouillement d'un genre de textes qui ne sont ni histoires ni chroniques à proprement parler mais des traités sur les antiquités de Constantinople. On ne trouve rien sur la fin du monde dans le texte d'Hesychius (sixième siècle), rien dans les *Enarrationes Breves Chronographicae* (huitième siècle). Il en est autrement de la *Narratio de aedificatione Templi S. Sophiae* (huitième ou neuvième siècle) où il est dit que Justinien avait eu l'intention de construire pour St. Sophie un plancher tout d'argent mais que des philosophes et astrologues Athéniens l'en dissuaderent en disant que «dans les jours finals des dynasties obscures viendraient et enlèveraient le plancher.»[13] Mais c'est dans les *Patria Constantinopoleos* du dixième ou onzième siècle, comme on le sait depuis un article magistral de Charles Diehl, que pullulent les croyances eschatologiques.[14] Ce sont tout particulièrement les statues de la capitale qui de par leurs figures et leur inscriptions sont censées de prédire les peripéties de l'âge final du monde. Telle cette fameuse base carrée de la cour du Taureau où etaient gravées les destinées finales de Constantinople «quand les Russes vont détruire la ville même.»[15] A noter aussi la mention du palais de Bryas d'où,

---

[11] Pseudo-Symeon p. 622; Theophanes Continuatus II 28 p. 84; Scylitzes — Cedrenus, vol. II, p. 99; Zonaras XV 24, vol. III, p. 400 ed. *Dindorf.* Le professeur *S. G. Mercati* a découvert, il y a bien des années, le manuscrit d'un poème en 180 vers dont les trois lignes citées par les chroniqueurs forment l'incipit (Sur une poésie inédite dont ou connait seulement les trois premiers vers relatés par le Pseudosiméon et par d'autres chroniqueurs au sujet de la révolte d'Euphemios, dans Actes du IIIᵉ Congrès International des Etudes Byzantines, Athènes, 1932, pp. 111—113). Il s'agit du Vatic. Gr. 1257 (le numéro 1234 donné dans le sommaire de la conférence du professeur Mercati est une erreur), folios 36—39. Je me propose de publier et d'étudier à fond ce texte intéressant.

[12] Photius, Bibliotheca, cod. 67, vol. I, p. 99 ed. *R. Henry.* Voir *F. Barišić,* Deux versions sur Thomas chef de l'insurrection de 821—823, dans Zbornik Radova Vizantološkog Instituta 6 (1960) 145—169.

[13] Narratio de aedificatione Templi S. Sophiae, fasc. I p. 97 ed. *Preger.* Sur la date voir *Th. Preger,* Die Erzählung vom Bau der Hagia Sophia, dans B. Z. 10 (1901) 455—476.

[14] *Ch. Diehl,* De quelques croyances byzantines sur la fin de Constantinople, dans B. Z. 30 (1929-30) 192—196.

[15] Patria II 47 (fasc. II p. 176 ed. *Preger*).

disent les *Patria* suivant une étymologie populaire, le dernier empereur de Byzance, avant de sortir de la ville et de se rendre à Jérusalem, devait entendre les lamentations des citoyens de Constantinople.[16]

Quelques conclusions générales se dégagent de notre étude de l'empreinte de l'eschatologie sur l'historiographie.

Premièrement, cette influence a été profonde à deux égards: elle a fourni tout un système de notions à l'opposition politique des empereurs byzantins et elle a déterminé le ton pessimiste de cette littérature historique puisqu'on croyait vivre dans le septième et dernier millénaire du monde.

Mais notons aussi, deuxièmement, une réserve marquée de l'historiographie byzantine à l'égard des croyances eschatologiques. Précisons tout d'abord que tandis qu'il est difficile de trouver un texte historique qui ne dise rien des idées eschatologiques, il est également difficile d'en trouver un qui en dise beaucoup. Ceci est d'autant plus surprenant que les apocalypses, homélies et autres sources primaires de l'eschatologie montrent que le sujet des temps finals n'était que très rarement absent de la pensée byzantine. De plus il est tout à fait remarquable que les historiens et chroniqueurs ne parlent pour ainsi dire jamais de l'eschatologie en leurs propres noms mais que normalement ils placent les allusions à l'eschatologie ou les oracles qu'ils citent dans la bouche d'un personnage de leur histoire ou les attribuent à un groupe plus ou moins précis, par exemple à la rumeur publique. C'est bien le cas dans tous les exemples mentionnés jusqu'ici[17], à l'exception des *Patria Constantinopoleos*. Cette exception pourrait bien nous aider à trouver les raisons de la réserve des autres sources au sujet de la tradition eschatologique. On sait bien que les *Patria Constantinopoleos* abondent en données légendaires, en miracles, en étymologies populaires et que cette oeuvre appartient à la littérature populaire.[18] On ne s'étonnera donc pas que l'historiographie officielle ou aulique ait hésité à faire trop de concessions aux vues populaires sur la fin du monde. La réserve de l'historiographie byzantine vis-à-vis de l'eschatologie s'explique donc par le caractère de la tradition historiographique byzantine. La distinction entre littérature aulique et littérature populaire n'étant guère précise et admettant plusieurs degrés de transition, on peut dire que plus un auteur historique est indépendant de la cour et des cercles officiels, plus il tendra à abandonner la réserve normale envers la tradition eschatologique.[19]

---

[16] Patria III 170 (fasc. II p. 268 s. ed. *Preger*).
[17] J'ai tenu à indiquer, ou dans le texte ou dans les notes de cette communication, les personnes auxquelles les auteurs cités attribuent des prophéties eschatologiques.
[18] Voir *Th. Preger* dans la préface à son édition, fasc. II, p. IV.
[19] La distinction entre littérature aulique et littérature populaire est due à *A. Pertusi*, L'Attegiamento spirituale della più antica storiografia bizantina, dans Aevum 30 (1956) 134—166, spécialement p. 142 n. 2.

Mais — et c'est la troisième conclusion générale qui se dégage, à mon avis, d'une étude de notre problème — c'est precisément cette réserve normale qui montre toute l'importance des mentions occasionelles et exceptionelles de la tradition eschatologique dans les sources historiques. Il fallait de très bonnes raisons pour qu'un Procope ou la source perdue sur la révolte d'Euphémius s'abaisse à recourir à la terminologie eschatologique: cette raison était certainement leur opposition à la politique impérialiste de Justinien d'une part ou à la politique religieuse des empereurs iconoclastes de l'autre. Mais il fallait aussi des circonstances extraordinaires pour qu'un Théophylacte Simocatta au temps d'Héraclius insérât dans son histoire des prophéties qui se rattachaient à la tradition eschatologique. Et si Léon le Diacre sous Basile II faisait mention de l'attente populaire d'une fin prochaine du monde dans la préface même de son histoire — place dont le caractère rhétorique et formel interdisait normalement toute concession aux tendances populaires — il devait avoir en effet des raisons puissantes pour agir d'une manière aussi extraordinaire. Il semble que sous Héraclius et Basile II les événements militaires — guerres contre Perses et Arabes sous Héraclius, contre Bulgares et Arabes sous Basile II — aient produit de tels bouleversements dans la structure sociale et intellectuelle de l'Empire que même l'historiographie officielle ne put se soustraire à leurs effets et fut forcée de prendre note des courants religieux populaires. Peut-être n'est-ce pas le moindre intérêt de l'étude des éléments eschatologiques dans l'historiographie byzantine qu'elle fournisse un baromètre assez précis pour mesurer la pression eschatologique éprouvée par la population de l'empire pendant les époques critiques de son histoire millénaire.

ADDITIONAL BIBLIOGRAPHY

On the career of the Byzantine general John Mystakon to
whom Chosroes II supposedly prophesied the end of the
Byzantine Empire and of the world (p.4 above), see Paul
Lemerle,"Notes sur les données historiques de l'autobio-
graphie d'Anania de Shirak",<u>Revue des Etudes Arménien-
nes</u>,N.S.1,1964,195-202,esp.197-199.M.Ia.Sjuzjumov,
"Mirovozzrenie L'va D'iakona" (=The World View of Leo
Diaconus),<u>Antichnaia Drevnost' i Srednie Veka</u> 7,1971,
127-143,esp.132 and 142 n.9,is of the opinion that while
Leo Diaconus was aware of contemporary expectations of
an imminent end of the world (p.5 above),he himself did
not share these views.However,inasmuch as in all the
instances discussed in this paper the Byzantine historians
ascribe eschatological expectations to persons other than
themselves (p.7 above),it seems likely that Leo Diaconus,
with his stylistically reserved attitude towards the imm-
inence of the Second Coming,is following a convention of
the hagiographic genre and that his personal attitude towards this view may have been more positive than his
words indicate.While I have not published the "prophesy"
on the revolt of Euphemius (p.5f. and p.6 n.11 above),
the reader will find further information on this text in no.
XIV,14.

HISTORICAL INTERPOLATIONS IN THE *ZBORNIK POPA DRAGOLIA**

L'appétit vient en mangeant — and most historical apocalypses owe their existence to the realization, on the part of a reader, that an earlier apocalypse or other prophecy is wholly or in part applicable to his own historical experience. An apocalyptist's literary activity may take various forms. Thus for example a monk Peter, perhaps a Greek living in seventh century Gaul, translated Pseudo-Methodius' famous prophecies from Greek into Latin because, he writes, "they were more aptly predicted for our own day ... so that we consider the predictions of our Fathers fulfilled by what we observe with our own eyes". [1] In other instances the reading of an earlier apocalypse inspired a reader to re-edit the original text and to adjust it, more or less radically, to the historical development known to him. [2] This paper will be concerned with a revision of earlier apocalypses by a reader who lived many centuries after the date of the original composition and who applied it to his own time and place by a series of additions and substitutions.

The earlier text, a *Vision of Daniel*, was composed in Sicily in 827/8 in the Greek language. [3] It is lost but a Slavonic translation survives in two manuscripts. One of them is *codex Athos Chilandar 24*, saec. XIII—XIV, from which the text was printed twice, first by V. Istrin in 1897

---

* The following paper was prompted by a question posed to me by the Very Reverend Dr. H. Chadwick, of . Christ Church . In 1966 I had the honour of addressing the Byzantine Society of Oxford University on the Arab conquest of Sicily. In the course of my talk I referred to the interpolations in the *Zbornik Popa Dragolia*, the subject of this paper. In the discussion Dr. Chadwick enquired after the date and circumstances of the interpolator. I could not satisfy him at the time, but the present paper is my long delayed answer and my grateful tribute to his stimulating remarks. I also wish to express my gratitude to Professor Roman Jakobson, of Harvard University, who with great kindness answered questions on the Slavonic text. The research for this paper was carried out partly during two semesters as member of the Institute for Advanced Study, Princeton, N. J., and under a generous grant from the Humanities Research Institute from the University of California, Berkeley. I wish to express here my gratitude to both these institutions.

[1] Ed. Ernst Sackur, *Sibyllinische Texte und Forschungen*, Halle a. S., 1898 (reprint Torino, 1964), 59 f. : nostris sunt aptius prophetata temporibus ... ut iam per ipsa que nostris cernimus oculis vera esset credamus ea quae praedicta sunt a patribus nostris.

[2] Examples in my article "Medieval Apocalypses as Historical Sources", "American Historical Review", 73, 1968, 997—1018.

[3] Some preliminary remarks on this text in the article cited in the preceding note. A fuller treatment will be found in my study entitled *Les Débuts des conquêtes arabes en Sicile et la tradition apocalyptique byzantino-slave*, in "Bollettino del Centro di Studi Filologici e Linguistici Siciliani", 12, 1973, 1—37.

and independently by P. A. Lavrov in 1899. [4] This manuscript is free
from the interpolations that form the subject of this paper. The interpolated text was part of a manuscript discovered in 1873 by P. Srechkovic
in an Albanian village near Skutari, the *Zbornik Popa Dragolia*, henceforth to be cited as *Zbornik*. It was lost during World War I, but fortunately the relevant part was published by its discoverer. A comparison
of the Chilandar text with Srechkovic' edition of the *Zbornik* reveals
clearly the nature and scope of the interpolations. [5]

The principal interpolations in the text of the *Vision of Daniel*
according to the *Zbornik* are the following:

1. In the Chilandar manuscript it was said that an Emperor "will
send envoys properly loyal to him to the regions of the West as well.
Those in the city called Rebel City who have rebelled will sally forth,
etc." In the *Zbornik* this passage appears in an abbreviated form : "And
he will send envoys to the regions of the West. Those of the city called
Rebel who have rebelled will sally forth", but after the words "city called
Rebel" the name Sredic is added. Thus the interpolator considered Sredic,
i.e. Sardica (modern Sofia), the Rebel City.

2. A few lines further down the Chilandar manuscript contained
the words : "And two rebels will arise, the first from the East of the city,
the other from the West". After the last words the *Zbornik* added : "from
Glavinica".

3. Somewhat later the Chilandar text mentioned a city "where
there stood in those days a sign". The *Zbornik* added at the end : "at
Pernik."

4. The Chilandar codex prophesied that "the Ismaelites will enter
the extremity of this island and take much booty". In the *Zbornik* the
genitive of the word "island" is followed by the name of the River Danube
in the genitive (*Dunaia*).

5. In the next sentence the original prophecy predicted that the
"Ismaelites" would come to a place called Marianii, to which the *Zbornik*
added the words : "and to Mraka" (*i na Mraka*).

6. According to the original, the "Ismaelites" would then come to
a place called Ieninei (Sicilian Enna). To this place name the *Zbornik*
added in the same case that of Veliblud (modern Küstendil).

---

[4] V. Istrin, *Otkrovenie Mefodiia Patarskago i Apokrificheskiia Videniia Daniila v Vizan-
tiiskoi i Slaviano-Russkoi Literaturakh*, Chteniia v Moskovskom Obshchestvie Istorii i Drevnostei Rossiiskikh pri Moskovskom Universitete, 1897, vol. 191 (henceforth to be cited as "Istrin,
Izsledovanie") and 192 (henceforth to be cited "Istrin"), pp. 156—158; P. A. Lavrov, *Apokrificheskie Teksty*, Sbornik Otdeleneiia Russkogo Iazyka i Slovesnosti Imp. Akademii Nauk 67,
no. 3, St. Petersburg, 1899, pp. 1—5.
[5] P. Srechkovic, *Zbornik Popa Dragolia*, Srpska Kralievska Akademija, Spomenik 5,
1890, p. 10 f. Srechkovich assigned the manuscript to the first quarter of the fourteenth century
while M. I. Sokolov, *Materialy i zametki po starinoi slavianskoi literature*, "Izvestiia Istoriko-
Filologicheskago Instituta Kniazia Bezborodko v Nezhine", XI, 3, 1887—1889, p. 19 f. placed
it on unspecified palaeographical grounds at the end of the thirteenth or beginning of the fourteenth century. It entered the National Library at Belgrade as no. 466 (632) and the catalogue
of that collection (Ljub. Stojanović, *Katalog Narodne Biblioteke u Beogradu*, vol. IV, Belgrade,
1903, pp. 290—294) assigned it to the thirteenth century. Istrin, Izsledovanie, 140 f. listed the
interpolations in the *Vision of Daniel* but did little or nothing for their historical interpretation.
He remarked, p. 268, n. 1, that they were written in the Bulgarian language. They were certainly
composed for the Slavonic rather than the Greek text, for the Chilandar codex shows that the
translator did not know them.

7. In the Chilandar text there followed several lines of eschatological prophecy and nothing here seems to have prompted the interpolator to intervene. However, in the very first sentence where the original once again "predicted" certain historical events, to the effect that "they (i.e. the inhabitants) will set forth from this city called Rebel", the *Zbornik* added the same place name as in item 1 : Sredic (modern Sofia).

8. The Chilandar text then mentioned a battle between an emperor, anointed in the Rebel City, with the "Ismaelites" in a place called Perton. "He will fight a fierce battle. And there is in that place a well with two mouths so that the blood of the Romans and Ismaelites is mingled". In the *Zbornik* a sentence was added after the name Perton : "there are two hills on one side of Sredic" (= Sardica, Sofia).

9. In the Chilandar codex there followed some eschatological material where no interpolations occur in the *Zbornik*. Then it was prophesied, in the original text, that "there will arise a tenth horn which will endure less than one year. And it will fight against the Ethiopian emperor and many of its princes will flee to him. And the tenth horn will be destroyed by the Ethiopian emperor". The *Zbornik* added a lengthy passage : "The first day of the present (or : coming) month of August will pass. Michael will take the imperial power (*cesarstvo*). And the mountains will begin to divide, the fish to die in the streams. And the Lord will be with him forever."

10. The sentence following immediately upon item 9 read in the Chilandar text : "And he will enter the (city of) the Seven Hills (*v ζ' vrekh*, i. e. Constantinople) from the West," but in the *Zbornik* the city of Thessalonica (*v Solun*) was substituted.

11. The original prophecy predicted that "the scepter will rule thirty-two years". In the *Zbornik* this sentence is modified :"the scepter will rule thirty-three years at Thessalonica (*v Solune*)."

12. Later it was prophesied in the original text that the Antichrist would be born "in the village of Khuz". Here the *Zbornik* added : "at Strumica" (*v Strumice*).

13. Another text contained in the *Zbornik* contains an interpolation so kindred in content and spirit to those in the *Vision of Daniel* that it is advisable to include it in this discussion. It occurs in the Slavonic translation of the *Revelation* of Pseudo-Methodius, the last item in the *Zbornik* separated from the *Vision of Daniel* by other materials of an eschatological character.[6] Here a lengthy passage was inserted in Pseudo-

---

[6] Analyses of the contents of the *Zbornik* in the works by Srechkovic and by Stojanović mentioned in the preceding note. In Srechkovic' description the *Vision of Daniel* has the number 32 and the translation from Pseudo-Methodius no. 38. The intervening twenty-three folios were filled with highly interesting material that deserves special study : a second "interpretation" of Daniel (no. 33); a fragment of St. Hippolytus of Rome's *Commentary on Daniel* (no. 34); a fragment of Hypatius of Ephesus on the subject : When will the end of the world occur? (no. 35); a Comprehensive Prophetic Narrative referring to the Byzantine Emperor Manuel (Comnenus, 1143—1180) and the Tatars (no. 36); and a Vision of the Prophet Isaiah on the Last Times (no. 37). All these texts were published by Srechkovic.

Methodius' description of the oppression of the conquered population by the "Ismaelites". It ran as follows [7] :

"And there will be great destruction of the land. And one man will set out from Sredic and another from Solun. And they will meet each other at Veteri carrying gold and will say to one another : Brother, how far is it go to Solun? He will say to him : The same (distance) as to go to Sredic. Woe to us, brother, the land has remained deserted. A sheep will fetch the price of an ox and an ox the price of a horse and a horse thirty pounds (*litrai*). And men will sell themselves for three or four gold pieces. And from hunger they will destroy each other. Great hostility will arise and cruelty and la wlessness. The entire land will be filled with injustice. Woe to us, brother, these days are cruel to us. Then there will be much sighing among men, and there will be no comfort for all types of injustice, and it will never end."

In these lines, there is the same geographical focus as in the interpolations found in the *Vision of Daniel*. There the "Ismaelites" are said to invade across the River Danube (item 4) as far south as Mraka and Veliblud (items 5 and 6), with a battle against them being fought near Sredic (Sofia, items 7 and 8). All these places were located in Northwestern Bulgaria, Southwest of Sofia more or less along the River Struma. Strumica (item 12) and Solun (items 10 and 11) lay to the South of that line.[8] The interpolator of the *Revelation* of Pseudo-Methodius envisaged the same region from Sofia to Thessalonica.[9] As item 13 was interpolated into the translation of Pseudo-Methodius at a point where the text described the effects of the Ismaelite invasions, it is probable that the interpolator considered the devastations of the land, the famine, the scarcity of domestic animals and the many injustices referred to in item 13 as the consequences of an "Ismaelite" invasion, just as the interpolator of the *Vision of Daniel* witnessed the southward march of "Ismaelites" and was prompted thereby to add to the original text. It is difficult to avoid the conclusion that the interpolator of the text of Pseudo-Methodius was identical with that of the *Vision of Daniel*.

---

[7] Istrin, Izsledovanic, 140 f. reprinted this interpolation but he did not relate it to the interpolations in the *Vision of Daniel*, which he discusses pp. 260—263, nor did he attempt a historical explanation. This was done, however, very briefly by C. Jireček, *Das christliche Element in der topographischen Nomenclatur der Balkanländer*, "Sitzungsberichte Wien", 136, 1897, 92.

[8] Most of these place names may be found on any map of medieval Bulgaria, for instance in the *Atlas po Bulgarska Istorica*, Sofia, 1963 and in *Grosser Historischer Weltatlas* II Teil: Mittelalter, Munich, 1970, map 91. Mraká is an area on the Struma between Radomir and Žabljano (C. Jireček, *Das Fürstenthum Bulgarien*, Prague, etc., 1891, 468 (with map). Only one place name points in another direction : Glavinica (item 2). There were several places of that name on the Balkan Peninsula, but since it said that it lay West of Sredic, the interpolator must mean the town of that name on the Bay of Vallona on the Adriatic, modern Balsha.

[9] He mentioned Veteri midway between Sofia and Thessalonica. Jireček, *loc. cit.* (note 7), 92, was unable to locate it. The Russian traveler Viktor Grigorovich, in his *Ocherk puteshestviia po Evropeiskoi Turcii*, Kazan, 1848, 146, noted in 1845 a village called Větren West of the River Struma and East of Valovishte, see also Wilhelm Tomaschek, *Zur Kunde der Hämus-Halbinsel*, "Sitzungsberichte Wien", 113, 1886, 285—373, esp. 364. It is questionable whether the interpolator's Veteri may be identified with Větren not only because the form of the name is different but also because it seems to lie closer to Sofia than to Thessalonica.

Is it possible to obtain an idea of the original form of the interpolations? In the *Zbornik* all of them, with one exception, appeared in the guise of additions to the original texts. [10] It will also be noted that nearly all of them are related syntactically to a word in the original text, either by being placed in the same case as a word of that text (items 1, 4, 6, 7) or connected with it by a preposition or conjunction (items 2, 3, 5, 10—12). Items 8, 9 and 13 are different in that respect as each of them consists of one or several independent clauses and the relationship with the original is therefore one of context and meaning rather than one of grammar. If one wishes to visualize the genesis of the interpolations, item 8 is instructive : "there are two hills on one side of Sredic". At first sight it would seem that exceptionally there is here no connection of either syntax or meaning between the interpolation and the passage of the original that precedes it. Yet the observation that all other interpolations are related, in one way or another, to the original makes it advisable to consider whether item 8 may have been misplaced by a copyist and originally have been meant to follow another phrase of the original. Indeed, two clauses later one reads in the *Vision of Daniel* : "and there is in this place a well with two mouths". Here therefore would be a definite relation of meaning between original and interpolation : two mouths — two hills. There can be little doubt that the interpolator saw the prophecy concerning the two mouths fulfilled by certain events that he knew to have taken place at two hills near Sofia. Now this inference of the displacement of item 8 shows that in the model of the *Zbornik*, or in one of its ancestors, item 8 stood in an ambiguous position, i.e. as a glose between the lines or in the margin, and could therefore be misplaced with relative ease by a scribe. What was true of item 8 was undoubtedly true also of the other interpolations. The conclusion emerges that the interpolations of the *Zbornik* originated as interlinear or marginal gloses. If the suggestion made before that the author of item 13 was identical with the interpolator of items 1—12 is correct, it would follow that these gloses were added to a manuscript that contained the Slavonic translations of both the *Vision of Daniel* and the *Revelation* of Pseudo-Methodius, perhaps also of all or some of the other eschatological pieces that in the *Zbornik* separate the two works.

It is extremely difficult to establish the date of the interpolator and of the events to which he referred. Clearly he wrote after the text that he interpolated was composed, that is to say after 827/8, and prior to the palaeographical date of the *Zbornik*, at the latest the fourteenth century. This, however, leaves an uncomfortably wide margin. It is important to get beyond these outer chronological limits and to identify the historical events which the interpolator evidently considered a fulfillment of the ninth century text. Several scholars have therefore attempted to establish a *terminus post quem*. Thus M. I. Sokolov was of the opinion that the ruler Michael of item 9 was the Byzantine Emperor Michael VIII Palaeologus (1259—1282) while A. A. Vasiliev seems to have thought of

---

[10] The one exception is item 10 where Thessalonica was substituted for Constantinople. The possibility cannot be excluded that the interpolator intended substitutions rather than additions also for items 1, 4, 6, 7 and 12, but that a copyist misunderstood his intentions.

Michael III (842—867), the last ruler of the Amorian house. [11] Both views were guesswork. C. Jireček, on the other hand, thought that in the items on the "Ismaelite" attacks (items 4—8, 13) the interpolator was referring to the Magyar and Pecheneg invasions of the Balkan Peninsula in the eleventh century. [12] As will be seen, he came close to the truth, but he offered no evidence for his view. It might also be tempting to derive a *terminus post* from the term "Ismaelites" used in the *Vision of Daniel*. It is true that it appears only in the original text and not in the interpolations, but the raison d'être for the interpolated item 4—8 and 13 is clearly the fact that in some sense the interpolator considered his contemporary invaders of Northwestern Bulgaria "Ismaelites". In Byzantine literature this is a normal designation for Arabs and Ottoman Turks. The Arabs never invaded Bulgaria and while the Ottomans did in the fourteenth century, they came from the South and not from the North, as suggested in items 4—6. One wonders whether the term "Ismaelites" could be applied to the Tatar invaders of Bulgaria in the thirteenth century because during that century these Mongols of the Golden Horde became converts to Islam. [13] If the Tatar converts to Islam were meant, this would date the interpolations late in the thirteenth century at the earliest but this *terminus post* proves invalid if one considers the usages not only of Byzantine but also of the Slavic literatures. Roman Jakobson has collected the evidence for the fact that the early Russian chronicles specifically interpreted Pseudo-Methodius' prophecies of an "Ismaelite" invasion as refering to Torkmens, Pechenegs, Torks and Kumans, all descended according to these texts from Ismael. [14] The same holds true of Bulgarian usage. A Bulgarian *Vision of Isaiah*, for exemple, composed in the second half of the eleventh century, mentions a legendary Bulgarian ruler Ispor, destroying many "Ismaelites". [15]

Thus attempts to establish a *terminus post* on the basis of any one specific feature in the interpolations have led to widely conflicting and insecure results. Undoubtedly, the reason for this unsatisfactory situation lies in the fact that no individual element mentioned by the interpolator is precise enough to permit reliable chronological conclusions. It seems, therefore, more promising to make the starting point for a chronological enquiry not a single aspect of the interpolations but the totality of the several historical circumstances to which he alludes. What are they? In the first place, a rebellion at Sardica (Sofia), but it is not clear imme-

---

[11] For Sokolov's view I rely on the remarks of Istrin, Izsledovanic, 268, as Sokolov's publication is not accessible to me. Istrin himself rejected Sokolov's identification but did not advance one of this own. In Vasiliev's remarks on the subject in *The Emperor Michael in Apocryphal Literature*, "Byzantina-Metabyzantina", 1, 1946, 237—248, esp. 244 (reprinted in his *The First Russian Attack on Constantinople in 860/1*, Cambridge, Mass., 1946, 152—164, esp. 161) it is not clear to me whether his identification of Michael III applies only to the interpolated Slavonic Pseudo-Methodius or also to the *Vision of Daniel*.

[12] Jireček, *Das Christliche Element*, (n. 7 above), 92.

[13] The parallel term Agarēnoi (= sons of Hagar, mother of the biblical Ismael) may have been applied, at least by one surce, the *Notitiae Sugdaeae* (in the Crimea), to the Tatars, see Gyula Moravcsik, *Byzantino-Turcica*, 2nd ed., Berliner Byzantinistische Arbeiten 10 and 11, Berlin, 1958, esp. vol. II, p. 55.

[14] Roman Jakobson, *La Geste du Prince Igor*, "Selected Writings", IV, The Hague and Paris, 1966, 245—249.

[15] C. Jireček, *Das Christliche Element*, etc. (n. 7 above), 87.

diately against whom it was directed.. Secondly, there is the reference to
an invasion of Northwestern Bulgaria, from the Danube southward via
Sofia at least as far as Küstendil accompanied by tremendous destruction,
famine, scarcity of domestic animals and cheapness of human liberty. [16]
Finally, there is the reality or expectation of a ruler called Michael who
would take the throne (*cesarstvo*) after a first day of August, enter Thessalonica from the West and rule there for thirthy-three years. Leaving
aside for the moment the third element relating to the ruler Michael, it
is noteworthy that the interpolator envisages a rebellion at Sofia and more
or less simultaneously an invasion of the country from the North. Now
the classical period in medieval Bulgarian history when rebellions and
Northern invasions occurred in combination with each other was the latter
half of the eleventh century. It will, therefore, be advisable to review
briefly the story of rebellions and foreign invasions in Western Bulgaria
during this period in order to ascertain whether and where the events
alluded to by the interpolator can be placed into an appropriate historical
context. [17] Naturally, this procedure cannot produce more than a plausible
working hypothesis, in particular it cannot exclude the possibility that
other periods in Bulgarian history witnessed a similar combination of
events. However, there is some hope that an hypothesis emerging from
a survey of rebellions and foreign invasions in eleventh century Bulgaria
may then be strengthened by an examination of the third historical element
in the interpolations, the figure of the ruler Michael.

Bulgarian rebellions against Byzantine rule as established by Basil
II in 1018 began only two decades after the subjugation of the country.
The first of them was directed principally against Byzantine fiscal oppression and was led by Peter Delian (1040/1). It began in the extreme Northwest of Bulgaria, in the valley of the Morava and around Belgrade, and
thence spread southward. Niš and Skoplje were captured, a rebel army
entered Dyrrhachium on the Adriatic Sea, another marched towards
Greece and the main body of the rebels moved against Thessalonica. At
the zenith of the revolt the rebels controlled the Balkan Peninsula from
the Danube to Attica and from Dyrrhachium to the neighborhood of
Thessalonica. There is explicit evidence that Sardica (Sofia), too, fell
into the hands of the rebels. [18] The rebellion eventually collapsed because
of disagreements and treachery in the camp of the insurgents and it was
finally quelled in a military campaign commanded personally by the
Byzantine Emperor Michael IV (1034—1041). In the course of it the
fortress of Boiana near Sardica was taken. [19]

---

[16] See item 13 where all these last features are mentioned. The price of thirty pounds,
evidently of gold, for a horse was exorbitant. G. Ostrogorsky, *Löhne und Preise in Byzanz*,
"Byzantinische Zeitschrift", 32, 1932, 293—333, esp. 328 f, collects three examples of prices
of horses from the tenth to the thirteenth centuries which range from 12 to 15 nomismata. The
price mentioned in item 13 is one hundred fourty-four times the larger of these two figures. For
the prices of slaves he cites only data for the late ancient period, but even in the Byzantino-
Russian commercial agreements of 911 and 944 there is no figure for the price of slaves as low
as 3 or 4 nomismata (*ibid.*, 300 and n. 3).

[17] The following survey will be based on the two works which I found most useful:
V. Zlatarski, *Istoriia na Bulgarskata Durzhava prez srednite vekove*, 3 vols., Sofia, 1918—1940,
esp. vol. II, 1934; G. G. Litavrin, *Bolgariia i Vizantiia v XI—XII vv.*, Moscow, 1960.

[18] Zlatarski II 41—80; Litavrin, 376—387. On Sardica: Zlatarski II 78.

[19] Zlatarski II 78; Litavrin, 393 f.

During the next three decades the Bulgarians as a people did not participate in military rebellions against Byzantium, not even in those of George Maniaces (1043) and Leo Tornices (1047) who traversed the country or at least passed not far from the borders of Bulgaria. However, it was during those decades that nomads of Turkish origin crossed the Danube into Byzantine territory. In 1048 the Emperor Constantine IX Monomachus (1042—1055) settled a force of twenty thousand Pechenegs as allies in fortresses on the right bank of the Danube with the mission of guarding the crossings against their kinsmen. [20] During the winter of 1048/9 eighty thousand Pechenegs marched across the frozen river, were defeated by the Byzantines, but once again this attack led to the assignment of land to thousands of Pechenegs, this time in the neighborhoods of Sardica, Niš and Ovče Pole. Gradually, Pechenegs occupied all of Northeastern Bulgaria between the Danube and the Balkan Mountains, from the River Osem in the West to the Black Sea. [21] From there they invaded and ravaged the Byzantine areas to the South, especially Thrace (1049). Fierce battles were fought between Pechenegs and Roman armies and the invaders penetrated to the suburbs of the capital, Constantinople (1050). [22] In the same year the Pechenegs suffered serious defeats and in 1051/2 there is no record of Pecheneg activities south of the Balkans. The five-year war between Pechenegs and Byzantines ended in 1053 with a peace treaty intended to last thirty years on the basis of the *status quo*. [23]

In 1059 Northwestern Bulgaria became the theater of a Magyar invasion commanded by King Andrew. The Byzantine Emperor Isaac Comnenus (1057—1059) advanced with a large army as far as Sardica but there peace was made. The Pechenegs exploited this situation to resume their raids but like the Magyars they were forced to make peace. In 1064 Bulgaria was invaded by another Turkish people, the Uzes. One of their armies marched through Bulgaria and Macedonia towards Salonica and captured enormous amounts of booty on its way; however after a series of natural disasters and of attacks by their enemies the people disappeared from history. [24] Four years later (1068) the extreme Northwest of Bulgaria was invaded by King Salomon of Hungary who for a brief time occupied Sirmium . King Salomon repeated his inroads in 1071 and again 1072 and in the latter year pushed southward as far as Niš.

As already pointed out, no major internal disturbances broke out in Bulgaria in the course of those early invasions by Pechenegs, Magyars and Uzes. When in 1066 the Bulgar and Vlach populations of Thessaly rose up in arms, they had reason to hope that large numbers of Bulgarians would join forces with them. The rebels were, however, liquidated before they could enter Bulgaria proper and thus realize the revolutionary potential of the country. [25] The second, truly formidable Bulgarian revolt erupted, however, in 1072 and was caused once again primarily by the economic policies pursued by Byzantium. Under the Emperor

---

[20] Zlatarski II 90.
[21] Zlatarski II 96.
[22] Zlatarski II 101—104.
[23] Zlatarski II 105, 108.
[24] Zlatarski II 116, 118.
[25] Litavrin 400 f.

Michael VII Dukas (1071—1078) his chief minister, the logothete Nicephoritzes, had imposed new taxes. The price of wheat rose at the rate of 1:18 and famine spread in the countryside. [26] At the head of the Bulgarian revolt stood Constantine Bodin, son of the prince of Serbian Zeta. The rebels proclaimed Constantine tsar of the Bulgarians and he established himself at Prisdiana (Priština) north of Skoplje. There the insurgents defeated a Byzantine army sent against them, captured Niš to the Northeast, as well as Skoplje and Ochrida to the South and laid siege to the fortress of Castoria. [27] Once again, however, the Bulgarian rebellion disintegrated because of disunity among the rebels. This second Bulgarian rebellion differed from the first led by Peter Delian, among other things, in geographic spread : it remained limited to the area from Macedonia in the South to Niš in the North and there is no evidence that it spread as far as Sardica. [28]

The government of Michael VII Dukas thus had succeeded in suppressing the second major revolt in Bulgaria. Towards the end of his reign, however, the desperate military and economic plight of the Empire, both in Asia and in Europe, produced a series of rebellions which led to his overthrow and also involved the Bulgarian territory and population. In 1077 the Byzantine governor of Dyrrhachium, Nicephorus Bryennius, rebelled and moved with his army eastward to Adrianople. The Pechenegs exploited the situation, laid siege to the city, committed massacres in the surrounding countryside and drove away large herds of cattle. [29] Bryennius was obliged to pay them a high ransom to persuade them to call off their siege of Adrianople and to withdraw to their settlements north of the Balkans. While Bryennius was still threatening Constantinople (November—December 1077), his successor as duke of Dyrrhachium, Nicephorus Basilaces, rebelled and seized Thessalonica. The Byzantine garrisons stationed in Illyricum and Bulgaria sided with him. Late in 1077 Nicephorus Botaneiates, *strategos* of the Anatolic theme in Asia Minor, also revolted, overthrew Michael VII Dukas and was crowned in his stead at Constantinople (2 June 1078).

The new Emperor sent an army against Basilaces to Thessalonica and ended the rebellions of both Bryennius and Basilaces, while the Pechenegs, in conjunction with another Turkish people, the Kumans, once again advanced through Southern Bulgaria to Constantinople [30]. In the same year 1078, there is again evidence for uprisings in Bulgaria proper. A certain Lekas, a native of Philippopolis and from a "Paulician" family, cooperated with the Pechenegs and threatened the Byzantine government. It is known that he was active in Sardica, for Scylitzes reports that Lekas "slew Michael, bishop of Sardica, who was a partisan of the Emperor

---

[26] Michael Attaleiates, *Historia*, p. 203 ed. Bonn.

[27] Zlatarski II 119—149; Litavrin 402—410.

[28] See Litavrin's instructive map entitled : Antifeudal movements of national liberation on Bulgarian territory in the eleventh and twelfth centuries.

[29] Michael Attaleiates, *Historia*, p. 262 ed. Bonn. : (the Pechenegs) πᾶσαν ὁμοῦ κατελωβήσαντο καὶ διήρπασαν, φόνον μὲν πολὺν τῶν ἐν ἀγροῖς ποιησάμενοι, κτηνῶν δὲ ἀμυθήτων ἀγέλας ἐλάσαντες καὶ οὐδὲ ἓν εἶδος κακώσεως παραλιπόντες τοῖς κάμνουσιν. Cf. also Scylitzes, vol. II, p. 731 ed. Bonn and Zlatarski II 160 f.

[30] Zlatarski II 161 f.

(Nicephorus Botaneiates) and who was exhorting the city to do the same"[31] This passage implies that a large part of Sardica's population was hostile to the Byzantine Emperor and therefore presumably sympathized with Lekas. In fact, it has been plausibly suggested that the rebellion at Sardica was related to measures of Byzantinization undertaken by Bishop Michael.[32] Simultaneously a certain Dobromir was agitating against Byzantium at Mesembria on the shore of the Black Sea. Both Lekas and Dobromir cooperated with the Pechenegs who ravaged the neighborhoods of Niš and Sardica. However, for reasons unknown, the two rebel leaders submitted before the Emperor carried out a plan of sending a military force against them. In the next year (1079) the general Alexius Comnenus, the future Emperor, marched against the Pechenegs as far as Sardica and forced them to return to their homes. In 1080 the new Byzantine governor of Mesembria made peace with both Pechenegs and Kumans. It lasted until 1087. [33]

The preceding survey of Bulgarian rebellions during the eleventh century and of Turkish depredations from the North should facilitate the solution of the chronological problem posed by the interpolations in the *Zbornik*. It should be clear that the rebellion of 1066 can be excluded from the beginning, for it never reached Bulgarian territory, let alone Sardica. The rebellion of Peter Delian in 1040/1, it is true, affected all of Bulgaria including Sardica. This rebellion may, however, be eliminated on other grounds. The interpolator knew of an invasion of Western Bulgaria from north of the Danube and it is most natural to assume that it occurred simultaneously with or at least not long after the rebellion at Sardica. However, the Pecheneg invasions of Bulgaria did not begin until 1048 while the rebellion of Peter Delian ended in 1041. The revolt led by Constantine Bodin is not likely to be meant either, for there is no indication in the sources that it affected Sardica. The situation is different for the period from the end of Michael VII Dukas' reign to the accession of Alexius I Comnenus, i.e. from 1077 to 1081. In those years there were a number of rebels with headquarters in or near Bulgaria : Bryennius, Basilaces, Lekas and Dobromir. As has been seen, Lekas in particular played a key role in Sardica. There he opposed the local bishop who tried to strengthen the Byzantine influence in the city. In addition, those years were a time of repeated inroads by Pechenegs, Kumans and Magyars. In 1078, in particular, the Pechenegs were active around Niš and Sardica and in the following year Alexius Comnenus led a Byzantine army into the same area and against the same enemy. A rebel-

---

[31] Scylitzes, vol. II, p. 741, Bonn : τότε δὴ ὁ Λέκας τὸν ἐπίσκοπον Σαρδικῆς Μιχαὴλ τὰ τοῦ βασιλέως φρονοῦντα καὶ τὴν πόλιν αὐτὸ τοῦτο ποιεῖν παραινοῦντα ἀνεῖλε κτλ. Cf. Litavrin, 415. Scylitzes and Attaleiates are the only sources to mention the rebellion of Lekas.

[32] Zlatarski II 163.

[33] Zlatarski II 163—165, 188.

lion at Sardica, an "Ismaelite" raid of a people from across the Danube
via Sardica and Mraka southward to Küstendil and their cooperation
with the rebel, as described by the interpolator, would fit well into the
history of the years 1077—1081. So would the description of famine,
scarcity of domestic animals, cheapness of human freedom and general
devastation (item 13), which agrees to a remarkable extent with the
reports of the Byzantine historians on the plundering habits especially
of the Pechenegs.

Can the third element in the interpolations, the data on the ruler
Michael, be fitted into the proposed solution? If it proves valid, the
Byzantine Emperor Michael VII Dukas cannot be meant, for he abdi-
cated in January 1078. A number of features are striking in the interpolator's remarks about Michael. In the first place, apart from the matter
of his accession after August 1, the interpolator evidently possesses little
hard information about him. "The mountains will begin to divide, the fish
to die in the streams" does not sound very persuasive. The statement on
the ruler enjoying divine protection clearly is no more than an expression
of a pious hope. This raises the possibility that Michael's accession to
the throne after August 1 may also be a piece of wishful thinking. In other
words, one wonders whether Michael was not a pretender rather than an
actual ruler. Secondly, it is surprising that in item 10 the interpolator
has Michael entering Thessalonica "from the West". It is true that the last
three words were part of the original prophecy, but it should be noted that
by interpolating item 9 on Michael and by changing in item 10 the City
of the Seven Hills (Constantinople) into Thessalonica the interpolator
destroyed the original context of the *Vision of Daniel* in which the eastward
march of the emperor from Rome to Constantinople was well motivated.
Yet it must have been precisely the mention of a ruler entering a city from
the West that gave the interpolator the idea of changing the name of the
city. Nothing else in item 10 can have struck him as applying to his own
time. By changing the name of the city the interpolator therefore appropriated the words "from the West". Finally, there is the problem of the
relationship of item 9 on the Emperor Michael to the original text. On the
analogy of the other interpolations one is inclined to suppose that the
words preceding the interpolation were responsible for the insertion.
There it was stated that an earlier ruler, who held his power for less than
one year, fought with an Ethiopian Emperor, was deserted by many of
the great men and was eventually "destroyed" by the Ethiopian Emperor.
But is is surely surprising that precisely in the sentence following item 9
the interpolator for the only time resorted to a change in the original text
rather than adding to it. His exceptional procedure seems to indicate that
he attached particular importance to the item. If that is so, one wonders
whether item 9 on the Emperor Michael and item 10 on an emperor's
entry into Thessalonica from the West do not belong together, in other
words whether item 9 is not just as exceptional as item 10 and was prompted
not by the preceding sentence about the Ethiopian Emperor but by the
following sentence about an Emperor entering a city from the West.
To put it differently, it would seem that the interpolator inserted the
passage about Michael (item 9) because without it the text would have

prophesied that the Ethiopian Emperor would enter Constantinople from the West. He found this prophecy meaningless and removed the stumbling blocks by two interventions, first by inserting the passage about Michael (item 9) and thereby making him rather than the Ethiopian Emperor the subject of the following sentence; and secondly, by transferring the scene of the Emperor's entry from Costantinople to Thessalonica (item 10).

It has been suggested so far that the interpolator was referring to a rebellion taking place in Northwestern Bulgaria between 1078 and 1081 as well as to a roughly contemporary Pecheneg invasion, that the Michael referred to in item 9 may have been not an actual ruler but a pretender and that the interpolator hoped that Michael would enter Thessalonica from the West. Was there in those years a pretender to the Byzantine throne called Michael?

Ever since in 1071 the Norman Duke of Apulia Robert Guiscard had conquered Bari from the Byzantines, he had developed plans for the conquest of the Byzantine Empire. The reasons for this project were manifold, among them the fact that his Italian enemies frequently found asylum on Byzantine territory across the Adriatic Sea. He searched for a pretext of intervening in the affairs of the Byzantine Empire, then hard pressed on all sides and especially by the Seljuq Turks in Asia Minor. The Emperor Michael VII Dukas was in desperate need of military assistance against the Seljuqs and for that purpose made several attempts to win a military alliance from the powerful Norman Duke by means of a dynastic marriage . He succeeded in the end and his son Constantine, a few months after his birth, was betrothed to a daughter of Robert Guiscard, called Helen by the Greeks [34]. In 1076 the little Norman princess arrived at the court of Constantinople. When in 1078 Nicephorus Botaneiates was proclaimed Emperor, he abrogated this betrothal and thus presented Robert Guiscard with his *casus belli*. War was delayed for a while by the revolt of several Italian cities, but in 1080 at the latest he began to make preparations, diplomatic as well as military. By the end of July of that year there is attested as being at his court a person claiming to be the dethroned Emperor Michael VII Dukas.[25] In fact, he was an impostor, as the real Michael VII Dukas continued to reside at Constantinople as a monk and later as metropolitan of Ephesus.[36] Anna Comnena, in her *Alexiad*, tells in detail the story of this political comedy.[37] The individual in question was a monk from Southern Italy named Rhaiktor. According to one

[34] Analysis of the terms of the alliance by Hélène Bibicou, *Une page d'histoire diplomatique de Byzance au XIe siècle : Michel VII Dukas, Robert Guiscard et la pension des dignitaires*, "Byzantion", 29—30, 1959—60, 43—75. On the betrothal see D. I. Polemis, *The Doukai, A Contribution to Byzantine Prosopography*, London, 1968, 60. On all aspects of Robert Guiscard's campaign against Byzantium see F. Chalandon, *Essai sur le règne d'Alexis Comnène*, Paris, 1900, 57—94; and *Histoire de la domination normande en Italie et Sicile*, 2 vols., Paris, 1907, especially I 258—284. See also G. Kolias, *Le Motif et les raisons de l'invasion de Robert Guiscard en territoire byzantin*, "Byzantion", 36, 1966, 424—430.

[35] See the letter of Pope Gregory VII, of 25 July 1080, addressed to the bishops of Apulia and Calabria. The Pope expresses no doubt as to the identity of the *Gloriosissimus imperator Constantinopolitanus, Michahel* (ed. E. Caspar, *Das Register Gregors VII*, MGH, Epistolae Selectae, tomus II, fasc. II, Berlin, 1923, 523).

[36] Polemis, *The Dukai*, 44.

[37] Anna Comnena, *Alexiad*, I 12 (vol. I, pp. 42—47, ed. B. Leib).

tradition, the initiative for the impersonation lay with Rhaiktor who appeared at the Norman court, claimed to be the ex-Emperor Michael VII Dukas and asked Robert Guiscard to help him recover the Byzantine throne and at the same time to free his own daughter. In the second version of the story, which Anna Comnena considered more likely, it was asserted that there had been, at the Norman court, a great deal of opposition to Robert Guiscard's project of an attack against Byzantium. He had, therefore, sought to fabricate a plausible pretext for war (βουλόμενος πιθανὴν τὴν πρόφασιν τοῦ πολέμου ποιήσασθαι) and sent agents to Cotrone in Southern Italy. They brought the monk Rhaiktor back to Salerno and produced him before the opponents of war against Byzantium as the ex-Emperor Michael VII. With the help of this Pseudo-Michael Robert Guiscard was then able to win over his barons to the military campaign which he had been contemplating. Whichever version of the episode may come closer to the truth, Anna Comnena is probably right in assuming that both protagonists counted on outwitting the other, Robert Guiscard on abandoning Pseudo-Michael after he had won the war and Pseudo-Michael on capturing the throne for himself in the conviction that the Byzantine people and army would never accept a barbarian like Robert Guiscard as Emperor. Meanwhile Robert Guiscard left Italy in May 1081 and "exhibited (Pseudo-Michael) to the cities and urged the inhabitants through whose territories he was passing and whom he could persuade to do so to revolt (against Alexius Comnenus)".[38] This occurred, for example, during the siege of Dyrrhachium. On one occasion, the inhabitants offered to surrender their city to Robert Guiscard if they would recognize the ex-Emperor Michael. Robert Guiscard immediately gave orders for Pseudo-Michael to be produced in a magnificent procession, to the sounds of musical instruments. This was done, but the people of Dyrrhachium did not recognize him and showered insults upon the pretender.[39] Yet even Anna Comnena told, in the paragraph immediately following, that some people believed that Pseudo-Michael was really the ex-Emperor Michael VII and added a little later that "from all sides innumerable forces flock to him (Robert Guiscard) like snowflakes in winter and the more lightheaded of them believe the impostor to be in fact (the Emperor) Michael and so join up with Robert".[40] This was the last time that Pseudo-Michael figured in the pages of the historians of the Norman war against Byzantium.

---

[38] Anna Comnena, *Alexiad*, I 15, 6 (vol. I, p. 56 ed. Leib) : (Robert Guiscard) διεδείκνυ τοῦτον (Pseudo-Michael) ταῖς πόλεσι καὶ πρὸς ἀποστασίαν ἐπῆρεν, ἐφ'οὓς ἂν παραγένοιτο καὶ συμπείθειν ἠδύνατο. Anna Comnena inserted this passage at a place in the narrative before the Duke left Italy, but the cities mentioned must be those of the Balkan Peninsula. She must be anticipating the routine followed by Guiscard whenever his army appeared before the walls of a Byzantine city.

[39] Anna Comnena, *Alexiad*, IV 1, 3 (vol. I, p. 144 Leib) : "Ἅμα δὲ τῷ τοῦτον θεάσασθαι ἄνωθεν μυρίαις ὕβρεσιν ἔπλυνον μὴ ἐπιγινώσκειν αὐτὸν ὅλως διισχυριζόμενοι. See the parallel and closely related account in William of Apulia, *La Geste de Robert Guiscard*, ed. M. Mathieu, Istituto Siciliano di Studi Bizantini e Neoellenici, Testi e Monumenti 4, 1961, IV 262—271 where one of the insults is specified : *iste solebat / Crateras mensis plenos deferre Lieo / Et de pincernis erat inferioribus unus*. William of Apulia did not mention that Pseudo-Michael was a monk.

[40] Anna Comnena, *Alexiad*, IV 2, 1 (vol. I, p. 146 Leib) : ἀπανταχόθεν ἀπειροπλήθεις δυνάμεις εἰς αὐτὸν συρρέουσι νιφάσιν ἐοικυῖαι χειμερίῃσι καὶ οἱ κουφότεροι τὸν ψευδώνυμον ἐπ' ἀληθείας Μιχαὴλ εἶναι τὸν βασιλέα πιστεύοντες προσέρχονται τῷ Ῥομπέρτῳ.

He may have died on the campaign, but it is also possible that he continued to play his role in persuading the inhabitants of Byzantine cities to surrender to the Normans. In 1082 Deabolis, Kastoria, Dyrrhachium and Ochrida were betrayed to the Norman army and because of the several crushing defeats suffered by Alexius Comnenus the inhabitants of many cities on the Balkan Peninsula despaired of the Emperor and wholeheartedly sided with Robert Guiscard's son Bohemond, as Anna Comnena said.[41] It is not impossible that Pseudo-Michael continued to be useful to the Norman cause until the time when in 1082 the Norman armies reached the easternmost points of their advance, Larissa in Thessaly and the River Vardar east of Moglena and not far north of Thessalonica.[42] In 1083 the fortunes of war began to turn in favor of the Byzantines and Bohemond was forced to return to Italy. In 1084 Robert Guiscard undertook a new campaign, but this time his forces did not get beyond the islands of Corfu and Cephalonia, as well as a few minor places on the Eastern shore of the Adriatic, and he died on Cephalonia on 17 July 1085. With his death the Norman campaign against the Byzantine Empire came to an end, to be taken up again only at a much later time within the context of the First Crusade.

Did the interpolator of the *Zbornik* mean Pseudo-Michael in items 9—11? He mentioned the ruler named Michael after his interpolations on the rebellion at Sardica and on the foreign invasion from the Danube southward to Küstendil. The rebellion at Sardica may have been that of Lekas in 1078, but given the chaotic conditions in the Empire under Nicephorus Botaneiates it would not be surprising if the disorders at Sardica continued or erupted once more after Lekas had made his submission. The foreign invasion envisaged by the interpolator will then be that of the Pechenegs in 1078, or that of 1079 when Alexius Comnenus marched against them to Sardica. Pseudo-Michael was certainly, as noted above, established at Salerno by 25 July 1080, but there is no way of knowing how much earlier he arrived there. As time went on, as the Norman armies landed on the Eastern shore of the Adriatic in 1081 and advanced in the next year as far as the River Vardar, it must indeed have appeared possible, even probable, to a Bulgarian observer that the man whom he considered to be the ex-Emperor Michael VII Dukas, supported by the Norman armies and by the "innumerable forces" from the Balkan Peninsula which, according to Anna Comnena, were flocking to the conquerors "like snowflakes in winter", might in the near future "enter Thessalonica from the West". Did he predict that Michael would take the throne (*cesarstvo*) after August 1 and rule "at Thessalonica" for thirty-three years because he expected Pseudo-Michael with his powerful Norman support to obtain for himself a position similar to the one that in 1081 the new Emperor Alexius I Comnenus offered as a compromise to the rebel Nicephorus Melissenos : the dignity of *caesar* and the rule of Thessalonica ?[43] Some expectation of this sort would be all the more plausible if what is stated by J. M. Hussey, unfortunately without citing

[41] Anna Comnena, *Alexiad*, V 4, 1 (vol. II, p. 17 Leib) : ἀπεγνωκότες γὰρ καθάπαξ τοῦ αὐτοκράτορος ὅλοι τῆς τοῦ Βαϊμούντου γεγόνασι γνώμης.
[42] Anna Comnena, *Alexiad*, V 5 (vol. II p. 22 ff. Leib.).
[43] Anna Comnena, *Alexiad*, II 8, 3 (vol. I, p. 89 Leib).

evidence, is true, namely that during the Norman-Byzantine war Alexius Comnenus "had to face opposition stirred up in the Balkans and in Dalmatia, where Bulgarians, Serbs and Ragusans were supporting a pro-Norman Ducas party led by a pretender claiming to be Michael VII".[44] If such a "pro-Norman Ducas party" existed, the interpolator of the *Zbornik* undoubtedly belonged to it.

Thus the events of the reign of Nicephorus Botaneiates and the earliest years of Alexius I Comnenus explain rather satisfactorily the interpolations in the *Zbornik*. To go beyond this chronological hypothesis and to decide on a particular year is difficult. On the one hand the interpolation on the rebellion at Sardica (items 1—2) would suggest the year 1078 and the rebellion of Lekas, although, as noted above, unrest in that city may have continued beyond Lekas' surrender. The interpolations on the foreign invasion (items 4—6) also point to the years 1078 or 1079. On the other hand, if Michael (item 9), is, as suggested, to be identified with Pseudo-Michael, one is inclined to think of a somewhat later date : 25 July 1080 when he is first attested or even later, in 1081 after the Norman armies had landed on the Balkan Peninsula or in 1082 when they were operating on the River Vardar not far from Thessalonica. Thus there exists the dilemma that within the context of the hypothesis here presented the interpolations regarding Michael are most easily explained by a date a year or two later than the one suggested by the rest of the information. The difficulty, however, is by no means unsurmountable and may be overcome by assuming that the interpolations were written at a time, say between 1079 and 1082 when it was known in Bulgaria that Pseudo-Michael had been recognized by Robert Guiscard as Michael VII Dukas and when the revolt of Lekas and the depredations of the Pechenegs in 1078 and 1079 were still fresh and painful memories.

Whatever the precise year of the interpolations, they were inserted in a Slavonic manuscript containing both the *Vision of Daniel* and the *Revelation* of Pseudo-Methodius. If the hypothesis presented in this paper is correct, the rebel from Glavinica west of Sofia (item 2) may have been one of several advance agents sent by Robert Guiscard to sow dissension in Byzantium's Western provinces. Nothing is known from the narrative sources of a victory of the inhabitants of Sardica over the "Ismaelites" near that city (items 7—8), unless perhaps this is a reference to an episode in Alexius Comnenus' military operations around Sardica in 1079. Why the interpolator expected the birth of Antichrist to take place at Strumica (item 12) is not clear, but the terrible destruction along the road from Sardica to Thessalonica, the scarcity of food and domestic animals and the cheapness of human freedom in the same area (item 13) are easily explained

---

[44] *Cambridge Medieval History*, vol. IV, part 1, Cambridge, 1968, 213. Ordericus Vitalis, *Hist. Eccl., P. L.* 188, 519 C-D reports that "Alexius Comnenus, together with the Patriarch of Constantinople and the wise men and senators of the Greek Kingdom, decreed that the sacred empire should not be given back to Michael, who had fled to the public enemy and entrusted all his belongings to the faithless Normans." Ordericus is clearly thinking of the man known to history as Pseudo-Michael, but it is questionable whether the "decree", if it is historical, was not in fact directed against the true Michael living in 1081 in a Byzantine monastery. If it envisaged Pseudo-Michael, it would be evidence that in 1081 the new government of Alexius Comnenus was afraid of his claims. Cf. V. Grumel, *Les Regestes des actes du Patriarcat de Constantinople*, vol. I, fasc. III, 1947, no. 916.

by the repeated inroads of Pechenegs, Magyars, Uzes and Kumans during the preceding decades.

The interpolator's identification of the "Ismaelites" in the *Vision of Daniel* with the Pechenegs is interesting from another point of view. Roman Jakobson has pointed out that the Russian chroniclers presented the events of A.M. 6600—6604 (= A.D. 1092—1096) in the language of Byzantine apocalypses and in particular identified the Kuman invaders of Russia with Pseudo-Methodius' Ismaelites. He has explained this striking fact by the ingenious observation that the end of the seventh millennium and especially the seventh century of that millennium, were considered the last age of the world.[45] The interpolations in the *Zbornik* show that in Western Bulgaria there existed similar expectations a decade or more earlier as A.M. 6600 (A.D. 1092) was approaching.

To re-emphasize what was stated at the beginning, the solution presented in this paper was not reached by a process of establishing secure *termini post* and thus excluding alternative explanations. Yet unless and until another conclusion is advanced that fits the data equally well or better, it may be stated with some confidence that the hypothesis of a Bulgarian adherent of Pseudo-Michael and of Robert Guiscard interpolating the Slavonic *Vision of Daniel* and the *Revelation* of Pseudo-Methodius around the years 1079 to 1082 has much in its favor.

---

[45] Roman Jakobson, *La Geste de Prince Igor*, "Selected Writings" IV, The Hague and Paris, 106—300, esp. 246 : "C'est le déclin du septième millénaire qu'on considérait comme le dernier temps du monde, et spécialement le septième siècle, les années sept-centièmes et sept-millièmes à la fois promettait d'être l'époque des terribles cataclysmes".

INDEX